Ideas and Data
The Process and Practice
of Social Research

THE DORSEY SERIES IN SOCIOLOGY

Editor   ROBIN M. WILLIAMS, JR.   *Cornell University*

Ideas and Data
The Process and Practice
of Social Research

SHELDON OLSON

University of Texas, Austin

 1976

The Dorsey Press   *Homewood, Illinois 60430*
Irwin-Dorsey International   *Arundel, Sussex*   *BN18 9AB*
Irwin-Dorsey Limited   *Georgetown, Ontario*   *L7G 4B3*

First Printing, March 1976

ISBN 0-256-01809-X
Library of Congress Catalog Card No. 75–35104
Printed in the United States of America

To my parents,
Oscar and Lauretta Olson,
for years of encouragement

Preface

If I have tried to do anything with this book, it is to get away from the notion that research methods are a series of disconnected tools. Rather research methods should always be viewed within the larger process of theory construction and theory testing. When viewed within this context the sometimes antagonistic stance between different styles of research disappears. Perhaps disappears is too strong a statement, but it is surely safe to say that the potential for mutual reinforcement becomes more readily apparent.

I take as a starting point that social theory can be roughly characterized as a statement about social life which applies to more than one situation. Thus a central task confronting social science is to move from information about a single setting to abstract principles which note similarities via the formation of more general concepts. As has been frequently noted the reverse flow, from general principles to concrete instances, is also central to the enterprise. It is in this sense that the analogy drawn between the methods of social science and the tasks of translating a language becomes appropriate. The "methods" of social science are largely means by which the translation from idea to data and data to idea is accomplished.

For heuristic purposes I have organized the book around the movement from the discovery of the folk system to the test of analytic propositions. Indeed, I toyed with the idea of using "From Discovery of the Folk to Test of the Analytic" as the title for the book. However, it was finally decided that this would place too much emphasis on a one way flow. It is the back and forth movement between idea and data that we are interested in.

Having finished the manuscript for this book I find myself indebted to a number of persons. For early stimulation and research experience I wish to thank Herbert Costner, Clarence Schrag, and L. Wesley Wager. For facilitating two enjoyable and stimulating years as a Russel Sage Fellow in the Law and Social Science Program at Yale Law School I am indebted to Stanton Wheeler. For listening, arguing, and providing friendship I thank my colleagues at the University of Texas. Without the flying fingers of Nancy Becker, Damon Bockoven, Sharon McMullen, Dianne Odegard, Connie Smyrl, and Jane Wootan this book would still be smudges on pieces of paper. Finally, I owe much to Cheryl, Scott, and Brooke for the companionship and enjoyment, as well as some night hours of proof reading, which allowed this book to be completed.

Austin, Texas   SHELDON OLSON
February 1976

Contents

Practical Exercises

Chapter 1

Introduction

A friend of mine, on hearing that I was writing a book on methods, left the following quotation in my mailbox as an ominous though friendly warning:

> Remember the observation of Frank Knight to this effect: A man writing on methodology is in the same position as one who plays the slide trombone; unless he is very good at it, the results are more likely to interest him than his audience. (Duncan, 1966, pp. 95–96)

There is much to warrant such skepticism. For one thing, learning the methods of social science is one of those occasions when you don't really learn without doing. The craft of using statistics, the interlaced processes of theory construction and theory testing, the task of designing and carrying out a survey become mastered and understood through actual practice. It is like learning to play tennis. You can read all day that you are to cock your wrist, take your backswing shoulder high, and shift your weight to the front foot, which is pointing at a 45-degree angle to the net, but until you get out on the court and begin to swing you never experience the movement and flow of the operation, nor do you start improving your skills.

So it is with the methods of social science. There are certain "strokes" that can be described in detail. But, until you begin to choose appropriate statistics and controls, until you begin to draw a sample, until you face the task of developing rapport with those you are to observe, you will not get a real feel for the process.

Why, then, write this text, much less expect you to read it? It is the case that a certain degree of preparatory knowledge may be helpful. By pointing to the elements that constitute the overall process, the reader may, hopefully, better anticipate what the game is all about. As you enter an actual study you will run into questions and develop problems. Foreknowledge may help avoid the severity of these problems and may serve as a guide when difficulties are to be corrected. In addition, an idea of what "good" research should look like allows a more discerning critique of works read.

Beyond these pragmatic reasons it is reasonable to examine the *methods* of social science in that they constitute a central struggle: How do we go about knowing? Regardless of our substantive aims, be they political alienation, family structure and conflict, or the dynamics of poverty, we are called upon to make informed judgments. By noting the potential as well as the limitations of gathering information on human activities we are in a better position to reach more reasonable conclusions.

Why write a methods book, then? If such things need further justification, it is just because I am interested in the topic. It is simply an intriguing question to ask, "How do we go about knowing?" When I began the project of writing I planned to learn a great deal. Now, as I write this introduction, I find that to be the case. But what of you? Surely the book is more than just a means to satisfy the author's interest and desire to learn. Hopefully, the book will do several things.

First, I hope you come away from each chapter with some "feel" for social research. It can be extremely interesting and, at times, even an exciting endeavor. Toward this end I have included a series of "practicum" (note I have avoided the duller label of "exercise") through which you can get at least a taste of what is involved. I also have tried to draw upon examples of research wherein the authors have struggled and, in some sense, come to terms with the difficulties encountered. Thus, you should obtain an idea of the difficulties ahead for those who would construct and test empirically based theories about social life.

A second, and no less important, goal is that the book helps you build certain research skills. You should acquire adeptness in the use of certain tools. Refinements in your skills, like refinements in all skills, must await practice, mistakes, and more practice. I have found great satisfaction in writing this book. I hope, in reading it, you gain as much. We shall see.

SOCIAL SCIENCE AS A PROCESS OF TRANSLATION

The view of social science to be pursued is one of a process in which we construct and test theories about social life. Such a process involves the continuing and reciprocal movement from one scheme—that of the theorist—to another—that of the observed phenomena—and back again. Becoming acquainted with the methods of social science, then, is much like learning to translate from one language to another.

Such translation is difficult in that gaps always remain. Something is always lost in translation. One language cannot completely express the nuances of another. These are frequently expressed difficulties for the linguist. So it is with theory construction. Such construction often involves the translation of the perspective of the participant into the perspective of the observer. In such a process something is always lost. Likewise with theory testing, the analytic concepts of the theorist are often quite complicated and multidimensional. To pin them down to a single item or even a number of items on a questionnaire or other systematic observation strategy often leaves the researcher with feelings of incompleteness. The questionnaire items may be accurate reflections of ideas as far as they go but they often do not go far enough.

This is not to say that translation is impossible. It is possible. It is also difficult, frustrating, and usually less than perfect. Strategies developed to handle these problems and the difficulties encountered will occupy our attention throughout.

We begin by examining the translation of the folk system, the world as seen through the eyes of the day-to-day participants, into an analytic system, the world as seen through a system of propositions designed by the observer to account for more than one situation. The second major section of the book starts where the first leaves off. Given an analytic system, the researcher is faced with the task of designing measurement strategies to discover whether or not the propositions within the analytic scheme are valid within particular settings.

The division of this book is made with the full realization that every investigator worth his or her salt is going to be interested in both the discovery and the test of hypotheses. Theory testing and theory construction, like the colors orange and red, shade into one another. This makes a distinction nonetheless useful. With this interlocking nature in mind, it will be argued that, within various projects, theory testing and theory construction are given differential emphasis. With this differential comes a number of differences in observation strategies. The choice of method is determined largely by how well it accomplishes the related translation.

Experiments are most powerful when translating the idea of cause. Participant observation studies are most powerful when translating the insider's perspective into a more general analytic scheme. We will have much more to say along these lines in the remainder of the book. The final chapter will deal with a somewhat distinct set of translation problems, that of the "is" into the "ought" and vice versa. Here, the issue is whether and to what extent social research can inform and be guided by policy concerns.

Without further preview, let us begin.

REFERENCES

Duncan, Otis Dudley
　　1966　"Methodological Issues in the Analysis of Social Mobility." In Neil J. Smelser and Seymour Martin Lipset (eds.), *Social Structure and Mobility in Economic Development*. Chicago: Aldine.

Contents

Chapter 2

Uncovering the Folk System: The Basic Plan and Problems

A BASIC DILEMMA

Assume for the moment that you wish to construct a theory about social life starting from the participants' point of view. You want to start fresh, unencumbered by existing "outside" theoretical preconceptions. Precoded, pretested questionnaires locked in by preselected concepts and indicators are out of place. What is most important is the point of view of those being studied. You want to know the world through their eyes. You want the "insider's point of view," and yet you are an "outsider." It is this problem of wanting in but being out that plagues the theory constructor, who starts by searching for the insider's perspective, as much as anything else.

On Being Out and Wanting In

James Spradley (1970) has attempted to gain such a view of those he calls the urban nomads; those whom others have called "wino," "derelict," "bum," "skid-row alcoholic." Spradley notes that, previous to his study, four models had been suggested for defining these men and their world. The first is the *popular model*. Here, the men ". . . are seen as people who fail abysmally, are dependent on society, lack self-control, drink too much, are unpredictable, and often end up in jail for their criminal behavior. In a word they are *bums*." A second model is a *medical model*. Here, the men are *alcoholics*. They are the victims of a disease. The alcoholic is incapable of planning for the future and unable to survive in society without the imposition of external controls. A third model focuses on *legal identity*. Here, the key word is *vagrant*. For police and court officials these men are a kind of petty criminal, guilty of committing a number of minor offenses, all stemming from their drinking problem. A final model, often "imposed" on the world of the urban nomad, is what Spradley calls the *sociological model*. Here, the important dimensions of identity are *age, race, sex, income,* and *drinking behavior.* In this regard Spradley quotes a rather cynical observer of this perspective:

> When the sociologist arrives on skid row with a precoded, pretested survey questionnaire in hand, every one of his questions implicitly assumes the person is a failure and asks why. Even though this question remains unstated, both questioner and questioned perceive its fundamental reality. (Wallace, 1965, p. 159; cited by Spradley, p. 68)

What all of these models have in common is that they view this world from the outside. Whatever else they provide, they do not take us very far into the insider's point of view. It is precisely this perspective that Spradley hoped to discover. Accordingly, the key question was: "How do members of the group being considered here classify and define themselves and the social identity of those with whom they interact?" In pursuit of this question the strategy was not to use questionnaires or a preselected interview format. Rather, "Initially the data were gathered by *listening* and *observing,* not to discover answers but to find which questions to ask" (Spradley, p. 69).

Thus, the initial picture of the research reported by Spradley is one of an observer peering in from the outside trying to grope for, to empathize with those who are the focus of interest. Still, even with this stance, Spradley was an outsider. He was faced with the problem of breaking through certain barriers and establishing certain bonds. He has to build trust; to establish rapport.

On Being In and Wanting Out

For other observers, seeking the insider's point of view, this is not so much of a problem. They find, for one reason or another, that they are part of the world they plan to study and thus can report on the world directly from the inside. Viktor Frankl (1959) provides one such example.

Frankl is a man who found himself incarcerated in a German concentration camp during World War II. "Discovery" was, in this sense, forced on him. Becoming part of the insider's world was not problematic; he was bombarded on all sides with its reality. The problem was just the reverse of that facing Spradley. Frankl had to find a way to step back. He had to get distance between his analysis and his experiences. In Frankls' own words: "To attempt a methodical presentation of the subject is very difficut, as psychology [add social science in general] requires a certain scientific detachment. But does a man who makes his observations while he himself is a prisoner possess the necessary detachment? Such detachment is granted to the outsider, but he is too far removed to make any statement of real value. Only the man inside knows. His judgments may not be objective; his evaluations may be out of proportion. This is inevitable. An attempt must be made to avoid any personal bias, and that is the real difficulty of a book of this kind" (p. 8).

Thus, a person attempting to construct a picture of the insider's world is faced with a kind of quandary. There are benefits and drawbacks for both the outsider and the insider. The outsider is too far removed from the data; the insider is ensnared. The outsider has the distance needed for objective observations; the insider has the experience needed for insightful discovery and analysis. To completely overcome this dilemma is perhaps impossible. To recognize its presence is imperative.

Between the time of getting in and the time of getting out there is a multiplicity of events that recurs as researchers go about the task of uncovering the "folk system." The remainder of this chapter is devoted to an exploration of these recurrences. First, we will look at the underlying current that pushes the research along. This is the current of initially uncovering the insider's perspective and then translating it into more abstract, and thus more generally applicable, terms. We will turn then to a number of whirlpools and crosscurrents that sometimes deflect and sometimes reverse the basic flow of events.

The underlying current as well as the sidetracks and reverses are important. Without some direction the study proceeds willy-nilly. Without unexpected changes and, at times, reversals the study becomes too rigid. Reflecting on his study of the folk inhabiting Street Corner Society, William Foote Whyte (1955) summarized this as follows:

> The ideas that we have in research are only in part a logical product growing out of a careful weighing of evidence. We do not generally think problems through in a straight line. Often we have the experience of being immersed in a mass of confusing data. We study the data carefully, bringing all our powers of logical analysis to bear upon them. We come up with an idea or two. But still the data do not fall in any coherent pattern. Then we go on living with the data—and with the people—until perhaps some chance occurrence casts a totally different light upon the data, and we begin to see a pattern that we have not seen before. This pattern is not purely an artistic creation. Once we think we see it, we must reexamine our notes and perhaps set out to gather new data in order to determine whether the pattern adequately represents the life we are observing or is simply a product of our imagination. (pp. 279–80)

In similar reflection, Hortense Powdermaker notes:

> Few practicing social scientists today believe their research resembles the orderly intellectual presentations in textbooks on method: choice of problem, formulation of hypotheses and testing of them, analysis and interpretation of data. All of these do occur, and, obviously, research

must be planned in advance. But, as Edward Shils has pointed out, the research process is often quite disorderly. (p. 10)

Keeping in mind the sometimes "disorderly" nature of uncovering the folk system we first look at the more orderly side.

UNCOVERING THE FOLK SYSTEM IN STAGES

Becker (1958) notes four progressive stages in this style of research, progressive in the sense that each succeeding stage depends on the previous one.[1] First is the selection and definition of the problems, concepts, and indices. Second is the check on the frequency and distribution of the phenomena. Third is the incorporation of individual findings into a model of the situation under study. The fourth stage is the presentation of evidence and support of their validity.

The Selection and Definition of Problems, Concepts, and Indices

Recall the early stance of Spradley in his study of the urban nomad. It was one of listening and observing, not to discover answers but to discover the appropriate questions. As time went on, the study began to take on a more directed nature. The men were asked specific questions to elicit certain answers. More particularly, the focus turned to perceptions of their identity.

> In order to further check the saliency of different identity terms two questions were asked a group of fifty men. First, they were asked to place in rank order those terms which they felt best described the men at the treatment center. They were presented with the words *inmate, tramp, bum, citizen, convict* and *prisoner* and instructed to include additional words which would better describe the population. (pp. 70–71)

This procedure not only allowed an initial assessment of the presence of the various labels but also elicited new information to the effect that there were "mission stiffs," "hustlers," "dingbats," and others. The question then became: "Which of these identities should be further explored?" With this decision the study necessarily narrowed. The relationship between the interests of the researcher and the focus of study began to intermesh. Spradley states, "Though all these identities are important, we shall focus upon only two: tramp and inmate. Their selection is partly determined by research interest in law and order for minority groups but it also reflects informants' feelings about the relative importance of their different identities" (p. 71).

Given this selection of the problem and concepts, the task became one of developing indices to allow the investigation of their meaning

[1] For a related, though in many ways more refined, discussion, see Diesing (1971).

and, thus, indirectly the outline of the urban nomad's perspective. To accomplish this, Spradley relied on established procedures employed most frequently by ethnographers. He began to develop *taxonomic* and *componential* definitions for the label "tramp." Taxonomic definitions simply name and categorize types into general and less general categories. By asking the men, "Are there different kinds of tramps?" and, then, given a positive response, asking, "What kinds of tramps are there?", Spradley came up with the taxonomy presented in Figure 2.1.

FIGURE 2.1
Taxonomic Definition of Tramp Domain

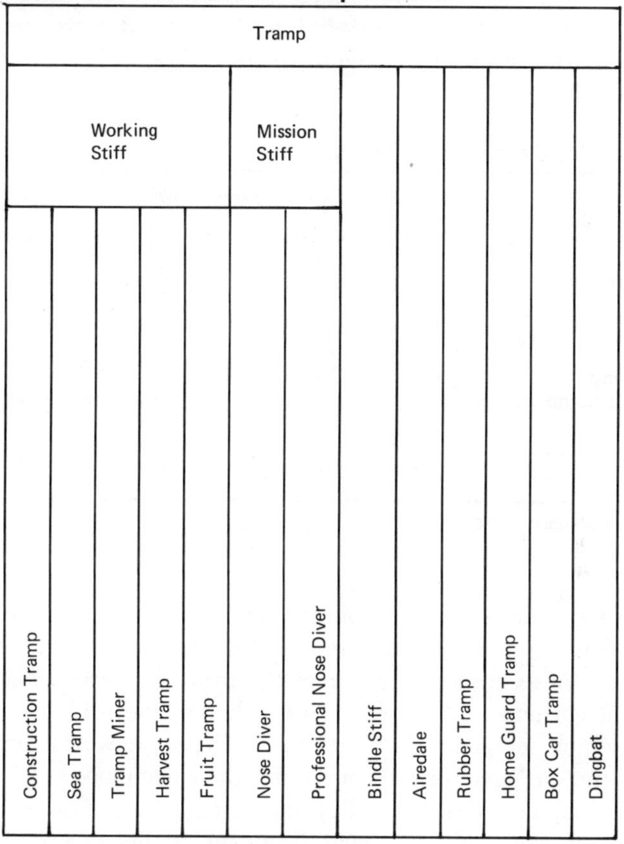

Tramp												
Working Stiff					Mission Stiff							
Construction Tramp	Sea Tramp	Tramp Miner	Harvest Tramp	Fruit Tramp	Nose Diver	Professional Nose Diver	Bindle Stiff	Airedale	Rubber Tramp	Home Guard Tramp	Box Car Tramp	Dingbat

Source: From Spradley, 1970, p. 75.

Thus, "tramp" turned out to be a "cover term," a term with a number of subcategories. There were "working stiffs" and "mission stiffs," which, in turn, were cover terms for a number of types of tramps such as the "sea tramp" and "harvest tramp," on the one hand, and the "nose diver" or "professional nose diver," on the other. Given this classification scheme, Spradley reasoned that further insight could be gained if the dimensions used to distinguish one type of tramp from another could be uncovered.

Toward this end of developing *componential* definitions, the men were presented with three labels at a time and asked which were similar and which different. They were then asked to elaborate on the basis of their decision. An example is the person given the terms "bindle stiff," "airedale," and "box car tramp." This elicited responses such as, "The first two are similar because they both carry a pack with them where they have a bedroll and other belongings, but a box car tramp travels streamlined" (p. 76). After a series of such comparisons the dimensions of definitions presented in Figure 2.2 were arrived at to differentiate the various meanings of the term "tramp."

FIGURE 2.2
Componential Definition of Tramp

	Mobile	*Mode of Travel*	*Home Base*	*Livelihood*
Working stiff.	Yes	Freight, commercial,	Job	Specialized – works
Mission stiff	Yes	Commercial	Mission	Specialized – missions
Bindle stiff.	Yes	Freight	Pack	Generalized
Airedale	Yes	Walk	Pack	Generalized
Rubber tramp	Yes	Car	Car	Generalized
Home guard tramp	No		Town and kinsmen	Generalized
Box car tramp.	Yes	Freight	None	Generalized
Ding	Yes	Freight	None	Specialized – begs

Source: Spradley, 1970, p. 76.

The four dimensions of mobility, mode of travel, home base, and livelihood were enough to differentiate one type from another. The box car tramp, for example, differs from the rubber tramp in that he travels by freight car and has no home base, whereas the rubber tramp travels by car, which serves as his home base. These types are similar in that they depend on "generalized" sources for their livelihood.

In this manner, then, Spradley increasingly honed in on his chosen definition of the problem—what it meant to be a "tramp" from the insider's perspective. The methods used have been elaborated in the works of Goodenough (1956), Lounsbury (1956), and Conklin (1962). There are, of course, a number of alternative strategies that Spradley might have chosen to develop indices of this meaning system. He might have relied on more informal observations after a long period of living with some of these men and taking field notes. He might have relied on less structured interviews. He might have utilized less direct methods, such as the interpretation of responses to Rorschach inkblots utilized by the Spindlers in their study of the Menomini Indians (1970). We will have a closer look at some of these strategies in Chapter 3. First, we move to the second stage of research suggested by Becker, that of checking the frequency and distribution of the phenomena chosen for study.

Checking the Pervasiveness and Pattern of the Phenomenon

As the outline of the insider's perspective begins to emerge, attention turns to its frequency and differential distribution. Is it a universally held perspective? Does it set one segment of the community apart from another? Does it change over time? Are there systematic changes?

Along these lines, Howard Becker, Blanche Geer, Everett Hughes, and Anselm Strauss (1961) have presented an excellent example of exploring the pervasiveness and changing nature of the perspective emerging as students pass through medical school. By comparing field notes and keeping track of such things as whether the information was elicited or volunteered, these observers of medical school were able to reach conclusions not only as to the pervasiveness of certain attitudes and behaviors but also as to the systematic changes occurring as students passed from the early stages of the experience to later stages. We will have occasion in the following chapters to return to this study a number of times.

In a similar manner, John Irwin (1970) discussed the changing nature of the "felon's" reaction to the experiences of passing through prison and reentry into the community, noting in the process that the changes paralleled those of other situations, such as returning war veterans or Peace Corps volunteers, where persons are faced with the problem of reorientation. It is when we begin to note similarities across situations that we move to the third stage in the process, that of putting the findings into a more general framework. This translation of the insider's perspective into an analytic perspective is the focus of Chapter 4. For now we turn to some of the problems of uncovering the folk perspective that commonly recur as you move from the choice of problem and indicators to the check on the pattern of distribution.

PROBLEMS ENCOUNTERED WHEN UNCOVERING THE FOLK SYSTEM

To some extent the problems you encounter are specific to the setting you are going to study. In this sense each project is a new experience. However, there are also certain repetitious patterns that emerge. The following discussion is based on an extensive examination of self-reports of persons who have returned from their studies and published their experiences. The general outline of uncovering the folk system, if not the specific events, should become clearer as we proceed.

The Spy Problem: A Matter of Secrecy

In some sense a folk system is a "system" by virtue of its autonomy from its surroundings. This autonomy is reinforced and maintained by various strategies of insulation. One of these strategies lies in the development of secrets that set "insiders" apart from "outsiders." That such processes exist is perhaps obvious when we consider certain "deviant" life styles where discovery frequently means punishment. See, for example, Becker (1963, ch. 9) and McCleery (1960). As Becker notes:

> If I wanted to study the splitting of fees between surgeons and general medical practitioners, how would I go about finding and getting access to the people who participate in such arrangements? Once found, one has the problem of convincing them that they can safely discuss the problem of their deviance with you. (p. 170)

In addition, it has been noted repeatedly that secrets are likely to develop in such "nondeviant" places as bureaucracies. Competitors want to keep secrets to maintain a market advantage. Units within corporations may develop secrets to maintain an edge in the struggle for company resources. Underlings may insulate themselves to avoid the watchful eye of the supervisor. Personnel may develop internal procedures to minimize hassles from clients. For discussions of these often subtle processes see such works as Merton (1952), Feld (1959), Gouldner (1959), Coser (1961), and Blumberg (1966). The term "secret" need not imply any sort of planned, sinister conspiracy but a more subtle form of adaptation to a frequently uncontrolled and unpredictable environment. As Blumberg has pointed out in his discussion of the "closed" courthouse community,

> Rather than any view of the matter in terms of some variation of a "conspiracy" hypothesis, the simple explanation is one of an ongoing system handling delicate tensions, managing the trauma produced by law enforcement and administration, and requiring almost pathological distrust of "outsiders" bordering on group paranoia. (pp. 21–22)

Perhaps even less obvious than these processes are parallel events in otherwise "open" and less formally organized communities. Suttles (1972) provides an enlightening discussion of a neighborhood in this regard.

> Perhaps the most subtle structural feature of the defended neighborhood is its shared knowledge of what might be called its underlife.

> People who share a residential identity are privy to a variety of secrets which range from the assured truths cf gossip to the collective myths of rumor. These bits and pieces of knowledge touch intimately on the lives of those who share a residential area because they add to the collective guilt or pride of coresidents. But they are also some of the surest markers which separate insiders from outsiders. (p. 36)

Nor is the suspicion of outsiders limited to "contemporary industrialized" society. As Freilich (1970, p. 500) has noted, when the anthropologist enters the field, "It is highly probable that many natives will be convinced that the anthropologist is a spy."

What you find, then, as you go about uncovering a folk system, is that you are quite predictably faced with a certain reluctance and suspicion. Before it is possible to move through the first stage of research it is necessary to overcome these frequently unseen barriers. One way in which this is accomplished is through a trusted sponsor, one willing to indicate that the researcher is O.K.

The Initial Sponsor: "She's O.K.—He's O.K."

An account of one of the more successful entrances into a community through a sponsor is that provided by Whyte (1955) and his initial relationship with "Doc." Entering the community through a settlement house, Whyte was introduced to Doc and began to relate his plans for a study.

> Doc heard me out without any change of expression, so that I had no way of predicting his reaction. When I was finished, he asked: "Do you want to see the high life or the low life?"
> "I want to see all that I can. I want to get as complete a picture of the community as possible."
> "Well, any nights you want to see anything, I'll take you around I can take you to the joints—gambling joints—I can take you around to the street corners. Just remember that you're my friend. That's all they need to know. I know these places, and, if I tell them that you're my friend, nobody will bother you. You just tell me what you want to see, and we'll arrange it. . . ."
> That was our beginning. At the time I found it hard to believe that I could move in as easily as Doc had said with his sponsorship. But that indeed was the way it turned out. (pp. 291, 293)

A similarly "lucky" contact was made by Powdermaker (1966) in her study of a small town in Mississippi. Describing her initial introduction at a meeting of the leading citizens, she notes, "The leading citizens of Indianola were completely unconvinced by Mr. Green's oration or few words. They were suspicious of a Yankee and did not want their 'niggers' studied by anyone. Their questions, the expressions of their

faces, and the tone of their voices indicated both fear and hostility"
(p. 139).

Following this initial encounter, Powdermaker goes on to relate,

> I was thoroughly depressed. I knew that I could not work with
> Negroes if everything had to be sieved through this group of white
> citizens and approved by them. . . . I was feeling desperate. Suddenly
> I remembered that Will Percy, the poet, lived in Greenville. (p. 140)

After visiting for a time, Mr. Percy called the mayor indicating that,
"Miss Powdermaker, an old friend of the family, is here with me in
my office. I understand she will be living in Indianola for awhile, and
I do hope you will make her comfortable" (p. 141). This was enough
to gain the confidence and cooperation of many of the former antago-
nists. As an "old friend of the family," Hortense Powdermaker was able
to move about more freely in an otherwise closed community.

Many entrances have not been so smooth as those of Powdermaker
and Whyte. The Spindlers (1970), for example, relate a stumbling experience into the world of the Menomini. The Spindlers were driving
down the highway one day and picked up a hitchhiker, who, in the
course of conversation, invited them to meet her relative medicine man.
Such an invitation is not to be bypassed, and the Spindlers gladly accepted. So far so good. Some two weeks after this meeting, they were
again driving down the highway and noticed a ceremony in the medicine
lodge. Whereupon,

> We pulled up, stopped our car, and listened to the muffled beat
> of the water drum and the tight-throated singing. No two more excited
> anthropologists ever sat listening to strange music. We wanted to get
> into the lodge. No one seemed to have the authority to let us in, or
> tell us whom to ask. George Spindler looked for the entrance, but none
> was visible. Finally, desperate to enter, he disregarded all rules of con-
> duct for field workers and slid through a narrow slit between two sections
> of canvas, tripped, and fell into the midst of action. (p. 277)

Luckily, their medicine man acquaintance was there and motioned for
the new arrival to come and sit by him. As the ceremony progressed,
however, a large Winnebago woman, "who had been glaring at George
Spindler, swung her (medicine) bag directly at him, hunched over it,
and danced by, shooting him with it several times. . . . At intermission
George left, feeling that he had been too forward, as indeed he had,
and that his absence might be appreciated more than his presence"
(p. 277).

As it turned out, George Spindler later became ill and was willing
to assert that his illness was due to the incident and, thus, that he
was in need of help. This became a basis for further entrance and acceptance by the people they were attempting to study.

An entry nearly fatal to the planned project is related by Whitten (1970) of his encounter with Nova Scotians. Following the advice of knowledgeable persons, Whitten decided to phone an official to introduce himself and his intentions. At which point, "I was told, politely, but firmly, that the people of the rural Dartmouth region had had enough of outsiders who insulted and hurt them under the guise of research, that the people of the region were as human as I and that I might turn my attention to other communities in the province" (p. 371).

Whitten later found out that this rather abrupt response was due in part to two misinterpretations arising from the lack of knowledge of the insiders' perspective. Thus, in this type of research, you frequently are faced with a rather difficult problem. Entry may depend on knowledge of the very thing entry is designed to uncover. In the initial stages it is likely that the information may not be totally candid and, in many cases, as reported by Hannerz (1969) and Dentan (1970), intentionally misleading.

Referring to his work with the Semai, Robert Dentan notes,

> They distrust outsiders (*mai*) so much that they use a special slang to conceal what they are talking about in the presence of an outsider who is familiar enough with them to have picked up a smattering of their language. They feel that most outsiders regard them as stupid savages, and they play "stupid savage" for an outsider, thus at one fell swoop giving the visitor what they think he expects, amusing themselves and each other, and exploiting his stereotype of them in order to avoid cooperating with him. (p. 92)

Discovery of a folk system is thus often viewed as an imposition, sometimes threatening and frequently as an attempt to turn a community into a zoo for observation. This is not to say that these are the most usual responses, or even likely, but they are possible. This being the case, when planning field work of this sort, you should be sensitive to the implications of these perceptions. This sensitizing may require a good deal of background research on the focus of the planned study. Failing this—and there may be little or no background material available—the only thing you can do is simply jump in and sink or swim. In the process of jumping, it is good advice to take a genuinely interested stance, a stance reflecting non-condescension, a stance reflecting a willingness to take on the role of the learner.

We find repeatedly in the reports of those returned from the field that their experiences run parallel to the early socialization of a child. It is a matter of reorientation, sometimes rather dramatic, sometimes only slight, sometimes a matter of hours, sometimes weeks or months, but always a time of transition. The researcher who is able to progress beyond this initial transitional stage is the researcher who is able to establish a degree of natural trust, respect, and understanding. This is often no easy task. This difficulty makes it no less important. On the other hand, research, on occasion, is welcomed by the insiders as part of their attempt and desire to "get their story out." On such occasions the problems of entry are greatly reduced.

The Solicited Entry

In his recount of the early days of studying the "Doomsday Cult," Lofland (1966) reports the enthusiastic response his planned investigation received.

> Lee already knew me as a "sociologist interested in social and religious movements." We had discussed other movements on several occasions, and at her request I had even loaned her monographs on several of them. Thus it was not difficult to say that I had become interested in studying her group. I was surprised (then, but not later) to find her not only receptive, but enthusiastic about the project. In fact she cast me in the role of chronicler of the beginning of the New Age in America. Although she kept brief notes in a diary, she felt the need of a more detailed account of what happened in the early last days. People in the New Age would want to know what things had been like in these times. (p. 272)

In similar fashion, Seth Searcy and I received initial support in a study of several trial courts. In an early conversation, a supporting judge indicated his interest by noting, "The thing you folk can serve us best is in how efficiently we bring them (the cases) on. If you folk have any interest in this, this study can be of great value to us and I would hope of some reward to you. . . . We have suffered from taking in our own washing, judging ourselves. . . . You come to the courthouse and your case is there and nothing happens, no judge is available, the court reporter is not available or all of the many reasons that cause delay in the judiciary crop up. People don't holler about it because they are, I suppose, overly kind to us and no one knows whether we need more courts. No one seems emboldened really to find out. . . . I'm not suggesting that the criticism be unfriendly. I am suggesting to you that it ought to be objective, it ought to be critical, it ought to be intelligent, it ought to be responsible, but it ought to be *coming.*"

Even with initial support, however, you must be careful to realize that early stages of most relationships, and especially those that involve potentially critical observation, involve a degree of cautious skepticism. Such became apparent in the study of the trial courts in an early meeting with the judges in which displeasure was expressed at an article in a local newspaper indicating that a study was to take place and that its purpose was to "scrutinize" the courts. For election- and image-conscious judges, bad publicity is nothing to toy with, and, thus, there was some concern that such publicity not occur in the future.

What we find, then, is that, when you enter the field with an eye on discovering the insider's perspective, you are faced with a time of transition. It is a time when your place in the world of the insider is being established. Much of the later success or failure of the study depends on these early events. Establishing a continuing relationship is problematic since, as an observer, you are neither totally in nor out. You are participating but still observing. As the title of a recent book on the topic indicates, you are a "marginal native" (Freilich, 1970).

On Being In and Out

How well you do in translating the world of the insider depends in part on the position you occupy in the social network of the setting being studied. We will look first at the overall marginality that characterizes the researcher's position, then turn to some strains that marginality may engender, and, finally, look at consequences of differential access to various segments of the network.

Growing out of a series of seminars held by Everett Hughes at the University of Chicago, Junker (1960) and Gold (1958) have presented a characterization of the field workers' role consistent with our previous discussion of gaining access to the "secrets" of the community. Marginality can be characterized by the degree to which you have access to the inner life of the community and to the individuals in that community.

For analytic purposes, Junker has divided this information into the categories of "public"—"What everybody knows and can talk about"; "confidential," or statements that, if used in the report, are not to be attributed to the source; "secret," which is information known to members of the in-group "who avoid letting it be known to any outsider, since its exclusive possession is important to the in-group's solidarity and continued existence"; and "private," or information that is personal to an individual.

It is the degree of access to these various types of information that partially defines the role you are likely to take. These roles, in turn, have been arranged along a continuum by Junker (1960) with the complete participant at one end, where "the field worker is or becomes a complete member of an in-group, thus sharing secret information guarded from outsiders," and the complete observer at the other, which Junker feels is "more imaginary than real or possible, although . . . it may be approximated in a laboratory or simulated in reflection" (38). Between these extremes are the roles of the participant-as-observer and the observer-as-participant.

Whatever the labels, as research progresses, successful projects find an increasing access to the inner life of the setting being studied. As you become part of the scene, as friendships and trust build up, more detailed and intimate information becomes available. Frequently the realization that one is now "in" is marked by some specific event. This may entail being asked to play in a baseball game, as was the case with Whyte (1955). It may be participating in a dance, which was the case with Powdermaker (1966). It may involve the assignment to a clan, such as that reported by Hart (1970). It may be signaled by an invitation to attend a planning session of a prison-guard union meeting, which was the case in our study of pretrial detention (Olson, 1974).

Each of these events signaled an acceptance into inner circles and yet, in each instance, a degree of distance remained. It is a rare event when the entrance is total. There most frequently remain various niches in the relationship that continue to mark the distinction between the researcher and the setting. Again, single events may symbolize or accentuate the remaining marginality.

After a period of restlessness in watching her friend Pulong become very sick and give birth to a dead baby, Powdermaker (1966) reports:

> I sat around the bed with the women, went back to my house, wrote up everything, wandered back to Pulong's bed again. The fact that I was getting good data did not take away restlessness. I felt all wrong during this crisis: outside it, though emotionally involved. Living in a culture not my own suddenly seemed unnatural. It was as if the group had withdrawn into itself, and I was left outside. Pulong recovered; the normal daily life was resumed and I lost this feeling. But during Pulong's illness and in similar emergencies, I knew that no matter how intimate and friendly I was with the natives, I was never truly a part of their lives. (p. 116)

Less dramatic, though nonetheless convincing, evidence that the researcher remains separate from the setting is available from the work of Whyte (1955) as he relates his experience of cutting loose with a string of obscenities and profanities, whereupon Doc shook his head and said, "Bill, you're not supposed to talk like that. That doesn't sound like you" (p. 304).

Indicators of continued marginality also may be directly connected with access to community secrets when it becomes apparent that persons are being less than candid. The experience of Jeremy Boissevain (1970) and his study of a village in Malta is instructive in this regard.

> After five months in Farrug, I assumed that the villagers accepted me well enough to give information freely on the delicate matter of political and band club rivalry. In retrospect it was too short a time to assume that sort of confidence. I was still an outsider peering in

at the private life of the village. There was still much that people did not care for me to learn. This was especially marked in regard to factional conflicts, which marred the image of village unity that they like to project to outsiders. (p. 75)

What emerges, then, from self-reports of workers in the field, is that there always remains a certain distance separating the field worker from the setting of research. Such a situation is not totally without benefit when it comes to later stages of analysis and a disconnected look at what has been gathered. It is in the ability to live close to people as they go about their lives and at the same time maintain a certain distance that a balance between being a participant and an observer is maintained. While noting that this balanced marginality may be of some use in later "objective" presentations, it should not be missed that, while in the setting, there are likely to be a series of strains emerging from being simultaneously in and out.

Implications of Marginality

This status of marginality has a number of implications that can be divided into *problems of integration, ethical issues,* and problems associated with *differential access.*

As you become integrated into the social setting, you will find yourself frequently judged by the standards of the community and expected to act like any "civilized" (read properly oriented) human being. This may mean that you will be asked to take sides, to help solve problems, to settle disputes, to participate in activities that you might otherwise shy away from. At the same time, as an observer, you may be concerned with minimizing the influence of your presence. By interjecting yourself into the situation, you may be carrying it in directions in which it would not otherwise go. To a certain extent some impact from your presence will be inevitable, but you may want to minimize this influence.

Thus, the requirements of participation often are at odds with the requirements of observation. One calls for detachment, the other for involvement. This tension between participation and observation is easily transformed into ethical dilemmas. Up to this point we have drawn on accounts of researchers who have left the "field." Equally important are accounts of the observed. For perhaps obvious reasons, these reactions to research by the observed are less available than accounts from the observer. Vine Deloria (1969) provides a useful exception to this. Pointing to the ethical problems generated from a totally observing stance, Deloria notes,

> Into each life, it is said, some rain must fall. . . . But Indians have been cursed above all other people in history. Indians have anthropologists. . . . They (anthropologists) are the most prominent members

of the scholarly community that infests the land of the free, and in
the summer time, the homes of the braves. . . . An anthropologist comes
out to Indian reservations to make *OBSERVATIONS*. During the winter
these observations will become books by which future anthropologists
will be trained, so that they can come out to reservations years from
now and verify the observations they have studied. . . . Thus go the
anthropological wars, testing whether this school or that school can
endure longest. And the battlefields, unfortunately, are the lives of Indian
people. . . . The fundamental thesis of the anthropologist is that people
are then considered objects for experimentation, for manipulation, and
for eventual extinction. The anthropologist thus furnishes the justification
for treating Indian people like so many chessmen available for anyone
to play with. (p. 78–81)

Deloria goes on to spell out how he feels the work of anthropologists,
governed as it is by self-interest, has reached erroneous and frequently
detrimental depictions of the contemporary American Indian.[2] To correct
this, Deloria suggests a less detached stance, one more sensitive to the
immediate and longer range needs of the various Indian communities.
A similar view is spelled out by Etkowitz and Schaflander (1968) in
conjunction with the concerns of sociologists. We will pursue these
"Knowledge for what?" questions in the final chapter. For now, we
note that involvement in the setting of study is frequently inviting and
perhaps compelling. This is particularly the case when the issues of
moral commitment and action are clearly drawn.

However, in some situations, factions are present and one's gain is
another's loss. Total involvement or commitment to one may mean total
alienation from another. In such situations the "right" thing to do in
terms of involvement is hazier. In addition, by participating to the fullest,
the researcher may find that the antagonistic factions have closed off
access and thus important information may be lost. The final picture
arrived at will be distorted to a greater extent than it would be otherwise
due to omission of alternative perspectives. To some extent such omissions are inevitable, but this is not to say that you should not attempt
to minimize their biasing influence.

Along these lines, one problem involvement may create is that of
differential access. There is flexibility in a degree of marginality that
allows you to move easily from one faction to another. To the extent
you become identified and involved with one segment of the social network is the extent to which others are closed off. This differential access

---

[2] For evidence that this exploitation is not altogether imagined, see Eggan (1954),
who notes: "While there are a few 'primitives' in our own backyard, there are the
new frontiers of Africa, India, Southeast Asia, Indonesia, and Melanesia to exploit.
Here is still a complete range in terms of cultural complexity and degree of culture
contact. Africa alone is a much more challenging 'laboratory' in many respects than
is the American Indian. And for those who like their cultures untouched there is
the interior of New Guinea" (p. 756).

need not emerge from a reasoned decision to become involved in one set of interests and activities rather than another. It may simply be due to ignorance. As Freilich (1970) reports, "Many of my initial problems with some members of the community stemmed from my habit of loafing at the post office (considered a lower-class hangout), and from my friendship with Rapas. Because of his constant fights with his brothers and his mother, Rapas was generally avoided by the prestigious Indians of Anamat. He was also disliked by most of the Negro peasants" (p. 22).

It is thus a good idea to keep an early eye out for problems developing in this regard. It may be necessary to break off initial contacts in order to avoid early identification with some faction or interest group. It may be necessary to remain sensitive to the implications of involvement as the project continues to unfold. As your research develops you are likely to find certain lines of communication that are more open than others and thus more likely to be used. In such a situation you are likely to develop certain friendship patterns that eventually will influence the available information. By maintaining a degree of marginal involvement, movement from one faction to another will be more easily accomplished.

SUMMARY

What have we seen? We have seen that gaining access to an otherwise foreign setting often means overcoming the problem of secrecy, the spy problem. This may be too dramatic a phrase for the situation, but the problems of entrance, of building trust and establishing a willingness to relate the less superficial aspects of a setting are those that recur again and again. In moving toward the "middle" of a setting, it is wise to keep close tabs on what your developing network of interaction implies for an overall grasp of the setting. Are there important segments that are closed off? Also, moving toward the middle of the setting increasingly means that ethical and interpersonal dilemmas are likely to arise. The importance of this is not to be minimized. In an attempt to observe, there is the tendency to objectify, to treat those being observed as objects. This may be acceptable behavior when experimenting with new strains of wheat, but rarely is it advisable in an interpersonal relationship.

Uncovering the folk system is an attempt to gain insight into the insider's perspective. In the process we find a frequent bind between the requirements of participation and the requirements of observation. This becomes evident in ethical dilemmas and the problem of differential access. The marginality implied in the bind, however, is not totally counterproductive. With marginality comes a certain flexibility. It is in the balance of living close to a setting and yet maintaining enough

distance to minimize a biased perspective that we gain understanding
that eludes the total insider and the total outsider.

In part, the balance is maintained by the reciprocal actions and attitudes of the researcher and those in the setting; in part, it depends
on technique. Participation and analysis may be separated in space and
time. Certain data-gathering techniques can be utilized that allow for
detection of bias, if not its elimination. It is to these techniques that
we turn in the next chapter.

KEY ISSUES

1. What is a basic dilemma confronting one who wants to analyze the insider's perspective or to construct a model of a particular setting?
2. Considering the orderly aspect of uncovering the folk system, discuss
   the various stages. In what sense are they progressive?
3. Briefly discuss the problems and potential resolutions you can expect
   to encounter as you move from one stage to the next.
4. Discuss the consequences of the marginality that characterizes the field
   worker's role.

REFERENCES

Becker, Howard S.
    1958   "Problems of Inference and Proof in Participant Observation."
           American Sociological Review, vol. 23, pp. 652–60.

Becker, Howard S.; Geer, Blanche; Hughes, Everett; and Strauss, Anselm
    1961   *Boys in White.* Chicago: University of Chicago Press.

Becker, Howard S.
    1963   *Outsiders: Studies in the Sociology of Deviance.* New York: Free
           Press.

Blumberg, Abraham
    1966   "The Practice of Law as a Confidence Game: Organizational Coop-
           tation of a Profession." *Law and Society Review,* vol. 1, pp. 15–39.

Boissevain, Jeremy
    1970   "Fieldwork in Malta." In George D. Spindler (ed.), *Being an
           Anthropologist: Fieldwork in Eleven Cultures.* New York: Holt,
           Rinehart and Winston Inc.

Conklin, Harold C.
    1962   "Lexicographical Treatment of Folk Taxonomies." In F. W. House-
           holder and S. Saporta (eds.), *Problems in Lexicography.* Indiana
           University Research Center in Anthropology, Folklore and Lin-
           guistic Publication 21, pp. 119–41.

Coser, Rose Laub
    1961   "Insulation from Observability and Types of Social Conformity."
           American Sociological Review, vol. 26, pp. 28–39.

Deloria, Vine
  1969   *Custer Died for Your Sins: An Indian Manifesto.* London: Macmillan Co.
Dentan, Robert K.
  1970   "Living and Working with the Semai." In George D. Spindler (ed.), *Being an Anthropologist: Fieldwork in Eleven Cultures.* New York: Holt, Rinehart and Winston Inc.
Diesing, Paul
  1971   *Patterns of Discovery in the Social Sciences.* Chicago: Aldine.
Eggan, Fred
  1954   "Social Anthropology and the Method of Controlled Comparison." *American Anthropologist,* vol. 56, pp. 743–63.
Etkowitz, Henry, and Schaflander, Gerald M.
  1968   "A Manifesto for Sociologists: Institution Formation—A New Sociology." *Social Problems,* vol. 15, pp. 399–408.
Feld, M. D.
  1959   "Information and Authority: The Structure of Military Organization." *American Sociological Review,* vol. 24, pp. 15–22.
Frankl, Viktor
  1959   *Man's Search for Meaning.* New York: Washington Square Press.
Freilich, Morris (ed.)
  1970   *Marginal Natives: Anthropologists at Work.* New York: Harper and Row.
Gold, Raymond L.
  1958   "Roles in Sociological Field Observations." *Social Forces,* vol. 36, pp. 217–23.
Goodenough, Ward H.
  1956   "Componential Analysis and the Study of Meaning." *Language,* vol. 32, pp. 195–216.
Gouldner, Alvin
  1959   "Organizational Analysis." In Robert K. Merton et al. (eds.), *Sociology Today.* New York: Basic Books Inc.
Hannerz, Ulf
  1969   *Soulside, Soulside: Inquiries into Ghetto Culture and Community.* New York: Columbia University Press.
Hart, C. W. M.
  1970   "Fieldwork among the Tiwi." In George D. Spindler (ed.), *Being an Anthropologist: Fieldwork in Eleven Cultures.* New York: Holt, Rinehart and Winston Inc.
Irwin, John
  1970   *The Felon.* Englewood Cliffs, N.J.: Prentice Hall Inc.
Junker, B. H.
  1960   *Fieldwork: An Introduction to the Social Sciences.* Chicago: University of Chicago Press.

Lofland, John
 1966 *Doomsday Cult: A Study of Conversion, Proselytization, and Maintenance of Faith.* Englewood Cliffs, N.J.: Prentice-Hall Inc.

Lounsbury, F. G.
 1956 "A Semantic Analysis of the Pawnee Kinship Usage." *Language,* vol. 32, 158–94.

McCleery, Richard
 1960 "Communications Patterns as Bases of Systems of Authority and Power." In Richard A. Cloward et al., *Theoretical Studies in Social Organization of the Prison.* New York: Social Science Research Council.

Merton, Robert K.
 1952 "Bureaucratic Structure and Personality." In Merton et al. (eds.), *Reader in Bureaucracy.* Glencoe, Ill.: Free Press.

Olson, Sheldon R.
 1974 "Minutes in Court, Weeks in Jail: A Study of Pretrial Detention." New York: MSS Modular Publications, Inc., Module 22.

Powdermaker, Hortense
 1966 *Stranger and Friend: The Way of an Anthropologist.* New York: W. W. Norton and Company, Inc.

Spindler, George, and Spindler, Louise
 1970 "Field work among the Menomini." In *Being an Anthropologist: Fieldwork in Eleven Cultures.* New York: Holt, Rinehart and Winston Inc.

Spradley, James P.
 1970 *You Owe Yourself a Drunk: An Ethnography of Urban Nomads.* Boston: Little Brown.

Suttles, Gerald D.
 1972 *The Social Construction of Communities.* Chicago: University of Chicago Press.

Wallace, Samuel E.
 1965 *Skid Row as a Way of Life.* Totowa, N.J.: The Bedminister Press.

Whitten, Norman E., Jr.
 1970 "Network Analysis and Processes of Adaptation Among Ecuadorian and Nova Scotian Negroes." In Morris Freilich (ed.), *Marginal Natives: Anthropologists at Work.* New York: Harper and Row.

Whyte, William Foote
 1955 *Street Corner Society: The Social Structure of an Italian Slum.* Chicago: University of Chicago Press.

Contents

Chapter 3

Uncovering the Folk System: The Techniques

There are two bread-and-butter techniques employed when searching out the boundaries and content of the folk system—interviewing and observation. There are, of course, variations on these procedures providing for adaptation to particular settings and problems. In part, the variation in strategy depends on the stage of your research, on how far along you are. It is frequently a matter of moving from an *early open-endedness* to a *midway focusing-in* to a *final refined probing*. We will first look at these shifting postures and, then, within these postures, the techniques employed.

SHIFTING POSTURES: SEMI-ORIENTED TO REFINED PROBING

Because books and articles are relatively polished and organized documents, it frequently is surprising to find research involving a time of wandering, a time of uncertainty as to where the findings were leading, a time when the study was guided to the next step by findings just collected. For example, Whyte (1955), in his study *Street Corner Society*, notes that it was after 18 months in the field that he finally realized where his study was going. In like fashion, if you read the findings of *Boys in White* before reading the chapter on the design of the study, you might be surprised to find the authors stating, "In one sense, our study had no design. That is, we had no well-worked-out set of hypotheses to be tested, no data-gathering instruments purposely designed to secure information relevant to these hypotheses, no set of analytic procedures specified in advance. Insofar as the term 'design' implies these features of elaborate prior planning, our study had none" (Becker et al., 1961, p. 17). You may indeed find, as Radcliff-Brown (1922) reports, that your preselected design is more a hinderance than a help.

Instead of a predetermined sampling and conceptual frame, the events and concepts to be developed and sought out emerge as the insider's perspective unfolds. This strategy is quite different from that utilized when the primary orientation is to test a theory. To test a theory, concepts are defined beforehand and translated into specific operations (e.g., items on a questionnaire or experimental manipulations). Events or persons are selected in a way to ensure representativeness of a predetermined population. This is not to say that the "hang loose" style of research allows a helter-skelter attitude. It is only to say that the direction of the study emerges as information is collected.

It is also not to say that you enter a project totally devoid of all orienting preconceptions and predispositions. Rare, if not nonexistent, is the person who enters a situation with such a blank slate. In *Boys in White,* for example, the authors proceeded from a series of assumptions embedded in symbolic interaction theory and paid particular attention to phenomena producing group conflict and tension. Whatever your predispositions and preconceptions, they most assuredly influence the direction and shape of the project. The early stages, then, involve a posture of semi-orientation. You have an operating framework but remain flexible in your design. With this posture of semi-orientation you are able to more readily accommodate new-found information and adjust plans accordingly.

As these adjustments occur and the shape of the findings emerges, you are likely to find yourself focusing on more limited and more specifically defined aspects of the setting. Such specification may come after analytic flashes, as was the case with Whyte (p. 328) and his recognition of the three-way connection between group position, performance, and mental health. It may be a more gradual evolution, with prolonged though sometimes wandering thought and periodic writing, which seems to have been the case with Powdermaker (p. 96) and her study in Lesu. It may entail a rather systematic search for progressively refined definitions, as is the case in Lindesmith's study of opiate addiction (1947) and Cressey's study of embezzlement (1953). Whatever the procedure, as the project proceeds into the later stages, you frequently find yourself bringing the ends together, honing in on specific aspects of the broader picture.

It is at this point that the project takes on a less open-ended and more structured nature, similar in many ways to the structure of the hypothesis-testing procedures to be discussed in the second half of this book. Indeed, in the latter stages that is precisely what you may be doing—checking on hypotheses concerning the nature of attitudes and actions, the structure and content of life in the setting you have chosen.

For example, in our study of pretrial detention (Olson, 1974) it was suggested that a high degree of ambiguity was the focal concern out of which emerged the perspective of persons detained prior to trial. It was hypothesized from conversations and observations that the degree of tension, both personal and collective, flowed primarily from the lack of communication links with the outside and the resulting uncertainty flowing from the progress and outcome of the case. To pursue this issue we devised a structured interview format, a portion of which is reproduced in Figure 3.1.

FIGURE 3.1
Portion of Interview Schedule Used in Latter Stages of Pretrial Detention Study

Do you feel more tense in jail than you did while on the streets?

How? What is the source of most tension in jail?

How much do each of the following affect you in terms of the amount of tension or problems they produce?

| | Very great deal | | | | | | | | | Hardly any at all |

A. Uncertainty about your case

   10 9 8 7 6 5 4 3 2 1 0

B. Lack of communication with outside friends or family

C. Access to drugs

(If answer is "Hardly any at all," ask: Were you ever addicted to drugs?)

D. Action or attitudes of fellow inmates

E. Actions or attitudes of guards

F. Physical conditions of jail

G. Loss of job

H. Services received from lawyer

I. Possibility of family trouble

With responses to these questions it was possible to assess the relative importance of isolation and uncertainty, compared with such other factors as the actions and attitudes of fellow inmates and guards, the physical condition of the jail, and the loss of a job. As it turned out, these interview schedules provided useful confirmation and refinement of our earlier observations and more loose-knit conversations.

In moving from a posture of semi-orientation to one of refined probing, it is advisable to go through a time of intermediate stock-taking. That is, it is advisable to periodically sit down and try to gather your many observations, conversations, and interviews; to cut out false leads and speculations; and to see where the information is heading. In this way you can more readily recognize emerging issues and blind alleys before it is too late. You may find, in a way similar to Boissevain (1970) and others, that such stock-taking forces you to rethink your problem and, in addition, provides a useful document from which you can get initial feedback from colleagues.

What we find, then, when we note the shifting postures of field work, is a close connection between observation and analysis. We find a process that has been labeled "theoretical sampling" by Glaser and Strauss (1967).

> Theoretical sampling is the process of data collection for generating theory whereby the analyst jointly collects, codes, and analyzes his data and decides what data to collect next and where to find them, in order to develop his theory as it emerges. This process of data collection is *controlled* by the emerging theory. . . . The initial decisions for theoretical collection of data are based only on a general sociological perspective and on a general subject or problem area. . . . The initial decisions are not based on a preconceived theoretical framework. (p. 45)

Given these shifting orientations, what of the mechanics? What should be recorded? How and when should it be recorded? How should it be organized once recorded? What should be included in the interviews? How structured or unstructured? How do you check on the validity of your observations and interviews? These are the questions addressed in the following.

FIELD OBSERVATIONS

Taking It Down

Once you have gained access to a setting, questions will arise. What and when should I record? Should I use a tape recorder, or perhaps videotape? Should I rely more heavily on memory? Should I take a note pad? Can I find time to jot down key words and phrases that will help me recall events more fully when I get away from the activity? How long should I wait before making the more detailed recordings? Most of these questions are not ones to be answered in a textbook. By and large they will depend on the setting being observed.

When reading accounts of field studies, we find persons employing various combinations of recording strategies with differential degrees of success. It will depend. You may find yourself in a situation similar to that of Norbeck (1970), where it is convenient to excuse yourself to go to the bathroom (to jot down notes)—willing to run the risk that others will think you have some sort of kidney problem.

You may find yourself in a situation similar to that of Powdermaker (1966) and her observations of mortuary rites, where overt notetaking is not only tolerated but also generates a degree of appreciation. On the other hand, pad and pencil may pose an immediate threat to those being observed (Blau 1964). These are things that are hard to anticipate. If you engage in an inappropriate strategy you will, in all likelihood, be rapidly informed. Perhaps the only thing to do in preparation is to be sensitive to the potential impact of your actions. Whatever your decision you must get the information down. It is amazing how things you "will never forget" somehow slip away. It is also evident that, as time passes, details are lost. From most accounts of field workers it appears that it is relatively safe to "sleep on it" if you write up a detailed account upon waking. If days pass, the amount of material lost seems to increase geometrically. Once you begin to write up your detailed notes, at least as much time must be spent on developing observations in some permanent fashion as was spent in the observation itself.

Example. The process of "getting it down" can be roughly divided into two segments—jotted notes and full field notes. If you have never engaged in this practice, an example may give you a feel for what is involved. The following are unedited jotted and full notes (except that names have been deleted and handwriting has been changed to print in the jotted notes). The jotted notes were recorded while sitting in a car, immediately after a "shift" of observation. The full notes were typed out, using the jotted notes as a guide, within a 24-hour period after the observations.

Jotted Notes:

Initial part in warden's office

_____ *quiet thinker somewhat of a dreamer*

Commissioner _____ 2 years still working on it.

Initial impression with haircut

bondsman needed

used to be one yr. now more like 6 mos.

Drunk hang around

single inmate long hair—lost when he gets upstairs

most time spent handing out razors

some kidding between kids and oldies—some not so funny.

_____ *walking around*
lot of card playing
separation——
start out tough and then ease up rather than vice versa
can't get too friendly w/inmates. Some do, it's bad. Firm but
cordial.
Throw guard right in w/o training.
Girls outside windows calling inside.
Hot in dayroom _____
water is shut off some disturbance.
20 day sentence rather than 20 and $20.
going to school during day, guard at night. Law enforcement.
Summer help.
Lock-up at night.
Let them stay a little past time to see movie. No problem.
Differential treatment, mainly by age, but might also
be by disposition, e.g. —— going through drawers.
"Have to know how far you can push a guy. Some older guards
very good at psychology—e.g. _____ *and* _____.
Hope I could be as good as they are some day. They have
worked here a long time and not too much gets by them."
Clean-up is something else. Mop dirty floors w/dirty
water and dirty mop.
Sat down w/_____ after. Said he didn't think would work
because they would con students. Some better off in
jail. Shouldn't mix. Sep. facility for drunks, garden
good idea.
New facility would improve things.
Kids thrown in w/other ought to bring kids through. Son
learns lesson. Release non-support and traffics.
_____ *says they do that to get sent to other places.*
Separation by races. Don't speak same language
Also blues and browns. Shows kid who sliced wrists.—
Some exaggeration of attacks _____
Opened one side of block to get more room.

Full Field Notes:

June 15   West Wing 4:00–12:00 P.M.
    Arrived about 4:00 Warden's office. Commissioner was with Warden talking about the construction of the jail in East Haven. He is still holding out for having it constructed in 2 to 2½ years. Warden would definitely be in favor of such progress but thinks it will be more like five years.

From Warden's office went out to the control room and talked with _____. *Just for a short time. Joked around about my not being there on the hot and humid Friday and waiting for the coolness of this Monday. Seemed to be a little more hesitant in conversation than before. Might have been because I came with the Warden both times. . . . .*

Warden is a little uptight about visit from Mrs. _____. *Did not know that we had been in contact but brought her up in the course of the conversation as a woman who called up indicating she wanted to talk to him about the narcotics program that they did or did not have at the jail. When she arrived she started right off about how she had heard the health conditions in general and the services provided by the Dr. in particular were abominable. Warden made point that sure Doc was tough, but you had to be (I'm not sure you have to be as "tough" as this doctor is) or the inmates would run all over you. In addition the Dr. with all his faults was perhaps the most regular and consistent in his treatment of the prisoners of any doctor in the system. Warden indicated* _____ *seemed to be on a witch hunt. (At this point I think we should definitely stay disconnected from their project.)*

Went down to the AP room. When I entered the guard (one I have not met before) wondered where my paper and pencil were. Apparently _____ *had been talking about the Yale people doing the study while I was on my way down. First wanted to know if I wanted to talk to the inmates. . . . . You want to talk to us. . . . . No I'm just here to get acquainted with the operation so as to better understand what is going on and help decide where law students might be most useful. Talked for about ten minutes about what we have in mind. Seemed to accept it but was still a little wary about (I think) people in general who come in to find out things. Later in the evening was somewhat surprised to see that I was still around at 11:30. (This I think shows as well as anything the value of the researcher or whoever spending the entire workday at any given session. You become somewhat more than a temporary fixture, in the time perspective of the workday, and the informal conversation that often develops in the lull periods is invaluable.) (Guard) . . . . as much as anything a bondsman was needed, i.e., should be readily available for these inmates. Either that or the bond should be lowered. A lot of inmates should not be in here at all. This point was demonstrated a little later when a boy with long hair came in by himself (with guards of course). Asked if he wanted to cut his hair . . . . yes . . . . emptied pockets (as I remember had small New Testament, handkerchief, a little small change, 35¢ or so, and that's it . . . .) first time in . . . . very unsure of himself . . . . walked over, took off clothes . . . . went into shower . . . . just about scalded himself with the hot water . . . . came back out . . . . put on the white jumper . . . . not his underwear socks or shoes . . . . apparently thought they were to be confiscated . . . . told that he could hang on to his underwear . . . . asked if he could keep his shoes too . . . . yes . . . . you'd also better hang onto your socks . . . . he picked up another inmate's socks by mistake . . . . set them down in a hurry when he found out what he had done . . . . apparently afraid the inmate would think that he was trying to steal them. Picked up his shoes put socks inside, wrapped his underwear up in his bed sheets . . . . told that he had better hold on tight to his sheets cause they were the only ones he would get . . . . walked around somewhat in a daze, finally asked where he should go . . . . told to go into the cage. . . . . (One wonders how this kid ever got plugged into what he was about to experience). . . . . Saw him after coming back from dinner . . . . apparently had just come up from the AP Room and was walking down the corridor along the West wing block. . . . . Still looked very lost and very out of place. . . . . Went into the barber's shop. . . . . _____ said watch this . . . . the before and the after . . . . he won't look like the same kid when he comes out . . . . saw him about an hour later. In one sense he did look different . . . . he looked much younger and much more vulnerable . . . . but in another he looked the same lonely, bewildered individual. . . . . Walked around the day room, where no one said anything and barely looked at him. . . . . Apparently he was looking for someone he might know . . . . everyone playing cards, looking at TV, shaving, standing by windows breathing, walking around or talking in groups. . . . . Finally came up to the guards desk . . . . didn't say anything but had that "what do I do next look." The guard took the cue and told him that if he wanted to he could go to his cell and directed him to its location. On the right side of the cell block first tier. . . . . Inmate appeared relieved that he could get out of the day room and headed immediately for his cell. Didn't come out for the rest of the night.*

The day room at night is pretty much like it is during the day. Much smoke . . . . about 200 inmates in room, hot and humid even though it was fairly cool outside, windows were open and the fans were on. . . . . That much body heat is enough to heat up any room that size. . . . . Most of the guards time at the desk was spent handing out razors and taking down inmate numbers then crossing them off when they brought the razor back . . . . several inmates young and old black and white, were asked to go back and clean out the razors. . . . . The evenness of applying standards was not apparent however in all areas of activity. . . . . Older inmates were allowed greater freedom around desk. . . . . _____, mentioned previously, started looking through the drawers of the desk for something, matches I think. . . . . Guard says. . . . . Go ahead and look you won't find anything . . . . (Same practice seemed to hold for most inmates say above the age of 50 both sentenced and unsentenced.) . . . . . However, when younger inmates especially _____ would even approach the desk they were asked to move so the guard could see or . . . . . "Get off the desk". . . . . One rather short black man (about 40 yrs) came up and asked about his sentence and wondered

why his name wasn't up on the court list for the next day. Guard said he would check out in front which he did. . . . . Your sentence is 20 days plus $20 you will probably serve 17 for the 20 days, and 4 for the $20. That makes a total of 21 . . . . had to explain this several times . . . . after the inmate left guard came up to me shaking his head and said . . . . man, some of these guys can't understand anything . . . . then proceeded to tell me what the problem was . . . . inmate came back after talking with some of his friends . . . . (all black, there is a definite split along racial lines in the day room. During the night blacks occupied the first front rows of the TV viewing area . . . . mixture the last rows. . . . . White young kids sitting along cabinets . . . . drunks along far wall talking to one another two "rovers" _____ and another I haven't seen before. . . . . Blacks and whites (in separate groups) playing cards on the floor and on the tables in middle of the room and along two side walls. . . . .) . . . . . Anyway, this inmate came back to the guard and insisted that he should have been out today and . . . . what's happening cause my name isn't up on the list again for tomor- row . . . . you'd better check again. . . . . The guard did and again tried to explain the situation to the inmate. . . . . When inmate left guard looked at me and shrugged his shoulders as if to say what do you do with a guy like that . . . . again the inmate is back . . . . look man I know I got 20 days or 20 dollars. . . . . Are you sure it was 20 or 20 and not 20 and 20. . . . . Yeah man I'm sure. . . . . Well I'll check once more but that's all. . . . . Called out in front and told them to check the record book and make sure this time. This they did and sure enough it was 20 or 20 and the inmate should have gone out today. . . . . Satisfied he had "Won" went back and told friends . . . . came back. . . . . Look man I'm the one who should be mad not you. . . . . It's my life that's being wasted in here not yours. . . . . (Guard had gotten mad or disgusted just before the last call). . . . . You guys fuck up in here and it's me who takes the rap. . . . . Guard smiled and tried to make the best of the situation in which he was obviously wrong. . . . .
_____ *(an older sentenced inmate) tries to get into cabinet. . . . . While he's in there young inmates try to shut him in. . . . . He came out and looked around as mean as he could look . . . . didn't say anything . . . . went back to his search . . . . again they tried to shut him in . . . . came out looked around again mad . . . . didn't say anything but walked off without finding what he was after. . . . . Another revolving door type was standing near the young inmates . . . . first tried to grab his shoestring . . . . next played like they were going to take his magazine out of his pocket. . . . . Told them to go to hell and walked off. . . . . One of the young inmates was one who tried to cut his wrists the night before (sgt_____ pointed him out earlier as one who tried to get sympathy so he could go to CVH. . . . .)*
A third revolving door type was sitting down by a young (maybe

22–23 yrs) black inmate . . . . (black inmate talking). . . . . Why
don't you go over there and sit with your friends . . . . what's the
matter with right here? There's plenty of room . . . . yeah but you
ought to be sitting over there. . . . . (About this time started getting
"flak" in the form of a toilet paper roll thrown from the next bench.)
R. D. stood up picked the roll up and threatened to throw it back . . . .
several times . . . . finally let fly . . . . missed the intended victim by
about 15 feet . . . . laughter about nice shot etc . . . . by the time
he went to sit down his place had somehow disappeared . . . . inmates
had spread out. . . . . Thus territory is maintained in the day room.
Guard told inmates to cut it out once.
_____ walking giving a lot of people bad time
. . . . stuck to white population (he is white) walked up to one guy
about same age (about 18–20) said come on . . . . stand up and I'll
break your nose . . . . inmate stood up "playful scuffle" for about 15
seconds. . . . . Most of the inmates just ignore him. . . . . Came up to
me started "question game" what do you do . . . . what do you mean
by that . . . . well what is that . . . . etc. . . . .
In earlier part of the evening _____ gave me a few lessions about
how to be a good guard . . . . . (Question . . . . About how long
would you say it takes for a new guard to get into the swing of things?
or something like that. . . . .) Well, the guard comes in cold . . . .
you know no previous training like on the police force. . . . . But
if you give me a man for about two months I can have him in pretty
good shape. . . . . The biggest problem with most new guys is that
they are too soft. . . . . You got to start out tough and then you can
slack off . . . . but if you start off nice like and always kidding around
then you ain't got a chance . . . . you notice that none of the guys
give me any trouble. . . . . I can walk anywhere in here and the only
guys that will come up are those that have a real problem. . . . .
That's cause I don't fool around with them. . . . . You got to keep
your distance or they will always be coming up to you. . . . . There
are a lot of guards in here who try to talk nice to the guys when
they want them to do something. . . . . Well that just doesn't work
most of the time. . . . . You got to talk their language. . . . . Some
of the administration have been down on us for using rough language
but man you got to if your going to get anything done. . . . . Instead
of saying would you please get to your cells . . . . in which case they
will give you a bad time . . . . you got to say get the fuck in
there. . . . . You talk any way else and it's too different from the
life outside. . . . . (In later conversation there appears to be a selective
use of language in this genre . . . . like he expressed sympathy for
persons who don't belong in jail and who don't know what is coming
off . . . . apparently meant young kids, and non-support cases. (Al-
though not entirely clear on this last category.) After you start out
tough then you can slack off a little but if you start off easy then
its a lot toughter to get hard. . . . . Some guys have done it though
and then they are tougher than I am. . . . . You know they started

out being nice and all and then some inmate takes them. After this happens they decide that this isn't the way to do things so they get real tough. . . . .

You take _____ now. (_____ is a student at New Haven College during the day, Law enforcement major, works and lives at the jail at other times. Is the man in the previous report that _____ and _____ were afraid of losing to go to guard school—thought he was a good man.) He's picked up real good? (At this point I had not met _____ and asked the sgt if he was the one studying to be a priest. . . . . Had heard earlier that this guy was real good with the inmates because he was willing to talk with the men. . . . . Many comments like . . . . . He'll know a lot more about the real world than he would learn at seminary. . . . . This experience will make him a lot better priest . . . . etc . . . . . I thought if this _____ was the student priest I had heard about the sgt was using an example which did not fit his previous description. . . . .) (Sgt) . . . . . No, that priest kid isn't here yet. . . . . I don't know if he's coming back or not this year. (They get some returning summer help.) But he was too soft on the inmates. . . . . (at least he isn't inconsistent). You got to be firm but cordial. . . . .

After staying in the day room for about hr and half, decided to go out and see what was going on in the cell block. Much cooler out there. Joking about couldn't take it anymore huh? . . . . . Started talking with _____ (young guard mentioned above). (First impression of this guard was during dinner when the guards were talking about their experiences with motorcycles. . . . . Some fantastic stories about how various crashes occurred . . . . and corresponding advice about how the disasters might have been avoided. . . . . _____ seemed to be the most competent, at least in the conversation, told of near miss last week with truck . . . . wouldn't have happened if I hadn't been in so much of hurry. . . . . Although he is young (22–24) more respect for him (in terms of listening without interruptions and number of degrading jokes than for other young guards. . . . .)

Asked me if I knew _____ . . . . . Said he had taken a class in constitutional law from him at New Haven College. . . . . In course of conversation came out he was majoring in Law Enforcement and interested in the area of corrections and so thought he would give this job a try. . . . . You learn a hell of a lot in a hell of a hurry in a place like this. . . . . Sometimes I'll be out with some guys and we'll start talking about jails and prisons and they'll tell me about stories they've heard about sexual attacks. . . . . Everyone knows that some of this goes on in a place like this . . . . you can't stop it all but most of the stories they tell are great exaggerations of the true picture . . . . regarding sexual "deviance" in jail. . . . . (When I first entered the cell block for the evening we walked past cell 5 West wing. . . . . Man in cell masturbating . . . . guard _____ didn't say anything to him . . . . as we were walking on down the block _____ (the above young guard) came up and

*was talking to guard about some other inmate and then asked
him . . . . did you see the man in cell five "beating his meat"? . . . . .
Yeah (It was not clear whether* _____ *had actually seen the man
or not) so what? . . . . (*_____*) Just thought I would ask . . . .
as we walked on into the day room sgt. says . . . . what do you
do? . . . . He's happy isn't he. . . . .*

    While talking to _____ *(the young guard above) water goes
off . . . . just before the 9:45 bell to return to cells, around 9:15.
Inmate comes and asks where the water is . . . . at this point* _____
*didn't know . . . . in a couple of minutes a couple of inmates (sen-
tenced) came up with pipe wrenches in their hands with one of the
guards who informed* _____ *that the water had been shut off so they
could fix one of the pipe's that had just broken. . . . . Some inconvenience especially at this time of the night when a lot of the inmates
were trying to shave, go to the bathroom, take showers, heat up their
coffee etc. . . . . Bell sounds to go in . . . . still no water. . . . .
One inmate starts hollering WATER . . . . WE WANT
WATER . . . . WATER . . . . WE WANT WATER. . . . . About
this time a lot of the other inmates were getting upset and started
to join in on the chant. . . . . With only three guards and 220 inmates
this was a little disconcerting. . . . . Then when the cresendo was
building there was a swish and all the faucets in the place started
working. . . . . They had all been turned on previously by the inmates. . . . . This quieted things down. . . . . On this particular night
the inmates were allowed to stay up past the closing hour 10:00 due
to a movie on TV (war story). This is not the usual procedure. . . . .
The previous night* _____ *indicated that they didn't make it the
usual practice but occasionally they made exceptions. . . . . One night
the inmates were watching some program and wanted to see the end
(was the Miss America pageant).* _____ *called out in front and
asked if the inmates could be allowed to stay up past the time . . . .
(indicated that he thought it would have been a good idea. . . . .)
Front office said no. . . . . So* _____ *walked over to the set and
was about to turn it off. . . . . (Inmate). . . . . Don't touch that
set. . . . .   "Well I turns around and Boom slammed the button
off . . . . turned around and said now who's man enough to come
up here and turn it back on. . . . . Well one man left then on-
other . . . . then another . . . . until the man who did the yelling
saw he was losing support so he went too. . . . . You've got to show
these men you're not afraid. . . . . If they detect one bit of hesitance
you're done for. . . . . Some guards get into a lot of trouble by hesitat-
ing and trying to reason with the inmates. . . . ." (At this point related
story reported earlier about the guard who was spat at . . . .)
then. . . . . now Me and* _____ *we get right in there cause, you
see, we feel we're as big and tough as any of these guys . . . . (and
they are). . . . . You like to work with a good man (determined by
his willingness to get into the middle of a fight or back you up if
in trouble) cause you know if anything happens they'll help you. . . . .
The other guys you have to carry the whole load. . . . .*

Back to this night . . . . allowed to stay up past time . . . . guards thought movie was to be over at 10:00. . . . . Was still going at 10:15 so they moved the remainder of the population back into the blocks before the movie was over. The procedure was rather interesting. . . . . When the 9:45 bell rang they (the guards) didn't tell the population that they could stay up. . . . . They just didn't say anything to the inmates who waited around the TV set until the last minute. . . . . Then let them stay up a little longer. . . . . The rationale being that if they would have announced it they would have had everyone up past the time. . . . . This way most of the day room was cleared out by shut down time. . . . . This is one of the occasions when there was a deviation from routine. . . . . Earlier in the evening was with _____ and were watching the men check out razors . . . . they were crowded around the desk in a haphazard manner. . . . . They shouldn't be like that. . . . . If we had an experienced man in here he would have them in a line. . . . . You've got to build up a routine and then all the men fall right into it and you don't have any trouble . . . .

While I was standing on second tier with _____ shortly before 10 . . . . men filing past . . . . an occasional hi how you doing . . . . most avoid eye contact. . . . . Inmate hollers. . . . . Hey look at the chicks out there. . . . . Hello honey how you doin' . . . . came down to the landing where we were standing grabbed another inmate and says . . . . look out there look at them chicks one brunette and one blond. . . . . No man you can't see them here the lights bother you (lights on outside used to light the side of the building during the night. . . .) come on down to this other window. . . . . See'm . . . . . Hey baby what's happenin'. . . . . Talked (or I should say yelled with them for about ten minutes). . . . . _____ said. . . . . They were here last night until finally we had to go out and tell them that if they didn't leave we would have them arrested. . . . . They had better watch it or they are going to get picked up. . . . . You know if you let something like that continue you get the men all worked up and then they are harder to control. . . . . (From what I could see the girls looked to be about 16–18 couldn't really tell though.)

Man comes by with bucket filled with soapy water, broom and mop . . . . walked by as if everything was normal.. . . . got up to the third tier and the guard down on the first tier called up to _____ and asked _____ what that guy was going to do with the pail. . . . . I don't know. . . . . Well we had better find out. He's not supposed to have that up there. . . . . _____ went up to inquire . . . . told that he was going to clean out his cell. . . . . At this time of night? yeah. . . . . What you going to do when you're done. . . . . Keep the stuff in my cell. . . . . _____ yells down to the other guard. . . . . He's going to clean his cell out sort of mumbles to me. These guys have all night to clean out their cells and they wait until the last minute. . . . . Well I guess that if he keeps it in his cell all night its O.K. . . . . . O.K. go on. . . . . (Man was black about 21–23.)

In conversation with _____ . . . . . *You got to know how far you can push a guy and when to let up. . . . . Some of the older guards like* _____ *and* _____ *are really good that way. . . . . You know they know how to handle a man when to get tough and when to let up. . . . . If you keep on a man too much he's likely to blow up. . . . . You've got to be able to walk a tight line. . . . . I hope I can be like them some day. . . . . Those guys have worked here a long time and not too much that goes on gets by them. . . . . I mean everything. . . . . Especially* _____. . . . .

(_____ *again*) *The clean up around here is something . . . . mop dirty floor with dirty water which is put on with dirty mop. . . . . It doesn't do a whole lot of good. . . . . Went down to the other end of the block to lock the men for the night . . . . couldn't get them closed. . . . . Locked by mechanical device consisting of a long lever attached to a gear-like device on the end of a long rod which runs the length of the block. . . . . Have trouble when one door is slightly ajar since it stops the long bar from closing. . . . . Had to walk down the block to see which one it was . . . . couldn't find anything wrong . . . . went back and tried again . . . . still wouldn't close. . . . . Finally found one that was slightly open . . . . shut it . . . . went back and locked them in. . . . . Then went along to make sure each door was closed . . . . done by pushing in on them. . . . . After all inmates were in the cells* _____ *went back up to make the count . . . . came back down. . . . . Then saw inmate on the third tier talking to some of the guys on the first who were cleaning up . . . .* _____ . . . . *what you doing . . . . aren't you on the third tier . . . . yeah. . . . . Well then why aren't you in your cell don't you know that I've already taken the count . . . . silence . . . .* _____ *went up and took the man to his cell . . . . or rather walked along with him. Some confusion is created by the fact that some inmates are able to stay out past the lock up time for clean up duty. . . . .*

Went back into the day room . . . . floors had been mopped. . . . . Other guard had gone and brought back some coffee . . . . asked if he had gone into the "hole" alone . . . . yeah . . . . you should have taken someone with you . . . . no man, its better to go by yourself. . . . . You take someone with you and the guy thinks . . . . look at me. . . . . I'm a big man it takes all these guys to handle me. . . . . You should have taken at least one man with you . . . . that guy is about to go off the deep end. . . . . He's been there about a week now. . . . . You could get hurt. . . . . (Apparently they go down and let the guy out to dump his bucket. . . . . While talking Summer guard tells _____ *to tell me about his "Nice experience" the week after he got here. . . . . Oh yeah, "knowing smiles" exchanged. . . . . Well we were having trouble with this one inmate one night and he got away from another guard and started running down the hall (corridor beside the cells) the guard he got away from grabbed him around the neck and I made a flying tackle at his legs. . . . . When I hit him I slid right off him like a greased pig. . . . . The jerk had taken his bucket and spread shit all over himself. . . . . Man, I got into the shower and stayed there for three hours. . . . . Took the man to CVH. . . . . Incidents like this seem to build solidarity among the guards. . . . .*

At about 11:10 went out in front and talked with _____ . . . . Wanted to know again what we were trying to do here. . . . . Said he didn't think it would work (before I got through the first sentence) because they would con the students too easily . . . . cited instance of divinity students coming about two years ago. . . . . The whole thing soon deteriorated and finally just stopped. . . . . (Another instance where "Yalies" are all lumped into one bunch. . . . .) Finally agreed that some good might come out of the program even if it was just the education of law students to the fact that everyone in jail is not a simon pure in need of help. . . . . Thought the idea of having the jail people have a second crack at determining bail was a good idea. . . . .

What to Include

Everything? Above all else the full field notes should include as complete an account of the observations as possible. This is especially essential in the early stages of semi-orientation. You may find it is easiest to use your jotted notes as mind joggers in developing a flow-of-consciousness report. When filling gaps in your jotted notes, you need not be concerned about style, grammar, or how what you say might sound to the outsider. Your field notes are for your own use.

When developing the account of previous observations, it is frequently useful to rely on a "sequence-of-events" style. It is amazing how much better you do if you sit down and try to recall events in sequence than if you try to simply recall, in any sequence, what happened. One event seems to lead to the recall of the next. An alternative to this strategy, which is most useful in later stages of observations, is one of specifying categories of information. You may even devise forms to be filled out similar in format to questionnaires. We will have more to say of this strategy shortly. Having asserted the utility of the "sequence of events" style of recall, it should not be concluded that the field notes stay in sequence come hell or high water. .

When events or thoughts that have nothing to do with the narration are recalled, go ahead and put them down. This is especially true when comments about the progress of the research or your own feelings are involved. Note, for example, comments in the above example about staying uninvolved with the concerned citizen, the attitudes of the jail personnel toward "Yalies," the importance of spending complete shifts in observations, and so forth. When you come back to your notes for later analysis, these "asides" may help you better understand the context in which the observations were made.

One important category of "asides" is reference to previous notes and anticipation of future developments. Not only do these allow you to tie one observation to another but, in later analysis, it also is frequently important to note such things as which persons were involved on different occasions or that the same story seemed to be slightly different when related in different contexts or by different persons. Referencing is thus one way of tying field notes together, as well as a device to check on the validity or reliability of the information recorded.

Checks for Bias. The related questions of reliability and validity are of utmost importance. You should make sure to build checks and safeguards into your field notes. A good model in this regard is the study of a medical school (Becker et al., 1961) referred to earlier. This study represents a sensitive attempt to check on the possibility that findings recorded in the field notes were due to the action and influence of the researchers. One focus of this study was on the collectively shared nature of the student perspective. The researchers recognized that actions or statements in this regard might reflect quite different things, depending on such influences as whether the actions or statements were volunteered or elicited by the researcher and whether the actions or statements occurred in the company of others or in more private settings. To check on this the scheme in Figure 3.2 was devised, whereby the findings were reported in the appropriate categories.

FIGURE 3.2
Scheme for Classifying Statements and Activities

		Volunteered	Directed by the Observer	Total
Statements	To observer alone			
	To others in everyday conversation			
Activities	Individual			
	Group			
Total				

Scheme as developed in research of Becker et al. (1961).

Still, given such a scheme, the question remains as to how to treat the findings. How should the categories of information be weighted in drawing conclusions? It is not possible to develop sharp boundaries. Rather, it is a matter of relying on rules of thumb. As reported by the investigators of the medical school,

We have not developed any formulas for interpretation of a table of this kind, but we can state a few ground rules. In the first place, the number of directed statements should be small in comparison to volunteered statements. Secondly, in the "Volunteered" column, the proportion of items consisting of statements made to the observer alone should not be overwhelming. This, of course, begs the question of just what proportion would be large enough to cause us to doubt our proposition that the perspective is collective. We are inclined now to think that any proportion over 50 percent would necessitate another look at the proposition, but we cannot state any rationale for this inclination. Third, there should be a reasonable proportion of activities as well as statements by students. Again, we cannot state any rigid formula, but we are inclined to think somewhere in the neighborhood of 20 or 25 percent would be an appropriate figure. (Becker et al., 1961, p. 43)

We are thus confronted with rather hazy zones where the findings seem to be more or less convincing. It is not totally unlike selecting a level of statistical significance to use when deciding to accept or reject a statistically tested hypothesis. You will have to devise your own scheme. In the process you can, fortunately, draw on the published experiences of others. See, for example, those reported in the January 1955 issue of the *American Journal of Sociology*, Dean and Whyte (1958), and Webb et al. (1966). Unfortunately, this question of the reliability and validity of observational techniques has not been systematically reduced to a set of procedures parallel to those available when checking on the reliability and validity of items on questionnaires used in the construction of an index. In part, this lack of systemization arises since observations in the field frequently are used in the construction of a concept, rather than as a reflection of concepts defined prior to research. In part, it flows from the fact that the observations gathered are not so susceptible to quantitative analysis, which makes statistical checks available in other styles of research.

Realizing that you are likely to be called on to invoke a good deal of ingenuity, there are certain categories of potential sources of bias you will want to note. These are biases arising from *differential access, selective perception,* and *observer impact.*

First, consider the problem of *differential access* to various portions of the social networks that define the setting you choose. Differential access arises most frequently from two related sources—the presence of factions in the setting and the characteristics of the observer. Most communities, organizations, and other settings of any size above three to five persons are characterized by factions or interest groups. This being the case, identification with one faction cuts off access to others. As Hart (1970) reports from his work among the Tiwi, there is a tendency for the stranger or outsider to be taken in, to have his or her time monopolized by one group or faction. In such a situation, if you are interested in the activities and attitudes of other factions, it is important that you maintain a certain degree of distance. Gusfield (1960) provides another enlightening example in this regard. As was noted in the last chapter, the quality and pattern of relationships is likely to change as time in the field accumulates. It thus becomes important to note these changes in your field notes so that, when you return for more detailed analysis, you will more readily recall just how representative your observations were at any particular time.

A second type of differential access arises from the way personal characteristics, such as sex, age, marital status, and race, interact with those being observed. Observers who are with their families may have a wider range of access than those who embark alone. Accompanied by children and spouse, the researcher may have a wider range of information according to sex and age than would otherwise be the case. Going into the setting alone, on the other hand, might provide access to activities and information that would be closed off to someone entering with other "outsiders." Whatever the case, it is important to keep notes on how your pattern of access is affected by your various attributes and to substantiate these notes with observations of concrete instances illustrating the state of and changes in orientation.

In addition to bias arising from differential access, a second set of biases may be introduced through selective perception. This problem of selecting out only partial information is, in one sense, inevitable. It simply is not possible to record every aspect of every situation observed. You must select. What we record is likely to be governed by our own perceptions of what is important, whether the importance flows from personal feelings or more general academic orientations. Whatever the source it is important to note, when possible, the state of your own thinking so as to more readily recognize, in later analysis, what kinds of things you were looking for. Even then it is likely that a degree of unnoticed bias will enter in. *It is not a matter of elimination but rather of defining and minimizing.*

In part, the selections of your perceptions will run with the developing attachments to persons and the setting being studied. These are likely to change as time passes and, if the social dynamics of this style of research are similar to other instances of situational adaptation (we will have more to say of this in the next chapter), the process of settling down is likely to occur in certain stages. You should note your changing orientations and at least the potential impact they seem to have. In the early stages there is likely to be a degree of anxiety and suspicion, a kind of cautious formality. As time progresses, differential attachments will develop, exhibiting the full range of openness, informality, and conflict that defines all ongoing social interaction. For example, in the early stages of research, when you are acquainting yourself with the setting, everything may seem new and important. As the research progresses and events recur, some may fade into the background as you begin to feel that "everybody knows that already." It is not that these events occur any less frequently but simply that you have recorded them less often.

Another source of selective perception is more temporary and less predictable in nature. It may be that certain events in a setting become temporarily so salient that they override others. To guard against the situational salience of certain events and the fading of others as familiarity breeds disinterest, a systematic reporting format is useful. In this regard the discussion of the systematic observation of natural social phenomena by Reiss (1971) is particularly noteworthy. Reiss and his students, in a study of police–citizen encounters, devised a series of observational forms similar in format to questionnaires, where the *observer* was the one answering "inquiries." Portions dealing with the nature of police behavior and citizen characteristics are reproduced in Figure 3.3.

By using the standardized format, the observer's attention was routinely drawn to similar aspects of police–citizen encounters. In this way, the danger of focusing on only one aspect of, say, an "agitated" encounter was avoided, since even in these extreme situations the observer would also record such relatively "uninteresting" facts as the sex, age, and income level of the participants. In later analysis this routine recording becomes very useful.[1]

In addition to the advantage of routine recording of specified types of information, the fixed format for observational forms also provides, as do direct observation techniques in general, a way to reduce the retrospective reinterpretation of events that frequently occur in the interview situation. Reiss (1971), for example, reports that, on returning to citizens within three months after they had been observed in encounters with police, ". . . almost four in ten citizens either did not recall their transactions with the police or reported the event that gave rise to it but denied having had any contact with the police" (p. 8). Field notes themselves are of course retrospective in the sense that the observer recalls what he or she saw. However, the time lag is generally shorter, hours compared to months, and thus less distortion is likely to enter in. For a general discussion of these issues Deutscher (1973) provides useful material.

Up to this point, we have suggested that you keep notes and develop techniques to check on the potential biasing impact of differential access and selective perception. A third source of possible distortion arises from what might be called the "third party" influence. We have just

---

[1] For an analysis of this information, see Black and Reiss (1970) and Black (1970).

FIGURE 3.3
Portions of Schedule Used by Observers of Police–Citizen Encounters
15. (continued)

	Complainant Group			Offender Group			Victim Group			Informant			Bystander			Don't Know		
Total Number																		
Sex: Male, Female, Both	M	F	B	M	F	B	M	F	B	M	F	B	M	F	B	M	F	B
Age: Juvenile, Adult, Both	J	A	B	J	A	B	J	A	B	J	A	B	J	A	B	J	A	B
Income:																		
High																		
Middle																		
Low																		
Mixed																		
Don't Know																		
Manner: General State																		
Agitated																		
Calm																		
Very Detached																		
Mixed																		
Don't Know																		
Toward Police:																		
Very Deferential																		
Civil																		
Antagonistic																		
Mixed																		
Don't Know																		
Other Pertinent Information: [specify]																		

argued that selective perception is in part a function of the interpersonal dynamics of the research process. So is the "third party" influence. When we speak of interpersonal impact in this latter sense, however, we are referring to the possible biasing influence of the observer, not because of distorting perceptions but because of the influence on events that

FIGURE 3.3 (*continued*)

17. Relationships between the citizens in the situation: [Specify the preexistent relationships between the incumbents of the various roles. Use the code below.]

<u>Code</u>

1. Family

2. Friend(s) or Acquaintance(s)

3. Neighbor(s)

4. Mixed: No. 1 – No. 4

5. Business Relationship

6. Other Formal Relationship (e.g., teacher–pupil)

7. No Apparent Relationship

8. Don't Know

9. Mixed: No. 1 – No. 8

0. Inapplicable

	Complainant								
Complainant		Offender							
Offender			Victim						
Victim				Complainant Group					
Complainant Group					Offender Group				
Offender Group						Victim Group			
Victim Group							Informant		
Informant								Bystander	
Bystander									Don't Know
Don't Know									

occur. It is not a matter of selective recording but of occurrence. As Schwartz and Schwartz (1955) have suggested, "The participant observer is an integral part of the situation he is observing. He is linked with the observed in a reciprocal process of mutual modification. Together the observer and the observed constitute a context which would be different if either participant were different or were eliminated" (p. 346).

Again, the difference between what would have happened had you not been there and what actually happened is likely to fluctuate with the stage of research. Recalling the discussion in the last chapter, as you move from a relationship allowing access to only public information

FIGURE 3.3 (*continued*)

29. Did the police comply with the central request or demand that was made in the situation?

_____ 1. Yes   _____ 2. No   _____ 9. Don't Know   _____ 0. Inapplicable

If "No," specify the discrepancy: _____

_____

_____

_____

_____

30. Manner of police behavior toward the primary and other citizen participants in the situation: [Use the same numbering system for primary citizens as was used in Items No. 12–14. For officers, use the same numbers as those used in the general (white) packet. Fill in the boxes with numbers from the appropriate codes.]

   a.   Control of Citizen [use one number per box]

   Code

   1.   Took Firm Control
   2.   Maintained Control
   3.   Acted Subordinate

Primary Citizens

Officers	No. 1	No. 2	No. 3	No. 4	No. 5
No. 1					
No. 2					
No. 3					
No. 4					

to one incorporating secrets and private thoughts of the setting, the difference should go down. This, of course, further underlines the importance of taking note of the changing nature of your integration into the setting.

In addition to differences that change with the stage of research, it also may be the case that the difference between the "would have been" and the "actually occurred" is influenced by the characteristics of the observer and the observed. Males observing females, older persons observing children, whites observing blacks, blacks observing whites, political activists observing policemen, and so forth are likely to produce

FIGURE 3.3 (concluded)

30. (continued)

    b.   <u>Control of Self</u> [use one number per box]

                <u>Code</u>
       1.   Had Firm Self-Control
       2.   Maintained Self-Control
       3.   Lost Self-Control

Officers

	No. 1	No. 2	No. 3	No. 4	No. 5
No. 1					
No. 2					
No. 3					
No. 4					

    i.   <u>General Manner</u> [use as many numbers as necessary]

                <u>Code</u>
       1.   Was Hostile, Nasty, Provocative
       2.   Was Brusque, Bossy, Authoritarian
       3.   Openly Ridiculed or Belittled
       4.   Subtly Ridiculed or Belittled
       5.   Was Businesslike, Routinized, Impersonal
       6.   Was Good Humored, Playful, Jovial

Other Citizens

Officers	Complainant Group	Offender Group	Victim Group	Informant	Bystander	Don't Know
No. 1						
No. 2						
No. 3						
No. 4						

results different from some other, more "congruent" combination. If your study calls for more than one observer, you can check for differential bias by comparing field notes. If there is just one observer, it is frequently difficult to assess the "absolute" level of bias.

It is likely that the impact of the observer changes with relative salience. For example, if your presence changes the context of interaction from a situation involving two persons to a situation involving three, the impact might be quite large. For a discussion of the sociological significance of the third element, see Simmel (1950, pp. 145–69). On the other hand, if it is a matter of entering a situation to observe, say a rock concert where there are numerous persons, then the impact may be negligible. Nevertheless, even in the rock concert-like situation, you are going to be interacting in smaller contexts within the larger setting. Thus, it is important to keep note of the *relevant* context of interaction as well as the larger picture.

What, then, do you include in field notes? Well, you include the substance of your observations. You include notes for tying different observations together. You include information on the stage of your interaction and adaptation to the setting. You include analytic jottings as organizing thoughts occur to you. You build in checks on possible sources of bias. We have tried to indicate some general forms your notes might take. All of this is to say that, whatever format you decide on, whether flexible or fixed, you must record your observations, feelings, and thoughts so that, when you move to more thorough analysis, you will not have to rely on total recall from your memory. Instead, you will be able to retrieve information from a more complete and permanent source.

> *Practicum 3.1*   If you know of a setting to observe relatively inconspicuously—a game, buying or selling in a department store, a court trial, a church service, a bar, registration procedures at a university, preexam behavior, and so forth—practice observing, going away to jot down notes, and, finally, either typing or recording and then transcribing full field notes. Failing the availability of a setting you feel comfortable observing, you may practice by going to a movie.
>
> Once completed, reflect on the problems encountered and the directions your observations would take if you were to continue.

INTERVIEWING

Closely linked to the process of observing is the process of interviewing. Your interpretation of what you observed will most assuredly be influenced by what you were told. In addition, interviews frequently are used as vehicles for indirect observation. Some events of interest occurred in the past and you need accounts from persons who were there. In like fashion, interviews can be used to check on your own interpretation of observed events. You may find yourself asking, "I saw the other day that such-and-such. Does this mean . . . ?" In reverse, observations can be used as checks on conversations or as the basis for probing for additional elaboration. "I saw the other day where. . . . You were saying. . . . How do these fit together?"

Interviews and what might more correctly be called conversations are interlocked with observations. They provide access to information that would be otherwise unavailable. They also provide the chance for elaboration and validation of your observations and interpretations of events. In a similar manner, observations supplement and guide material gained through interviews and conversations. In combination, then, you will be able to expand your data beyond that available if you relied totally on interviews or on your own observations.

Types of Interviews

It was around 10:00 in the morning, early in October, when the initial rush of classes was over and persons at the university were settling in for the duration of Fall semester. It was the first chance a seasoned survey researcher, whom we shall call Carolyn Crampyourstyle, had to drop by to see her friend and sociological colleague, whom we shall call Harold Hangloose. On entering Harold's office with her cup of coffee, Carolyn noticed that Harold had a rather perplexed look on his face. "How's it going? Have you had coffee this morning?" "No, come on in." Harold was more than happy to have someone to share his misery with. Nodding at what looked like some 500 double-spaced typed pages, Harold sighed, "I've been trying to figure out what to do with these transcripts from the interviews we did last summer. How the hell do you organize this material? I have a good feel for what I think are the important patterns, but, man, this stuff is unmanageable."

Recalling their conversations of the previous year and leaping at the I-told-you-so opportunity, the smug Carolyn said, "I told you so. I told you that you would have this problem. You should have been more specific. You should have precoded your responses and been more routine in the way you presented the questions. You could have had all this on computer tape by now and been well on your way to analysis."

"Ah, go jumpnalake. You know as well as I do that I don't need that kind of advice right now. Besides, we've been through it all before. It's not like I was conducting a survey on how mad you were at Nixon, from very mad to not mad at all. I wanted to get a broad picture of how people perceived the world, how they acted day to day, and what kinds of tensions they faced. If I had done what you were suggesting last year, you're right, I wouldn't have all this material. I would have nothing."

With that the conversation turned to the problems of classes and a new movie that had just come to town.

This fictitious, though commonly heard, argument points to differences in the purpose and style of interviewing. If you are in a situation where you have limited knowledge about the setting to be studied, if you are interested in accounts of interpersonal activities, certain events, or other information that could potentially yield a wide range of responses, then you should opt for an unstructured format. This means that you will end up with what appears at times to be a morass of material. With a good indexing scheme, however (we will discuss this in more detail shortly), you can turn this morass into organized elaboration.

If, on the other hand, you are interested in the degree of agreement or disagreement with certain statements, with specified political leanings or other attitudes, if you are interested in the relative ranking of specified objects or persons, if you are interested in specific information like the number of persons in a household, if you already know a good deal about the setting you are going to study, then you should opt for a more structured format. You will lack in elaboration but you will be in a much better position for concise analysis of the way in which attitudes, opinions, and reported actions seem to be patterned. We will have more to say of this type of interview in Chapter 8.

When considering the "structure" of an interview, two separable parts—the schedule of questions and the interview itself—should be kept in mind. Each can be more or less structured, depending on the thoroughness of the instructions and specification of the questions. For example, Figure 3.4 reproduces a portion of an interview schedule used in a survey of Seattle, Washington residents concerning their attitudes toward the police. The larger study actually contained a wide range of questions on victimization and attitudes toward various offenses as well.[2] This represents an instance in which the questions, potential responses, and instructions to the respondent were all routinized. By being specific it is possible to hone in on concrete aspects of the respondent's attitudes and opinions. This makes coding and later analysis substantially easier. It also presupposes that the researcher has decided beforehand what the important elements of attitudes and opinions are.

By way of contrast, Figure 3.5 contains an outline used as an interview guide in a series of conversations with former drug dealers (Lieb and Olson, 1975). Here, the strategy was to cover each of the areas, but not necessarily in that particular order, and to frame the questions as the flow of conversation dictated. The material thus gathered was fuller in detail and, as a result, more difficult to pigeonhole. Take, for example, the following excerpt from one of the interviews.

---

[2] For an analysis of some of this information, see Hawkins (1973) and Smith and Hawkins (1973).

FIGURE 3.4

Portion of Interview Schedule Used in Study of Attitudes toward Police

VI. POLICE QUESTIONS

For this part of the interview I am going to read to you some statements that include things that some people are saying about the police. (*Hand Respondent Card.*) Please indicate how you personally feel about each of the statements by telling me whether you "Strongly Agree," "Agree," "Disagree," or "Strongly Disagree" with each of the statements. There is not a "right" or "wrong" answer—each statement is a matter of opinion.

(Interviewer: Circle appropriate responses)

Now, here is the first statement.

Card 9		IBM Cols.	
IBM Cols.	1. While the term "dumb cop" is generally unfair, most policemen are somewhat less intelligent than the general public. SA. . 2 D. : 1 A. . 2 SD. . 1 U. . _ NR. . 9		4. The police are greatly underpaid today. SA. . 1 D. . 2 A. . 1 SD. . 2 U. . _ NR. . 9
11		14	
	(code) 2. If a person breaks the law, he shouldn't be entitled to the same rights he had before he became a criminal and shouldn't complain about how the police treat him. SA. . 1 D. . 2 A. . 1 SD. . 2 U. . _ NR. . 9		(code) 5. People who know the ropes and have money to afford good lawyers don't really have anything to worry about from the police. SA. . 2 D. . 1 A. . 2 SD. . 1 U. . _ NR. . 9
12		15	
	(code) 3. A young man who has a choice between becoming a policeman and getting a job paying just as much in the construction business would be making a mistake if he became a policeman. SA. . 2 D. . 1 A. . 2 SD. . 1 U. . _ NR. . 9		(code) 6. There seem to be a lot of policemen who just enjoy pushing people around and giving them a hard time. SA. . 2 D. . 1 A. . 2 SD. . 1 U. . _ NR. . 9
13		16	
	(code)		(code) 7. The police ought to have leeway to be tough with people when they have to. SA. , 1 D. . 2 A. . 1 SD. . 2 U. . _ NR. . 9
		17	
			(code)

FIGURE 3.5
Conversation Guide Used in Study of Drug Dealers

I.   Background Information

Age
Place of birth
Where did you grow up?
What kind of place was it?
How large a place?
Marital Status
Length of time
Children—ages and sex
Occupation
What do you do for money?
Are you currently employed by someone other than yourself?
Educational Background
High school
Where and when
College
Special schooling
Military background
Family Background
Father
Occupation
Education
Mother
Sisters
Brothers
What position are you in the family?
Does it mean anything to you?
Does your father
mother
sister   Drink and to
brother   what extent?
Does your father   Take pills for
mother   medication, pleasure,
sister   assistance, or any
brother   other reason?

II. Current Situation

Where do you live?
In what kind of dwelling?
Are you buying, leasing, or renting?
What kind of neighborhood is it?
How long have you lived there?
Where did you live before that?

FIGURE 3.5 (*continued*)

What kind of neighborhood?
How long have you lived there?
Why did you move?
Why do you normally move?
Do you live alone or with others or another?
Do you normally live alone or with others—Why?

III. Drug Background

When did you first become aware of the so-called illicit drugs, such as marijuana, LSD, mescaline, hashish, psylocybin, speed, etc.?
How old were you?
Where?
What was the occasion—setting?
When did you first experiment with drugs?
Which drugs?
Why?
Where were you?
What were you doing?
When was the next time?
What was it?
Why?
Was your drug usage casual and infrequent or more serious and involved?
What does that mean?

IV. Drug Dealing: General

How involved did you get?
What does dealing mean to you?
When did you first get involved in dealing?
How does one get involved?
What transpires?
Have you dealt more than one drug?
Which drugs?
Is there any difference in dealing different drugs?
Why have you or do you deal these drugs?
Do you or did you support yourself dealing?
For how long?
How much money is involved in dealing?
Are you dealing drugs now?
What?
Did you ever work with others as partners—associates—cohorts, etc.?
Possession of a controlled substance is a felony in Texas punishable by a 2–10 year sentence.

FIGURE 3.5 (*continued*)

It is highly illegal and severely punished by law—Why do you deal?

Is it for money?
social   position?
prestige?
thrill?
independence?
power?
ideology?

Has dealing affected your concept of law and law enforcement?

V.   Patterns of Social Involvement as Drug Dealer

How much of your time is involved in dealing?
When do you work at dealing?
Who are your friends?
Has it affected the type of friends you have?
Does it affect the type of neighborhood you live in?
Are you integrated into your neighborhood?
Do you know your neighbors?
Why not?
Do you have a sense of community?
Do you feel that you are a part of your city or state?
Has dealing altered, developed, or otherwise changed your concept of society-at-large?
What roles do you identify with a society?
Has dealing affected your concept of time?
Do you make future plans?
Do you consider yourself a functioning member of society?
Do you when you deal?
Do you vote or otherwise have political affiliation?
What lasting effects—concrete and abstract—has dealing had on your life?

VI.   Dealing as Social Encounter

Typical kind of deal
What went on?
Location?
Trust?
Rules?
Difference by type of drug?
Persons involved? (number and type)
Partnership?
Dangers?
Hassles?

FIGURE 3.5 *(continued)*

VII. Dealing as Economic Encounter

    Getting supply
    Determining price
    Costs incurred
    Determining quality
    Marketing
    Profit

VIII. Dealing as an Illegal Activity

    Potential of being caught
    Paranoia involved
    Strategies used to avoid detection
        Social (rules of dealing, etc.)
        Technical (modes of transporting, etc.)
    Getting busted
        Ever been busted?
        What happens?
        Where, when, why, who?
        Result of carelessness, informer, etc.?
        What were you thinking?
        Attitude taken?
    Being incarcerated
        Ever been in jail, prison?
        What happened?
        What were you thinking?
        Attitude taken?
    Reentry
        Did you find community, friends, contacts, etc., changed?
        Did jail/prison have lasting impact?
    Impact of being busted?
        On self-conception
        On social contacts
        On later dealing
        On perceptions of legal system

IX. Getting out of Dealing

    Still dealing?
    (If not) Why did you stop?
        Legal hassles
        Social hassles
        Economic hassles
    Would you deal again?
        Full time
        Part time
        Circumstances

FIGURE 3.5 (*concluded*)

X.   Looking Back

Has context of dealing changed?
What ways?
Economic
Social
Legal
What difference do these changes make?
Profit margin
Dangers
Hassles
Social (prestige, etc.)
Would you recommend it as of now?
To whom
What circumstances

INTERVIEWER: How has dealing developed or otherwise changed your self-concept in relation to society at large?

FORMER DEALER: Well, that's a big question because it has changed my view of myself and shaped it quite a bit. But it's given me, in a certain fashion, just the thing that everyone needs to develop—the fact that I can take care of myself, you know, I can be independent, and I can swallow a minimum of bullshit doing it. Which, I think, you know, everybody in some way or another is going to do in some fashion or another. . . . They're going to go out and "make it," so to speak. As far as with others, it's given me—I don't know if it's the dealing experience or my own interpretation of the actual drug experience—but it's given me a view of myself, as you know, having to relate to people and friends in some way other than a pure, mutual, beneficial kind of arrangement which I see a lot of people fall into. . . . (At this point this person began to ramble and then said) . . . Maybe you ought to ask the question again 'cause there were several things and I've forgotten the question.

INTERVIEWER: Has it altered, developed, or otherwise changed your self-concept in relation to society at large? Has it changed your concept of society?

FORMER DEALER: I didn't have all that well-formed opinion before I started dealing. It's hard to separate it out.

INTERVIEWER: Did you develop a concept of society? Such things like family, class?

FORMER DEALER: Class, more or less. Not specifically—not as far as family goes, I don't think. . . . You know, I was pretty rebellious as far as family went before I got involved in drugs. You know, it was one of those chicken-and-egg things—whether or not I went into drugs to rebel from my family or whether. . . . It was involved in it somehow but I don't think it was a cause and it may have just been a symptom. As far as self-concept in relation to society, it was on some sort of microsystem level. I mean, you know, it's like it's us against them, that sort of game. You know, we're all in this together. It's like an early Christian trip. You sit around, smoke your dope behind locked doors, worry about the man that might come. On that kind of level it has, not on a broader spectrum, I don't think it has.

At this point the interviewer began to probe into other specific aspects of the relationship between the individual and society—political affiliation, patterns of residence, friendships, and, then, finally, attitudes toward law and its enforcement.

What should be noted from this is the flexibility of format and the wording of questions. There was little concern that the questions be worded in a precise, preselected manner, as was the case in the interview in Figure 3.3. It was a matter of forming questions according to the dictates of the conversation. When the respondent did not understand, the interviewer felt free to specify and even change the thrust of the question. This is a matter of interpersonal sensitivity.

Designing a Schedule

As a rule of thumb, it is a good idea, when conducting a rather open-ended conversation interview, to move from the general to the specific. For example, in the above interview the interviewer moved from the relationship of the individual and society, as broadly conceived, to more specific relationships in the realm of social, political, and legal areas, followed finally by specific instances of concrete events. This movement is not in one direction, however. In many instances you will find that clarifying a question about a specific event calls for reference to more general ideas. Again it is a matter of conversational flow.

When proceeding with the conversational interview, you should have some idea as to where you are going and where you have been. In this sense you should spend time designing an interview outline and revising it as additional information accumulates. This implies that you spend a good deal of time going over the collected interviews. Since, by their very nature, these interviews almost ensure that topics will be covered in various orders, it is important that you keep track of topics that have been covered and those that are still undeveloped.

This strategy also implies that you have access allowing for follow-up interviews, interviews that allow you to pursue omitted topics and new leads. With the single-shot conversation, it frequently is advisable to proceed with more structure to ensure that each of the topics is covered. Without this structure you eventually may find that various crucial pieces of information have been omitted.

Once again, when proceeding with interviews in an ongoing project, it is important to take some assessment of the research in terms of moving from a position of marginal semi-orientation to one of a more assimilated, refined probing. In the process you will encounter a time of transition, a time of false security arising from assumed understandings.

You may find yourself in a position similar to that of Hannerz (1969), who encountered unexpected hostility from a seemingly innocent question. "I tried to be very careful not to do anything which could be misinterpreted, but obviously even a very innocent remark could be seen in an unexpected light. Jimmy, for instance, noted before for his hot temper, was upset when I made a complimentary remark about his new sweater and asked where he had got it. 'What the hell do you mean, where did I get it? This is my own sweater, I bought it. Why do you ask? I don't know if we can trust you'" (p. 209).

In a like fashion, Keiser (1970) reports,

> Whenever I thought I was really "hip," that I really "knew what was happening," something would occur that brought home the extent of my ignorance. For example, on the very last night of my first summer's field work I mistook a challenge to fight for a friendly warning. A Vice Lord said to me, "Hey man, you better walk light." Because a gang fight had taken place a few hours earlier, and because I had heard "walk light" used in previous contexts as a friendly warning, I completely misunderstood and responded most inappropriately, "Yeah I'm hip." Actually I could not have been more unhip for "You walk light!" or "You better walk light!" is usually a challenge to fight, while simply "Walk light!" is used as a friendly warning. Because of the complete inappropriateness of my response, my would-be protagonist did not know how to proceed. (p. 235)

You must, then, be on the lookout for miscues. This note of caution points to the utility of combining the techniques of direct observation with those of interviewing. One of the problems of interviewing persons from settings with which you have little contact is that you run the danger of misinterpretation. By preselecting wording and substantive content of questions, you run the risk of faulty translations. This obviously is the case when the setting includes a "foreign" language where our ignorance is readily apparent. It is more subtly the case, as Becker and Geer (1957) have pointed out, and as the above examples illustrate, when there is partial familiarity. In such situations "we often do not understand that we do not understand and are thus likely to make errors in interpreting what is said to us" (p. 29). When designing a schedule and conducting interviews, then, you must recognize that settings that are distinct from their surroundings, whether this involves a work group in a steel plant or drug dealers on a college campus, often develop an "argot," which, as any dictionary will tell you, is a language of a particular group. This is easy enough to detect when unfamiliar words are used. It is more difficult and subtler when otherwise familiar words take on different meanings.

When designing an interview plan, you will have to decide how structured to make the schedule of questions and mode of presentation. When guiding the conversation from one topic to another, a useful rule of thumb is to move from the general to the specific. Now, this will not always be the case and you may have to make adjustments, but it is a good starting point. When framing questions and interpreting answers, you should be on the lookout for special meanings of words and phrases. This may be especially tricky in a setting where you are at least partially familiar with the language being used.

Finally, a topic that we have skipped is how to record. This is something you will have to decide for yourself, depending on the impact you think various recording devices such as pad and pencil, tape recorders, and even video tape will have. In some settings or situations within settings even the most seemingly obtrusive device may have little impact on the events that occur. In others, even the most innocuous pad and pencil tucked away in a pocket or purse may change the course of the outcome. In any event, as was the case for field notes from observations, you must get it down. This may entail going home or to an available car, office, or room to jot down, dictate, or otherwise record what was said.

> *Practicum 3.2* **If you are able to use recording devices, your problems of getting the material down are greatly reduced. If, however, the use of such devices is not feasible, then you will have to develop your recall capabilities. One way to do this is to have a friend or someone else engage in a recorded conversation or interview. After the interview is over sit down and try to reproduce verbatim the topics covered and answers given. Then check what you have written by playing back the conversation. Keep practicing until your skills are such that you are confident you will at least not be in the position of distortion and, hopefully, in a position to remember comments as they were made. You may want to vary the length of the interview and the length of time between the conversation and your later recall to get a feel for how much is lost as "lag" time increases.**

Once the conversations and interviews are recorded, you face the problem of what to do with them. How do you glean what is important? How do you organize the material to make sense within some framework? It is to these problems of retrieval that we now return.

HOW TO RETRIEVE

Consider the following: The example of full field notes on pages 32–41 represents approximately 11 pages of double-spaced typed comments. This represents one session of observation. On some days the observations were longer, on others shorter. Nevertheless, assume an average of 10 pages and a total of 100 observation sessions, not an unusually long study; in fact, rather short. This gives 1,000 pages of field notes. What are you to do with this material? How are you going to find the portions relevant to the various topics you decide on? You are faced with a problem of indexing.

In the study of pretrial detention, from which the above field notes were taken, we developed an indexing scheme that was partially descriptive and partially analytic. It emerged as the study progressed. We read the field notes and jotted the relevant categorization in the margins. These locations then were entered by day and page number on 3x5 cards, which were filed according to appropriate topic. For example, we had cards for staff/inmate relations, physical facilities, trouble, uncertainty, stigmatization, bonding, disciplinary hearings, informal reactions to deviance, mail, relations with outside agencies, the observer's role, and so forth. Later on, as we began the more detailed analysis of the data, this indexing scheme became indispensible.

One idea we became interested in was that of the "multiplicity of legal levels" developed by Pospisil (1967). Building on the work of others, it is Pospisil's position that "every functioning subgroup of a society regulates the relations of its members by its own legal system, which is of necessity different, at least in some respects, from those of the other subgroups." (3) Within this scheme, families, industrial organizations, and universities all have "legal" machinery. This seemed to be a very useful insight for any attempt to understand and predict the impact of *the* criminal justice system. The criminal-justice system is actually a sequence of interdependent, relatively autonomous subunits—police, court, and correctional personnel and facilities. Each has developed somewhat different working perspectives of the world and the administration of justice. Each has its own legal system, its own way of handling trouble. Persons passing through the criminal-justice system are thus confronted with a multiplicity of legal systems.

Defining "law" in part as a system set up to straighten out "trouble," it became important to ferret out the meaning of trouble within the context of life in a pretrial detention facility. In pursuit of this we examined our notes for occasions on which the topic of "trouble" came up. These conversations and observations included such diverse situations as fights, riots, red tape, cliques, hassles, and tip-off events, and such labels as "non-thinkers," "organizers," "jokers," "con-artists," and persons who were "spaced out" or who were "antiadministration." Clearly, *trouble* is a cover term in the same sense as *tramp* discussed by Spradley (1970). There are a number of shapes that trouble takes on. The job became one of attempting to make some sense of the multitude of meanings. Clearly, there was a degree of severity involved; but what were the dimensions of a situation or the characteristics of an individual that defined qualitative differences?

Following further discussions with persons working on the project and persons working at the jail, the scheme presented in Figure 3.6

FIGURE 3.6
Scheme for Categorizing Trouble Within a Jail

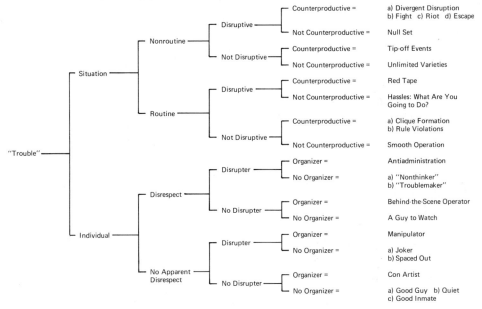

evolved. Clearly, an initial dimension was whether the reference point was an individual or a situation. Troublesome situations were distinguished from one another according to whether they were routinely encountered, whether they were immediately disruptive, and whether they were counterproductive in terms of posing a threat for future order within the jail.

Troublesome individuals were distinguished from one another according to whether they exhibited a degree of disrespect, whether they were at the moment disrupting the operation and routine of jail life, and whether they appeared to be organizers. In this way the significance of labeling a person as "Anti-administration" as opposed to a "'Manipulator" or a "Joker" takes its shape.

These dimensions of trouble become particularly important when discussing the allocation of justice within the pretrial detention facility. (See Olson, 1974b.) It was not so much the crime the individual was charged with on the outside—burglary, theft, drunkenness, and so forth; rather, it was how he or she was labeled within the context of jail life and what type of situation was involved. "Rule violations" called for less severe punishment than fights, primarily because fights were viewed as being nonroutine, disruptive, and potentially counterproductive (pushing and shoving might turn the fight into a brawl or a riot). "Rule violations," then, were routine, nondisruptive events, such as not getting up for breakfast, not wearing an identification band, or being in the wrong cell, which were only potentially counterproductive for the continued ordered flow of events.

Justice also was allocated differentially, depending on the combination of type of individual and type of situation involved. "Jokers" and persons labled "Operators" were treated differentially, although they were both involved in "Hassles," primarily due to the fact that "Operators" showed disrespect and organized behind the scenes, whereas jokers were neither disrespectful nor did they engage in "organizing" activities. In a parallel manner, justice involved the same treatment for the seemingly very distinct events of clique formation and rule violations. Both were handled in a nonformal manner. Persons were moved to another cell block or another facility. Sentences were suspended after lectures about the possible counterproductive nature of violating rules.

Looking at the data with an eye on the multiplicity of legal systems is, of course, only one way in which this information could have been organized. Any number of alternative themes might have been chosen. The point is that, whatever the framework, you will have to come up with some sort of indexing or filing scheme that allows you to pull out relevant information. This scheme takes its form as the study progresses and, thus, you may find yourself reading and rereading your field notes in repeated attempts to categorize in insight-producing ways. Filing and indexing often involve rather tedious procedures and hours of work. They also involve a time in which the data collected begin to make sense. It is thus at once boring and exciting. It is also crucial. Without some organizing scheme you will be buried in material.

Practicum 3.3 **Take some detailed account of a particular situation, such as Oscar Lewis' *Children of Sanchez*, and develop an indexing scheme for the material. In the case of *Children of Sanchez*, you might note the discussions of being a "man" in this setting. There are, of course, many other themes you might choose. Once you have developed a scheme, go back and analyze the data, reporting what the setting reveals on the topic you chose. For additional help along these lines, see Holsti (1969). We will deal in greater detail with many of these issues in Chapter 7.**

SUMMARY

Looking back on the last two chapters we see that research of this type is embedded in a time of settling down, a time when the researcher and the setting reach some sort of equilibrium. The state reached is characterized, in large measure, by the degree of access to various types of information. Complete participants share even the guarded secrets of the setting. Others are restricted to "public" information. Even with access to the inner secrets, however, there is a sense in which the researcher remains apart, what anthropologists are inclined to call "marginal natives."

It is from this position that observations are collected, interviews conducted, and tentative analysis done. We have discussed two of the more frequently employed techniques in this regard—field observations and interviews. There are variations on these techniques you may want to explore. For example, there is a series of "projective techniques," originally designed by clinical psychologists, which have been employed in field research. The Spindlers (1958), for example, employed the Rorschach ink blot test in their study of the Menomini to discover differences among various subgroupings. Others have employed sentence-completion tests and variations on the Thematic Apperception Test. For a discussion of the utility and drawbacks of using these and other, normally considered clinical, techniques in field settings, see Pelto (1970).

By employing these techniques, sometimes in ways that make field research more an art than a cookbook operation, you should be in the position of having a good deal of information shedding light on the situation you have chosen. When you move to the final stages of analysis, after your data have been collected, you may find yourself making sense out of the material by referring to similarities exhibited with other settings you have observed or read about.

It is when you begin to move beyond a particular setting to similarities with otherwise distinct settings that you begin the translation from a folk system to an analytic system. You begin to rely on more abstract concepts that may be completely foreign to those in the setting you have studied but encompass and make sense out of events or thematic patterns that otherwise appear as disconnected tidbits of information.

The next chapter explores this movement from the folk to the analytic in some detail. Specifically, drawing on such diverse settings as prisons, hospitals, concentration camps, medical schools, law schools, and the process of "reentry," we will move toward an analytic framework of "situational adjustment" as applied to the process of "passing through."

KEY ISSUES

1. Discuss the relationship between analysis and data collection as reflected in the process of shifting postures.

2. Discuss the types of material that should be included in field notes.

3. What sources of biases are likely to permeate your research? How are these sources best handled? How do they differ from one stage to the next?

4. Discuss the pros and cons of using structured and unstructured interview formats.

REFERENCES

Becker, Howard S., and Geer, Blanche
    1957 "Participant Observation and Interviewing: A Comparison." *Human Organization*, vol. 16, pp. 28–32.

Becker, Howard S.; Geer Blanche; Hughes, Everett; and Strauss, Anselm
    1961 *Boys in White*. Chicago: University of Chicago Press.

Black, Donald J.
    1970 "Production of Crime Rates." *American Sociological Review*, vol. 35, pp. 732–48.

Black, Donald J., and Ries, Albert J., Jr.
    1970 "Police Control of Juveniles." *American Sociological Review*, vol. 35, pp. 63–77.

Blau, Peter
    1964 "The Research Process in the Study of the Dynamics of Bureaucracy." In Phillip Hammond (ed.), *Sociologists at Work*. New York: Basic Books.

Boissevian, Jeremy
    1970 "Fieldwork in Malta." In George D. Spindler (ed.), *Being an Anthropologist: Fieldwork in Eleven Cultures*. New York: Holt, Rinehart and Winston.

Cressey, Donald R.
    1953 *Other People's Money: A Study in the Social Psychology of Embezzlement*. Glencoe, Ill.: Free Press.

Dean, John P., and Whyte, William Foote
    1958 "How Do You Know if the Informant is Telling the Truth?" *Human Organization*, vol. 17, pp. 34–38.

Deutscher, Irwin (ed.)
    1973 *What We Say/What We Do: Sentiments and Acts*. Glencoe, Ill.: Scott, Foresman and Co.

Glaser, Barney M., and Strauss, Anselm M.
    1967 *The Discovery of Grounded Theory: Strategies for Qualitative Research*. Chicago: Aldine Publishing Co.

Gusfield, Joseph
    1960 "Fieldwork Reciprocities in Studying a Social Movement." In Adams and Priess (eds.), *Human Organization Research*. Homewood, Ill.: Dorsey Press.

Hannerz, Ulf
    1969 *Soulside, Soulside: Inquiries into Ghetto Culture and Community.*
        New York: Columbia University Press.

Hart, C. W. M.
    1970 "Fieldwork among the Tiwi." In George D. Spindler (ed.), *Being
        an Anthropologist: Fieldwork in Eleven Cultures.* New York: Holt,
        Rinehart and Winston.

Hawkins, Richard O.
    1973 "Who Called the Cops?: Decisions to Report Criminal Victimiza-
        tions." *Law and Society Review,* vol. 7, pp. 427–44.

Holsti, Ole R.
    1969 *Content Analysis for the Social Sciences and Humanities.* Reading,
        Mass.: Addison Wesley Publishing Company.

Keiser, R. Lincoln
    1970 "Fieldwork among the Vice Lords of Chicago." In George D.
        Spindler (ed.), *Being an Anthropologist: Fieldwork in Eleven
        Cultures.* New York: Holt, Rinehart and Winston.

Lewis, Oscar
    1961 *The Children of Sanchez.* New York: Random House.

Lieb, John, and Olson, Sheldon R.
    1975 "Prestige, Paranoia and Profit: On Becoming a Dealer of Illicit
        Drugs in a University Community." Paper presented at Society
        for Study of Social Problems Meetings, San Francisco.

Lindesmith, Alfred
    1947 *Opiate Addiction.* Bloomington, Ind.: Principia.

Norbeck, Edward
    1970 "Changing Japan: Field Research." In George D. Spindler (ed.),
        Being an Anthropologist: Fieldwork in Eleven Cultures. New
        York: Holt Rinehart and Winston.

Olson, Sheldon R.
    1974a "Minutes in Court, Weeks in Jail: A Study of Pretrial Detention."
        New York: MSS Modular Publications, Inc., Module 22.

Olson, Sheldon R.
    1974b "Patterns of Infarctions and Official Reactions to Institutional
        Regulations." *Social Science Quarterly,* vol. 54, pp. 815–26.

Pelto, Pertti J.
    1970 *Anthropological Research: The Structure of Inquiry.* New York:
        Harper and Row.

Pospisil, Leopold
    1967 "Legal Levels and the Multiplicity of Legal Systems in Human
        Societies." *The Journal of Conflict Resolution,* vol. 9, pp. 2–26.

Powdermaker, Hortense
    1966 *Stranger and Friend: The Way of an Anthropologist.* New York:
        W. W. Norton and Company Inc.

68   *Ideas and Data*

Radcliff-Brown, A. R.
  1922   *The Adaman Islanders.* Glencoe, Ill.: Free Press. (Reprinted 1948.)
Reiss, Albert J., Jr.
  1971   "Systematic Observation of Natural Social Phenomena." In Herbert Costner (ed.), *Sociological Methodology 1971.* San Francisco: Jossey-Bass Publishers.
Schwartz, Morris S., and Schwartz, Charlotte Green
  1955   "Problems in Participant Observation." *American Journal of Sociology,* vol. 60, pp. 343–53.
Simmel, Georg
  1950   *The Sociology of Georg Simmel,* Kurt H. Wolff (trans.). New York: Free Press.
Smith, Paul E., and Hawkins, Richard O.
  1973   "Victimization, Types of Citizen-Police Contacts and Attitudes Toward the Police." *Law and Society Review,* vol. 8, pp. 135–52.
Spindler, George, and Spindler, Louise
  1958   "Male and Female Adaptations to Change." *American Anthropologist,* vol. 60, pp. 217–33.
Spradley, James P.
  1970   You Owe Yourself a Drunk. Boston: Little, Brown and Company.
Webb, Eugene, Campbell, Donald T.; Schwartz, Richard D.; and Sechrest, Lee
  1966   *Unobtrusive Measures: Nonreactive Research on the Social Sciences.* Chicago: Rand McNally.
Whyte, William Foote
  1955   *Street Corner Society: The Social Structure of an Italian Slum.* Chicago: University of Chicago Press.

Contents

Chapter 4

Translating from the Folk to the Analytic

Once your pursuit of the folk system nears completion and patterns begin to emerge, you will be faced with a crucial decision: how to best present the findings. Should the participants speak in their own terms with little emphasis on analyzing these thoughts, attitudes, and actions—an approach similar to that of Chambliss (1971) in his study of a professional thief?

> At some point we decided to use the materials he was giving me for a book. . . . I had been agonizing with most of these materials for some time. How could they best be organized? Should Harry's story and his philosophy of life be expressed as a biography or as an autobiography? Should I tell the story as he gave it to me with generous quotations from him or keep it all in his own words? . . . It became clear to me that I had been so close to Harry King, the man, that it was difficult to consider him the "object" or "subject" of a book. Once I realized the problem it became easier to cope with. In the coping I came to the obvious conclusion that the story should be told in his own words. (X)

Alternatively, you may feel some "manipulation" of the information is called for. You may feel the setting is best presented by analyzing interlocking *themes*. Themes may be combined in the form of a *model* to summarize what appear to be the crucial elements and their interconnections.

THEMATIC ANALYSIS OF THE FOLK SYSTEM

Along these lines, recall the theme of "trouble" in a pretrial detention institution developed in the last chapter. This study also revealed that pretrial detention was permeated by a number of additional focal concerns. "Keeping the lid on," "Dealing or copping a plea," "Ambiguity," "Isolation," "Transition," "Personal and social disruption" were all part of the pretrial experience viewed from the inmates' and officials' stand-point. In schematic fashion these themes were interlocked as presented in Figure 4.1.

The transition theme was signaled by arrest (Link A). In addition to its legal definition, arrest is a time when the formerly free become

FIGURE 4.1

A Model Presenting the Interconnections Among Themes Defining Pretrial Detention

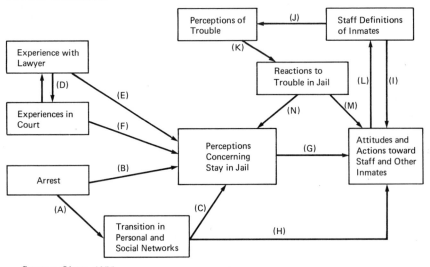

Source: Olson, 1975.

the suspected and restrained. The implications of this have been captured by Solzhenitsyn (1973): "Arrest! Need it be said that it is a breaking point in your life, a bolt of lightning which has scored a direct hit on you? . . . Arrest is an instantaneous, shattering thrust, expulsion, somersault from one state into another. . . . That's what arrest is: it's a blinding flash and a blow which shifts the present instantly into the past and the impossible into omnipotent actuality" (pp. 3–4). In similar fashion, Irwin (1970) noted the disruptive nature of the time from arrest to conviction in a setting closer to the pretrial detention study being "modeled."

> One's identity, one's personality system, one's coherent thinking about himself depend upon a relatively familiar, continuous, and predictable stream of events. In the Kafkaesque world of the booking room, the jail cell, the interrogation room, and the visiting room, the boundaries of the self collapse.

> While this collapse is occurring, the prisoner's network of social rela-

tions is being torn apart. The insulation between social worlds, an insulation necessary for the orderly maintenance of his social life, is punctured. Many persons learn about facets of his life that were previously unknown to them. . . . Furthermore, a multitude of minor exigencies that must be met to maintain social relationships go unattended. Bills are not paid; friends are not befriended; families are not fed, consoled, advised, disciplined; businesses go unattended; obligations and duties cannot be fulfilled—in other words, *roles* cannot be performed. Unattended, the structure of the prisoner's social relations collapse. (pp. 39–40)

This personal and social disruption is easily translated into perceptions of life in jail: how disruptive, how smooth, how fair or unjust (Links B and C).

In a parallel fashion, perceptions of jail life are influenced by contacts with lawyers, both direct and through stories related by persons in similar situations (Links D, E, and F). On one hand, such contacts frequently generated perceptions that all dealings were part of a large game embedded in a sea of bargained justice of negotiated pleas, and any other view of the judicial proceedings was simply a farce. Given that large portions of the individual's current life, reputation, and later life chances were at stake, these perceptions readily translated into increased alienation from the "justness" of the proceedings. Lawyer contacts were also at times the source of increased respect and perceptions of fairness. Whatever the direction of the impact, the theme of dealing or copping a plea clearly influenced orientations of those passing through the pretrial detention facility.

As persons entered and left the pretrial detention facility, they were faced with forming and breaking relationships with fellow inmates and guards. The character of such relationships was, in part, a function of perceptions of fairness and harshness, as well as the transitional nature of both personal and social networks (Link G). Along these lines it should not be missed that social disruption was accompanied by a process of social integration (Link H). This dual process of integration into jail life and disruption of community ties is sometimes referred to as prisonization, or, more generally, institutionalization.

Such shifting relationships, with their accompanying attitudes and actions, were perhaps most graphically reflected in the study of pretrial detention when we looked at changing patterns of institutional offenses related to the length of time the offenders had been in jail. When infractions of institutional rules were separated according to whether the victims of the infractions were staff or inmates and then these categories plotted against time the offender had been in jail, the patterns in Figure 4.2 emerged. Offenses involving fellow inmates decreased in probability and those against the staff increased. Thus, as inmates adjusted to life in jail, their patterns of attitudes and actions changed.

FIGURE 4.2
The Changing Nature of Institutional Crime with Increasing Time Spent in Jail at Time of Offense

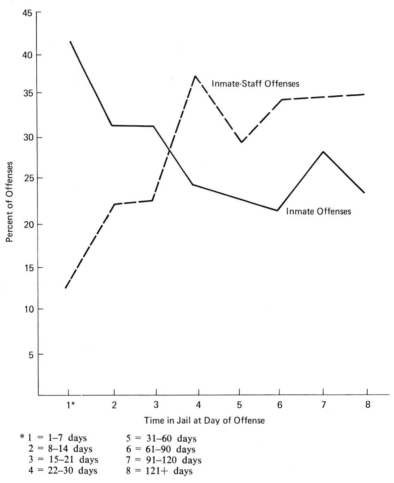

*1 = 1–7 days   5 = 31–60 days
2 = 8–14 days   6 = 61–90 days
3 = 15–21 days   7 = 91–120 days
4 = 22–30 days   8 = 121+ days

Further evidence that life in jail involved marching to a different drummer is available in the rhythm of the rate of infractions during the week. Contrary to the pattern of street crimes, where infractions cluster around the weekend, beginning with Friday night, infractions of institutional rules were at their peak on Monday, Tuesday, and Wednesday, as Figure 4.3 shows. Drawing from the widely held idea that rates of deviance fluctuate with times of transition, we can speculate that the patterns of transition during the week are different in jail than on the streets. Indeed, we found that in jail going and coming was

FIGURE 4.3
Volume of Institutional Crime by Days of the Week

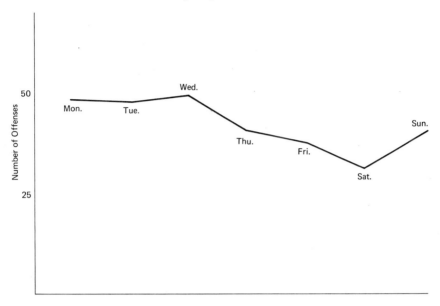

at its peak on Monday, Tuesday, and Wednesday, when inmates were shuttled back and forth to court appearances.

We find, then, that life in jail—the patterns of attitudes and actions, the perceptions of fairness or harshness—has an integrity of its own. We can go on to note that this integrity is in part maintained by reactions to and perceptions of "trouble" (Links *I, J,* and *K*). As Figure 4.1 depicts, these reactions to trouble, both formal and informal, feed back on perceptions of the stay in jail and further tendencies for various attitudes and actions directed toward other inmates and staff members (Links *L, M,* and *N*). To understand the impact of *the* criminal-justice system in terms of increasing or decreasing feelings of injustice or fairness, of avoidance and attraction, we must realize that *the* system is more correctly depicted as a series of social situations to which persons adjust in a number of ways. In discussions of the deterrent impact of the criminal-justice system, such segmentation should not be overlooked.

Neither should we overlook the fact that, in part, the shape and meaning of pretrial detention is formed by anticipations of imprisonment. For this reason the scheme in Figure 4.1 is incomplete. This is not a special problem with this particular model. Rather, it is inherent in the case-study method. Just as you think you have pinned it down, you find a loose end, a link to portions of the broader setting.

One of the uncertainties of case studies is that they always remain open and changing. There is always the chance that the model you choose only partially represents the elusive character of an ongoing system. You may find, in addition to linkages with some broader whole, that the setting is not standing still while you analyze. You are likely to find yourself in a setting similar to that described by Diesing (1971).

> Human systems are always developing and always unfinished; they always retain inconsistencies, ambiguities, and absurdities. Belief systems never achieve complete rationality and consistency; personalities and groups are always in the process of resolving old conflicts and sharpening new ones; accumulations of power are always crumbling and being rebuilt; ceremonies are being elaborated or simplified. Consequently a faithful model of a particular system at a particular time will itself include inconsistencies, ambiguities, and exceptions. (p. 165)

Nevertheless, you must stop the motion long enough to "get it down." In so doing something is lost. Even if you supplement your written account with videotape or film, much will be left out. The translation of reality will always be less than perfect. The alternative, however, is to not communicate your findings. Work at it. Organize and reorganize. Write and rewrite. You will be surprised how much you can do.

Such elaborations of the insider's world are useful and insight-producing. They uncover what is perhaps a latent structure of meaning among the participants. They are essential in understanding the "folk system." However, some social scientists do not want to rest there. They would push us still further—beyond the folk system to an *analytic system*. See, for example, the discussion of Paul Bohannan (1957). Unlike the folk system, the analytic system belongs to the researcher. It represents his or her scheme for interpreting the world. It may incorporate, but is not limited to, conceptualizations of insiders. Once again the methods of social science call for translation. This time it is a translation of the *concepts* of the "insiders" into concepts of a more general scheme—a scheme applicable to a number of situations.

Some persons are turned off by such an enterprise. For some the search for regularity across situations destroys what is important—those characteristics that are unique to the situation. Analytic "theory" is just that and nothing more—an exercise in abstraction. Besides, the argument continues, every situation, every individual is different. To create a scheme that treats them as similar is to miss the point. From this stance, unique details are important, not commonalities. This position has been elaborated and criticized by Karl Popper (1957).

In what follows we will set these objections aside. If you are an anti-analytic individual, interested in exploring the world from a situational point of view, the material presented may seem useless. However, three considerations may pull you through. First, it is at least arguably the case that one should know alternative research strategies. One should be familiar with strategies employed in developing and exploring analytic schemes if only to know the "enemy." It is difficult to criticize if you are not acquainted. Second, the world of theory testers and constructors is a world to be explored in its own right. Even for the antagonist, this is best done from the insider's point of view. Third, the development of thematic models of insider perspectives and the application of analytic schemes are not altogether separate enterprises. It is frequently difficult to develop the insider's perspective without reference to more general statements and how this setting is similar in many ways to other situations. You may find yourself drawing on other research, such as the above reference to the discussion of arrest and conviction by Solzhenitsyn and Irwin. Such comparisons may involve concepts of the same generality. You are not claiming that the experience of, say, arrest is a special case of a more general phenomenon, such as negative reinforcement. Rather, such comparisons are used to lend credence to the basic characterization of the setting.

The link between the illumination of the folk system and the development of a theoretical framework is not limited to using concepts on the same level of generality, however. It is frequently useful to shed additional light by noting how events in a setting reflect more general processes. In the above discussion of pretrial detention, we drew on the idea that times of transition are related to increases in deviant behavior in order to explain the pattern of offenses within the walls of the jail. We also referred to the increasingly general concepts of prisonization, institutionalization, and situational adjustment.

When we speak of generality, in this context, we are speaking of the relative *scope* of a concept. The scope of a concept is in turn determined by the range of situations to which it applies. "Prisonization" is less general than "institutionalization," since the former refers to a process of reorientation within prisons, whereas the latter refers to events in prison as well as to events in high schools, universities, mental institutions, military posts, and so forth. "Situational adjustment" is a more general concept than either prisonization or institutionalization, since it encompasses these latter two terms as well as a large number of other settings.

Construction of an analytic framework, then, involves the construction of increasingly general concepts. Once these concepts have been fashioned the task becomes one of relating the concepts to one another and specifying when these linkages will hold and when they will not. In so doing we arrive at a theoretical network that is used not only to illumine one particular setting but also to anticipate or predict events not yet explored. It is at this point we begin the task of deciding how to best test a theory. But this is getting ahead of the game. We will have more to say of testing strategies in later portions of this book.

First, the process of theory construction. You will soon recognize, without too much thought, that construction and testing are not mutually exclusive.

Since the initial goal is to develop concepts that apply to a number of situations, it should not be surprising to find a useful strategy comparing a number of situations to locate similarities. It is to this process of what has been called controlled comparison (Eggan 1954) that we now turn.

CONTROLLED COMPARISONS: TOWARD A THEORY OF PASSING THROUGH

When we speak of *controlled* comparison we refer, in part, to the criteria used in the choice of settings. In terms of an efficient selection of settings, it is advisable to move in short steps from similar settings to those with greater diversity. Such a procedure minimizes the chance of premature conclusions. As patterns emerge from slightly different settings, say, the comparison of medical schools and law schools, concepts of slightly broader scope can be fashioned. These concepts then can be tried out in still more distinct settings, say, prisons or hospitals, where the similarities are defined by the fact that each setting involves people-processing. Finally, noting, for example, that the process of passing through people-processing institutions involves a pattern of reorientation, the basic findings can be explored within the context of a still broader framework of the acquisition and extinction of behavior.

This process of moving from the characterization of the folk system to a conceptual system of broader analytic scope thus may be conceived as a progression toward generality. Such progression frequently is visited with a good deal of disorder and chance. Chance flashes of enlightenment are not to be discounted. They often provide much needed fresh insight into an otherwise closed system of thought. The actual process of moving from the folk to the analytic may involve contact with or knowledge of a number of different settings where the pieces are apparently unrelated, until, suddenly, they fall into place. For purposes of present elaboration, however, the process will be put forth in an orderly fashion, moving from comparisons of settings similar in nature to those that, at least on the surface, are more distinct.

Adjusting to Medical School and Law School: An Initial Comparison

Passing through medical school has been characterized by Becker et al. (1961) in what is becoming a classic study of a social system from an insider's perspective. These authors were interested, among other things, in presenting a picture of changing student perspectives as early contact with school turned into later semesters of anticipating entrance into actual practice. A perspective was defined as "a coordinated set of ideas and actions a person uses in dealing with some problematic situation . . . a person's ordinary way of thinking and feeling about and acting in such a situation." It arises "when people see themselves as being in the same boat and when they have an opportunity to interact with reference to their problems" (pp. 34, 36).

In medical school the pattern of changing perspectives seemed to be divisible into three stages. The initial perspective, summarily characterized as an effort to "learn it all," was a time when the students seemed to be saying, "We want to learn everything, as we will need it when we become physicians. There is a tremendous amount to learn. We have to work very hard—that is, many hours. If our present hours are not enough for us to get everything, we'll do whatever we can to increase them—but how?" (p. 94). In short, "The students define their situation in medical school as one in which there is an almost overwhelming amount of material to be learned. Their goal is to 'learn it all' (and thus become good physicians) by working hard."

After about two and a half weeks or so, the students moved to the next stage, the provisional perspective of "you can't do it all." Unlike the initial perspective, the provisional perspective "is not something each individual student brought with him to medical school, but a collective development" (p. 107). As for the substance of the perspective, "In the initial perspective they agree on the need for long hours of work; in the provisional perspective they agree on the existence of an overload and the necessity of selecting the important things to study. They do not agree, however, on the proper criterion to use in deciding what is important" (p. 135).

In the third stage, agreement began to emerge. This third stage was a time of learning "what they want us to learn."

> The student's premise in the final perspective is that there are many things to learn and many ways of demonstrating learning on examinations. . . . Quite aside from the question of their own abilities they believe they must make every effort to find out what an instructor wants in order to study intelligently for an examination and do themselves justice in taking it. They see it as part of their job as students to understand a teacher's perspective on his subject, and they direct their efforts toward this end. (178)

In this sense the students moved from an early phase of unsettledness and tension when their expectations of medical school were only partially met, to a time of transition, and, finally, to a time of adjustment to the immediate demands and rewards of the situation. It was a process of reorientation. In part it is a process captured by the more general concept of passing through. The picture we get of "passing through" is a process in which there is a high level of activity and emotional energy aimed at locating benchmarks, at deciding what the new situation calls for. As time progresses this activity and emotional energy decreases, until a stable level of apparent equilibrium or a kind of acquiescence is reached.

In our study of law schools, similar patterns emerged (Stevens, 1973 and Olson, 1971). In a series of interviews reported in Stevens' article, the phases of passing through law school were recorded as follows. The initial period, when the new surroundings were still strange and to a degree threatening, was noted by one student suggesting,

> And so you come in here and bang, you are thrown into a big class where you sort of stick your neck out when you say something, you don't know very much about the law, so intellectually you are sticking your neck out. . . . So what happens to a lot of people—I sort of have been looking at this lately; I see this happening—you learn not to open your mouth.

Thus, one early adaptation to the initially threatening strangeness may be withdrawal. However, in law school, a predominant mode of teaching is the Socratic method, wherein participation in class is forced. It is, as the following interview indicates, a matter of sink or swim. It is also a time similar in terms of emotional tension to the learn-it-all phase described by Becker et al.

> I think everybody is sort of a little overwhelmed to start with. You're sort of thrown into a pool and made to swim. There is no real effort to try and point out to you, point by point, what's going on. You just sort of dump yourself into the whole environment and try to find your way out.

As time progressed, the boundaries of learning to think like a lawyer became clearer.

> Most of the time, when I've seen my fellow students at the beginning of the year make really interesting comments about the relationship of the course to outside problems, to social problems, or to larger philosophical questions, they were usually ignored, or put down or by-passed. . . . There is a conscious desire to mold our thinking into being more precise and more legalistic.

Thus, as in medical school, part of the process of passing through involved turning from the concerns of the outside to those more specific to the immediate situation, and the students began to think like lawyers. Some facets of learning to "think like a lawyer" are reflected in the following:

> You're taught to think in terms of specific rules that you're supposed
> to apply to cases: how these rules are developed, how to get to them,
> what they mean. There's a kind of reasoning, a process of reasoning,
> a way of asking questions. I mean, postulating . . . taking a position,
> and then examining alternate consequences of that position. I mean,
> it sounds like, you know, writing a program for a computer. I mean,
> you try and follow one point to the next point and the next point
> and then you see what you've got.

As experiences in the law school accumulated, the importance of legalis-
tic thinking increasingly became part of the student's own perspective.

> I think more of the nitty-gritty that is actually going on. I think
> beforehand I had the general impression of this dealing with wider
> social policies. . . . I have come to the realization that this sort of
> view of wider social policies is impossible without first understanding
> the basis of court cases, that you have to go through the nuts and
> bolts to get to the larger picture.

Finally, this increasing tendency toward a more precisely defined view
of what it means to think like a lawyer, to perform well in law school,
and the implications this has for the diversity of perspectives among
those passing through the institution was noted in the following:

> When I first arrived I thought they (students) were very diverse,
> but it could just be they were being worn down by just being here,
> the amount of work and the fact that people talk about the law a
> lot. Our interests are being reduced to the lowest common denominator,
> so to speak.

Thus, although different in many respects, attending law school involves parallel phases to passing through medical school. Additional
documentation of this point is available in Olson (1971).

It appears that the ideal typical pattern for this process of situational
adjustment is something like that depicted in Figure 4.4. There is an
initial stage, apparently related to either expectations and background
experiences persons bring with them or to perspectives arrived at during
initial contact. This period of high activity and emotional involvement
is followed by a time of transition, a time when adjustments in perspectives are taking place. Finally, there is a period of restabilization. Going
to law school and going to medical school are both rather specific processes, processes that can be incorporated under the more general concept of "passing through." Passing through is a process in which initial
patterns of attitudes and behavior gradually are extinguished while other
perspectives, more directly attuned to the immediate surroundings, are
acquired. This said, we can move to more distant comparisons.

FIGURE 4.4

Hypothetical Curves for Acquisition and Extinction of Behavior While "Passing Through"

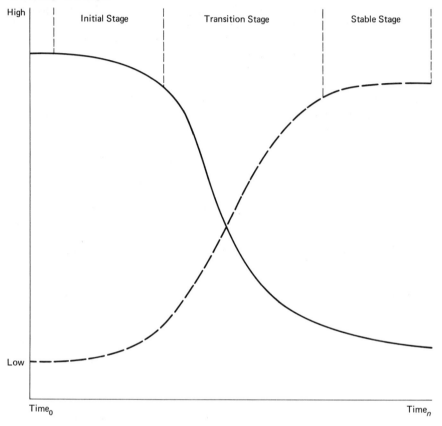

Adjusting to Prison: A Slightly Larger Conceptual Leap

Medical and law schools have some obvious similarities. Less obvious, perhaps, are the similarities these institutions have with institutions designed to incarcerate people. Nevertheless, prisons, like medical and law schools, are settings through which persons pass, settings that call for adjustments in perspectives. This being the case we can broaden the information base by comparing the process of passing through prisons with the processes just discussed.

Scaff (1949) and Frankl (1959) have provided useful information in this regard in their discussions of the Japanese internment camps and German concentration camps of World War II. The same pattern of behavior and attitudinal changes are noted. Scaff's summary of the

situation is: "The early days were characterized by confusion and uncertainty. . . . This was a time of restlessness marked by feelings of
anticipation. . . . Soon, however, the initial enthusiasm wore off . . .
replaced with a more sober and realistic but also more reliable attitudes
that characterized internment morale" (pp. 14–15).

In more detail, Frankl describes the changing orientations while passing through concentration camps.

> The newly arrived prisoner experienced the tortures of other most
> painful emotions, all of which he tried to deaden. First of all, there
> was his boundless longing for his home and his family. This often could
> become so acute that he felt himself consumed by longing. Then there
> was disgust; disgust with all the ugliness which surrounded him, even
> in its mere external forms. (p. 31)

> At that moment I saw the plain truth and did what marked the
> culminating point of the first phase of my psychological reaction: I
> struck out my whole former life. (p. 21)

> The prisoner who had passed into the second stage of his psychologi-
> cal reactions did not avert his eyes anymore. By then his feelings were
> blunted, and he watched unmoved. . . . Disgust, horror, and pity are
> emotions that our spectator could not really feel anymore. The sufferers,
> the dying and dead, became such commonplace sights to him after
> a few weeks of camp life that they could not move him any more.
> (pp. 32–33)

Like life in medical and law schools, life in concentration camps,
when viewed as a process of passing through, is characterized by an
early unsettledness, followed by a period of transition, and, finally, a
kind of acquiescence, a reorientation to the new situation. We noted
earlier, in the work of Irwin (1970) and our study of a pretrial detention
institution, how this same process of reorientation was found in prisons
incarcerating persons either charged or convicted of a crime. The process
of prisonization, then, appears to be a special case of a more general
process of passing through and situational adjustment.

If this is the case, we would expect that the perspectives gained
while in prison would be rather flexible, amenable to change as persons
approach release and reentry to the community. The process of anticipatory change in perspective is noted most graphically in the work of
Wheeler (1961). Noting that the degree to which a person is "prisonized"
depends on the phase of his incarceration (early, middle, or late),
i.e., "inmates who are soon to return to the community are more frequently oriented in terms of conventional values. Inmates conform least
to conventional standards during the middle phase of their institutional

career. These inmates appear to shed the prison culture before they leave it, such that there are almost as many conforming inmates at time of release as at time of entrance into the system" (p. 706). Wheeler goes on to suggest, "If observations could be made on parolees, it is possible that we could locate other points in the cycle. The results suggest a complex process of socialization and resocialization as offenders move into and out of the correctional community" (p. 708).

Information on these other points, information supporting the situational nature of the adjustment, is available in the work of Irwin (1970) and Erickson et al. (1973) in their discussions of the process of reentry into the community. This process is once again ushered in by a time of initial unsettledness.

> The ex-convict moves from a state of incarceration where the pace is slow and routinized, the events are monotonous but familiar, into a chaotic and foreign outside world. The cars, buses, people, buildings, roads, stores, lights, noises, and animals are things he hasn't experienced at first hand for quite some time. The most ordinary transactions of the civilian have dropped from his repertoire of automatic maneuvers. Getting on a streetcar, ordering something at a hot dog stand, entering a theater are strange. Talking to people whose accent, style of speech, gestures, and vocabulary are slightly different is difficult. The entire stimulus world—the sights, sounds, and smells—is strange. (Irwin, p. 114)

In a more abbreviated fashion, one of the persons interviewed by Erickson et al. suggested, "The best way to describe getting out is what it would be like for a cat that's penned up all the time. Let it out and it sees a mouse, and it don't know whether to catch it or run from it. He's sort of lost" (p. 115).

Like the process of passing through an institution, the process of reentering the community can be divided into stages. Irwin has labeled these the time of "settling down," "making it," and "doing good." The initial phase is relatively short, a matter of weeks or perhaps a month or two. It is a time when persons become reacquainted with the physical and social world that has not remained constant during the time of incarceration. The second stage of "making it" is a time of establishing survival capabilities, a time of finding a job, a home, transportation, and, perhaps, former friends. Finally, assuming the person makes it, the process continues as attention turns more to the standards of success as defined by life in the community—to the good life. The parallels between this process and those already discussed should be obvious. The time of early unsettledness is followed by a transitional time of locating appropriate strategies of action and, finally, by a time of adjustment to the standards of the new setting.

Adjusting to Death and Dying: A Larger Leap Yet[1]

We come now to an even larger analytic step—the comparison of death and dying with our previous examples of situational adjustment. Although dying may appear to be quite different from passing through medical school, law school, or even concentration camps, from an *analytic* point of view there are important similarities. Death, in social terms, is a process in which existing networks of relationships are disturbed. Preexisting normative expectations are dissolving. Behavioral anticipations are changing. The social bonds that unite and guide persons are in a state of flux. From the vantage point of shifting social networks, then, there are similarities. There also are similarities in terms of the context in which the process of reorientation occurs.

There is general agreement that the social context of dying has changed in recent years due to advances in medical knowledge and technology. Whereas most persons died in their homes during less technologically advanced times, it has been estimated that now some two-thirds of all deaths in the U.S. occur in hospitals (Glaser and Strauss, 1970). Moreover, the average length of time between the onset of a fatal illness and death has lengthened substantially due to sophisticated life-prolonging techniques. As a result, death and dying, like education and imprisonment, occur largely within the context of organizations that process people (Brim et al., 1970, p. 303).

This process has been explored by Kübler-Ross (1969) in a series of interviews with dying patients. On analysis of these interviews, it was concluded that the process of adjusting to the experience of dying occurred in five stages. The first of these was one of denial and isolation. Apparently the denial functions as a buffer after unexpected shocking news, allows the patient to collect himself or herself, and, with time, to mobilize other less radical defenses (p. 35).

When the first stage of denial cannot be maintained any longer, it is replaced by feelings of anger, rage, envy, and resentment. This second stage can be seen as the beginning of the transition period in which the patient searches for an understanding of the new experience. The third stage, "bargaining," also can be viewed as falling into this time of transition. It is a time when persons pray for an extension of life, sometimes in exchange for good behavior or other services, such as donating parts of their bodies to science or for transplants. The goal is an extension of life, modified by a wish for a few days without pain.

The fourth stage is one of depression, which is viewed as preparatory grief—grief in preparation for impending loss of social contact. Though depression certainly occurs in all the various stages of dying, Kübler-Ross

[1] Many of the ideas discussed in this section were first developed with Linda Aiken. See Olson and Aiken (1973).

differentiates between the reactive depression occurring in early stages as a result of a past loss and the preparatory depression of the final stages of adaptation that takes into account impending losses.

This preparatory depression, a kind of anticipatory withdrawal, leads into the final stage of adjustment that Kübler-Ross labels acceptance, which is really a kind of provisional adjustment, provisioned on the sometimes remote hope of recovery. Acceptance is a stage almost devoid of feelings, where the patient seeks less and less company from family and others. There is neither depression nor anger. The patient is tired and, in most cases, quite weak and will contemplate the situation with a certain degree of quiet expectation.

Comparing these observations on the process of dying in a hospital with our other examples of passing through people-processing organizations, we find familiar stages: (1) high emotional involvement and restless anticipation; (2) a transitional settling down; and (3) acquiescence or adjustment to the demands of the situation. The similarities with still other instances of situational adjustment are suggested by Kübler-Ross (1972), when she notes,

> The "stages of dying" affect not only terminally ill patients. You can apply these lessons to everyday living. If a man loses a girlfriend, he may deny it at first; then he becomes angry at the other suitor. Then he sends her some flowers to bargain, and if he cannot get what he wants, he becomes depressed. Eventually, he reaches the stage of acceptance, when he finds another girlfriend. (178)

Other comparison points can be found. We might look at community disaster studies, where the process of situational adjustment is perhaps best captured in the novel *The Plague*, by Albert Camus (1960), who wrote of the townspeople:

> In this respect they had adapted themselves to the very conditions of the plague, all the more potent for its mediocrity. None of us was capable any longer of an exalted emotion; all had trite, monotonous feelings. "It's high time it stopped," people would say, because in time of calamity the obvious thing is to desire its end, and in fact they wanted it to end. But when making such remarks, we felt none of the passionate yearning or fierce resentment of the early phase; we merely voiced one of the few clear ideas that lingered in the twilight of our minds. *The furious revolt of the first weeks had given place to a vast despondency, not to be taken for resignation though it was nonetheless a sort of passive and provisional acquiescence.* (p. 164. Emphasis added)

We have thus moved a good distance from our original comparison of medical and law schools. In each case we have seen that the process of "passing through" is a process of reorientation. The old set of expectations and definitions are set aside. Social networks are shifting. This leaves a state of limbo, a state of transition. As the characteristics of the new setting are mapped, a new order emerges as individuals settle into the new context.

> **Practicum 4.1** Take a critical stance toward the comparisons and ideas just discussed. Have we jumped too far in our attempt to note similarities? If so, what are the important differences that have been overlooked? How would you modify the ideas discussed? What clarification is needed? What additional settings might shed light on your speculations? What additional information would you like to have from the settings discussed? Think of your own experiences. Do they yield any relevant information?

At this point you may be saying, "Look, you are equating the experience of going to medical school with that of dying. That is simply foolish." When we approach the setting from the insider's point of view, such a criticism has obvious merit. Death for the dying person certainly involves different perspectives than passing through medical school. However, for the outsider, in this case the social theorist, both situations have vestiges of similarities. Each involves adjustment to problematic circumstances. It is this general concept of *adjustment* that allows us to move from the "folk system" to the "analytic system" and thus treat the situations as similar.

But still, the critic responds, even in terms of social science the structure of these situations differs. On the one hand, you have a setting in medical school where large numbers of persons are passing through together, having contact with others who have already gone through similar experiences. On the other hand, you have the dying patient who, from the various practices of doctors and nurses as well as from hospital policy, passes through in isolation. In addition, the settings differ in terms of their "closure," in terms of the degree of contact with other settings. Prisons and concentration camps are certainly more closed than, say, a law school. After all, the process of adjustment is, in part, going to depend on how much adjustment is called for, on how totally the present context is cut off from former perspectives, on how much discontinuity and, therefore, reorientation is called for.

It is when we begin to note general differences, as well as similarities, that we move on to refine our analytic framework, on to conditions likely to affect the initial generalizations. This frequently involves a construction of typologies for classifying settings and thus anticipating differences likely to occur.

BACK TO THE BUSINESS AT HAND

What does all this imply for the process of theory construction? Many "purists" would scoff at the idea that the above discussion is by any stretch of the imagination a "theory." It is too loose, too fuzzy. Perhaps we can clear things up a little. To this point we have noted the following: (1) The pattern of reorientation is dependent on the information flow within the interpersonal setting. (2) The pattern of reorientation is dependent on the degree of disruption or disjuncture between the past and the present setting. (3) Related to both of these points is the idea that the pattern of reorientation is dependent on the "closure" of the setting being adjusted to. We would anticipate, for example, that the process of reorientation in a minimum-security institution, where family and friends are permitted freer visists, would be substantially different than the process of reorientation in a totally isolated block of a maximum-security institution.

We arrived at these generalizations in a process of comparing a variety of situations. From the insider's perspective they may be quite different; for analytic purposes they exhibit important similarities. From these comparisons we began looking at the situations through theoretical glasses provided by concepts of increasing scope. Still there is a kind of looseness. Have we been biased in our look at the information? Have we selected only those aspects of reorientation patterns that supported our ideas, at the expense of disconfirming observations? How might we use these ideas? If we wanted to see if the ideas have any validity, how might we set up a study to test them? Given different settings, how might we devise indicators that would be parallel across settings? Can we be more specific about predictions concerning the shape of the reorientation curves? We have sometimes simply suggested that "A" is somehow related to "B." At other times, we have been more specific and suggested that "A," the reorientation process, is speeded up by factors that increase the flow of information. Is it possible to continue our fashioning of theory still further?

For many social scientists, theoretical parsimony—the concise, non-repetitive presentation of ideas—is highly desirable. To accomplish this, ideas often are translated one step further into the analytic language of mathematical models. Verbal and sometimes rambling presentations are summarily symbolized by one or more mathematical equations. For example, the process of situational adjustment can be seen as the change in behavior or attitudes per unit change in time. As time in the new setting increases, changes in behavior and attitudes take place. When our ideas reach a more refined stage, these curves can be linked to mathematical equations. The acquisition of new behavior patterns (Y) after repeated encounters with the circumstances of a situation (X) can be represented by a general equation $Y = aX^n$ where the values of a and n, and thus the shape of the curve, depend on the characteristics of the situation.

For those of you interested in further discussion of these possibilities,

Hamblin et al. (1973) have provided a discussion of the process of social adaptation in their attempt to construct a mathematical theory of social change. We will postpone discussion of the use of mathematical models until a later chapter.

Uncontrolled Aspects of Controlled Comparisons

The strategy of controlled comparisons, as we have been using the term, refers to the process of collecting and comparing findings available from any number of sources. We relied on information collected by others for purposes other than our own. The task was to find similarities and locate potential sources of differences. This done, we find a substantial degree of ambiguity remaining in the looseness of the ideas and tentativeness of the conclusions. It is difficult to move beyond this looseness utilizing the procedures discussed to this point. We have discussed the methods of exploring situations in their own terms as they naturally occur. This means, to an important extent, that control is only partial.

For one thing, we are constrained by the availability situations. We may suspect that an important variable is the degree of closure of a particular setting and yet be unable to gain access to a totally closed insitition, or be unable to find a totally open institution or institutions with various degrees of closure inbetween. Also, once located, we may find that settings with varying degrees of closure differ in any number of additional ways. Administrators may be different. Persons selected to pass through a maximum-security institution are likely to differ in a number of ways from persons going to a prison farm or to a model-community-based correctional program. We are thus left with the question of whether observed differences in the patterns of situational adjustment are due to the structure of the situation, to the actions of administrators, to the types of persons involved, or to some combination of factors.

Additional lack of control in the above comparisons lies in the lack of parallel indicators for various ideas. The studies cited measured the dimensions of the process of situational adjustment in a number of ways. Emotional change was captured in each study. Each reported a change from tense uneasiness to settled acquiescence. What about other dimensions? What about normative orientations, behavior patterns? Not having designed the studies, leaves us with a number of unanswered questions. How might we go about designing a study to make comparisons more controlled?

Developing Predictive Propositions

Without turning the discussion into a cookbook, consider the following: First, think about the problem of interest in terms of *variables,* i.e., things that vary. We have discussed the following sets of variables: (1) There are the patterns of reorientation. How steep or level are the curves representing the acquisition and extinction of behavior, attitudes, and feelings? (2) Then, there is the structure of the situation. Here, there is the degree of information flow and the degree to which it is closed off from other settings. (3) We have considered variation in the type of persons involved in the sense that the setting represents varying degrees of disjuncture from past experiences.

Second, think about the problem in terms of how the variables are related to one another. A rough summary of the situational adjustment discussion could be that presented in Figure 4.5. For one thing, we

FIGURE 4.5
Initial Diagram of Relationship Between the Structure of Situations, the Types of Persons Passing Through, and the Pattern of Reorientation

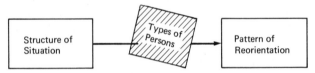

have the variable we are trying to explain, the pattern of reorientation. On the other hand, we have the variables we are suggesting as the source of explanation, the various dimensions of the structure of the situation and past orientations of individuals. These explanatory variables are themselves linked in that individuals act as filters through which the impact of the structure of the situation passes. This is an oversimplified representation of the argument, but for the time being that is what we want.

Further specification is possible. The stages of reorientation can be seen as a series of sequentially arranged acquisition and extinction curves where, taking the case of dying in a hospital as an example, the behavior and attitudes in question are those defining the stages of denial, anger, bargaining, depression, and acceptance. Parallel stages in the process of reentry are those of settling down, making it, and doing good. Those in passing through medical school are learning it all, provisional strategies, and learning just what "they" want us to. The *content* of the stages will differ from one setting to the next. It is the *pattern* of reorientation we are interested in.

It is not that manifestations of each stage of reorientation, say, anger, are absent from each succeeding or preceding stage, say, barganing. It is rather that each of the stages is defined by the predominance of a certain kind of behavior and attitudinal orientation. Again drawing on the example of the stages suggested by Kübler-Ross, we can characterize the reorientation process as that in Figure 4.6, where time is plotted along the bottom and changes in the frequency of behavior on the vertical axis. When the acquisition and extinction curves cross,

FIGURE 4.6

Stages of Reorientation to Dying Represented by Frequency of Behavioral Manifestations

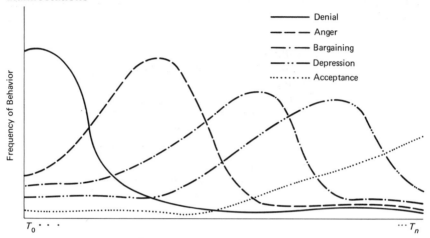

we say a new stage is entered. Additional research into situational adjustment might thus focus on the length of stages, the shape of the acquisition-extinction curves, the sequence in which the stages occur, and factors that might influence various patterns.

We have hypothesized, for example, that the pattern of reorientation is contingent on the degree of disjuncture the present setting represents from the past. Given a certain level of disjuncture, we have further hypothesized that the process of reorientation is greatly influenced by access to relevant information about the new setting. Understanding of the new setting, and thus the speed of reorientation, is in part dependent on whether others in the setting have been in similar positions and thus able to provide relevant information. We found, for example, that contact with upperclassmen during the initial semesters of law school sped up the process of reorientation among law students (Olson, 1971).

Keeping in mind the desire to predict the shape of the curves and using access to information as a guiding variable, the typology suggested by Wheeler (1966) for categorizing interpersonal settings provides a useful framework. In Wheeler's scheme there are four types of interpersonal settings. Settings are categorized according to where they fall along two dimensions, which in turn are dichotomized. The first dimension is separated according to whether the individual passing through is accompanied at the same time by others—whether the setting is "collective" or "individual." The second dimension is divided depending on whether those passing through have contact with "experienced" others who have already been through earlier stages—the "disjunctive/serial" dimension. When these dimensions are combined, they form what is referred to in the general case as the property-space of a typology. See Figure 4.7.

FIGURE 4.7
Property–Space for Interpersonal
Setting

	Individual	Collective
Disjunctive	Type I	Type II
Serial	Type III	Type IV

Source: Wheeler, 1966.

Drawing from the previous examples, the settings characterized by Type I parallel that facing the dying patient in a hospital. For a number of reasons, dying persons pass through hospitals largely in isolation. They do not have contact with persons who have already experienced the situation. In addition, doctors and nurses as well as relatives often act as if normal life continues. There are often attempts, sometimes subtle, sometimes direct, to hide the fact of impending death from the patient.

An example of the Type II situation is provided by the first group to enter a newly formed concentration camp. There are no experienced persons who have been through the experience, but persons are able to communicate with each other. The fourth type is exemplified by the situation in educational institutions. Not only are persons able to communicate with others at approximately the same stages as themselves, but they also have contact with others at more advanced stages in the process. We have not considered settings that parallel the third type. However, it is approximated by the individual taking on a new job and having contact with the outgoing occupant.

This typology of interpersonal settings in Figure 4.7, then, allows us to further specify and refine our ideas regarding the process of "passing through." It might also serve as a future guide for choosing additional settings. We might, for example in a study of the reentry process, search out cities or states where parole programs differ along these dimensions. In some locations, persons no longer in prison readjust to community life in a system approaching the individual disjunctive context. They are asked to report to their parole officers by themselves and are required to stay away from "shady" company, which means persons who have been to prison and have reentered community life. In other cities, programs might approach the collective serial setting, in which ex-convicts get together in groups with other persons experienced at reentering community life from prison.

It should be noted, before we move on, that, although the typology characterizes settings as a whole, persons passing through might be encountering different degrees of "collectiveness" or "disjuncture." This being the case, we would predict that their reorientation patterns would vary accordingly.

Given this means for categorizing settings, where do we go? We have already mentioned that interest, in terms of future predictions, lies with the shape of the acquisition and extinction curves. The shapes of the curves, i.e., the speed of reorientation, should fluctuate according to the characteristics of the interpersonal settings being passed through. From this, we might hypothesize, for example, that the transitional portion of the process would be reached sooner and be of shorter duration (i.e., the curve would be more "peaked") in the collective-serial setting than in the individual-disjunctive setting. The role of certain "transitional units," such as halfway houses for ex-convicts, can be viewed in these terms. The nature of parole progress, i.e., the speed and probability of moving from the settling-down stage to the stages of making it and doing good, is contingent in part on various sources of information and support provided by halfway houses.

Thus, the curves representing the patterns of reorientation should change in shape depending on the structural characteristics of the situation through which persons pass. In addition, the shape of these curves will vary with the *substance* being acquired or extinguished. By this we mean, for example, that the acquisition of normative orientations, like idealistic beliefs about the medical profession, may differ from the acquisition of behavior patterns or emotional reaction patterns. We found in the law-school study that the changing emotional reactions, in terms of the degree of tension, differed substantially from behavior changes, such as the percentage of assignments done on time. Apparently, emotional changes occur at a more rapid rate than do behavior or normative orientations. Little can be said with precision beyond this. Nevertheless, the acquisition of various social substances appears to involve different mechanisms and, therefore, varying models would be applicable. Once we are able to distinguish various "substances," the original differential predictions for varying social settings should again enter the picture.

Since the substance of any set of stages will differ from one reorientation process to the next, the remainder of the present discussion will
focus on one reorientation process, that of dying. We do this primarily
because Kübler-Ross has elaborated the stages with relative clarity.
Throughout the remainder of the discussion you may want to periodically refer to Figure 4.6 to remind you of what we mean when referring
to the shape and sequence of stages.

Given present practices in the majority of hospitals, dying occurs
within an individual-disjunctive setting. That is, persons usually do not
share the experience of dying with others who are dying, and they
do not have the benefit of consulting with those who have passed
through the experience before them. There will, of course, be variation
along these lines. It is this variation in the patient's awareness of his
or her situation and the degree of openness among the hospital staff
with the information they possess that become crucial factors in terms
of predicting the patient's reorientation pattern.

Along these lines, Glaser and Strauss (1964, 1965) define the concept
of awareness context. Awareness contexts are divided into four types,
ranging from "open awareness" to "closed awareness." Based on the
above discussion, we would hypothesize that an open-awareness context
facilitates passage through the stages of reorientation reflected by the
shorter length of time it takes to reach the final stage, while a closed-
awareness context slows adaptation and results in prolongation of the
reorientation process, a prolongation of the denial and anger and bargaining stages.

Tentative support is available in the work of Fox (1959). In a study
of the seriously ill patients on an experimental metabolic research unit,
Fox provides one of the few published examples of dying patients within
an open, collective social context. Patients on this unit appeared to pass
through all of the previously mentioned stages under more open circumstances than normally are found within hospitals. First, there was a
sense of community within the research unit, with patients feeling a
sense of commitment to each other. Second, open awareness existed
in terms of each patient knowing that there was not yet a cure for
his or her illness. Both physicians and patients coped with this uncertainty by sharing what was known about the illness and prognosis; patients took pride in that they knew as much as the doctors. Third, patients exchanged medical information that helped offset some of the
uncertainty. It would appear that both the open-awareness context and
the opportunity to share experiences with other dying people facilitated
the process of adaptation in the sense that the latter portion of the
reorientation process was more quickly reached.

Further research in this area might fruitfully pursue the more precise
variations in the patterns of acquisition and extinction curves. Behavioral

as well as attitudinal measures of the various stages will be needed. We will have more to say of this process of developing indicators in Chapters 5 through 8. Once indicators have been worked out, it remains to link variations in the patterns of change to variations in such things as information flows and social support. For anyone who has given thought to these matters, the difficulties are not small.

In addition to the structure of the setting in terms of information flow, we have argued that the pattern of situational adjustment depends on the degree of disjuncture or disruption the new situation presents. Persons with prior contact with prison or other state institutions, persons for whom prison does not represent such a drastic break with the past, are likely to exhibit different patterns of reorientation than those with little or no prior contact. In the case of death and dying, this degree of disjuncture, this degree of disruption to existing social networks is captured in the idea of the degree of social loss. The impact of death and dying, in social terms, is an impact on various connections binding the social actors together. Death, like other disruptive experiences, disturbs existing networks of exchange, as well as normative and affective orientations. It is in this sense that death involves a "social loss." The anticipation, as well as the immediate existence of this social loss, has direct effects on the behavior of the hospital staff and the family as well as the patient.

We can predict, then, that the greater the social loss the less likely individuals involved are to move to the acceptance stage of the reorientation process. If we view the hospital staff and family as also "passing through," as also adjusting to the situation, we can say the greater the social loss the longer it will take for *them* to reach the "acceptance" stage of the process.

Interesting insights along these lines are provided by Glick, Weiss, and Parkes (1974) in their study of the reorientation process among a sample of widows. These authors suggest that the "process of recovery" occurred in the phases of (1) early disbelief, shock, anger, and grief; (2) the closely linked transition time of keeping busy, engaging in activity primarily to divert thinking about the loss; and (3) a time of activity with "a purpose," as the widows began adjusting to role changes called for in the shifts from "wife" to "provider," from being a marriage partner to being alone. With this third phase came the development of new skills and a return to full social participation. This study of widows also is relevant to the present discussion in that the authors point to a number of factors, such as the anticipation of the death, that influence the speed and "substance" of the reorientation process.

In addition, the reorientation pattern of the dying individual will be influenced by the amount of cost the departure involves. For those who are integrated into their social setting, those in the "prime" of their lives, the emotional reaction should be more pronounced and prolonged, as should the bargaining stage. Acceptance, if ever reached, should be slow in appearing. By contrast, those persons who have retired and thus already disengaged, to a certain extent, should more readily move to the acceptance stage and have less of an emotional reaction. The pattern for children is more difficult to predict, though it will be related if the present discussion is used to guide our thinking, to the degree of existing attachments to family and peers, as well as to anticipations that might surround the future.

Thus, it is through this route of social loss that the variables of age, occupation, fame, accomplishments, education, and family stability enter the picture as important conditioning factors. If Glaser and Strauss are correct, the single most important characteristic on which social loss is based is age (1964b). Children and adolescents represent a higher social loss than old persons. Adults in their prime are in the midst of their contributions to their families, occupations, and society and are often considered the greatest loss, for they are depended upon by most others. Age, then, becomes a readily available indicator of the degree of disruption that death and dying signal. Thus, we expect the patterns of reorientation to vary accordingly. It is from specifications such as these that we move to the next step in designing a study, that of translating ideas into concrete indicators.

We might, for example, design a survey or interview study where the ideas become reflected in items on a questionnaire or questions on an interview schedule. We might, as an alternative, attempt to construct our own settings and conduct an experiment, varying the degree of information flow, the degree of openness in terms of the awareness, the degree of closure, and so forth. There is an impressive tradition of experimentally pursued learning psychology to draw upon. Learning, after all, is a kind of adjustment.

Through studies such as these we can further refine and change our ideas about the process of passing through. This brings us to the important point. *The processes of theory construction and theory testing are integrated enterprises.* Differences lie in the degree to which the problem is formulated in general terms prior to the study and the degree to which this prior formulation guides the information sought. As Selvin and Stuart (1966) have suggested, it is possible to "hunt," "snoop," and "fish" to varying degrees with survey results. Novel ideas, unexpected patterns, and completely new theoretical schemes may emerge from experimental studies, as well as from studies designed to include a time of participant observation. It is just that the experiment and survey strategies allow for greater control and precision and thus are most useful when pursuing a preselected set of ideas calling for concrete indicators, experimental manipulation, and random selection of the individuals, groups, organizations, or nation/states you wish to study. In the next chapters we begin to explore these more controlled alternatives in some detail. For now, it is time to summarize.

SUMMARY

One style of research, variously called qualitative research, participant observation, or ethnographic research, has been pursued in the first portion of this book. A frequent goal of this research is to capture the "folk system," the insider's perspective. Once this is done, a decision must be made as to how to best present the findings: in their own terms, within the context of a thematic model; or within the context of a more general analytic framework. In the process you will encounter a number of problematic situations.

One of these problems is the quandry of being in and wanting out or being out and wanting in; the problem of needing the insider's insight and the outsider's distance. You will have to plan to a certain degree, but you also will have to remain flexible enough to change directions if the situation confronts you with unanticipated findings. In all likelihood you will be confronted with the "spy problem." The eventual detail of your data will depend on how far you progress toward the inner circles of the setting. At the same time you may find yourself confronted with a segmented setting wherein access to one segment means isolation from another. This, of course, has implications for the representativeness of your findings and the generality of your conclusions. In addition, in your role as "marginal native," you will find a series of ethical decisions that must be made. These decisions will have implications not only for your study but also for the lives of those you are studying and your relationships with them.

Beyond this we can say little. Spend time acquainting yourself with the experiences of others. Accounts of the sociologist and anthropologist at work are increasingly available. We have referred to several throughout. Develop your skills in note taking and interviewing before you get too far into your study. Pay attention to details—they are sometimes boring, but they provide more than ample dividends. However, don't lose sight of the forest. Search for overarching patterns, for ideas allowing for the understanding of the immediate situation as well as anticipation of patterns in other settings.

KEY ISSUES

1. Discuss the process of thematic analysis.
2. How does the thematic analysis of the folk system differ from the development of analytic concepts through controlled comparisons?

3. What are some key controlled aspects of controlled comparisons?
4. Discuss the pros and cons of developing predictive propositions.

REFERENCES

Becker, Howard S.; Geer, Blanche; Hughes, Everett; and Strauss, Anselm
    1961   *Boys in White*. Chicago: University of Chicago Press.
Bohannan, Paul
    1957   *Justice and Judgment Among the Tiv*. London: Oxford University Press.
Brim, Orville; Freeman, H. E.; Levine, Sol; and Scotch, N. A. (eds.)
    1970   *The Dying Patient*. New York: Russell Sage Foundation.
Camus, Albert
    1960   *The Plague*. New York: Knopf.
Chambliss, Bill (ed.)
    1971   *Box Man: A Professional Thief's Journey*. New York: Harper and Row.
Diesing, Paul
    1971   *Patterns of Discovery in the Social Sciences*. Chicago: Aldine.
Eggan, Fred
    1954   "Social Anthropology and the Method of Controlled Comparison." *American Anthropologist*, vol. 56, pp. 743–63.
Erickson, Rosemary J.; Crow, Wayman J.; Zurcher, Louis A.; and Connet, Archie V.
    1973   *Paroled But Not Free: Ex-offenders Look at What They Need to Make it Outside*. New York: Behavioral Publications.
Fox, Reneé
    1959   *Experiment Perilous: Physicians and Patients Facing the Unknown*. Glencoe, Ill.: Free Press.
Frankl, Viktor
    1959   *Man's Search For Meaning*. New York: Washington Square Press.
Glaser, Barney, and Strauss, Anselm
    1964   "Awareness Contexts and Social Interaction." *American Sociological Review*, vol. 29, pp. 669–78.
Glaser, Barney, and Strauss, Anselm
    1964b   "The Social Loss of Dying Patients." *American Journal of Nursing*, vol. 64, pp. 119–21.
Glaser, Barney, and Strauss, Anselm
    1965   *Awareness and Dying*. Chicago: Aldine.
Glaser, Barney, and Strauss, Anselm
    1970   *Anguish: A Case History of a Dying Patient*. San Francisco: Sociology Press.
Glick, Ira O.; Weiss, Robert S.; and Parkes, C. Murray
    1974   *The First Year of Bereavement*. New York: John Wiley and Sons.

Hamblin, Robert L.; Jacobson, R. Brooke; and Miller, Jerry L.
 1973 *A Mathematical Theory of Social Change*. New York: John Wiley and Sons.

Irwin, John
 1970 *The Felon*. Englewood Cliffs, N.J.: Prentice-Hall.

Kübler-Ross, Elizabeth
 1969 *On Death and Dying*. New York: Macmillan.

Kübler-Ross, Elizabeth
 1972 "On Death and Dying." *Journal of the American Medical Association*, July 10, Vol. 221, 174–79.

Olson, Sheldon R.
 1971 *The rise and Fall of Student Involvement in Law School*. Unpublished Ph.D. dissertation, University of Washington, Seattle.

Olson, Sheldon R., and Aiken, Linda
 1973 "Dying as a Socially Disruptive Experience: Some Predictive Implications." Paper read at Southwest Social Science Association meetings, Dallas.

Olson, Sheldon R.
 1975 "Patterns of Interpersonal Conflict and the Process of Prisonization." Paper presented at conference on prison violence, New England Center for Continuing Education, Durham, N.H.

Popper, Karl
 1957 *The Poverty of Historicism*. New York: Harper and Row.

Scaff, Alvin H.
 1949 *The Internment Camp: A Sociological Analysis of Collective Behavior in the Civilian Internment Camps in the Philippines*. Unpublished Ph.D. dissertation, University of Texas.

Selvin, Hanan C., and Stuart, Alan
 1966 "Data Dredging Procedures in Survey Analysis." *The American Statistician*, vol. 20, pp. 20–23.

Solzhenitsyn, Aleksandr
 1973 *The Gulag Archipelago*. New York: Harper Row.

Stevens, Robert
 1973 "Law Schools and Law Students." *Virginia Law Review*, vol. 59, pp. 551–707.

Wheeler, Stanton
 1961 "Socialization in Correctional Communities." *American Sociological Review*, vol. 26, pp. 697–712.

Wheeler, Stanton
 1966 "The Structure of Formally Organized Socialization Settings." In Orville Brim and Stanton Wheeler, *Socialization After Childhood: Two Essays*. New York: John Wiley and Sons.

Contents

PERFORMANCE LEVEL

Performance Factor	Outstanding	High Satisfactory	Satisfactory	Low Satisfactory	Unsatisfactory
Quality	Leaps tall buildings with single bound	Needs running start to jump tall buildings	Can leap only small buildings	Crashes into buildings	Cannot recognize buildings
Timeliness	Is faster than a speeding bullet	Only as fast as a speeding bullet	Somewhat slower than a bullet	Can only shoot bullets	Wounds self with bullets
Initiative	Is stronger than a locomotive	Is stronger than a bull elephant	Is stronger than a bull	Shoots the bull	Smells like a bull
Adaptability	Walks on water consistently	Walks on water in emergencies	Washes with water	Drinks water	Passes water in emergencies
Communication	Talks with God	Talks with the angels	Talks to self	Argues with self	Loses those arguments
Relationship	Belongs in general management	Belongs in executive ranks	Belongs in rank and file	Belongs behind a broom	Belongs with competitor
Planning	Too bright to worry	Worries about future	Worries about present	Worries about past	Too dumb to worry

Source: *Footnotes*, vol. 1, no. 2, February 1973.

Chapter 5

Translating Analytic Concepts into Observation Strategies: Some General Considerations

TESTABLE THEORIES AS INTERLOCKING NETWORKS

One view of theory, the view to be pursued in the remaining chapters, sees a theory as a collection of interconnected hypotheses. Hypotheses, in turn, are seen as interconnected concepts. By connecting concepts you get hypotheses. By connecting hypotheses you get theories. In addition, hypotheses are assumed to be *testable*. They must be subject to some kind of observation. These statements are somewhat oversimplified in that theories generally incorporate several levels of abstraction. However, the criteria of connected concepts and hypotheses are enough for present purposes.

One way to picture a testable theoretical scheme is to think of two interconnected networks, such as presented in Figure 5.1. See Blalock

FIGURE 5.1
A Testable Theoretical Scheme

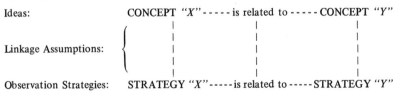

| Ideas: | CONCEPT "X" - - - - - is related to - - - - - CONCEPT "Y" |

Linkage Assumptions:

Observation Strategies: STRATEGY "X" - - - - - is related to - - - - - STRATEGY "Y"

(1968) for a more detailed discussion along these lines. One network is comprised of interconnected *ideas* about how the world works. The other network consists of interconnected *strategies* for translating these abstract ideas into "observable" information. Tying these ideas and strategies together is a series of *assumptions* the researcher makes concerning the correspondence between concept and data. Observation strategies may include, among other things, items on a questionnaire to be answered by respondents, planned observations to be made by the participant observer, elements of an experiment in the laboratory, manipulation of census data, FBI reports, or other available documents. The "nodes" of each network represent the *substantive* aspects of the theory, for example, a theory about minority relations. The "fibers" represent the *relational* aspects, for example, prediction or cause.

Suppose a hypothesis suggests that we can predict the rate of crime from the degree of societal transition.

$$+$$
SOCIETAL TRANSITION............CRIME RATE

This is read—the greater the degree of societal transition the greater the crime rate. Each of the substantive concepts—societal transition and crime rate—can be measured or observed in a number of ways. To measure societal transition we might go to legal statutes and look at such things as changing zoning laws for various areas of a city. Alternatively, we might conduct an attitude survey in which we group individuals according to the degree they feel their social surroundings are changing. Further, we might look for patterns of activities, changes in these patterns and note, for example, that there seems to be a period of transition during the weekend. The number of ways to measure societal transition is limited largely by the imagination of the researcher.

Likewise with the crime rate. Here, we could conduct a "victim" survey to find who had been victimized by what kind of offense and offender in the past year. We could conduct a similar study and instead ask persons what offenses they, themselves, had committed during the past year. Being skeptical of the validity of these techniques, we might rely on official records of police arrests or court convictions. We might want to rely on direct observations of the legal process. Finally, whatever the source of information, we might want to focus on specific types of crimes and thus concentrate on murders, robberies, thefts, drug offenses, or some combination of these.

Diagramatically, the translation of the substantive aspect of this hypothesis can be presented in a fashion similar to that in Figure 5.2.

It takes only a little thought to realize that, when we change translation procedures, i.e., when we change the indicators of concepts, we may alter the substantive aspects of the hypothesis being tested. Thus, it is crucial to be very clear as to the linkage between concepts and observation strategies.

A second translation task attaches to the conceptual link *between* concepts—the relational aspect. Most often one of two links is considered: prediction, or cause. It is one thing to assert that the crime

FIGURE 5.2
**Diagram of Ways to Translate Societal Transition Explanation
of the Crime Rate**

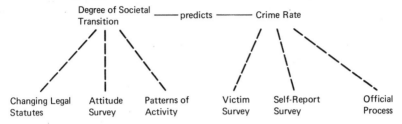

rate can be predicted from the degree of societal transition. It is another to assert that the crime rate is caused by transition.

Procedures for translating each of these relational concepts have been devised. We can compare percentage differences, examine various summarizing measures of association, employ certain control procedures to establish sequence and eliminate alternative explanations. Some of these possibilities will be explored in Chapters 10 and 11, when we turn to the question of analyzing the information gathered. For now it is enough to note the importance of making explicit the observational strategies for establishing and exploring the idea of "relationship."

One of the most crucial stages in any research project designed to test hypotheses, then, is "tooling-up," deciding what data-gathering operations are to be performed. Whatever the measurement strategy employed, as a rule of thumb it is a good idea to include more than one indicator for each concept if space, time, and monetary considerations allow. With a number of indicators for a single substantive concept, the sometimes multidimensional aspects of a single idea can more readily be explored. Thus we are able to more thoroughly investigate the theory under consideration. In addition we are able to more easily detect problem areas such as unreliable or invalid indicators.

RELIABILITY AND VALIDITY

Reliability and validity are frequently discussed topics, both simple and complex. They are simple in definition and complex in determination. Reliable strategies of observation are strategies that can be trusted. They are strategies that will measure phenomena in a consistent fashion, regardless of who is employing them or to whom they are applied. Valid strategies are also strategies we can trust. They are strategies that measure what we think they are measuring. How do you decide?

When considering reliability as well as some meanings of validity, three factors must be kept in mind: the observer or observers employing the strategy, the setting being studied, and the strategy being employed. For the sake of a manageable discussion we have limited attention to two possibilities for each factor in Figure 5.3. It is possible, of course,

FIGURE 5.3
Depicting Aspects of Study Entering into Determination of Reliability

	Situation I				Situation II	
	Strategy I	Strategy II			Strategy I	Strategy II
Observer I	A	B		Observer I	A'	B'
Observer II				Observer II		
Observer *N*	C	D		Observer *N*	C'	D'

that more complex circumstances could be imagined, such as five observers employing three strategies in eight settings. But never mind that for now. The principles developed below will be applicable to these more complex situations.

Inter-Observer Comparisons

A frequently encountered means for determining reliability is to compare two or more observers employing the same strategy within the same situation. When we discuss content analysis of available documents in Chapter 7, we will have occasion to explore a means of determining whether observers are consistent in applying the same coding scheme to the same set of documents. In Situation I the appropriate comparisons are between *A* and *C* or *B* and *D* in Figure 5.3, depending on the strategy in question. The parallel comparisons in Situation II are, of course, also appropriate. In this manner you can detect whether documents are being ordered in the same fashion, whether situations are being characterized in similar ways, whether different interviewers are producing comparable results, and so forth.

What do you do to minimize unreliability in the inter-observer sense of the term? To ward off unreliable results it is wise to spend time before beginning the collection of information, not only designing your strategies but also familiarizing those who will be implementing these strategies with what is expected. It is for this reason that careful survey research involves a time of orientation for the interviewers before sending them into the field. It is for this reason that persons are asked to take dry runs at using a coding scheme for analyzing available documents.

And, it is for this reason that persons are given explicit instructions concerning categorization of events when observing a process such as police-citizen encounters or the emergence of communication patterns within a group in the laboratory setting.

Still, even with these warding-off practices, you may find that inconsistent results are being produced within your study. The first thing to do is to begin looking for more specific sources of the trouble. The disturbance may be arising from a limited number of questions in an interview or just one aspect of the overall coding scheme. It may be limited to only a minority of your observers or even to a single observer. Given the locus of disturbance the question becomes what to do. It is not safe to simply throw the apparently disturbing observers out. It may be that they are the best users of your scheme. It may be that the consistent observers have gotten together when employing a coding scheme and have thus failed to reach independent judgments.

The solution, then, is to examine the disturbance carefully to detect any obviously biasing factors, such as some observers producing consistently more negative responses for what appear to be personal predisposition reasons. Once these systematic sources of bias are eliminated—or you may find no consistent pattern, and you end up with what appear to be honest differences of opinion—another strategy is to "average" responses across observers. Through averaging, assessments given to magazines, newspapers, historical documents, or contemporary settings can then approach a more reliable, i.e., less observer specific level. We will return to these matters in Chapter 7.

Inter-Strategy Comparisons

A second situation involves comparing results obtained by different observation strategies within the same study. This includes comparisons of single items on a questionnaire designed to tap the same concept and what is generally referred to as the "split-half" method of item comparison, where a pool of items that have been combined to form a scale is compared with another pool designed to tap the same concept. Inter-strategy comparisons also include the comparison of divergent techniques, such as the examination of records, on the one hand, and responses to questionnaire items, on the other, again designed to tap the same concept.

When constructing an interview or questionnaire format, the initial period spent designing items and then pretesting them to see which are ambiguous and which produce results consistent with other items is a time spent to reduce later unreliable results. We will have more to say of this in Chapter 8. After you have decided on a pool of items and after you have collected the data, you still will want to look at the degree to which items designed to tap the same concept are in fact correlated. You also will want to determine the degree to which scores obtained from individual items correlate with overall scale values obtained after pooling various items. We will also have more to say of this topic, which can become rather complex, in Chapter 8. The practice of pooling items to form a scale arises largely from the desire to increase the reliability of a research strategy through averaging. Assuming that individual items will have a degree of random flux, by combining items we get a more stable, and therefore more reliable, measure of the concept we are interested in.

When we address the issue of inter-strategy comparisons, we come to an area in which the questions of reliability and validity run together. Validity also is frequently determined by comparing one strategy with another. As an example, Pennings (1973) compares various measures of bureaucratic centralization and formalization listed in Figure 5.4. As can be seen, these strategies were grouped into the questionnaire approach and the institutional approach, which actually was an examination of records and interviews with a few "experts" within the organization. Penning's results must be viewed with some caution, since his sample size was rather small—ten organizations. Nevertheless, the procedures employed are instructive.

Pennings set out to determine the convergent and discriminant validity of the measures, using a strategy referred to as the multitrait-multimethod procedure, a procedure developed by Campbell and Fiske (1959) for the validation of measures of more than one trait by more than one method. Convergent validity is determined, as one might expect, by the degree to which measures designed to tap the same concept converge. This is established by comparing the size of the correlation between pairs of measures of the same concept with the size of correlations between pairs of measures tapping different concepts. We might compare the size of the correlation between the autonomy aspect of centralization, measured by the institutional approach and the personal-participation aspect of centralization as measured by the questionnaire approach, on the one hand, with other correlations between variables tapping different aspects of bureaucracy using the same two general strategies, on the other. As you can readily see, this procedure may become rather complex rather quickly. If you are going to employ more than one general strategy of observation, and if you have a number of substrategies within these major strategies, you should consult the Campbell and Fiske article, as well as more recent elaborations contained in Althauser and Haberlein (1970), Alwin (1974), and Althauser (1974). As you will see when you examine these chapters, most of the more refined issues in this area take us beyond the present treatment.

In addition to allowing discovery of difficulties, differing observation approaches frequently complement one another in that what is available

FIGURE 5.4
Alternative Measures of Bureaucracy

Institutional approach

A₁.   Centralization

Autonomy – This scale consists of 23 issues to measure whether decisions on these issues are made inside or outside the organization.

Chief executive span of control – This indicates the number of subordinates who report directly to the chief executive, regardless of the hierarchical position of the subordinates.

Worker/supervisory ratio – This value indicates the number of subordinates in production departments per first-line supervisor.

Number of direct supervisors (%) – This indicates the number of first-line supervisors in production departments, including the assistants and deputies.

B₁.   Structuring of Activities (formalization)

Formalization: role definition – This scale measures the degree to which rules and procedures are written.

Specialization – This scale measures the extent to which one or more individuals occupy a non-work-flow function on a full-time basis, regardless of the number of specialists.

Questionnaire approach

A₂.   Centralization

Personal participation in decision making – This is a Likert scale measuring how much the individual participates in decisions about the allocation or resources and the determination of organizational policies.

Hierarchy of authority – This scale measures the degree to which the organization member participates in decisions involving the tasks associated with his or her position.

Departmental participation in decision making – This Likert scale measures how much an individual "and his colleagues" participate in decisions involving their work and work environment.

B₂.   Formalization

Job codification – This is a scale measuring the degree of work standardization, that is, how many rules define what organizational members are to do.

Job specificity – This scale measures the degree to which procedures defining a job are spelled out.

Strictness – This scale measures a dimension related to rule observation: the degree to which existing rules are enforced.

Rule observation – This is a measure of whether rules are employed and enforced.

Written communication – This is a rating scale measuring the frequency of written communication as reported by individuals.

Source: Pennings, 1973.

FIGURE 5.5
Utility of Alternative Data-gathering Strategies for Various Research Goals

	Participant Observation (Including Unstructured Interviews as Well as First-hand Observation)	Records	Structured Questionnaires and Interviews	Experiments
Contemporary Setting	Best type	Useful but may be mis- or unrecorded	Useful as supplement	Not useful since artificial
Historical Events	Useful but susceptible to retrospective reinterpretation	Useful and sometimes only source	Not too useful and sometimes impossible	Limited use in "Natural Ex-Experiment" sense
Description of Distribution	Useful but susceptible to much bias due to nature of observation	Somewhat useful but may be biased	Best strategy since can be guided by principles of random sampling	Not useful
Causal Analysis	Not too useful given lack of observer control	Not too useful	Somewhat useful but limited	Best strategy due to maximum control

through one means might not be through another. Figure 5.5, an expanded version of the suggestions of Zelditch (1962), suggests some of the possibilities. In a study relying primarily on participant observation, you may find it useful to supplement your findings with a survey if you desire a representative description of the distribution of particular traits. In like manner, if you desire historical context for a contemporary examination of public opinion, you may be called upon to develop indicators from available documents. If you find correlations between certain variables in a survey but are unable to control for all contending explanations for this finding, you would do well to devise an experiment that allows you to isolate the relationship of interest more thoroughly. The reason, as well as the necessity, for these possibilities will become clearer as we proceed through the following chapters. Here, it is enough to note that the validity of your study is often enhanced by the use of more than one basic data-gathering strategy. What eludes you in one way is generally available in another.

Two additional inter-strategy comparisons have been devised to handle the problem of never being able to finally decide whether we are actually measuring what we think we are measuring. It is impossible, in the last analysis, to bridge the gap between indicator and concept. When all is said and done, it is a matter of assumption. We rely on what has been called face or logical validity: Does the measurement strategy we are using make sense; does it seem reasonable to assume that it measures what we are claiming?

In some situations this decision is handled by definition. We simply state that the concept is what we say it is via our measurement. The problem with this approach is that, frequently, there is a nagging feeling that our measurement strategies do not tap what we really mean. The number of times an individual goes to church, coupled with the amount of money given to that church, may not tap even the most important aspects of being religious. Indeed, as many writers have suggested, we may want to look at what appear to be more secular activities to determine involvement with the sacred. We want in some sense to tap what is "really" meant by the idea of being religious. It is in this real definitional sense that we can never be sure that our efforts at turning ideas into data have been successful. To help us in this regard, inter-strategy comparisons are made.

One type of inter-strategy comparison involves the examination of how closely the measurement technique in question matches up with some standard, a technique designed to measure the same concept, in which we have a great deal of faith. For example, when using scale "A," designed to tap the amount of conflict in a particular group, do we come up with the same categorization of groups as that obtained through direct observation of the groups?

A second type of inter-strategy comparison, designed to estimate the validity of a measure, is seeing if it works within the context of some well-established theory. Does a new scale of alienation or job satisfaction correlate with the same variables, say, position in the hierarchy, as do other measures that have been employed in numerous other studies? The problem with this approach is that, if different patterns of findings emerge, you are left with the decision as to whether the theory itself is erroneous or whether your new measure is invalid. This is no clear-cut situation. It will involve you in a good deal of thought and additional research, as well as speculation. Perhaps all that can be said in this regard is to not get so tied to your new measure that you hold on, come hell or high water. Neither should you abandon your own ideas, however, just because they are out of line with previous findings. It may be that you have hit on something others have missed. It is in the quandry of making these decisions that we come to the conclusion that perhaps we will never know for sure. The best we can do in most problematic situations of this sort is wait for additional research to take us in one direction or another.

Inter-Situation Comparisons

Reliability also is frequently determined by comparisons across situations. This may involve comparisons of the same sample of persons or setting at two or more points in time with the same strategy and researcher. It may involve different situations or sets of persons being studied by the same observer with the same strategy. It may involve different research sites being studied with the same techniques but by different observers.

Take the first situation, where the same site of research is examined two or more times via the same strategy and observer. Suppose you find that the results differ. Is this due to changes in the setting? Is it due to an unreliable scale or coding scheme that produces one set of responses one time and another on a different occasion? Has the research site become test-wise, in that the respondents remember their responses from the first time and thus answer in such a way to "improve" their scores? Has the fact that research was conducted previously sensitized the population in such a way to make them actually change? These are alternatives that can, under most research conditions, not be separated satisfactorily. It is possible through various quasi-experimental designs (see Campbell and Stanley, 1963) to examine certain possibilities, but, in many situations, the demands of these designs cannot be met. What to do?

When faced with alternative explanations for results that differ when replicating the study on the same population, you frequently are left with deciding what is the most plausible explanation. Are the differences consistent with what you might expect under the hypothesis that the setting has in some sense become test-wise or undergone some real change? Are the findings instead mixed up in such a way that no apparent explanation can account for the differences other than the unreliability of your strategies? To answer these questions you are called upon to examine your data rather closely and perhaps investigate what has transpired between the time of the first study and its replication.

What about the second situation, where the research is replicated by the same researcher but in a different context? If the settings are truly independent, there will be no chance for becoming test-wise. If the study is conducted at the same point in time, historical events usually can be eliminated also. Settings frequently are coming out of a different tradition, but, hopefully, your instrument will not be affected by such differences. This tradition or cultural-background difference, however, is just the sort of thing that frequently plagues the researcher trying to apply the same questionnaire, interview schedule, or coding scheme in different settings. Some words or ways of presenting questions signify different things in different settings. You are well advised to spend some time before conducting any research, even if it is replication, familiarizing yourself with the setting so as to avoid unreliable responses. Indeed, it can be argued that situation free scales are impossible to develop.

This situation specific nature of scales is at the heart of the controversy over the reliability (and validity) of certain IQ tests. It is simply difficult to tap a person's abilities without also tapping, in some sense, cultural background. Thus, items that make one kind of sense to some persons may signify nothing or something entirely different to others without ever tapping any innate ability resource. We may not want to argue that situation free scales and measurement strategies are impossible to devise. It is easier to establish that such development frequently is no small task.

The final aspect of reliability in the inter-situation sense of the term couples variation of situation with variation in observers. Here, you have all the difficulties of inter-situation reliability plus variation in observer. As noted, it is to facilitate replication, regardless of observer, that there is a call for explicitly defined data-gathering procedures. It is one thing to say in a vaguely defined fashion that you are going to conduct a survey of public attitudes toward drug abuse, or governmental corruption, with a general interest in the impact of age on the degree of negative attitudes. It is another, and more reliable, procedure to make sure that each of the interviewers conducts himself or herself in a similar manner, asking the questions in the same fashion.

Once again this is a deceptively simple solution. You must remember that data gathering is a social activity and that certain actions, certain ways of self-presentation, like the items on a questionnaire, may be interpreted differently in different settings. In some interpersonal settings, a tie and coat may put the interviewee at ease. In other settings, less formal appearance may more readily signal approachability. The important thing is not consistency in the outward mode of dress but rather the production of the image of approachability. What this means, again, is that you spend some time familiarizing yourself with the research setting with an eye to producing consistent interpretations of cues in the context of the interpersonal interaction that characterizes the data-gathering situation. For some findings along these lines, see Gordon (1969), especially Chapter 6.

It also should be remembered of course that, if your strategies differ too much from those used in the study you are replicating, the comparability of your results will come into question. We are once again in the area where social research comes closer to a craft than an exercise in using a cookbook. Rarely is it a good idea to throw away the cookbook until you have become quite familiar with the process. Neither is it a good idea to slavishly refuse to make innovations if the resulting stew will taste better.

Excellent guidelines and first-hand experiences are reported in Converse and Schuman (1974). One interviewer suggested the following dual, and partially conflicting, role for the interviewer:

> The interviewer is required to be *two* things to all people. First, he must be a *diplomat:* warm, sympathetic, sensitive to the respondent—

just the sort of person who in ordinary social life does not go about asking embarrassing questions because, through sensitivity and tact, he knows how to avoid them. But, at the same time, he must be something of a *boor:* no sympathetic understanding of the respondent will prevent him from elbowing his way right in with questions that might embarrass or discomfort the other person. (p. 31)

If you are going to conduct an interview study, this book is well worth your time.

Practicum 5.1   **To get these various meanings of reliability and validity in mind, refer to Figure 5-3. Assume that each cell represents results from a particular combination of observer, strategy, and setting. What comparisons are appropriate in the inter-strategy sense of the term? What difficulties do you foresee in comparing the results collected by different observers in different settings using different strategies but aiming at examining the same hypothesis or set of hypotheses?**

LEVELS OF MEASUREMENT

We come now to what is, along with questions of reliability and validity, perhaps the most frequently discussed issue under the general considerations of translating ideas into data. This is the level of measurement you attain with your strategies of observation. Were it not for its importance, we could skip this topic, since it has been discussed so frequently elsewhere. However, when we turn to strategies for translating the relational aspects of a theory into data in Chapters 9 nd 10, the level of measurement will in large part determine the available statistical techniques. Thus, it needs to be understood.

A point that should be emphasized at the outset, a point that is frequently glossed over, is this: *The level of measurement attained cannot be determined independently of the conceptual framework in which you are working.* When considering the nature of the scales you construct, you must keep in mind what concepts you are tapping. Consider the following questions taken from a study of law students:

1.   Your religious persuasion is:
     A.   Catholic
     B.   Jewish: Orthodox
     C.   Jewish: Conservative
     D.   Jewish: Reform
     E.   Atheist
     F.   Agnostic
     G.   Protestant _____
                         (Please specify denomination)

    H. Other _____

                     (Please specify)

2. Was your high-school education primarily in:
    A. Public schools
    B. Nonsectarian private schools
    C. Parochial or denominational schools

3. What was your major(s) in college

_____

4. Have you ever been on full-time active duty in the armed services for a period of at least four months?
    A. Yes
    B. No

Each of these is an example of a question used to construct a nominal scale. All provide a means of categorizing respondents into mutually exclusive and exhaustive categories. The categories do not arrange themselves in any kind of order, and to talk of distances between categories does not make any sense. Nominal scales, as the name implies, are means of naming. They allow us to categorize persons, events, organizations, societies, or whatever into distinct classes. Now, consider the following questions taken, with slight modification, from a study of managerial personnel and their staff meetings.[1]

1. You may recall occasions when there have been disagreements, arguments, or open conflict in staff meetings you have attended. As you think about it now, which *one* of the following best describes the most typical staff meetings you have attended which are held by the supervisor or manager to whom you now report?
    A. Occasional open conflict and frequent disagreement
    B. Seldom open conflict but frequent minor disagreements and arguments
    C. Occasional minor disagreements and arguments but not often
    D. Rarely disagreements or arguments of any kind

2. In general, how much of your worktime would you judge is spent handling unexpected disruptions and emergency situations?
    A. Hardly any at all
    B. Not much
    C. Some
    D. Quite a bit
    E. A very great deal

---

[1] These questions were taken from a questionnaire administered to managerial personnel of the Boeing Company. The larger study was directed by L. Wesley Wager.

3. How often does your immediate supervisor or manager circulate an agenda *before* the day of the staff meetings?
   A. Always
   B. Usually
   C. Sometimes
   D. Seldom
   E. Never
4. Rate the most typical staff meetings held by the supervisor or manager to whom you now report as a place where you can get support from others when you most want it.
   A. Good
   B. Fair
   C. Poor

Each of these is a question used to construct an ordinal scale. Not only do the questions allow you to categorize the respondent's work setting into separate categories but it is also possible to arrange these categories in order. That is, we can assert that work setting A has more of a given characteristic than setting B, that setting B has more than setting C, and that, consequently, setting A has more than setting C. What we cannot say is that the difference between A and B is the same as, larger, or smaller than the difference between B and C. That is, we can arrange categories in order but are unable to further specify distances between categories.

Finally, consider the following questions, again taken from the study of managerial personnel.

1. How many persons usually attend the crew meetings or staff meetings you hold for persons who report directly to you? _____
2. What is your age (to your nearest birthday)? _____
3. In your present position, how long have you been working under and reporting to the supervisor to whom you now report?
   _____ years _____ months

Each of these questions is used to construct an interval scale. Not only are you able to categorize respondents and their staff meetings, not only are you able to arrange these categories in order, but you also are able to ascertain the distance between one category and another. It is possible to say that the difference between meetings with 10 and 15 persons is the same as the difference between those with 15 and 20 persons. In both cases one group has 5 more persons than the other. As we will see, the *meaning* of this difference may shift from one theoretical problem to the next, and, so, things often are not quite so simple.

As it turns out it also is possible to use the final set of questions in the construction of a ratio scale. With a ratio scale you are not only able to categorize, arrange in order, and determine differences between categories, but you also are able to assert that one category is some ratio of another. In the above instances it is possible to say that Sam, who is 35, is half as old as Mary, who is 70. In parallel fashion, it is possible to make such assertions in the case of the size of meetings and length of time with the present supervisor. What allows these ratio assertions is the presence of a zero point. Ratio scales, then, involve ordered categories with additive distances between categories and with a zero point. Hamblin (1971, 1974) presents interesting examples of additional ratio scales and their utility.

The relationship between these types of scales can be seen in Figure 5.6. Scale I represents a nominal scale. You have information on whether

FIGURE 5.6
Relationship between Levels of Measurement

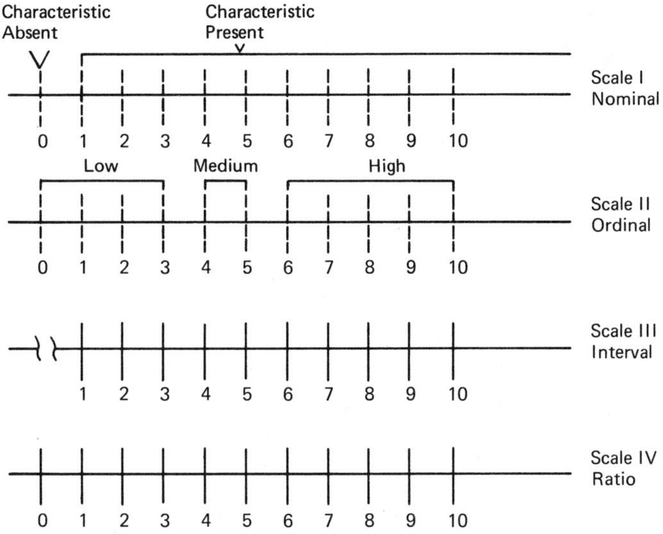

the individual does or does not like a given attitude object. It is a matter of categorization. The "do not like" persons correspond to those who "score" zero on the ratio scale (Scale IV). The "do like" persons correspond to all the rest. Scale II represents an ordinal scale. Persons who report a low degree of liking correspond to those who, if it were known, would score 0, 1, 2, or 3 on the ratio scale. Persons who report a medium amount of liking correspond to those who, if it were known, would score 4 or 5 on the ratio scale. Persons with a high degree of affinity for the attitude object would, again, if the more detailed information were available, score 6, 7, 8, 9, or 10. Given this type of scale it is possible to rank persons but it is not possible to determine distances between responses, since, for example, you do not know whether a "high" response represents individuals with a score of 6, 7, 8, 9, or 10. Finally, the only difference between an interval scale and a ratio scale is that in the former it is not possible to determine the zero point and in the latter it is.

These, then, are the basic scale types. Types are determined by the arrangement of and distances between categories and the presence or absence of a zero point. If this were all there was to it, the determination of a scale type would be a simple matter. There are, however, complications. A scale with one level of measurement in one theoretical context can be at another level given another theoretical issue. Age is one example. If we are interested in chronological age, then the number of years a person has lived can be considered an interval, and even a ratio scale, in that not only is it possible to say, for example, that the distance between 15 and 21 is the same as the distance between 45 and 51, but it is also legitimate to assert that being 60 years of age is twice as old as being 30 years of age.

Assume, however, as is often done, that we use age, not simply as an indicator of chronological age but as a proxy for another conceptual variable. We might, for example, use age as a proxy for maturity. In such a case the interval and ratio assumptions break down. No longer is the distance between 15 and 21 the same as the distance between 45 and 51 in terms of the degree of maturity. No longer is it safe to assume that a person of 60 is twice as mature as a person of 30. Even the assumptions of ordinality may break down. The person who is 16 is not always more mature than the person of 15, nor is this person always less mature than the person of, say, 19.

The assumptions break down for two reasons. First is that there may not be a linear relationship between age and level of maturity. Rather, the level of maturity may fluctuate with age as indicated in Figure 5.7. Thus, a change in age, say, from 25 to 30, where maturity is rising relatively rapidly, does not accompany the same change in maturity as the change from 55 to 60, where the change in maturity is slight. Also, as the distribution of dots, which signify persons, around the line indicates, some persons at younger ages are more mature than persons at older ages and vice versa. This is just another way of saying that the relationship between age and maturity is not perfect. Thus, by using age, even in the ordinal sense, we will run the risk of miscategorizing some individuals.

To make the point further, age may turn out to be a nominal variable in a theoretical context of life stages such as that suggested by Erickson (1968). Ages defining infancy, early childhood, play age, school age, adolescence, young adulthood, adulthood, and old age become important

FIGURE 5.7
Hypothetical Relationship between Age and Maturity

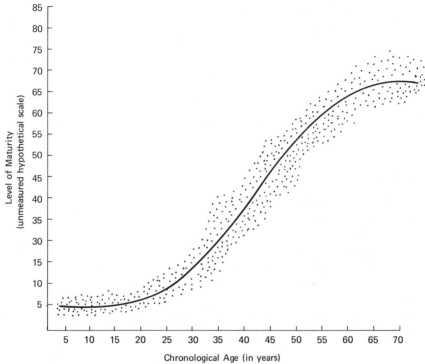

not for the continuous progression but for the discrete categories they signal in terms of psychosocial crises and resolutions thereto. Play age is a time when initiative confronts guilt; school age finds industry developing in the face of inferiority; in adolescence it is a matter of identity versus confusion; and so on. The point is that in such theoretical contexts to speak of even the order of age categories makes less sense when we consider that stages are in part considered to be independent of one another, each constituting a "new drive-and-need constellation."

Another commonly encountered instance of this questionable, but rarely questioned, attribute of certain scales is when income and education are used to tap the conceptual idea of "status." As Carter (1971) has amply documented, differences between categories defined by dollars and years of education are not equal in the implications they have for "status." To assume they are is to assume that the difference between persons making $1,000 and $10,000, on the one hand, has the same status implications as the difference between persons making $201,000 and $210,000, on the other. This is clearly a questionable assumption and amounts to assuming "as much difference between the privileges of two independently comfortable career diplomats as between a physician and a *poor* migrant laborer" (16).

What you need to do, then, is to clearly think through and, where possible, test your assumptions about the links between your concept and data before making any assertions about the nature of the scale you have constructed. Dealing with these links between concept and data, links referred to as epistemic correlations, is one of the more intriguing, important, and, at times, difficult aspects of social research. For discussion of possibilities in a midrange of complexity, see Costner (1969).

SUMMARY

These, then, are the general issues in the process of translating concepts into strategies of observation. Always keep in mind the assumptions you are making about the connection between concept and data. Always be in a position to check on the reliability and validity of the measures you devise. A useful rule of thumb in this regard is to develop more than one indicator for the concepts in question. Not only will this multiple-indicator approach allow you to more readily check on the reliability and validity of your strategies; it will also lead you toward a more thorough conceptualization of what turn out to be multidimensional ideas.

Chapters 6 through 8 explore the general issues we have been discussing in the present chapter in more concrete situations. Chapters 6 and 7 explore the manipulation of "available" data. Chapter 8 explores the design of questionnaires. In Chapter 11, when we turn to the translation of the idea of cause into data, we will have occasion to examine the design of experiments. As we have briefly suggested, each set of strategies has its benefits and drawbacks.

A chief factor recommending the use of available sources of data is one of cost. It is simply a very expensive operation to collect data, especially when we want to explore questions of national or international scope. A second, but no less important, attribute of available data is its availability. When we want to explore trends of the past, we must rely largely on already existing documents. These documents may range from such things as novels, films, newspapers, and legislative hearings to various statistical records. The richness of available data is impressive.

On the negative side, available documents have been produced by others with purposes generally different from those that guide a given research project. Difficulties arise from the way in which questions have been asked, the way in which statistics are compiled, the samples drawn, the coverage of topics, the clarity of expression, and so on. Worse still, the purpose for producing statistics may sometimes make these statistics suspect when it comes to the purposes of research. Organizations frequently produce statistics that place them in the most favorable light. So do national governments. The fact that data are available does not absolve you of the responsibility of knowing how they were collected, what the possible sources of bias might be, and what controls are needed to at least partially check on the validity of the information.

A study is only as good as its data. Weak or misleading data mean a weak or misleading study. It is not the case that some information is better than no information. Misleading information can result in faulty conclusions just as good data can bring us closer to a valid picture of what is going on. In most situations, when called upon to use available information, we "make do." We attempt to specify the limitations of the information and thereby avoid claiming too much from our results. We also strive, however, for sometimes ingenious reshaping of the information to shed light on what might otherwise remain dark regions of our experiences and the structure of society.

KEY ISSUES

1. Why is it important to develop a number of alternative measures for single concepts?
2. Discuss the various meanings of reliability and validity.
3. Why is it difficult to determine the "level of measurement" irrespective of the theoretical context?

REFERENCES

Althauser, Robert P.
    1974   "Inferring Validity from the Multitrait-Multimethod Matrix: Another Assessment." In Herbert Costner (ed.), *Sociological Methodology 1973–1974*. San Francisco: Jossey-Bass.
Althauser, R. P., and Haberlein, T. A.
    1970   "A Causal Assessment of Validity and the Multitrait-Multimethod Matrix." In E. F. Borgatta and G. W. Bohnstedt (eds.), *Sociological Methodology 1970*. San Francisco: Jossey-Bass.
Alwin, Duane F.
    1974   "Approaches to the Interpretation of Relationships in the Multitrait-Multimethod Matrix." In Herbert Costner (ed.), *Sociological Methology 1973–1974*. San Francisco: Jossey-Bass.
Blalock, Hubert M., Jr.
    1968   "The Measurement Problem: A Gap Between the Languages of Theory and Research." In Hubert M. Blalock, Jr., and Ann B. Blalock (eds.), *Methodology in Social Research*. New York: McGraw-Hill.

Campbell, Donald T., and Fiske, D. W.
  1959 "Convergent and Discriminant Validation by the Multi-trait, Multi-method Matrix." *Psychological Bulletin,* vol. 56, pp. 81–105.
Campbell, Donald T., and Stanley, Julian
  1963 *Experimental and Quasi Experimental Designs for Research.* Chicago: Rand McNally and Company.
Carter, Lewis
  1971 "Inadvertent Sociological Theory." *Social Forces,* vol. 50, pp. 12–25.
Converse, Jean M., and Schuman, Howard
  1974 *Conversations at Random: Survey Research as Interviewers See It.* New York: John Wiley and Sons.
Costner, Herbert L.
  1969 "Theory, Deduction and Rules of Correspondence." *American Journal of Sociology,* vol. 75, pp. 245–63.
Erickson, Erik H.
  1968 "Life Cycle." In *International Encyclopedia of the Social Sciences,* vol. 9. New York: Macmillan and The Free Press.
Footnotes, vol. 1, no. 2, February, 1973.
Gordon, Raymond L.
  1969 *Interviewing: Strategy, Techniques and Tactics.* Homewood, Ill.: Dorsey Press.
Hamblin, Robert L.
  1971 "Ratio Measurement for the Social Sciences." *Social Forces,* vol. 50, pp. 191–206.
Hamblin, Robert L.
  1974 "Social Attitudes: Magnitude Measurement and Theory." In Hubert M. Blalock, Jr. (ed.), *Measurement in the Social Sciences: Theories and Strategies.* Chicago: Aldine.
Pennings, Johannes
  1973 "Measures of Organizational Structure." *American Journal of Sociology,* vol. 79, pp. 686–704.
Zelditch, Morris
  1962 "Some Methodological Problems of Field Studies." *American Journal of Sociology,* vol. 67, pp. 566–67.

Contents

Chapter 6

Translating Ideas into Data, I: Developing Indicators from "Available" Information

As data archives from national and local surveys accumulate, as census material becomes more complete and widely available, as economic and social indicators are systematically developed and published, the possibilities of exploring "available" data expand geometrically. We are not yet at a point where a wide range of systematically collected information on the movement of society over long periods of time is available, but we are definitely moving in that direction. Increasingly, then, to become aware of possibilities along these lines is to take a productive path. The present chapter considers some of the possibilities.

We will first consider the construction of population indicators, such as size, age and sex distribution, dependency ratios, sex ratios, and birth and mortality rates, using census publications as the source of data. We will then shift attention to the process of capturing one aspect of officially defined deviance as reflected in the FBI's *Uniform Crime Reports*. In the next chapter we will examine strategies for exploring nonstatistical documents, using a series of techniques roughly characterized as content analysis. We will then turn to the use of the *Human Relations Area Files*, an indexed system of studies from a wide range of cultures.

Such available sources of information can be very useful. They have the common drawback, however, of already being collected and put together in certain ways. If these are useful for your purposes, well and good. If they are not, and frequently you will find a question or mode of presentation is not quite what you wanted, then there are difficulties. You make do with what you can find. In Chapter 8 we will consider the construction of indicators beginning before the "raw" data, the items on a questionnaire, the statistics compiled, and so forth are fixed.

Regarding the process of theory construction and testing, the present chapter shifts perspective slightly. In Chapters 2 through 4, we discuss a process of concept formation—a process in which the researcher is totally immersed in the initial collection of information, fashioning concepts as data take shape and comparisons are made. The emphasis is on moving from the gathered information to ideas about that information. It is, of course, the case that the process is more complex. You will at most times be gathering data, guided by the ideas you hold about the setting. Once again we have been describing the overall flow.

In this chapter we begin examining the reverse flow, that of moving from concept to indicator. Here, too, we will find that, as indicators are fashioned and as patterns emerge, there is an opportunity for fashioning concepts. Nevertheless, when you have some idea as to how you want to manipulate the data prior to your study, your strategies will differ somewhat from the situation where you are most interested in letting the data collected be fashioned by an ongoing process of situational discovery.

You may simply want to get a reading. Unguided by theoretical concerns, i.e., general explanations, you may want to estimate the size of a community or society and how its growth has changed over time. You also may be interested in the composition of that society in terms of age and sex, the proportion of "dependent" persons to "productive" persons, and the patterns of mortality and migration. Alternatively, you may want to look at the crime, economic, or educational pictures.

Given these readings, it is easy, almost natural to begin wondering— wondering what factors are linked with certain outcomes, e.g., differential crime rates; wondering what implications certain patterns, e.g., changing dependency ratios, might have for the future. In such a case you begin to look for indicators of possible explanatory factors, such as lower access to material goods or adaptive changes in the economy, possibly linked with higher dependency ratios. In such explorations we again find theory testing and theory construction as closely interlocked processes. Indeed, at times the shades of difference, like the shades of orange and red, are so slight there is no important difference at all.

EXPLORING CENSUS REPORTS

In the hands of a skilled craftsman, data obtained from census reports and surveys can yield highly useful information about societies and subportions of societies. In the following sections we will consider some of the more basic, i.e., uncomplicated, techniques for manipulating population data. In such manipulations we come to the reason for placing quotes around "Available" in the title of this chapter. Data are rarely "available" like so many stones on the beach. Rather, data must be combined in a number of ways to yield desired information.

First, of course, the information must be collected. By way of example the questionnaires used in the 1970 U.S. Census are included in Appendix A. Additional examples can be found in Shryock and Siegel (1973, Chapters 2 and 3). In the 1970 U.S. Census there were actually four pools of items. Some information was collected from all persons.[1] A second set of information was obtained from a 20-percent sample;[2] a third from a 15-percent sample;[3] and a fourth from a 5-percent sample.[4]

From information such as this a number of interesting and important questions can be pursued. Perhaps most obvious is the question of size. Although at first glance the size of a population may appear to be a rather dull piece of information, many have found quite the opposite. On the national level, for example, Davis (1958) has argued that size is an indispensible asset if a nation is to be powerful. Sawyer (1967) has underscored this point by showing the close linkages between size of the national population and GNP and arable land and energy resources. Whatever the reasons for these linkages, when we look at sources such as the United Nations *Demographic Yearbook,* we find wide variations in the size of national populations. In 1967, for example, we find variation from 14,000 persons in Andorra, on the one hand, to an estimated 720 million in China, on the other.

Age-Sex Pyramids

Once size is estimated, additional strategies are called for as the composition of the population is explored. To develop "composition" indicators you begin to disaggregate the raw-population totals. Age and sex breakdowns are two obvious criteria. Race, place of origin, level of education, and place of residence are others. To keep things manageable, consider the age–sex breakdowns for five census periods in Table 6.1, where both numbers and percentages are presented. From this table

---

[1] This included address, name, relationship to the head of household, sex, race, age, month and year of birth, marital status, and, if American Indian, name of tribe.

[2] This included information on place of birth, educational attainment, number of children ever born (for women), employment status, hours worked in week preceding enumeration, year last worked, industry, occupation and class of worker, state or country of residence five years ago, activity five years ago, weeks worked last year, and earnings last year from wages and salary, from self-employment, and from other income.

[3] Here, information on country of birth of parents, county and city or town of residence five years ago (and whether within or without the city limits), length of residence at present address, language spoken in childhood home, school or college attendance (and whether public, parochial, or other private school), veteran status, place of work (including street address, which city or town, which county, state, and ZIP code, and whether in city limits or outside), and means of transportation to work.

[4] These included information of Spanish descent, citizenship, year of immigration, whether married more than once and date of first marriage, whether first marriage ended because of death of spouse, vocational training, presence and duration of disability (for persons of working age), industry, and occupation and class of worker five years ago.

TABLE 6.1
Population, By Age and Sex: 1900–1970

Age	1900 Male	1900 Female	1920 Male	1920 Female	1940 Male	1940 Female	1960 Male	1960 Female	1970 Male	1970 Female
Number of Persons (thousands)										
All ages	38,969	37,243	54,086	51,935	66,350	65,815	88,331	90,992	98,912	104,300
Under 5 years . . .	4,643	4,546	5,880	6,738	5,379	5,210	10,330	9,991	8,745	8,409
5 to 9 years	4,487	4,402	5,771	5,663	5,444	5,291	9,504	9,187	10,168	9,788
10 to 14 years. . . .	4,089	4,003	5,383	5,285	5,980	5,820	8,524	8,249	10,591	10,199
15 to 19 years. . . .	3,759	3,811	4,687	4,767	6,209	6,178	6,634	6,586	9,634	9,437
20 to 24 years. . . .	3,643	3,718	4,544	4,761	5,728	5,917	5,272	5,528	7,917	8,454
25 to 29 years. . . .	3,348	3,214	4,552	4,560	5,482	5,664	5,333	5,536	6,622	6,855
30 to 34 years. . . .	2,921	2,660	4,147	3,950	5,095	5,186	5,846	6,103	5,596	5,835
35 to 39 years. . . .	2,632	2,352	4,090	3,710	4,767	4,813	6,080	6,402	5,412	5,694
40 to 44 years. . . .	2,267	1,994	3,301	3,067	4,435	4,379	5,676	5,924	5,819	6,162
45 to 49 years. . . .	1,844	1,619	3,132	2,651	4,221	4,055	5,358	5,522	5,851	6,265
50 to 54 years. . . .	1,569	1,380	2,546	2,203	3,765	3,511	4,735	4,871	5,348	5,756
55 to 59 years. . . .	1,148	1,067	1,887	1,671	3,021	2,838	4,127	4,303	4,766	5,207
60 to 64 years. . . .	920	875	1,587	1,402	2,406	2,335	3,409	3,733	4,027	4,590
65 to 69 years. . . .	669	636	1,082	990	1,902	1,913	2,931	3,327	3,122	3,870
70 to 74 years. . . .	450	435	707	689	1,274	1,300	2,185	2,554	2,315	3,129
75 to 79 years. . . .	262	259	421	437	725	781	1,360	1,694	1,561	2,274
80 to 84 years. . . .	122	129	186	217	360	416	665	915	876	1,409
85 years and over. . .	54	68	91	119	157	208	362	567	542	968

Percent of Total Population

	51.1	48.9	51.0	49.0	50.2	49.8	49.3	50.7	48.7	51.3
All ages	51.1	48.9	51.0	49.0	50.2	49.8	49.3	50.7	48.7	51.3
Under 5 years	6.1	6.0	5.5	5.4	4.1	3.9	5.8	5.6	4.3	4.1
5 to 9 years	5.9	5.8	5.4	5.3	4.1	4.0	5.3	5.1	5.0	4.8
10 to 14 years.	5.4	5.3	5.1	5.0	4.5	4.4	4.8	4.6	5.2	5.0
15 to 19 years.	4.9	5.0	4.4	4.5	4.7	4.7	3.7	3.7	4.7	4.6
20 to 24 years.	4.8	4.9	4.3	4.5	4.3	4.5	2.9	3.1	3.9	4.2
25 to 29 years.	4.4	4.2	4.3	4.3	4.1	4.3	3.0	3.1	3.3	3.4
30 to 34 years.	3.8	3.5	3.9	3.7	3.9	3.9	3.3	3.4	2.8	2.9
35 to 39 years.	3.5	3.1	3.9	3.5	3.6	3.6	3.4	3.6	2.7	2.8
40 to 44 years.	3.0	2.6	3.1	2.9	3.4	3.3	3.2	3.3	2.9	3.0
45 to 49 years.	2.4	2.1	3.0	2.5	3.2	3.1	3.0	3.1	2.9	3.1
50 to 54 years.	2.1	1.8	2.4	2.1	2.8	2.7	2.6	2.7	2.6	2.8
55 to 59 years.	1.5	1.4	1.8	1.6	2.3	2.1	2.3	2.4	2.3	2.6
60 to 64 years.	1.2	1.1	1.5	1.3	1.8	1.8	1.9	2.1	2.0	2.3
65 to 69 years.	0.9	0.8	1.0	0.9	1.4	1.4	1.6	1.9	1.5	1.9
70 to 74 years.	0.6	0.6	0.7	0.6	1.0	1.0	1.2	1.4	1.1	1.5
75 to 79 years.	0.3	0.3	0.4	0.4	0.5	0.6	0.7	0.9	0.8	1.1
80 to 84 years.	0.2	0.2	0.2	0.2	0.3	0.3	0.4	0.5	0.4	0.7
85 years and over	0.1	0.1	0.1	0.1	0.1	0.2	0.2	0.3	0.3	0.5

Note: Data do not include Armed Forces overseas.
Source: Bureau of the Census, 1920 Census of Population, Abstract of the Fourteenth Census of the United States; 1940 Census of Population, vol. IV, part 1; 1960 Census of Population, vol. 2, part 1; 1970 Census of Population, vol. 1, part 1; and unpublished data. Reprinted in Social Indicators (1973), Social and Economics Administration, U.S. Department of Commerce, p. 255.

a number of additional indicators can be devised. The most direct translation of the table is into what are called *age–sex pyramids*. These "pyramids" are simply a series of bar graphs sometimes representing the absolute numbers and sometimes the proportion of the total population that each age–sex category represents. Figure 6.1 represents the age–sex pyramids for each of the time periods shown in Table 6.1. The bars to the left of center represent the proportion of males in various age categories and those on the right, females.

By "eyeballing" these pyramids one gets a much quicker feel for the composition of society than is available from tables such as Table 6.1. We might, for example, note certain "holes" or "bulges" that have distinct implications for past, present, and future events. Such variations in the shape of the population pyramid are graphically illustrated in the detailed information contained in Figure 6.2 depicting the population of France, 1967. A baby boom becomes a "bulge." As years pass and the bulge moves up the age categories, certain demands are placed on the educational, marriage, housing, and retirement institutions as persons pass from one stage in the life cycle to the next. By way of illustration, consider the hypothetical demand curves in Figure 6.3, reprinted from Corsa and Oakley (1971).

From considerations such as these it is readily apparent that the numbers in Table 6.1 are not just so many statistics. They have important implications for the quality of life within society. Your job as a researcher is to turn these raw figures into indicators shedding light on issues of theoretical and policy importance. The population pyramid is one possible manipulation of the information. There are others.

Sex Ratio

The sex ratio is simply the number of males per 100 females. It is calculated by dividing the number of males in the population of interest by the number of females and multiplying this ratio by 100. For example, consider the population in the United States in 1900 as represented in Table 6.1. There were approximately 38,969,000 males and 37,243,000 females when all age categories are combined. To calculate the sex ratio for the total population, you perform the following manipulation.

$$\frac{38,969,000}{37,243,000} \times 100 = 104.6$$

Simple.

Practicum 6.1 To get the feel for it, calculate the sex ratios for the remaining census periods in Table 6.1, using the total population as your focus.

FIGURE 6.1
Population by Age and Sex: 1900–1970

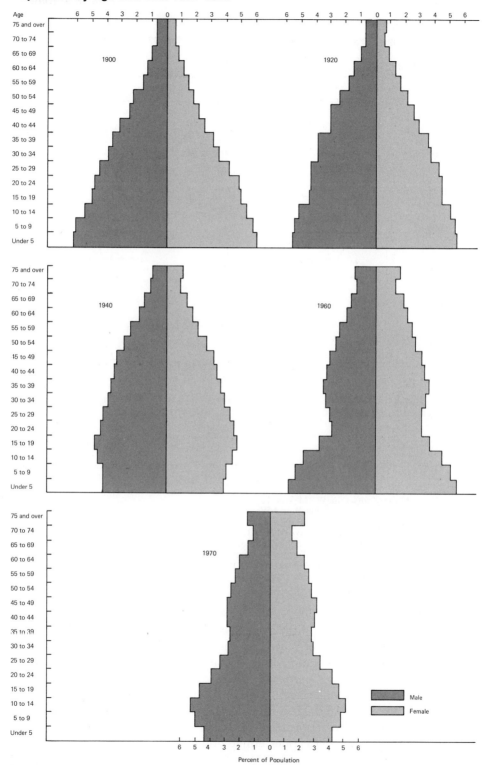

Reprinted, *Social Indicators,* 1973 U.S. Department of Commerce, p. 238.

Ideas and Data

FIGURE 6.2
Population of France, by Age and Sex: January 1,1967

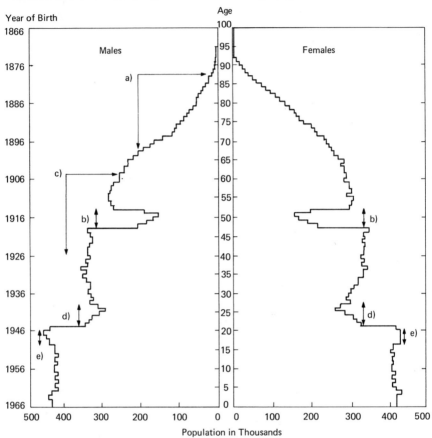

(a)   Military losses in World War I
(b)   Deficit of births during World War I
(c)   Military losses in World War II
(d)   Deficit of births during World War II
(e)   Rise of births due to demobilization after World War II
    Source: Based on France. Institut national de la statistique et des études économiques, *Annuaire statistique de la France, 1967,* 1968, p. 33. Reprinted from Shryock and Siegel, 1973, p. 242.

There are a number of reasons why you might want to change focus and calculate sex ratios for segments of the population. You might want to reflect the impact of a war on the balance between the sexes and thus calculate the sex ratio within certain age categories. Assuming that, on the average, in a particular society, males marry females 3 years younger and that marriage generally occurs between the ages of 20 and 28 for males and 17 and 25 for females, you could calculate the sex ratio among "marriageables." Alternatively, you might be interested in the sex ratio among various ethnic groupings in society and calculate

FIGURE 6.3
Time Relationships between a Birth and Future Service Requirements

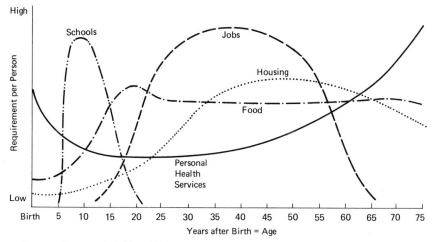

Source: Corsa and Oakley, 1971.

a set of sex ratios such as those in Table 6.2. Such calculations, of course, will call for additional data to that in Table 6.1. The principle remains. First, specify the target population. Next, divide the number of males by the number of females within that population and multiply by 100. That's all there is to it.

TABLE 6.2
Sex Ratios by Nativity and Race, the United States: 1960 (sex ratios are shown as males per 100 females)

Race/Nativity	*Sex Ratio*
Total.	97.1
White	97.4
Native	97.5
Foreign-born	94.2
Nonwhite	94.3
Negro	93.4
Indian	101.2
Japanese	93.9
Chinese	133.2
Filipino	175.4
All other	111.4

Source: Adapted from *U.S. Census of Population: 1960,* vol. 1; Characteristics of the Population, Part 1, United States Summary, 1964, tables 44, 45, and 156. Reprinted from Shryock and Siegel (1973) p. 194.

Dependency Ratio

A manipulation of data closely linked with the sex ratio, in terms of calculations, is the dependency ratio. This time, instead of comparing males and females, we compare those who are "dependent" with those who are "supportive" or in the "working ages." We need first specify what we mean. Being in the dependent ages is frequently taken to mean those under 15 and those 65 and over. Persons between these ages are considered in the supportive or working years. These age categories might change from one society or one time period to the next, depending on the length of productive years. Thus, when working cross-culturally, some thought will have to be given to appropriate age categories. However, for the time being, let's settle on this definition. The total-dependency ratio is simply the number of persons in the dependent years per 100 persons in the supportive or working years. More specifically, you add those under 15 to all those 65 and over, divide this figure by the number aged 15 to 64, multiply the result by 100, and you have what is called the total-dependency ratio—the number of dependent persons per 100 supportive persons.

You may have already thought that this total-dependency ratio could be fruitfully broken down into two separable ratios, one for those in the youth category and one for those in the old-age category. You are right. The first of these, naturally enough, is referred to as the *child-dependency ratio*, while the latter is called the *aged-dependency ratio*. They are both calculated in a parallel fashion to the total-dependency ratio. That is, the child-dependency ratio is the number of persons under 15 divided by the number of supportive persons, the result once again being multiplied by 100. The aged-dependency ratio is defined by the number of persons 65 and over divided by the number of supportive persons, multipled by 100.

> *Practicum 6.2* Take the data in Table 6.1 and construct the total-, child-, and aged-dependency ratios for each time period. As a check, the total-dependency ratio for 1900 is 62.3. If available, go to census publications and construct dependency ratios within various segments of the population of your own chosing.

Once again, such calculations are not just a bunch of statistics. The dependency ratio has definite implications in terms of the drain on and potentialities of a society. For an interesting discussion in this regard see Keyfitz (1971) and his discussion of societal development, comparing the developing Honduras of 1966 and the developing Sweden of 1800. Although both countries are mountainous, face the ocean, and had labor forces engaged largely in agriculture, the fact that in 1966 Honduras had a total-dependency ratio of 113.89 whereas Sweden in 1800 had a total dependency ratio of 61.53 has definite implications concerning the relative possibilities for development and the pattern of drain on societal resources.

Birth and Death Rates

The *crude birth rate* is yet another commonly employed indicator. Here, the total number of births in a year is divided by the total midyear population. As you can readily see, with only little thought, this is indeed a "crude" indicator, since the birth rate is going to be greatly influenced by the age and sex structure of a society. One remedy to this has been devised and referred to as the *general fertility rate*, the number of births in a year per 1,000 women in the child-bearing ages (generally taken to mean 15 through 44). Still further refinement is provided with what is called the *age–specific fertility rate*. This is defined by the number of births to women in a narrower age category (Say, 20–24) per 1,000 women in that category.

On the other side of the ledger, what is called the *crude death rate* is simply the number of deaths in a year per 1,000 of the midyear population. Category specific death rates, such as rates by sex, occupation, age, state, region, race, and so forth also may be constructed. Again, you simply specify the relevant population and time period, divide the number of deaths by the population, and this time multiply the result by 1,000 to get the number of deaths per 1,000 persons in the category being focused on. Along these lines, a commonly used indicator, because many feel it is closely linked with the overall "health" of the community, is the infant mortality rate. The number of infants who die before their first birthday is divided by the total number of live births during that year and the result multiplied by 1,000.

> **Practicum 6.3** Death rates, of course, can be related to certain factors such as age or race or the degree of development in a society. Along these lines translate the information contained in Figures 6.4 and 6.5 into a paragraph explaining what these figures show.

Life Tables

Closely linked to the calculation of death rates is the *life table*. One type of life table, the *generation life table*, follows a given birth cohort, say, those persons born in 1900, and records the age specific death rates until no one remains in the cohort. A much more frequently used life table is the *current life table*. The current life table is hypothetical in that it does not reflect the experiences of an actual birth cohort but, instead, is constructed from age specific mortality information during a specified time period. For example, the current life table presented

FIGURE 6.4
Death Rates: 1940–1971, by Race and Sex

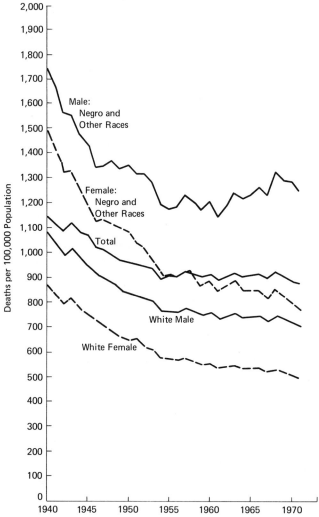

Source: *Social Indicators*, 1973, U.S. Department of Commerce, p. 242.

in Table 6.3 was constructed from data on age specific mortality rates and the midyear U.S. population in 1971. Although it is hypothetical in nature, the current life table offers the not-small virtue of more efficient calculation than a generation life table. You need not follow an entire cohort through an entire life span to get some idea of average life expectancy and age-related patterns of dying.

Given the rather forbidding appearance of the life table, it is important

FIGURE 6.5
Infant Mortality Rates: 1940–1971, by Race

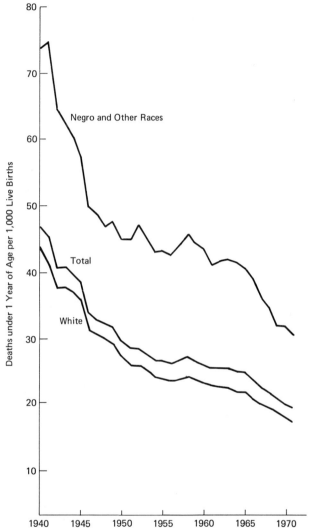

Source: *Social Indicators,* 1973, U.S. Department of Commerce, p. 246.

to realize that once again we are not dealing with just another mountain of statistics. Indeed, as Browning (1968) has convincingly argued, information obtainable from a life table has a multitude of implications for the quality and dynamics of societal processes. We will have more to say about this shortly. First, how to interpret the numbers.

It should be noted initially that a current life table generally represents

TABLE 6.3
Abridged Life Tables by Color, United States, 1971

Age Interval (1) Period of Life Between Two Exact Ages Stated in Years x to $x+n$	Proportion Dying (2) Proportion of Persons Alive at Beginning of Age Interval Dying During Interval nq_x	Of 100,000 Born Alive (3) Number Living at Beginning of Age Interval l_x	Of 100,000 Born Alive (4) Number Dying During Age Interval nd_x	Stationary Population (5) In the Age Interval nL_x	Stationary Population (6) In this and All Subsequent Age Intervals T_x	Average Remaining Lifetime (7) Average Number of Years of Life Remaining at Beginning of Age Interval e_x
Total						
0–1	0.0190	100,000	1,902	98,310	7,103,518	71.0
1–5	.0032	98,098	312	391,645	7,005,208	71.4
5–10	.0020	97,786	200	488,390	6,613,563	67.6
10–15	.0020	97,586	196	487,488	6,125,173	62.8
15–20	.0056	97,390	543	485,704	5,637,685	57.9
20–25	.0072	96,847	701	482,514	5,151,981	53.2
25–30	.0071	96,146	684	479,044	4,669,467	48.6
30–35	.0085	95,462	812	475,374	4,190,423	43.9
35–40	.0122	94,650	1,151	470,563	3,715,049	39.3
40–45	.0184	93,499	1,718	463,507	3,244,486	34.7
45–50	.0278	91,781	2,547	453,001	2,780,979	30.3
50–55	.0425	89,234	3,795	437,243	2,327,978	26.1
55–60	.0637	85,439	5,439	414,348	1,890,735	22.1
60–65	.0959	80,000	7,674	381,738	1,476,387	18.5
65–70	.1361	72,326	9,844	337,953	1,094,649	15.1
70–75	.2023	62,482	12,641	281,720	756,696	12.1
75–80	.2844	49,841	14,173	214,375	474,976	9.5
80–85	.3845	35,668	13,714	143,360	260,601	7.3
85 and over	1.0000	21,954	21,954	117,241	117,241	5.3
White						
0–1	0.0179	100,000	1,788	98,373	7,170,645	71.7
1–5	.0030	98,212	294	392,153	7,072,272	72.0
5–10	.0020	97,918	195	489,066	6,680,119	68.2
10–15	.0019	97,723	188	488,192	6,191,053	63.4

Age					
15–20	.0051	97,535	502	486,518	5,702,861	58.5
20–25	.0065	97,033	631	483,602	5,216,343	53.8
25–30	.0060	96,402	580	480,569	4,732,741	49.1
30–35	.0070	95,822	672	477,509	4,252,172	44.4
35–40	.0102	95,150	970	473,497	3,774,663	39.7
40–45	.0161	94,180	1,515	467,407	3,301,166	35.1
45–50	.0259	92,665	2,401	457,783	2,833,759	30.6
50–55	.0402	90,264	3,632	442,794	2,375,976	26.3
55–60	.0623	86,632	5,394	420,464	1,933,182	22.3
60–65	.0917	81,238	7,451	388,535	1,512,718	18.6
65–70	.1343	73,787	9,911	345,189	1,124,183	15.2
70–75	.1937	63,876	12,374	289,453	778,994	12.2
75–80	.2879	51,502	14,827	221,136	489,541	9.5
80–85	.4076	36,675	14,949	145,242	268,405	7.3
85 and over	1.0000	21,726	21,726	123,163	123,163	5.7

All Other

Age					
0–1	0.0312	100,000	3,117	97,300	6,528,792	65.3
1–5	.0054	96,883	518	386,240	6,431,492	66.4
5–10	.0027	96,365	261	481,110	6,045,252	62.7
10–15	.0027	96,104	256	479,938	5,564,142	57.9
15–20	.0077	95,848	736	477,589	5,084,204	53.0
20–25	.0133	95,112	1,267	472,561	4,606,615	48.4
25–30	.0155	93,845	1,450	465,752	4,134,054	44.1
30–35	.0194	92,395	1,794	457,710	3,668,302	39.7
35–40	.0269	90,601	2,437	447,262	3,210,592	35.4
40–45	.0386	88,164	3,402	432,772	2,763,330	31.3
45–50	.0533	84,762	4,522	413,143	2,330,608	27.5
50–55	.0734	80,240	5,888	387,223	1,917,465	23.9
55–60	.0997	74,352	7,413	353,887	1,530,242	20.6
60–65	.1326	66,939	8,879	312,966	1,176,355	17.6
65–70	.1767	58,060	10,259	264,899	863,389	14.9
70–75	.2386	47,801	11,404	210,252	598,490	12.5
75–80	.2962	36,397	10,781	154,751	388,238	10.7
80–85	.3480	25,616	8,913	105,274	233,487	9.1
85 and over	1.0000	16,703	16,703	128,213	128,213	7.7

Source: *Vital Statistics of the United States,* 1971, Department of Health, Education, and Welfare.

a hypothetical birth cohort of 100,000. Each of the numbers in the table takes on meaning only when this is kept in mind. Consider column 2 in Table 6.3, the "Proportion Dying" column. This is the column from which the remaining information is derived. The numbers here represent the proportion of the hypothetical cohort dying before reaching the end of the age interval. For example, we see estimates that out of every 100,000 births, 1,900 infants (actually it is 1,902 as column 4 shows) will die before the first year is up when we consider the population as a whole. When we break this total down by "color," we find further estimates that approximately 1,790 white infants and 3,100 infants of other "color," again out of 100,000 births, will die during the first year. Thus, this column represents *probabilities* of death during specific age intervals.

> **Practicum 6.4** **Compare the proportion of persons dying in the age intervals 20–25, 35–40, 55–60, and 70–75 for "White" and "All Other."**

Remembering that the life table presented in Table 6.3 represents a hypothetical population of 100,000 births, column 3 presents the number of individuals living at the beginning of the specified age interval. Think for a moment and you will realize how this column is related to column 2. Also, since the base number is 100,000, column 3 can be readily translated into the proportion of the original cohort still alive at the beginning of the specified age interval. For example, looking at the total population, approximately 85.4 percent are still alive at the beginning of the 55 to 60-year interval. When broken down by whites and others, the comparable figures are 86.6 percent and 74.3 percent, respectively.

> **Practicum 6.5** **Compare the percentage of persons still alive at the beginning of the 15–20, 35–40, and 80–85 age intervals for whites and others.**

Column 4 represents the number of persons dying during a specified age interval, assuming an original birth cohort of 100,000 live births. Again, a little thought will reveal how this column is related to columns 2 and 3.

> **Practicum 6.6** **Compare whites and others in terms of the numbers dying in a birth cohort of 100,000 for the 0–1, 15–20, 65–70, and 75–80 age intervals.**

For the present discussion the figures in columns 5 and 6 are best interpreted as the total amount of time lived by those in the specified time intervals. Column 5 tells us, for example, that in a cohort of 100,000 under the death-rate assumptions of the table, 470,563 total years will be lived between the ages of 35 and 40 by those 94,650 persons (out of the original 100,000) who reach their 35th birthday. Column 6 represents the estimate of the total number of years remaining in life from the beginning of the specified age interval. For those 94,650 persons who reach their 35th birthday, it is estimated that a total of 3,715,049 years remain.

In terms of how they are most frequently used, the figures in column 6 are most useful in the calculation of the last column, the "Life Expectancy" column. This gives an estimate of the average number of years remaining from the beginning of the specified age interval. For example, average life expectancy from birth is estimated to be 71 years for the total population, 71.7 for whites, and 65.3 for others. These average life-expectancy figures are calculated by dividing the figures in column 6 by the corresponding figures in column 3. Thus, for the 86,632 whites who reach their 55th birthday, there is an estimated total 1,933,182 years remaining in life, for an average (total number of years divided by the total number of persons) of 22.3 years remaining. It is this average number of years remaining that is referred to as the life expectancy of a given group of individuals.

> **Practicum 6.7** What is the life expectancy (years remaining) for the total population among those who have reached their 15th birthday? What is the comparable figure for whites and others. Given an estimated total of 3,120,511 years remaining for 93,933 persons reaching their 45th birthday, what is the average remaining life expectancy?

It should be kept in mind that these figures are estimates of probabilities. Nevertheless, they provide much grist for speculation regarding not only the existing quality of life but also concerning societal changes that might take place given differing death-rate patterns and life expectancies. Noteworthy in this regard is the work of Browning (1968) and his discussion of the interrelationship between life expectancy and various events in the life cycle, such as age at marriage, the number and spacing of children, the prevalence of orphans and orphanages, education and career orientations, and the presence of extended family relationships. The fact that persons can expect to pass through all of the major phases in the life cycle with some certainty has definite implications when we consider family-planning practices, care and socialization of children, postponement of immediate gratification for more long-run-career concerns, the eventual spacing of the otherwise "crowded" events of marriage, entrance into a career, and the birth of the first child.

Were there little variation across societies in this regard, there would be only theoretical reasons for interest. However, when we realize that there have been, or continue to be, societies represented by the life-table figures reprinted in Table 6.4, we can begin to glimpse some of the

TABLE 6.4
Survivors to Certain Ages for Five Model Life Tables (Males)

	Model Life Expectancy at Birth				
	I 22.851	II 32.484	III 47.114	IV 61.228	V 73.899
Age	*Number Surviving*				
0	100,000	100,000	100,000	100,000	100,000
5	50,957	64,242	79,961	91,744	98,510
15	46,151	60,000	77,147	90,444	98,273
25	40,254	54,520	73,107	88,240	97,723
35	33,087	47,598	67,851	85,429	97,079
45	25,149	39,332	60,979	81,255	95,876
55	16,955	29,623	51,289	73,412	92,076
65	8,963	18,343	37,047	58,427	81,150
75	2,706	7,232	18,685	34,223	56,701
	Percent Surviving from Age 15 to Selected Age				
25	87.2	90.9	94.8	97.6	99.4
35	71.7	79.3	88.0	94.5	98.8
45	54.5	65.6	79.0	89.8	97.6
55	36.7	49.4	66.5	81.2	93.7
65	19.4	30.6	48.0	64.6	82.6

Source: Browning, 1968: Adapted from the "West" series of model life tables
given in Ansley J. Coale and Paul Demeny, *Regional Model Life Tables and Stable
Populations* (Princeton, N.J.: Princeton University Press, 1966).

probable differences between a society in which almost half of the population (Model I) alive at age 15 is dead by age 45, when compared to another society with a nearly 98-percent (Model V) comparable survival rate.

What we have in these indicators—the crude birth rate, the sex ratio, the age–sex pyramid, the life table, and so forth—is a series of readings on the nature of the population of a specified society or community. The amount of useful information derivable from these and other indicators is impressive. We can begin to better understand some of the problems facing developing countries when we note, over time, certain changes in birth and death rates. We find that with "development" comes a movement from the relatively inefficient pattern of high birth, high death rates; to a period of low death, high birth rates; and, finally, to a period of low birth, low death rates. While this is occurring and countries move through the second stage of low death, high birth rates, rapid increases in population occur—more births, fewer deaths, larger totals. For some countries such a process may eventually help supply needed labor forces. For others the rapid rise in population can be disastrous. For the world community there are most assuredly limits. Food, shelter, and health resources may be strained to the breaking point.

Density and Social Pathology

A growing population, coupled in many regions with a process of population concentration, has additional implications for the social, cultural, and political institutions, as well as customs and patterns of interactions. It is Konrad Lorenz (1966) who suggested, "The close crowding of many individuals in a small space brings about a fatigue of all social reactions" (p. 244). To explore this hypothesized impact of density on interpersonal relations, and it has been suggested by many more persons than Lorenz, we might construct an indicator such as the number of persons per acre, square mile, kilometer, or other measure of area. Given this we might then devise additional measures of the quality of life to see whether as density goes up the social "health" of a community goes down.

The examination of *relationships between* indicators gets us slightly ahead of ourselves, but a preliminary look at some of the issues will be instructive. Galle, Gove, and McPherson (1972) provide a useful study in this regard in that they show, among other things, the importance of a close link between indicator and idea and the utility of having a number of indicators for a single concept. These researchers set about exploring the human implications of studies on animals, showing the close connection between high density and such "unhealthy" or "pathological" behavior as increased mortality, neglect of young by mothers, overly aggressive and conflict-oriented behavior, a breakdown in social order, and various sexual aberrations.

Utilizing the *Local Community Fact Book for Chicago*, an initial examination of the idea that high density is linked with rates of "unhealthy" responses received little support when the measure of density was the number of persons per acre. Reasoning that the concept of density within the context of the theoretical ideas being pursued really meant something akin to "interpersonal press," and that even in high density areas, as measured by the number of persons per acre, "escapes" into privacy are possible, Galle, Gove, and McPherson devised a number of additional indicators of density—persons per room, rooms per housing unit, housing units per structure, and structures per acre.

As expected, they found the closest link when the density indicators were more directly connected with "interpersonal press." That is, they found the strongest relationships when using the number of persons per room and the number of rooms per housing unit. Thus, in addition to providing interesting information on the density-social pathology question, this study illustrates the importance of devising alternative measures for concepts. This is especially true when ideas are only crudely formed. Differences in findings, using different indicators, frequently lead to important refinements in theoretical ideas. The moral is, do not restrict yourself to a single indicator; whenever possible, devise alternatives.

Practicum 6.8 Referring to published government documents, devise at least four indicators for the "health" of a community. Let your imagination run free. If you were in a position to generate new information for additional indicators, that is, information not at the present time published, what would you call for? Again, let your imagination run free.

When we begin to consider additional measures, it soon becomes apparent that the amount of "available" information is almost unending. To be sure the specific information desired is sometimes hard to come by, but the volume of statistics put out by the federal government of the United States alone is mountainous, to say nothing of newspapers, news broadcasts, legislative hearings, and historical documents. Some of this information will be more useful to social scientists than others. The Consumer Price Index, the National Health Survey Program, and the Current Population Survey will probably be more useful than, say, studies of the vanishing whale. Given ecological interconnections, many would argue that even this is a bad example.

It is safe to say that there is a good deal of data to be mined, the widely publicized secrecy of bureaucracies in general and the federal government in particular notwithstanding. Particularly useful in this regard is the *American Statistics Index: A Comprehensive Guide and Index to the Statistical Publications of the U.S. Government*, published by the Congressional Information Service. It is always necessary when using available information to be aware of limitations. At times, organizations release records that put them in the most favorable rather than the most enlightening light. Therefore, be cautious. In the following section we will consider available crime statistics. This discussion should be instructive in pointing both to the possibilities and problems of using available records.

EXPLORING THE UNIFORM CRIME REPORTS

The most frequently used and widely cited source of crime statistics in the United States is the *Uniform Crime Reports*, published by the Federal Bureau of Investigation. This practice of publishing statistics on the crime picture of the United States was begun on a continuous basis in 1930. Since that time, various changes in the reporting practices have been made. In addition, a number of "irregularities" have been noted over the years (see Wolfgang, 1963). Even with these changes and limitations, however, these documents yield some indication as to changes taking place in a series of crimes selected for their seriousness, frequency of occurrence, and likelihood of being reported. The 1973 report, portions of which are reproduced in Appendix B, represents the picture of crime as reported to the FBI by law-enforcement agencies with jurisdiction over 93 percent of the total national population.

The most complete information is presently reported on the seven "Part I Index Crimes." These include criminal homicide (murder, nonnegligent and negligent manslaughter), forcible rape, robbery, aggravated assault, burglary, larceny-theft (except auto theft), and auto theft. Figure 6.6 contains the definitions in use as of the 1973 report.

FIGURE 6.6
Definitions of Part I Index Crimes used in 1973 *Uniform Crime Report*

1. Criminal homicide—(a) Murder and nonnegligent manslaughter: All willful felonious homicides as distinguished from deaths caused by negligence. Excludes, attempts to kill, assaults to kill, suicides, accidental deaths, or justifiable homicides. Justifiable homicides are limited to: (1) The killing of a person by a law enforcement officer in line of duty; and (2) The killing of a person in the act of committing a felony by a private citizen. (b) Manslaughter by negligence: Any death which the police investigation established was primarily attributable to gross negligence of some individual other than the victim.

2. Forcible rape—The carnal knowledge of a female, forcibly and against her will in the categories of rape by force, assault to rape, and attempted rape. Excludes statutory offenses (no force used—victim under age of consent).

3. Robbery—Stealing or taking anything of value from the care, custody, or control of a person by force or violence or by putting in fear, such as strong-arm robbery, stickups, armed robbery, assault to rob, and attempts to rob.

4. Aggravated assault—Assault with intent to kill or for the purpose of inflicting severe bodily injury by shooting, cutting, stabbing, maiming, poisoning, scalding, or by the use of acids, explosives, or other means. Excludes simple assaults.

5. Burglary—breaking or entering—Burglary, housebreaking, safecracking, or any breaking or unlawful entry of a structure with the intent to commit a felony or a theft. Includes attempted forcible entry.

6. Larceny-theft (except auto theft)—The unlawful taking, carrying, leading, or riding away of property from the possession or constructive possession of another. Thefts of bicycles, automobile accessories, shoplifting, pocket-picking, or any stealing of property or article which is not taken by force and violence or by fraud. Excludes embezzlement, "con" games, forgery, worthless checks, etc.

7. Auto theft—Unlawful taking or stealing or attempted theft of a motor vehicle. A motor vehicle is a self-propelled vehicle that travels on the surface but not on rails. Specificaly excluded from this category are motor boats, construction equipment, airplanes, and farming equipment.

As an examination of Appendix B will show and as a more detailed look at the total report will substantiate, these publications yield a good deal of information on offenses known to the police and subsequently reported to the FBI. Along with such breakdowns as urban, suburban, rural, and region of the country, these reports also document changes over time. Table 6.5 presents the changing crime picture as reflected by these reports from 1960 through 1973.

It is from such data that a good deal of theorizing has been done concerning the sources or causes of crime, on the one hand, and policy decisions designed to carry out the demand for "Law and Order," so frequently heard during the 1960s and early '70s, on the other. The suggestion that there has been an 86-percent increase in the *rate* of murder and non-negligent manslaughter, a 204-percent increase in the *rate* of robbery, and a 140-percent increase in the *rate* of burglary during this 14-year span is not a finding to be taken lightly. It bears close examination. In the process of examination, we will learn more about the utility of the crime reports, alternatives in the calculation of rates, and restrictions on conclusions that might be drawn.

First, although the data in Table 6.5 might suggest an unrelenting rise in the crime rate, an examination of longer range trends, such as that presented by Schrag (1971), suggests otherwise. For example, it was not until 1972 that the murder rate reached the figure of 8.9 per 100,000 inhabitants, which was the rate reported in 1930. Indeed, the data reported by the FBI show a rather consistent decline in the homicide rate from 1930 until about 1960, at which time it began to rise as shown in Table 6.5.

Calculating Crime Rates

Whatever the fluctuations, the conclusions drawn are only as good as the indicators devised. Although there is no necessary connection between the size of the population and the volume of crime, it is widely accepted that we should pay greatest attention to the rate of crime rather than its simple volume. Thus, the bottom half of Table 6.5 presents the rate per 100,000 inhabitants. The calculation of these rates is exactly parallel to our previous discussion of other rates. But, is the total population the appropriate reference point? Would it be better to calculate more specific rates? Should we focus on the "at risk" population and calculate rates based on the potential-victim population? Such a practice would take into account the idea that crime may be as much a function of available opportunities as increased "potential" within individual offenders or groups of offenders. Rising crime rates may not reflect a process wherein the fabric of society is breaking down so as to produce more rape-oriented persons but rather rising rates may be indicating

TABLE 6.5
Index of Crime, United States, 1960–1973

Population*	Total Crime Index	Violent† Crime	Prop-erty‡ Crime	Murder and Nonnegligent Manslaughter	Forcible Rape	Rob-bery	Aggra-vated Assault	Burglary	Larceny–Theft	Auto Theft
Number of offenses:										
1960 — 179,323,175.	3,352,800	286,220	3,066,600	9,050	17,050	107,410	152,720	903,400	1,836,800	326,400
1961 — 182,953,000.	3,455,500	287,120	3,168,400	8,680	17,080	106,240	155,130	940,400	1,893,800	334,200
1962 — 185,822,000.	3,717,400	299,150	3,418,200	8,480	17,410	110,410	162,850	984,800	2,068,700	364,800
1963 — 188,531,000.	3,756,700	314,490	3,756,700	8,580	17,510	116,000	172,400	1,076,000	2,274,800	406,000
1964 — 191,334,000.	4,522,300	361,350	4,161,000	9,300	21,250	129,860	200,940	1,201,600	2,489,300	470,200
1965 — 193,818,000.	4,695,500	384,340	4,311,200	9,900	23,230	138,130	213,090	1,270,200	2,546,900	494,100
1966 — 195,587,000.	5,175,200	426,830	4,748,300	10,970	25,620	157,350	232,800	1,396,500	2,793,700	558,100
1967 — 197,864,000.	5,849,200	496,150	5,353,000	12,160	27,410	202,100	254,490	1,616,500	3,080,500	656,100
1968 — 199,861,000.	6,658,900	590,640	6,068,200	13,720	31,410	261,780	283,720	1,841,100	3,447,800	779,300
1969 — 201,921,000.	7,343,300	657,050	6,686,200	14,670	36,880	297,650	307,850	1,962,900	3,849,700	873,600
1970 — 203,184,772.	8,024,100	733,530	7,290,500	15,890	37,690	348,460	331,480	2,183,800	4,183,500	923,200
1971 — 206,256,000.	8,509,800	810,680	7,699,100	17,670	41,940	386,150	364,920	2,376,300	4,379,900	942,900
1972 — 208,232,000.	8,173,400	828,820	7,344,600	18,550	46,480	374,790	389,000	2,352,800	4,109,600	882,200
1973 — 209,851,000.	8,638,400	869,470	7,768,900	19,510	51,000	382,680	416,270	2,540,900	4,304,400	923,600
Percent change 1960–1973‡	+157.6	+203.8	+153.3	+115.6	+199.2	+256.3	+172.6	+181.3	+134.3	+183.0
Rate per 100,000 inhabitants:										
1960	1,869.7	159.6	1,710.1	5.0	9.5	59.9	85.2	503.8	1,024.3	182.0
1961	1,888.8	156.9	1,731.8	4.7	9.3	58.1	84.8	514.0	1,035.2	182.7
1962	2,000.5	161.0	1,839.5	4.6	9.4	59.4	87.6	530.0	1,113.3	196.3
1963	2,159.4	166.8	1,992.6	4.5	9.3	61.5	91.4	570.7	1,206.6	215.3
1964	2,363.6	188.9	2,174.7	4.9	11.1	67.9	105.0	628.0	1,301.0	245.7
1965	2,422.6	198.3	2,224.3	5.1	12.0	71.3	109.9	655.4	1,314.0	254.9
1966	2,646.0	218.2	2,427.7	5.6	13.1	80.4	119.1	714.0	1,428.4	285.3
1967	2,956.2	250.8	2,705.4	6.1	13.9	102.1	128.6	817.0	1,556.9	331.6
1968	3,331.8	295.5	3,036.2	6.9	15.7	131.0	142.0	921.2	1,725.1	389.9
1969	3,636.7	325.4	3,311.3	7.3	18.3	147.4	152.5	972.1	1,906.5	432.7
1970	3,949.2	361.0	3,588.1	7.8	18.6	171.5	163.1	1,074.8	2,059.0	454.4
1971	4,125.8	393.0	3,732.8	8.6	20.3	187.2	176.9	1,152.1	2,123.5	457.2
1972	3,925.2	398.0	3,527.1	8.9	22.3	180.0	186.8	1,129.9	1,973.6	423.7
1973	4,116.4	414.3	3,702.1	9.3	24.3	182.4	198.4	1,210.8	2,051.2	440.1
Percent change 1960–1973‡	+120.2	+159.6	+116.5	+86.0	+155.8	+204.5	+132.9	+140.3	+100.3	+141.8

* Population is Bureau of the Census provisional estimates as of July 1, except April 1, 1960 and 1970, census.

† Violent crime is offenses of murder, forcible rape, robbery, and aggravated assault. Property crime is offenses of burglary, larceny-theft, and auto theft.

‡ Percent change and crime rates calculated prior to rounding number of offenses. Revised estimates and rates based on changes in reporting practices.
Source: *Uniform Crime Reports* for the United States, 1973, Federal Bureau of Investigation, U.S. Department of Justice, p. 59.

an increase in opportunities. Or so might go the argument. To take this into account the FBI began reporting the rate of rape per 100,000 females. These figures are presented in Table 6.6 for the period between 1965 and 1973.

TABLE 6.6
Rape Rate per 100,000
Females for the Years
1965 to 1973

1965	23
1966	25
1967	27
1968	30
1969	35
1970	36
1971	40
1972	43
1973	47

Still, one might argue it is not the total female population that is important but rather the population of "real" potential victims. Very young and very old females are not highly vulnerable to this crime. Indeed, a recent study of victimization (U.S. Department of Justice, 1974) shows a quite restricted range in this regard. It is only between the ages of 16 and 35 that the risk is of significant proportions. Given this, we might want to calculate age specific victim rates using the total number of females between the ages of 16 and 35 as the base population and calculate the rate per 100,000 females in this age bracket.

Practicum 6.9 **Using the figures in Tables 6.1 and 6.5, calculate the age specific rape rate for 1960 and 1970 for females between the ages of 15 and 34 years.**

Continuing this line of reasoning, crime victims are not always persons. There are also crimes "against" households, businesses, and automobiles. Adjusting for the increase in opportunities then becomes a matter of constructing rates based not on the population of individuals but on the increasing presence of households, businesses, and cars. We might then explore whether there are any differences in the trends depending on the prevalence of types of households, for example, apartments as opposed to separate units. Such differences might account, in part, for the differences between types of areas noted in Appendix B, where we see burglary rates per 100,000 inhabitants of 1,949 in large core cities with over 250,000 inhabitants, 1,054 in suburban areas, and 564 in rural areas.

The general point is this. In many situations you should shift from rates per 100,000 inhabitants to rates per units of opportunities. In this way you can better estimate changing potentials to take advantage of the opportunities and thus better tap any basic "cultural" changes taking place in society over and above such things as the age–sex composition or the increasing number of housing units, businesses, or cars and their degree of concentration.

Rates per units of opportunity do not exhaust the possible alternatives. You might instead calculate the rates per offender population. Sellin (1951) has argued that the rape rate should be calculated on the basis of the male population, always excluding children under the ages of 10 or 12 years. The argument also might be extended to older ages as well. We might thus define the "rape-prone" years in a manner parallel to the way in which we defined the "supportive" years when calculating the dependency ratio. We might, for example, calculate the rate of rape per 100,000 males between the ages of 15 and 50.

Similar reasoning can be employed when we realize that other crimes such as robbery, assault, and burglary are also age- and sex-related. By calculating sex and age specific rates, we can more directly reflect the changes taking place, say, among males between the ages of 15 and 55. The age categories might of course change by the type of crime involved. It has been shown repeatedly that the ages surrounding the 15th year to the 26th year are high robbery prone years. The age specific category, then, might include this interval. For other purposes we might shift still again.

It also is possible to combine adjustments in the rates for both offenders and opportunities. We might calculate, for example, the number of offenses per 100,000 males in a certain age bracket and then divide this rate by the number of opportunity units and then multiply the result by 100,000 to get the number of offenses per 100,000 offenders per 100,000 opportunities. This is easier to represent by way of formula than by words.

$$\left(\frac{\text{Number of offenses/Number of potential offenders} \times 100,000}{\text{Number of opportunity units (Persons, females, cars, and so forth)}} \right)$$
$$\times 100,000 = \text{Rate per 100,000 high-potential offender per 100,000 opportunity units}$$

Practicum 6.10 (a) **Referring to Tables 6.1 and 6.5, calculate the rape, robbery, and assault rates per 100,000 males in the age categories 15 to 35 for 1960 and 1970. (b) Calculate the same rape rate per 100,000 offenders, adding adjustment for rate per 100,000 females between ages 15 to 35.**

We find, then, when using available documents such as the *Uniform Crime Reports,* that you should not feel constrained to use exactly what the reports yield directly. You should be prepared to construct indicators more closely representing the concepts you are translating. If, for example, you are trying to portray the crime *potential* among a certain group, you may want to construct your rate per units of opportunity. Changes in your indicator over time will then more directly represent changes in the tendency to take advantage of the available opportunities. Such remanipulation of the data will frequently necessitate looking for additional sources of information, such as the changes in housing units or number of cars, when constructing an opportunity based rate for auto theft or burglary.

Exploring the Correlates of Crime

Once you settle on an appropriate indicator and note various patterns of difference, it is almost natural to begin wondering and constructing possible explanations for the patterns. For example, we note from Appendix B that homicide rates were highest in the Southern states during 1973. This region-related pattern is consistent with previous findings and has taken on the label of the "Southern factor" in discussions of homicide. Given this, you may begin to wonder why. Is it a matter of a Southern cultural factor, the pattern of law enforcement, the weather, reporting patterns of police departments, or what?

The question becomes, for present purposes: Is there available data that allow us to pursue some of these issues? Is there, for example, any relationship between the prevalence of capital punishment and the rate of homicide? We find from an examination of the maps reprinted from Harries (1974) in Figures 6.7 and 6.8 that, indeed, there seems to be a fairly close relationship. The regions with the highest number of executions are generally the regions with the highest rate of homicide. But, what conclusions can be drawn from these indicators? Relatively few. We will see in later chapters that the fact that we can predict something from something else need not imply anything about a causal linkage.

Just because we can predict high homicide rates from high frequency of capital punishment does not mean that capital punishment causes high rates of homicide. They might both be reflecting a violent aspect of a more deeply rooted cultural trait. It might be that it is the certainty of capital punishment rather than its mere frequency, in which case we should construct a rate of executions per crimes committed. It may be that the swiftness of justice is the key factor. If states that have invoked the death penalty are states where appeal procedures are the most intricate, then, justice may be delayed. If the swiftness of punishment is the deterrent rather than its severity, then, the higher homicide rate may be due to slow rather than harsh justice.

To pursue these alternatives with thoroughness we need more powerful

FIGURE 6.7
Prisoners Executed under Civil Authority in the United States, by State, 1930–1967

Source: Harries, 1974.

tools than simply a visual examination of two maps such as those in
Figures 6.7 and 6.8. We need knowledge of techniques that are discussed
in Chapters 10 and 11. If you are interested in this particular topic
and want to examine more sophisticated techniques before we get to
later chapters, see Bean and Cushing (1971) and then read Cousineau
(1973) for a critical appraisal of the conceptual ideas and the way
in which they have been translated into data.

What we have to this point, then, is a series of rather enticing clues
as to the nature of the crime picture in the United States. The available
data take us a good distance, but, sometimes, just to the brink of solid
insight. Having noted these sources of information, and there are others
we might have pursued, it is time to note some limitations.

Limitations

If we can say that a test of a theory is only as good as the link
between its indicators and concepts, then it is doubly the case that

FIGURE 6.8
Regional Homicide Distribution, 1968

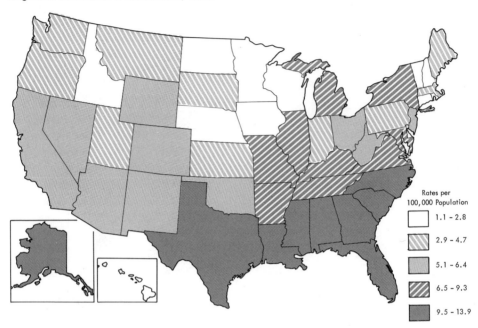

Rates per
100,000 Population

☐ 1.1 - 2.8

▨ 2.9 - 4.7

▨ 5.1 - 6.4

▨ 6.5 - 9.3

■ 9.5 - 13.9

Source: Harries, 1974.

indicators are only as good as the data from whence they come. As a researcher you are called upon to account for the quality of the data you use, even when you have not initially collected the data yourself. In the present context the question can be raised as to how well the *Uniform Crime Reports* reflect the actual prevalence and patterning of crime in the United States. We began this section by noting that these documents are the most frequently used and cited sources of information on crime in the U.S. These same reports are also the most severely criticized.[5]

When local law-enforcement departments are reporting the crimes

_____
[5] Along these lines, see Wolfgang (1963). There is continual effort to improve the quality and utility of the *UCR* but these have met with only limited success. In Appendix B you will find a discussion of verification procedures used. However, as is noted in this section of the 1973 *UCR*, "Regardless of the extent of the statistical verification processes used by the FBI, the accuracy of the data assembled under this Program depends upon the sincere effort exerted by each contributor to meet the necessary standards of reporting. For this reason, the FBI is not in a position to vouch for the validity of individual agency reports." Wolfgang's article provides some interesting historical instances when the reporting agencies were making less than sincere efforts to provide valid statistics. These historical "quirks" in the data should be considered if you plan to use the information for longitudinal studies.

known to the police, do they inflate their numbers when going before the city governing body for more money? Do these same departments deflate their rates when they are trying to establish the deterrent impact of a recent crackdown? As is always the case, persons gathering information are very much at the mercy of those furnishing information when it comes to the truthfulness of responses.

Even if we assume total candor on the part of local law-enforcement officials, the rates include only those offenses reported to the police. What of the real volume and distribution of crime? We know from a number of studies of victims that only a small portion of some crimes are reported to the police. We know also from a number of "self-report" studies, that is, studies asking respondents to report their own past criminal behavior, that criminal activity is much more evenly distributed across social-class categories than is indicated by official data.

To obtain this information, researchers have had to devise studies that have gone beyond the "available" information. Scales were devised and included as part of larger survey studies to examine correlates of real as opposed to officially recorded delinquency. For the first time, a report was issued in 1974 by the Department of Justice, from a continuing survey of households and commercial establishments, designed to tap the pattern of crime as reported by the victims. As this source of data builds up a history similar to the *Uniform Crime Reports*, another rich source of information will become available. In addition, as more and more studies by social scientists are stored in data banks, increasing analysis will be possible.

Still, even with these newly accumulating sources of information, it will no doubt be found that available questions and statistics do not always fit the purposes of the research at hand. In such cases a new study is called for. We will have more to say of this in Chapter 8. However, given the costly initial collection of information, it is very likely that we will continue to "make do" in many cases. We will continue to fashion indicators from the data available. In the process it is important to keep in mind the limitations this places on our conclusions.

In addition to the *Uniform Crime Reports*, other documents published by the Federal Bureau of Prisons and more recently by the Law Enforcement Assistance Administration provide information on other portions of the criminal-justice system. It is important, when using these documents, to keep in mind the rule of thumb that as you move away from the scene of the offense the statistics become less and less representative of the nature of the event and the persons involved. Thus, as a general rule, prison documents are less representative of the offender population than are court records. Court records are less representative than police arrest records. Arrest records are less representative than crimes reported. Crimes reported to the police are probably less representative than independent surveys of victims. These differences become important when we begin to shape explanations of crime based on the patterns reported. Not only do many cases and persons get screened out of the process as depicted in Figure 6.9 but also the reported nature of the case may change as lawyers bargain pleas of guilty for reductions in charge. The resulting screening process is governed by a series of factors such as the characteristics of the defendant, the nature of the offense, the current level of tolerance in the community for such offenses, the backlog of cases on the court docket, the quality of evidence gathered by the police, the amount of space available in the local jail or state prison, and so forth.

It is from considerations such as these that many have argued that understanding the crime picture must be grounded in understanding the operation of the criminal-justice system. Without the insight that arrest rates, court convictions, and prison sentences are social activities—the result of an interaction of forces rather than a simple, unvarying reaction to an illegal action committed—the official publications lose a good deal of their utility.

You may be wondering at this point, "If this is a methods book, why all the specifics on the production of crime statistics?" The general point is this. All production of available data is a social activity. Statistics are useful not only for the researcher but they also can be tools of support or difficulty for the organizations and individuals whose behavior they represent. Thus, when utilizing available material, it is incumbent upon you to familiarize yourself with the specifics of how the statistics are gathered and reported, what the possible sources of bias might be, and what precautions have been taken to ensure the quality of data.

A WORD ABOUT SURVEY DATA ARCHIVES

In recent years, what could turn out to be revolutionary sources of information on trends in society have been developed in the form of data libraries. These centers, such as the Roper Center at Williams College, the National Opinion Research Center at the University of Chicago, the Inter-University Consortium for Political Research at the University of Michigan (Ann Arbor), and the International Data Library and Reference Service at the University of California (Berkeley), provide valuable sources of survey data collected over a period of years on a wide range of topics.

The Roper Center, for example, which contains the largest collection, recently published a listing of questions, by subject matter, which have been asked in the same way over a period of years. It is possible to write the Roper Center, conveying the topic you have in mind, and receive back a listing of relevant questions and, if you desire, data decks

FIGURE 6.9
Criminal Justice System Model
(with estimates of flow of offenders for Index Crimes in the United States in 1965)

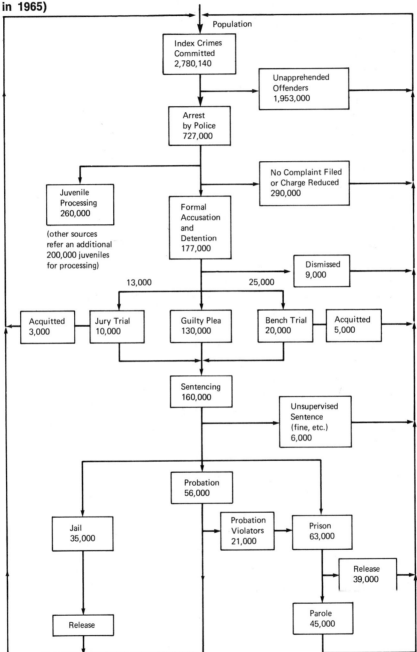

Source: Schrag, 1971. Adapted from the President's Commission on Law Enforcement and Administration of Justice, *The Challenge of Crime in a Free Society* (Washington, D.C.: Government Printing Office, 1967), pp. 262–63.

for your own analysis. Such a resource cuts the cost of survey studies to a fraction of what they would be if you had to collect the data yourself. Since they provide data from a number of points in time, these sources of information provide access to information that would otherwise be unavailable.

As with other sources of available data, you should acquaint yourself with the limitations and points of caution, as well as potential. Along these lines the introduction to the *Roper Manual* by Glenn (1975) and the lengthier general discussion of Hyman (1972) are very useful. Techniques relevant to the analysis of such survey information are discussed in Chapters 10 and 11 of this book.

Once you acquaint yourself with the type of data available, the questions asked, the samples drawn, and so forth, you will be confronted with a search for questions relevant to your concerns. It is possible, when scanning the available data, that previously unthought of studies will occur to you. In addition to these expanded horizons, however, you also will begin to realize that available questions will not always be phrased in just the way you would have preferred. You also will begin to realize that subtle and not-so-subtle changes in the wording of questions have been made over time and, thus, comparisons between surveys may not be possible. Once again you will be confronted with what to do with less than perfect indicators for the concepts you have in mind. Don't let this lack of perfection totally thwart your efforts. Be aware of the limitations and proceed with caution.

In addition to the data available through the various centers, summary results from some public-opinion polls are widely available in the form of the *Gallup Index* and the section on "The Polls" published at the end of issues of *Public Opinion Quarterly*. Again, pay attention to the wording of the questions and the sources of the data, especially the types of samples from which the information has been gathered. With this information in hand, use these sources of information; they provide no small resource.

> *Practicum 6.11* In Appendix C there is a copy of the survey instrument used in the 1974 National Opinion Research Center's poll of public opinion. Taking the questions used, what kinds of studies might be conducted? A) Specify the concepts that five different questions tap. B) What problems do you see with the way the questions are worded? C) What alternative questions might be devised to tap the same concepts?

SUMMARY

We have considered three sources of information that can be used in the construction of indicators for a wide range of topics. In each case we have noted such available sources can provide rich information about the structure and dynamics of society. These same data also have what are at times severe limitations. The information gathered has most frequently been organized for purposes other than those of social-science research in general and your study in particular. Be aware of the limitations. Also be aware of the potential that lies in reshaping the information provided. If you proceed with an eye only on perfection, you would stop before leaving the starting gate. If, however, you proceed with informed caution, you can make some inroads into areas that would otherwise be untouched. In the next chapter we will examine additional sources of available information, less statistical in nature.

KEY ISSUES

1. When using "available" data, what precautions should you take?
2. What limitations do you see in the use of the *Uniform Crime Reports?* How might these be lessened?
3. What is meant by category specific rates? Give some examples of how these are calculated and why they are more useful than more crudely constructed rates.
4. How are population indicators, which for the most part are static "snapshots," useful in making predictions about processes of social change? Give two examples.

REFERENCES

Bean, Frank, and Cushing, Robert
     1971   "Criminal Homicide, Punishment, and Deterrence." *Social Science Quarterly*, vol. 52, pp. 277–89.
Browning, Harley
     1968   "Life Expectancy and the Life Cycles—Some Interrelations." In Richard N. Farmer, John D. Long, and George J. Stolnitz (eds.), *World Population—The View Ahead.* Bloomington: Indiana University, Foundation for School of Business.
Corsa, Leslie, Jr., and Oakley, Deborah
     1971   "Consequences of Population Growth for Health Services in Less Developed Countries—An Initial Appraisal." In Study Committee of the Office of the Foreign Secretary National Academy of Sciences, *Rapid Population Growth: Consequences and Policy Implications.* Baltimore: Johns Hopkins Press.
Cousineau, Douglas F.
     1973   "A Critique of the Ecological Approach to the Study of Deviance." *Social Science Quarterly*, vol. 54, pp. 152–58.
Davis, Kingsley
     1958   "Population and Power in the Free World," in Philip M. Hauser (ed.) *Population and World Politics*, New York, the Free Press.

Galle, Omer R.; Gove, Walter R.; and McPherson, J. Miller
    1972   "Population Density and Pathology: What are the Relations for
            Man." *Science,* vol. 176, pp. 23–30.

Glenn, Norval
    1975   "Trend Studies with Available Survey Data: Opportunities and
            Pitfalls." In Philip K. Hastings and Jessie Southwick (eds.), *Survey
            Data for Trend Analysis: An Index to Repeated Questions in
            U.S. National Surveys held by the Roper Public Opinion Center.*
            Williamstown, Mass.: Roper Public Opinion Research Center.

Harries, Keith D.
    1974   *The Geography of Crime and Justice.* New York: McGraw-Hill.

Hyman, Herbert H.
    1972   *Secondary Analysis of Sample Surveys.* New York: John Wiley
            and Sons Inc.

Keyfitz, Nathan
    1971   "Changes of Birth and Death Rates and Their Demographic
            Effects." In Study Committee of the Office of the Foreign Secretary
            National Academy of Sciences, *Rapid Population Growth: Conse-
            quences and Policy Implications.* Baltimore: Johns Hopkins Press.

Lorenz, Konrad
    1966   *On Aggression.* New York: Harcourt, Brace and World Inc.

Sawyer, Jack
    1967   "Dimensions of Nations: Size, Wealth and Politics." *American
            Journal of Sociology,* vol. 73, pp. 145–72.

Schrag, Clarence
    1971   *Crime and Justice: American Style.* National Institute of Mental
            Health, Publication No. HSM-72-9052.

Sellin, Thorsten
    1951   "The Significance of Records of Crime." *The Law Quarterly Re-
            view* vol. 67, pp. 489–504.

Shryock, Henry S., and Siegel, Jacob S.
    1973   *The Methods and Materials of Demography.* U.S. Department
            of Commerce.

U.S. Congressional Information Service
    1974   American Statistics Index: A Comprehensive Guide and Index to the
            Statistical Publications of the U.S. Government (Retrospective).

U.S. Department of Health, Education, and Welfare
    1971   *Vital Statistics of the United States 1971,* vol. 2, Section 5, Life
            Tables.

U.S. Department of Justice
    1974   *Criminal Victimization in the United States: January–June 1973,*
            vol. 1, November.

Wolfgang, Marvin E.
    1963   "Uniform Crime Reports: A Critical Appraisal," *University of
            Pennsylvania Law Review,* vol. iii, pp. 708–38.

Contents

Chapter 7

Translating Ideas into Data, II: Exploring Available Documents

In the present chapter we will examine two additional sources of documents available for secondary analysis. The first section focuses on considerations of content analysis as it applies to more "popular" documents, such as newspapers, films, novels, and television programs. The second section focuses on the use of the *Human Relations Area Files* as an organized set of reports on cultures throughout the world.

CONTENT ANALYSIS AND THE EXPLORATION OF AVAILABLE "DOCUMENTS"

Available data need not be "statistical." There are other "documents," such as magazines, newspapers, books, personal memoirs, speeches by public officials, television shows, laws, films, art, legislative hearings, and so forth. To explore these, we are once again called on to analyze content, to reshape available information. This time, however, content analysis does not involve constructing numerical indicators from other numbers but, instead, most frequently involves an assessment (sometimes numerical, sometimes not) of linguistic symbols. This assessment may be an overall impression or feeling, as when we say the major theme of a novel is the "eternal triangle." This general, impressionistic assessment will not be our major concern, though we will most certainly be considering various "impressions."

The present section is concerned with the topic of content analysis as it involves the construction and application of coding schemes designed to translate verbal or other nonmathematical symbolic statements into overall indexes of what has been said or more generally portrayed. Given the range of available documents considered here, it is not surprising that topics pursued through "content analysis" differ widely. They include evidence introduced in court for criminal-sedition trials (Laswell, 1949); analysis of changing trends in popular religion (Schneider and Dornbusch, 1958); motivation reflected in suicide notes (Osgood and Walker, 1959); assessment of the salient issues of the 1960s (Funkhouser, 1973); the content of comic strips and fiction novels (Berelson and Salter, 1946, and Spiegleman et al., 1953); correlates of the concerns of 17th-century English scientists (Merton, 1957); as well as many others.

A prime virtue of content analysis is that it allows access to past events that might otherwise be unavailable. Historical events by their very nature are not subject to contemporary direct observation. We must rely on accounts of these events. One way to gather information is through interviews that produce retrospective interpretations by persons who were there. Another way is through analysis of "artifacts" left behind. Part of these artifacts are documents. By analyzing the content of historical documents, broadly considered, we can begin to get an idea of past events, perspectives, values, and so forth, reported as they occurred. We need not rely on retrospection, which many times produces a reinterpreted past. Also, by relying on documents, we are not interjecting ourselves in such a way as to influence the course of events. We thereby avoid the obtrusiveness that plagues the participant observer and the survey researcher.

Analysis of "primary" documents, then, has the dual virtue of allowing unobtrusive access to otherwise unavailable information. There are also drawbacks. The material reported rarely if ever captures the totality of the setting we are trying to depict. As any observer of contemporary news reporting knows, documents do not always provide information in the form you would like. You make do. You attempt to garner as much insight from the information as possible, realizing that many times there will be holes.

You try to plug the holes. You try to ensure reliable and objective analysis on your part. Your efforts will be less than perfect, but they also will avoid total neglect. You will make headway. Once again the success of a project depends on rational planning seasoned with a strong measure of ingenuity and intuition born out of familiarity with the material and experience with problems encountered.

Developing the Coding Strategy

One way to ensure reliability, that is, one way to ensure results that can be replicated by others, is to develop an explicit coding scheme. At times this is no easy task given the complexity of the material. How do you study the multiple dimensions of changing religious trends? How do you capture the "tenor" of the times in a decade such as the 1960s? How can you represent, by way of indexes, the complexities and subtleties of a novel like Tolstoi's *War and Peace?* Questions such as these have created a good deal of discussion concerning the viability of the process we are about to pursue. Like attempts to translate the nuances of a concept such as alienation via items on a survey questionnaire, our attempts to capture much of the richness of documents via a coding scheme will be only partially successful. This said, it is equally the case that systematic attempts to pursue the content of written documents yield insights that escape efforts producing a vaguely defined feel for what is being portrayed. Consider some examples.

A Study of Popular Religion

If ever there was a multifaceted, complex, subtle concept it is the idea of religion. Yet Schneider and Dornbusch have set out a coding scheme to analyze the changing trends in popular religion within the Judeo-Christian tradition. The major thematic categories of their coding scheme are: (1) Functions of religious faith; (2) Mutual relations of God, Man, and Nature; (3) Changing the self and the world; (4) Salvation—Rationale; and (5) Salvation—attitudes and techniques. Within each of these major categories there are breakdowns for characterizing the thrust of the books being analyzed. Figure 7.1 presents the subcategories for the major category of "Salvation—Rationale."

These categories and subcategories were devised in discussions among those who eventually coded the material. After initially reading many of the books, trial runs with various alternative categories were made. Following progressive refinement, the scheme was "frozen" for the complete study. This initial period of discussion provided not only a more refined scheme but also developed intimate knowledge of the scheme's meaning among those recording their observations.

In addition to developing a coding scheme, Schneider and Dornbusch had to decide on the appropriate pool from which to draw their material. Wanting to depict changes in popular religion within the Judeo-Christian tradition, they chose best selling inspirational books published between 1875 and 1955, employing the following definition: "Inspirational religious literature assumes the general validity of the premises of the Judeo-Christian religious tradition; it is designed to inspire with the sentiment of the possibility of salvation here or in the afterlife; and it presents techniques for attaining the salvation it sets out, at the same time addressing itself to the ordinary problems of everyday people." The criteria of "best selling" was decided on the basis of books appearing in three published listings of best sellers. See Appendix C of *Popular Religion* for further elaboration.

The validity of the idea that these books represent popular religious

FIGURE 7.1
Portion of a Coding Scheme Used in *Popular Religion*

D. Salvation—Rationale:
   D1.   Man can be saved in the next life:
       D1.1—by religious means (intercession of an objective God).
       D1.2—by spiritual means (being in tune with the infinite or the divine).
       D1.3—by religious and psychological means.
       D1.4—by spiritual and psychological means.
       D1.5—by psychological means (conquering the enemy within: fear, hate, anxiety, etc.).
   D2.   Man can be saved in this life:
       D2.1—by religious means (intercession of an objective God).
       D2.2—by spiritual means (being in tune with the infinite or the divine).
       D2.3—by religious and psychological means.
       D2.4—by spiritual and psychological means.
       D2.5—by psychological means (conquering the enemy within: fear, hate, anxiety, etc.).
   D3.   The essential nature of man:
       D3.1—is evil.
       D3.2—is evil but perfectible.
       D3.3—is good but subject to sin or error.
       D3.4—is good.
   D4.   Happiness in this world:
       D4.1—cannot be expected.
       D4.2—cannot be expected by most men.
       D4.3—can be expected by most men.
       D4.4—can be expected.
   D5.   Significance of suffering or pain (physical or emotional).
       D5.1. Suffering has divine significance, sent by God for his purposes.
       D5.2. Suffering is a sign of divine displeasure.
       D5.3. Suffering is a sign that you are out of tune with the divine.
       D5.4. Suffering is part of man's lot on earth (religiously neutral).
       D5.5. Suffering should be assiduously avoided and fought (religiously neutral).
   D6.   Relation of faith and reason.
       D6.1. Faith alone is necessary for salvation.
       D6.2. When faith and reason conflict, faith should rule.
       D6.3. Reason should be mistrusted, in whole or in part.
       D6.4. Reason supports faith.
       D6.5. Both faith and reason are necessary.

FIGURE 7.1 (*continued*)

D6.6. When faith and reason conflict, reason should rule.

D6.7. Reason alone is necessary.

D7. Faith and works as means to salvation.

    D7.1. Faith is more important than works.

    D7.2. Works are more important than faith.

    D7.3. Works and faith are of approximately equal importance.

D8. Dogma, subjective religious experience, and ritual [preferred code order: .5, .6, .7 over .1, .2, .3, .4].

    D8.1. Favorable mention of systematic doctrine or dogma.

    D8.2. Favorable mention of subjective religious experience.

    D8.3. Unfavorable mention of systematic doctrine or dogma.

    D8.4. Unfavorable mention of subjective religious experience.

    D8.5. Dogma is more important than subjective religious experience.

    D8.6. Dogma and subjective religious experience are of equal importance.

    D8.7. Subjective religious experience is more important than dogma.

    D8.8. Favorable reference to ritual (ceremonies, liturgies, sacraments, music, use of vestments, etc.).

    D8.9. Unfavorable reference to ritual.

D9. Presence or absence of denominationalism.

    D9.1. The dogma (and/or ritual) of a particular church is favorably mentioned.

    D9.2. The dogma (and/or ritual) of a particular church is unfavorably mentioned.

    D9.3. Participation in *some* (any) church is necessary.

    D9.4. Belief in God suffices.

D10. Signs of salvation or damnation.

    D10.1. Riches signify:

        D10.1.1—you are in some way good.

        D10.1.2—you are in some way evil.

        D10.1.3—neither; both good and bad people are wealthy.

        D10.1.4—nothing; riches are an illusion.

    D10.2. Poverty signifies:

        D10.2.1—you are in some way good.

        D10.2.2—you are in some way evil.

        D10.2.3—neither; both good and bad people are poor.

        D10.2.4—nothing; poverty is an illusion.

FIGURE 7.1 *(concluded)*

D10.3. Physical health signifies:
  D10.3.1—you are in some way good.
  D10.3.2—you are in some way evil.
  D10.3.3—neither; both good and bad people are healthy.
  D10.3.4—nothing; health is an illusion.

D10.4. Physical illness signifies:
  D10.4.1—you are in some way good.
  D10.4.2—you are in some way evil.
  D10.4.3—neither; both good and bad people are ill.
  D10.4.4—nothing; illness is an illusion.

D10.5. Emotional adjustment signifies:
  D10.5.1—you are in some way good.
  D10.5.2—you are in some way evil.
  D10.5.3—neither; both good and bad people are emotionally adjusted.
  D10.5.4—nothing; emotional adjustment is an illusion.

D10.6. Emotional maladjustment signifies:
  D10.6.1—you are in some way good.
  D10.6.2—you are in some way evil.
  D10.6.3.—neither; both good and bad people are emotionally maladjusted.
  D10.6.4.—nothing; emotional maladjustment is an illusion.

D11. Level of aspiration in this world (*not* religious, spiritual, or psychological).
 D11.1. Be satisfied with what you've got (support of status quo).
 D11.2. Set your sights moderately higher.
 D11.3. Set your sights according to your capabilities.
 D11.4. Set your sights according to your capabilities and to social situation (environmental realities and limitations).
 D11.5. Set your sights very high.

D12. Source of testimonials or case histories:
 D12.1. People successful in business.
 D12.2. Scientists.
 D12.3. Popular heroes (e.g., sports, entertainment, etc.).
 D12.4. Ordinary people.

thinking rested on several additional assumptions. It was assumed that the books bought were indeed read. It also was assumed that either the books represent the beliefs of the readers or that the books were influential in shaping those beliefs once they were read. There obviously was no direct way to confirm these assumptions. The authors reasoned, however, that even if they proved to be false in part, the material selected deserved study in its own right in that it represented an important segment of the surrounding cultural setting.

With their coding scheme, their sample of books, and their rationale in hand, the task of pursuing changing trends in popular religion could begin. One more decision had to be made, however. What was the appropriate "unit" to which to apply the coding scheme? Should they analyze words, sentences, paragraphs, chapters, thematic sections of books, or should they simply score the entire book once on each of the dimensions? The major strategy chosen was one where paragraphs were the units of analysis. Paragraphs were first read and then "scored" according to their content. The proportion of paragraphs on a particular theme then became a basic piece of information used to characterize literature and locate changing trends.

But what of the changing trends? Could changes noted simply be due to progressive familiarity with the coding scheme? As the research progressed, "artificial" trends, that is, trends due to changing coding practices rather than changes in the literature, might be noted. To avoid this possibility Schneider and Dornbusch randomly allocated the books by time. Thus, books written early in the period between 1875 and 1955 were just as likely to be read late in the research as were books written more recently.

What we find in this study of popular religion, then, in addition to the rather interesting characterization of an aspect of popular culture, is a carefully designed and executed study employing the technique of content analysis.

What are the benchmarks of a careful study? First, there is the development of the coding scheme. When developing a coding scheme, you should be willing to spend some initial time "playing" with the material to be coded, trying out alternatives, deciding on what categories best fit your purposes while at the same time maintaining the integrity of the material. There should be a stance similar to that period of semi-orientation we noted in the process of uncovering the folk system. Indeed, there are some important similarities in the two endeavors. Your sources of information are different, but in both cases you are trying to come up with some way to capture the sometimes elusively rich information about a setting.

As you become familiar with the material, as your own interest takes on more definite shape, the coding scheme will become more specific and fixed. Schneider and Dornbusch talk of "freezing" their scheme. This, too, has its counterpart in participant observation. There, we noted the strategy of refined probing as familiarity with the setting and its possibilities for yielding information became clear. The coding scheme is only part of the research, albeit an important part. You must also develop criteria for selecting your material. You must develop definitions of what "units" within this material are to be analyzed. Then you are ready to proceed. As you proceed you should make provisions to ensure that the patterns you note are not artificial. One recurring possibility is differences that might creep into your analysis via differential application of the coding scheme.

When analyzing trends, one way to minimize the impact of differential application is to randomize the examination of material so that coded information is in no way connected with your increasing familiarity with the coding instructions. However, this problem might emerge even when time trends are not involved. It is thus important that you spend some initial time practicing so as to equilibrate before the actual research begins.

Even with the best laid plans you should also build checks into your study. Of prime importance is the question of how reliable your coding scheme is. You can proceed along at least three lines in this regard. Two have to do with cross-checking the coders. You can get at least two persons to code the same material and then compare their results. If no one is willing or able to spend the time, you might check on yourself by going back at the end of the study and recoding some of the material to see if any changes have taken place in your own orientation. More will be said of reliability shortly.

In addition to cross-checking coding, you can frequently gather additional information that may confirm or disconfirm your results. Funkhouser (1973), for example, used available Gallup Polls to cross-check his ranking of salient issues on the basis of analyzing three popular news magazines. This study of the rather turbulent '60s was in many ways simplistic—frequency counts were made on the basis of various summary listings—but, by checking with independent sources of information from the same period, Funkhouser built up greater confidence in the findings than would otherwise be warranted.

In brief, take time to develop the coding scheme. It's your most important tool. Familiarize yourself and those working with you with the scheme before the actual study starts. Define the body of material you will be studying. Define the "units" within this material you will be examining. We will have more to say of these "sampling" issues in Chapter 9. Check on yourself while the project is progressing and once it is finished. With these words of advice for developing your own devices, we can point to some additional work of others that might be helpful.

A Scheme for Analyzing Newspapers

One widely available document is the newspaper. Klein and Maccoby (1954), in the context of examining newspaper coverage of the Stevenson–Eisenhower election, devised a general scheme for assessing various dimensions of newspaper coverage. Basically, the scheme suggested by them provides a set of coding instructions for stories according to how the stories occupy "prime" space in the newspaper format. When analyzing the content of front-page coverage over time, six general categories of information should be kept in mind.

1. The number of stories on a given topic
2. The type of headline coverage
3. Story placement
4. Story content
5. Picture and cartoon coverage
6. Total space allocation

Each of these categories was developed further. The first, the number of stories, is relatively straightforward. It is simply a matter of obtaining the appropriate newspapers and counting the material. The type of headline coverage is a little more complicated. Working with the assumption that the "importance" given a particular issue or story is reflected in the placement and size of the headline, Klein and Maccoby suggested a threefold scheme for categorizing headlines. Type A headlines are those four or more columns wide appearing above the "fold" of the newspaper. Type B headlines are those two or three columns wide appearing either above or below the fold. Type C headlines are one-column headlines appearing above or below the fold. One measure of news coverage, then, becomes the space given the story for each type of headline. Although Klein and Maccoby failed to pursue the issue, you might arbitrarily weight the various types of headlines and then combine the coverage to obtain a weighted average per news issue over a number of issues. Failing this weighting procedure, you might proceed as the authors did and construct the simple average headline space allocated.

In addition to length and location, headlines also differ according to type size. Thus, average type size might be a useful index. You will frequently want to devise coding schemes for the content of the headlines. These can range from simple characterizations of the "slant" of the headline—favorable or unfavorable—to more elaborate analysis of the intensity of wording. We will have more to say of this question of coding "intensity" and direction shortly.

In addition to the size, location, and content of headlines, another indicator of story importance is its column location. It is generally agreed that stories in column eight above the fold have the best location, i.e., the most attention-getting. Column one above the fold is next, followed by other locations in less-agreed-upon order. Like the content of headlines the content of stories can also be coded. Again the specifics of this coding scheme will depend on the nature of your research. Your scheme might include substance issues—what topics were covered, issues of bias, or issues of intensity.

Pictures and cartoons are yet other indicators of news coverage. Again the number, size, and location of the pictures will be important. Analyzing the content of pictures will call for a good deal of ingenuity on your part. Your scheme might again range from some assessment of the slant of the picture to more elaborate characterizations of its content. Finally, as an overall indicator of coverage, you might want to calculate a total space indicator, including in your calculations headline, story, and pictorial material.

> *Praticum 7.1* **Using the above discussion as a rough guide, what parallel indicators of news coverage might be devised for television? For example, what is the counterpart to column inches, to front-page coverage, and so forth? Assuming you wanted to assess the orientation of a newspaper in terms of its being oriented toward local, state, national, or international issues, how would you proceed?**

Coding Direction and Intensity

We come now to perhaps the most debated aspect of content analysis—that of characterizing evaluation, its direction and intensity. To understand the difficulties involved we need only recall our previous discussion of how the participant observer frequently misinterprets the meaning of various comments, gestures, or events within the setting being studied. It will be recalled that Keiser (1970), in his study of the "Vice Lords," reported a misinterpretation of a threat, "You better walk light," for a friendly warning. Keiser not only had words at his disposal but also voice tone and body gesture. Thus, it should not be surprising that there is substantial risk of misinterpretation when you have only the written word of a document.

When we attempt to analyze the direction and intensity of communication, we frequently are attempting to uncover the intentions of the writer. Yet we have only information on our own impressions of what he or she wrote. It is in this sense that evaluative characterizations of material may be a better predictor of the "message's" impact on the "receiver" than it is an estimate of the intentions of the "sender."

Keeping the frequent appearance of ambiguity in mind, consider the following examples of evaluative statements:

1. Abortions are an abomination, an affront to mankind and to the value of human life.

2.   Abortions seem to raise troublesome issues in that they involve the right of a woman to control her own body, on the one hand, and the snuffing out of a human life, on the other.

3.   Abortions are an essential right of a woman in that they protect the inalienable right to decide the fate of one's own life and the state of one's body.

As for the first statement, there would be widespread agreement that the direction is negative and the intensity is high. The second might be considered neutral. The third is surely positive and the intensity will depend on how "inalienable" the right is considered. So far so good.

But how does the second statement differ from one that might be considered neutral in the sense of apathetic? To say that abortions are troublesome is surely different than saying, "Abortions are once again in the news." In some situations it may be enough to note that communications are either pro, con, or neutral. In others you will want to develop your categories to reflect differences between a concerned, balanced treatment and one that might be considered unconcerned or apathetic.

A frequently cited technique for more elaborate analysis of evaluative content is "evaluative assertion analysis" developed by Osgood (1959) and others. This technique first involves making distinctions between what are called attitude objects (AO) and common meaning terms. Attitude objects are those focuses of evaluation—dogs, coffee, criminals, conservatives, Italians, militarization, and, as in the above example, abortions. The "meaning" assigned to these various terms will differ from one individual to the next, depending on background, predisposition, particular situations, and so forth. Common meaning terms, by contrast, have more agreed-upon meaning. It is generally agreed that "abomination" is a stronger word than "troublesome," that "compassionate" is good while "unjust" is bad, and so forth. There will, of course, be differences of opinion when comparing various words, such as when we say X is ambitious. For some, "ambitious" will signal a person who is willing to step on others for personal gain. For others, it will signal a person who is single-minded in purpose, willing to put out a good deal of effort for what is being sought.

A third task for the coder using the evaluative assertion technique is perhaps the most ambiguous. Here, it is a matter of assessing the meaning of the "connectors," those words that link the attitude object with the common meaning term. For a more detailed elaboration of the procedures involved and various rules for coding, you should refer to Osgood and various articles cited therein. Using the above sentences about abortions as examples, this procedure involves the following:

First, locate the attitude objects. In this case—abortions, troublesome issues, right of a woman to control her own body, inalienable right to decide fate of one's own life, snuffing out human life, and the inalienable right to decide fate of one's body. To ensure objectivity by coders when they come to the task of assigning values to the connectors and the common meaning terms, the attitude objects are assigned masking codes—abortions becomes Z, for example. Once the attitude objects are isolated and masked, they are combined with the connectors and the common meaning terms in the following format:

1.   Attitude object/Connector/Common meaning term
2.   Attitude object$_1$/Connector/Attitude object$_2$

The above sentences become a set of assertions:

Abortions/are/an abomination.
Abortions/are/an affront to mankind.
Abortions/are/an affront to the value of human life.

Abortions/seem to raise/troublesome issues.
Abortions/involve/right of woman to control own body.
Abortions/involve/snuffing out human life.

Abortions/are/an essential right of a woman.
Abortions/protect/inalienable right to decide fate of one's own life.
Abortions/protect/inalienable right to decide fate of one's body.

Once words are isolated and assertions reconstructed, the task is to assign values to the various elements of the assertions. Osgood and fellow workers suggest a seven-point scale ranging from —3 to +3. For full details of constructing value scores, you should refer to the work of Osgood, but an examination of the above assertions about abortions will provide some insight into what is involved.

The first sentence has been broken down into three assertions. The task is to come up with a score for the sentence regarding the intensity and direction of the attitude toward abortions. One way to proceed is to give a score ranging from —3 to +3 for the connector and the common meaning term or second attitude object; multiply these scores; sum the resulting scores for each assertion; and then divide by the number of assertions for an overall average score. Figure 7.2 illustrates this procedure. The overall average score for the first sentence is —9. The issues and decisions involved in the first sentence are rather straightforward. Now, consider the second sentence. Parallel scores for the second sentence and its assertions are presented in Figure 7.3. The average score, —.67, is very close to 0, or a neutral assertion score. Its "negative" component comes from the word "troublesome." Had the sentence read "seems to raise issues" as opposed to "troublesome issues," its neutrality would have been further enhanced. What of the attitude object regarding the right of a woman to control her own body? Here, we get into the feelings or evaluations of the coder as much as the intentions of

FIGURE 7.2
Example of Evaluative Assertion Score

Attitude Object₁	Connector	Score	Common Meaning Term or Attitude Object₂	Score	Assertion Score Total
Abortions	are	+3	Abomination	−3	−9
Abortions	are	+3	Affront to mankind	−3	−9
Abortions	are	+3	Affront to value of human life	−3	−9
				Total	−27
				Average	−9

FIGURE 7.3
Example of Evaluative Assertion Score

Attitude Object₁	Connector	Score	Common Meaning Term or Attitude Object₂	Score	Assertion Score Total
Abortions	Seem to raise	+1	Troublesome issues	−2	−2
Abortions	Involve	+2	Right of woman to control own body	+3	+6
Abortions	Involve	+2	Snuffing out	−3	−6
				Total	−2
				Average	−.67

the writer. If the coder perceives this to be a highly important right, the score will be higher. If not so important, the score goes down accordingly. To make the decision to score such ambiguous phrases, the evaluative assertion analysis technique involves further searching for the same attitude object in other portions of the document, scoring in a manner similar to the above figures, and then substituting this score each time the attitude object appears connected with the attitude object in question. You should consult the more detailed discussions of these procedures if you run into this problem.

> **Practicum 7.2** Referring above to the third sentence evaluating abortion, construct a score parallel to those in Figures 7.2 and 7.3. What problems do you see with this method?

At times, methods such as the evaluative assertion analysis place one in the position of killing a mosquito with a cannon. You can get by with much less with no significant change in the result. In addition, Osgood found, "In a rough check on the speed with which sets of three coders (one masking, another translating into assertions, and a third giving ratings and computing evaluative locations) could handle material, it was found that it takes about one hour of coder time for each 133 words of material (one triple-spaced page). This is certainly laborious" (p. 52). Thus, before you begin developing your coding scheme, consider the degree of complexity you need. In some cases you may want even more complex measures than the ones just discussed, though it is doubtful that they would be much more complex. In other situations you may be able to get by with simple summary measures of the evaluative direction.

A Word about Reliability

Whatever the complexity of your scheme, there is always the element of coder predisposition, selective perception, and so forth. On the basis of the discussion thus far, it should be clear that, in many situations, it never will be possible to eliminate observer "distortion" completely. What you want to do, then, is develop some check on the consistency of application from one observer to the next. With such a check you can first determine the presence and degree of variation from one coder to the next and, then, if appropriate, explore factors such as attitudes, age, and so forth that might be related to systematic patterns in the variation. These questions center around what is generally referred to as the reliability of the coding scheme.

There are a number of alternatives for checking. Consider one for the situation where you are having coders rank entire news magazines on the degree of support for the vigorous prosecution of the Watergate defendants. So that we can better build toward more complex situations, first assume that your budget or number of submissive friends made it necessary to limit the number of coders to two. Figure 7.4 represents the situation in which there was perfect agreement between your two friends-turned-coders. Figure 7.5 reflects a slight bit of disagreement;

FIGURE 7.4
Showing Total Agreement between Two Coders

Magazines	Rank by Coder A	Rank by Coder B	D_i	D_i^2
A	1	1	0	0
B	2	2	0	0
C	3	3	0	0
D	4	4	0	0
E	5	5	0	0
F	6	6	0	0
G	7	7	0	0
H	8	8	0	0
I	9	9	0	0
		Total	0	0

FIGURE 7.5
Showing Slight Disagreement between Two Coders

Magazines	Rank by Coder A	Rank by Coder B	D_i	D_i^2
A.	1	2	−1	1
B.	2	1	1	1
C.	3	4	−1	1
D.	4	3	1	1
E.	5	5	0	0
F.	6	6	0	0
G.	7	7	0	0
H.	8	9	−1	1
I	9	8	1	1
		Total	0	6

Figure 7.6 still more disparity, and, finally, Figure 7.7 represents a situation where the rankings are reversed.

How can we reflect these various situations in a summary measure of agreement or disagreement? First, we need some indication as to

FIGURE 7.6
Showing Substantial Disagreement between Two Coders

Magazines	Rank by Coder A	Rank by Coder B	D_i	D_i^2
A.	1	7	−6	36
B.	2	4	−2	4
C.	3	3	0	0
D.	4	5	−1	1
E.	5	2	3	9
F.	6	1	5	25
G.	7	6	1	1
H.	8	9	−1	1
I	9	8	1	1
		Total	0	78

the amount of disparity between the items being ranked, in this case news magazines. One way is to subtract the rankings of the two judges for each item. This gives us individual item disparity. For a total measure we might add these disparity scores; but, as figures 7.4 through 7.7 illustrate, this will always yield a total score of 0. This situation can be remedied by squaring the difference in ranking scores and then adding to get the D_i^2 total in figures 7.4 through 7.7.

A problem with this latter total, as an overall measure of judge disparity, is that it varies not only with the degree of disparity between items but also with the number of items being ranked. Thus, it makes

FIGURE 7.7
Showing a Reversal of Rankings between Two Coders

Magazines	Rank by Coder A	Rank by Coder B	D_i	D_i^2
A	1	9	−8	64
B	2	8	−6	36
C	3	7	−4	16
D	4	6	−2	4
E	5	5	0	0
F	6	4	2	4
G	7	3	4	16
H	8	2	6	36
I	9	1	8	64
		Total	0	240

interpretation of scores difficult. What is needed is some measure that varies within a specified range, regardless of the number of ranked items, showing total agreement on one end and total reversal on the other. Spearman's r_s has been devised for just this situation. Without going into the derivation of the formula, we can see how it works very simply by applying it to Figures 7.4 through 7.7. The formula is as follows:

$$(1) \qquad r_s = 1 - \left(\frac{6 \sum_{i=1}^{N} D_i^2}{N(N^2 - 1)} \right)$$

First, the symbol $\sum_{i=1}^{N}$ simply means sum up the items, beginning with the first and going to the Nth, in this case, difference scores squared for nine magazines. N equals the number of items being ranked. In the first situation, where there is total agreement, represented by Figure 7.4, we find the following result:

$$(2) \qquad = 1 - \left(\frac{6(0)}{9(80)} \right) = 1.0$$

Perfect agreement is reflected in a positive 1.0 value. In the second and third situations we have the following:

$$(3) \qquad \text{For Figure 7.5} = 1 - \left(\frac{6(6)}{9(80)} \right) = .95$$

$$(4) \qquad \text{For Figure 7.6} = 1 - \left(\frac{6(78)}{9(80)} \right) = .35$$

Thus, as the degree of agreement goes down the size of the summarizing measure goes down, until we reach the value of -1.0 as illustrated by a reversal of rankings in Figure 7.7.

$$\text{For Figure 7.7} = 1 - \left(\frac{6(240)}{9(80)}\right) = -1.0$$

Practicum 7.3   Calculate Spearman's r_s for the following situations:

	Situation I			Situation II	
	Coder A	Coder B		Coder A	Coder B
A	1	9	A	1	7
B	2	7	B	2	5
C	3	8	C	3	4
D	4	5	D	4	9
E	5	4	E	5	8
F	6	6	F	6	6
G	7	2	G	7	1
H	8	1	H	8	2
I	9	3	I	9	3

Spearman's r_s, then, is useful when a measure of overall agreement is desired and when two judges are doing the ranking.

Two complications are commonly encountered using this measure of agreement. The first is what to do when there are more than two judges. The second is what to do with tied rankings by a single judge. Taking the second problem first, it is frequently found that the material is such that the overall impression or the single quantitative score, if you are using something like the evaluative assertion techniques, leads to an identical ranking for two items. In such a situation, you simply average. You assign adjoining ranks to the items, take the average, and assign the average to each item. Say, you are ranking and find, when you come to the seventh and eighth items, that no discernible difference exists. You assign 7.5 (the average of 7 and 8) to each of the items and then move to "9" for the next item ranked. If three items are tied, the principle remains. You assign three adjacent numbers, say, "4," "5," and "6"; take the average, 5; give each of the items this rank; and then move on to the next rank for the next item, "7" in this case.

Figure 7.8 illustrates the situation where items "2" and "3," and items "5," "6," and "7" are tied by the coder.

Complications arise when there are a large number of tied items in relation to the total number of items being ranked. Of course, it may be that a large number of items are identical. It also may be the case, however, that your coding scheme is simply not very sensitive to differ-

FIGURE 7.8
Illustration of How to
Treat Tied Ranks by a
Single Coder

	Item	Rank
	A	1
Tied	{ B	2.5
	{ C	2.5
	D	4
	(E	6
Tied	{ F	6
	(G	6
	H	8
	I	9

ences. In such a case the value of Spearman's r_s will be "inflated" by the disproportionately large number of ties. In this event, adjustments are called for. If you find yourself in this situation, consult Kendall (1955) for the appropriate adjustments.

In addition to the problem of tied rankings, the question frequently arises as to how to measure the disparity between more than two judges. Equation (1) is appropriate for two sets of rankings. One way to handle more than two sets of rankings is to take the mean measure of agreement with all possible combinations of rankings. Say you had four coders. There are six combinations of two: I-II, I-III, I-IV, II-III, II-IV, and III-IV. You simply calculate the measure of agreement for each of these pairs, as outlined above, add the resulting measures of agreement (make sure you observe the positive and negative signs), and take the average.

Practicum 7.4 To the situations presented in Practicum 7.3, add a third coder who ranked the same items as follows:

Coder C

Item	Rank
A	1.5
B	1.5
C	3
D	4
E	5
F	6.5
G	6.5
H	9
I	8

Calculate the overall measure of agreement for the three coders. Given that two of the coders are in fairly close agreement and one is "out of line," what ambiguities do you see in relying only on the final average degree of agreement among the coders?

Frequently, if you rely only on the final summarizing measure of agreement, you will miss important information. You may, for example, have seven coders; five are in close agreement, the remaining two are not. Instead of throwing this information away by simply mixing it into the overall measure of agreement, take a close look to see if you can discern any reasons why. It may be that only a couple of items are out of line. It may be that the two coders simply were not taking the task seriously. It may be that they were given inappropriate instructions. It may be that they are your best independent coders; the remaining had gotten together and worked out their differences while coding the material. Rarely is it a good idea to rely only on the single summary measure. Look for disparities between individual items and between coders before you come to any conclusions about the meaning of your summary measure. This is not only a good principle in the present instance. It is also appropriate strategy when we get to later chapters exploring the statistical translation of the ideas of prediction and cause.

Practicum 7.5 What we have outlined to this point are a series of objectives and guidelines to keep in mind when doing "content analysis." If you have never engaged in this activity you may still be unaware of some of the difficulties that arise, as well as much of the gain to be had from analyzing documents in this fashion. To remedy this I have included a historical document, the *Code of Hammurabi*, an ancient legal code, in Appendix C. Either alone or with some classmates or friends, devise a coding scheme to analyze this document. Include in your study a strategy for checking on the reliability of your coding.

To give you an idea of the possibilities, you might classify the events represented by each of the statements into various classes—say, criminal offenses, service activities, and specifications of procedures for carrying out reactions to criminal behavior or for handling ambiguous situations. Within each of these types of events you will need additional categories for classifying the component parts. For example, within the criminal-offense category you might include a scheme for classifying the action in question, the offender, the victim, the object involved, the reaction specified, and the actors who are to carry out the reaction. There are, of course, other possibilities.

Once you have decided on your coding scheme, what kinds of questions might be interesting to pursue? What problems do you foresee in such a study?

EXPLORING THE HUMAN RELATIONS AREA FILES

When carrying out research calling for cross-cultural data, a valuable document resource is the *Human Relations Area Files* (*HRAF*). These files contain primary sources of information on cultures throughout the world. The range of topics that might be pursued is almost unending.

To be sure, as we will shortly see, there are limitations and notes of caution that must be observed. However, once you become aware of these limitations, the available material promises much by way of return.

Before delving into the use of the *Files*, we should understand their plan of organization. Basically, the *HRAF* system is a means of cataloging material by culture and subject matter. To accomplish this purpose, two "outlines," the *Outline of World Cultures* (*OWC*) (Murdock, 1972) and the *Outline of Cultural Materials* (*OCM*) (Murdock et al., 1971), serve as frameworks.

The Outline of World Cultures and the Human Relations Area Files

The *Human Relations Area Files* are organized in conjunction with a scheme for cataloging the known cultures of the world developed through several revisions by George P. Murdock. This scheme is the *Outline of World Cultures*. The *OWC* scheme has the dual virtue of being simple to understand and highly flexible for further expansion. Its purpose is to allow researchers to consistently catalog societies according to a system of numbers and letters. There are nine major breakdowns, each signified by a letter.

W — World
A — Asia, not including Indonesia, the Middle East, and Asiatic Russia.
E — Europe, exclusive of the portion ruled directly by the Soviet Union.
F — Africa, excluding northern and northeastern portions that belong culturally to the Middle East.
M — Middle East, made up of southwestern Asia and northern and northeastern Africa.
N — North America, including the northen portion of Central America.
O — Oceania, made up of Australia, Indonesia, the Philippines, and the islands of the Pacific.
R — Russia, including the portions of Europe and Asia ruled directly by the Soviet Union.
S — South America, including the West Indies and the southern portion of Central America.

Within each of these major regional breakdowns there are subcategories for cultures within that region. Each category and subcategory is assigned a letter and number. An excerpt from the *OWC* is reproduced in Figure 7.9.

The *OWC* is designed to be an exhaustive cataloging scheme. The *HRAF* system includes information on only a portion of this total. Cultural material in the *HRAF* available as of January 1, 1975 is listed in Figure 7.10. It is from material on these cultures upon which your study will be based when using the *Files*. Efforts have been made,

FIGURE 7.9
Excerpt From *Outline of World Cultures*

Africa

F1.　*Africa.* General data on Africa south of the Sahara (or on the continent as a whole), on its geography, natural resources, and demography, and on the history of European exploration, economic penetration, including the slave trade, and colonial expansion. For general data on northern or Islamic Africa see M1.

F2.　*Black Africa.* General data on the indigenous peoples, languages, and cultures of Africa south of the Sahara from the beginning of recorded or oral history, including ethnological and archeological generalizations, linguistic classifications, human biology, ethnic and culture history, and changes related to Arab, European, or other contacts. For general data on Blacks of African descent in the New World see N5.

F3.　*Prehistoric Africa.* General data on Africa south of the Sahara, its peoples and cultures, from the earliest evidences of man to the beginning of recorded or oral history. For general data on the prehistoric periods in North Africa see M6-M8.

F4.　Deleted.

West Africa

FA1.　*French-speaking West Africa.* General data on the history, geography, demography, non-indigenous inhabitants, economy, and politics of French-speaking West Africa (or of West Africa as a whole), either exclusive or inclusive of its Islamic northern section, and specific data on the government of the former Federation of French West Africa. For general data on the history of the Sahara and Muslim Sudan see MS2. For data on the specific countries of Dahomey, Guinea, Ivory Coast, Togo, and Upper Volta see FA38-FA57. For data on the specific countries of Mali, Mauritania, Niger, and Senegal see MS34-MS37.

FA2.　*West Africa Peoples.* General data on the indigenous peoples and cultures of West Africa, either exclusive or inclusive of its Islamic northern section, from the beginning of recorded or oral history, including their ethnic and culture history, and changes related to North African, European, or other contacts, and general and specific data on the history, polity, and economy of the "medieval" West African empires of Ghana, Mali, and Gao or Songhay. For specific data on the dominant ethnic group of each of these empires respectively see MS21 Soninke, FA27 Malinke, and MS20 Songhai. For general data on the peoples of the Sahara and the Muslim Sudan see MS1.

FIGURE 7.9 *(continued)*

FA3. *Prehistoric West Africa.* General data on the prehistoric peoples and cultures of West Africa, either exclusive or inclusive of the northern Sudan. For general data on the prehistoric Sahara and northern Sudan see MS3.

FA4. *Guinea Coast Peoples.* General data on the indigenous peoples and cultures of the West African coastal zone from Cameroon to Gambia.

FA5. *Anyi-Baule.* Specific data on the Abure (Akapless, Assini, Issinese), Afema, Ahanta, Anno (with the Gan), Anyi (Ndenie), Attie (Kuroba), Baule, Betie, Menyibo (Vyetre), Safwi, and Sanwi tribes of the Ivory Coast. For data on the related Twi see FE12.

FA6. *Atakpame.* Specific data on the Atakpame or Ana tribe of Togo, including the related Tsha of Dahomey. For data on the Yoruba peoples in general see FF62.

FA7. *Baga.* Specific data on the Baga tribe of Guinea.

FA8. *Bambara.* Specific data on the Bambara or Banmana tribe of Mali, including the kindred Kagoro.

FA9. *Bargu.* Specific data on the Bargu (Bariba) nation of northern Dahomey, plus the related Besorube, Dompago, Kilinga, Namba, Pilapila, Somba, and Tamberma.

FA10. *Basari.* Specific data on the Basari tribe of Togo, including the related Chamba or Akasele.

FA11. *Bobo.* Specific data on the Bobo people of Mali and Upper Volta, comprised of the Bua (Black Bobo, Bobofing, Boua), Kian (Bobo-zbe, Tian, White Bobo), Nienige (Nieniegue), and Tara (Bobo-oule, Red Bobo).

FA12. *Busansi.* Specific data on the Busansi (Busanse) tribe of Upper Volta, including the Bisa.

FA13. *Chakossi.* Specific data on the Chakossi tribe of Togo. For data on the kindred Twi see FE12.

FA14. *Diola.* Specific data on the Diola (Jola) peoples of the Casamance region of Senegal, comprised of a number of subgroups including the Bayot, Bliss-Karone, Diamat, Dyiwat, Felup, Fogny, and Her.

FA15. *Diula Tribes.* Specific data on a group of dispersed mercantile tribes of presumable Soninke origin scattered throughout West Africa and variously known as Dafi, Diula, Huela, Ligbi, Marka, Mau, Sia, and Yarse. For data on the Vai see FD9.

FA16. *Dogon.* Specific data on the Dogon (Dogom, Habe, Kado, Tombo) nation of Mali, including the related Deforo.

FA17. *Ewe.* Specific data on the Ewe nation of Togo, including the Anglo, Glidyi, Ho, and other component tribes.

FIGURE 7.10
Human Relations Area Files Available as of January 1, 1975

OWC Code	Name of Society	Number of Sources	Number of Pages
AU1	Afghanistan (M)	74	6,234
AV1	Kashmir (M)	6	2,006
AV3	Dard	4	711
AV4	Kashmiri (M)	5	893
AV7	Burusho (M)	8	2,157
AW1	India (M)	41	14,980
AW2	Bihar	1	619
AW5	Coorg	4	802
AW6	East Panjab (M)	3	1,106
AW7	Gujarati (M)	4	627
AW11	Kerala (M)	13	989
AW17	Telugu	1	265
AW19	Uttar Pradesh	4	255
AW25‡	Bhil (M)	8	1,175
AW32	Gond (M)	4	1,552
AW37	Kol (M)	1	347
AW42*	Santal (M)	5	1,318
AW60	Toda (M)	13	1,553
AX4*‡	Sinhalese	7	1,004
AX5	Vedda (M)	5	776
AZ2*	Andamans (M)	11	1,229
AA1*‡	Korea (M)	58	6,148
AB6‡	Ainu	11	1,571
AC7‡	Okinawa	3	817
AD1	<u>Formosa</u>	40	1,836
AD4	<u>Formosan Aborigines</u>	Subfile	
AD5*	Taiwan Hokkien	4	1,387
AE3	Sino-Tibetan Border	7	529
AE4	Lolo	5	564
AE5	Miao (M)	12	1,182
AE9	Monguor (M)	5	1,221
AF1	China (M)	80	19,442
AF12	North China (M)	8	2,595
AF13‡	Northwest China	3	1,299
AF14	Central China (M)	2	1,130
AF15	East China (M)	3	1,384
AF16	Southwest China (M)	7	2,800
AF17	South China (M)	8	1,846
AG1‡	Manchuria (M)	7	1,820
AH1	Mongolia (M)	9	1,358
AH6‡	Inner Mongolia (M)	13	1,840
AH7‡	Outer Mongolia (M)	4	2,821
AI1	Sinkiang (M)	3	860
AJ1‡	Tibet (M)	26	6,831
AI4	West Tibetans (M)	22	1,905

* HRAF Probability Sample Files.
† New file in process.
‡ New additions in process to existing files.
Underlining indicates a file made up substantially of old-form file slips.
Files also included in HRAF-Microfiles Collection are indicated by the letter M in parentheses.

FIGURE 7.10 (*continued*)

OWC Code	*Name of Society*	*Number of Sources*	*Number of Pages*
AK5	Lepcha (M)	11	1,038
AL1	Southeast Asia (M)	22	3,851
AM1	Indochina (M)	153	19,633
AM4	Cambodia (M)	Subfile	
AM8	Laos (M)	Subfile	
AM11	Vietnam (M)	Subfile	
AN1	Malaya (M)	193	10,142
AN5	Malays (M)	Subfile	
AN7	Semang (M)	3	786
AO1	Thailand (M)	40	6,114
AO7*	Central Thai	7	1,199
AP1	Burma (M)	31	4,680
AP4	Burmese (M)	Subfile	
AP6	Kachin	Subfile	
AP7	Karen	Subfile	
AR5*	Garo	9	1,169
AR7*‡	Khasi (M)	21	998

Europe

E1	Europe	9	1,599
E16	Slavic Peoples	7	903
EA1	Poland (M)	31	3,940
EB1	Czechoslovakia (M)	75	6,491
EC1	Hungary	16	1,401
ED1	Rumania	9	1,245
EE1	Bulgaria	7	998
EF1	Yugoslavia (M)	13	2,765
EF6*	Serbs (M)	19	3,450
EG1	Albania (M)	9	1,975
EH1	Greece (M)	10	1,153
EH14	Sarakatsani	2	441
EI9‡	Imperial Romans	3	740
EK1	Austria	6	1,334
EO1	Finalnd	1	402
EP4*‡	Lapps (M)	17	3,915
ER6	Rural Irish (M)	17	1,673
ES10*†	Highland Scots	5	1,045
EZ6	Malta (M)	9	1,069

Africa

F1	Africa	1	2,339
FA8	Bambara (M)	4	1,127
FA16*	Dogon (M)	7	1,132
FA28	Mossi (M)	12	942
FC7	Mende (M)	8	605
FE11	Tallensi (M)	10	954
FE12*‡	Twi (M)	27	3,523
FF38	Katab (M)	4	252
FF52	Nupe (M)	9	858
FF57*	Tiv (M)	30	2,891
FF62	Yoruba (M)	45	1,637
FH9	Fang (M)	8	1,117
FJ22	Nuer (M)	16	1,541

FIGURE 7.10 (*continued*)

OWC Code	Name of Society	Number of Sources	Number of Pages
FJ23	Shilluk (M)	29	1,073
FK7*	Ganda (M)	16	2,261
FL6	Dorobo	14	354
FL10‡	Kikuyu (M)	9	1,950
FL11	Luo (M)	21	463
FL12*	Masai (M)	19	2,095
FN4	Chagga (M)	6	1,986
FN17	Ngonde (M)	14	1,474
FO4*‡	Pygmies	5	1,350
FO7*	Azande (M)	68	3,264
FO32	Mongo (M)	9	773
FO42	Rundi (M)	10	1,314
FP13	Mbundu (M)	6	847
FQ5*	Bemba (M)	10	830
FQ6	Ila (M)	6	998
FQ9*	Lozi	10	1,635
FR5	Ngoni (M)	14	1,123
FT6	Thonga (M)	3	1,231
FT7	Yao (M)	11	555
FX10	Bushmen (M)	16	1,259
FX13	Hottentot (M)	14	1,359
FX14	Lovedu (M)	5	455
FY8	Tanala (M)	1	334
M1	Middle East (M)	72	13,908
MA1	Iran (M)	72	7,000
MA11*‡	Kurd (M)	11	1,018
MB1	Turkey (M)	14	1,493
MD1	Syria	11	1,395
MD4	Rwala (M)	2	1,042
ME1	Lebanon	11	657
MG1	Jordan (M)	22	3,358
MH1	Iraq	8	1,825
MI1	Kuwait	7	877
MJ1	Saudi Arabia (M)	30	3,371
MJ4	Bedouin (M)	Subfile	
MK2	Maritime Arabs	4	103
MK4	Trucial Oman	3	256
ML1	Yemen	14	446
MM1	Aden	8	683
MM2	Hadhramaut (M)	23	765
MO4*	Somali (M)	31	2,194
MP5*‡	Amhara (M)	13	1,851
MR13	Fellahin (M)	9	1,262
MR14	Siwans (M)	7	518
MS12*‡	Hausa (M)	18	2,118
MS14*	Kanuri	4	902
MS25	Tuareg (M)	8	1,225
MS30*‡	Wolof (M)	46	2,026
MS37	Senegal (M)	23	849
MT9*†	Libyan Bedouin	9	938
MW11*‡	Shluh	4	1,321
MX3	Rif	4	379
MZ2	Bahrain (M)	8	428

FIGURE 7.10 (*continued*)

OWC Code	Name of Society	Number of Sources	Number of Pages
	North America		
NA6‡	Aleut (M)	70	2,253
NA12*‡	Tlingit (M)	19	1,778
ND8	Copper Eskimo (M)	29	2,277
ND12	Nahane (M)	7	758
NE6	Bellacoola (M)	8	1,561
NE11	Nootka (M)	19	1,547
NF6*†	Blackfoot	4	1,047
NG6*	Ojibwa (M)	26	4,354
NH6	Montagnais	18	1,013
NJ5	Micmac (M)	8	1,016
NL7	Historical Massachusetts	1	533
NM7	Delaware (M)	15	1,733
NM9*	Iroquois (M)	40	2,704
NN11	Creek (M)	3	757
NO6	Comanche	10	745
NP12	Winnebago (M)	10	915
NQ10	Crow (M)	24	1,479
NQ12	Dhegiha (M)	33	1,968
NQ13	Gros Ventre (M)	8	1,085
NQ17	Mandan (M)	10	1,297
NQ18*	Pawnee (M)	14	1,703
NR4	Plateau Indians	4	303
NR10*‡	Klamath	9	1,617
NR13	Northern Paiute	15	910
NR19	Southeast Salish	7	945
NS18	Pomo (M)	22	1,220
NS22	Tubatulabal	4	180
NS29	Yokuts (M)	16	975
NS31	Yurok (M)	13	1,101
NT8	Eastern Apache (M)	4	589
NT9*†	Hopi	6	1,026
NT13	Navaho (M)	146	11,626
NT14	Plateau Yumans (M)	14	927
NT15	River Yumans	6	561
NT18	Tewa (M)	15	1,274
NT20	Washo	9	521
NT23	Zuni (M)	16	2,842
NU7‡	Aztec (M)	18	1,942
NU28	Papago (M)	19	2,183
NU31	Seri	12	616
NU33*	Tarahumara (M)	13	2,055
NU34	Tarasco (M)	11	655
NU37	Tepoztlan (M)	5	859
NV9*‡	Tzeltal	9	1,109
NV10	Yucatec Maya (M)	11	1,870
	Oceania		
OA1	Philippines (M)	58	7,451
OA5	Apayao (M)	Subfile	
OA14	Central Bisayan (M)	Subfile	
OA19*‡	Ifugao (M)	29	2,983
OB1	Indonesia (M)	18	4,367
OC6*‡	Iban (M)	18	1,655

FIGURE 7.10 (continued)

OWC Code	Name of Society	Number of Sources	Number of Pages
OF5	Alor (M)	3	726
OF7	Bali (M)	9	1,297
OF9	Flores	Subfile	
OG6	Makassar (M)	1	379
OG11*	Toradja	5	2,391
OH4	Ambon	Subfile	
OI8*	Aranda (M)	40	3,259
OI17	Murngin (M)	15	1,731
OI19	Tasmanians (M)	1	293
OI20	Tiwi (M)	13	563
OJ13‡	Kwoma	2	501
OJ23	Orokaiva (M)	4	652
OJ27‡	Wogeo (M)	15	678
OJ29*	Kapauku (M)	5	869
OL6*	Trobriands (M)	24	2,991
OM6	Manus (M)	7	1,639
OM10	New Ireland (M)	5	457
ON6	Buka (M)	5	721
ON13	Santa Cruz	6	420
OO12	Malekula (M)	3	883
OQ6*	Lau (M)	10	997
OR11	Marshalls (M)	21	2,199
OR19*‡	Truk (M)	25	2,208
OR21	Woleai (M)	41	2,665
OR22‡	Yap (M)	21	1,951
OT11*‡	Tikopia (M)	26	2,727
OU8	Samoa (M)	19	3,008
OX6	Marquesas (M)	13	1,163
OY2	Easter Islanders (M)	15	960
OZ4	Maori (M)	10	3,257
OZ11	Pukapuka (M)	12	860
	Russia		
R1	Soviet Union	81	11,987
RB1	Baltic Countries	3	211
RB5	Lithuanians	11	990
RC1	Belorussia	5	191
RD1	Ukraine (M)	20	2,219
RF1	Great Russia	4	386
RG4	Estonians	5	615
RH1	Caucasia	4	1,500
RI1	Georgia	5	759
RI3	Abkhaz	4	207
RL1	Turkestan	4	707
RL4	Turkic Peoples	1	235
RQ2‡	Kazak	7	969
RR1	Siberia	4	609
RU4‡	Samoyed	35	2,073
RV2*	Yakut	32	933
RX2	Gilyak (M)	13	2,281
RY2*‡	Chukchee (M)	22	2,240
RY3	Kamchadal	11	840
RY4	Koryak	5	810

FIGURE 7.10 (*concluded*)

OWC Code	Name of Society	Number of Sources	Number of Pages
	South America		
SA15	Mosquito (M)	3	263
SA19	Talamanca (M)	6	479
SB5*	Cuna (M)	34	3,932
SC7*	Cagaba (M)	7	1,134
SC13	Goajiro (M)	10	724
SC15	Paez	8	700
SD6	Cayapa (M)	4	747
SD9	Jivaro (M)	34	1,426
SE13	Inca (M)	13	2,646
SF5*	Aymara (M)	14	1,772
SF10	Chiriguano (M)	7	1,570
SF21	Siriono	5	692
SF24	Uru (M)	9	434
SG4	Araucanians (M)	12	1,397
SH4*‡	Ona	4	2,198
SH5	Tehuelche (M)	6	611
SH6	Yahgan (M)	3	1,700
SI4	Abipon (M)	2	452
SI7*	Mataco (M)	8	595
SK6	Choroti (M)	2	523
SK7	Guana	6	407
SM3	Caingang (M)	4	308
SM4*‡	Guarani	6	484
SO8	Timbira	2	379
SO9	Tupinamba (M)	26	1,637
SO11	Bahia Brazilians	5	1,333
SP7	Bacairi (M)	6	1,085
SP8*‡	Bororo	9	1,041
SP9	Caraja (M)	9	687
SP17	Nambicuara (M)	8	436
SP22	Tapirape (M)	13	369
SP23	Trumai	1	120
SQ13	Mundurucu (M)	14	649
SQ18*‡	Yanoama	15	1,284
SQ19*‡	Tucano	7	1,320
SQ20	Tucuna	5	259
SR8	Bush Negroes (M)	6	1,411
SR9	Carib (M)	2	532
SS16	Pemon	4	602
SS18	Warao	6	722
SS19	Yaruro	7	284
ST13	Callinago (M)	13	524
SU1	Puerto Rico (M)	3	1,750
SV3	Haiti (M)	3	1,052
SY1	Jamaica	2	459

Total number of Major Files available (including in process)	294
Total number of text pages	500,107
Total number of sources in Files	4,290
Total number of File slips in each set (estimate)	3,010,000

when selecting cultures for inclusion in the *Files*, to maximize cultural diversity and geographical dispersal and to include societies that have been adequately reported on. See Figure 7.11.

As described in Lagace (1974), in an excellent guide to the use of these files, "The ideal source from the standpoint of the *Files* consists of a detailed description of a culture, or of a particular community or region within that culture, written on the basis of prolonged residence among the people studied by a professional social scientist having a good knowledge of the language of these people" (p. 28).

Even with these efforts to maximize the scope and quality of coverage, there are limitations. We will examine some ways to maximize the quality of your specific study shortly. Before this, however, you should keep in mind that the *Files* are not exhaustive, either of the total known cultures or the material available on a given culture. Unfortunately, there are reasons to believe that inclusion or exclusion is not random. There are biases introduced via the difference in probability that certain societies will be selected for study. Naroll (1967, 1968) has suggested that we are more likely to have information on cultures that are warlike, colorful, resistant to colonial intrusions, large, and near transcontinental routes of communication than information from cultures with the opposite traits. Such selection bias may be influencing our conclusions in cross-cultural research. We will have more to say of this when we take up sampling in Chapter 9.

Within their limitations, however, the *Files* can be quite useful. They may be approached in a number of ways. You may be interested in a comprehensive examination of a single culture. In this case you begin with your chosen culture, see if it is included in the *Files*, and begin exploring available materials. You may be interested in more restricted substantive questions and want to pursue, say, divorce patterns, or family structures, or political practices in a sample of societies. In the discussion that follows we will assume this latter stance and explore the strategies for translating your ideas into the conceptual scheme used in organizing the *Files*.

Translation of Your Ideas into *HRAF* Terms

Whereas the cultures contained in the *HRAF* system are classified according to the *Outline of World Cultures*, the content of culture— such as child-rearing practices, death rituals, political customs, family structure, types of physical artifacts, types of economic institutions, and so on—are categorized according to the *Outline of Cultural Materials* (Murdock et al., 1971). Your task thus becomes one of translating your chosen topic into terms used in this outline.

FIGURE 7.11
Human Relations Area Files Map

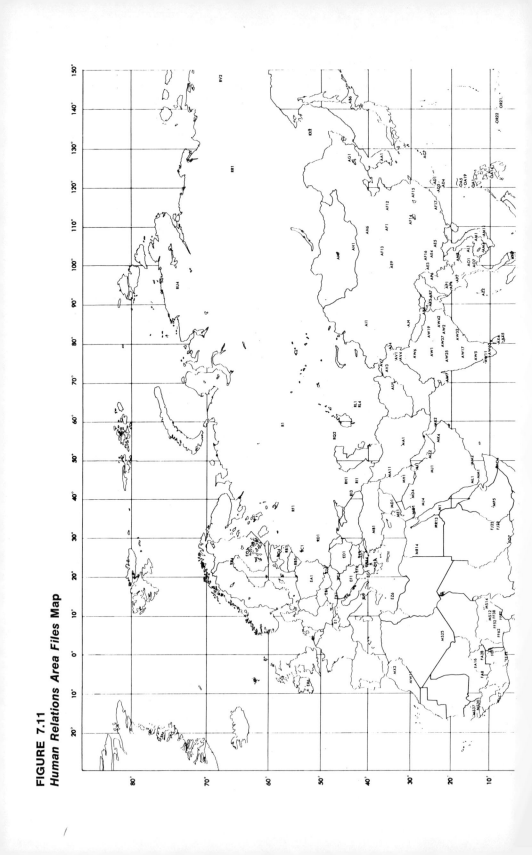

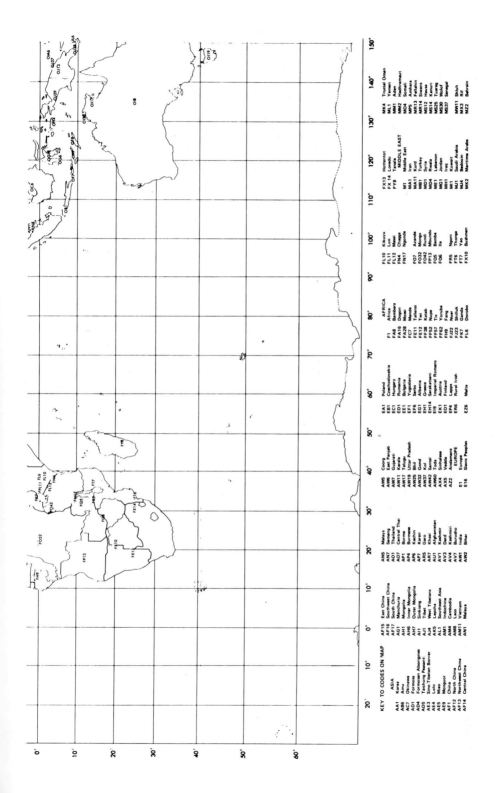

FIGURE 7.11 *(concluded)*

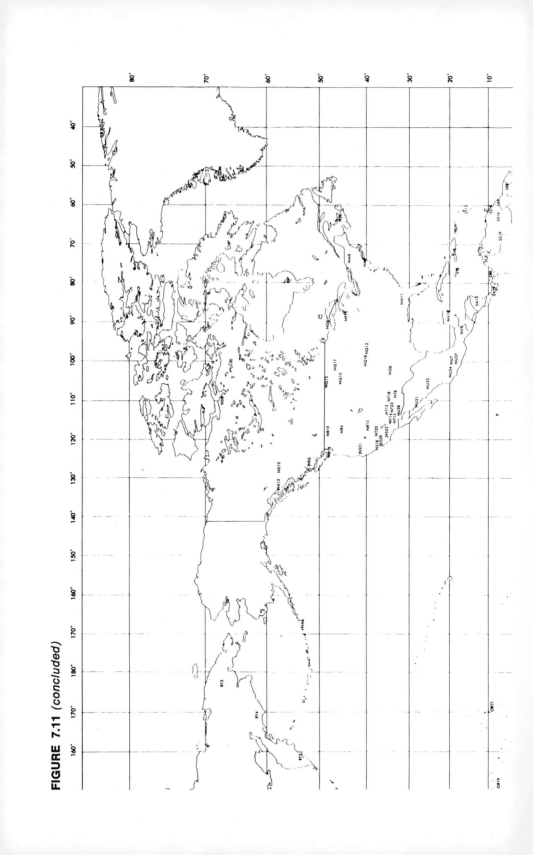

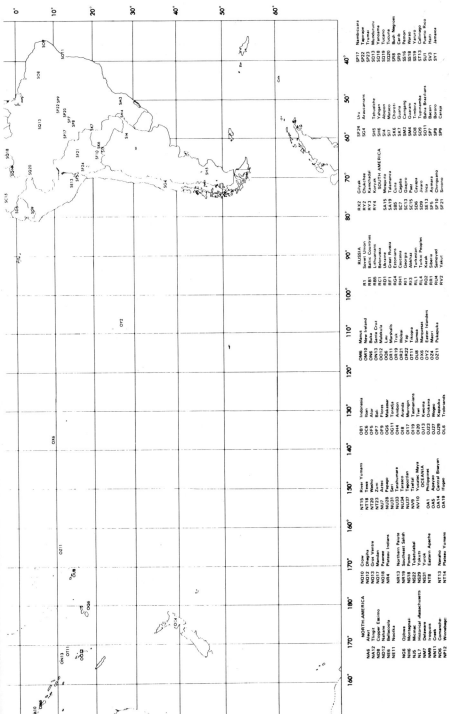

Source: Published by Human Relations Areas Files, Inc., with permission of American Geographical Society, New Haven, 170.

FIGURE 7.12
Portion of Table of Contents from *OCM*

63 TERRITORIAL
    ORGANIZATION
    631 Territorial Hierarchy
    632 Towns
    633 Cities
    634 Districts
    635 Provinces
    636 Dependencies

64 STATE
    641 Citizenship
    642 Constitution
    643 Chief Executive
    644 Executive Household
    645 Cabinet
    646 Parliament
    647 Administrative Agencies
    648 International Relations

65 GOVERNMENT
    ACTIVITIES
    651 Taxation and Public
        Income
    652 Public Finance
    653 Public Works
    654 Research and
        Development
    655 Government Enterprises
    656 Government Regulation
    657 Public Welfare
    658 Public Education
    659 Miscellaneous
        Government Activities

66 POLITICAL BEHAVIOR
    661 Exploitation
    662 Political Intrigue
    663 Public Service
    664 Pressure Politics
    665 Political Parties
    666 Elections
    667 Political Machines
    668 Political Movements
    669 Revolution

67 LAW
    671 Legal Norms
    672 Liability
    673 Wrongs
    674 Crime
    675 Contracts
    676 Agency

68 OFFENCES AND
    SANCTIONS
    681 Sanctions
    682 Offenses against Life
    683 Offenses against the
        Person
    684 Sex and Marital Offenses
    685 Property Offenses
    686 Nonfulfillment of
        Obligations
    687 Offenses against the State
    688 Religious Offenses
    689 Social Offenses

69 JUSTICE
    691 Litigation
    692 Judicial Authority
    693 Legal and Judicial
        Personnel
    694 Initiation of Judicial
        Proceedings
    695 Trial Procedure
    696 Execution of Justice
    697 Prisons and Jails
    698 Special Courts

70 ARMED FORCES
    701 Military Organization
    702 Recruitment and
        Training
    703 Discipline and Morale
    704 Ground Combat Forces
    705 Supply and Commissariat
    706 Navy
    707 Air Force
    708 Auxiliary Corps

FIGURE 7.12 (*continued*)

71 MILITARY TECHNOLOGY
    711 Military Engineering
    712 Military Installations
    713 Ordnance
    714 Uniform and
        Accouterment
    715 Military Vehicles
    716 Naval Vessels
    717 Military Aircraft
    718 Special Military
        Equipment
    719 Munitions Industries

72 WAR
    721 Instigation of War
    722 Wartime Adjustments
    723 Strategy
    724 Logistics
    725 Tactics
    726 Warfare
    727 Aftermath of Combat
    728 Peacemaking
    729 War Veterans

73 SOCIAL PROBLEMS
    731 Disasters
    732 Defectives
    733 Alcoholism and Drug
        Addiction
    734 Invalidism
    735 Poverty
    736 Dependency
    737 Old Age Dependency
    738 Delinquency

74 HEALTH AND WELFARE
    741 Philanthropic
        Foundations
    742 Medical Research
    743 Hospitals and Clinics
    744 Public Health and
        Sanitation
    745 Social Insurance
    746 Public Assistance
    747 Private Welfare Agencies
    748 Social Work

75 SICKNESS
    751 Preventive Medicine
    752 Bodily Injuries
    753 Theory of Disease
    754 Sorcery
    755 Magical and Mental
        Therapy
    756 Psychotherapists
    757 Medical Therapy
    758 Medical Care
    759 Medical Personnel

76 DEATH
    761 Life and Death
    762 Suicide
    763 Dying
    764 Funeral
    765 Mourning
    766 Deviant Mortuary
        Practices
    767 Mortuary Specialists
    768 Social Readjustments to
        Death
    769 Cult of the Dead

77 RELIGIOUS BELIEFS
    771 General Character of
        Religion
    772 Cosmology
    773 Mythology
    774 Animism
    775 Eschatology
    776 Spirits and Gods
    777 Luck and Chance
    778 Sacred Objects and
        Places
    779 Theological Systems

78 RELIGIOUS PRACTICES
    781 Religious Experience
    782 Propitiation
    783 Purification and
        Expiration
    784 Avoidance and Taboo
    785 Asceticism

FIGURE 7.12 (*concluded*)

786 Orgies
787 Revelation and Divination
788 Ritual
789 Magic

79 ECCLESIASTICAL ORGANIZATION
791 Magicians and Diviners
792 Holy Men
793 Priesthood
794 Congregations
795 Sects
796 Organized Ceremonial
797 Missions
798 Religious Intolerance

80 NUMBERS AND MEASURES
801 Numerology
802 Numeration
803 Mathematics
804 Weights and Measures
805 Ordering of Time

81 EXACT KNOWLEDGE
811 Logic
812 Philosophy
813 Scientific Method

814 Humanistic Studies
815 Pure Science
816 Applied Science

82 IDEAS ABOUT NATURE AND MAN
821 Ethnometerology
822 Ethnophysics
823 Ethnogeography
824 Ethnobotany
825 Ethnozoology
826 Ethnoanatomy
827 Ethnophysiology
828 Ethnopsychology
829 Ethnosociology

83 SEX
831 Sexuality
832 Sexual Stimulation
833 Sexual Intercourse
834 General Sex Restrictions
835 Kinship Regulation of Sex
836 Premarital Sex Relations
837 Extramarital Sex Relations
838 Homosexuality
839 Miscellaneous Sex Behavior

The organization of the *OCM* has emerged in a trial-and-error fashion as social scientists, travelers, missionaries, and government officials, among others, have called for and produced various reports on the cultures of the world. Portions of the Table of Contents for the *OCM* are reproduced in Figure 7.12. As is readily apparent the scheme is based on a numbering system, each topic receiving a unique number. It should also be apparent that there is overlap between categories. To deal with this overlap, additional cross-references have been devised. Examples of the descriptions of categories and cross-references to other relevant topics taken from the body of the *OCM* are given in Figure 7.13. In this instance they deal with cross references and topics under the general heading of "Religious Beliefs." What you have, then, in the body

FIGURE 7.13
Categories and Cross-References from *OCM*

77 RELIGIOUS BELIEFS

77   RELIGIOUS BELIEFS—general statements about several types of religious beliefs and ideologies. The behavioral and organizational aspects of religion are treated, respectively, under 78 and 79.

771   GENERAL CHARACTER OF RELIGION—conception of what constitutes religion; differentiation of the sacred and the profane; distinctions drawn between religion and superstition; relation of religion to the unknown and the unpredictable; relative prominence of magical and anthropomorphic elements; evidence of the expression of projective mechanisms in religious beliefs; primary orientation of the religious system (e.g., ancestor worship, nature worship, totemism, ritualism, mysticism, redemptive religion); social and individual role of religion (e.g., services and disservices); incidence of faith, indifference, and skepticism; existence of non-supernatural ideologies supported with a faith akin to that in religion (e.g., ethical systems, political philosophies); etc. See also:

Personality.	15	Magic.	789
Integration of religion with		Religious sects.	795
other aspects of culture	182	Philosophy.	812
Ethical ideals	577	Ideas about the social role	
Ancestor worship	769	of religion	829
Extended discussions of		Inculcation of religious	
theological systems	779	beliefs	869

772   COSMOLOGY—conception of the universe; cosmological systems (e.g., heavens and hells); universal categories (e.g., dualism of nature); etc. See also:

Realm of the dead	775	Ideas about cosmic	
Conception of a moral order		phenomena	821
of the universe.	812		

773   MYTHOLOGY—cosmogony (e.g., theories and accounts of the creation of the world and of man); mythical epochs (e.g., golden age, age of the gods, age of animals); cataclysms (e.g., mythical floods and conflagrations); culture myths (e.g., accounts of a culture hero, mythical explanations of culture traits); myths about the origin of evil and death; nature myths; totemic myths; theogonic myths; ancestor myths; etc. For texts of myths see 539. See also:

Historical traditions. 173

FIGURE 7.13 (*continued*)

774 ANIMISM—conception of the soul; number of souls; location in the body; characteristics (e.g., shape, visibility, separability); relation of the soul to the body, to the name, to the breath, to dreams, to shadows and reflections, and to life and death; notions of the temporary departure of the soul from the body; attribution of souls to animals and inanimate objects; etc. See also:

Personality. 15	Spirit possession and dream	
Names 551	interpretation 787	
Conception of conscience . . . 577	Interpretation of shadows	
Theories of disease and	and reflections. 822	
death 753, 761	Ethnozoology 825	
Concepts of soul-stuff	Ideas about breathing. 827	
and animated fetishes. 778	Ideas about abnormal	
	mental states. 828	

775 ESCHATOLOGY—conception of the survival of the soul; career of the soul after death (e.g., mode of departure from the body, temporary sojourn near place of death, indefinite sojourn as a disembodied soul or ghost, journey to a realm of the dead); notions about ghosts, specters, apparitions, and phantoms (e.g., shape, substance, propensities); behavior of departed souls or ghosts (e.g., haunting of houses and cemeteries, visitations); spiritualistic beliefs; conception of a realm of the dead (e.g., place, mode of life, rewards and punishment); duration of afterlife; belief in immortality; ideas of transmigration and reincarnation; conception of the survival of the body (e.g., resurrection); etc. See also:

Belief in witches, vampires,	Communication with spirits . . 787
and werewolves 754	Notion of death and rebirth in
Cult of the dead. 769	initiation ceremonies 881

776 SPIRITS AND GODS—conception of supernatural beings of a higher order than disembodied souls; indications of their genetic relationship to ghosts; prevalent types of supernatural beings (e.g., guardian and familiar spirits, tutelary divinities, tribal gods, nature spirits and gods, angels, animal and totemic divinities, fairies and spirtes, demons, mythical monsters, deified heroes and saints, divine tricksters, occupational or functional deities, creator gods, rulers of the spirit world, high god or supreme being); attributes of individual deities and of categories of divine beings (e.g., name, sex, form, character, powers, functions, symbols); hierarchial arrangement (e.g., polytheistic pantheon, dualism, henotheism, monotheism); etc. See also:

Totemic beliefs associated	Hero worship 769
with kin groups 61	
Religious practices 78	

FIGURE 7.13 (*concluded*)

777 LUCK AND CHANGE—concept of good and back luck; ideas about chance and probability; things associated with good or bad luck (e.g., lucky objects, luck-bringing formulas, lucky and unlucky numbers, propitious and unlucky days); techniques for controlling luck (e.g., wearing of luck amulets, reciting of lucky formulas); conception of fate; etc. See also:

Insurance. 456	Divination 787
Gambling. 525	Pattern numbers. 801
Protective amulets 751	Calendar 805
Theory of accidental injuries . 752	Scientific theory of chance . . 813

778 SACRED OBJECTS AND PLACES—conception of sanctity (e.g., possession by an indwelling or frequenting spirit, infusion with impersonal supernatural power); idols and fetishes; extraordinary objects (e.g., bezoar stones, albino animals, mandrake roots); sacred places (e.g., shrines, altars); places of asylum and sanctuary; notions of impersonal supernatural power (e.g., mana, soul-stuff); animatism; beliefs and practices of consecration and desecration; etc. See also:

Churches and temples 346	Luck amulets 777
Heirlooms 523	Notions of uncleanness. 783
Asylum. 696	Taboos 784
Protective amulets 751	Phallic rites 786
Relics. 765	Conception of magic force. . . 789
Conception of the sacred and	Holy men 792
the profane 771	

779 THEOLOGICAL SYSTEMS—elaborated systems of religious beliefs (e.g., totemism, pantheism); state religions; revealed religions (e.g., Buddhism, Christianity, Mohammedanism); sacred books; content of complex systems of dogma and theology; asociation of theological systems with ethics and philosophy; etc. See also:

Totemic kin groups. 61	Statements on the general
Ethical ideals 577	character of religion 771
Ancestor worship 769	Sects 795
	Theologians 812

of the *OCM*, is a series of interlocking, numerically coded references to various substantive topics.

When you examine the Table of Contents of the *OCM*, something of a flow is detectable. The scheme seems to move from overall characterization of available material, to issues of simple survival and day-to-day activities, to more complex issues of societal organization, and, finally, to afterlife and problems of societal perpetuation. This is only a rough flow, however. In the Preface to the 1971 edition (xxi, xxii), the categories are broken down into seven theoretically relevant types and you may want to refer to this discussion. However, in large measure the *OCM* has been devised to allow categorization of a wide range of material gathered from reports from persons with widely divergent backgrounds. Thus, it is not theoretically tight. Rather, it has emerged in a trial-and-error fashion aimed at devising a scheme for classifying available materials.

If your chosen topic is not listed in the Table of Contents, it may be obtainable in the Index. It is from these two sources, the Table of Contents and the Index, that you proceed in search of information relevant to your research. You may be saying at this point, "Well, so far all I have is a listing of numbered topics. What do I do with them? Where do I go to find the appropriate material? What do I do with the sources once they are located? How do I know what quality of information I am dealing with? How do I put specific bits of information, say, about child-rearing or suicide or political intrigue, into context?" Answers to these questions and perhaps others are best pursued by way of example.

An Example: Cross-Cultural Material on Political Corruption

Given widely publicized events in the political system of the United States, you may want to investigate the cross-cultural appearance and correlates of other "Watergates." Clearly, Watergate is too specific a topic for a general categorizing scheme such as the *OCM*. Political corruption is a more likely possibility. In the Table of Contents you will find categories of Political Behavior (66), including Exploitation (661); Political Intrigue (662); Pressure Politics (664); Political Machines (667); as well as others. In turning to the Index you will find no listing under Political Corruption, but you will find cross-references under Corruption, Political. The Index will refer you to categories 662 and 667, Political Intrigue and Political Machines, respectively. In turning to these categories you will find the following descriptions:

> 662 POLITICAL INTRIGUE—use of the techniques of manipulative mobility to wrest favors from the holders of power or to obtain political preferment; flattery and ingratiation; use of bribery; deals; palace intrigue; opportunism; "playing politics"; etc. See also:
>
> Manipulative mobility 557   Punishment of bribery 687
>
> 667 POLITICAL MACHINES—special organizations for the control of elections and office and the distribution of spoils; personal and party machines; rewards to members and controlled voters

(e.g., jobs, contracts, favors, police protection, petty graft); mechanisms of mobility within the machine (e.g., ward heeling, getting out the vote); relations with the underworld; extent of political corruption; attempts at reform; etc. See also:

Police. 625   City government 633

Thus, under Political Intrigue you get an additional lead through the category "Manipulative Mobility" (557), which appears as follows in the *Outline:*

557 MANIPULATIVE MOBILITY—extent to which desirable statuses and the prestige they bring can be achieved by opportunistic manipulation of social relationships (e.g., cultivation of persons in authority, political machinations, exploitation of friends and relatives, backslapping, marriages of convenience); prominence and relative effectiveness of manipulative techniques as compared with acquisition of skills and wealth; desirable statuses achievable thereby (e.g., political preferment); etc. See also:

Interpersonal relations 57   Traits of leadership 157
Political behavior 66

What you end up with, then, is a series of leads, categories that may be instructive in pursuing your chosen topic. In this case, category 662, Political Intrigue, appears to be the most promising. The others should be investigated, of course, but, for present purposes, consider only category 662. How much information is available in the *Files?* How representative is the information for various regions of the world and types of cultures? If your desire is to do a truly cross-cultural study, these are not unimportant questions. To get an initial feel for the range and depth of information contained in the *Files,* you consult the *HRAF Index.* This *Index* is a series of volumes (eight at the present time) cataloging the available material in the *Files.* It is organized first by *OCM* code, then by *OWC* codes within each of the topics, and, finally, by author and page number of the relevant works. A reproduction of the initial listings under *OCM* category 662 is reproduced in Figure 7.14. In the complete listing you will find material for the major regions as follows: Asia, 19 cultures; Europe, 5 cultures; Africa, 14 cultures; Middle East, 12 cultures; North America, 6 cultures; Oceania, 9 cultures; Russia, 5 cultures; and South America, 2 cultures. Thus, there is at least some material available from each of the major regions. However, when you compare this distribution of material with the overall distribution of the *Files* in the total *HRAF* system, you find that North America, Oceania, and South America are under-represented.

In this initial perusal of available material, you should begin to get

FIGURE 7.14
Listings under Category 662 from *HRAF Index*

662	POLITICAL INTRIGUE								
AA01	1.HULBERI	81	133	−135	169	175	179	−180	182 343
AA01	2.GRIFFIS	16	224	−225					
AA01	4.MOOSE.......	41							
AA01	6.GRAJDANZE ...	38	45	−46	58	−59			
AA01	22.OSGOOD......	134	207						
AA01	36.KENNAN......	310	312						
AA01	46.BISHOP.......	256	282	368	431	−432	446	−449	
AA01	49.DALLET	23	−25	126					
AA01	51.CARLES	290	−299						
AA01	52.SAVAGE	162							
AA01	54.ANONYMOUS...	11							
AE04	3.MA	7							
AE09	4.SCHRAM......	16	−18	24	26	66	−67		
AE09	5.SCHRAM......	40	47	56	−57				
AF01	8.LEVY........	222	−223						
AF01	12.CHIEN	128	−132	173	176	194			
AF01	21.FRIED	215	−217						
AF01	25.LEE.........	494							
AF01	29.LEVY........	14	−16	45	48	−49			
AF01	35.THOMAS......	99	−100						
AF01	40.ROSTOW......	254							
AF01	44.FEI	26	−27						
AF01	74.INSTITUTE	43	−44	177	−178				
AF12	3.CHAO........	152	−153						
AF14	1.STANFORD	537	−539						
AF16	6.LIAO	169	−170						
AH01	10.KRADER......	168							
AI01	1.LATTIMORE ...	111	219	−220					
AJ01	2.MACDONALD...	46	53						
AJ01	4.BELL........	158	160	171	−172				
AJ01	8.KAWAGUCHI ...	318	−319	381	−382	421	−424	432 −433 511 −512	
		620	627	−629	638				
AJ01	9.DAS.........	52							
AJ01	10.WADELL......	234	−235						
AJ01	16.BELL	36	50	−52	54	56	125	127 −129 140	
AJ01	20.TSYBIKOV.....	508							
AJ01	24.PETER	447							
AJ04	1.CUNNINGHA ...	266							
AJ04	2.RAMSAY......	59	64	66	81				
AJ04	13.HEBER	203	−204						
AM01	1.GOUROU......	309	−310	400	−401				
AM01	8.LANGRAND....	37							
AM01	10.ORLEANS	88	92	95	300				
AM01	22.WHITE	266	279	310	324				
AM01	23.FRANCK......	84							
AM01	24.DORGELES	179							
AM01	28.CRAWFURD....	417	422	428					
AM01	33.THOMPSON	36							
AM01	48.PASQUIER.....	163							
AM01	55.PETIT........	90	−92						
AM01	56.KRESSER	71	80						
AM01	65.LURO........	79							
AM01	69.LEWIS........	165	−166	170	175	−176			
AM01	88.MAYRON	439							
AM01	93.AUBARET.....	241	−242	270	−271				
AM01	98.JEANSELME....	4							
AM01	110.DUTREUIL	65	−67	148	157				

some feel for the scope of the task that lies ahead.[1] You also get a feel for some of the limitations. Some cultures, such as AHl (Mongolia), have only one source and one page within that source listed. Others have multiple listings with a number of pages within the listed source. What the *Index* gives you, then, is a quick glimpse at how feasible, in terms of available information, your topic is.

The next task is to select the cultures. You may decide to examine all information. You may choose only those cultures with "reasonable" amounts of available material. Geographic distribution also may be a consideration. Whatever the choice, once selected, you go to the *File* slips, which are reproductions of pages from the source material, and begin examining what the authors have to say. For example, pages 177 and 178 from "AFOl (China) 74. Institute" is reproduced in Figure 7.15. In the margins you will find the *OCM* categories next to the relevant passages.

As is apparent, more than one topic is covered on each page and thus a reproduction of the page is contained under each topic in the *Files*. When examining these slips, several questions emerge. Perhaps most readily apparent is that the material is taken out of a broader context. You have the immediate material surrounding the passages, but what of the more complete work? You should always make an effort to set the findings within the context of the more complete material. To do this you can refer to category 116 (Texts) in the *File,* wherein a complete copy of the material is contained. Also useful in terms of getting a relatively quick view of the total amount of information available in a file is category 10 (Orientation). Here, in addition to a general orientation, you will find information identifying the society or cultural group (category 101), maps (102), names of places within the culture (103), a glossary designed to define native terms frequently used (104), and a general cultural summary (105). Also useful is the information contained in category 11 (Bibliography) and its various subdivisions (111–117).

A second question that might arise has to do with the quality of the material. Who wrote it? What kind of data is being drawn on? You can, of course, decide this for yourself by referring to the complete text and summaries discussed above. However, for quick reference, the staff of the *HRAF* has provided you with its assessment in the heading of the *File* slip. For example, in Figure 7.15 you will find the following headnote: 74:Inst. of Pac. Rel. U-4,5 (1935–1937) 1938 AFl China AFl. The initial portion should be familiar from your reference work in the *HRAF* Index. "74:Inst. of Pac. Rel." is the number (74) and title of

---

[1] This Index, when used in conjunction with the *HRAF Source Bibliography,* also allows the researcher, who does not have access to take *HRAF* files, to pursue topics anyway.

FIGURE 7.15
Reproduction of File Slips

74: Inst. of Pac. Rel. U-4, 5 (1935–1937) 1938 AF1 China AF1

FOREIGN CAPITAL AND PEASANTRY IN HONAN

tobacco company, called Nanyang Bros., reaped a huge profit | **276**
during this period, and the influence of the latter on the Honan
leaf market began to increase. But the British-American Tobacco | **471**
Company did its best to negotiate with the Chinese Government
and to find a more capable and shrewd Chinese chief compradore
to succeed Jen Pei-yen, and after 1929 the company again opened
its business in Hsuchang with new vigor and plans.

In re-establishing its business in Honan, the company spent a
great deal of money in order to bribe the governmental authorities | **276**
in Hsuchang as well as the rotten gentry in the surrounding dis-
tricts. In the meantime the company secured Oo Ting-seng as | **471**
their compradore. Oo derives his prestige from the fact that he
was once the Chairman of the National Association of the Tobacco | **662**
Business, in Shanghai, and is still an important official in the
Chinese Ministry of Finance; and it seems that no one can better
handle the process of bribery in order to pave the way for the new
plans and success of the company.

Upon Oo's arrival in Honan, he induced both politicians and
powerful gentry to participate in carrying out the company's pro-
gramme. Soon reports were circulated that the land property of
Yung-an-tang, formerly managed by Jen Pei-yen, was to be sold to
a new company called the Hsuchang Tobacco Company, which
was really just as much of a facade to camouflage the company as
the Yung-an-tang. The total price given for several hundreds of
mow was only $9,000 but of course the bribery and other extra-
ordinary items in the transaction amounted to over ten times this
sum.

Oo's successful intrigue with the bureaucrats and gentry gave
satisfaction to one group but aroused the jealousy of another. This
latter group sued Oo and the former group for the illegal sale of land
to foreigners. This attempt was defeated by a skillful counterattack
from Oo who again bribed the Court and manoeuvred through
influential elements in Nanking. He also established a newspaper—
The Agricultural and Commercial Daily—in Hsuchang as a vocal
organ of the company. There was widespread public hatred of the
company because nearly half a million tobacco peasants in over
ten districts round Hsuchang had not been given a square deal
for their products, and hundreds of leaf merchants had been deprived of their business after the company had arranged with the

FIGURE 7.15 (*continued*)

74: Inst. of Pac. Rel. U-4, 5 (1935–1937) 1938 AF1 China AF1

AGRARIAN CHINA

276 | Ministry of Railways for the monopoly of leaf transportation. But the group which originally sued Oo had no intention of fighting
471 | a public cause and indeed they were out to make trouble for the company in order to reap selfish gains for themselves. Thus when a part of that group also received money from Oo, and when the judge had been bribed with $5,000 the company finally won the case.

Since 1934, the Hsuchang Tobacco Company has been the tool
276 | of the British-American Tobacco Company in securing its monopoly
471 | of leaf collection in Honan. The new compradore, Oo, succeeded in suppressing all the minor leaf collectors in Hsuchang, and there-
661 | fore the tobacco peasants round Hsuchang have no alternative but to sell their products to the foreign company. With the middle-men eliminated, the peasants have to carry their own leaves to the door of the company's building, sometimes covering a distance of 70 or 80 miles, and often in quantities of less than 100 *catties*. This in itself is difficult enough, but on arrival they have to line up in queues and sometimes wait for over a day without leaving the spot.

Immediately after entrance into the tobacco shed the peasant is given a number, after which the grading price of his leaves are recorded, but the prices accorded are almost invariably those of an inferior grade to that submitted. This in itself is unfair enough, but what is worse is the great price reduction in general since 1934. Whereas formerly one *catty* of leaves was given to the company for from 80 cents to $1.20 it is now given for from 10 to 30 cents. This refers only to the first grade and the present price for the inferior grades range anywhere from three to ten cents.

The production figures round Hsuchang show that even on the best soil only a little over 200 *catties* can be obtained from one *mow* and out of these not more than 40 or 50 *catties* on the average are first grade. Thus 6 cents per *catty* is the average price received by the peasants, or in other words the income from one *mow* is about $12. This is such a meagre income that it cannot cover all the necessary expenses of production. In many cases what the peasant receives for his leaves is not enough to cover the accumulated debt incurred on coal used for the baking process.

The increased poverty in the tobacco districts has been clearly reflected in the wholesale closing of the middle schools where the

the reference source. The next entry is the assessment of the author and quality of material. "U" is the author designation, "Unknown" in this case, taken from the following author identification scheme:

A	Archeologist, Antiquarian	O	Lawyer, Judicial Personnel
B	Folklorist	P	Psychologist
C	Technical Personnel (engineers, agricultural experts, foreign-aid advisers, etc.)	Q	Humanist (philosopher, critic, editor, writer, etc.)
D	Physician, Physical Anthropologist	R	Artisan (artist, musician, architect, dancer)
E	Ethnologist, Social Anthropologist (formerly used also for Sociologist, see Z)	S	Social Scientist (other than those designated)
F	Foreign Resident	T	Traveler (tourist, explorer)
G	Government Official (administrator, soldier, foreign diplomat)	U	Unknown
H	Historian	V	Political Scientist, Propagandist
I	Indigene	W	Organizational Documents and Reports (constitutions, law codes, government or UN reports and documents, censuses)
J	Journalist		
K	Geographer	X	Economist, Businessman
L	Linguist	Y	Educator (teacher, school administrator)
M	Missionary, Clergyman		
N	Natural or Physical Scientist	Z	Sociologist

On other occasions you might find entries such as "H" for Historian, "K" for Geographer, "L" for Linguist, "E" for Ethnologist, Social Anthropologist, and so forth.

The "4,5" designates a characterization of the quality of the material, in this case Excellent, in terms of the following scheme:

1   Poor sources
2   Fair sources
3   Good, useful sources, but not uniformly excellent
4   Excellent secondary data (e.g., compilations and/or interpretations of original data and primary documents)
5   Excellent primary data (e.g., travelers' accounts, ethnological studies, etc., as well as primary documents such as legal codes, other legal documents, autobiographies, etc.)

With this information—i.e., the information gleaned from an initial estimate of how broadly the *Files* cover your chosen topic, from an initial reading of the characterization of the various cultures you will focus on, and an initial assessment as to the quality of the data—you are ready to proceed. When looking at the information from the file slips, such as that in Figure 7.15, you are called upon once again to develop what amounts to a coding scheme for notetaking. What information is available? What categorization scheme might be useful? What problems do you encounter when reading the material? What crucial bits of information are unavailable? Does this unavailability mean that the trait is absent from the particular society, or is it simply an oversight on the part of the persons reporting?

It is when you come upon this problem of desiring information on topics not covered that you should recall that the *Files* are not exhaustive of either the known cultures of the world or of the information available on cultures incorporated into the *Files*. You should at all times be ready to look beyond the *Files*. The bibliographic information contained in categories 112 (Sources Consulted) and 113 (Additional References) will provide you with useful leads. Even then, however, you should remind yourself that additional searching may be called for. The *Files* are not designed to end your research tasks; they are designed to make them somewhat easier.

What you end up with when mining the *HRAF* system is information on a sample of societies relevant to your chosen topic. We already have mentioned that this information is incomplete in many ways. Not only are just a portion of the known cultures included in the *Files*, not only is the information on the included cultures just part of the total amount of information available in many cases, but, even when you have all available studies on cultures, many gaps may remain due to the focus of particular studies.

Does absent information indicate that the trait is absent from the particular culture, or does it mean that persons reporting on that culture simply have not included it in their scheme of analysis? The study may have had the structure of the family and how this relates to the economic system as its focus. In such a research project the researcher may or may not have gotten into the area of political intrigue or manipulative mobility.

Such omissions and ways of structuring information plague secondary analysis of available data as much as anything else. You simply become aware of the possibility, try to sensitize yourself by relating the file slips to the broader context, and then proceed with some caution. The alternative is not to do the research. Although it is incorrect to assume that any analysis is better than no analysis, it is equally the case that substantial gains can be made from less-than-ideal circumstances. To repeat a point, you should approach secondary analysis of available information, not with demands for perfection but with an eye on how ingeniously you can refashion the information to suit your own purposes.

The Quality Control Sample

Anthropologists, who have been the primary persons involved in the construction and use of the *Files*, are not unmindful of these problems. In 1967 a conference was held that had, among other things, the task of designing a sample of cultures that would maximize the quality and representativeness of coverage for cross-cultural research. With such a sample, users of the *Files* could proceed with greater efficiency and the certainty that their chosen sample represented the broader universe of cultures.

In the past, most judgments for including cultures have paralleled those outlined above in that, in the last analysis, they depended on the judgments of the researcher, and, thus, unknown sources of bias were introduced. It is well known that such subjective sources of sampling bias can be handled through the use of random techniques. We will pursue these in greater detail in Chapter 9. But simple random samples in the cross-cultural arena produce their own difficulties. Murdock (1957) has been among those noting the problems.

> Random sampling of all the world's known cultures must unfortunately be excluded for several reasons. In the first place, this would result in the inclusion of many cultures for which the descriptive information is very incomplete and in the exclusion, through chance, of a substantial proportion of the richest and most dependable ethnographic literature. In the second place, it would yield only a percentage of all the world's cultures without reference to their distribution by types. Areas like Europe and the Far East with a few large and culturally homogeneous nations, for example, would tend to be heavily under-represented as compared with areas like aboriginal Australia with hundreds of discrete but not notable divergent tribal cultures. . . . Third, purely random sampling would inevitably omit many of the truly unique cultures of the world, each the sole known representative of a distinctive type. (p. 9)

As a means of synthesizing the virtues of both random and purposefully selected samples, Naroll (1967) outlines the procedures used in constructing what is referred to as a "stratified random sample from a bibliographically defined universe." Initially, the procedure involved the selection of societies whose technical literature met the criteria listed in Figure 7.16. This resulted in two types of cultures—those that met the minimal criteria and those that met more stringent criteria.

Using these criteria, there were 58 societies on the Top Quality list and 146 societies on the Quality list. This pool of cultures was then "stratified" into 60 sampling groups, and one society was selected randomly from these groups to yield the following distribution: 12 from Africa; 8 from the Circum-Mediterranean and Europe; 10 each from Asia, Oceania, and North and South America. When possible, the random selection was taken from societies that met the criteria for *Top Quality Files*. When these were unavailable, the shift was to societies that met the less stringent standards for a *Quality File*. There were four departures from this procedure, which are relatively minor. These have been

FIGURE 7.16
Standards for Quality Control Sample

Minimum for *Quality File:* (B level)

1. At least 1,200 pages of cultural data, focused on a community or other delimited cultural unit, regardless of size, on which accounts by different authors overlap.
    Coverage of additional subgroups or entire culture area is highly desirable. This total must include 1,000 pages, exclusive of texts, myths, physical anthropology, or archeology.
2. Substantial contributions from at least two different authors (at least one monograph or the equivalent from one author and 100 pages or more of articles from the second), one of whom must be a professional anthropologist with formal training in ethnology. The work of a nonprofessional whose work is regarded as meeting accepted standards of ethnographic description may also be acceptable.
3. The basic ethnographic account must be considered reliable by the profession, i.e., reviews should not have questioned basic data nor subsequent work revealed fundamental flaws.
4. Rounded coverage of basic economics, sociopolitical organization, and life cycle. Rounded coverage implies basic description of all or most aspects of these subjects.
5. A major portion of the ethnographic evidence must have been gathered while the group was a viable functioning culture. A viable functioning culture is defined as one in which (a) the group is large enough to continue as a functioning social unit and (b) the aboriginal economic system has not been fully replaced.
6. Historical depth should be available (record extending back at least 100 years from the time of major observation).

Minimum for *Top Quality File:* (A level; in addition to above qualifications)

1. An additional 1,000 pages of cultural data, including above restrictions on focus and nature of data.
2. At least two professional anthropologists (as qualified above).
3. At least one of anthropologists must have spent a minimum of 12 months in the area and have had a working knowledge of the native language. This requirement may be reduced when three or more anthropologists have worked in the area for varying periods.

Source: Naroll, 1967, pp. 82–83.

detailed in Naroll's article (1967). The final 60 *Files* chosen are indicated by asterisks in Figure 7.10.

Using this stratified sample of *Files*, it is possible to move more quickly to the chosen topics with the assurance that the *Files* included represent the major regions of the world with high quality. Still, however, there are problems. In no way is the Quality Control Sample a random sample of the larger universe of known cultures. Rather, it is a random sample of cultures that have been well documented. As we have already noted this tendency to describe one culture or one class of cultures rather than others appears to be associated with a number of factors. Instead, the Quality Control Sample represents a thoughtful effort by well-informed individuals to create a source of data that will allow more careful treatment of topics than would be possible without such effort. As we learn more about the sources of bias in the Sample, we can make further refinements. For now it is a useful source of information. On occasion the Sample will not include information on selected topics. This, of course, adds yet another difficulty. In such situations you must decide whether to simply do without the information or search for a replacement in the original pool of Quality and Top Quality Files. A listing of the original pool can be found in *Behavior Science Notes* (1967, pp. 84–88).

SUMMARY

This, then, is the structure of the *Human Relations Area Files*. It is a collection of material from a wide range of cultures throughout the world that has been thoroughly indexed and assessed in terms of quality. It does not represent anywhere near the total number of known cultures. It represents, instead, a set of cultures that have been selected in such a way as to produce possible distortions in cross-cultural conclusions. To minimize these distortions in your study, familiarize yourself with various discussions cited throughout. In addition, a second type of difficulty is encountered when you find that the *Files* do not contain information in quite the form you would like. The conceptual schemes used by the authors may be different from your own, material may have been left out, and you may be unable to determine whether this omission signals an absence of the trait or simply a point of neglect in the material being examined.

These difficulties are not minor. Neither are they usually totally devastating. You are again faced, as you are in any use of available material, with working with what is available, noting the difficulties, claiming neither too much nor too little for your study.

Having noted the potential and problems with available materials, we will return in the next chapter to the initial production of your data.

This time we will consider the process of translating ideas into items on a survey questionnaire. In Chapter 11 we will consider some aspects of this translation process as they relate to the development of experiments and the pursuit of casual relationships. Although this generation of new data is frequently a costly enterprise, it pays dividends in a closer link between the concepts and data than is frequently possible when you are limited to available resources of information.

KEY ISSUES

1. What considerations should be made when developing a coding strategy?
2. What difficulties are likely to be encountered when coding the direction and intensity of communication?
3. How does one go about establishing the reliability of a coding scheme?
4. How is the *HRAF* system organized?
5. What difficulties are likely to be encountered in the use of the *Files?*
6. What is meant by the Quality Control Sample?

REFERENCES

Berelson, Bernard, and Salter, Patricia
    1946   "Majority and Minority Americans: An Analysis of Magazine Fiction." *Public Opinion Quarterly,* vol. 10, pp. 168–90.
Funkhouser, G. Ray
    1973   "The Issues of the Sixties: An Exploratory Study of the Dynamics of Public Opinion." *Public Opinion Quarterly,* vol. 37, pp. 62–75.
Kendall, Maurice G.
    1955   *Rank Correlation Methods.* London: Charles Griffin.
Keiser, R. Lincoln
    1970   "Fieldwork among the Vice Lords of Chicago." In George D. Spindler (ed.), *Being an Anthropologist: Fieldwork in Eleven Cultures.* New York: Holt, Rinehart and Winston.
Klein, M. W., and Maccoby, N.
    1954   "Newspaper Objectivity in the 1952 Campaign." *Journalism Quarterly,* vol. 31, pp. 285–96.
Lagacé, Robert O.
    1974   *Nature and Use of the HRAF Files: A Research and Teaching Guide.* New Haven, Conn.: Human Relations Area Files, Inc.
Laswell, Harold D.
    1949   "Detection: Propaganda Detection and the Courts." In Harold D. Laswell et al., *The Language of Politics: Studies in Quantitative Semantics.* New York: George Stewart.
Merton, Robert K.
    1957   "Science and Economy in 17th Century England." In *Social Theory and Social Structure.* New York: The Free Press.

Murdock, George P.
  1957   "World Ethnographic Sample." *American Anthropologist,* vol. 59,
         pp. 664–87.
Murdock, George P.
  1972   *Outline of World Cultures.* New Haven, Conn.: Human Relations
         Area Files, Inc.
Murdock, George P., et al.
  1971   *Outline of Cultural Materials.* New Haven, Conn.: Human Rela-
         tions Area Files, Inc.
Naroll, Raoul
  1967   "The Proposed HRAF Probability Sample." *Behavior Science
         Notes,* vol. 2, pp. 70–80.
Naroll, Raoul
  1968   "Some Thoughts on Comparative Method in Cultural Anthropol-
         ogy." In Hubert M. Blalock, Jr., and Ann B. Blalock (eds.), *Meth-
         odology in Social Research.* New York: McGraw Hill.
Osgood, C. E.
  1959   "The Representational Model and Relevant Research Methods."
         In I. de S. Pool (ed.), *Trends in Content Analysis.* Urbana: Uni-
         versity of Illinois Press.
Osgood, C. E., and Walker, Evelyn G.
  1959   "Motivation and Language Behavior: Content Analysis of Suicide
         Notes." *Journal of Abnormal Serial Psychology,* vol. 59, pp. 58–67.
Schneider, Louis, and Dornbusch, Sanford
  1958   *Popular Religion: Inspirational Books in America.* Chicago: Uni-
         versity of Chicago Press.
Spiegleman, M.; Terwilliger, C.; and Fearing, F.
  1953   "The Content of Comics: Goals and Means to Goals of Comic
         Strip Characters," *Journal of Social Psychology,* vol. 37, pp.
         189–203.

Contents

Chapter 8

Translating Ideas into Data, III: Developing Structured Interviews and Questionnaires

There are times, when devising observation strategies, that existing data simply will not be sufficient. The measures available may not portray the dimension of a trait you have in mind. The reports may not combine the data in the way you need. You may not have access to the raw data from which summaries have been drawn, and, thus, reworking the basic information may be out of the question. In short, you are faced with creating the initial building blocks for a study. In the present chapter we will consider one style of research quite useful in many situations—survey research with questionnaires.

The survey questionnaire has been a workhorse in sociological research. What the experiment has been to psychology, what field observations and more open-ended conversations have been to anthropology, is what the survey questionnaire has been to sociology. We already have considered field research. We will turn to experiments in Chapter 11. We turn now to the benefits and difficulties of the use of the structured questionnaire.

SOME GENERAL CONSIDERATIONS

As noted in Chapter 5, the situation in which structured questionnaires are most useful is when a description of the distribution of certain predetermined traits of a specified population is desired. This is particularly the case when the traits involve current individual attitudes, opinions, and factual status, such as number of persons in a household and the number of cars, television sets, etc., that are owned. Although in many circumstances there is ample reason to believe that persons might not be totally candid, either intentionally or unintentionally, there seems to be no better way to get a reading on the collective opinion climate

than to ask the persons involved. This, coupled with their relative efficiency, has led to a blossoming of public-opinion polls.

Measuring Anticipated Behavior

Structured questionnaires are less useful, though frequently used,
when tapping behavior. This difficulty emerges when asking about anticipated future behavior—What do you think you would do if you found
yourself in the following circumstances?—and when asking about recol-
lected past behavior—During the past year have you ever . . . ? In
the first situation it is frequently difficult for the respondent to know
for sure just how she or he would act. The intensity of the moment
might be different. The presence of certain friends or, for that matter,
strangers might make a good deal of difference. In the context of the
structured questionnaire it is difficult to spell out all the contingencies
that might occur. This point was made some time ago by La Piere
(1939) in the context of discussing responses to the question, "Would
you get up to give an Armenian woman your seat in a street car?"
Attempts to assess the validity of responses to questions such as this,
either in terms of the attitudes they reflect or in terms of actual future
behaviors, are problematic at best. As La Piere suggests:

> Now the question may be constructed with elaborate skill and hidden
> with consummate cunning in a maze of supplementary or even irrelevant
> questions, yet all that has been obtained is a symbolic response to
> a symbolic situation. The words "Armenian woman" do not constitute
> an Armenian woman in flesh and blood, who might be tall or squat,
> fat or thin, old or young, well or poorly dressed—who might, in fact,
> be a goddess or just another old and dirty hag. And the questionnaire
> response, whether it be "yes" or "no," is but a verbal reaction and
> this does not involve rising from the seat or stolidly avoiding the hurt
> eyes of the hypothetical woman and the derogatory stares of other
> street-car occupants. (p. 230)

Reports of anticipated future behavior must be viewed with a good
deal of caution when based on this type of data. The same holds when
we are speaking of anticipated feelings—How would you feel if . . . ?

The problem with this anticipation of future behavior and feelings
is somewhat lessened when asking the respondent to think of situations
similar to those encountered in rather structured and routine ways in
day-to-day living. In such situations a good deal of past experience is
available to inform the imagination. It is one thing to ask a judge what
action he or she would take in a criminal case given certain characteristics of the defendant, the prosecution, and the offense. It is a similar thing
to ask employment officers whether they would hire an individual with certain employment and personal background. It is quite another to ask the

respondent to step into an imagined situation never before encountered and anticipate his or her own behavior or feelings. The correlates of misreported anticipated reactions are not well understood at this point. Even in the structured setting the problem of invalidity remains, as evidenced by the previously noted study of La Piere. Many of the issues concerning the connection between what we say and what we do are discussed in Deutscher (1973).

Measuring Past Behavior

Questionnaires also have proven to be frequently misleading when *past* behavior is reported. As noted in an earlier chapter, this once again proved to be the case in a study of police-citizen encounters. Reiss (1971) reports the following in this regard:

> In our attempts to use surveys to estimate victimization from crime and mobilization of the police, we observed police and citizen transactions, and, then, within three months, interviewed citizens about their experience. Our studies show that almost four in ten citizens either did not recall their transactions with the police or reported the event that gave rise to it but denied having had any contact with the police. (p. 8)

Almost 40 percent—this is no small slippage.

Biderman (1967) has discussed this problem in some detail, noting differences which occur as questions become more specific and the tendency of some respondents to "telescope" time periods. Questions which included reference to specific time periods, specific types of events, and specific persons proved more effective mind-joggers than more general attempts simply to ask, "Were you ever . . . ?" Also noted was a tendency of persons to extend ("telescope") the time frame of the question so as to include events that happened before or after the time interval. Given the need for question specificity and the time consuming nature of such concrete detail, Biderman concludes, "Although it is theoretically possible to use the survey method for a measure of the entire life experience of each respondent . . . in practice this would presumably require, to say the least, very time consuming interview methods." (p. 23)

Thus, questionnaires should be used (if at all) with extreme caution and with built-in checks on the validity of responses when dealing with actual behavior. Without such checks the evidence may be highly suspect.

A peculiar problem frequently emerges when dealing with past behavior and the degree to which that behavior is related to attitudes. It frequently is assumed that attitudes lead to or, put more strongly, cause certain behavior. As we will discuss in a later chapter, to assert a causal linkage is to assume that the cause does not follow the effect in time. And, yet, in survey studies we sometimes find that research involves reports of *past* behavior and *present* attitudes. That is, we find the survey questionnaires asking the respondent to report on past voting behavior or delinquent acts and then asking about current level of alienation or attachment to parents, and so forth.

An example is once again in order. Travis Hirschi (1969), in a carefully conceived and executed study of juvenile delinquency, wanted to pursue the basic hypothesis that the lack of certain bonds to society is a cause for committing delinquent acts. Realizing that official records introduce certain biases, there was an attempt to get the respondents to report their own delinquent activities using the following items:

1. Have you ever taken little things (worth less than $2) that did not belong to you?
2. Have you ever taken things of some value (between $2 and $50) that did not belong to you?
3. Have you ever taken things of large value (worth over $50) that did not belong to you?
4. Have you ever taken a car for a ride without the owner's permission?
5. Have you ever banged up on purpose something that did not belong to you?
6. Not counting fights you may have had with a brother or sister, have you ever beaten up on anyone or hurt anyone on purpose?

The response categories for each of the items were: (1) Never; (2) More than a year ago; (3) During the last year, and (4) During the last year and more than a year ago. Further recognizing the problems with the validity of reports of past behavior, especially in what might be sensitive areas, Hirschi went to some lengths to establish the validity of the self-reports as reflected in their correspondence with official records. So far so good.

A problem arises when the basic hypothesis—that lack of bonds to society is causally linked to delinquent acts—was pursued. To assume this is to assume that the bonds, which are partially defined in terms of certain attitudes and opinions, either precede or occur at the same time as the delinquent acts. As measured, the attitudes and opinions referred to a time *after* the commission of the delinquent acts. Such questions as "Do you care what teachers think of you?" "Do you like school?" "Would you like to be the kind of person your father is?" "Do you respect your best friends' opinions about the important things in life?" refer to current states of mind. The reported behavior measures refer to past action. This clearly presents some difficulty when exploring the causal linkage between attitudes and behavior. It would be less of a problem if interest was simply in prediction. We will have more to say of the distinct, but related, strategies employed when exploring predictive as opposed to causal linkages in Chapters 10 and 11.

Systematic Sources of Bias

It is troublesome enough to note that such misreporting of behavior has been detected in a number of studies. It is additionally disturbing to note that similar misreporting has been uncovered in the context of using less behavior-oriented measures. In both cases there have been attempts to uncover the sources of the invalidity. Among the possible sources, two have received a good deal of attention. The first, which frequently is referred to as response acquiescence, is a tendency of some respondents to consistently answer either negatively or positively no matter what the question. To detect these "naysayers" and "yeasayers" is a relatively simple matter when compared to the second source of invalidity. You can simply reverse the direction of some of the questions that make up your index and then look to see which respondents answered "no" or "yes" to items in both directions.

The second frequently cited source of response invalidity is the tendency of some persons to respond in ways perceived to be socially desirable. Regardless of the amount of a particular trait a person actually possesses, there sometimes is a tendency to respond in ways that put him or her in the most favorable light. Phillips (1973) has explored the apparent impact of social desirability within the context of measuring mental illness and the degree to which certain traits, such as the level of happiness and the number of friends, were reported. These results are worth noting.

In one study, six areas were explored. The level of reported *general happiness* was determined by asking, "Taking all things together, how would you say things are these days—Would you say you're very happy, pretty happy, or not too happy these days?" The level of *involvement with religion* was determined by asking, "How religious would you say you are—very religious, somewhat religious, or not at all religious?" The *number of friends* was ascertained by the question, "Think of people, including relatives, whom you consider really good friends—that is, people you feel free to talk with about personal things—About how many such friends would you say you have?" *Martial happiness* was measured by asking, "Taking all things together, how would you describe your marriage? Would you say that your marriage is very happy, pretty happy, or not too happy?" The *level of prejudice* was determined by asking, "If you went to a party and found that most of the people were of a racial or ethnic group different from your own, would you be very bothered, somewhat bothered, or not bothered at all?" Finally, the *extent of doctor visits* was indicated by, "I visit my doctor at least once a year—Yes, No."

Clearly, in light of our just-completed discussion, there are problems with some of these indicators. For now, however, we are interested in the degree to which responses to these items were patterned around the degree of perceived desirability of the traits in question. To ascertain the level of desirability, Phillips asked his respondents to rate each of the above traits on a nine-point scale from low to high desirability. The relationship between perceived desirability and the reported possession of the trait is presented in Table 8.1.

TABLE 8.1
Responses on Six Measures by Social Desirability of Traits

	Trait Desirability		
	High	Medium	Low
1. % very happy	36.5	29.6	15.6
	(249)	(108)	(45)
2. % very religious	38.2	22.5	6.2
	(149)	(102)	(145)
3. % seven or more friends	39.1	31.5	31.2
	(166)	(111)	(112)
4. % very happily married	78.6	72.2	25.0
	(248)	(86)	(16)
5. % nonprejudiced	82.5	62.2	63.3
	(252)	(82)	(60)
6. % visited a doctor	83.4	79.4	44.3
	(229)	(97)	(77)

Source: Phillips, 1973, p. 46.

In each case there is a connection. For each of the traits, the higher the perceived desirability of the trait, the more likely the report of a high degree of possession. There are at least two possible reasons for this finding, as Phillips points out. One might be the "invalidity hypothesis." Here, the suggestion is that respondents report those traits they perceive will place them in the best light, whether or not they actually possess the trait. The second explanation suggests that the higher the perceived desirability of a given trait, the higher the probability that that trait will be developed and thus the higher the actual level of possession. This latter explanation, of course, suggests the respondents are reporting the correct level. The former hypothesis suggests a misleading response.

To determine which is the case, the actual behavior would have to be observed. This would involve no simple study. However, in suggesting that the findings reflect misreporting in part, Phillips notes that just because persons find a happy marriage desirable is no reason to believe they will actually end up with a happy marriage.

This kind of speculation, however, is just that—speculation. We simply are not in a position, given these findings, to decide with much degree of certainty. Given the nature of the interpersonal interaction in the interview situation, however, there is reason to believe that the degree of perceived desirability will have an impact on response patterns. It is to minimize this possibility that respondents are assured that there are no right or wrong answers, that responses will be anonymous, and that it is important to be completely candid. Most of the time you simply will be unable to determine the degree to which these strategies have eliminated inaccurate responses. You are always at the mercy of the candor of those answering your questions.

The implications of this misreporting will be different, depending on whether you are interested in explanation or simply a description. If description is the goal, any distortion will yield misleading results in terms of characterizing a community in, say, the overall level of happiness. If explanation is sought, the impact is more subtle. The impact of misreporting is perhaps most important when it is linked with both the variable you are attempting to explain and the variable used to explain.

In this regard, Phillips explored the link between the socioeconomic status of the respondent and various traits used to define mental illness. In part, his argument is that the frequently noted relationship between socioeconomic status and mental illness is brought into question, since socioeconomic status is related to both perceived desirability of certain traits and to positive responses to a number of mental-illness items. However, after controlling for contending factors (we will explore the meaning of control in Chapter 10), he concludes that "the existence of a relationship between socioeconomic status and mental disorder is *not* just an artifact of the hypothesized distortions arising from response bias."

The point for present purposes is not whether there is or is not a relationship between socioeconomic status and mental illness, but, rather, that response biases are possible alternative explanations for findings and, thus, when possible, you should build checks into your study to eliminate or reduce this possible distorting influence.

These, then, are some general considerations to keep in mind when constructing a structured interview or questionnaire. Be cautious when measuring behavior, either past or future. There is ample evidence to suggest that distortions are commonplace. Whenever possible, check. In the case of behavior, direct observations are always better. When opinions, beliefs, attitudes, and, in the general case, various states of mind are being measured, direct observation is impossible. Short of various chemical and electronic devices, you must rely on reports from respondents. In this situation a key factor to keep in mind is what various responses mean within the social context of the interview situation. Some responses might signal that the respondent is less or more "desirable" as a person. When faced with a stranger (in this case, the interviewer) there may be a tendency for the respondent to project a more favorable image than is a true reflection.

It is at this point that the interpersonal skills of the interviewer, and in the case of a mailed questionnaire, various convincing assurances, come into play. At times you will find the role of the interviewer split in conflicting directions. You are at once a diplomat and a boor, a technician and a human being. You are called upon to be tactful and pushy. You have to develop some sensitivity as to when to be what and what sorts of compromises should be reached. Excellent suggestions along these lines are contained in Converse and Schuman (1974).

In a parallel fashion, when a mailed questionnaire is used, you will find yourself assuring the respondents that their responses will be treated in an impersonal manner and, at the same time, convincing them that it is their opinion that matters. Personal involvement is needed to complete the task of answering all the questions. Impersonal assurances sometimes are called for when dealing with what might be sensitive matters. Again, you will have to decide within the context of your own study which of these alternatives should be emphasized and what sort of balance should be struck. Pretesting your instrument on persons before the study often provides much by way of useful guidelines.

THE CONTENT OF QUESTIONS

Keeping these general considerations in mind, we come to the issue of question content. This is the crucial step in any translation of concepts into items on a questionnaire. Have you captured the idea? Once again, it is best to consider come concrete examples.

Measuring Social Bonds

Perhaps there is no more powerful concept in social science than the idea of social integration or alienation—the way in which individuals, organizations, socioeconomic classes, or nations are bound to one another in what is referred to as social order or structure. The ways in which the bonds between units in a given social system are strengthened, weakened, formed, and reformed are central to any discussion of the dynamics of social organization and individual action.

It is within this general theoretical context that Hirschi devised the previously noted study of juvenile delinquency. The task was to translate this idea of "bonds to society" into items on a questionnaire administered to junior and senior high-school students in Western Contra Costa County, California. The way in which this was accomplished is instructive.

The first task was one of determining various ways in which persons, in general, and junior and senior high-school students, in particular, are bound to society. The second task was to locate various "connection points"—parents, school, friends, the legal system, and so forth—to which persons are bound. The bonds to society were divided into four types: attachments, commitments, involvement, and beliefs. The items on the questionnaire were used according to the degree to which they reflected these concepts. It thus became crucial to carefully spell out what was meant by attachments, commitments, involvement, and beliefs.

Attachment was taken to mean "sensitivity to the opinions" of others. Individuals are bound to one another and to broader social units to the degree to which the actions of those others make a difference. To the extent that this bond to others is missing or weakened is the extent to which the potential for "deviance" (in the case of Hirschi's study, delinquent acts) goes up. As elaborated in the context of attachments to parents, "The important consideration is whether the parent is psychologically present when temptation to commit a crime appears. If, in the situation of temptation, no thought is given to parental reaction, the child is to this extent free to commit the act" (p. 88).

This hypothesis concerning the connection between attachment and delinquency seems quite plausible. How was the idea of attachment measured? The reasoning went as follows: "Which children are most likely to ask themselves, 'What will my parents think?' Those who think their parents know where they are and what they are doing" (p. 89). Four items, two given once for mother and once for father, on the questionnaire were used to tap this perceived supervision: "Does your mother (father) know where you are when you are away from home?" And, "Does mother (father) know whom you are with when you are away from home?" The response categories were: "Usually," "Sometimes," and "Never."

Clearly, these questions are only indirect measures of the sensitivity to the opinions of parents. We can only speculate as to why more direct measures were not used. Additional measures of attachment to parents were used to replicate a test of the hypothesis. Once again the items on the questionnaire seem to only indirectly tap sensitivity to others. In this second situation the items tapped the "intimacy of communication." The rationale for their use was elaborated as follows: "(T)he more the child is accustomed to sharing his mental life with his parents, the more he is accustomed to seeking or getting their opinion about his activities, the more likely he is to perceive them as part of his social and psychological field, and the less likely he would be to neglect their opinion when considering an act contrary to law" (p. 90).

The questions emerging from this line of reasoning were as follows: "Do you share your thoughts and feelings with your mother (father)?" "How often have you talked over your future plans with your mother (father)?" "When you don't know why your mother (father) makes a rule, will she (he) explain the reason?", and "When you come across things you don't understand, does your mother (father) help you with them?" The first two questions were combined to form an index of the intimacy of communication flowing from the respondent to the parents. The second two were combined to measure the reverse flow. Yet a third line of reasoning led to another question: "Would you like to be the kind of person your mother (father) is?" Here the response categories were, "In Every Way," "In Most Ways," "In Some Ways," "In Just a Few Ways," and "Not At All." In these distinct ways, then, Hirschi translated, through sometimes indirect means, the basic idea that attachment to parents involved being sensitive to their opinions.

> *Practicum 8.1* **Keeping in mind the conceptual definition of attachment, what problems do you see with these measures of attachment? What questions might have tapped the same idea in different ways? Do you see any problems with the measures you devised?**

What of the second bond to society, that which Hirschi labeled "commitment"? The conceptualization of commitment involves the rational component of the ways in which we are bound to society. As suggested by Hirschi,

> Few would deny that men on occasion obey the rules simply for fear of the consequences. This rational component in conformity we label commitment. . . . The idea, then, is that a person invests time, energy, himself, in a certain line of activity—say, getting an education, building up a business, acquiring a reputation for virtue. When or whenever he considers deviant behavior, he must consider the costs of this deviant behavior, the risk he runs of losing the investment he has made in conventional behavior. (p. 20)

The basic hypothesis, then, is that the greater the level of existing commitments, the less the probability of delinquent acts. What were the measures of commitment? One measure used was, "What period of your life do you think will turn out to have been the happiest part of your life?"

A. Grade-school years	E. Age 20 to 30
B. Junior high-school years	F. Age 30 to 40
C. High-school years	G. Over age 40
D. Between high school and age 20	H. None of my life has been or will be happy

A second set of questions, combining involvement in various "adult activities," was used to construct an index in the following way. The respondent received a score of 0 if he did not smoke, drink, or date;

a 1 if he dated but did not drink or smoke; a 2 if he smoked and drank but did not date; a 3 if he smoked or drank and dated; a 4 if he smoked and drank but did not date; and a 5 if he smoked, drank, and dated.

How, you might be asking, do these questions tap the bond to society labeled commitment? Again the link requires some rather indirect connections. Reasoning that the adolescent can be located on the three interrelated career lines of education, occupation, and passage to adult status, Hirschi suggests the following rationale:

> (G)iven the age requirements of the occupational system, many adolescents in effect complete their education without at the same time being able to begin their occupational careers. Being no longer tied to an educational career, they become in one sense adults, yet, being free of an occupation, they remain in one sense children. . . . The adolescent caught in this situation tends to develop attitudes and behave in ways "appropriate" only to an adult; his structural position at the same time guarantees him the freedom appropriate only to a child. The consequence is a high rate of delinquency. . . . The adolescent caught in this situation should see the period between the two careers as one of relative ease and pleasure. He is free to enjoy some of the privileges of adulthood without being burdened by work and family responsibilities. This period is, as he sees it, and will always see it, the "happiest time of his life." (p. 163)

If this line of reasoning is correct, we should find that those who perceive the years between high school and age 20, as well as those who engage in a series of premature "adult activities," are those most likely to engage in delinquent activities. In fact, this is what Hirschi found.

> *Practicum 8.2* **Just because the findings were in line with Hirschi's rationale does not mean that the items were tapping the commitment bond. Do you see any fault in the measures designed to tap commitment as defined by Hirschi? What might be some alternative, more direct measures for the same concept? What problems do you see with your measures?**

In addition to the two measures just discussed, Hirschi also employed a composite achievement orientation index made up of the combined responses to three items: "I try hard in school," "How important is getting good grades to you personally?" and "Whatever I do I try hard." Thus, a prime virtue of Hirschi's study, even if we disagree with his measures, is that multiple indicators were used, allowing what amount to multiple tests of the same hypothesis. The consistency of findings yielding support over each of the indicators yields greater confidence in the conclusions than might otherwise be the case.

Practicum 8.3   The two remaining bonds to society—involvement and belief—were defined by Hirschi as follows: The idea that involvement constitutes a bond to society rests on the hypothesis that time and energy are inherently limited and thus, "a person may simply be too busy doing conventional things to find time to engage in deviant behavior." Beliefs are considered bonds to society in the sense that they constitute a link to a broader value system. How might these ideas be turned into questions on a structured questionnaire administered to junior and senior high-school students? Design separate questions for the bond to a general value system, to the value system of the educational system, and to the value system of parents. What problems did you encounter?

In completing the above exercises you may have had some difficulty in deciding on certain response categories, on deciding whether to use a single item or a series of items in the construction of composite index, or on deciding just how to word questions. Fortunately, there are some general categories and considerations that may prove useful.

Some Useful General Strategies

Given a concept of interest, the task becomes one of formulating questions. In this regard, it is a good idea to spend some time exploring what others have done in similar situations. Compilations of existing scales have been published, such as the work of Bonjean, Hill, and McLemore (1967); Robinson, Rusk, and Head (1969); Robinson and Shaver (1969); and Robinson, Athanasiou, and Head (1969); and Chun et al. (1975). Time spent exploring these existing scales provides much by way of suggestions. Still, you will frequently be faced with reworking existing scales. This may entail only slight modifications of wordings and rearrangement of items, such as was the case with Olsen (1969) and his development of alternative indicators of political alienation. It may involve more extensive changes as you discover outdated phrases like "zoot-suiters" or references to problems that at one time were pressing but in the current situation are meaningless. Indeed, you may find either that there is no appropriate question related to your conceptual framework or that existing questions require so much reworking that it is better to begin from scratch.

In such a situation it is a good idea to spend time in brainstorming sessions, trying out a wide range of alternatives. Such sessions will not only broaden your eventual pool of items but you will also most likely sharpen your conceptual thinking in the process.

When designing questions, avoid overly complicated questions, such as asking respondents to rank 25 items in order of preference. When questions must be complicated, such as with "screening" questions that ask for certain information and then ask separate questions according to responses, make sure your directions are clearly spelled out. This is important when interviewers will be asking the questions. It is doubly important when you are mailing or otherwise self-administering a questionnaire that requires the respondent to determine the next step. An example of such a multistep question designed to tap the managerial position of the respondent follows:[1]

In general, what is the nature of your supervisory or managerial work?
1. . Technical or staff work only, do not supervise other people at all
2. . First-line supervisor
3. . Other————→If Other, do you have supervisors reporting to you?
                4. . No
                5. . Yes————→If yes, are you at a *section managerial level or above?*
                          6. . No
                          7. . Yes

If you are including a number of questions designed to tap the same concept, avoid phrasing that yields questions all in the "same direction." The most frequently encountered instance of this situation is when you are tapping individual opinions by asking respondents to agree or disagree with certain statements. Design the statements so that agreement signals acceptance of a certain stance in some instances and rejection in others. In this way you will be able to partially check on the degree to which persons are simply responding positively or negatively regardless of the content of the items.

Yet another guidepost, which hardly needs stating, is—clear up ambiguities. Some ambiguities may be in the choice of words. Some ambiguities show up in multifaceted questions—questions that incorporate more than one part but allow only one overall response. For example, Olsen incorporated the following item into his scale of political dissatisfaction: "These days the government is trying to do too many things, including some activities that I don't think it has the right to do." Responses to this item are ambiguous in that it is unclear whether agreement or disagreement refers to the first portion of the statement, the second, or both. You might agree with one part and disagree with the other.

Such ambiguities can sometimes be detected in the early stages of editing. Further refinements, however, are almost always necessary after a few dry runs with the questionnaire. It is for this reason that "pretests" of the research instrument are conducted. In these pretests the respondents should be encouraged to ask questions and to respond in critical fashion to the items included. In this way the final version will be more

---

[1] This was part of a larger study of the Boeing Company's managerial personnel, directed by L. Wesley Wager, at the University of Washington.

usable and free of measurement error due to ambiguous wording and question format. Above all, when designing questions, keep in mind the concepts you are measuring. Slippage in the linkage between data and concept can lead to a good number of headaches when it comes to later analysis.

In addition to the "substance" of the question, there is the response format. This may be either open-ended or structured. For example, you will recall that Hirschi, when asking respondents about the happiest days of their lives, presented the respondents with a series of times that were informative within the context of the theoretical framework. This question might have been structured so that the respondents filled in anything that came to their minds in this regard. Open-ended questions have the virtue of uncovering unanticipated responses. They have the frequent drawback of making greater demands on the respondent and being more difficult to handle in later analysis. It is one thing to ask a series of structured questions designed to tap specific dimensions of opinions. It is another to simply ask a respondent to elaborate on how he or she feels about such-and-such. If you find yourself asking a number of open-ended questions in either one-shot interviews or self-administered questionnaires, you should reassess whether the interview-questionnaire approach might better be replaced with a more qualitative multistage interview/observation study.

When you decide that the closed-end or structured format is better, design your response categories so as to avoid ambiguities. In some situations you will be asking respondents to check only one response; in others they should be checking more than one. If there is any am-biguity—specify. In some situations, for example, when you are asking respondents to respond on a continuum of agreement, a single response is almost automatic. In other situations, when the response categories do not represent a continuum, multiple responses will be possible. In such situations tell the respondent what to do. You might instruct the respondent to circle the number that *best* represents his or her position. It might be a case of circling the *three most* important reasons. You may want respondents to rank only the top four responses. The key in such situations is to specify. Never assume that what to do is obvious.

Some Standardized Response Formats

When designing response formats for structured questions, there are a number of commonly encountered situations. Frequently the interest is in opinions on certain matters—the degree of agreement or disagree-ment with certain points of view. In other situations you may be asking the respondent to estimate the extent of certain activities, the frequency of certain feelings or actions, or the probability of certain outcomes.

Fortunately, there are a number of alternative response formats that have proven rather successful in the past.

Perhaps the most commonly encountered set of responses is "Strongly Agree," "Agree," "Undecided," "Disagree," and "Strongly Disagree." Instead of asking respondents an open-ended question on how they feel about welfare, crime, drinking, drug usage, Democrats, politicians, religion, work, and so forth, questions are designed to tap specified aspects of the attitude object and then ask the respondent to agree or disagree with these statements. Questions take forms such as, "My job offers ample opportunity for advancement." "Politicians are responsive to persons like myself." "Religion is the major hope of mankind." "My parents are generally willing to listen to my point of view." "The dangers of drug usage have been underestimated." "Persons who commit crimes are generally caught." "Persons who commit crimes are generally punished."

The list could go on and on. This format is indeed a useful method of proceeding. In some instances, when you want to force respondents to take a stand, you may leave out the "undecided" category. In other instances you may find that a continuum of agreement/disagreement is more useful than the five-category format. In such a situation you can follow each statement with the following continuum, asking the respondent to check the point along the continuum that best represents his or her position.

Complete Agreement ———/——/——/——/——/——/——/——/ Complete Disagreement

Another situation is when you are after the frequency, extent, or probability of certain outcomes or feelings. Frequency is often tapped with some variation of the following format: "Always," "Usually," "Sometimes," "Seldom," "Never." Variations might include: "Usually," "Sometimes," "Never," or, again, a continuum from "Always" to "Never." Also, percentage categories such as "90 to 100," "80 to 90," and so forth are useful in this regards.

The range of questions that can utilize these formats also is wide. "How frequently are persons who rob a store caught?" "How frequently does religion occupy an uppermost position in your thinking?" "How frequently are you able to talk over things that are important to you with your parents?" "Political decisions are made with persons like myself in mind." As should be apparent, some of these questions also might be followed by the agree/disagree format. You will have to decide which best fits your purpose.

It is the response format that determines the level of measurement within a given conceptual framework. Given that certain statistical techniques are in some sense more powerful and/or more efficient (a point to which we will turn in Chapters 10 and 11) than others, the arrangement and spacing of categories become important considerations. In this regard one technique devised to tap concepts at the ratio level of measurement (you will recall that ratio measures are measures with numerically determined distances between categories and a zero point) are available. Hamblin (1971, 1974) developed a series of "liking" and "disliking" items designed to tap the perceived attraction or repulsion from various hypothetical situations. By asking the respondents to report "0" if they liked or disliked the hypothetical outcome, a zero point was established. By asking respondents to assign numbers, fractions, or decimals indicating how much something was liked or disliked, Hamblin was able to determine the proportional degree of liking or disliking. Similar techniques can be utilized when obtaining estimates of likelihood of certain outcomes. For example, in a survey of the Seattle area,[2] respondents were asked the following:

> Some people feel that they themselves are very likely to suffer losses because of the theft or illegal destruction of their possessions. Others feel that it is very unlikely that they will suffer such losses. How do you feel? How likely do you think that it is that you yourself will suffer any kind of property crime *over the next year?* Make a short mark crossing the line below to record your judgment.

Almost certainly	Almost certainly
will not be a	will be a
victim of a crime	victim of a crime
against property	against property

0   10   20   30   40   50   60   70   80   90   100

Obviously, this does not measure the actual threat. Rather, it is tapping perceptions. By noting the position of the marks, it is possible to assign numbers to the respondents according to the level of perceived threat.

In a number of ways, then, response formats can be designed to yield differing levels of measurement. These measurement strategies will become important when you later choose from a wide range of statistical techniques, the appropriate analytic strategy for translating the ideas of prediction and cause into data. As a rule of thumb, design your response formats so as to maximize the available degree of distinction. For example, degrees of agreement are more useful than simple "yes" or "no" responses. There are, of course, limits to this rule of thumb. In some instances it will be strained to ask respondents to make refined judgments, such as those necessary in the construction of ratio scales.

---

[2] This question is taken from a Seattle Area Crime Survey, conducted at the University of Washington under the direction of Herbert Costner.

Nevertheless, when appropriate, maximize your information. It will be possible to reduce certain categories of responses in later analysis. It will not be possible to expand the information beyond that which you have obtained from the initial response formats.

There are a number of advantages to be gained from consistent response formats. Not the least of these is the added efficiency of questionnaire construction that is possible by combining questions using the same response format in the same location on the questionnaire. This not only makes it easier to avoid a cluttered appearance of the questionnaire but also makes it easier for the respondent to go through the questionnaire swiftly.

An example of this strategy is reprinted in Figure 8.1, which is a portion of a questionnaire given to high-school teachers by Helen Bernal (1974) in a study of school structure and teacher characteristics. It is, of course, the case that too much repetition is boring as well as efficient. Hence, when designing your questionnaire, you should balance these sometimes competing demands for efficiency and interest. You are saved from a large amount of grief in this regard since respondents generally find efficient designs the least bothersome.

Single Items or Composite Indicators

Given a number of items designed to tap what are perhaps different dimensions of a rather complex concept, the issue becomes whether or not to combine items into one overall indicator or to examine each of the items separately. There are pros and cons for each decision. On the one hand, by combining items, you may end up with a more reliable indicator in that variations produced by single items can be averaged out to give a more stable measure. Also, by including differing aspects in a single index, you more closely approximate the complexity of the "true" state of affairs. In this sense, composite indicators are perhaps more valid indicators as well as more reliable.

On the other hand, it may be the case that different dimensions of a single concept, such as alienation, are related in distinct ways to various outcomes, such as participation in radical politics. By combining items in a single index, some of these item differences may be missed. By exploring a number of items and their relationships with other variables instead of a single relationship, further refinements in ideas are possible as you find your hypothesis supported in one test and drawn into question in another. It is, of course, the case that, if you find items are highly related to one another and are producing consistent results, the items should be combined to take advantage of the benefits of composite indicators. We will have more to say about relationships among items in Chapters 10 and 11.

FIGURE 8.1
A Portion of a Questionnaire Used in a Study of
High-School Teachers

II. ACTUAL CONDITIONS IN THIS SCHOOL

I want you to think about your present situation in the school in which you are actually teaching right now. For each question asked below place an X in the box beneath the phrase which best describes how you act or what conditions are like for you right now in this school.

WOULD YOU SAY THAT	Quite Often	Sometimes	Rarely	Never
You feel teaching facilities and materials are adequate	□	□	□	□
You feel your teaching load is manageable and your preparation time adequate	□	□	□	□
You can schedule class activities in a way that will best help students achieve course objectives	□	□	□	□
You are developing your own style as a teacher	□	□	□	□
You are fulfilling yourself as a person through your teaching.	□	□	□	□
The principal tells you exactly what is expected of you in your teaching	□	□	□	□
You teach students all that you think is important for them to know	□	□	□	□
You train students so that they can get into a good college or get a good job when they graduate.	□	□	□	□
You help students discover things for themselves.	□	□	□	□
You help students learn things that are important to themselves	□	□	□	□
The principal evaluates your work and discusses it with you	□	□	□	□
You teach interested students.	□	□	□	□
You help students to understand themselves and other people.	□	□	□	□
The principal allows you to evaluate your own work	□	□	□	□
You have time to relax during the school day when you don't have to teach or prepare classes	□	□	□	□
You teach in the same room or area throughout the day	□	□	□	□

Source: Bernal, 1974.

The construction of composite indicators can range from the rather technical procedures and rigid assumptions of what is referred to as factor analysis, to the more commonsense and intuitive combination of items, such as the construction of an index designed to measure the intimacy of communication between parent and child and involvement in adult activities discussed above. In the present discussion we will limit ourselves to less technical matters. The basic outline of what follows, the idea that you first examine inter-item correlations and then make decisions as to which items to combine, applies as well to the more technical procedures.

PROPERTY SPACE REDUCTION AND THE CONSTRUCTION OF TYPOLOGIES

Given responses to two or more questions, we are able to locate a respondent in what has been referred to as *property*, or *attribute, space*. By combining categories emerging from the property space, we are able to construct a typology though a process that, logically enough, is referred to as the reduction of property space. Lazarsfeld (1937) and Barton (1955) have been instrumental in developing these procedures.

Types of Reduction

Examples taken first from Barton's chapter, then from a study of law students, and, finally, from the previously noted study of juvenile delinquency provide useful discussion touchstones. Barton, drawing on the earlier work of Lazarsfeld, suggests a typology for categorizing individuals in terms of their usual political-party affiliation and their degree of political interest. The original property space constructed by the combination of these two trichotomized variables is presented in Figure 8.2.

FIGURE 8.2
Property Space for Each of Nine Categories
Emerging when Party Affiliation and Political
Interest Are Combined

Degree of Political Interest	Usual Party Affiliation		
	Republican	Democrat	Independent
High	Partisans		Independents
Medium	----------Habituals----------		Apathetics
Low			

In certain conceptual frameworks it is useful to combine those who identified with either political party and compare them with Independents. It is also useful to compare those with a high degree of interest with those reporting either medium or low interest. When these two "reduced" variables are combined, they yield the four categories given in Figure 8.3. Thus, the original nine-category property space has been

FIGURE 8.3
Property Space after Reduction of Original Categories

Degree of Political Interest	Usual Party Affiliation		
	Republican	Democrat	Independent
High	A	B	C
Medium	D	E	F
Low	G	H	I

reduced to the four-category typology made up of "Partisans" (those party identifiers with high interest), "Independents" (those nonparty identifiers with high interest), "Habituals" (those who identify with either party but have low or medium interest), and, finally, "Apathetics" (those who neither identify nor report a high degree of interest).

The reduction thus accomplished not only yields a less complex typology; it also yields a theoretically more useful one. The idea is that the sources and impact of political involvement are better understood within the context of the four new categories. This reduction of property space for practical research purposes has been called pragmatic reduction.

Another type of property space reduction—functional reduction—can be accomplished according to the pattern in which individuals fall. Categories with few or no persons can be eliminated and various other combinations combined. An example is available in our study of the rise and fall of student involvement in law school (Olson, 1971). It will be recalled from the discussion in Chapter 4 that, when persons pass through various institutions, there is a tendency to settle down, a tendency to come to terms with the new setting. To explore this within the context of law school, students were asked to estimate their degree of involvement along nine dimensions over five semesters. One of these dimensions was emotional reaction. Persons were asked to report whether they were tense, nervous but not tense, or relaxed during each of the first five semesters of law school. If the ideas discussed in Chapter 4 are correct, we should find that most persons tended to collect in the "settling-down" combinations within the property space defined by the

FIGURE 8.4
Property Space for Emotional Reactions during First Five Semesters of Law School

2nd			First Semester									
			Tense			Nervous			Relaxed			
		5th	Ten	Ner	Rel	Ten	Ner	Rel	Ten	Ner	Rel	Total
3rd	4th	T	11	1	0	1	2	0	0	0	0	15
T	T	N	7	0	0	1	0	0	0	1	0	9
		R	3	0	0	1	0	0	0	1	1	6
	N	T	0	0	0	0	0	0	0	0	0	0
		N	8	1	0	0	1	0	1	0	0	11
		R	8	0	0	0	2	0	0	0	0	10
	R	T	0	0	0	0	0	0	0	0	0	0
		N	1	0	0	0	0	0	0	0	0	1
		R	1	3	0	0	3	0	0	0	1	8
N	T	T	1	0	1	1	1	0	0	0	0	4
		N	1	0	0	0	0	0	0	1	0	2
		R	1	1	0	1	0	0	0	0	0	3
	N	T	1	1	1	1	1	0	0	0	0	5
		N	33	16	1	4	17	0	2	3	2	78
		R	23	11	0	2	7	1	1	0	0	45
	R	T	0	0	0	0	0	0	0	0	0	0
		N	4	1	0	0	1	0	1	0	0	7
		R	31	23	1	4	11	0	1	2	3	76
R	T	T	0	0	0	0	1	0	0	0	0	1
		N	0	0	0	0	0	0	0	0	1	1
		R	0	0	0	0	0	0	0	0	0	0
	N	T	0	0	0	0	0	0	0	0	0	0
		N	1	1	0	0	1	0	0	1	0	4
		R	4	1	0	0	0	1	0	0	0	6
	R	T	1	2	0	0	2	0	0	0	0	5
		N	3	1	0	0	1	2	0	1	1	9
		R	14	48	12	7	64	44	0	1	37	227

five trichotomized variables. We should also find that there were few persons who became increasingly tense as the semesters passed.

The actual findings are presented in Figure 8.4 within the 243-category property space defined by the unreduced combination of the five trichotomized emotional reactions. By including only those categories that had more than ten persons, we are able to reduce this property space into the 15 categories in Figure 8.5. Allowing for differences in interpretations in the meanings of "Tense" and "Nervous," this 15-category property space can be reduced further to the 3 categories defined by consistently "up-tight" individuals, consistently "relaxed" individuals, and individuals who exhibited the hypothesized "settling-down" pattern.

By noting frequently occurring patterns, then, we have moved from an original classification scheme with 243 categories to one with 3 categories. Not a bad reduction in complexity. Such reduction is not neces-

FIGURE 8.5

Categories within Reduced Property Showing Most Prevalent Patterns of Changing Emotional Reactions

	Pattern					
Semester	1	2	3	4	5	Number of Students
	N	N	R	R	R	64
	T	N	R	R	R	48
	N	R	R	R	R	44
	R	R	R	R	R	37
	T	T	N	N	N	33
	T	T	N	R	R	31
	T	T	N	N	R	23
	T	N	N	R	R	23
	N	N	N	N	N	17
	T	N	N	N	N	16
	T	T	R	R	R	14
	T	R	R	R	R	12
	T	N	N	N	R	11
	N	N	N	R	R	11
	T	T	T	T	T	11

T–tense; N–nervous but not tense; R–relaxed.

sarily a good thing if we end up missing a large number of the units we are analyzing. In this case, however, the 15-category property space includes 74 percent of the total. Among these 395 persons, 330, or 83 percent, were categorized as "settling down." No pattern, which might be defined as the "increasingly tense," had more than 10 persons, as shown in Figure 8.4. By employing the three-category typology it is possible to go back to the original unreduced property space and increase the number of persons who might be categorized as "settling down." For example, there are eight persons who reported being tense through the first three semesters, nervous during the fourth, and relaxed during the fifth. In addition to highlighting patterns of involvement, the functional reduction of property space also emphasizes the degree to which the "settling-down" view of the process of passing through has a good deal of validity.

Yet a third mode of property space reduction is what Lazarsfeld refers to as the arbitrary numerical procedure. The degree of arbitrariness can vary. The items combined may be arbitrarily chosen. The values given categories and the weights given items can be arbitrarily arrived at. It is the latter form of arbitrariness that appears most frequently. The formerly noted construction of the intimacy of communication index between child and parent provides an example. It will be recalled that in the construction of this index there were two variables involved, each with three categories. The resulting property space is presented in Figure 8.6. The responses have been replaced with the numbers "2,"

FIGURE 8.6
Property Space for Index of Intimacy of
Communication with Mother

Do You Share Your Thoughts and Feelings with Your Mother?	How Often Have You Talked Over Your Future Plans with Your Mother?		
	2 *(Often)*	1 *(Occasionally)*	0 *(Never)*
2 *(Usually)*	4	3	2
1 *(Sometimes)*	3	2	1
0 *(Never)*	2	1	0

"1," and "0." By combining categories with the same "scores" we reduce a nine-category typology into one with five categories ranging from 0 through 4.

In this particular instance the element of arbitrariness is at a minimum. The scores have been arbitrarily arrived at in that the weighting of the items was equal, as was the "distance" between categories. This element of arbitrariness became less severe in the context of the actual analysis in that the scores were generally treated as ordinal rather than interval level measurement. The items were combined into an index only after a check had been made on the degree to which they were related to one another. The check points, then, when constructing a "numerical" index are (1) see if the items are correlated with one another, (2) decide what values to assign to the categories within the items being combined, and (3) decide what "weight" to give each item. In the above example, Hirschi gave equal weight. He might just as easily have doubled the "scores" on the "share your thoughts and feelings" question under the assumption that general communication is (arbitrarily) twice as important as communication about plans for the future when it comes to predicting delinquency.

What we have seen up to this point, then, are three methods of constructing and reducing property space. First, there is what has been called pragmatic reduction. Here, categories are combined for *conceptual* reasons to yield a new typology. Less attention is paid to the actual distribution of cases or to whether the items are highly correlated. The items may be correlated, but not necessarily. In the second procedure, functional reduction, it is the distribution of cases that determines the resulting reduction. Categories are eliminated and combined according to the frequency with which the units of analysis exhibit certain combinations of attributes. As we have seen, the resulting reduced property space may be further reduced for conceptual reasons. It is thus possible to combine procedures. The third procedure is referred to as the arbitrary numerical procedure. Categories within the variables are assigned numbers. The variables are assigned weights. The reduction of property space takes place according to the combined "scores" received. It is this latter type of reduction that generally characterizes the construction of indexes from multiple items on questionnaires. Up to this point we have considered primarily the combination of two items. It is possible, of course, to extend the procedure to more than two items, as the law school example indicates. It is to some of these multiple item procedures that we now turn.

Summated Rating Scales

Adapting the numerical approach to property space reduction, we come up with summated rating scales, which combine the numerically coded responses to single items. These techniques involving more than two items are straightforward extensions of what we have discussed up to this point. You look for correlations among items. You combine those items that yield clusters of high correlations. Once combined, you examine the correlations between the individual items and the composite scores. Much of the mechanics of these operations will have to wait for Chapters 10 and 11. For now, assume you have a pool of items correlated with one another, and you want to combine responses for one composite index of the concept you are interested in.

Olsen used the following four items to construct a composite index of what he called political incapability/futility:

1. I believe public officials don't care much what people like me think.
2. There is no way other than voting that people like me can influence actions of the government.
3. Sometimes politics and government seem so complicated that I can't really understand what's going on.
4. People like me don't have any say about what the government does.

Though it diverges from the procedures followed by Olsen, assume you have a response format of "Strongly Agree," "Agree," "Disagree," and "Strongly Disagree" for each item, to which you assign the values of $+2$, $+1$, -1, and -2, respectively. The resulting summation of scores will range from $+8$, indicating high alienation in the political incapability sense of the concept, to -8, indicating lack of alienation from the political system in this same sense. What you have done is to reduce a rather large property space (256 categories, resulting from the combination of 4 categories within 4 items) to one of more modest proportions—17 categories.

What you have done to accomplish this is to treat a number of distinct patterns of responses as representing the same level of alienation. This procedure of treating a number of distinct response patterns as the same involves the assumption that items included are identical in the sense that they represent the same intensity of the concept being tapped. In the present instance the second question is a less harsh judgment against the political system than the fourth in that the second allows the voting influence and the fourth suggests no impact from individuals like the respondent. Hence, a problem.

In addition to this problem of differing intensity, the scale includes items designed to tap different dimensions of political incapability. Items 1, 2, and 4 seem to be tapping influence; item 3 taps level of understanding. When qualitative differences such as this are introduced into a scale, it is possible that the same "score" can cover up important differences in patterns. A score of $+1$ can indicate strong disagreement with item 3 and agreement with the remaining items. It also can represent strong disagreement with the second item and agreement with the rest. In the first instance we have individuals who feel quite confident of their ability to understand what is going on but feel it makes little difference in that persons like themselves have little influence on the outcome of governmental activities. In the second instance we have what appears to be a partially inconsistent response. Persons with this pattern are disagreeing with the statement that there is no other way except through voting that persons like themselves can influence outcomes and, at the same time, agreeing with the statement that persons like themselves don't have any say at all about what the government does.

In part, such an apparent inconsistency may be due to the dual nature of the second item. On the one hand, it asserts that voters have some influence. On the other, it asserts that there is no other route for such influence than through voting. Some persons might disagree with this statement because there are additional routes to influence or because they feel there are no routes, including voting, that influence outcomes.

Whatever the interpretation, it is clearly arguable that patterns of responses are equally important to overall scores in many situations. To ignore such distinctions is to introduce what might turn out to be important sources of measurement error. In some cases such sources of measurement error may turn out to be minor in terms of their implications for eventual findings. This is not the point. The point is that, before you simply fall into the trap of combining items into a composite numerical index, think through the implications of treating different patterns of responses as the same. The danger in this regard is perhaps greatest when you are combining items that are designed to tap qualitatively different dimensions of the underlying concept.

Practicum 8.4 **Prepare four items in the agree/disagree format that tap alienation from the respondent's own** *family.* **Design your items** so as to tap the influence and understanding dimensions of alienation in a fashion parallel to the scale utilized by Olsen for tapping alienation from the political system. Now, add two additional items in the same format designed to tap what you consider to be another important dimension of alienation. What problems do you foresee when you combine the items into one overall summated index? What important response pattern differences are likely to be covered up by such a procedure?

Scalogram Analysis

Another commonly employed method of property space reduction, when multiple items are involved, is *Guttman Scaling* (Guttman, 1950). The reduction is accomplished according to a combination of pragmatic and functional assumptions as discussed above. Scale types are determined by noting frequently occurring patterns that are predicted in line with certain conceptual assumptions.

Consider the following:

1. Homosexuals should not be allowed to hold important positions in running the country.
   A. Agree
   B. Disagree
2. Homosexuals should not be allowed to hold any elected office, even when the position is not influential.
   A. Agree
   B. Disagree
3. Homosexuals should not be allowed to get involved in political campaigns.
   A. Agree
   B. Disagree
4. Homosexuals should not be allowed to influence the political process in any way.
   A. Agree
   B. Disagree

As we will now explore, one advantage of the Guttman scaling techniques is that they allow you to establish the *pattern* of responses as well as a single score. This is possible since the assumption is that the scale items can be arranged along a single continuum according to their "intensity." In the above example the questions can be arranged according to the degree of permissiveness or restrictiveness they reflect in terms of political power and influence allowed to a certain category of persons—homosexuals. Using parallel questions it would also be possible to obtain readings on such other groups as drug addicts, ex-convicts, Protestants, Catholics, blacks, John Birchers, and so forth. However, this gets us ahead of ourselves.

The conceptual assumption is that these questions can be arranged along a single continuum from permissive to restrictive boundaries in terms of political influence. It is this assumption of the unidimensional ordering of questions that allows the prediction of certain *patterns* of responses given certain "scores."

Persons at the restrictive end of the continuum are not going to allow any influence in the political process. Hence, they are not going to allow involvement in political campaigns, minor office-holding, or major office-holding. They will thus agree with all of the statements, giving a pattern of + + + +. See Figure 8.7. Persons agreeing with three of the items will be located further toward the permissive end of the continuum and thus will disagree with the "No Influence" item, given a pattern of − + + +. Persons unwilling to cut off involvement in political campaigns may still restrict holding of even minor elective offices, but, if they restrict minor offices, they surely will restrict major offices. Thus, agreement with two items will involve the pattern − − + +. A fourth pattern of responses involves agreement with one item. Since, as we have seen, agreement with the minor office, the political campaign, and the "No Influence" items implies agreement with at least one additional item in the battery of questions, the pattern of response with one agreement is − − − +. Finally, there are those who would not put any of the listed restrictions on homosexuals, yielding the − − − − pattern.

Thus we end up with a property space of 5 scale types. This is a reduction from an original 16- ($2 \times 2 \times 2 \times 2$) celled matrix. Any departures from these patterns are treated as "errors," evidence that the assumption of a unidimensional ordering of questions was unwarranted. It is the degree to which errors of this type are made that determines whether or not a number of items in a given pool are scalable.

If we are working from a conceptual foundation rather than attempting to discover which items "scale" for whatever reason, the procedure for determining the degree to which the items fall as predicted is rather simple. First, based on your conceptualization, you list the scale types, as has been done in Figure 8.7. Next, you determine the number of positive responses each respondent has. Referring to your predicted patterns you obtain the appropriate prediction for the pattern of responses. Patterns that vary from the predictions, such as − + + −, are treated as containing errors. The number of errors contained will depend on the rules you use. If, for example, you predict according to the number of positive responses, the above pattern would contain two errors. It is compared with Scale Type III in Figure 8.7 since there are two positive responses. An error is made with the final − and the + under item 3. The rules of prediction differ when items are not assumed in a priori fashion to fall in a certain order. These calculations are based on the marginal distribution of cases, that is, on the percentage of persons answering in the affirmative to certain items. Items toward the

FIGURE 8.7
Patterns of Predicted Responses Given Four Scalable Items

		Item*	4	3	2	1
Most Restrictive	Scale Type V (4 positives)		+	+	+	+
	Scale Type IV (3 positives)		−	+	+	+
	Scale Type IV (2 positives)		−	−	+	+
	Scale Type II (1 positive)		−	−	−	+
Least Restrictive	Scale Type I (0 positives)		−	−	−	−

* 4: allow no influence.
  3: no involvement in political campaigns.
  2: allow no minor office holding.
  1: allow no major office holding.

extremes will have the highest proportion of positive or negative responses, depending on the "direction" of the wording.

A problem with this latter procedure, a problem that is dealt with in some detail in Maranell (1974), is that chance factors operate in such a fashion when coupled with these after-the-fact predictions that almost any set of items, especially when there are less than five, form some sort of scale. Thus, unless you hypothesize the appropriate patterns beforehand, the Guttman scaling techniques should be used with a good deal of caution.

Further considerations that make this strategy for combining items somewhat less than ideal is the consideration that approximately the same outcome frequently can be obtained with far fewer questions. When you are concerned with efficient questionnaire design, and you should always be concerned with these matters, this may turn out to be a major shortcoming. Recall that the assumption under which the Guttman scaling techniques operate is unidimensionality and ordered intensity of items. Why not construct a single unidimensional question with a detailed response format that categorizes individuals the same as would be accomplished with the more numerous items? You might, for example, simply ask a single question something like, "How much influence would you allow homosexuals to have in political life?" "A very great deal," "Quite a bit," "Some," "Hardly any at all," or "None."

In some situations a single item will handle your measurement problems quite adequately. In others multiple items will seem more appropriate. Keeping in mind what has been said to this point, you will have to balance the demands for space in your questionnaire against the sometimes more detailed analysis that multiple questions, taken by themselves or in the form of a composite index, allow.

Practicum 8.5 Construct a five-item *Guttman Scale* for a concept of your choosing. What ambiguities, if any, are there in your arrangement of the items? What are the hypothesized patterns of response?

OVERALL FORMAT

The content of questions, the structure of responses, and the use of individual items or composite indicators are important considerations. Equally important is the overall format of the questionnaire—whether it appears cluttered or open, whether it appears complex or simple. Guides in terms of section headings, instructions as to how to mark questions, and coding facilitators for transfer of the material to computer cards can minimize errors and ambiguities in later analysis. It is to the overall format that we now turn.

Question Order

The ordering of questions is one of the most important issues in any questionnaire or interview format. It is also one of the more ambiguous to resolve. Fortunately, there is some useful folk-wisdom. The ordering of questions can be important for a number of reasons. Presenting one set of questions before another may "lead" respondents into certain later responses. In a long list of questions using the same response format, a strategy designed to make the questionnaire look less cluttered and more efficient in terms of how long it takes to answer may contain some quite distinct questions and this may "jog" the attention of the respondent. In the questionnaire reproduced in Figure 8.8, for example, there is the statement, "I feel at ease when I am at home." This is followed directly by the statement, "Teenagers who break the law are caught." On the other hand, question similarity may be the problem. You will recall that certain very similar items frequently are included in a questionnaire to check on yeasayers and naysayers, as well as other sources of measurement error. If these are close in the questionnaire, much of their utility is lost.

Unfortunately, any order of questions has certain limitations when it comes to leading patterns and mind-jogging discontinuities. If you think there may be problems in this regard, devise more than one format and try out each one to see if systematic differences in the patterns of responses occur.

Another important consideration is what questions to ask at the outset. Here, there is a good deal of folk-wisdom which indicates that you should ease into it. Begin with questions that are interesting enough to keep the conversation moving but not too sharp so as to be offensive. It is one thing to open the questionnaire reprinted in Figure 8.8 by asking the respondent to agree or disagree with the relatively inoffensive statement, "Life usually hands me a pretty good deal." It would have been quite another matter to begin with the question contained in a later portion, "Have you ever used a needle to inject (or had someone else inject) yourself with opiates, speed, or similar drugs?" In a similar fashion it is not a good idea to begin an interview on attitudes toward changing laws with, "Hello, how are you? What are your attitudes toward abortion." Again it is a matter of interpersonal sensitivity. It is certainly not a matter that should be neglected as unimportant. You may want to spend some time during your pretesting trying out alternatives. The way an interview or questionnaire-answering session is initiated is closely tied to the eventual quality of the data collected. Create and maintain interest, but do not pose an immediate threat.

Guideposts

There are a number of ways to improve questionnaires through the use of periodic guideposts. Initially, it is a good idea to include a brief section giving an overview of the study and what will be expected of the respondent. Throughout the questionnaire it is also a good idea to break the schedule into sections with brief notes on the mechanics of answering the questions—to "circle" or "x" and so forth. These intermediate summaries and directions foster a feeling for what is about to be covered as well as a feeling of completion in that a section has been finished.

It is also a good idea to include a set of guideposts on the questionnaire page for later use when the information is transferred to computer cards. Appendix E includes a more detailed discussion of this translation of information into a form processable by the computer. For now it is enough to note that, by including such guidelines, later difficulties with keypunching can be minimized. Here, again, your judgment will be called for. It is possible to include "coding" information with each question. Such a procedure, indicating which column on the computer card responses to given questions are to entered, however, may give a cluttered appearance to the questionnaire. Hence, it is a more esthetically pleasing and no less efficient method to incorporate periodic checkpoints, say, at the beginning and end of each page, to allow the keypuncher to make periodic checks. Also, where possible, you should include the numbers to be used as codes with your responses to the questions. For example, in Figure 8.8, respondents were asked to circle the appropriate numbers that could later be transferred directly to the computer cards.

An Example

Some of these points are best understood by referring to an actual questionnaire. For this purpose we have included a modified version of a questionnaire developed in part with Ronald Akers. This questionnaire was designed for administration to senior high-school students.

FIGURE 8.8

The following is a short questionnaire (it will take about 45–50 minutes) designed to tap feelings and experiences of persons like yourself. We are interested in how you feel at the present, some of your past experiences, and what you anticipate your life will be like in the future. These questions are designed to see how *you* feel. There are no right or wrong answers. You are to place your questionnaire through the slot in the box at the front of the room when you are finished. Thus, your answers will be anonymous. Thank you for your considered opinions and answers.

-1-

244 Ideas and Data

FIGURE 8.8 (*continued*)

YOUR PRESENT VIEWS

> In this first section we are interested in your views of your
> family, school, the law, and life in general. Some questions may
> seem repetitious. However, please consider each one separately.
> The responses are Strongly Agree (SA), Agree (A), Disagree (D),
> and Strongly Disagree (SD). Please *circle* the number that
> corresponds to your answer.

card 1,6

		SA	A	D	SD
1.	Life usually hands me a pretty good deal.	1	2	3	4
2.	I often feel like I would like to leave home	1	2	3	4
3.	School is a waste of time	1	2	3	4
4.	Most of my teachers try to help me when I need it	1	2	3	4
5.	My mother doesn't understand me	1	2	3	4
6.	My father doesn't understand me	1	2	3	4
7.	We are close to one another in my family.	1	2	3	4
8.	Persons who break the law are generally caught	1	2	3	4
9.	Laws are generally fair	1	2	3	4
10.	I have a good deal of respect for my father	1	2	3	4
11.	Most of my friends understand me	1	2	3	4
12.	I am anxious to get out on my own	1	2	3	4
13.	If you study hard it will pay off	1	2	3	4
14.	I have a good deal of respect for my mother.	1	2	3	4
15.	I find it easy to talk to one or both of my parents about matters that are important to me.	1	2	3	4

column 20

-2-

FIGURE 8.8 (*continued*)

> We shift slightly in this next section and ask you to report *how frequently* you feel in particular ways. Again, please *circle* the number corresponding to your answer.

	Most of the Time	*Some- times*	*Hardly Ever*	*Never*
1. I feel happy	1	2	3	4
2. I feel like I really don't belong.	1	2	3	4
3. I like school.	1	2	3	4
4. I feel at ease when I am at home	1	2	3	4
5. Teenagers who break the law are caught . .	1	2	3	4
6. My mother is a fair person when she dis- agrees with something I have done	1	2	3	4
7. When I try something, I try my best	1	2	3	4
8. Teenagers who are caught for breaking laws are treated fairly.	1	2	3	4
9. I feel I am just no good	1	2	3	4
10. My father is a fair person when he dis- agrees with something I have done	1	2	3	4

column 30

FIGURE 8.8 (*continued*)

YOUR ANTICIPATED FUTURE

> In this section we shift from how you feel to how you see your future turning out. Estimate what you see the chances are and then *circle* the number for the appropriate response.

	Quite High (90–100%)	Pretty High (60–80%)	About 50/50	Pretty Low (10–40%)	Very Low (less than 10%)
1. What are the chances you will do things that *could* get you into serious trouble with the law by the time you are 21.	1	2	3	4	5
2. What are the chances you will eventually end up in a good paying job.	1	2	3	4	5
3. What are the chances you will eventually end up in an interesting job	1	2	3	4	5
4. What are the chances your future life will be happy	1	2	3	4	5
5. What are the chances you will get married by the time you are 25	1	2	3	4	5
6. What are the chances you will take an active role in community affairs after you are 21	1	2	3	4	5
7. What are the chances you will get as much education as you want.	1	2	3	4	5
8. If you broke the law for something other than a minor traffic violation, what are the chances you would get caught.	1	2	3	4	5

column 38

-4-

FIGURE 8.8 (*continued*)

DURING THE PAST YEAR

The focus of the next questions is on the past. Please think back carefully over the past year and indicate how many times you found yourself in the various situations. Some of the questions deal with activities that many would consider to be wrong. We are not trying to make you feel uncomfortable. We are simply trying to see how widespread some of these activities and feelings are. Please be straightforward in your answers. *Circle the number that corresponds to the number of times listed above these numbers.*

During the Past Year	Never	Once	Two to Five Times	More than Five Times
1. How often have you had a good talk with one or both of your parents	0	1	2	3
2. How often have you gotten into trouble at school.	0	1	2	3
3. How often have you *actually* gotten into trouble with the police.	0	1	2	3
4. How often have you had a serious argument with one or both of your parents	0	1	2	3
5. How often have one or more of your *close* friends done things that *could* have gotten them into trouble with the police.	0	1	2	3
6. How often have you felt unfairly treated. . . .	0	1	2	3
7. How often have one or more of your *close* friends *actually* gotten into trouble with the police for more than a minor traffic violation	0	1	2	3

column 45

FIGURE 8.8 (*continued*)

During the Past Year	*Never*	*Once*	*Two to Five Times*	*More than Five Times*
8. How often have you done things that could have gotten you into trouble with the police	0	1	2	3
9. How often have you felt really guilty for things you have done.	0	1	2	3
10. How often have you beaten up on someone other than your brothers or sisters	0	1	2	3
11. How often have you taken something worth more than $5.00 that didn't belong to you	0	1	2	3

Again, during the Past Year . . .

	Never	*Hardly Ever*	*Sometimes*	*Most of the Time*
12. How often have you felt really good about yourself	0	1	2	3
13. How often have you felt the world was a good place to be in	0	1	2	3
14. How often have you resented having to go to school.	0	1	2	3
15. How often have you felt things in general were getting worse rather than better	0	1	2	3
16. How often have you felt close to your mother or father.	0	1	2	3
17. How often have you felt close to one or more of your friends	0	1	2	3
18. How often have you felt you really didn't "belong"	0	1	2	3
19. How often have you felt really "free".	0	1	2	3

column 57

FIGURE 8.8 (*continued*)

DRUG USAGE

The questions in this section ask about attitudes, opinions, and practices relating to the use of drugs. Throughout this section this means *use of drugs without medical supervision or for purposes other than medication.* All of the questions in this section should be *answered by drawing a circle around the number* of the answer in the same way you answered the questions in the previous sections.

1. About how many persons do you know personally who have ever used marihuana, LSD, or any other drugs?
   1. None
   2. One or two
   3. Three or four
   4. Five or more

2. About how many of the friends with whom you associate *most* often have ever used marihuana, LSD, or any other drugs?
   1. None
   2. One or two
   3. Three or four
   4. Five or more

	Never	Once or Twice	Several Times	Often
3. Have you ever sampled or tried marihuana (taken at least a drag or two) even if you felt no effects.	0	1	2	3
4. Have you ever used enough marihuana at one time to feel the effects from it.	0	1	2	3
5. How often have you used, at least sampled, or tried opiates (heroin, smack, etc.).	0	1	2	3
6. How often have you used LSD	0	1	2	3
7. How often have you used amphetamines (speed, pep pills, etc.)	0	1	2	3
8. How often have you used barbiturates for purposes other than medication (reds, yellow jackets, etc.).	0	1	2	3

column 65

-7-

FIGURE 8.8 (*continued*)

---

card 2,6

9. How often have you sniffed glue?
    1. Never
    2. Once or twice
    3. Several times
    4. Often or regularly

10. Have you used a needle to inject (or had someone else inject) yourself with opiates, speed, or similar drugs?
    1. Never
    2. Once or twice
    3. Several times
    4. Often

11. If you have ever used drugs, even if just a sample or try, how old were you when you first tried any drug?
    1. Have never used drugs
    2. Less than 10 years old
    3. 11–12 years old
    4. 13–14 years old
    5. 15–16 years old
    6. 17 years or older

12. What was the very *first* drug you ever used? (circle only one)
    1. Have never used drugs
    2. Amphetamine
    3. Barbiturates
    4. LSD
    5. Marihuana
    6. Opiates
    7. Other

13. If you have tried more than one kind of drug, what was the *second* drug you ever used? (circle only one)
    1. Have never used drugs
    2. Amphetamine
    3. Barbiturates
    4. Marihuana
    5. Opiates
    6. LSD
    7. Other

column 10

-8-

FIGURE 8.8 (*continued*)

14. How long have you used drugs, or how long did you use drugs if you have now stopped?
    1. Have never used drugs
    2. Used once or twice and have not used since
    3. Used drugs less than three months
    4. Used drugs three to six months
    5. Used drugs six months to a year
    6. Used drugs more than a year

15. Who was with you at the time you first tried any drug? (circle *any* that apply)
    1. Have never used drugs
    2. Friends
    3. Brothers or sisters
    4. Other people
    5. No one

16. Which one of the following best describes the *most important* reason for taking your first drug? (circle only *one*)
    1. Have never used drugs
    2. To see what it was like
    3. I was dared or urged to
    4. I was tricked into thinking it was something else
    5. I was rebelling against always being told not to do things
    6. To be sociable or part of the group

17. If you have ever used drugs, regardless of which kind or how much, have you used them at any of the following places?

    Yes No
    1   2   At home
    1   2   At a friend's home
    1   2   In or around cars
    1   2   On or around school grounds
    1   2   Any place where adults are not likely to be
    1   2   Other places (specify)_

    _____

    1   I never use drugs

column 24

-9-

FIGURE 8.8 *(continued)*

---

18. Are your *friends* likely to use drugs in any of the following places?

    Yes No
    1   2   At home
    1   2   At a friend's home
    1   2   In or around cars
    1   2   On or around school grounds
    1   2   Any place where adults are not likely to be
    1   2   Other places (specify)

        1   Friends never use drugs
        _____

19. Are other *teenagers* who use drugs likely to use them in any of the following places?

    Yes No
    1   2   At home
    1   2   At a friend's home
    1   2   In or around cars
    1   2   On or around school grounds
    1   2   Any place where adults are not likely to be
    1   2   Other places (specify)

        _____

20. If you use drugs, with whom are you *most* likely to do so? (circle only *one*)
    1. With friends
    2. With teenage relatives
    3. With adults
    4. With anyone who wants to
    5. Alone
    6. I never use drugs

21. With whom are your *friends* who use drugs most likely to use them? (circle only *one*)
    1. With friends
    2. With teenage relatives
    3. With adults
    4. With anyone who wants to
    5. Alone
    6. Friends never use drugs

column 39

FIGURE 8.8 (*continued*)

22. With whom are other *teenagers* who use drugs most likely to use them? (circle only *one*)
    1. With friends
    2. With teenage relatives
    3. With adults
    4. With anyone who wants to
    5. Alone

23. If you use drugs, are you likely to use them on any of the following occasions?

    Yes No
    1 2   Before or after going to a movie, party, show, sports event, etc.
    1 2   On single or double dates
    1 2   At teenage parties where there are no adults supervising
    1 2   Anytime I can get them and a chance to use them
    1 2   At home or elsewhere when parents or other adults are present
    1 2   Whenever I can get together with one or more friends
    1   I never use drugs

24. Are you friends likely to use drugs on any of the following occasions?

    Yes No
    1 2   Before or after going to a movie, party, show, sports event, etc.
    1 2   On single or double dates
    1 2   At teenage parties where there are no adults supervising
    1 2   Anytime they can get them and a chance to use them
    1 2   At home or elsewhere when parents or other adults are present
    1 2   Whenever they can get together with one or more friends
    1   Friends never use drugs

25. Are other *teenagers* who use drugs likely to use them on any of the following occasions?

    Yes No
    1 2   Before or after going to a movie, party, show, sports event, etc.
    1 2   On single or double dates
    1 2   At teenage parties where there are no adults supervising
    1 2   Anytime they can get them and a chance to use them
    1 2   At home or elsewhere when parents or other adults are present
    1 2   Whenever they can get together with one or more friends

column 60

-11-

FIGURE 8.8 (*continued*)

---

card 3,6

26. Here is a list of statements sometimes made about drugs. If you personally would make that statement about drugs, circle the ① under *Yes*. If you would not make that statement, circle the ② under *No*.

Yes No

1   2   Drugs help me enjoy a party
1   2   Using drugs often leads to trouble
1   2   Drugs help me forget my problems
1   2   Drugs help me feel at ease at social gatherings
1   2   Drugs are entirely and completely a social evil
1   2   Drugs help me feel more satisfied with myself
1   2   Drugs are bad for one's health
1   2   Drugs give me confidence in myself
1   2   Drugs always cause problems for the user and his or her community
1   2   Drugs help me feel better when I'm sad
1   2   Drugs help me get along better with people
1   2   People often do things while using drugs that they would not do ordinarily
1   2   Drugs help me do things more easily
1   2   Drugs help me bear doing certain unpleasant things

27. In your opinion, what are the main reasons *adults* who use drugs do so? (circle *no more than three*)
    1. To celebrate some occasion
    2. Because they like the effects of drugs
    3. Because it is a habit with them
    4. To be sociable or part of the group
    5. Because they are unhappy, worried, or have problems
    6. Because it makes them feel smart or important
    7. To change their mood (to feel better, confident, relaxed, pepped-up, etc.)

28. In your opinion, what are the main reasons *teenagers* use drugs? (circle *no more than three*)
    1. To celebrate some occasion
    2. Because they like the effects of drugs
    3. Because it is a habit with them
    4. To be sociable or part of the group
    5. Because they are unhappy, worried, or have problems
    6. Because it makes them feel smart or important
    7. To act adult or grown up
    8. To change their mood (to feel better, confident, relaxed, pepped-up, etc.)

-12-   **column 34**

FIGURE 8.8 (*continued*)

29. In your opinion, what are the main reasons your friends who use drugs do so?
    (circle *no more than three*)
    1. Friends never use drugs
    2. To celebrate some occasion
    3. Because they like the effects of drugs
    4. Because it is a habit with them
    5. To be sociable or part of the group
    6. Because they are unhappy, worried, or have problems
    7. Because it makes them feel smart or important
    8. To act adult or grown up
    9. To change their mood (to feel better, confident, relaxed, pepped-up,
       etc.)

30. If you have never used drugs of any kind, which of the following describe
    your reasons for not using drugs? (circle the ① under *Yes* if the reason
    applies to you; circle the ② under *No* if it does not)

    Yes No
    1   2   Because my parents don't want me to
    1   2   Because my friends don't want me to
    1   2   Because I dont't think I am old enough yet
    1   2   Because it is against my religion or it is morally wrong
    1   2   Because I think drug use is bad for one's health
    1   2   Because I have seen what happens to addicts and people with drug
             problems and I don't want that to happen to me
    1   2   Because it is against the law and I might get caught
    1   2   Because I think the first time is the one that starts you on the road
             to a habit
    1   2   Because I have never had a chance to try drugs
         1   I have used drugs

column 53

-13-

FIGURE 8.8 *(continued)*

31. If you have used any drug at least once or twice but no longer use it, which of the following describe your reasons for not using that drug anymore?

Yes No

1 2 Because my parents didn't want me to use the drug
1 2 Because my friends didn't want me to use the drug
1 2 Because I didn't like the effects of the drug
1 2 Because I felt that I wasn't old enough to keep using the drug
1 2 Because I felt it was bad for my health
1 2 Because I was afraid that if I kept using it I would get a habit
1 2 Because I have seen what happens to addicts and people with drug problems and I didn't want that to happen to me
1 2 Because it is against the law and I was afraid I might get caught
1 2 Because I have not had the chance anymore
1 2 Because I stopped getting the effects I wanted
   1   I have not used any drug

32. If you are using any drug now, which of the following describe your reasons for doing so? (if you do not now use drugs, go to question 34)

Yes No

1 2 To celebrate certain occasions
1 2 To rebel against always being told not to do things
1 2 Because I like the effects
1 2 To be sociable or part of the group
1 2 To change my mood (to feel better, more at ease, relaxed, pepped-up, etc.)
1 2 Because I think I am old enough
1 2 No special reason; I just think "Why not?"
1 2 Because there is nothing else to do

column 72

FIGURE 8.8 (*continued*)

---

card 4,6

33. If you now use drugs, would any of the following reasons probably cause you to stop using drugs?

Yes No

1	2	If using drugs made it difficult to study
1	2	If my friends didn't use drugs
1	2	If my parents found out
1	2	If I got arrested for using drugs
1	2	If I no longer got high using drugs
1	2	If my health was being harmed
1	2	If I thought I was getting a habit
1	2	If using drugs made it difficult to get into college
1	2	If using drugs made it difficult for me to get a job
1	2	If using drugs made it difficult for me to be good at the work I want to do

34. Think of *adults* (including parents and other adults) *whose opinions you value* or think are important. As far as you know, what is the attitude most of them have toward the use of *marihuana*? (circle *one*)
    1. Most of them think it is alright. They *approve*
    2. Most sometimes approve and sometimes disapprove, *depending upon the circumstances*
    3. Most think it is wrong. They *disapprove*
    4. Most don't seem to care one way or the other. They *don't have definite ideas about it*

35. What is the attitude most of these adults have toward use of other drugs? (circle *one*)
    1. Most of them think it is alright. They *approve*
    2. Most sometimes approve and sometimes disapprove, *depending upon the circumstances*
    3. Most think it is wrong. They *disapprove*
    4. Most don't seem to care one way or the other. They *don't have definite ideas about it*

column 18

FIGURE 8.8 (*continued*)

36. Think now of the *teenagers whose opinions you value.* As far as you know,
    what is their attitude toward use of *marihuana?* (circle *one*)
    1. Most of them think it is alright. They *approve*
    2. Most sometimes approve and sometimes disapprove, *depending upon
       the circumstances*
    3. Most think it is wrong. They *disapprove*
    4. Most don't seem to care one way or the other. They *don't have definite
       ideas about it*
37. What is their attitude toward use of other drugs? (circle *one*)
    1. Most of them think it is alright. They *approve*
    2. Most sometimes approve and sometimes disapprove, *depending upon
       the circumstances*
    3. Most think it is wrong. They *disapprove*
    4. Most don't seem to care one way or the other. They *don't have definite
       ideas about it*

What is *your* attitude toward the use of the following drugs?

38. *Marihuana*
    1. I think it is alright. I *approve*
    2. I sometimes approve and sometimes disapprove, *depending upon the
       circumstances*
    3. I think it is wrong. I *disapprove*
    4. I don't care one way or the other. I *don't have definite ideas about it*
39. *Opiates* (heroin, heavy drugs, etc.)
    1. I think it is alright. I *approve*
    2. I sometimes approve and sometimes disapprove, *depending upon the
       circumstances*
    3. I think it is wrong. I *disapprove*
    4. I don't care one way or the other. I *don't have definite ideas about it*
40. *LSD*
    1. I think it is alright. I *approve*
    2. I sometimes approve and sometimes disapprove, *depending upon the
       circumstances*
    3. I think it is wrong. I *disapprove*
    4. I don't care one way or the other. I *don't have definite ideas about it*
41. *Other Drugs* (goof balls, reds, crystals, bennies, etc.)
    1. I think it is alright. I *approve*
    2. I sometimes approve and sometimes disapprove, *depending upon the
       circumstances*
    3. I think it is wrong. I *disapprove*
    4. I don't care one way or the other. I *don't have definite ideas about it*

column 24

-16-

FIGURE 8.8 *(continued)*

42. What are your ideas about when it is wrong and when it is all right to use drugs? (circle the ① if you agree with the statement; circle the ② if you do not agree)

Dis-
Agree agree

Agree	Disagree	
1	2	It is alright if a person doesn't get the habit
1	2	It is alright as long as it doesn't hurt anyone
1	2	It is alright for adults but not for persons under 15
1	2	It is alright for teenagers but adults should leave drugs alone
1	2	It is alright for someone underage with parents' permission
1	2	It is wrong, but I don't condemn persons who can't help themselves
1	2	It is wrong, but it is a person's own business
1	2	It is never right to use drugs (other than for medication)

43. Have your parents ever found out you were using marihuana?
    1. Yes
    2. No

44. If yes, what did they do? (circle as many as apply)
    1. They *approved*
    2. They disapproved but *did nothing*
    3. They disapproved and *discussed* it with me
    4. They disapproved and *scolded or punished* me for it
    5. They turned me over to the officials
    6. I never use marihuana

45. Have your parents ever found out you were using drugs other than marihuana?
    1. Yes
    2. No
    If yes, what did they do? (circle as many as apply)
    1. They *approved*
    2. They disapproved but *did nothing*
    3. They disapproved and *discussed* it with me
    4. They disapproved and *scolded or punished* me for it
    5. They turned me over to the officials
    6. I never use drugs

column 46

-17-

FIGURE 8.8 *(continued)*

46. If you were to use marihuana and your parents were to find out about it, what do you think they *probably would do*? (circle as many as apply)
    1. They would probably *approve*
    2. They would probably disapprove but *do nothing* about it
    3. They would probably disapprove and *discuss* it with me
    4. They would probably disapprove and *scold or punish* me for it
    5. They would probably turn me over to the officials

47. If you have ever used marihuana, what has been the reaction of most of your *friends who also use marihuana*?
    1. They approve and *encourage* me
    2. They approve but *don't encourage* me
    3. They disapprove but *do nothing* about it.
    4. They disapprove and *discourage* me
    5. I never use marihuana
    6. My friends never use marihuana

48. If you have ever used other *drugs* (other than marihuana), what has been the reaction of most of your friends who also use other drugs?
    1. They approve and *encourage* me
    2. They approve but *don't encourage* me
    3. They disapprove but *do nothing* about it
    4. They disapprove and *discourage* me

49. If you have ever used marihuana, what has been the reaction of most of *your friends who do not use any drugs*?
    1. They approve and *encourage* me
    2. They approve but *don't encourage* me
    3. They disapprove but *do nothing* about it
    4. They disapprove and *discourage* me

50. If you have ever used *other* drugs (other than marihuana), what has been the reaction of *your friends who do not use any drugs*?
    1. They approve and *encourage* me
    2. They approve but *don't encourage* me
    3. They disapprove but *do nothing* about it
    4. They disapprove and *discourage* me

column 55

FIGURE 8.8 *(continued)*

For each statement below, please circle whether you strongly agree, agree, disagree, strongly disagree with, or have no opinion on it.

	Strongly Agree	Agree	No Opinion	Dis-agree	Strongly Disagree
51. The laws against the use of marihuana should be obeyed. . . .	1	2	3	4	5
52. The laws against the use of other drugs should be obeyed . . .	1	2	3	4	5
53. The fact that it is against the law does not necessarily make the use of drugs wrong.	1	2	3	4	5
54. Penalties for marihuana should be lowered.	1	2	3	4	5
55. Marihuana use should be legalized	1	2	3	4	5
56. Other drug use should be legalized	1	2	3	4	5
57. Teenagers who use drugs really shouldn't be held responsible since they are under too much pressure to resist.	1	2	3	4	5
58. People shouldn't condemn teenagers for using drugs since it really doesn't hurt anyone	1	2	3	4	5
59. Adults have no right to con-demn teenagers for using drugs since they do things just as bad or worse	1	2	3	4	5

column 64

FIGURE 8.8 *(continued)*

---

card 5,6

60. Have any of the following happened to you while or soon after using drugs? (if you do not use drugs, go on to next question)

Yes No

1	2	Been worried about your drug use
1	2	Gotten high but not really loaded
1	2	Gotten really loaded
1	2	Passed out
1	2	Gotten into a fight
1	2	Been picked up by the police on a drug charge
1	2	Been picked up by the police but for something other than drugs
1	2	Had a traffic accident
1	2	Gotten into trouble with teachers or other adults
1	2	Been unable to remember what happened while using drugs

61. How likely is it that a teenager who uses drugs will get into trouble with parents for it?
    1. Very likely
    2. Likely
    3. As likely to get into trouble as not
    4. Unlikely
    5. Very unlikely

62. How likely is it that a teenager who uses drugs will get into trouble with the police for it?
    1. Very likely
    2. Likely
    3. As likely to get into trouble as not
    4. Unlikely
    5. Very unlikely

How often have you had any of the following?

	Never	Sipped, or Sampled	Once in a While	Several Times	Often or Regularly
63. Beer	1	2	3	4	5
64. Wine.	1	2	3	4	5
65. Whiskey, gin, vodka, mixed drinks, or other liquor	1	2	3	4	5
66. Tobacco	1	2	3	4	5
67. Coffee	1	2	3	4	5

column 22

-20-

FIGURE 8.8 *(continued)*

GENERAL INFORMATION

Finally, we would like some general information about your background. Again, let me emphasize your responses will be kept anonymous. However, if you feel you do not want to answer these questions, just leave them blank and turn in your questionnaire through the slot in the box at the front of the room.

1. When were you born? _____
                      (month)   (day)   (year)

2. What is your sex?
   1. Male
   2. Female

3. Which group is closest to your own heritage?
   1. Blacks/Negro
   2. Mexican-American/Chicano
   3. White/Anglo
   4. Oriental
   5. Native American/Indian
   6. Other

4. How frequently have you moved in the past five years?
   1. None
   2. Once
   3. Twice
   4. Three or more times

5. When was the last time you moved?
   _____ months/years ago (circle appropriate time frame)

6. How long have you gone to this school?
   _____ months/years (circle appropriate time frame)

7. Are your parents living?
   1. Both are living
   2. Only father is living
   3. Only mother is living
   4. Neither is living

column 36

-21-

FIGURE 8.8 (*continued*)

8. If both parents are living are they
   1. Living together
   2. Separated
   3. Divorced
9. If both parents are living, how long have they been married, separated, divorced?
   1. Less than three months
   2. Three months to a year
   3. One to three years
   4. Three years or more
10. What class or grade in school are you in now?
    1. 9th
    2. 10th
    3. 11th
    4. 12th
11. What kind of grades do you usually make in school?
    1. Mostly A's
    2. Mostly B's
    3. Mostly C's
    4. Mostly below C
12. Do you have or have you had a part-time or full-time job during the current school year?
    1. Yes
    2. No
13. Have you had at least a 20-hr/week summer job between school years?
    1. Yes
    2. No
14. Write the number of older or younger brothers and sisters you have. (if you have none, write none)
    _____Younger brothers and sisters
    _____Older brothers and sisters
15. If you could go as far as you want, how much education do you hope to get?
    1. Less than high school
    2. Finish high school only
    3. Technical or business school
    4. Some college
    5. Finish college
    6. Beyond college

column 47

FIGURE 8.8 *(concluded)*

16. How much education do you *actually* expect to get?
    1. Less than high school
    2. Finish high school only
    3. Technical or business school
    4. Some college
    5. Finish college
    6. Beyond college
17. Which of the following best describes what kind of job you probably will get immediately upon leaving high school (not counting summer jobs)?
    1. Will probably get a *full-time job* after leaving high school
    2. Will probably get a *part-time job* after leaving high school
    3. Will probably *not* get a job right after leaving high school
    4. Will probably enter the *Armed Forces* after leaving high school
    5. Don't know
18. Regardless of your education and job plans, do you plan to get married after leaving high school?
    1. I plan to get married before finishing high school
    2. I plan to get married *within a year or so* after leaving high school
    3. I plan to get married *later than three years* after leaving high school
    4. Don't know

Thank you for your considered opinions. Place the completed questionnaire through the slot in the box in the front of the room.

column 50

Practicum 8.6   Take the questionnaire in Figure 8.8 as if you were a respondent. Keeping in mind the material covered in this chapter, what problems do you see in the questionnaire? How might these be remedied? What problems seem to be insoluble if we want to maintain the same focus of the study?

SUMMARY

In this chapter we have noted both the potential and the limitations of structured questionnaires and interviews when it comes to translating analytic concepts into concrete research operations. Questionnaires are most useful when tapping present opinions and attitudes. They are less useful and, at times, misleading when tapping behavior, either past or future. When you desire measures of anticipated or past behavior, you should, whenever possible, build in checks. You should be particularly concerned with checking on the "socially desirable response" syndrome. There are ways through assurances of anonymity to partially deal with this problem. Nevertheless, the interview situation remains a social occasion guided by the same interpersonal dynamics that operate in day-to-day life. Hence, interpersonal sensitivity is also called for. Again, whenever possible, check.

The content of questions and the format of responses remain at the heart of the instrument. Spend time gleaning from the work of others, modifying and replacing where necessary. Develop your theoretical rationale as you go along. Given demands for concise designs, it is rarely a good idea to simply throw in a few extra questions because they sound good.

When designing the overall format, pay attention to details. Avoid a cluttered appearnce. Work on question ordering. Work on introductions and periodic guideposts. Be explicit in your directions to respondents and interviewers. Keep in mind that later analysis on the computer can be facilitated by minor checkpoints for the keypuncher and "coder." Much improvement along these lines can be gained through pretesting the format.

KEY ISSUES

1. What are points of caution that should be noted when designing a survey study?
2. What are the reasons you should pretest your research instrument?
3. What is meant by the property space of a concept?
4. What are the various types of property space reduction? How are these related to summated rating scales and scalogram analysis?
5. What are the pros and cons of using composite indexes and individual items?

6. What assumptions are made about the nature of individual items when combining them into a single summated index or when combining them for the purposes of scalogram analysis?

REFERENCES

Barton, Allen H.
   1955 "The Concept of Property Space in Social Research." In Paul F. Lazarsfeld and Morris Rosenberg (eds.), *The Language of Social Research.* New York: The Free Press.

Bernal, Helen Hazuda
   1975 Climate of Perceived Organizational Control and Student Self Expression in a School Setting, unpublished Ph.D. dissertation, University of Texas, Austin.

Biderman, Albert D.
   1967 "Surveys of Population Samples for Estimating Crime Incidence." *The Annals of the American Academy of Political and Social Science,* vol. 374, pp. 16–33.

Bonjean, Charles; Hill, Richard; McLemore, Dale
   1967 *Sociological Measurement.* San Francisco: Chandler Publishing Co.

Chun, Ki-Taek; Cobb, Sidney; and French, John R. P., Jr.
   1975 *Measures of Psychological Assessment: A Guide to 3,000 Original Sources and Their Applications,* Survey Research Center, Institute for Social Research, University of Michigan, Ann Arbor.

Converse, Jean M., and Schuman, Howard
   1974 *Conversations at Random: Survey Research as Interviewers See It.* New York: John Wiley and Sons.

Deutscher, Irwin (ed.)
   1973 *What We Say/What We Do: Sentiments and Acts.* Glenview, Ill., Scott, Foresman and Co.

Guttman, Louis L.
   1950 "The Basis for Scalogram Analysis." In Samuel A. Stauffer et al., *Measuring and Prediction,* vol. 4 of *Studies in Social Psychology in World War II.* Princeton, N.J.: Princeton University Press.

Hamblin, Robert L.
   1971 "Ratio Measurement for the Social Sciences." *Social Forces,* vol. 50, pp. 191–206.

Hamblin, Robert L.
   1974 "Social Attitudes: Magnitude Measurement and Theory." In Hubert M. Blalock, Jr. (ed.), *Measurement in the Social Sciences: Theories and Strategies.* Chicago: Aldine.

Hirschi, Travis
   1969 *Causes of Delinquency.* Berkeley: University of California Press.

La Piere, Richard T.
   1934 "Attitudes Vs. Actions." *Social Forces,* vol. 13, pp. 230–37.

Lazarsfeld, Paul F.
    1937   "Some Remarks on the Typological Procedure in Social Research."
            Zeitschrift fur Sozialforchung, vol. 6.

Maranell, Gary M. (ed.)
    1974   *Scaling: A source Book for Behavioral Scientists.* Chicago: Aldine.

Olsen, Marvin
    1969   "Two Categories of Political Alienation." *Social Forces,* vol. 47,
            pp. 288–99.

Olson, Sheldon R.
    1971   *The Rise and Fall of Student Involvement in Law School.* Unpub-
            lished Ph.D. dissertation, University of Washington, Seattle.

Phillips, Derek L.
    1973   *Abandoning Method.* San Francisco: Jossey-Bass Publishers, Inc.

Reiss, Albert J., Jr.
    1971   "Systematic Observation of Natural Social Phenomena." In Her-
            bert Costner (ed.), *Sociological Methodology.* San Francisco:
            Jossey-Bass Publishers, Inc.

Robinson, John P.; Athanasiou, Robert; and Head, Kendra.
    1969   *Measures of Occupational Attitudes and Occupational Characteris-*
            tics, Survey Research Center, Institute for Social Research, Univer-
            sity of Michigan, Ann Arbor.

Robinson, John P., and Shaver, Phillip R.
    1969   *Measures of Social Psychological Attitudes.* Survey Research Cen-
            ter, Institute for Social Research, University of Michigan, Ann
            Arbor.

Robinson, John P.; Rusk, Gerald G.; and Head, Kendra B.
    1969   *Measures of Political Attitudes.* Survey Research Center, Institute
            for Social Research, University of Michigan, Ann Arbor.

Contents

Chapter 9
The Selection of Units for Analysis

In addition to developing observation strategies, the researcher is faced with the decision of choosing research sites and elements within these sites: In which country or countries is the study to be conducted; in which locations within the country? If these smaller locations are cities, which areas of the city are most appropriate; which set of individuals or events within these areas? In short, since we cannot study the entire world, we must sample, we must select "units" from a larger "population." In the process our ability to translate the findings of the study is restricted accordingly. Basically, the translation facilitated by various sampling techniques is one of relevance. It is a question of external applicability: To whom or to what broader arena does the study apply?

SAMPLING STRATEGIES: POINTS FOR SPECIFICATION

In planning your sampling strategy, the key word is *specify*. It is a rare instance in social research when you are able to "cookbook-it," but, in the process of designing a sampling strategy that will facilitate later translation of the results, it is a good idea to cover the following points.

When thinking ahead to your analysis of the data, *specify the population or populations to which you want to generalize when you are done*. It may be to a single population. It may be to a series of subpopulations. You may want to generalize to a culture as a single unit. You may want to generalize to various groups within a community. You may be studying an organization and desire to generalize to various levels of management.

Whatever the case, you should specify the population to which you want to generalize and then *specify your definition of the units within that population*. Sometimes this is rather straightforward. Often, when we think of the "cases" or "units" of analysis, we think of individuals. However, this need not be. You may be interested in "episodes," such as revolutions or historical cycles. You may be interested in the characteristics of "relationships," such as the balance of power between nations or the network of communication within various neighborhoods. You may want to study trends in certain bodies of literature. You may be interested in the characteristics of organizations, such as churches, industrial plants, hospitals, prisons, courtrooms, and so forth. Whatever the "unit" of analysis, an initial step is to be explicit in the criteria used to recognize a unit. In some cases this is not much of a problem. Organizations and individuals often have fairly clear-cut boundaries separating them from their surroundings. On the other hand, events, episodes, neighborhoods, and cultures often shade into their surroundings, and it becomes difficult to determine where the surroundings stop and the unit begins.

Once definitions of the population and units for analysis are in hand, probability sampling techniques require that you *specify a listing*. Again, the ease with which this is accomplished varies from one research setting to another. It is rarely something that can be assumed to be lying around somewhere. If persons are the units to be analyzed, then such things as voter-registration lists or telephone directories come to mind. It is readily apparent, however, that, if we are interested in generalizing to the total community of persons rather than just to registered voters or persons with listed telephones, these listings omit important segments of the population. Thus, when constructing your list, it is important to spend some time thinking about how to *specify possible omissions from the listing*.

Once a listing is in hand, you need to *specify some sort of selection strategy*. The eventual statistically based implications of the study in terms of its applicability depend on knowing the chances each of a number of units has of being included in the study. The reason interviewing passers-by on a street corner is usually a poor sampling technique is that you simply are not in a position to specify the applicability of the results. You know that persons on one street corner will differ from those on another in any number of ways. You do not know the total range or dimensions of this variation. Thus, you are not in a position to specify either the population from which the sample was drawn or the portion of that population that has been included. In this case, you are unable to say anything, with statistical backing, about anybody beyond those persons interviewed.

For the selection of probability samples, that is, samples that allow you to specify the probability of units of the population appearing in the sample, a commonly used device is the table of random numbers. In the next section, where simple random samples are discussed, we will look at these tables. Your selection strategy may be rather straightforward in that it involves only one stage. It may be more involved. You may want to first define segments of the broader population and then sample within all or some portion of these segments. Stratified and cluster strategies are examples of these multistage operations and will be discussed shortly.

Once you have settled on a sampling strategy, you should *specify the size of sample you will need.* This decision is based on three considerations; the degree of sampling error you are willing to tolerate; the sampling strategy you intend to employ; and the type of analysis you plan to pursue once the information has been collected.

When considering the sample size in terms of the probability of error, the general rule of thumb is that, until the sample comes close to including the total population, it is the sample size and not the sample-to-population ratio that is important. It is this rule that allows pollsters to generalize to the population of the United States from samples as small as 1,500. The exact size of the desired sample is, in the last analysis, a reasoned estimate in the sense that it most frequently depends on the researcher making guesses about information not available prior to the study. Nevertheless, there are procedures that allow approximation. Useful, relatively nontechnical discussions are available in a number of places, such as Lazerwitz (1968). In brief, the desired sample size depends on the anticipated heterogeneity among the units in the population from which the sample is drawn and the degree of error you are willing to tolerate.

The size of the sample also will depend on the design, whether you decide to take a simple random sample or some more complex strategy, such as a stratified or clustered sample. These are discussed in some detail below. Stratified samples, as a rule, are more efficient in terms of the number of cases needed for a given level of error. This is so since strata are selected to include cases similar to one another in terms of some criterion variable, e.g., sex, race, or religion in the case of individuals, or size, resources, and function in the case of organizations. Given this lowered variation within strata, fewer cases are needed to get an accurate picture. In an extreme example, where each case is identical to every other case, a sample of one would represent that stratum.

In cluster sampling, on the other hand, the initial population is first subdivided into categories that contain heterogeneous elements. A sample of clusters is drawn and then these selected clusters are used for further selection of units. This dual (sometimes triple or quadruple) level sampling generally yields greater sampling error than simple random samples of the same size. The question might occur to you, "Well, why use a cluster sample if they require more cases?" The answer lies in monetary and time rather than numerical costs. By first selecting clusters it is possible to concentrate interviewers in a more restricted geographical region. When faced with polling the attitudes of an entire country or even a state or metropolitan region, such considerations are by no means trivial.

A final consideration when deciding on sample size is the type of analysis that will be performed once the data are in. Certain statistical techniques are more efficient than others when it comes to the number of cases required for a given level of analytic complexity. For example, multiple-regression techniques are more efficient than cross-classification tables including the same number of controls. You may notice that "multiple regression" and "cross-classification with controls" are concepts we have not yet discussed. This situation will be remedied in Chapters 10 and 11.

Nevertheless, if, after reading the following chapters, you decide you want to present your data in cross-classification form—the least efficient in terms of number of cases required—there are certain rules of thumb that allow you to estimate the needed sample size. Consider Figure 9.1, where the focus is on the relationship between the socioeconomic

FIGURE 9.1
Number of Cells Contained in a Three-variable Situation with Seven Categories in Two Variables and Three in the Third

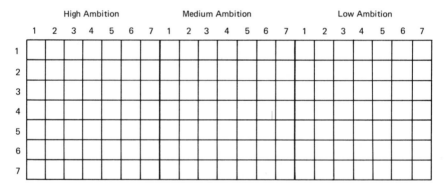

status of the parents (seven categories) and the first job obtained after completion of formal education (seven categories), controlling for the degree of ambition (three categories).

There are thus 147 ($7 \times 7 \times 3$) cells in this figure. A rule of thumb is that there be an *average* of 20 cases per cell. This does not mean there must be 20 cases in each cell. Thus, the needed sample size is 2,940 (147×20). The procedure, then, is to first calculate the "area" (number of cells) in the most complicated table you anticipate and then multiply this number by 20. This, of course, is susceptible to change as your analysis progresses, but it will give you a ball-park figure to work with.

Initially you may want to oversample since, for various reasons, there will be an attrition rate: people on your list may have died, they may not return the questionnaire or they may not agree to an interview; organizations may not allow access; there may not be enough available information on certain units; and so forth. This fact in the researcher's life brings us to an important point. Even with the most carefully designed sampling procedures, you are often left with ambiguity. How do the nonrespondents differ from the respondents? How does this affect the findings in terms of their applicability and validity? There are ways to lessen these problems, but rarely are they completely eliminated.

By way of summary, the goal of any sampling strategy is to come up with a sample that is an accurate representation of some defined population. Thus, whether a sample is good or bad depends, in the last analysis, on how well the sample does in this regard. It is frequently not possible to specify exactly how well you have done, but, by using certain principles of probability and by drawing samples on a probability basis, you are at least able to specify the chances of error more accurately than would otherwise be the case as you translate findings to some larger arena.

SIMPLE, STRATIFIED, AND CLUSTERED RANDOM SAMPLES

Given these rules of specification, consider some details of three of the more commonly used probability sampling techniques: simple, stratified, and clustered random samples. In a simple random sample, each combination of cases from the population has an equal opportunity of appearing in the final sample. To draw a simple random sample, there are three requirements. First, there must be a listing of the larger population from which the sample is drawn. Second, there must be some random device for selecting the various "units"—a table of random numbers or a rotating drum with numbered, equally weighted balls will do. Third, the "units" must be independent of one another; that is, the selection of one should not affect the selection of another.

Suppose you choose as your random selection device a table of random numbers similar to the segment in Figure 9.2. The procedure would be to assign a number to each of the "units" in the population from which the sample is to be drawn. Suppose, further, that there are 850 "units" in this broader population. How do you utilize the table of random numbers?

Since 850 has three digits, you decide to utilize three columns at a time. You might decide to start in the left-hand corner and work down. The first unit in the sample would be the one to which the number 740 has been assigned; next would be 483, 095, 516, 133, 599, 986—but wait a minute, there are only 850 units. When this situation

FIGURE 9.2
Segment from Table of Random Numbers

7408398490	4245589650	5703233029
4830617578	2950486497	7778174390
0952279504	7769078646	0662997628
5167687683	1358475280	2699794873
1330406751	4178273499	6252562465
5995470264	8214417457	7040573871
9861030941	3260659038	5781845841
1454171996	8796931699	1913866036
2548059155	4815161801	3894890939
0527641391	7455300653	1039755324
1260721609	3439181310	0376851175
0637893572	4900959770	6083019818
0265053433	3358409015	4356067684

arises you simply skip to the next number. The seventh case then would be 145; the eighth, 254; and so forth. When you reach the bottom of the table, you may shift over to the next three columns. You may want to shift to the next "segment" of the table. It makes no difference. If you come to a number that has already been included, you again simply skip to the next number. The procedure is continued until you reach the desired sample size of, say, 400 "units."

A frequently used alternative to the table of random numbers is what is sometimes referred to as systematic sampling, starting randomly and then taking every *nth* case. This procedure is somewhat easier to follow and will yield a random selection of cases if the original listing has not been based on some criteria that bias the results. The most frequently cited example in this regard is the listing based either on the rank of various individuals included or perhaps the apartment numbers of dwelling units, or every *nth* day of the week. In such cases a random start and then a selection of every *nth* case might result in quite different samples. For example, one study might include all top 10-percenters or all corner units in an apartment building. Another study with another random start might include all middle-of-the-roaders and all middle-of-the-hall units. In most instances these situations are easily detectable and readily remedied. You need only "shuffle" the listing if you are in doubt. After the shuffle you are then picking, for all intents and purposes, every *nth* case from a random listing.

Stratified simple random sampling is parallel to simple random sampling, except this time the original population of units from which the sample is drawn is divided into a series of subpopulations before sampling takes place. This strategy is employed most frequently when you feel certain strata differ from others and you want to make sure a representative picture of each is obtained. First-line supervisors will differ from vice presidents and mid-level managers along a number of dimensions. Vice presidents are fewer in number than other levels and thus have a smaller chance of appearing in a random selection from the total pool. To ensure a sample in which vice presidents are included, the researcher may first "stratify" the original population. This simply means that each group of individuals, in this case managers, is treated as a separate universe from which to sample. A sample is then drawn from each of these stratum in the same manner as that employed for a simple random selection discussed above.

The general principle when creating strata from which to sample is heterogeneity between and homogeneity within. The strata should be selected so the units within each strata are similar to one another and different from units in other strata on variables of interest. Since you sometimes do not have advance knowledge of these traits, difficulties emerge. A feel for this kind of design perhaps is best obtained by way of example. Travis Hirschi (1969), in his study of juvenile delinquency, described his sampling strategy as follows.

> The sample on which the present study is based was drawn as part of the Richmond Youth Project from 17,500 students entering the 11 public junior and senior high schools of this area in the fall of 1964. This population was stratified by race, sex, school, and grade, producing 130 subgroups, such as seventh-grade non-Negro boys at Granada Junior High School and tenth-grade Negro girls at Richmond High School. In most cases, 85 percent of the Negro boys, 60 percent of the Negro girls, 30 percent of the non-Negro (largely Caucasian but with some Oriental and Mexican American) boys, and 12 percent of the non-Negro girls were selected randomly for inclusion in the sample. In a few schools, where these sampling fractions would not produce 25 Negro boys or 25 Negro girls, all Negro boys and girls in the school were included in the sample. This procedure produced a stratified probability sample of 5,545 students: 1479 Negro boys, 2126 non-Negro boys, 1076 Negro girls, and 864 non-Negro girls. Of the 5,545 students in the original sample, complete data were eventually obtained on 4,077, or 73.5 percent. (pp. 35–36)

This example is instructive in that it not only illustrates a set of criteria used to define various strata but also represents an instance in which a *disproportionate* sample was taken from each of the strata. For example, each respondent who was a non-Negro male represented approximately 3.3 non-Negro males in the population, whereas each non-Negro female represented about 8 non-Negro females. This disproportionate selection was done primarily to ensure enough cases within each stratum for later analysis.

If you wanted to compare strata or to analyze data within strata, this disproportionate strategy would not present a problem since each sample of the strata is representative, within specifiable limits. If, however, we wish to construct a picture of the total population of youths attending senior and junior high school in the Richmond, California area, each of the subsamples would have to be weighted according to the proportion with which they were included. Assuming that each non-Negro male represented approximately 3.3 persons in the population and each non-Negro female represented 8 persons in the population, you weight each sample by a factor of 3.3 and 8, respectively.

The actual mechanics and precision of this weighting operation will vary according to the kind of tools available during analysis. If computer programs are available or if you can write your own program, the weighting can be rather precise. If you must rely on a counter sorter or other manual counts, then you might randomly duplicate or discard cases by a factor closest to the appropriate proportion. The implications of this weighting in terms of later statistically based inferences are rather complex. If you are actually conducting a study in which disproportionate sampling is necessary, you would do well to consult Kish's *Survey Sampling* (1965).

Of course, if proportionate samples from each of the stratum are selected, you need not be concerned with these differential weighting considerations. Each strata is included in the estimate of the total population according to the proportion of the total population it represents.

A third type of sampling is cluster sampling. Cluster samples and stratified samples are similar in that each involves an initial construction of subgroups from the larger population. However, unlike stratified samples, where a selection is made from *each* of the strata, cluster sampling involves a sampling of the subpopulations and then a resampling of elements within these clusters. You might, for example, want to study faculty members in the colleges in the United States, in which case you first select institutions (clusters) and then faculty members. Similar strategies would be followed in the selection of church members, city residents, and so forth, where the procedure would be to first select churches, then members, city blocks, and then residents or households.

In each instance there are two or more sources of sampling error—one in the selection of clusters and the other in the selection of elements within the clusters. It is this multiheaded sampling error that makes cluster samples, as a rule, less accurate than stratified or simple random samples of the same size. A second problem in this regard frequently emerges when clusters are selected by some sort of proximity criteria—students in a single large introductory class or residents of a certain area of the city. Proximity is often associated with similarity due to any number of factors and thus the clusters may not be the microcosms of the broader population the researcher thinks they are. This being the case, and if the researcher is interested in studying individuals within clusters to reach generalizations about the broader population, sampling error is multiplied. As Kish (1957) has pointed out, this biasing factor is not insignificant. Thus, if you decide that clustering is necessary, you should first check your clustering criteria with some thoroughness and be aware of the consequences in terms of later generalizations.

Researchers frequently find themselves confronted with a study that calls for some combination of the stratified, clustered, and simple or systematic probability techniques. Suppose you wanted to sample the students, faculty, and administrators of colleges and universities throughout the United States. Realizing the difficulties of selecting your subjects from a single total listing of all students, faculty, and administrators, you might develop something like the following.

You might decide to go the cluster route by selecting institutions from a listing such as that provided in *American Universities and Colleges*. Realizing that colleges and universities differ along such dimensions as size of the student population and available resources, you might decide to first stratify according to these criteria to ensure that the numerically small but functionally and theoretically important large universities would be included in your sample. Using data such as those presented by Cohen and March (1974) (see Figures 9.3 and 9.4), the proportion of schools to draw from each stratum could be decided. Once the disproportionate random sample of institutions was drawn, it would become apparent that to list the faculty, students, and administrators in a single compilation of the university population would be unwise, and, thus, you would stratify accordingly. Given these strata of faculty, students, and administrators, further stratification of each of these according to such criteria as college major in the case of students, or department in the case of faculty, might be useful. Finally, the strategy might call for the drawing of a proportionate or disproportionate sample from these strata within strata according to anticipated plans for analysis and the desirable number of cases.

What you end up with, then, is a disproportionate stratified sample of institutions coupled with a disproportionate stratified sample of persons within these institutions. In reconstructing the picture of students, faculty, and administrators in the United States, each of these stages would have to be taken into account.

Yet another example of complex sampling designs is provided by the strategies used by national polling institutes. The sampling strategy used by the National Opinion Research Center for their Spring 1974 General Social Survey is reprinted in Figure 9.5. Here the strategy was to first select Standard Metropolitan Statistical Areas, then block groups

FIGURE 9.3
Frequency Distribution of Full-Time Students (in hundreds)

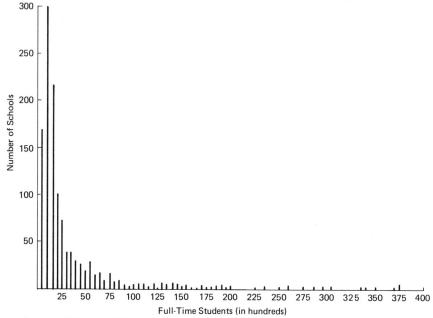

Source: Cohen and March, 1974.

or enumeration districts within those areas. Within these groups specific blocks were selected, and then, through instructions to the interviewers, quotas—specified proportions of respondents with specified characteristics—were gathered. This last step of obtaining quotas, rather than purely random selection, necessitates adjustments in the estimates of the sampling error.

Yet another type of complexity sometimes is introduced when the larger sample is used for a number of studies. In this case it may be necessary to draw out only a portion of the sampled respondents for analysis. This, of course, restricts the applicability of the smaller study, but the gains in terms of the theoretical utility of the results may be worth the reduction in later statistically based generalizations.

For example, the present writer once was involved in a study of the management of the Boeing Company. The sample for the larger study was a disproportionate, stratified random sample. Given this broader study, a decision was made to study factors related to tendencies to avoid or pursue managerial meetings. It thus became necessary to select a subsample of managers who spent a good deal of time together. This subsample was determined not by probability techniques but by

FIGURE 9.4
Frequency Distribution of Income/Full-time Student (in thousands of dollars)

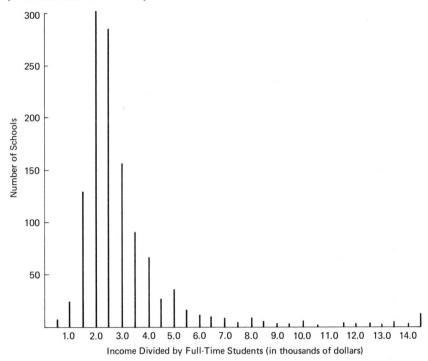

Source: Cohen and March, 1974.

responses to one of the items on the questionnaire. This question asked for the relative amount of time the respondent spent with various categories of persons. Respondents were included in the smaller study if they reported having contact "at least once a week" or "many times a day" with (1) persons who reported directly to them; (2) others at about the same level who reported to the same supervisor; and (3) those persons to whom they reported and, in addition, reported a low degree of contact ("no more than several times a month at most" or "practically never") with other categories of persons. With this group of respondents in hand it was possible to pursue a theoretical idea that meetings that accentuated inconsistent status rankings would be avoided, while situations that reduced the inconsistency of status rankings would be pursued. The theoretical rationale for this hypothesis can be found in Sampson (1963) and Kimberly (1966). For present purposes, however, we are not so much interested in the reasons persons with inconsistent rankings might avoid or pursue interaction but rather with various sampling strategies that might be employed.

FIGURE 9.5

Sampling Design for NORC Spring 1974 General Social Survey

The universe sampled in this study is the total noninstitutionalized population of the continental United States, 18 years of age or older.

The sample is a multistage area probability sample to the block or segment level. At the block level, however, quota sampling is used with quotas based on sex, age, and employment status. The cost of the quota samples is substantially less than the cost of a full probability sample of the same size, but there is, of course, the chance of sample biases mainly due to not-at-homes that are not controlled by the quotas. However, in order to reduce this bias, the interviewers are given instructions to canvass and interview only after 5:00 p.m. on weekdays or during the weekend or holidays.

This type of sample design is most appropriate when the past experience and judgment of a project director suggest that sample biases are likely to be small relative to the precision of the measuring instrument and the decisions that are to be made.

Selection of PSU

The Primary Sampling Units (PSU) employed are Standard Metropolitan Statistical Area (SMSA) or nonmetropolitan counties selected in NORC's Master Sample. These SMSA's and counties were stratified by region, age, and race before selection.[1]

Selection of Sample within PSU

The units of selection of the second stage were block groups (BG) and enumeration districts (ED). These ED's and BG's were stratified according to race and income before selection.[2]

The third stage of selection was that of blocks. The blocks were selected with probabilities proportional to size. In places without block statistics, measures of size for the blocks were obtained by field counting.

The average cluster size is five respondents per cluster. This provides a suitable balance of precision and economy.

Interviewer Instructions

At the block or segment level, the interviewer begins a travel pattern at the first DU (dwelling unit) from the northwestern corner of the block and proceeds in a specified direction until the quotas have been filled.

The quotas call for approximately equal numbers of men and women with the exact proportion in each segment determined by the 1970 Census tract data. For women, the additional requirement is imposed that there be the proper proportion of employed and unemployed women in the location. Again, these quotas are based on the 1970 Census tract

Source: National Opinion Research Center, 1974.

[1] For selection procedures, see "The 1972 NORC National Probability Sample," Benjamin King and Carol Richards, unpublished preliminary draft, 1972.

[2] Ibid.

FIGURE 9.5 *(continued)*

data. For men, the added requirement is that there be the proper proportion of men over and under 35 in the location.

These particular quotas have been established because past experience has shown that employed women and young men under 35 are the most difficult to find at home for interviewing.

Sampling Error

Although the mean squared error cannot be estimated directly from a quota sample, one can make estimates if sampling variability using procedures such as those outlined by Stephen and McCarthy.[3] Past experience would suggest that, for most purposes, this sample of 1,500 could be considered as having about the same efficiency as a simple random sample of 1,000 cases. In making this judgment concerning the design effect, we are concerned with the "average" effect upon a large set of different variables by the clustering of households at the last stage of selection. Any statement of sampling error assumes that the bias in quota sampling due to the lack of control over respondent availability is slight for the study under consideration.

For those persons interested in investigating the within sample variability of this data, we have included a "sampling error code." Information about the use of this code is available from the Sampling Department of NORC.

[3] Frederick Stephen and Philip McCarthy, *Sampling Opinions* (New York: John Wiley & Sons, 1958), Chapter 10.

In this particular instance the strategy involved a number of stages. The final stage involved actions that yielded a nonprobability sample and thus generalization beyond the study was problematic. It was felt that the gain in the theoretical applicability of the results was worth the cost in representativeness.

When developing your own strategy, similar decisions will have to be made and subsequent precautions taken. Frequently, the definitions of units for analysis will be vague, listings will be unavailable, and accessible data will be incomplete. In such cases, you must make decisions and draw cases on purposive rather than probabilistic grounds.

Practicum 9.1 Take a box and fill it with known numbers of objects—kernels of corn, rice, and beans, for example. Mix these thoroughly and draw repeated samples. Determine how far the sample proportions of rice, beans, and corn vary from what you put in. This is what is known as sampling error. By noting results for various sample sizes, you can get a feel for the importance of sample size. By changing the proportions of objects, say 10 beans, 2,000 kernels of corn, and 3,000 kernels of rice, you can get a feel for how "unusual units" in the population, e.g., deviant events or persons or numerically minor groups such as vice presidents of a company, might be missed without purposefully including them by first stratifying the population into subpopulations and then selecting a sample from each of these.

Practicum 9.2 Think of persons associated with your school as a single community. Specify how you would draw a simple random sample of this community. Is there reason to construct subsamples, either by clustering or stratifying? What are the relevant strata? What are the relevant clusters? What are the omissions likely to be? Now, think of residents in your state as the population you wish to sample. How would you construct a listing? What are the likely omissions? What are the useful strata and clusters? Finally, think of drawing a sample of neighborhoods of a city or town with which you are familiar. How would you define the units of analysis, "neighborhoods"? Specify the details of a sampling strategy that would allow you to choose a representative sample of *neighborhoods* in the city or town chosen.

SAMPLING MORE NEBULOUS UNITS

As useful as these probability techniques are, they are most often applied and most applicable when the "units" to be studied are relatively well-defined, independent wholes, such as individuals, organizations, or city blocks. They are less applicable when these conditions of closure and independence are not present. Two situations calling for the sampling of more nebulous units, commonly encountered by social scientists, are when the study calls for the analysis of either "cultures" or "events."

Cross-Cultural Sampling

One situation in which researchers have found themselves, where probability sampling is very problematic, is when cultures and cultural traits—their distribution and intercorrelations—are the focus for study. If you are interested in doing a case study of a single society where the attention is on specific details of that society and its development, then the sampling of cultures is not so severe. Considerations of availability, interest, and policy implications become relevant criteria. The sampling of events, individuals, or traits *within* that culture remains a problem if a representative picture is wanted, but the selection of the culture itself can be done for any number of reasons.

When you want to make statements concerning the degree to which certain characteristics of societies in general tend to appear singly, together, or in sequence, it then becomes important to draw a sample of cultures that represents some defined whole. In such research it becomes important to be in a position to specify the points previously outlined. At every turn, cross-cultural research runs into difficulty. We have already discussed some of these in Chapter 7.

Driver (1973) points to the rather impressive difficulties when attempting to construct a listing of human societies.

> It is impossible to draw a simple random sample from a roster of all human societies because no such list exists. If the standard is lowered to a universe of all societies adequately described, a closer approach to an operational parameter is achieved, but the unevenness of such descriptions still makes it impossible to draw a simple random sample and obtain the desired information on every society drawn. If the researcher finds the information on half the societies he chooses, he is doing well. (p. 333)

If the correlation among cultural traits is at issue, an initial difficulty in constructing a list is to find relevant criteria for determining the boundaries that separate one unit from another.

> When it is remembered that the human populations in ethnic units vary from a couple of dozen persons in the smallest "primitive" groups to 700 million in China, and from the simplest levels of subsistence exclusively on wild plants and animals to the wide choice of nationally marketed foods in the United States, it is easy to see why anthropologists and other social scientists are not very happy with the great variety of ethnic units used so far in statistical studies. . . . It is impossible or next to impossible to determine where one culture bearing unit stops and another begins on the basis of culture alone. The skin of a culture is extremely hard to find. (p. 331)

This, of course, is not to say that efforts are lacking in the direction of constructing relevant criteria for locating the "skin" of culture.

One of the more systematic attempts can be found in the work of Naroll (1964, 1968). Noting that certain criteria of the distribution of particular traits being studied—territorial contiguity, political organization, language, ecological adjustment, and local community structure—have been used to define cultural units, Naroll (1968) suggests that three of these be combined to form the definition of what he calls the cultunit. "A cultunit is defined as people who are domestic speakers of a common distinct language and who belong either to the same state or the same contact group" (p. 248).

While noting its potential utility, Naroll also suggests the cultunit's shortcomings. "The cultunit concept is far too awkward and cumbersome for most people. Most people would like something simpler, more elegant. So would I. . . . The urgent need now is for a new concept of a culture bearing unit—perhaps one fairly similar to the cultunit. This new concept should be simple and clear. It must be a concept which can be easily used to sort out tribes and cultures, using the kind of information now usually found in books about primitive tribes" (p. 251).

In the final analysis, then, researchers desiring to analyze cultures and their traits are left with available data, data that have been gathered for a wide range of purposes and thus presenting sometimes widely divergent sets of information. It remains, in such a situation, to attempt some specification of the possible biasing factors that might be influencing the listing, as well as the eventual sampling from the listing.

It is difficult to come up with a rule of thumb since the quality, distribution, and amount of available information will depend on the problem at hand. Nevertheless, it appears that certain patterns are discernible. As Naroll (1968) notes,

> While the *Human Relations Area Files* tried to follow a purposive sampling plan originally drawn up by Murdock, inspection of the list of societies shows that the Soviet Union and its immediate neighbors are disproportionately overrepresented, as is Southeast Asia. Clearly, one of the factors influencing the selection of societies for inclusion in the *Files* has been their interest to officials in Washington, D.C. (254)

This same anthropologist goes on to note further biasing factors, less political in nature.

> I would guess that larger societies are more likely to be studied and described than smaller ones, warlike societies more than less warlike ones, societies with highly elaborate ceremonials more than societies without them, societies near main routes of transcontinental or overseas travel more than societies distant from these routes, societies regarded as relevant to current anthropological theory . . . more than those societies considered less relevant, and, finally, societies that are relatively hostile to and resistant to European influence and colonial administration more than societies that are relatively docile and yielding. (pp. 256–57)

Keeping these difficulties in mind, some of the major sources of societal listings can be found in the work of Murdock (1972) and the *Northwestern University Permanent Ethnographic Probability Sample*. In addition, publications of the United Nations are useful in this regard. Whatever the listing, if you are considering a cross-cultural study with societal phenomena as your focus, you would do well to consult the works of Driver and Naroll cited above, as well as other works cited therein. By doing so you should be in a much better position to be sensitive to the boundaries of your conclusions.

Sampling Events and Other Naturally Occurring Social Phenomena

Another commonly encountered nebulous unit is when the researcher is interested in studying events as they occur in their natural setting. A problem that relentlessly plagues researchers of "naturally occurring social phenomena" is one of external validity. To whom or to what portions of a setting do the results apply? Which segments of the setting are represented in the findings? Whose point of view has been taken?

Some have argued that the observation of naturally occurring phenomena is necessarily biased (e.g., Becker, 1967). Whether bias is inevitable or not is not at issue here. What we are interested in is whether we can specify the limits and direction of the bias when the strategy for gathering information is the first-hand observation of events and the perceived source of bias is the representativeness of our sample.

In this regard Reiss (1971) has specified some issues that must be addressed if one is to systematically study social phenomena as they occur. Drawing from his study of police/citizen encounters, Reiss suggests, "The main procedures incorporated into a systematic social observation actually are homologous to those of survey research" (p. 4). As we have seen, sampling for observation is fundamental to survey research. When the question of translating the results of a study arise, sampling should be such that it provides the researcher with a small piece of the population that ". . . mirrors, with known precision, the various patterns of subclasses of the population" (Lazerwitz, p. 279). What happens when we apply probability sampling considerations to the observation of interlocking events?

An initial problem arises when we compare the interpersonal dynamics of an observation study with those of the survey questionnaire or interview study. When observing ongoing events, the researcher is often involved in an intricate relationship with the source of information, more intricate than with the mail-out questionnaire or administration of an interview. In the observation study the somewhat dictatorial structure of probability sampling—this is included, this is not—is often somehow alien to the enterprise. By definition, when observing naturally occurring social phenomena, we strive to let life unfold naturally, unencumbered by our methodological requirements.

For the person observing events as they occur, it is often self-destructive to establish or cut off relationships or participation simply because the segment of the scene is not part of the sample. Such practices can easily lead to charges of self-serving behavior and lack of interest in the "true picture." Unlike the relatively brief encounter involved in administering a questionnaire or conducting an interview, gathering information in first-hand observation studies often involves more extensive personal involvement and commitments. Thus, to cut off or establish research sites according to the dictates of a probability sample is a more delicate operation than beginning or ending an "interview." This is not to say that it is impossible or totally undesirable. Rather, it should be recognized that it is simply a more delicate situation.

In addition to the problems of interpersonal dynamics that make probability sampling somewhat less attractive when observing naturally occurring social phenomena, there are additional considerations that make the procedures difficult, even when desired. As useful as probability sampling is, it will be recalled that it is generally applied and most applicable when the units sampled are well-defined, independent wholes, such as individuals or relatively closed collectivities. What happens to these considerations when we want to sample—the more elusive, less well-bound "event"?

Suppose you want to study the interconnecting *events* that occur in the processing of legal cases through the court system. More so than individuals, events tend to fade into one another and thus it is often difficult to tell when one ends and another begins. As indicated, when drawing a probability sample, some sort of listing of the universe of the units is needed. When events are involved, usually no listing is available. However, for relatively well-structured and planned events, like court proceedings, you are sometimes aided by a published agenda. For example, courts often publish the schedule of the upcoming jury and non-jury weeks. Thus, if you are interested in the jury-trial event, you might want to use this listing as a starting point.

A problem arises when you realize that this provides only the crudest of estimates of the events occurring in the court. Cases are settled out of court. Unanticipated charges and countercharges will be filed with the clerk of the court. Pretrial conferences are held. The attorney general's office may decide that enough is enough and file large numbers of delinquent-tax cases. These, in turn, will overload the system and postpone many events.

To deal with this listing difficulty you might shift your focus slightly and suggest, since events occur in space and time, that you sample these units. Days of the week, times of the day, rooms in buildings, and so forth become our sample units. Still, we are faced with a series of questions. "What is the appropriate time frame?" "How long do events last?" "What happens if we break into the middle of an event?" Each of these questions only emphasizes that events are sometimes rather nebulous phenomena and thus not susceptible to the rigors of probability sampling.

In addition to the requirement of a listing, random sampling is such that the selection of one event should not affect the selection of another. Frequently, in the observation of events, the situation is complicated in that the researcher is led from one event to another in snowball fashion, later events becoming available according to what has been seen or experienced in the past.

An example will perhaps clarify the difficulties. You may recall the study of the pretrial detention setting cited earlier (Olson, 1974). The initial design of the study was grand. We were initially seduced by the possibility of uncovering both sides of the picture—the side of the rule breakers and the side of the enforcers. The overall objective was to get a full view of a jail in terms of its culture and social structure.

Thus, we spent time with the warden, the counselor, the guards, both inside and outside the cell block, as well as with the inmates.

In one sense the broader project offered a rather unique opportunity to come up with access to these various, sometimes conflicting segments of the setting. The research was undertaken within the context of a larger project designed not only to develop an understanding of the system of justice but also to enter that system in the form of legal aid. It was the dual nature of this quasi-attorney's role that made access to both sides somewhat less problematic than it otherwise might have been. On the one hand, the attorney acts as an officer of the court and thus bears certain public responsibility. At the same time, the attorney is adviser, advocate, and confidant to the client and thus develops certain obligations in that direction. Early in the project this rather ambiguous status was enough to facilitate contacts with both sets of actors and, thus, an observation of events and perceptions from both perspectives. As the research progressed, however, we found that inordinate time spent with one group or the other was frequently taken by the slighted group to indicate a movement to the "other side."

For example, following a period of perhaps four months involving some success in maintaining contacts with both staff and inmates at the pretrial detention facility, we decided to carry out a series of more systematic interviews with the guards. These were to pursue, in greater detail, issues raised in our earlier conversations and observations. About this same time, a suit developed in the local legal-aid office that eventually was filed on behalf of the inmates against the administration. Although we had little formal contact with the legal-aid office, the fact that we had been spending time with the inmates as well as with a group of antagonistic lawyers was enough to make the administration of the jail less candid than they had been previously and more rigid as to the events we might observe. In like manner, the initial cooperation of the administration at the pretrial detention facility created certain suspicions among some inmates, leading them to ask "who we knew" to be able to move in and out of the cell blocks with such ease.

In the end, the rather ambiguous status associated with the role of lawyer opened many doors that otherwise might have been closed. This same ambiguity created strain, closing some avenues that otherwise might have remained open. We thus ended up with a picture less complete than we would have liked.

As has been described by Howard Becker (1963),

> It is in the nature of the phenomenon of deviance that it will be difficult for anyone to study both sides of the process and accurately capture the perspectives of both classes of participants, rule breakers and rule enforcers. Not that it is impossible, but practical considerations of gaining access to situations and the confidence of the people involved

in any reasonable length of time mean that one will probably study
the situation from one side or the other. (p. 173)

The problem is that naturally occurring phenomenon are intertwined
in a number of ways. When sampling or observing events, the individual
often is part of the scene—either as a participant observer or as an
observer with certain degrees of access. A problem arises when we realize that segments of the structure will open and close accordingly. This
is an especially distinct possibility when the "niches" of the structure
represent conflicting interests. Given these interconnections among
events, we are led from one to another not so much through random
choice as through necessity, convenience, or availability. What we end
up with resembles more a "snowball" sample than a probability sample.
Whatever it is, it certainly does not meet the criteria of a simple random
sample.

When ingenuity has been exhausted in this situation, you simply recognize that when claiming representativeness for your study you should
tread softly. This, of course, does not mean that the study is invalid;
only that it is sometimes not possible to specify validity with any degree
of statistical precision.

Once strategies for gathering information have been devised, the units
sampled, and the information gathered, the researcher is faced with
the problem of translating the bits of information into a form that ad-
dresses the focus of the study. It is the problem of how to analyze
the data. Actually, the total picture is more involved. Most of the time
the researcher is engaged in analysis or considering potential analytic
strategies throughout the enterprise. In the final stages, however, analytic
concerns become paramount. In general, the path this analysis takes
when you are testing a theory will be guided by the initial set of theoretical ideas. However, even if hypothesis testing is your only goal,
you should always be on the lookout for surprising findings, findings
that may lead you into unforeseen analytic strategies and new theoretical
frameworks. Keeping this "discovery" posture in mind, we can proceed.

One initial aspect of analysis closely tied to sampling and the collection of information, and thus treated in this chapter rather than the
next, is the question of biased findings due to incomplete data. How
do you check on this nonresponse bias and limit its impact on your
study?

THE PROBLEM OF NONRESPONSE

Item: Slamming Doors

Hardly a new soap or politician gets off the ground these days without
a thorough poll of what the public reaction will be. But the nation's
pollsters—commercial, political, sociological—are running into an epi-

demic of taciturnity, especially among oversurveyed blacks. According to a recent report for the National Science Foundation, about 40 percent of recent surveys had to be dropped uncompleted because too few folks would answer questions. "We constantly have to exhort the public that we're not making sales pitches for encyclopedias and dance studios," sighs Mervin Field, operator of the respected California Poll. "It's too bad, because there's no better way to find out how the public thinks." (*Newsweek*, March 25, 1974)

No matter how carefully designed the sampling strategy is, there is always the problem of access. Individuals may refuse to be interviewed or to return the questionnaire. Organizations may refuse access to their files or personnel. Research utilizing "available" data in cross-cultural studies may find that, for some countries or cultures, data simply are not available or were collected in a manner that makes comparisons problematic. If this nonresponse were random in nature it would be of little concern. The nonrespondents are like the respondents. It is generally the case, however, that nonresponse, like other social activities, is patterned. We have already seen how the collection of data on cultures is patterned in a number of ways. So it is with interviewing.

In a most interesting and enlightening discussion of interviewing, Converse and Schuman (1974) have presented a number of comments and generalizations from the experiences of former interviewers in the Detroit Area Studies. For one thing, the unwillingness to respond to interviewers appears to be quite closely linked with the social context in which the respondent lives. In communities of varying sizes and within certain segments of communities, persons may be differentially willing to speak with strangers. Turning to this element of distrust and caution, Converse and Schuman note, "Some interviewers interpret it as a literal fear of crime; others see in it a more diffuse malaise—a desire to retreat into the relative privacy and security of one's own home as one's place in the broader society becomes more and more uncertain." In this regard, the experiences of one interviewer were related as follows:

In one building I rang a bell and distinctly heard someone come to the door. I rang again, but no response—other than the sound of someone, there, breathing, on the other side of the door. Suddenly an amazing thought struck me. Here was I, quaking in my boots, imagining that the whole neighborhood knew I was here and was out to get me, when actually the people were more afraid than I was. People were refusing to answer the door because *they* were terrified of *me*. The picture of two people, both perfectly friendly, standing wide-eyed and shaking on either side of a door was both tragic and comic. It altered my outlook considerably. I began to arrange interviews by first talking to people standing outside or sitting on stoops talking to one another—people for whom those doors would open. (pp. 39–40)

In addition to lack of response due to fear or distrust, there may be a reluctance springing from exasperation due to previous interview sessions that turned into sales pitches. The comment noted above by one of the more well-known pollsters that "We constantly have to exhort the public that we're not making sales pitches for encyclopedias and dance studios" is widespread. Additional reluctance might emerge from the degree of interest the interview holds for the respondent. It might also be a function of the way in which characteristics of the interviewer and respondent intermesh. Persons of the same sex or race as the respondent may be more effective interviewers in some situations and less effective in others. Persons who appear as well-dressed officials may be denied access in areas accustomed to the hassles of being investigated by social workers and welcomed with open arms in areas where such appearances signal more congenial familiarity.

The problem is that it is most frequently the case that the exact pattern of nonresponse and its sources are unknown. It has been suggested by Converse and Schuman that this unwillingness to respond to strangers be used as some measure of social fear and correlated with traditional variables in urban research. Thus, if the original study stalls, the researcher is left with at least something to look at. Failing this, and assuming that we maintain interest in the study that initiated the interviewing process, it becomes incumbent on the analyst to pursue the impact on nonresponse if at all possible.

For an instance of this checking, we can turn again to the study of juvenile delinquency done by Hirschi. It will be recalled that this study involved a questionnaire administered to junior and senior high-school students and aimed at locating the sources of juvenile-delinquent acts. Such studies can and have been dismissed by critics on the ground that they so severely underrepresent juvenile delinquents that they could not possibly be valid. Counter to this, it also has been argued that the lack of representativeness in the direction of not including enough delinquents has the effect of increasing confidence in the results since their inclusion would tend to strengthen the relationships found between delinquency and various social variables. By omitting extreme cases we reduce the size and probability of finding the theoretically predicted association.

To check on these possibilities Hirschi explored two questions with the data. First, is there a relationship between nonresponse and the probability of delinquency? Then, given a relationship, how does it influence the results? To approach this problem he constructed a listing of the original sample and one for the final respondents. He then went to the official records to see if one group was differentially represented in the official statistics and found, as expected, that delinquents tended to be underrepresented.

This being the case, the next task became one of examining the relationship between completion of the questionnaire and variables that were themselves related to the probability of committing delinquent acts. An example of this checking technique is presented in Table 9.1,

TABLE 9.1
Percent Completing the Questionnaire by Average Grade in English and Police Record—Non-Negro Boys Only

	English Weighted Average Mark				
Official Record	*Low* *1*	*2*	*3*	*4*	*High* *5*
No police record	54 (121)*	67 (220)	66 (232)	69 (240)	79 (247)
Police record	38 (133)	55 (157)	55 (76)	62 (69)	71 (28)

* Numbers in parentheses represent the total number of cases upon which the percentages are based. In this case, the table shows that 54 percent of the 121 boys who had no police record and the lowest average mark in English completed the questionnaire. When only one percentage figure is given, the complementary percentage can be directly inferred. Thus, the table also shows that 46 percent of the 121 boys who had no police record and the lowest average mark in English failed to complete the questionnaire.
Source: Hirschi (1969, p. 46).

which presents the percentage of respondents for each category of persons. From this table you can detect that in every category of academic achievement those students with no police record were more likely to be respondents than persons with some sort of official record with the police. Compare, for example, 54 percent with 38 percent in the first category.

The question remains as to whether this differential response rate affected the findings when it came to the strength of the direct relationship between such factors as race, academic achievement and academic ability, and the probability of delinquency. Portions of Hirschi's findings in this regard are reported in Table 9.2.

Here we see that the impact is small or absent when we compare the size of the percentage differences in the respondent and nonrespondent groups. It is the case, of course, that for other variables there may be a differential bias. Thus, even with these checks, the findings of this particular study must be treated with some caution. However, based on the checks carried out, we can be more certain that dismissal of the results simply because there was a higher nonresponse rate among delinquents than nondelinquents would be an ill-advised decision.

Nonresponse or lack of access, then, is always a troublesome fact in the life of the social researcher. When anticipating this problem it

TABLE 9.2
Official Delinquency by English Weighted Average Mark—
Non-Negro Boys Only (in percent)

	English Weighted Average Mark				
	Low 1	2	3	4	High 5
Official Record, Original Sample:					
No police record	48	58	75	78	90
Police record—no offenses in previous two years	13	13	7	7	4
One offense	18	14	10	11	5
Two offenses	7	7	4	3	1
Three or more offenses	15	8	4	1	. . .*
Totals	101	100	100	100	100
	(254)	(377)	(308)	(309)	(275)
Official Record, Final Sample:					
No police record	56	63	79	79	91
Police record—no offenses in previous two years	12	12	6	7	3
One offense	14	14	10	8	5
Two offenses	8	7	3	5	1
Three or more offenses	10	3	2	1	. . .*
Totals	100	99	100	100	100
	(117)	(234)	(196)	(208)	(215)

* Less than one-half of 1 percent.
Source: Hirschi (1969).

is a good idea to sit down and try to think of the possible reasons that might be given for denying access, refusing to be interviewed, or failing to fill out a questionnaire. When thinking about gaining access to some ongoing operation, your thoughts might run something like this. Is the study going to be threatening to those being studied? Is there any way this perceived threat can be diminished? Will this involve an element of deception? Are there ethical problems with this deception? Is there some contact person or issue that can be used to gain entry? Is there something about the study that might be helpful? Can some sort of trade-off be worked?

When designing a mail-out questionnaire you might well consider its attractiveness. Are the respondents going to be interested? How can the questionnaire be packaged to increase its attractiveness? How long should it be? What should be the sequence of questions to avoid boredom? Is there any payoff, like offering a copy of the results, that might be given the respondent? Will the information gathered be in any way a threat to the respondent? How can anonymity be maintained while at the same time keeping track of those who have not responded? Frequently, a separate postcard indicating completion, which can be mailed back separately, will help. When conducting an interview, what might be the reluctance of persons to allow strangers into their houses? How might this reluctance be overcome? How much inconvenience will be involved? How can this be lessened?

There are few well-charted strategies that can be assumed to hold across various research situations. What is called for is a sensitivity to the implications of the research operation and results for the sources of information. It is largely a matter of empathy. Beyond this it is also largely a matter of craftsmanship. Some difficulties might be avoided or more easily anticipated by reading accounts of studies similar in research style, if not in substance, to the one you are planning. By so doing you will not only be in a better position to "up your returns" but also to build in checks so that, when analyzing the results, you can better specify the possible biasing influence of omissions.

SUMMARY

When designing a sampling strategy, keep the following in mind. Be precise when specifying the units of analysis and the population to which you want to generalize. With such precision you will be in a better position to further specify the needed sample size, the complexity of the sampling design, the available listings, the probable omissions, and the potential for bias in your conclusions.

KEY ISSUES

1. What are the aspects of a sampling design that need specification?
2. What factors should be considered when settling on the appropriate sample size?
3. What are the characteristics of simple, systematic, clustered, and stratified probability samples?
4. What are the pros and cons for each type of sample?
5. What difficulties can you expect when sampling "cultures"?
6. What difficulties are likely to be encountered when sampling events?
7. What is to be done with the problem of nonresponse? When is nonresponse particularly troublesome?

REFERENCES

Becker, Howard S.
   1963   *The Outsiders: Studies in the Sociology of Deviance.* New York: The Free Press.
Becker, Howard S.
   1967   "Whose Side Are We On?". *Social Problems*, vol. 14, pp. 239–47.

Cohen, Michael D., and March, James G.
   1974   *Leadership and Ambiguity: The American College President.* New York: McGraw-Hill.

Converse, Jean M., and Schuman, Howard
   1974   *Conversations at Random: Survey Research as Interviewers See It.* New York: John Wiley and Sons.

Driver, Harold E.
   1973   "Cross Cultural Studies." In John J. Honigmann (ed.), *Handbook of Social and Cultural Anthropology.* Chicago: Rand McNally and Company.

Hirschi, Travis
   1969   *Causes of Delinquency.* Berkeley: University of California Press.

Kimberly, James C.
   1966   "A Theory of Status Equilibrium." In Joseph Berger, Morris Zelditch, Jr., and Bo Anderson (eds.), *Sociological Theories in Progress.* New York: Haughton-Mifflin Co.

Kish, Leslie
   1957   "Confidence Intervals for Clustered Samples." *American Sociological Review,* vol. 22, pp. 154–65.

Kish, Leslie
   1965   *Survey Sampling.* New York: John Wiley and Sons.

Lazerwitz, Bernard
   1968   "Sampling Theory and Procedures." In Hubert M. Blalock, Jr., and Ann B. Blalock (eds.), *Methodology in Social Research,* New York: McGraw-Hill.

Murdock, George P.
   1972   *Outline of World Cultures.* New Haven, Conn.: Human Relations Area Files, Inc.

Naroll, Raoul
   1964   "On Ethnic Unit Classification." *Current Anthropology,* vol. 5, pp. 283–312.

Naroll, Raoul
   1968   "Some Thoughts on Comparative Method in Cultural Anthropology." In Hubert M. Blalock, Jr., and Ann B. Blalock (eds.), *Methodology in Social Research.* New York: McGraw-Hill.

Olson, Sheldon R.
   1974   "Minutes in Court, Weeks in Jail: A Study of Pretrial Detention." New York: MSS Modular Publications, Module 22.

Reiss, Albert J., Jr.
   1971   "Systematic Observation of Natural Social Phenomena." In Herbert Costner (ed.), *Sociological Methodology 1971,* San Francisco: Jossey-Bass.

Sampson, Edward E.
   1963   "Status Congruence and Cognitive Consistency." *Sociometry,* vol. 26, pp. 146–62.

Contents

Chapter 10

Translating the Concept of "Prediction" into Data

In Chapters 6 through 8 we discussed the translation of the substantive aspects of a theory into concrete indicators. In the present chapter we turn to the translation of one type of hypothesized relationship, that of prediction. Desiring to translate this idea that you can predict the occurrence of Y given knowledge of X, you must decide which of a wide range of statistics best reflects the type of relationship you have in mind. This chapter is designed to facilitate this decision. In the next chapter we will turn to the issue of how to explore the proposition that X causes Y.

TRANSLATING THE CONCEPT OF PREDICTION

The case for evaluating a theory in terms of its predictive power has been made recently by Gibbs (1972), who claims, "In examining test results one question should be paramount: What do the results suggest about the predictive power of the theory? As the question indicates, predictive power should be the primary criterion by which sociological theories are assessed" (p. 64). And, on the next page of his book, "Regardless of the field, the purpose or function of theory need not be described in terms of causation or explanation; it can be taken as the identification or creation of order, and success can be judged by predictive power" (p. 65). If, for the moment, we use this criterion for judging a theory, the question becomes—How do we translate the idea of predictive power into data? What statistics most closely represent what we have in mind?

Percentage Differences

One way to get an indication of whether knowledge of one factor, say, degree of societal transition, allows prediction of another, say, the

crime rate, is to examine percentage differences. There are a number
of ways to calculate percentages. Thus, it is important, when dealing
with prediction, that the percentages chosen correspond to the question
being asked.

There was once a man who went to a doctor for a routine checkup.
In the ensuing conversation concerning the patient's health, the doctor
suggested that all was fine except for one thing. The man had all but
one of the symptoms associated with a rare and fatal disease. In caution-
ing the patient about this the doctor said, "If you notice anymore spots
appearing, be sure to let me know since recent studies have shown
that 80 percent of the persons with this disease have these spots." Going
home somewhat disturbed the patient began reading an article the doctor
had given him. In the process, his mind was eased somewhat when
he came upon the information shown in Figure 10.1. He saw, as the

FIGURE 10.1
Hypothetical Data Showing Frequency of Symptoms
and Disease

Symptoms	Disease		
	Yes	*No*	*Total*
Yes	4,000	25,000,000	25,004,000
No	1,000	175,000,000	175,001,000
Total	5,000	200,000,000	200,005,000

doctor had indicated, that 80 percent (4,000 out of 5,000 known cases)
did indeed exhibit the symptoms. What the doctor had failed to indicate
was that there were some 25,000,000 persons with the same symptoms
without the disease. The disease was indeed a rare one, much rarer
than the occurrence of the symptoms. Predicting the presence of the
disease from the symptoms, we find that only a tiny fraction of 1 percent
of the persons with the symptoms actually had the disease.

This example, while extreme and hypothetical, points to an important
consideration when setting up your data. If you are predicting a characteristic of some variable, such as the disease above, from another characteristic, symptomatic spots above, then you should percentage in the
direction of the prediction. The way in which these considerations become rather confusing is illustrated when we note that we can make
sense out of percentaging within categories of having or not having
the disease. When this is done, however, we are predicting the symptoms
of the disease rather than predicting the occurrence of the disease.

Practicum 10.1 Consider Figures 10.2 and 10.3, which present hypothetical data on the relationship between the age of prisons and rioting in prison and between training practices of parents and the history of the respondent's treatment of his or her own children. Now, state in the form of prediction, the questions that might be answered by (1) percentaging within columns and comparing across columns; (2) percentaging within rows and comparing across rows; and (3) percentaging using the total number of cases and the cell frequencies as the category number.

FIGURE 10.2
Hypothetical Data Showing Frequency of Riots in Prison and Physical Age of Prison

Physical Age of Prison	Rioting		
	Yes	No	Total
Old	75	50	125
New	30	47	77
Total	105	97	202

FIGURE 10.3
Hypothetical Data Showing Frequency of Training Practices of Parents and History of Child Abuse

Training Practices of Parents	History of Child Abuse		
	Yes	No	Total
Authoritative	600	220	820
Permissive	140	410	550
Total	740	630	1,370

The key to the appropriate presentation of percentage differences is to first think about the question you want answered and then make sure your presentation illustrates the relevant answer. This would hardly need saying if it were not for the frequent errors in translation that occur in this regard.

The Odds Ratio

A useful measure, closely linked to the examination of percentage differences, has been called the "odds ratio" (Goodman, 1969). It is calculated by examining the relative "risk" of exhibiting certain characteristics given certain other characteristics. For example, take the data presented in Figure 10.3. From this we find that for persons with parents who were authoritarian the odds are 600 to 220, or 2.73 to 1.00, that they will have a history of abusing their own children. By contrast, this same hypothetical data shows a 140 to 410, or .341 to 1.00, "risk" that persons with permissive parents will have a history of child abuse. Comparing these two risk factors we see that the relative risk, or the "odds ratio," is 2.73 to .341, or 8 to 1. This is interpreted to mean that the relative risk of child abuse is eight times as great for those with authoritarian parents as it is for those with permissive parents.

For a detailed treatment of the calculation rules for 2×2 tables, as well as more complex data, you should refer to Goodman's article as well as more recent elaborations (1972, 1974). Davis (1974) also provides a useful discussion. In brief, what you do is to first calculate the "risk" within each category of interest and then examine the relative risks by dividing the risk factors obtained for each category of the variable used for predicting.

Practicum 10.2 Using the following data from a study of rape and the imposition of the death penalty in the South during 1945–1965 (Wolfgang and Riedel, 1973), calculate the risk ratio, showing the risk of death for black defendants as compared to white.

	Death	*Other*	*Total*
Black	110	713	823
White	9	433	442
Total	119	1,146	1,265

Proportional Reduction in Error Measures

In addition to percentage differences and odds ratios, there are additional convenient and illustrative summary indicators of the degree of predictive relationship between variables. This "family" of statistics is referred to as the proportional reduction in error—PRE—measures. For detailed discussions of the statistics included in this family, see Costner (1965) and Mueller, Schussler, and Costner (1970, pp. 239–66).

To get a feel for the construction of these measures, consider the following. Suppose you are given information about a sample of teenagers. You know that half of them are delinquent and half nondelinquent. You are asked to predict which individuals are which. Without any additional information you might decide to play it safe and predict that all persons are nondelinquent. In this way you assure yourself of 50-percent success. If there are 100 persons in the sample, you will end up with 50 errors. Just before you make the prediction, however, you are given one additional piece of information: the degree of respect each individual has for the law. This respect is dichotomized into "high" and "low" categories. Hypothesizing that attitudes affect behavior, you decide to make your prediction on the basis of this attitude. For those with high respect you predict they are nondelinquent; for those with low respect you predict delinquent.

On inspection you find that, indeed, all persons with low respect for the law have committed at least one delinquent act and all persons with high respect have not, as shown in Figure 10.4. This being the

FIGURE 10.4
Hypothetical Data Showing Perfect Relationship between Respect for the Law
and Delinquency

Respect for Law	Delinquency	
	Yes	No
High	0	50
Low	50	0

case, all errors have been eliminated. The predictive power of "respect for the law" is high indeed. There has been a 100-percent gain in predictive power over predictions made without knowledge of respect for the law. This is reflected in a measure of association 1.0.

Rarely will we be in such a "lucky" position. Usually the prediction will be less than perfect. This reflects, in part, that delinquency, like other phenomena in society, is associated with a number of factors. To consider these more complicated and more realistic situations, two additional illustrations (Figures 10.5 and 10.6) are presented showing progressively weaker relationships between delinquency and respect to-

FIGURE 10.5
Hypothetical Data Showing Strong but
Not Perfect Relationship between Re-
spect for the Law and Delinquency

Respect for Law	Delinquency	
	Yes	No
High	5	45
Low	45	5

FIGURE 10.6

Hypothetical Data Showing Weak Relationship between Respect for the Law and Delinquency

Respect for Law	Delinquency	
	Yes	*No*
High	23	27
Low	27	23

ward the law. These fictitious data reflect the repeated finding that, although respect for the law is important, other factors are at work. Some persons with high respect will be delinquent; some with low respect will be totally law-abiding.

In Figure 10.5 we see that, by predicting delinquent when respect is low and nondelinquent when respect is high, we will be correct 90 percent of the time. However, .90 is not a satisfactory indicator of the relative *gain* in predictive power since we would have been correct 50 percent of the time on the basis of chance alone. We want some indicator of the *improvement* in predictive power attained from knowledge about respect for the law. To obtain this we can subtract the number of errors made when we know the degree of respect from the number of errors we make with no additional knowledge. This is divided by the number of errors made with no knowledge to obtain an indication of the *proportional reduction* in error produced when we predict from knowledge of respect for the law.

This new measure, .80 for Figure 10.5, is an example of a proportional reduction in error measure of association. In the general case, members of this family of measures are defined by four elements (Costner, 1965). First, there is a rule for predicting some characteristic from knowledge of its own distribution. In the above examples this was done by noting that there were 50 delinquents and 50 nondelinquents. Noting this, we decided to always predict nondelinquent and live with a sure 50-percent error. Had we known that 80 percent of the sample were nondelinquents, we would have predicted nondelinquent for each individual and settled for a 20-percent error.

The second element is a rule for predicting some characteristic of one variable from knowledge of another. In the above cases we worked from the hypothesis that the greater the respect for the law, the higher the chances of being nondelinquent. The third element is a definition of what constitutes error. In the above examples this was simply the number of cases that had been misclassified. Thus, we were in error for delinquents with high respect for the law and for nondelinquents with low respect.

The specific provisions of these rules will differ for each of the PRE measures. However, each can be expressed as a function of a combination of these elements. The way in which these elements are combined brings us to the fourth element, the defining formula.

$$\frac{E_1 - E_2}{E_1} = \text{PRE measure of association}$$

In this equation, E_1 is the number of errors made when predictions are based on the first rule. E_2 is the number of errors that will be made when predicting from the second rule.

Since each measure in this family differs in the specifics of calculation, you should familiarize yourself with the differences and their implications. These differences in calculation rules lead to a problem if we want to compare the results of one study with those of another. Frequently, one study will rely on one measure of association while a second study, dealing with the same substantive problem, relies on another. The apparent differences in results may be due in part to this switch in statistics.

A measure of association frequently used in conjunction with variables measured by interval scales and interpretable as a proportional reduction in error measure is the *correlation coefficient squared*, represented as r^2.

Take as an example the case where we are interested in the allocation of resources in a society in terms of who gets how much money. E_1 might be constructed in the following manner. First, you predict a value for each individual equal to the mean income. You will make mistakes unless everyone makes the same amount, but your mistakes will be minimized. E_1 is defined by first subtracting from the mean the actual amount the individual made and then squaring this figure. The total amount of error is then calculated by adding these errors for the total sample. This total, E_1, is referred to as the Total Sum of Squares (TSS).

Now, suppose you are given one additional piece of information—the sample was drawn from the community Schooltopia, where it had been decreed that each man, woman, and child be rewarded with $1,000 for each year of schooling completed, no more and no less, except that a basic figure of $3,000 would hold even if persons had never set foot inside a classroom. With this additional piece of information your best prediction for any given individual would be the formula:

$$\text{Income} = 3000 + (1000 \times \text{Years in School})$$

This is a specific instance of a more general set of equations, of the form $Y = a + bX$, referred to as linear regression equations. They are linear since, by plotting values of X and Y, we get a line. If the money were being distributed as planned, a plot of years in school and income for individuals in the sample would look like that in Figure 10.7. In

FIGURE 10.7
Relationship between Income and Years in School Using
Income = 3000 + (1000 × Years in School)
As Prediction Equation. Perfect Relationship in That All Persons Fall on the Line

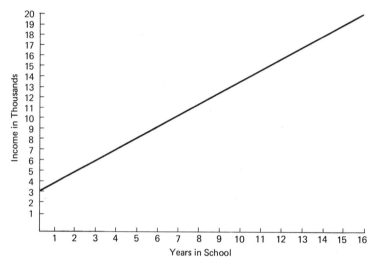

such a smooth-running community you would eliminate errors using the second prediction rule, E_2 would be zero, and thus arrive at a measure of association $E_1 - 0/E_1 = 1.0$, which indicates a perfect prediction of income from education.

Now, suppose that, after some ten years of rather smooth operation, this allocation plan began to falter. Persons began to obtain additional wealth from their parents through wills and influence. Some factory managers began differentially rewarding persons for showing initiative. Schools began selectively admitting persons based on past performance and thus it was not only the number of years in school that mattered but also how well they did during those years. Initiative and accomplishment, in turn, were found to be a function of childhood training and influence of certain significant others. It also was found that, as the years progressed, the availability of high-paying jobs was governed by the connections one had in terms of the prestige of one's college and the social network of one's professors. In short, it soon became evident that the money available was being allocated for a whole series of reasons other than the years of school completed.

Realizing that the allocation procedures were not working so well as planned, the government of Schooltopia formed a commission that in turn hired social researchers to find out just how far awry the system had gone. Once again this commission gathered data on income and education. Once again it based its original prediction on the mean level of income and its second prediction on the formula

$$\text{Income} = 3000 + (1000 \times \text{Years in School})$$

This time they found there were deviations around the line predicted on the basis of the decree. See Figure 10.8, wherein a dot represents

FIGURE 10.8
Relationship between Income and Years in School Using

Income = 3000 + (1000 × Years in School)

As Prediction Equation. Imperfect Relationship in That All Persons Do Not have the Income Predicted.

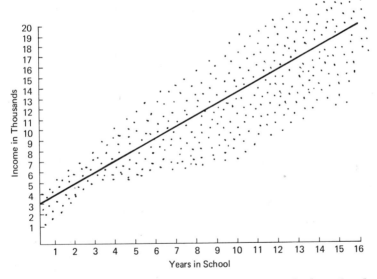

a value for one person's education an income. To calculate the degree of error in the system (E_2), they constructed a series of vertical lines from each individual to the predicted line defined by the decree formula. These distances, measured in terms of dollars, were then squared and added, as was done for deviations about the total mean. This done, it was found that $E_1 - E_2/E_1 = .35$. Knowledge of years in school was still of some help when predicting income, but over the years other factors had entered in.

In addition to illustrating the meaning of r^2, this example also can be used to point out the elements of regression equations, which also are important in prediction. These elements include the *intercept* ($3,000 above), which is defined as the point at which the line defined by the prediction formula crosses the vertical axis. That is, the intercept is the value of the *dependent variable* (in the above example, "Income") when the *independent variable* ("Years of Schooling" above) is at the minimum. Another element is the *slope coefficient* ($1,000 for each year of school above), which indicates the predicted change in the dependent variable per unit change in the independent variable.

Given the state of knowledge in the social sciences, we are rarely in such an advantageous position as that outlined above. We are still refining our measurements and ideas about the relationship between certain variables. We do not have kingly decrees to work with. However, some progress is being made. What is called for in this regard is a set of standardized measures of variables so that estimates of the slope coefficients can be applied across a number of research settings. Without standardized measures the slope coefficients, which indicate the change per unit change, will vary according to the scales being used. With standardized measures in hand we can begin to talk about deviations around some specific predictive model. By and large, however, what is normally done is to assume that the variables are linearly related and then look for the best-fitting line, that is, the line that minimizes the E_2 term. This is only in some rough sense of the term "prediction." Rather, we generally are coming up with a statement as to how close some general linear model comes to fitting the data, given measures of the variables and estimates of the slope coefficients from the data in hand.

Practicum 10.3 Assume you are reading a study of the relationship between group conflict and the degree of open and free discussion. In this study the degree of hostile group conflict (Y) has been measured with an interval scale from one to ten. The degree of open discussion (X) also has been measured on an interval scale from one to ten. The best fitting predictive equation for the relationship is as follows:

$$Y = 8.7 - .5X$$
$$r^2 = .37$$

Now, translate this equation into sentence form. Note (1) the amount of conflict when open discussion is at a minimum, (2) the predicted change in the degree of conflict as the discussion moves toward openness, and (3) the degree to which the equation allows us to accurately predict the amount of conflict from the degree of discussion.

The criteria governing the selection of a measure of association are only partially spelled out. Some measures are used for "nominal data," which simply categorize individuals—e.g., male, female. Other measures are used where the categories are ordered, e.g., high, medium, and low respect. Still others are used for interval data, where the categories are not only ordered but also equidistant from one another, e.g., age, years of education, amount of income in dollars. Beyond this, the criteria for selection are blurred. A step toward clarification has been taken by Leik and Gove (1971), but much remains to be specified. For the interested student this can be taken as uncharted ground to be explored.

A key point to keep in mind is to realize that measures of association vary not only according to the strength of the association between variables but also with the specific calculation rules defining their value. This being the case, it is important to acquaint yourself with the specifics of the statistics you propose to use to ensure that your presentation of the data is in line with your conceptualization of the problem.

ELABORATING OUR ABILITY TO PREDICT

Once association between pairs of variables has been explored, you may find yourself wondering further. You may, for example, find that support for capital punishment can be predicted with some success from political-party preferences and wonder if this is due to the attraction of authoritarian personalities to one party and not the other.

Cross-Classification with Controls

Suppose that, unknown prior to your study, the dynamics of personality traits, party selection, and support for capital punishment operated as indicated in the "probability tree" in Figure 10.9. This tree is read starting at the left and following the various limbs to the end. For example, it represents a society in which there is an 80-percent chance that persons with authoritarian tendencies will choose Party X. Within this 80 percent there is a 90-percent chance that those persons will support capital punishment, giving an overall tendency of 72 percent. In parallel fashion, there is a 50-percent chance that nonauthoritarians will choose Party X and a 40-percent chance that those persons will support capital punishment, giving an overall tendency of 20 percent.

With this picture of the process, what would data look like if you were to select a representative sample from this population. Assume a sample size of 2,000, which includes 1,000 authoritarians and 1,000 nonauthoritarians. Given the above probabilities, this would result, within limits of sampling error, in Figure 10.10 representing the relationship between party preference and support for capital punishment. You should satisfy yourself as to where the cell frequencies came from. For example, the 920 cases in the Party X/Support for Capital Punishment

FIGURE 10.9
Data Showing Probabilities Linking Personalities, Party Preferences, and Support for Capital Punishment in Hypothetical Population

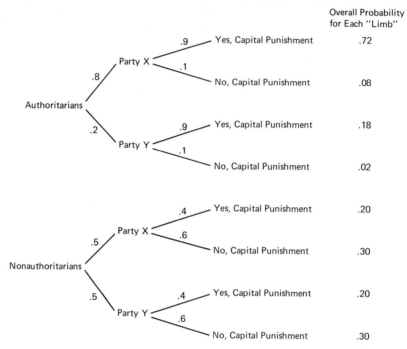

Overall Probability for Each "Limb"

.9 — Yes, Capital Punishment	.72
.1 — No, Capital Punishment	.08
.9 — Yes, Capital Punishment	.18
.1 — No, Capital Punishment	.02
.4 — Yes, Capital Punishment	.20
.6 — No, Capital Punishment	.30
.4 — Yes, Capital Punishment	.20
.6 — No, Capital Punishment	.30

FIGURE 10.10
Hypothetical Data from a Sample Drawn from a Population Represented in Figure 10.9, Showing Relationship between Party Preference and Support for Capital Punishment

Party Preference	Support Capital Punishment		
	Yes	*No*	*Total*
X	71% (920)	29% (380)	100% (1,300)
Y	54% (380)	46% (320)	100% (700)

cell came from the 720 persons who were authoritarians in Party X, supporting capital punishment, and the 200 nonauthoritarians in Party X, supporting capital punishment. This, of course, is information you did not have prior to your study. Upon examination of the data you find that members of Party X are more likely than members of Party Y to support capital punishment.

Given these findings, you continue the investigation by first examining the relationship between personality trait and party preference to uncover the findings in Figure 10.11. In like manner you rearrange the

FIGURE 10.11
Hypothetical Data from a Sample Drawn from a Population Represented in Figure 10.9, Showing Relationship between Party Preference and Personality Trait

Personality Trait	Party		
	X	Y	Total
Authoritarians	80% (800)	20% (200)	100% (1,000)
Nonauthoritarians	50% (500)	50% (500)	100% (1,000)

data to find the relationship between authoritarianism and support for the death penalty as indicated in Figure 10.12. Given this initial support for your hunch that the relationship between party preference and support for capital punishment was due to the tendency for certain personalities to gravitate to certain parties, the next step is to "control." To

FIGURE 10.12
Hypothetical Data from Sample Drawn from a Population Represented in Figure 10.9, Showing Relationship between Authoritarianism and Support for Capital Punishment

Personality Trait	Support for Capital Punishment		
	Yes	No	Total
Authoritarians	90% (900)	10% (100)	100% (1,000)
Nonauthoritarians	40% (400)	60% (600)	100% (1,000)

control, you look within categories of your control variable, in this case the personality trait authoritarianism, to see if the relationship between party preference and support for capital punishment remains.

Given a representative sample of a population that operates as indicated in Figure 10.9, you would find something like Figure 10.13.

FIGURE 10.13

Hypothetical Data from a Sample Drawn from a Population Represented in Figure 10.9 Showing Relationship between Party Preference and Support for Capital Punishment Controlling for Whether or Not Individuals Were Authoritarians or Nonauthoritarians

Authoritarians

Party Preference	Support for Capital Punishment		
	Yes	No	Total
X	90% (720)	10% (80)	100% (800)
Y	90% (180)	10% (20)	100% (200)

Nonauthoritarians

Party Preference	Support for Capital Punishment		
	Yes	No	Total
X	40% (200)	60% (300)	100% (500)
Y	40% (200)	60% (300)	100% (500)

Thus, when we separate authoritarians and nonauthoritarians, there is *no* relationship between party preference and support for capital punishment. Members of each party within each personality category are equally likely to support the death penalty. From this the conclusion is that the original finding of a relationship between party preference and support of the death penalty emerged from the common grounding in the personality trait, authoritarianism.

The process of elaborating our ability to predict, then, is one in which we rearrange data to get a different vantage point. Given a relationship between two variables, it is frequently the case that a series of "explanations" come to mind. To pursue these alternatives it becomes necessary to look at the same data in different forms. The form in any situation will depend on the "explanations" suggested. Again, the process of social research can be thought of as a process of translation.

Although you will have to decide for yourself which of a range of possibilities best represents your ideas, when examining possible explanations for your findings, a general format is frequently helpful. This is the format we called "control" above. The general format is represented in Figure 10.14. The basic pattern is to separate your cases according to some category on your control variable and then examine the initial relationship again.

By examining information as represented in the foregoing illustrations,

FIGURE 10.14
General Format for Control Using Cross-Classification Tables

	Control Category A Dependent Variable	
Independent Variable		

	Control Category B Dependent Variable	
Independent Variable		

we can seê in what way our ability to predict has been affected by the control. Showing that the original association between two variables was due to a common grounding in a third variable is only one among several prototypes of potential interconnections between three variables. In addition, you may uncover a third variable that has no effect on the original relationship. Still further, you may find that, when you control for a third variable, a relationship that originally appeared as negligible becomes strong. In this case the third variable is referred to as a suppressor variable, a variable that, when not controlled, hides the "real" relationship. You may find that the third variable is a "conditioner"; that is, the relationship between two variables is strong only within one category of a third variable. For example, imprisonment might be related to a decrease in future criminal behavior but only among certain individuals—those who view the legal system's reaction as legitimate. For those who do not view the law's reaction as legitimate there may be no relationship between incarceration and future behavior, or the relationship may be in the opposite direction.

Practicum 10.4 You probably have felt or heard at one time or another that success breeds ambition. Assume that you draw a representative sample from the population represented by the probability tree in Figure 10.15. Assume further that there is no sampling error. What will the overall relationship between success and ambition look like when you construct a table predicting ambition from success? What will this same relationship look like when you control for sex? Assume that you have the same number of males as females. State in your own words what the findings indicate.

Practicum 10.4 Now, suppose you are involved in a study to uncover factors related to the commission of delinquent acts. You read the literature on the subject and find that at various times persons have hypothesized delinquency to be related to a number of factors, among which are style of parental supervision, degree of respect for parents, grades in school, and friends who have committed delinquent acts. These are only a few of the factors that others have found to be associated with delinquency, but you decide to concentrate your efforts on these variables. Suppose, further, that, unknown to you, prior to your study, these factors are related to one another as depicted in

FIGURE 10.15

**Hypothetical Picture of Population, Showing Relationship
between Sex, Success, and Increased Ambition**

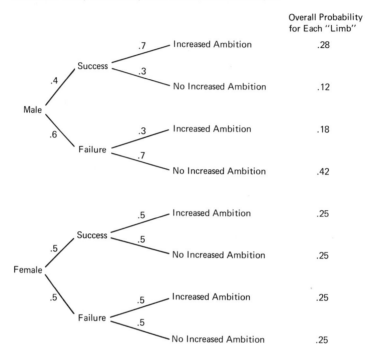

Overall Probability
for Each "Limb"

Figure 10.16 in the population from which you are going to sample.
Assume a random sample size of 2,000, with an equal number of respondents in both of the parental supervision categories. Set up a table
that allows you to pursue the hypothesis that parental supervision is
a good predictor of whether persons will commit delinquent acts. Write
out a summary statement of what you find. Now, introduce the control
variable "Respect for Parents." Again, summarize your findings. Finally,
and notice the additional complexity, introduce a second control for
grades and continue to examine the relationship between parental practices and delinquency controlling for respect. Summarize your findings.
This final step involves what are referred to as simultaneous controls.

Multiple and Partial Regression

You may have noted when setting up the final set of tables in the
above problems that, even with an original sample of 2,000, the number
of cases in cells was getting rather small. With one or more additional
controls, even fewer cases would have been available. You might also
have realized that the measurement employed was rather crude. Persons

FIGURE 10.16
Overall Probability of Delinquency

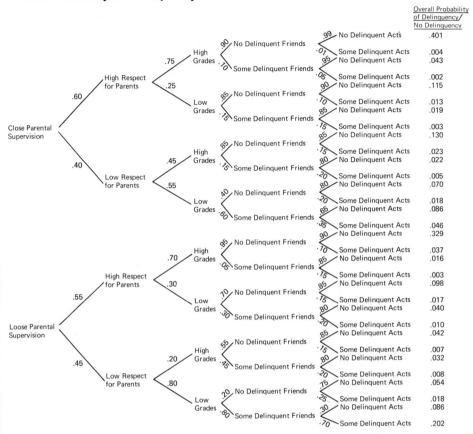

either had respect for their parents or they did not; they either had delinquent friends or they did not; and so forth. Better measurement devices might have indicated the number of friends and the degree of respect instead of just presence or absence.

Fortunately, there are techniques that allow us to rearrange data in such a way as to take advantage of more refined measures of concepts and at the same time get away with using fewer cases. These techniques already have been introduced when we discussed the prediction of income from education, where the sample was drawn from a society in which each member received $1,000 for every year of school completed, with a minimum wage of $3,000. It will be recalled that the equation for this situation was referred to as the regression equation, $Y = 3,000 + 1,000X$, where Y was an income and X the years of school completed. The measure of the degree to which this gave an accurate prediction was referred to as the correlation coefficient squared. As Figure 10.17 shows, regression equations and cross-classification tables are closely related. The major differences lie in the fact that, when cross-classification tables are used, measurements are collapsed. This, of course, reduces the precision of our prediction. With cross-classification

FIGURE 10.17
Relationship between Regression Line and Cross-Classification Table

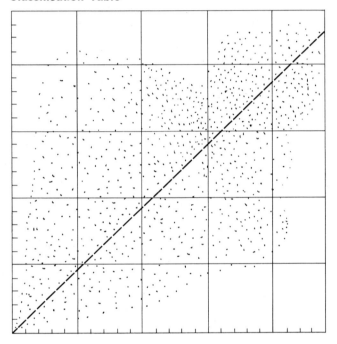

tables we predict the direction of the relationship between variables. With regression equations we also predict the form of the relationship. That is, with regression equations we predict to the line; with cross-classification we predict to the cells.

Given this relationship between regression equations and cross-classification tables with two variables, it should not be surprising to find there is also a close relationship between cross-classification tables with controls and what is called multiple regression, regression equations with more than two variables, and multiple and partial correlation coefficients.

First, the idea of multiple regression. With multiple regression we simply predict a variable with knowledge of two or more variables. In equation form this becomes $Y = a + b_1X_1 + b_2X_2 + e$. Referring back to our previous example, this can be translated to read that we predict income (Y) from knowledge of education (X_1) and a second variable (X_2), such as time on the job, age, or the income of parents at an earlier time. The idea that our predictions will be less than exact is represented by e, which reflects the probable finding that the values of income will cluster around the predicted values for Y rather than landing exactly on them. The b's in front of the X's allow us to translate the idea that each of the predicting variables is related to the predicted variable, controlling for the other. Years in school is related to income, even when controlling for X_2. In turn, X_2, time on the job, for example, is related to income controlling for years of education.

In this case, controlling for a variable and examining a relationship between the remaining two variables can be thought of as a repeated look at the relationship between the two variables within a large number of categories of the control variable and then pooling the results. This assumes that the relationship within categories of the control variable is the same. If it is not, that is, if the relationship between X_1 and Y depends on the value of X_2, then this pooled estimate will be misleading. Fortunately, there are also techniques that allow us to pursue this alternative. Unfortunately, once we get into these questions of uncovering conditional relationships between variables within various categories of the control variable, we get beyond the scope of the present discussion. You should be advised, however, that it is possible to translate these more intricate ideas into data. For discussions, the books by Hu (1973) and Kerlinger and Pedhazer (1973) provide clear presentations.

The regression equation, then, can include more than one predictor variable. How well we do in terms of accurate prediction, given this more complex regression equation, is once again reflected in what are referred to as correlation coefficients. In this case there are two different coefficients. One, the *partial correlation coefficient squared*, reflects the predictive power of a variable or set of variables, controlling for the remaining predictor variables in the equation. The second, the *multiple correlation coefficient squared*, reflects the total proportional reduction in error accomplished when employing each of the predictor variables simultaneously.

Examining the partial and multiple correlation coefficients, then, we are able to pursue the amount of income attributable to years in school and years on the job taken by themselves (the partials), as well as the allocation of income explained when they are combined (the multiple). This is not simply a matter of adding the respective partials since, among other things, the predictor variables may themselves be related. Again, we find that the plot thickens beyond the scope of the present discussion. Again, we are in the position of saying that techniques are available and that, if your problem calls for them, some effort will have to be expended on gaining the necessary skills. In addition to Hu and Kerlinger and Pedhazer mentioned above, Hayes (1973) provides more detailed discussion of the calculations and rationales involved.

SUMMARY

What this chapter has done is provide a quick overview of a number of statistical techniques for translating the idea of prediction into data. It has been too quick an overview for anymore than a tentative grasp of the issues involved. For more thorough knowledge you should consult the texts cited.

What you should come away with is some grasp of the proportional reduction in error criterion. Successful prediction means that we eliminate errors by having certain knowledge. The degree of error elimination is what this PRE family of measures reflect. This, as much as anything else, speaks to their utility.

Throughout this book we have referred to situations where you want to examine the correlation between certain traits. These may include cultural traits uncovered from data in the *Human Relations Area Files.* It may be the relationship between city size and rate of crime. It may be the situation where you are predicting certain behaviors from attitudes reported on a questionnaire. In each of these situations the question is: Can we predict *Y* from *X*? You should now be in a beginning position to present data relevant to this general set of predictive questions. In the next chapter we will turn to the slightly more complex issue of translating the idea of cause into statistical information.

KEY ISSUES

1. What is the important thing to keep in mind when using percentage differences to translate the idea of prediction?
2. What is meant by the "odds ratio"?
3. What is meant when we say a measure of association is a member of the PRE family?
4. What are the important elements of a regression equation and its PRE measure of association?
5. What is the difference between a multiple correlation coefficient and a partial correlation coefficient?

REFERENCES

Costner, Herbert L.
      1965 "Criteria of Measures of Association." *American Sociological Review*, vol. 30, pp. 341–53.

Davis, James A.
1974 "Hierarchical Models for Significance Tests in Multivariate Con-
tingency Tables: An Exegesis of Goodman's Recent Papers." In
Herbert L. Costner (ed.), *Sociological Methodology 1973–1974*,
San Francisco: Jossey Bass, Inc.

Gibbs, Jack P.
1972 *Sociological Theory Construction*. Hinsdale, Ill.: The Dryden
Press, Inc.

Goodman, Leo A.
1969 "How to Ransack Social Mobility Tables and Other Kinds of
Cross-Classification Tables." *American Journal of Sociology*, vol.
75, pp. 1–40.

Hayes, William L.
1973 *Statistics for the Social Sciences*. New York: Holt, Rinehart and
Winston.

Hu, Teh-wei
1973 *Econometrics, An Introductory Analysis*. Baltimore: University
Park Press.

Kerlinger, Fred N., and Pedhazur, Elazar J.
1973 *Multiple Regression in Behavioral Research*. New York: Holt,
Rinehart and Winston.

Leik, Robert K., and Gove, Walter R.
1971 "Integrated Approach to Measuring Association." In Herbert L.
Costner (ed.), *Sociological Methodology 1971*, San Francisco.
Jossey Bass Inc.

Mueller, John K., Schussler, Karl F., and Costner, Herbert L.
1970 *Statistical Reasoning in Sociology*. Houghton Mifflin Company.

Wolfgang, Marvin E., and Riedel, Marc
1973 "Race, Judicial Discretion, and the Death Penalty." *The Annals
of The American Academy of Political and Social Science*, vol. 407,
pp. 119–33.

Contents

Chapter 11

Translating the Concept of "Cause" into Data

CAUSE AND PREDICTION

For many theorists, prediction is not enough. Causal explanation is what we are after. Assertions about cause are central to theories of deviance, political behavior, occupational mobility, kinship structures, personality types, family stability, religious practices, and, more generally, to the sources and consequences of social order and organization. We can predict the joint occurrence of phenomenon all day and still not investigate the more complicated question of cause. As a leading proponent of "causal analysis" has reiterated, "It would be misleading to confuse causal notions with those of prediction. . . . The mere fact that X and Y vary together in a predictable way, and that a change in X always precedes the change in Y, can never assure us that X *produced* a change in Y" (Blalock, 1961, pp. 9–10; emphasis added). This same proponent is quick to recognize that "Strictly speaking, causal arguments cannot be verified empirically as they are not on the operational level. They involve purely hypothetical if—then statements and require simplifying assumptions that are inherently untestable" (Blalock, 1968, p. 155).

We are left, then, in somewhat of a bind. We have a central and pervasive theoretical idea and, yet, we are without the ability to observe. For a scholarly endeavor claiming uniqueness on its ability to observe, this is no small matter. It has led at least one sociological theorist to advocate abandonment of the pursuit of cause. "A causal language may or may not be feasible in other disciplines, but a mode of theory construction should be consistent with the conditions of work in a field, and in sociology those conditions are alien to a causal language" (Gibbs, 1972, p. 815). In even stronger language, Bertrand Russell (1918) suggested that causation is "a relic of a bygone age."

Nevertheless, since the issue remains unresolved and since much of the existing social-science literature is in causal terms, it is instructive to examine some potential solutions devised to move us from the *idea* of cause to its *observation*. We will first examine observable criteria that have been suggested. We will then turn to four classes of variables created when employing these criteria. Finally, we will examine strategies devised to handle these classes of variables. The close connection between elaborated prediction and causal analysis should become evident in the process.

CRITERIA FOR A CAUSAL LINKAGE

As summarized by Hirschi and Selvin (1967), three criteria must be met if a causal linkage between two variables is to be established: (1) The variables must be statistically related. (2) The cause must not follow the effect. (3) The association between the variables must be such that it does not disappear when the effects of "other variables causally prior to both of the original variables are removed."

The connection between these criteria and our previous discussion of prediction should be noted. The first criterion is directly transferred. In order to infer both cause and prediction, we must establish some association between variables. Thus, the measures of association discussed in the previous chapter should be equally useful here.

The second criterion is different. To explore predictive power we may be interested, though not necessarily, in the timing sequence. For prediction, we are interested in the state of one variable given knowledge of another. This may or may not imply that the predictor variable preceded the predicted variable. To establish cause, the timing must be such that the effect does not precede the cause. The effect may occur instantaneously or it may occur some years later, but the time sequence must be such that that which is doing the producing is not preceded by that which is produced. This is not to say that a variable that is at one time an effect cannot itself become a later cause of its original source. Deviant behavior may be a source as well as a consequence of alienation. What it does imply is that, when speaking in causal terms, the time sequence for any given hypothesized relationship must be specified. Frequently, this is no easy task. How long do we wait? How do we separate the timing of variables when feedback is involved? These are questions that have not yet been totally solved in many research projects.

The third criterion is related to the previous discussion of prediction in that it is a special type of elaboration. It involves strategies similar to the procedures for control presented in the last chapter. It is this quest for "spurious" or artificial relations that most readily gives the researcher ulcers. Trouble emerges in two forms. First, it is always possible to assert that the observed relationship is the artifact of some unnoticed preceding variable. This is particularly the case when analyzing survey data. It is also problematic, as we will soon see, when we are able to set up a situation for experimental manipulation. The second source of trouble emerges as one tries to separate "spurious" relations, that is, relationships that result from a common grounding in a third variable, from the specification of intervening variables, which do not deny the causal linkage between the original variables but rather specify the mechanism through which the causal linkage works. The spurious relationship is diagrammed in Figure 11.1. The intervening relationship

FIGURE 11.1
Showing Spurious Relationship between Y and Z.
Both Y and Z flow from X

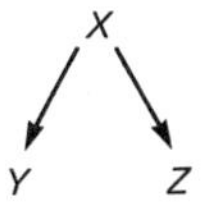

FIGURE 11.2
Showing Indirect Relationship between Y and Z
with Intervening Variable X

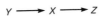

is shown in Figure 11.2. As these figures show, the difference lies in the sequence of variables.

Keeping in mind these three criteria, we are left, as Kish (1959) has suggested, with four types of variables. Class I variables are those of primary interest. They are labeled the independent (that which is causing or predicting) and the dependent (that which is caused or predicted). Class II variables include those variables controlled either through statistical or experimental manipulation. Class III variables include those confounding variables that are not controlled but are influencing the relationship between the variables of primary interest. Class IV variables are those variables the effects of which are randomized. Class IV variables may be influencing the relationship of primary interest but their effects cancel one another and thus the conclusions should not be biased.

The task is to move as many variables as possible into the controlled category. Failing this, and it is always possible that some variables will escape control, the job is to transfer as many of the confounding influences from variables in Class III into the randomized influences of Class IV. The most useful available strategy to accomplish these tasks is the experiment. The investigatory power of an experiment in terms of reflect-

ing cause comes from its control. This control manifests itself in randomization and manipulation. To explain these strategies, an example should
be useful.

THE EXPERIMENT

Example: Stephan and Tully (1973) have provided an interesting experiment
designed to investigate factors related to juror decisions in civil-suit trials.
The experiment was set up in the following way: Subjects for the experiment
were students enrolled in upper-division social-psychology classes in a large
Southern university. An equal number of these students was randomly assigned
to one of eight groups. These eight groups were defined by the information
given regarding the characteristics of the plaintiff in terms of age, sex, and
physical attractiveness:

	Attractive		*Unattractive*	
Sex	*25 yr*	*8 yr*	*25 yr*	*8 yr*
Male	1	2	3	4
Female	5	6	7	8

Thus, one group of students (cell 1) was presented with an attractive 25-year-
old male plaintiff, while another group (cell 8) was presented with an unattractive 8-year-old female plaintiff, and so forth. Each student was presented
with a packet containing a picture of the plaintiff, his or her age, and a
synopsis of the accident. After reading the synopsis the students were asked
to record their decision, acting as if they were jurors. Splitting the subjects
into those with "attractive" (cells 1, 2, 5, and 6) and those with "unattractive"
(cells 3, 4, 7, and 8) pictures of the plaintiff, it was found that, when
the decision was for the plaintiff, the attractive plaintiffs were awarded more
money (mean value $49,457.88) than unattractive plaintiffs (mean value
$34,779.83). There were other findings but these are enough to serve discus-
sion purposes.

In addition to the rather interesting findings, we should note the
random assignment of subjects to different groups and the *symmetry*
of design in terms of equal number of students assigned to each group.
Random assignment is the procedure that allows us to rule out, on
statistical grounds, the confounding influence of additional neglected
variables. It is a way to move Class III variables to Class IV. Symmetry
of design allows us to eliminate the confounding influence that might
occur from the interrelationship of independent variables. It is a way
to move Class III variables to the controlled category, Class II.

In more detail, the purpose of randomization is to ensure, with specifiable statistical probability, that the groups have similar distributions
of persons in terms of such things as years in school, psychological

predisposition, social-class background, bias toward experiments, and the like. Looking at a group as a whole, say, those students with unattractive 25-year-old female plaintiffs, and comparing this group with others, differences in the amounts awarded should not be due to composition differences since the groups are assumed to have the same distribution of individual characteristics. It may be, of course, that the workings of chance have produced such differences. However, by random assignment, we are at least able to specify the probability of this happening. With this procedure, then, we are able to handle the third criteria for establishing cause, namely, the elimination of alternative explanations from otherwise neglected variables that precede both the hypothesized cause and effect. It is this lack of random assignment to categories of the independent variable in analysis of survey results that makes the survey a less powerful tool in this regard.

The purpose of symmetry in terms of equal numbers in each experimental condition is to eliminate the intercorrelation that might otherwise occur among the specified independent variables. Suppose, for example, that "attractive" plaintiffs were also predominantly young. The findings of differential awards to the plaintiff according to attractiveness might then have been due to age differentials rather than attractiveness. By assuring an equal number of subjects in each experimental situation, this possibility was eliminated. When differences are found between awards to attractive and unattractive plaintiffs, these differences cannot be attributed to the age or sex of the plaintiff since these differences have been eliminated within categories of attractiveness. In this manner, Stephan and Tully moved potentially confounding variables into the controlled variable class.

These, then, are the benefits of experiments when pursuing the idea of cause: (1) Experiments allow the researcher to manipulate the independent variable in such a way as to ensure the appropriate time sequence between dependent and independent variables. (2) Experiments allow the researcher to analyze results to see if there is an association between the dependent and independent variables controlling for possible neglected as well as suspected confounding alternatives.

What are the drawbacks? To discuss this question a useful distinction has been made by Campbell and Stanley (1963) between the *internal validity* and *external validity* of a study. Internal validity of a study is determined by the extent to which alternative explanations of the findings have been eliminated. It is to this end that the procedures of random assignment to experimental groups and the symmetry of design are employed. The external validity of a study is determined by the extent to which the results are applicable outside the given experimental setting.

Returning to our example, we saw that random assignment and symmetry of design reduce the probability that the findings were due to some third variable. In the process, however, the experiment may have created new, contending explanations for the findings. Three notes of caution are sounded by Stephen and Tully concerning the potential influence of the simulated jury in this regard. The first arises when simulated jurors realize their decisions will not affect human lives. If the perceived importance of a decision influences the probability of using superficial cues, such as physical attractiveness, when decisions are reached, this will create an artificial relationship between physical attractiveness and the amount awarded. A second potential artificial source for the findings resides in the scope of the information provided the jurors. As Stephan and Tully note, "The simulated juror in this study viewed only a short transcript. This situation may be so limiting in richness and depth of detail that decisions reached would have little correlation with verdicts in an actual case of the same nature." Thus, again, the experiment may be generating its own competing explanations. A third possibility arises as the simulated jurors reached their decisions in isolation. If the collective nature of the decision is related to the probability of using superficial information, we are again confronted with a finding that might have been artificially produced.

We find, then, that in the process of setting up an experiment we frequently generate our own competing explanations. Problems similar to those discussed above have been variously labeled the "guinea-pig effect," the "reactive effect of measurement," and "role selection." These and other threats to both the internal and external validity of a study are discussed in Campbell and Stanley (1963), Webb et al. (1966), Ross and Smith (1968), and Burgess and Bushell (1969). There are various experimental designs that allow control or at least the examination of various categories of problems in this regard. Unfortunately, a detailed discussion of these problems and suggested solutions would carry us too far afield at this point. If you are considering setting up an actual experiment, you should consult these or similar discussions.

The external and internal validity of a study are related in that, when the experiment creates its own confounding conditions, the results *may* not apply outside the setting. The importance of this lack of generalizability differs in part with the nature of the concepts being investigated. When we are dealing with relatively concrete concepts, such as juror decisions in civil suits as opposed to the more general concept of, say, decision making in general, then the applicability of the results becomes more problematic.

In the above experiment it would be risky, indeed, to jump from these results to suggestions that the 12- or 6- person jury with real-life situations and more complete information would reach decisions in the same pattern. Not only is the contrived trial different in content and form but the subjects as well are in no way representative of the total pool of registered voters who might be selected for an actual jury.

If, on the other hand, we are interested in treating the results at a more general level, we become more interested in isolating lawlike relationships rather than replicating specific situations. In the more general situation we are concentrating on internal validity suggesting that *if* conditions in the real world are like those in the laboratory we will find similar results. We are in the same position as those formulating laws governing the movement of falling bodies, relying on results carried out in a vacuum. There is no claim that objects in the real world fall in a vacuum without obstruction, only the claim that, if they did, the results would be similar to those experimentally derived. Now, these laboratory laws are not insignificant or irrelevant to the real world. They allow us to more easily locate the existence and direction of differences between the real world and that of the laboratory and, in this way, move to a more complete elaboration of what is going on.

Whether or not we are concerned with external validity, experiments need not be limited to the "laboratory." They may be designed to more closely represent the "real" world. Consider the following example of a study designed to investigate the impact of passing through the criminal-justice system.

Example: In an experiment to investigate the impact of passing through the criminal-justice system on subsequent employment opportunities, Schwartz and Skolnick (1962) set up a study in the following manner: Through an "employment agent," who was actually a law student working in the area of the study during the summer, potential employers were presented with a folder of a prospective employee. As Schwartz and Skolnick reported it, "Four employment folders were prepared, the same in all respects except for the criminal court record of the applicant. In all of the folders he was described as a 32-year old single male of unspecified race, with a high-school training in mechanical trades and a record of successive short-term jobs as a kitchen helper, maintenance worker, and handyman. These characteristics are roughly typical of applicants for unskilled hotel jobs in the Catskill resort area of New York State, where employment opportunities were tested." The folders differed only in the reported contact with the criminal process. One folder noted that the applicant had been convicted and sentenced for assault. The second folder indicated that the applicant had been tried for assault but acquitted. The third folder presented an applicant who had been tried and acquitted for assault but also contained a letter from the judge certifying the finding of not guilty and reminding the reader of the presumption of innocence. The fourth folder contained no mention of a criminal record. A sample of 100 actual potential employers was used, with 25 being randomly given one of the four folders for consideration.

Looking at this experiment for its strategies of observation, you should note the random assignment of employers to the categories of the independent variable, the four folders. You should also note that the folders were alike in every respect except for the record of the applicant. The results are reprinted in Table 11.1.

TABLE 11.1
Effect of Four Types of Legal Folders on Job Opportunities (in percent)

	No Record	Acquitted with Letter	Acquitted without Letter	Convicted	Total
	(N = 25)	(N = 25)	(N = 25)	(N = 25)	(N = 100)
Positive response	36%	24%	12%	4%	19%
Negative response	64	76	88	96	81
Total	100%	100%	100%	100%	100%

Source: Schwartz and Skolnick, 1962.

Contact with the criminal-justice system clearly enters into the decision to offer a job, even when the applicants have been acquitted. Compare percentage differences across columns. There is a smooth progression from those with no record to those with a conviction in terms of a positive response to a job inquiry. Since this study was carried out under "natural" conditions, Schwartz and Skolnick can more readily discuss its implications in terms of the dynamics of community life and what might be the actual impact of changing policy. For example, they note:

> Two legal principles conflict in practice. On the one hand, "a man is innocent until proven guilty." On the other, the accused is systematically treated as guilty under the administration of criminal law and until a functionary or official body—police, magistrate, prosecuting attorney, or trial judge or jury—decides that he is entitled to be free. Even then, the results of treating him as guilty persists and may lead to serious consequences. . . . The courts have done little toward alleviating the post-acquittal consequences of legal accusation. One effort along these lines has been employed in the federal courts, however. Where an individual has been accused and exonerated of a crime, he may petition the federal courts, for a "Certificate of Innocence" certifying this fact. Possession of such a document might be expected to alleviate post-acquittal deprivations. (136)

Experiments in natural settings, then, are possible and frequently enlightening. Unfortunately, from a methodological point of view, but, fortunately, from a number of other vantage points, it is not always possible for the researcher to manipulate the natural setting in such a way as to accomplish random assignment to categories of the independent variable, symmetry of design, and manipulation of the independent variable.

Take, for example, the study of housing regulations discussed in Lemperts' article (1966) on "Strategies of Research Design in the Legal Impact Study." This study, done on the island of Oahu, Hawaii, by Ikeda, Ball, and Yamamura, sought to determine effects of different *housing regulations* on the *mobility patterns* among housing-project families. Initial examination of data showed that mobility was higher among families in projects with no income limits than among families living in projects having low- or moderate-income limits.

Consider the limitations, arising from the lack of initial random assignment to the projects, that must be placed on these findings concerning the impact of the *regulations* on *mobility.* As Lempert points out, these findings might have been due to any number of plausible alternatives. Families in the projects with no income limits may have started with higher incomes. Income and not regulations might have accounted for the difference in mobility. Also, families in the different projects may have been in different stages in their life cycle and thus more or less likely to move for any number of reasons. It might have been that family members in different projects differed in any number of ways in terms of social psychological characteristics. Although Ikeda, Ball, and Yamamura were well aware of these limitations and were able to control for some by examining income differentials, life-cycle data, and so forth, the point is that it is always possible that some neglected variable accounts for the finding. Such is the inherent hazard of inferring cause without the ability to randomly assign to the experimental condition, in this case to the different housing projects.

For additional examples of studies and discussions of this type of research, you might refer to Becker (1969), Krislov et al. (1972), Muir (1967), and Dolbeare and Hammond (1971).

Practicum 11.1 (A) Design an experiment, specifying the dependent and independent variables and the means of controlling for alternative explanations that might be advanced for the hypothesized findings. (B) What are some of the possible shortcomings of the study you have designed? (C) If the study you have proposed is to take place in a "laboratory," what benefits or drawbacks might there be in moving the experiment to the "field"? If the study you have proposed is to take place in the "field," what benefits or drawbacks might there be in moving the experiment to the "laboratory"? Is such movement from the field to lab or vice versa possible? If not, why not?

Quasi-Experimental Data

The type of nonexperimental research in which possibly neglected confounding variables most frequently lurk in the background is survey research. The problem is the same as that faced in the study of the relationship between housing regulations and mobility patterns. Persons or other units of observations have not been randomly placed in categories of the independent variables. They are what they are for systematic and uncontrolled reasons. Suppose, for example, we wanted to conduct a study of the relationship between respect for the law and deviant behavior. Persons who report high respect for the law on a survey may be different in any number of ways from persons reporting low respect. These differences may be the source of any relationship found between respect and deviant behavior.

Not to be deterred by this unresolvable problem in causal analysis, many researchers develop and use *path diagrams* and *path analysis*. These strategies take us to the fringes of some of the more technical areas of social science. They involve the learning of refined statistical principles. Nevertheless, by noting their existence, at this point we can at least realize that there is some way out of the wilderness. As we will now see these strategies of analysis are directly linked with the multiple regression equations discussed in the last chapter.

Basically, there are two steps.

1. Summarize your ideas of the way variables are causally linked in a diagram, showing the direction of cause by way of arrows.

2. Translate this diagram into a series of regression equations, putting the dependent variable, that which is caused, on the left and the independent variables on the right. This method of translating the idea of cause is justified in the following way: By looking at the value of the slope coefficients (in most cases it is actually a standardized coefficient adjusted for standard deviations in the dependent and independent variable, but this is taking us beyond the scope of the present discussion), we get an indication of the causal relationship in the sense that this measure reflects an attempt to deal with the three criteria of cause discussed earlier. It will be recalled that slope coefficients in regression equations can be interpreted as the change in the independent variable per unit change in the dependent variable, controlling for the remaining variables in the equation. Thus, the first criterion, that of establishing association, and the third criterion, that of controlling for alternative explanations, are handled. What about the second criterion, that of time sequence? This becomes reflected in the fact that the slope coefficients for any given regression equation are asymmetrical. That is, they reflect time sequence in the sense that they represent a change in the dependent variable per unit change in the independent variable, but not the reverse. If the variables were reversed in causal sequence, the slope coefficient might be quite different. For a relationship that is one way, the *assumption* is that the slope coefficient for the reverse direction is zero. It is this asymmetric character that allows translation of the time-sequence

criterion. Unfortunately, this remains only an assumption in much research in that there is no clear-cut a priori time sequence and data are
gathered at one point in time.

Take the following example. Suppose that we are interested in the
relationship between parents' socioeconomic standing and the respondent's occupational attainment. The idea that occupational attainment
is caused by parents' socioeconomic standing plus other factors is reflected in Figure 11.3. It will be recalled that the regression equation

FIGURE 11.3

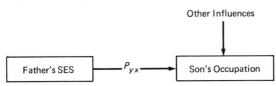

representing this relationship is Respondent's Present Job $(Y) = b$
Father's SES $(X) + e$. To repeat, the slope coefficient is interpreted
as the change in the respondent's education per unit change in the
father's education. When this is standardized, it is referred to as the
path coefficient (P_{yx}), which has been entered above the arrow. By
convention, the first subscript represents the dependent variable and
the second the independent.

Now, suppose that we are also interested in the "other" variables,
represented by the error term. More specifically, we are interested in
the mechanism through which the socioeconomic standing of the parents
becomes translated into occupational attainment. From reading the literature and drawing on our own experience, we hypothesize that two
additional variables, encouragement from significant others and the resulting occupational aspirations of the respondent are important and
linked in the larger process as presented in Figure 11.4.

How is this conceptual model reflected in a series of equations? At
first glance we might say that, since occupational attainment is a function
of aspirations, encouragement of significant others, and socioeconomic

FIGURE 11.4

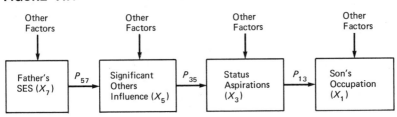

standing, the multiple regression equation should include each of these,
factors. On further reflection, we realize that, since the slope coefficients
reflect changes in the dependent variable *directly* linked to the relevant
independent variable, other factors held constant, then the coefficients
for socioeconomic standing and the influence of significant others should
be zero. Since these latter variables only work through the respondent's
own aspirations, when we control for aspirations they should, if the
model is correct, go to zero. In this case each variable becomes a function
of the single preceding variable. As a system of equations this model
is translated in the following manner:

$X_7 = e$	Parental socioeconomic standing is a function of unexplored factors in the present model.
$X_5 = bX_7 + e$	Influence of significant others is a linear function of parental socioeconomic standing plus other unexplored factors.
$X_3 = bX_5 + OX_7 + e$	Occupational aspirations are a function of unexplored factors plus significant others influence, controlling for socioeconomic standing of parents. The impact of socioeconomic standing goes to zero when controlling for the influence of significant others.
$X_1 = bX_3 + OX_5 + OX_7 + e$	Occupational attainment is a function of occupational aspirations plus other unexplored variables, controlling for the influence of significant others and the socioeconomic standing of parents. The influence of these latter variables goes to zero when controlling for the remaining variables in the equation.

It should be noted that the influences of significant others and socioeconomic standing have been maintained in the last two of the above equations even though their slope coefficients are hypothesized to be zero.
This is done to reflect the idea that the slope coefficient of the remaining
variable has been adjusted by controlling for these variables. These
zero values allow us to examine how well the model fits the data. If
it turns out, for example, that the slope coefficient for the influence
of significant others is larger than some agreed-upon standard, then
the model will have to be revised to include a direct link between
significant-others influence and occupational attainment.

Now, hold on to your hats and consider the following. Suppose you
are in a position to explore some of the unexplored sources in Figure 11.4.

For example, you might hypothesize that encouragement from significant others (X_5) is caused not only by the socioeconomic standing of parents but also by the mental ability (X_8) of the respondent and the respondent's academic performance (X_6) (see Figure 11.5). You might further

FIGURE 11.5

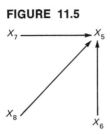

expect that academic performance (X_6) is caused in part by mental ability (X_8) and is itself a source of occupational (X_3) and educational (X_4) aspirations and educational attainment (X_2) (see Figure 11.6). In

FIGURE 11.6

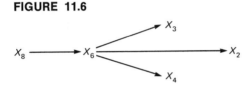

addition, you hypothesize that these occupational (X_3) and educational (X_4) aspirations are causes of occupational attainment (X_1), occupational aspirations directly and educational aspirations through the mediating variable of educational attainment (X_2) (see Figure 11.7). Finally you

FIGURE 11.7

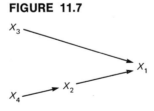

hypothesize that educational (X_4) and occupational (X_3) aspirations and educational attainment (X_2) are caused in part by the influence of significant others (X_5) (see Figure 11.8). When each of these hypotheses are combined into a single set of hypotheses, you get a model in which occupational attainment is directly "caused" by educational attainment and occupational aspirations with the remaining variables connected as

FIGURE 11.8

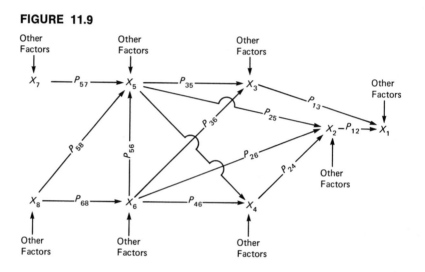

FIGURE 11.9

depicted in the path diagram (Figure 11.9). This is actually a slightly simplified version of what has been called the Wisconsin model of early occupational attainment. It is useful to consult the article of Haller and Portes (1973) to get a feel for the way in which a group of scholars progressively arrived at the above model, building on the work of previous writings and reformulating according to additional findings.

Given the basic procedure of first constructing a path diagram to represent the set of causal ideas and then a set of predictive equations to translate these ideas into data, we are in a position to infer cause from nonexperimental observations. There are a series of *assumptions* crucial for this translation and, if violated, make any causal inference very problematic at best. To label these assumptions, such as the idea that a "closed" system is involved and that the error terms are assumed to be uncorrelated, would be too bald a statement to do much good. To explain these assumptions would be beyond the present purposes. Once again, then, we are in a position to reaffirm the introductory nature of the present work and to suggest that further development of more advanced analytic skills will depend on your digging into more advanced treatments. For now you should be in a position to at least have some feel for the utility of path diagrams and path analysis. Their primary purpose is to translate the idea of cause into concrete form so that causal inferences can be made from nonexperimental data.

> *Practicum 11.2* (A) Translate the following statement regarding the causes of delinquency into a path diagram. It has been asserted that delinquency is primarily the function of birds of a feather flocking together. That is, it has been asserted that delinquency is most immediately the result of association with delinquent friends. This has been elaborated by noting that persons tend to spend time with their friends as a result of lack of attachment to their parents. The question then becomes whether the resulting delinquency is due primarily to the contact with delinquent friends, lack of attachment to parents, or some combination of the two. (B) Now, translate your diagram into a set of regression equations that could be used to shed light on the possible causes of delinquency. (C) What additional variables might be added?

SUMMARY

This chapter has explored a problem—the problem of translating the idea of cause into observable information. Three criteria have been suggested as the best approximation of this elusive idea. These three criteria leave us with four types of variables. The power of experiments lies in their ability to manipulate these variables in such a way as to meet the three criteria for establishing cause. In many situations it is either impossible or undesirable to conduct experiments. In such situations, techniques have been devised to draw causal inferences from nonexperimental data. The full discussion of these details requires more space than is appropriate here. In this instance, perhaps more than any other in this book, you are required to strike out on your own to find additional assistance.

We are left with the following key issues.

KEY ISSUES

1. What are the observable criteria for determining if X causes Y?
2. What is the difference between a spurious relationship between X and Y and a relationship between X and Y that is mediated through an intervening variable?
3. When employing the observable criteria of cause, what *general types* of variables are there?
4. What makes an experiment such a useful device for exploring causal relationships?
5. What is the purpose of random assignment in experiments?
6. What is the difference between internal and external validity?

7. What steps are taken in constructing a path diagram for causal analysis of nonexperimental data?

A BRIEF RECAP

In the chapters of this book, we have moved from the discovery of a folk system to the test of an analytic set of propositions. In the process we have noted a series of problems you can expect to encounter as you engage in the process and practice of social research. As we have moved through various issues, we have also explored a number of tools—tools that have been developed for a wide range of specific research projects.

One further point has been implicit throughout. This is the idea that social research can be potentially quite useful in the exploration of questions that confront those who would struggle for a better world. It was Albert Einstein who wrote—"Concern for man himself and his fate must always form the chief interest of all technical endeavors. . . . Never forget this in the midst of your diagrams and equations."

In the final chapter we will examine this last and in some ways most difficult, perplexing, and intriguing translation—the translation of empirical findings and theoretical generalizations into assertions about what ought to be. We also will consider the reverse translation—the movement from value positions to the selection and pursual of research topics. There are those who assert that the realm of the "ought" and the realm of the "is" are forever separated, that no bridging the gap is possible. There are others who would assert that such reciprocal interplay between these issues of value and fact form the core of the pursuit for knowledge. You will have to decide for yourself.

REFERENCES

Becker, Theodore L. (ed.)
  1969 *The Impact of Supreme Court Decisions.* London: Oxford University Press.
Blalock, Hubert M., Jr.
  1961 *Causal Inferences in Nonexperimental Research.* Chapel Hill: The University of North Carolina Press.
Blalock, Hubert M., Jr.
  1968 "The Measurement Problem: A Gap Between the Languages of Theory and Research." In Hubert M. Blalock, Jr., and Ann B. Blalock (eds.), *Methodology in Social Research.* New York: McGraw Hill.
Burgess, Robert L., and Bushell, Don
  1969 "Characteristics of the Experimental Analysis." In Robert L. Burgess and Don Bushell (eds.), *Behavioral Sociology: The Experimental Analysis of Social Process.* New York: Columbia University Press.

Campbell, Donald T., and Stanley, Julian C.
  1963 *Experimental and Quasi-Experimental Designs for Research.* Chicago: Rand McNally and Company.

Dolbeare, Kenneth M., and Hammond, Phillip E.
  1971 *The School Prayer Decisions.* Chicago: University of Chicago Press.

Gibbs, Jack P.
  1972 *Sociological Theory Construction.* Hinsdale, Ill.: The Dryden Press., Inc.

Haller, Archibald, and Portes, Alejandro
  1973 "Status Attainment Process." *Sociology of Education,* vol. 46, pp. 51–91.

Hirschi, Travis, and Selvin, Hanan C.
  1967 *Delinquency Research: An Appraisal of Analytic Methods.* New York: The Free Press.

Kish, Leslie
  1959 "Some Statistical Problems in Research Design." *American Sociological Review,* vol. 24, pp. 328–38.

Krislov, Samuel et al.
  1972 *Compliance and the Law: A Multidisciplinary Approach.* Beverly Hills, Cal.: Sage Publications.

Lempert, Richard
  1966 "Strategies of Research Design in the Legal Impact Study: The Control of Rival Hypotheses." *Law and Society Review,* vol. 1, pp. 111–32.

Muir, William K.
  1967 *Prayer in the Public Schools: Law and Attitude Change.* Chicago: University of Chicago Press.

Russell, Bertrand
  1918 *Mysticism and Logic.* London: George Allen and Unwin Ltd. Especially Chapter IX.

Ross, John, and Smith, Perry
  1968 "Orthodox Experimental Designs." In Hubert M. Blalock, Jr., and Ann B. Blalock (eds.), *Methodology in Social Research.* New York: McGraw-Hill.

Schwartz, Richard D., and Skolnick, Jerome H.
  1962 "Two Studies of Legal Stigma." *Social Problems,* vol. 10, pp. 133–42.

Stephan, Cookie, and Tully, Judy
  1973 "The Influence of Physical Attractiveness of a Plaintiff on the Decisions of Simulated Jurors." Paper presented at the North Central Sociological Association meetings, Cincinnati, May.

Webb, Eugene J.; Campbell, Donald T.; Schwartz, Richard D.; and Sechrest, Lee
  1966 *Unobtrusive Measures: Nonreactive Research in the Social Sciences.* Chicago: Rand McNally and Company.

Contents

Chapter 12

Research for What

We come to a final consideration: the role of social research in the context of broader society. Which problems should we select for research? How should we analyze the collected information? What role should and what role does social science take in policy questions? Once again these questions can be fruitfully pursued as a problem of translation. To what extent are policy concerns translated into research and theorizing? To what extent can empirical research and theorizing be used to make policy judgments?

A DEBATE

This relationship between policy and research, between value and fact, has been hotly debated. For some, it is a matter of putting on different hats; the roles of scientist and advocate should be clearly separated. For others, it is a matter of inseparable human responsibility and perhaps pragmatic utility; the roles of scientist and advocate should be inextricably linked.

Consider the following points and counterpoints:

> *Point:* The ultimate test of scientific statements is their reliability and validity in the prediction of observable phenomena. Scientific methods have been designed to eliminate, insofar as possible, the influence of personal beliefs or desires in the observation and analysis of empirical evidence. The language of science is descriptive, logical, and informative. Scientific statements are sharply distinguished from the emotional expression of esthetics, the value judgments of ethics, and the dictates and commands of persons in authority. (Lundberg et al., 1968, p. 740)

> *Counterpoint:* In neither case will it be possible simply to assume that the only important question is the empirical validity or factuality of the intellectual systems involved and that the viable parts of each theoretical system can be sifted out by "research" alone. The question here is not simply which parts of an intellectual system are empirically true or false but also which are liberative and which repressive in their consequences. In short the problem is: What are the social and political

consequences of the intellectual system under examination? Do they liberate or repress men? Do they bind men into the social world that now exists or do they enable men to transcend it? (Gouldner, 1970, p. 12)

Point: Should the American Sociological Association take a stand on social, economic, and political issues beyond those directly affecting the craft of sociology as an academic discipline? It is my contention, based on the premises above, that the answer must be decisively in the negative. For to pursue such a course is to confuse the roles of the scientist and the citizen or social engineer. It necessitates a value judgment that the science of sociology cannot produce, on which sociologists may and do disagree, and which perverts the role of sociologists as scientists. (Hauser, 1969, p. 141)

Counterpoint: Almost all of American sociology has abdicated the responsibility for finding solutions to the more urgent problems facing our society. . . . We believe, as human beings and as sociologists, that we have a deep moral responsibility to go far beyond mere objective analysis of our society. . . . We believe it is imperative for sociologists to analyze precisely what is sick in American society and then to act to try to change and heal American society. (Etkowitz and Schaflander, 1968, p. 399)

In both theoretical and action concerns, there is disagreement. Many of these issues were argued and reargued with renewed fervor during the late 1960s when attention turned to questioning a wide range of governmental actions and the role of the academic community in general and social science in particular in shaping the direction of those actions. There were calls for and resolutions to boycott cities symbolizing the repressiveness of governmental action. There were calls for and resolutions to set up alternative institutions to combat the plight of poverty and ghetto living. There were calls for and resolutions to maintain professional separation from the transient conflict of the moment so that the longer range goal of accumulated knowledge might be more readily achieved. There were charges and countercharges of radical destruction and reactionary petrifaction.

The times have changed since then. So has the intensity of the debate. We are left, however, with the issues.

Part of the conflict in this split between "pure" and "applied" interests can be summarized in what might be called the fiddler's dilemma, a dilemma of irrelevance and cooption. On the one hand, social science has been accused of fiddling while Rome burns. Social scientists, at times, seem to be detached from the surrounding world, interested only in their own closed system of thought and professional advancement. On the other hand, social scientists are found still "fiddling," but this time in the affairs of the community. We find social science not only concerned about but also taken in and directed by interest groups involved in various "crises."

Increasingly, the techniques of social science are emerging in nonacademic settings. Politicians use public-opinion polls to shape their campaigns. Attorneys use polls to help select jurors sympathetic to their cases. Marketing firms conduct experiments and commission polls to fashion favorable sales techniques. U.S. Supreme Court decisions speak of evidence needed in terms of levels of significance and various forms of validity. It is perhaps an understatement to say that the techniques of social science are beginning to pervade our culture.

One avenue through which the interconnection between policy and social science is being most solidly established is through what is generally called evaluation research. Evaluation research ranges from descriptions of broad trends and how these align with expectations or certain goals to more detailed attempts to explore the impact of "programs" and legal decisions.

EVALUATING BROAD SOCIETAL CHANGES

One type of evaluation research focuses not so much on specific programs as on broad societal changes that are supposedly taking place as an aggregate result from changing attitudes, legal statutes, court decisions, institutional arrangements, hiring practices, and so forth. In such research the attempt is not necessarily to locate the "responsible" causes or predictive factors but simply to examine data with an eye on changes taking place.

An example of such research is provided by Butler (1974) in his examination of the changing patterns of participation in the Armed Services by race. After having noted that, as of November 30, 1973, blacks were underrepresented in the upper enlisted grades (see Table 12.1), the question became whether there were any changes in this pattern over time. To examine this question, summarizing rank order correlations[1] between

TABLE 12.1
Percentage of Blacks, Whites, and Others in Each Enlisted Grade (as of Nov. 30, 1973)

Grade	White	Black	Other	Total
E-9	88.7	9.7	1.7	100
E-8	82.9	15.0	2.1	100
E-7	77.9	20.4	1.7	100
E-6	75.1	23.7	1.2	100
E-5	80.1	18.6	1.2	100
E-4	83.8	15.0	1.2	100
E-3	81.9	17.0	1.1	100
E-2	76.2	22.6	1.2	100
E-1	68.8	29.5	1.7	100
Total	81.1	17.7	1.2	100

Source: Butler (1974): The Office of Equal Opportunity and Programs—The Pentagon.

FIGURE 12.1
**Enlisted Personnel—Rank Order Correlations between Grade and
Percentage of Blacks in Grade in the Four Services for the
Years 1962 through 1972**

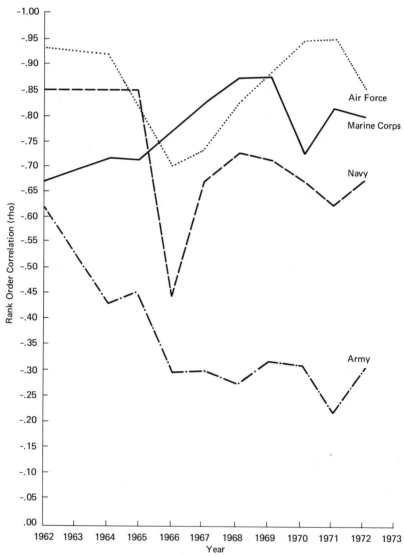

Source: Butler, 1974.

enlisted grades and the percentage of blacks in a given rank were used. A negative correlation indicated that the higher the rank, the lower the percentage of blacks. The extent to which the absolute size of this correlation goes down is the extent to which representation is equalized. As shown in Figure 12.1, this trend toward equalization is noted most markedly in the Army.

Findings such as these led to a kind of cautious optimism. Keeping in mind that the correlation has always been negative between percentage black and rank, the trend, in the Army at least, has been toward equalization. The reasons for this trend might be multiple. In the evaluation of broad changes it is frequently difficult to pin down the precise sources of change. It is a matter of evaluating the overall pattern and noting whether it is in line or out of line with certain expectations.

Such attempts to monitor changes in society immediately confront the problem of choosing indicators. What are the important factors that need to be tapped? In practice it generally has been a matter of developing some idea of the "health" of the community or society being examined. Jones and Flax (1970), for example, suggest the concerns and

FIGURE 12.2
Quality Areas and Selected Indicators

Quality Areas	*Indicators Used*
Income	Per-capita money income adjusted for cost-of-living differences
Unemployment	Percent of labor force unemployed
Poverty	Percent of households with less than $3,000 income
Housing	Cost of housing a moderate-income family of four
Education	Selective Service mental test rejection rate
Health	Infant (i.e., under 1 year) deaths per 1,000 live births
Mental health	Suicides per 100,000 population
Air pollution	A composite index of pollutants
Public order	Reported robberies per 100,000 population
Racial equality	Ratio between nonwhite and white unemployment rates
Community concern	Per-capita contributions to United Fund appeal
Citizen participation	Percent of voting-age population that voted in recent presidential elections
Social disintegration	Known narcotics addicts per 10,000 population

Source: Jones and Flax, 1970, p. 6; Reprinted from Fox, 1974.

indicators reprinted in Figure 12.2. Cohen (Department of Health, Education, and Welfare, 1970) goes a step further and suggests not only indicators of important societal health concerns but also a series of goals that should be aimed at. These are reprinted in Figure 12.3.

---

[1] It is interesting to note as a methodological sidetrack that this is the same measure used in conjunction with comparing raters of documents discussed in Chapter 7.

FIGURE 12.3

Indicator	Present Experience	1976–79 Goal
1. Infant mortality (per 1,000 live births)	22.1 (1967)	12
2. Maternal mortality (per 100,000 live births)	28.9 (1967)	15
3. Family planning services (for low-income women 15–44)	1 million (1968)	5 million
4. Deaths from accidents (per 100,000 population)	55.1 (1967)	50
5. Number of persons in state mental hospitals	426,000 (1967)	50,000
6. Expectancy of healthy life	68.2 years (1966)	70.2 years
7. Three- to five-year-olds in school or preschool	35.2% (1967)	95%
8. Persons 25 and older who graduate from high school	51.1% (1967)	65%
9. Persons 25 and older who graduate from college	10.1% (1967)	15%
10. Persons in learning force	100 million (1967)	150 million
11. Percent of major cities with public community colleges	66% (1968)	100%
12. Number of first-year students in medical schools	10,000 (1967)	18,000
13. Handicapped persons rehabilitated	208,000 (1968)	600,000
14. Average weekly hours of work— manufacturing	40.6 (1967)	37.5
15. Labor-force participation rate for women aged 35–64	48% (1967)	60%
16. Average annual paid vacation— manufacturing	2 weeks (1967)	4 weeks
17. Housing units with bathtub or shower	85% (1960)	100%
18. Percent of population illiterate	2.4% (1960)	0
19. Voters as a percentage of voting-age population	63% (1964)	80%
20. Private philanthropy as a percent of GNP	1.9% (1967)	2.7%
21. Public and private expenditures for health, education, and welfare as a percent of GNP	19.8% (1968)	25%
22. Percent of population in poverty	12.8% (1968)	0
23. Income of lowest fifth of population	5.3% (1967)	10%
24. Persons who work during the year	88 million (1967)	110 million
25. Life expectancy	70.2 years (1966)	72 years

Source: Department of Health Education and Welfare (1970).

A listing such as Cohen's provides a set of standards against which we can judge discrepancy. In 1967 there were 22.1 infant deaths per 1,000 live births; we should try to bring this down to 12 by 1979. There were 100 million persons in the learning force in 1947; we should shoot for 150 million by 1979. Almost 13 percent of the population was in poverty in 1968; we should attempt to eliminate poverty by 1979. In such concrete proposals we move from abstraction to specification.

We also move into the arena of controversy and analytic complexity. Which of these goals should be given highest priority? What additional goals should be added? Which should be dropped? What is the most efficient means to reach these goals? Before moving toward incorporating more persons into the learning force, should we concentrate on changing the nature of the learning process? What about racial discrimination, alcoholism, suicide, violent crimes? And so it goes. These questions of value priority are those that cannot be answered by data alone. Nevertheless, perhaps we can inform such judgments by developing a less haphazard approach to the development of social indicators.

To bring some theory-based plan into the selection of social indicators, Gross (1966) has argued for the development of a social systems accounting within the context of a "general systems model." Gross suggests,

> According to this model, the state of any nation at any period of time —past, present, or future—can be analyzed in terms of two interrelated, multidimensional elements: system structure and system performance. The elements of the system structure deal with the internal relations among the system's parts [and] the elements of system performance with the acquiring of inputs and their transformation into outputs. Both involve relations with the external environment. This model, or any part thereof, may be flexibly applied to describe the unique characteristics of any country whatsoever, no matter what the level of industrial development or the type of political regime. (p. 155)

Even with the specification of system structure and system performance, this scheme remains very abstract. It is indeed applicable to a wide range of settings. Further translation is needed if we are to employ the ideas in concrete research. Happily, such further specification is provided by Gross. The elements of system performance are further translated into more concrete form in Figure 12.4.

Still, you are probably saying (if you have taken time to examine Figure 12.4) that even at the intermediate level of abstraction you have concepts such as "good government," "due process," "law enforcement," or "fair employment." What do these mean in concrete terms? Further specification is called for.

Such issues of translation from the abstract to the concrete do not take place in an academic vacuum. They have been grappled with for years in the political arena, and, recently, the U.S. Supreme Court has taken an active role in deciding just what kinds of evidence will be required to establish "fair employment" practices.[2] As we move from grand abstractions such as "fairness" and "rational behavior" to concrete

---

[2] See, for example, Note, "Employment Discrimination: Statistics and Preferences under Title VII," *Virginia Law Review*, vol. 59, pp. 463–91. U.S. *v* Georgia Power Co., 5th 474, Fed. Rep., 2nd, March 1973. Griggs *v* Duke Power Co., 401, U.S. 424, 1971.

FIGURE 12.4
National Performance Abstractions: Grand and Intermediate

	Grand Abstractions	Intermediate Abstractions
Satisfying interests	Peace, security, freedom, liberty, autonomy, self-determination, equality Tolerance, dignity, honor, prestige, pride Progress, culture, beauty, the arts, self-development	Full employment Fair employment Equitable income distribution Higher living standards
Producing output	Abundance	Growth in national output Output of specific services or goods Price stability
Investing in system	Expansion, unity, national con-sciousness Saving free enterprise, building socialism or a new or great society	Investment in hard goods Investment in people or institutions Conservation and development
Using inputs efficiently.		Productivity ratios Balanced budget
Acquiring resources.	Economic independence or self-sufficiency	External assistance Economic independence or self-sufficiency Favorable balance of payments
Observing codes	Justice, equity Democracy Order, duty Obedience to God or gods	Law enforcement Due process Fair procedures
Behaving rationally	Reason Wisdom	Scientific or technological progress Good government or administration

Source: Gross, 1966.

indicators such as percentage differences in the racial composition of the available labor force compared with a particular company's work force, we also move to an area where we may miss a major point. We may rely too heavily on readily available indicators and neglect the more intricate mechanisms through which various discrepancies emerge.

It is important that we make efforts to keep in mind the broader picture. It is not a good idea to remain entirely in the ether of abstraction or the gravel of concrete indicators. Rather, reciprocal movement is called for. "Any rich understanding of a past or present system state or any rich portrayal of future purpose requires one to run up and down the abstraction-specificity ladder. This is the only way to escape the 'slippage' resulting from decreased precision as one goes up, and of increasing multiplicity and decreasing relevance as one moves down-ward" (Gross, p. 266).

One way to handle this balancing between abstract richness/meaninglessness and concrete precision/irrelevance is to develop intermediate models for portions of the broader system. We might examine, as has Anderson (1973), factors related to the workings of the health-care sector of society. Relying on data available from the U.S. Bureau of the Census, the U.S. Center for Health Statistics, and publications from the American Hospital Association and the American Medical Association, Anderson constructed a causal model for the prediction of infant mortality rates, parallel to the path models discussed in Chapter 11.

A problem plaguing Anderson was one confronting most efforts in this direction—reliance on available material. Given past practices, records are kept in such a form that they include only partial information on factors of interest. Theories are fashioned from what is available rather than from what might be most theoretically relevant. It is for this reason that many have called for reexamination of existing practices in the publication of social indicators. It is for reasons similar to this that writers such as Gross (1966) and Fox (1974) have pushed for theory-grounded approaches to the development of indicators.

Progress in this area has been and continues to be rather slow. The problems push us to the edge of how far we can go given existing practices. No doubt, progress in the future will depend upon a good deal of tenacious groping for the most appropriate theoretical framework or frameworks and the accompanying concrete indicators. It also will call for cooperation among "academics" and persons directly responsible for gathering such information. It is at once a most interesting and difficult predicament. It also is a predicament in which the value questions of policy and the factual questions of social research join hands. Given limited resources, which directions do we take? Do we examine participation in existing institutions, or do we make these institutions problematic and ask what changes might be called for? Is it governmental stability that is important, or is it the correlates of revolution?

Should our major efforts be concentrated on the examination of education, the labor market, health-delivery systems, or justice-delivery systems; or should we recognize the interconnections among these and spread the limited resources evenly throughout each of the sectors? Surely we can do better than superficial assertions that each of the major institutions is somehow interlocked with others. Surely we can do better, but what of the specifics? These issues of evaluating ongoing systems in light of general social-science theory are very much open at this point. They are, indeed, at the frontiers of our efforts.

EVALUATING PROGRAMS

Another type of evaluation research, less broad in scope, is program evaluation. As societies become increasingly involved in active intervention in the lives of individuals, questions arise concerning the impact of various "programs." Who is involved? What kinds of activities are going on? What impact is the program having? What is the comparative impact of two alternative lines of action? These are clearly important questions in a setting where there is some commitment to the rational model for change, wherein feedback concerning results is called for.

In reading evaluation reports it soon becomes apparent that two related but distinct types have emerged. One is largely *descriptive* in nature. Here, it is a matter of explaining how the program works, who is involved, and what the results have been. The second is based on the *experimental* model. There is an attempt to not only describe how the program works, who is involved, and what the results have been but also an attempt to systematically compare the results obtained with results obtained employing various alternatives. In this latter instance the demands of study design are more stringent. There is some attempt to develop "control" groups. As discussed in Chapter 11 this ideally involves the random assignment of "cases" to one treatment or another. Since these programs generally take place in the real world, where it may be ethically and/or legally questionable to withhold or impose action on a random basis, compromises in the study design are frequently made, yielding what generally are referred to as quasi-experimental evaluations.

We will first consider the descriptive style of evaluation and then turn to evaluations based on the experimental model.

Descriptive Evaluations

Before discussing the general issues addressed in descriptive evaluations, it is useful to have a specific reference point. For this reason we have included a brief description of a program set up in a criminal-court system in an attempt to divert certain types of individuals from the normal flow of proceedings.

SUMMARY MANHATTAN EMPLOYMENT PROJECT

One hundred and three thousand arrested persons came into the Manhattan Criminal Court in 1968. Most were young, uneducated, unskilled, unemployed members of a minority group from one of the city's ghettos. In the normal course of events, this would not be their last arrest. Statistics vary, but at least one expert has concluded that "the average man who is arrested once will be arrested seven times." (James Q. Wilson, *New York Times Magazine*, May 11, 1969). It is likely that the only successful people most of these defendants had ever known were people beating the system: gamblers, pimps, numbers-runners, narcotics dealers. People from the ghetto who make a legal success of themselves do not remain in the ghetto as examples for the young.

Federal, state, city, and private programs have been developed in an attempt to counteract some of the disabilities faced by the young ghetto resident; welfare assistance, remedial education, addiction treatment, employment guidance, job training, health programs, legal services, are all available. But few reach a person when he may need them most—at the time of arrest—and even fewer focus specifically on people accused of a crime.

The Manhattan Court Employment Project (MCEP) is an experimental attempt to intervene in the usual court process just after a defendant's arrest, to offer him counseling and job opportunities and, if he cooperates and appears to show promise of permanent change, to recommend that the prosecutor (District Attorney) and the judge dismiss the charges against him without ever deciding whether he is guilty. Thus, the MCEP attempts to convert a participant's arrest from a losing to a winning experience. The system stands to benefit from this conversion as much as the defendant. Successful participants leave the project working and earning an honest living, the community gains a taxpayer, and the resources of the overburdened criminal justice system are freed to attend to serious cases.

In brief, the MCEP operates as follows: Shortly after each arrested man is brought to the Manhattan Criminal Court for arraignment (appearance before a judge, setting of bail, and assignment of counsel), our screening unit reviews his papers, checks his prior record, and interviews him to see whether he is eligible to take part in the project under standards drafted by project staff and the prosecutor's office. If he is eligible and he and his lawyer agree to his participation, we ask the prosecutor to request the judge to adjourn his case for 90 days and release him on recognizance, i.e. without bail. The court and District Attorney approve about 70 percent of these requests.

A new participant, frequently coming straight from the court's detention cells, is taken to the MCEP office in the court building and is assigned to a Representative (counselor), who will take prime responsibility for him throughout his time with the project. If he needs money or immediate services of some kind, he is sent to the Social Services Unit, which consists of two employees of the city's Department of Social Services (formerly the Department of Welfare) who have been assigned to work with project participants.

The project offers participants two basic services: counseling with their Representatives, or Reps, and job placement through the Career Development Unit. The Representatives, who are nonprofessionals and ex-convicts, go to participants' neighborhoods regularly to talk over problems, meet their families, and just spend time with them. The Reps also see participants at the project offices and in group counseling sessions one evening a week at the project's clubhouse. A majority of participants also develop a continuing relationship with the project's Career Developers, who help prepare them for interviews and for jobs, set up appointments for them, and follow their progress by keeping in close touch with employers and project Reps.

At the end of 90 days, when the participant must appear for his adjourned date in court, we recommend that the District Attorney make one of three possible requests to the court: (1) dismissal of charges (if the defendant has met the basic requirements of the program); (2) a second adjournment to give us more time to work with him; or (3) in the case of defendants we have been unable to work with successfully, return of the case to the normal court processes. This last recommendation, by agreement with the District Attorney, carries no implication that will be used to the defendant's disadvantage in the continued prosecution of his case.

The project was designed in 1967 under the auspices of the Vera Institute of Justice, a private organization in New York City formed to test and bring about changes in the criminal justice system of the city, and was funded by the Manpower Administration of the United States Department of Labor under a three-year contract.

The MCEP has been envisaged as working in two stages. The first, which this report covers, was the developmental period, in which the chief questions to be explored were the basic ones: whether the project was feasible at all; whether the court would accept and ultimately cooperate with it; whether it was possible to produce and observe a change in a significant number of participants in a three-month period; whether it was possible to predict what kinds of people might be most receptive to treatment based on jobs; whether our staff—particularly the nonprofessionals—would perform effectively; whether a data system could be designed for supervision and analysis of results. The project's work in the first phase answered these questions in the affirmative. The second phase, while we continue to take in and work with new participants, will be directed at answering four new questions: First, we will look at defendants who have been out of the project for some time to see if the project has had any apparent effect on their job situations and on their rate of recidivism (repeated commission of crime). Second, we will further define the types of defendants who can benefit from the project's services and try to estimate how many there are in the court population. Our experience during the first phase indicates that substantially more defendants than we accepted were eligible under the existing criteria and that the criteria might be expanded. Third, we will take steps to institutionalize the project in the operation of the criminal court so that our services become a standard part of the criminal justice process. Fourth, by demonstrating the effectiveness of our intervention immediately after arrest, we hope to make the point that other kinds of treatment—for addicts, alcoholics, prostitutes, and others—could be used to great advantage at this point in the court process.

Source: Vera Institute of Justice, 1970.

Although this description is for one program in a single court system, it contains elements general to most descriptive evaluations. We read first of the *need* for and *general purpose* of the program. Statistics show that persons arrested once will be arrested, on the average, seven times. Few existing programs are designed to reach persons at the time of arrest. Thus, the Manhattan Court Employment Project (MCEP) was designed to intervene at this stage with the general goal being to turn a "losing" experience into a "winning" one. In more concrete terms, it is the goal of the project that persons will leave "working and earning an honest living." The community gains in that taxpayers are added to the tax rolls and "resources of the overburdened criminal justice system are freed to attend to serious cases."

Clearly, there are value judgments embedded in these statements of need and goals. It is in the debate of these values that questions arise concerning the extent to which social scientists should become involved in such applied research. As it turns out, however, there are value judgments involved in any selection of problems. Some select problems for long-range theoretical importance. Some select problems for personal interest. Some select problems because "that's where the money is." Some select problems through personal commitment to immediate involvement. Most choose their focus of research for some combination of these reasons. As long as there are differences of opinion in this regard there are going to be debates on whether social scientists are acting as they should.

In addition to describing the need for and goal of a program, descriptive evaluations spend time *outlining the mechanics* of the program. We find from the above account that the MCEP intervened in court proceedings on the basis of standards specified in conjunction with the prosecutor's office. Once selected, clients of the program are offered counseling and job-placement services. At the end of 90 days, recommendations are made to the district attorney for either dismissal of the charges, continuation of services, or return to the normal court process. In the fuller report on the program, additional detail is provided on each of these points. The additional narrative is accompanied by statistics showing the characteristics of persons involved, recommendations made, and outcome observed.

It is at this point, also, that debate emerges on the propriety of the social scientist's involvement in such projects. Those against such involvement charge that, by selling technical skills, the social scientist is being coopted for purposes other than social science. If social science is an endeavor in which we attempt to construct and test general theories about social life, spending time gathering and publishing what often turns out to be public-relations information on specific projects is spinning our wheels. We learn nothing from this particular situation in terms of more general theoretical issues.

Recognizing that persons involved in purely technical-assistance roles may indeed miss opportunities for theoretical contributions, due to time constraints as well as other reasons, there is still much potential for mutual benefit in such research. The key to mutual benefit lies in a modification of a point previously made. We previously noted (Chapter 5) that several empirical indicators can be employed to measure a single theoretical concept. I now suggest that a single indicator or set of indicators can be treated in different ways at different times and thus related to diverging theoretical and action-oriented purposes.

For example, take the following possibilities, beginning with a quotation from a *Law Review* article aimed at accentuating the policy significance of certain events within prison.

> The disciplinary process is viewed by correctional authorities as an important phase of the treatment program of the institution. However, the procedures presently followed in disciplinary cases are not designed to produce justice or even an appearance of justice, and, as a result, the present process may significantly undermine the treatment objectives of an institution. *This aspect of current correctional-administrative law and practice, more than any other, stands in urgent need of reform.* (Jacob and Sharma (1970). Emphasis added)

Being attuned to legal matters, the lawyer's attention turns to those events that parallel judicial proceedings in the community—prison disciplinary hearings.

Such attention to the multiplicity of legal levels within the criminal-justice system is easily incorporated into existing schemes of social scientists. We find, for example, sociologist Selznick (1969) and anthropologist Pospisil (1967) referring to the importance of this idea. Further, it has long been asserted by observers of social life that examination of cases of conflict provide insight into the workings of any particular community. Thus, disciplinary hearings within penal institutions provide an opportunity for fruitful cooperative research. For the policy-oriented practitioner, the important dimensions of disciplinary hearings may be considerations of procedural due process and types of punishment for types of crimes. With some modification the data useful in reaching policy conclusions become useful to the social scientist concerned with theory construction and verification.

As noted earlier, in a study of institutional disciplinary hearings we found that the rhythm of institutional crime was a rather interesting variation of the rhythm of crime in the community (Olson, 1974). One of the more consistent findings regarding crime in the community is that it tends to reflect a kind of cyclical rhythm. Weekends and night hours are times of high activity for the police on the streets. Generally, this fluctuation is attributed to a kind of community transition period when the pace as well as the substance and location of activity is changing (Cumming, Cumming, and Edell, 1965).

By comparison, we found that infractions of institutional rules were concentrated most heavily in the first three days following the weekend. In the context of life within this particular institution, which housed men awaiting the outcome of their trials, these offense rates paralleled those times when activities were in a state of change. Monday, Tuesday, and Wednesday were days when going to and arriving from court appearances reached their maximum. Saturday, the day furthest removed from court appearances, had the lowest rate of institutional crime.

Within the time span of each day, the rates of infractions peaked when the inmates were asked to "reenter" the life of jail (morning); when the inmates were asked to return to their cells for the night; and when there was a grouping and regrouping of inmates in the cell blocks and mess hall for meals. Thus, support is gained for the theoretical proposition that the crime rate will vary in direct proportion to the degree of societal transition or reorganization taking place.

A second example of the theoretical relevance of this applied research is available. Some attention has been given by social scientists interested in prisons to what has been called the phases of prisonization. The idea is that various phases of prisonization involve differing degrees of conformity to staff norms and assimilation into the inmate culture.

Supporting information was obtained from the disciplinary records when we found that there was a consistent overrepresentation of institutional crime among those who had spent longer periods of time in the institution, thus indicating inmate movement away from the staff. Further evidence of assimilation into an inmate culture was discovered when we examined the occurrence of various "types" of institutional crimes as related to the length of time the charged individual had been in jail. Here, the finding was that offenses against fellow inmates (fights, kangaroo courts, assaults) predominanted in the early stages of incarceration but steadily decreased as time passed. By contrast, offenses where the staff was the apparent victim (insubordination, disrespect, threatening an officer) steadily increased as time passed and were predominant by the fourth week (Olson, 1974).

These are only two examples of the general idea that information gathered for one purpose often can be used for another. This being a book on the workings of social science, we have emphasized the relevance of policy-related information for the formation and test of general propositions about the regularities in social life. An easy case can be made for the relevance of these same data for policy questions. It is in this working and reworking of information that the investigation of social life becomes a craft.

Once the need for, the goal, and the mechanics of a program are described, attention frequently turns to the implications of the program for other settings and times. We find in the closing paragraph of the

above description of MCEP that the second stage of the project is aimed
at determining the longer range impact of the project in terms of job
situations and recidivism rates. We also find concern for expanding the
program to a wider range of defendants. Finally, we find an attempt
to establish the program as a permanent part of the criminal-justice
system.

Given these latter goals, attention focuses on the effectiveness of the
program and whether it is worth the necessary resources. In such situations, where resource commitments are called for, it frequently is necessary to establish not only the effectiveness of a particular program but
also its relative effectiveness over alternative lines of action. This entails
comparisons with other programs; it may entail comparisons with alternatives involving no "program." In either instance, such need for comparison requires that we be in a position to examine alternative explanations
for emerging differences. In such situations experimental and quasi-experimental designs prove useful.

Experimental Evaluations

The basic strategy in the experimental design is to compare two or
more groups that are similar except for the "treatment" received. As
we saw in Chapter 11, similarity often is achieved through the random
assignment to one category or another. When this relatively straightforward design is embedded in the "natural setting" where it sometimes
interrupts the normal flow of events, difficulties easily arise. Again, consider a specific example before we move to the general issues. This
example is taken from a study (Kassebaum, et al., 1971) designed to
evaluate the effectiveness of various treatments within a prison.

❋   ❋   ❋

FORMULATING THE STUDY DESIGN

Early studies of treatment outcome and the general literature on methodological problems of evaluation provided us with guidelines for making research
decisions. A fundamental decision was to impose an experimental design on
the existing program. That is, not to set up a specially staffed and temporarily
heavily subsidized program that could reach only a small number of inmates
and would be unrealistic in terms of departmental and prison budgets. Underlying this decision was one assumption of the group counseling program,
namely, that nonprofessional group leaders could elicit attitude and behavioral
changes in inmates.

A longitudinal design was selected in preference to a cross-sectional one.
The principle issues here concerned the initial comparability of inmates who
did and did not have counseling experience, the precision of the description
of the counseling experience, and the identification of factors that accounted

for individual differences in response to treatment. Although the techniques of partial correlation used in cross-sectional analyses might clarify the comparability problem, we believed that more conclusive evaluation could be obtained by a longitudinal experiment in which initially comparable groups of men were assigned to treatment or to control conditions (with other aspects of imprisonment kept as constant as possible) and in which subjects were studied over time.

At least six characteristics of longitudinal experimental designs are required to accomplish the aims of an evaluation study like this one:

1. An adequate control group.
2. The controlled selection and assignment of subjects to the treatment and control conditions to ensure initial comparability.
3. The spatial separation of subjects in the different treatment settings to minimize contamination of the independent variable.
4. A range of types of persons to permit the generalization of findings.
5. A uniform follow-up of all experimental and control subjects after release.
6. The instruments for observation and measurement of independent and dependent variables.

Our efforts to meet these requirements follow the specification of hypotheses to be tested.

The Formal Structure of Theory to be Tested

Our review of the literature dealing with group treatment and our discussions with prison-staff members led us to establish several hypotheses based on the assumed importance of group counseling in facilitating communications between inmates and staff. Communication should be, according to the theoretical basis of the program, subject to fewer conventional restrictions and should encourage confrontations and disclosures between leaders and group members which are tabooed by those tenets of the inmate code that value the withholding of information. The virtue of inmate solidarity should be called into question by inviting inmates' criticism of other inmates in the counseling session. In these terms, what was anticipated was not depth psychology but the lessened endorsement of values that sanction further antisocial behavior. We thus were led to suppose that, if adherence to the inmate code were weakened, there would be less resistance to the acceptance of conventional alternatives to post-release crime.

The twofold notion that treatment might affect inmate values and that this in turn might result in the lessened sanction of illegal behavior was phrased as testable hypotheses.

First, it is argued that participation in group counseling changes attitudes, specifically, that it alters allegiance to inmate norms.

> *Hypothesis 1.* Participation in treatment results in lessened endorsement of the inmate code.

But it is said that more occurs than just a shift in inmate values. (For example, staff–inmate communication is facilitated, and there is more of it.) And, hence, participation and all that it implies results in lowered *resistance* to accepting conventional alternatives to illegal or antisocial behavior (which, in turn, affects the incidence of the behavior itself). Treatment, then, affects not only attitudes but also affects acts. Although the link between them might seem causal (attitude changes make a change in behavior possible), apparently one is not a necessary antecedent of the other according to Fenton. He merely suggests that they are two consequences of group counseling.

Proponents assert that behavioral changes are both short- and long-term, and thus we have separated immediate from post-release effects. Both are operationalized in negative terms, that is, positive impact is defined as the absence of certain behaviors (trouble with authorities), not the presence of certain acts. More specifically:

> *Hypothesis 2.* Inmates who participated in the group-counseling program will receive fewer prison disciplinary reports.

> *Hypothesis 3.* Parolees who participated in the prison group-counseling program will have lower recidivism rates than controls.

The independent variable is differential exposure to the treatment program (group counseling); dependent variables are attitudinal and behavioral and reflect short- and long-term effects. Measures of in-prison response to treatment are the endorsement of inmate norms and the breaking prison rules. End result measures are post-release behavior—conformity to parole regulations and recidivism. These criteria were selected to empirically support one of the following eight outcome possibilities:

Outcome	Accept	Reject
I	1, 2, 3	
II		1, 2, 3
III	1, 2	3
IV	1, 3	2
V	1	2, 3
VI	2, 3	1
VII	3	1, 2
VIII	2	1, 3

The Selection of a Site

It was apparent from the earliest discussions of this project that the research operation could not be statewide. The ten prisons, which comprised the Department of Corrections in 1961, differed too greatly in terms of the architectural design, the size and makeup of inmate population, the size and makeup of staff, and the industrial, work, and treatment programs to allow the simple summing of information from all facilities. Also, because of the size of the state, repeated visits to monitor widely dispersed study operations were prohibitively costly.

Even the selection of several institutions from the department posed problems. Two of the ten prisons were classified as maximum security, two as medium security, two as minimum security, one housed aged inmates, another contained only youth offenders, another was for men with medical and psychiatric problems, and the tenth prison was for women. Eliminating the last four as special-purpose institutions, we were left with six possibilities. The difficulty with four of these prisons was in the ability to generalize from findings based on the extreme populations of inmates in the maximum- and minimum-security settings. Custodial and security considerations dominated institutional life at the maximum-security prisons, whereas the most elaborate treatment programs in the Department of Corrections characterized the minimum-security institutions.

We thus decided to focus our study on the impact of group treatment on men in a medium-security-prison setting. Studies focused on this population permitted a greater power of generalization because of the more equal distribution of custodial and treatment concerns in institutional operations. Second, although it is true that only about 30 percent of the men in California prisons are housed in medium-security prisons at any one time, a figure of upward of 40 percent represents the real proportion of California prisoners who have been confined in medium-security prisons during their terms. Some of the inmates who end up at San Quentin and Folsom were management problems at medium-security prisons. Many inmates who end up at medium- and minimum-security facilities earned their transfers after a period of testing their institutional adjustment at a prison higher in the security ratings. Other men, originally committed to minimum-security institutions, are transferred to medium-security prisons after demonstrating their inability to "go along with the program."

A third reason for selecting a medium-security-prison population is that a better representation of offenders is found in these institutions. A disproportionate number of men convicted of crimes of violence are housed in maximum-security prisons, but men who have committed property offenses (nonsufficient-funds checks, larceny, fraud, embezzlement, and the like) are overrepresented in minimum-security facilities. Inmates of maximum-security prisons have the most extensive criminal careers; inmates of minimum-security institutions have the least extensive. A mixture of all types of offenders and careers is found in the medium-security-prison population.

At the time our study was to be initiated, there was one medium-security prison in operation and another under construction. The selection was made following the inspection of the prison site at San Luis Obispo. (Inspection is, perhaps, too serious a term. Superintendent John Klinger and Dr. Kassebaum floundered through the mud and looked into the still-bare concrete and steel shell of the partially completed California Men's Colony—East Facility.) Most of the initial information about the new prison came from Mr. Klinger, who was to administer both the East Facility and California Men's Colony—West (known throughout the department as "the old men's home"). The new prison was to house 2,400 men in a medium-security setting containing the most recent innovations in architectural design and institutional operation. Housing, recreation, and dining facilities were organized on a quadrangle basis, with each quad being a semiautonomous unit of 600 men. It was apparent that the total number of inmates and staff would be sufficient for adequate statistical analysis; furthermore, the structure of the physical plant would permit the operation of several different treatment conditions. The random assignment of inmates to the four quads would result in four samples more comparable in both population characteristics and prison environment than would be possible if the samples were drawn from separate prisons in the state. Finally, because at the time of planning the institution had not yet been opened, the introduction of special assignment procedures and treatment and research operations would pose fewer problems than at long-established institutions.

Problems Posed for Institutional Operations

A research design was drawn up that capitalized on the flexibility inherent in the fact that CMCE was a new prison. Initially it called for a control group and three varieties of group counseling, to be distributed among the four quads. To achieve comparable subsamples, the random assignment of inmates to each was necessary. In addition, large samples of the prison population would take questionnaires and tests and would be interviewed. Background data would have to be gathered from inmate records, and the access to group sessions and important institutional committee meetings would be required.

All of this implied extensive interference in the programming of the institution and strongly suggested the advisability of joint planning with the staff prior to the opening of the prison to its first inmates. Accordingly, several planning sessions were held at the prison before a final design was decided on.

The first formal meeting on the design took place in February 1961 at the prison with representatives of the Department of Corrections, including J. Douglas Grant, Chief of the Research Division and the Men's Colony—East administration. After hearing about the preliminary plans, the institution staff raised these questions:

1. Would the research plan be adversely affected by constant and even rapid turnover if Men's Colony inmates were sent out to a new minimum-security facility at Susanville, which also was nearing completion?
2. Would it be possible to maintain a completely undifferentiated type of population distribution in the four quadrangles, inasmuch as a recent departmental decision had been made to place in one of the quadrangles a number of psychotic inmates in the stage of "partial remission," some aged inmates with arson histories (which prevented their being housed in the wooden barracks of Men's Colony—West), some young "management problems," and some particularly troublesome homosexuals?
3. Would the integrity of the design be compromised by the prison administration's need to transfer men from one quadrangle to another for security and control reasons?

The first question was resolved by the department's agreement to our request that transfer to fill the new Susanville facility be temporarily suspended at Men's Colony until data collection at the prison was completed. We might note that the Men's Colony staff found the research project to be an advantage to them in, at least, this regard, because "good" inmates would be kept at the institution instead of continually being transferred. The department did not draw on the study population to fill fire-camp or conservation assignments during the first year of the study and only to a minimal degree during the second year, selecting only those men whose date of entry into the program or parole eligibility obviated their being included in the follow-up sample.

Second, in the light of the institution's need to house "special" categories of inmates in one quad, we decided to restrict our study population to three of the four quadrangles (A, B, and C) rather than sacrifice random assignment. (Notice that designations of "special" were made in departmental headquarters, not at CMCE.) This was the most important modification of the research design made for the benefit of institutional needs. It should be noted that not all "problem" inmates were assigned to D Quad. For example, inmates transferred to Men's Colony because they were management problems elsewhere became part of the regular prison population and, thus, were eligible for participation in the study.

The third question was not easily answered. To persuade the Adult Authority that it was warranted to deny group counseling to a sizable number of inmates was not a simple task. At that time, about 12,000 inmates and hundreds of staff members were involved in group-counseling programs, and the Adult Authority, and to some extent the department, had become convinced during the preceding years of the soundness of the program. This, despite the fact that there was *no* systematically collected evidence that such participation, in fact, had changed in-prison or post-prison behavior. Our argument was that only through maintaining a control group for a specified period of time would it be possible to assess the impact of group counseling on inmate attitudes and parolee behavior. We pointed out that there was only one prison in California where all inmates were enrolled in counseling, and, after some discussion, the advantages of the control-group feature of the design were seen to outweigh the disadvantages of the denial on a random basis of any program that might benefit an inmate. Finally, it was noted that if group counseling was found to make for positive changes in inmates, then, perhaps, all inmates should be enrolled in the program.

In regard to the problem that was posed by the transfers within the institution, it was agreed that the administrator of each of the quadrangles could, at his discretion, reassign to a different program group or housing assignment up to 5 men out of 100. Thus, if the initial assignment procedure resulted in the placement of an uncooperative person in mandatory group counseling, the administrator could transfer the inmate to the voluntary-program assignment if, in his judgment, this would clearly be more beneficial to the inmate and to the other members of the group to which he originally was assigned. Those transfers could be made only *from* compulsory group-treatment programs and only to voluntary programs. The superintendent could make transfers at his discretion without limitation or restrictions. In view of the implications of transfers for the research effort, however, the superintendent agreed to try to limit transfers between the quadrangles or out of prison to cases in which the transfer necessity clearly overrode the implications of the move for the research design.

In May 1961, a second meeting was held. Its purpose was to set forth a reasonably detailed statement of the inmate assignment plan, the definition of the varieties of treatment, and the staffing required. This plan was designed to meet research requirements within the limits of prison staffing and program capabilities.

Varieties of Treatment and Control

It was agreed that the group-treatment varieties would constitute additions to the usual programs of religion, recreation, academic schooling, and vocational training. Three conditions of group counseling and two control groups were established as follows:

Condition 1. Voluntary Small Group Counseling. This condition consisted of small groups of men (10 to 12) who met weekly for an hour. Inmate participation was voluntary. Group leaders represented all segments of the staff and had the usual training provided by the department for all group counselors. This option created a second self-selected control group (see Condition 5).

Condition 2. Mandatory Small Group Counseling. In Condition 2, group counseling was required for all inmates in one building of one quadrangle. As in Condition 1, groups were small and not necessarily based on common housing units. Groups met more often than in Condition 1—twice weekly, each meeting was one hour. Group leaders were correctional counselors (caseworkers), lieutenants, and correctional officers. One other element that distinguished this variety from Condition 1 was that all group leaders received supplementary training in group-counseling techniques (provided by research funds). This training was supplementary to the training some leaders had received in their formal education in social work and to the training that all leaders had received from the Department of Corrections. . . .

Condition 3. Mandatory Large Group Counseling. This variety of group treatment, which centered around men from a common living unit, such as a hall or wing of a cell house, was referred to as Community Living. At Men's Colony the physical layout of the prison divded the men into groups of 50—each quadrangle had two buildings each housing 300 men, with each building comprised of three floors of 100 men, divided again into two groups of 50 by means of a central control area. Each 50-man section had its own dayroom, and it was in these rooms that the entire group was required to meet four times each week for one-hour sessions. The three leaders were members of the custodial and treatment staff attached to that unit, at least one of whom was required to be a senior administrative official, such as the quadrangle's administrator, or a senior custodial officer or a treatment specialist, such as the senior caseworker with group counseling experience. In addition to daily meetings, on the fifth day the large group split into three smaller groups, each with one group leader. Each of these group leaders received the supplementary training in group-counseling methods described above for the leaders of mandatory small group counseling.

Condition 4. Mandatory Controls. The only difference between the mandatory controls (men in C Quad) and the other treatment conditions was that participation in any type of organized group counseling was not part of the total quad program. All other elements of the institutional program were available.

Condition 5. *Voluntary Controls.* By implication, the units of A and B Quads, in which group counseling was voluntary, also had a self-selected (voluntary) control sample.

IMPLEMENTING THE DESIGN

Staffing of the Group Treatment Program

The Men's Colony staff believed that they could cope with the requirements of time, effort, and manpower involved in the operation of all of the programs except the one in the community living units. The extra burden imposed on institution resources by mandatory counseling was met through the addition to the prison staff of two additional counseling specialists (caseworkers who

FIGURE A

had had graduate training in social work and counseling experience) paid for from UCLA project funds. In addition to leading a counseling group in a community living unit, both of these extra staff members were: (1) to substitute for leaders who might be unable to meet with their groups because of illness, vacations, or other reasons; (2) to be available to assist any group leader who was having problems in conducting his group; (3) to assist other caseworkers in their normal duties; and (4) to keep daily logs of events and issues that occurred in their counseling sessions. The men selected to fill these positions were recruited for work at CMCE through the usual selection procedures.

Here we also must point out another important decision in regard to staffing that had been made earlier as a result of discussions with representatives of the National Institute of Mental Health, who posed the question of whether a project that evaluated group counseling as it was operated in the department was really a fair test of this counseling. If the outcome was negative, it might be argued that the group programs would have shown positive results "if only they had been run the way they should be run," that is, with more highly trained leaders. Hence, we revised an earlier decision to only evaluate an ongoing program by establishing variations of the group-counseling program whose leaders participated in an intensive training program. Thus, we raised the level of training for some group leaders above the limits of departmental funding.

Briefly, leaders were selected from the mandatory group-counseling conditions and met in two groups of 16 each for a three-day workshop at a site away from the prison. Nine follow-up sessions were held biweekly in a recreation center on the grounds of CMC—West Facility. This supplementary training was directed by William C. Schutz, a psychologist with considerable experience in similar training efforts. . . .

Inmate Assignment Procedure

With the cooperation of the superintendent and his staff, an inmate assignment procedure was developed that was unambiguous to the officers making assignment decisions and that assured unbiased election to the treatment and control conditions. Because the quadrangles were sequentially activated—first A Quad, then B, then C—housing was assigned to incoming inmates as the quads were readied for occupancy. The procedure is described and diagrammed below (see Figure B).

Two categories of inmates had to be identified and then assigned to housing units on a somewhat different basis than the study eligibles. These were "special" category cases and men who were ineligible for the parole follow-up study. The research team had agreed to the institution's request that men sent to CMCE who were designated "special" would be assigned directly to D Quad. This designation was made by departmental headquarters not by CMCE staff and included post-psychotic cases, aged, arsonists, transients, and the so-called management cases. This does not mean that all "trouble-makers" were sent to D Quad.

The other category (men who were not eligible for parole follow-up) were assigned to voluntary counseling units. Ineligibility was defined as not being in the prison long enough to meet the minimum criterion for treatment exposure (six months) or having no chance of parole prior to the cutoff date for institutional data collection, or being over the age of 65 at admission. In other words, men whose terms had been set by the parole board and had less than six months remaining to be served in the prison and men who would not be eligible for parole for at least three years were part of all phases of the study, except the parole follow-up. Housing assignment was based on the last digit of their departmental serial number: if it was even, they went to A Quad; if odd, to B Quad.

All incoming inmates who did not fall into one or the other of the above

FIGURE B
The Inmate Assignment Procedure (depending on inmate's choice)

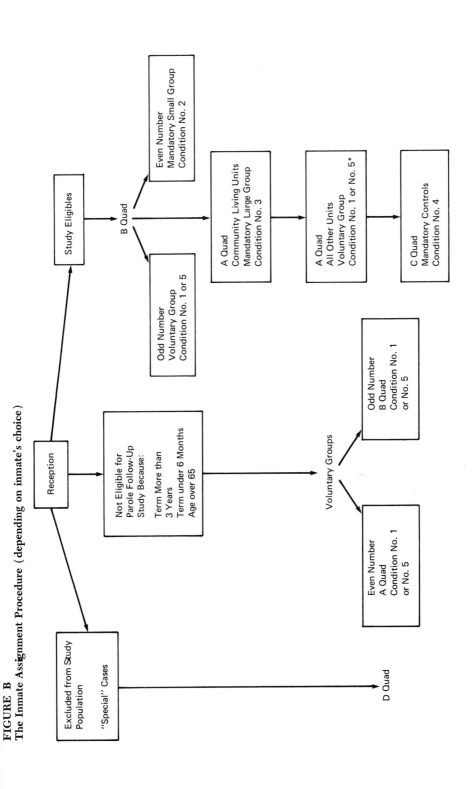

two categories were assigned to one of the treatment conditions on a random basis without further consideration of individual characteristics. Since new inmates arrive in groups, it first was necessary to specify a systematic way to list them for the assignment procedure. This was done by ranking the men in each group in order of the last two digits of their departmental serial number—men then were assigned to the first vacancy in accord with the following plan:

1. The first assignment was to B Quad. If the last digit of the inmate's serial number was even, he was assigned to one of the units where counseling was mandatory (Condition No. 2). If his number was odd, he went to housing units in which ccunseling was voluntary. That is, he became part of either condition No. 1 or No. 5, whichever he elected.
2. Next came the assignment to the Community Living Units of A Quad, where he became part of Condition No. 3 (mandatory large group counseling).
3. Then came assignment to the units with voluntary counseling in A Quad. Depending upon the inmate's choice, he became part of Condition No. 1 or No. 5.
4. Next was the assignment to Condition No. 4—Mandatory Controls in C Quad.

As was observed earlier in this chapter, treatment effect often has been obscured by either the lack of, or biased assignment to, a control group. At this point it is useful to consider data on how well the assignment system worked in producing comparable treatment and control groups.

An examination of five variables—type of primary offense, prior commitment, race, base expectancy, and intelligence quotient—shows *no* significant differences between our treatment and control groups. The first four were selected because they were known to be related to parole success, and we believed that IQ might effect the desire or abililty to participate in the treatment program.

· · · · ·

Data Collection at Men's Colony

Project funds provided for a full-time sociologist and a half-time research assistant to reside at the study site. In addition, we and other project staff from UCLA made biweekly trips of several days each. During the 18 months of the institutional phase, many kinds of data were collected from hundreds of inmates using a number of different techniques. These instruments are summarized below. They include an abstract of prison records prepared for every inmate released to parole supervision; questionnaires dealing with inmate values, the first of which was given to a 50-percent random sample of inmates and the second of which was administered six months later to all men who had taken the first; a questionnaire dealing with group counseling that was given to participants in the program; and a psychological inventory that was given to a sample of men who were about to be paroled. In addition, interviews were conducted with 75 inmates selected on a random basis.

Since at the time that these instruments were administered we were not able to identify which inmates would be released to parole, that is, who would become part of the parole follow-up cohort, we therefore do not have all data possible on every parolee. For example, some men who ultimately became part of the parole cohort had not taken the inmate attitude questionnaire or the group counseling questionnaire. In the summary that follows the extent of the overlap for the parole cohort will be detailed descriptions of instruments, and their analyses make up the bulk of the remaining chapters.

1. *Prison Record Abstract.* An abstract from official records of 59 items was prepared for 968 inmates who met study requirements for inclusion in the follow-up study. Coded information was gathered about treatment exposure, criminal career, personal and family background, psychiatric diagnosis, prison activities, prison rule violations, and release plans. Additional written commentaries supplied illustrative and anecdotal materials. . . .

    In connection with an analysis of inmate types, a shortened version was completed for an additional 217 inmates.

2. *Inmate Values Questionnaire.* This questionnaire contained measures of inmate code endorsement, several standardized scales, and many items related to group counseling. It was administered to a 50-percent random sample of all inmates (1,800) in the three study quadrangles. This resulted in a total of 871 usable forms. To assess change over time, there was a second administration six months later to all men remaining from the original sample. Five hundred and sixty-seven usable forms were obtained. . . . Two hundred and eighty-seven men in the parole cohort took the first questionnaire, and 150 were still in the prison for the second.

3. *The Group Counseling Questionnaire.* This questionnaire, referred to as the "Group Opinion Inventory" (GOI), was administered only to participants in group counseling.
    Because of the fact that this inventory was given late in the institutional phase of the study, only 96 men in the parole cohort had taken it.

4. *California Psychological Inventory.* A 40-percent sample of men ready for release were given the CPI. . . .

5. *Interviews.* Seventy-five interviews were conducted with a randomly selected sample of inmates on a variety of topics that ranged from inmate adjustment to feelings about the treatment program. . . .

Parole Follow-Up

Following a large number of subjects for several years is a difficult, time-consuming, and costly proposition. Our decision to have a three-year follow-up for nearly 1,000 subjects was possible only because of California law and departmental operations. Attrition is a major issue in any longitudinal design, but in our study this problem was minimized because the penal code provides indeterminate sentences for all offenders and because the policy of the State Board of Corrections is to release all inmates to parole supervision. That is, the flexibility of the sentencing law gives the paroling body (the Adult

Authority) the opportunity to impose fairly long periods of parole, during which regular reporting of whereabouts, job, and the like is required.

In addition, we were able to obtain arrest data and Adult Authority actions for all subjects from two correctional data collection operations: the California Bureau of Criminal Identification and Investigations runs an efficient centralized arrest reporting system and the Research Division of the Department of Corrections conducts a well-organized follow-up system.

Conclusion

A delay in final funding arrangements was responsible for a corresponding delay in the full implementation of the design until June 1962. During the interim period, however, the prison assigned incoming inmates to housing and treatment programs in accordance with the research formula. It was an indication of the strength of commitment of Superintendent Klinger and the Sacramento Central Office that, during a period of several months of uncertainty about ultimate funding, the prison maintained the scheduled program. After funding was definite, a final meeting was held with the members of the prison staff, the Department headquarters staff, and the Adult Authority. The principal issues were again concerns about "the denial of treatment" (group counseling) to men in C Quad and the rumored plans for shifts in prison populations throughout the department, which would affect the population at CMCE. Of additional concern, was the need to obtain the cooperation of the Adult Authority in not giving preferential treatment in parole decisions to men participating in the group-treatment programs. At the conclusion of this meeting, the Adult Authority, the department, and the institution reaffirmed their support of the study as originally planned. The Adult Authority also agreed to omit discussion of group-treatment participation with prospective parolees and, in the granting of paroles, to try not to discriminate against men in control samples.

The essential phases of the study can be summarized as follows.

June 1961 to December 1961. The prison opened, and the assignment of inmates to housing units was made according to the research design. There was no group-treatment plan in operation.

January to August 1962. The regular group-counseling program began, as did the regular institutional training program for group leaders. Although one community living unit and the mandatory group-counseling programs had begun, the supplemental training for group leaders was not yet in operation. (During this period, funds were not in hand to enable either supplemental training for group leaders or for an increment of staff.) Operation of C Quad was the same as the other quadrangles, with the exception of a group-counseling program. The institution staff maintained the procedures for the random assignment of incoming men to housing and treatment and control varieties.

September 1962. Enabling funds permitted the start of the supplemental training program, the establishment of two additional community living units, the increment in prison staff, and the assignment of research-project personnel to resident status on the site.

July 1962 to December 31, 1963. The release of study subjects on parole.

October 1962 to December 1963. Institutional data-collection phase (including data on men released since July) and the operation of the experimental programs as designed.

March 1963 to December 1965. Data collection from parolees and parole-agent records.

December 31, 1966 to June 1967. Last date for the inclusion of arrest and disposition data on men in follow-up, providing a minimum of 36 months follow-up on all cases. Approximately five months' additional time was required for the CDC Research Division to receive parole agents' reports and to gather arrest data from the Bureau of Criminal Identification.

July 1967 to August 1969. The analysis of masses of data collected over the preceding five years, the critique of analysis and manuscript drafts by the California Department of Corrections personnel, the staff members at Men's Colony—East, and our colleagues in sociology and psychology.

Despite a delay in getting the research design underway and the loss of one quadrangle from the original study plan, the Men's Colony project approximates more closely the requisite conditions for an experimental longitudinal study of correctional treatment outcome than do most of the earlier studies that came to our attention.

❀   ❀   ❀

By considering the facets of this attempt to evaluate the impact of various treatments, we are able to locate a series of general issues that emerge when using the experimental model for evaluation. First is the selection of the research site. As indicated in Chapter 11, two different types of validity—internal, where the concern is with eliminating alternative explanations for the findings, and external, where the concern is with the general applicability of the findings—need to be considered. Both types become points of concern in the selection of the prison for study.

Architectural design became important in that the various treatment groups were to be separated from one another. This was to avoid contamination effects of attempting to run several different programs in the same unit. The organization of the prison into separate quads provided the architectural facilities for experimental demands. Transfers within the institution and the presence of "special" inmates put restrictions on the eventual utility of the prison design. Through meetings between researchers and staff of the institution, compromises were worked out. In addition, the presence of four quads (eventually the study was limited to three) in a single institution made the groups more comparable than similar groups from separate institutions. The planned architecture of the institution, then, offered substantial benefits in terms of maximizing the comparability of groups and minimizing contamination of experimental conditions across groups.

Other factors were noted when considering the applicability of the results. Minimum- and maximum-security institutions were rejected due to the "extreme" nature of their populations and programs. Medium-security institutions, by contrast, were more attractive because of a wider variety of inmates and programs more toward the middle of the spectrum.

The general point is that, when designing an evaluation project on the experimental model, you should make efforts to identify threats to the internal and external validity of your study and then attempt to eliminate or minimize these threats. Certain experimental designs are more useful than others (Campbell and Stanley, 1963). Certain characteristics of the setting to be studied may be more or less conducive for the demands of a carefully controlled study.

Part of the control inherent in the experimental model is that provided by the random assignment of "units" to one treatment or another. This is also a facet of the experimental design that frequently produces conflict between the demands of an ongoing operation and the demands of a carefully designed study. Again, these become apparent in the above example. Randomly deciding who is to be treated in what ways involves obvious ethical problems. Transferring persons out of one quad to another or out of the institution altogether for administrative reasons produced problems of group comparability and attrition for the experiment. These conflicting demands of the simultaneous operation of a study and a prison eventually were compromised. Such compromises are the rule rather than the exception. It is simply the case that the demands of operating a "program" are different than the demands of a study. It is at this point of compromise that persons involved in such studies have to walk a tight line between irrelevance and cooption.

On the one hand, researchers who devote their attention solely to esoteric theoretical gaps are likely to find themselves either out of a job or relegated to the "back wards" of the operation. In parallel fashion, persons "taken in" by the program may find they are pumping out public-relations information for the program and thus neither conducting a useful evaluation study nor gathering information for broader theoretical issues.

Two additional points should be made. One, when conducting an evaluation of a program using the experimental model, explicit identification of the independent and dependent variables is called for. This is frequently no easy task in that "programs" are multifaceted phenomena. "Success" or "impact" also must be translated into concrete research operations. Given the multiplicity of goals and value orientations that accompany any ongoing operation, this is no small portion of the eventual success of the study.

The second point is less difficult to solve; indeed, it is more a matter of recognition and commitment. Such evaluation research often involves large amounts of time. The lag time between the onset of a program and its eventual impact or determination of success is frequently substantial. We find in our example that the program got off the ground in June of 1961 and the writing and analysis took place from July 1967 through August 1969. Such commitments are not for the fainthearted.

Practicum 12.1 One type of evaluation we have not dealt with explicitly is the examination of the impact of changing laws. Design a study to examine the impact of U.S. Supreme Court decisions. You might look at police control or capital-punishment rulings, prayers in school, or busing for racial-integration decisions. What different demands will be placed on your study depending on whether you select the descriptive or the experimental model of evaluation?

SOME FINAL THOUGHTS

All of this attention to the issues of evaluation research in the last chapter should not be taken as an attempt to convince you that evaluation research is the only appropriate mode of proceeding. Don't be afraid to strike out on seemingly irrelevant paths if you think the long-range payoff is great. Spin-offs and unexpected dividends from basic research are well-documented. In addition, "programs" and "problems" are frequently the result of political maneuverings. If we become program or problem chasers we are likely to find a great deal of spasmodic movement and little else.

Develop a perspective of what you perceive the central issues to be and proceed accordingly. In the process, keep in mind that social science and society are intertwined in a number of frequently quite subtle ways. The problems you select and the ways in which you proceed will in many ways reflect the values you hold. In this sense there is no value-free research. The virtue of social-science research methods is that they are designed to minimize the impact of preconceptions and prejudices. Perfection in this regard is not possible. Improvement is. Finally, in reporting your findings, remember that the findings of social science become incorporated into the folk-wisdom of society in ways that may have both detrimental and beneficial effects. Once these effects are perceived, they are likely to have their own reciprocal impact on social science as either a thriving or barely surviving enterprise.

REFERENCES

Anderson, James G.
    1973   "Causal Models and Social Indicators: Toward the Development of Social System Models." *American Sociological Review*, vol. 38, pp. 285–301.

Butler, Johnny S.
    1974   *Unsanctioned Institutional Racism in the U.S. Army,* unpublished
            Ph.D. Dissertation, Northwestern University, Evanston, Illinois.
Campbell, Donald T., and Stanley, Julian C.
    1963   *Experimental and Quasi-Experimental Designs for Research.* Chi-
            cago: Rand McNally and Company.
Cumming, Elaine; Cumming, Ian; and Edell, Laura
    1965   "Policeman as Philosopher Guide and Friend." *Social Problems,*
            vol. 12, pp. 276–86.
Etkowitz, Henry, and Schaflander, Gerald M.
    1968   "A Manifesto for Sociologists: Institution Formation—A New
            Sociology." *Social Problems,* vol. 15, pp. 399–408.
Fox, Karl A.
    1974   *Social Indicators and Social Theory.* New York: John Wiley and
            Sons.
Gouldner, Alvin W.
    1970   *The Coming Crisis in Western Sociology.* New York: Basic Books.
Gross, Bertram M.
    1966   "The State of the Nation: Social Systems Accounting." In Raymond
            A. Bauer (ed.), *Social Indicators.* Cambridge, Mass.: M.I.T. Press.
Hauser, Philip M.
    1969   "On Actionism in the Craft of Sociology." *Sociological Inquiry.*
            vol. 39, pp. 139–47.
Jacob, Bruce R., and Sharma, K. M.
    1970   "Justice After Trial: Prisoners Need for Legal Services in the
            Criminal-Correction Process." *Kansas Law Review,* vol. 18, pp.
            493–628.
Jones, Martin V., and Flax, Michael J.
    1970   *The Quality of Life in Metropolitan Washington, D.C.: Some
            Statistical Benchmarks.* Washington, D.C.: Urban Institute.
Kassebaum, Gene; Ward, David A.; and Wilner, Daniel M.
    1971   *Prison Treatment and Parole Survival: An Empirical Assessment*
            New York: John Wiley and Sons, pp. 69–85.
Lundberg, George A.; Schrag, Clarence C.; Larsen, Otto N.; and Catton,
            William R.
    1968   *Sociology.* New York: Harper and Row.
Olson, Sheldon R.
    1974   "Minutes in Court, Weeks in Jail: A Study of Pretrial Detention."
            New York: MSS Modular Publications, Inc. Module 22.
Pospisil, Leopold
    1967   "Legal Levels and the Multiplicity of Legal Systems in Human
            Societies." *The Journal of Conflict Resolution,* vol. 9, pp. 2–26.
Selznick, Philip
    1969   *Law, Society and Industrial Justice.* New York: Russell Sage
            Foundation.

U.S. Department of Health, Education and Welfare
1970   *Toward a Social Report.* Ann Arbor: University of Michigan Press.
Vera Institute of Justice
1970   The Manhattan Court Employment Project: Summary Report on Phase One, November 1, 1967 to October 3, 1969. New York: The Vera Institute of Justice.

Appendix A

Questionnaire from 1970 U.S. Census

This leaflet shows the content of the questionnaires being used in the 1970 Census of Population and Housing. See explanatory notes on the page 1 flap.

UNITED STATES CENSUS

This is your Official Census Form

Please fill it out and mail it back on Census Day, Wednesday, April 1, 1970

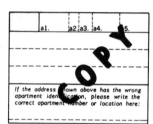

If the address shown above has the wrong apartment identification, please write the correct apartment number or location here:

How To Fill This Form

1. **Use a black pencil to answer the questions.**

   This form is read by an electronic computer. Black pencil is better to use than ballpoint or other pens.

   Fill circles "○" like this: ●

   The electronic computer reads every circle you fill. If you fill the wrong circle, erase it, mark completely, then fill the right circle.

   When you write an answer, print or write clearly.

2. **See the filled-in example on the yellow instruction sheet.**

   This example shows how to fill circles and write in answers. If you are not sure of an answer, give the best answer you can.

   If you have a problem, look in the instruction sheet.

   Instructions are numbered the same as the questions on the Census form.

   If you need more help, call the Census office.

   You can get the number of the local office from telephone "Information" or "Directory assistance."

3. **Your answers are CONFIDENTIAL. The law (Title 13, United States Code) requires that you answer the questions to the best of your knowledge.**

   Your answers will be used only for statistical purposes and cannot, by law, be disclosed to any person outside the Census Bureau for any reason whatsoever.

   The householder should make sure that the information is shown for everyone here.

   If a boarder or roomer or anyone else prefers not to give the householder all his information to enter on the form, the householder should give at least his name, relationship, and sex in questions 1 to 3, then mail back the form. A Census Taker will call to get the rest of the information directly from the person.

4. **Check your answers. Then, mail back this form on Wednesday, April 1, or as soon afterward as you can. Use the enclosed envelope; no stamp is needed.**

   Your cooperation in carefully filling out the form and mailing it back will help make the census successful. It will save the government the expense of calling on you for the information.

U.S. Department of Commerce
Bureau of the Census
Form D-60

PLEASE CONTINUE

5. Answer the questions in this order:

Questions on page 2 about the people in your household.

Questions on page 3 about your house or apartment.

6. In Question 1 on page 2, please list each person who was living here on Wednesday, April 1, 1970, or who was staying or visiting here and had no other home.

EXPLANATORY NOTES

This leaflet shows the content of the 1970 census questionnaires. The content was determined after review of the 1960 census experience, extensive consultation with many government and private users of census data, and a series of experimental censuses in which various alternatives were tested.

Three questionnaires are being used in the census and each household has an equal chance of answering a particular form.

80 percent of the households answer a form containing only the questions on pages 2 and 3 of this leaflet.

15 percent and **5 percent** of the households answer forms which also contain the specified questions on the remaining pages of this leaflet. The 15-percent form does not show the 5-percent questions, and the 5-percent form does not show the 15-percent questions. On both forms, population questions 13 to 41 are repeated for each person in the household but questions 24 to 41 do not apply to children under 14 years of age.

The same sets of questions are used throughout the country, regardless of whether the census in a particular area is conducted by mail or house-to-house canvass. An illustrative example is enclosed with each questionnaire to help the householder complete the form.

80, 15, and 5 percent (100 percent)

DO NOT MARK THIS COLUMN

LINE NO.

1. WHAT IS THE NAME OF EACH PERSON who was living here on Wednesday, April 1, 1970 or who was staying or visiting here and had no other home?	2. HOW IS EACH PERSON RELATED TO THE HEAD OF THIS HOUSEHOLD?	3. SEX	4. COLOR OR RACE	5. Month and year of birth and age last birthday	6. Month of birth	7. Year of birth	8. WHAT IS EACH PERSON'S MARITAL STATUS?

Print names in this order

Head of the household
Wife of head
Unmarried children, oldest first
Married children and their families
Other relatives of the head
Persons not related to the head

Column 2:
Fill one circle.
If "Other relative of head," also give exact relationship; for example, mother-in-law, brother, niece, grandson, etc.
If "Other not related to head," also give exact relationship; for example, partner, maid, etc.

Relationship options per person:
- Head of household
- Wife of head
- Son or daughter of head
- Other relative of head— *Print exact relationship*
- Roomer, boarder, lodger
- Patient or inmate
- Other not related to head— *Print exact relationship*

Column 3: *Fill one circle* — Male / Female

Column 4: *Fill one circle.* *If "Indian (Americ.)," also give tribe. If "Other," also give race.*
- White
- Negro or Black
- Indian (Amer.)— *Print tribe*
- Japanese
- Chinese
- Filipino
- Hawaiian
- Korean
- Other— *Print race*

Column 5: *Print* — Month / Year / Age

Column 6: *Fill one circle*
- Jan.-Mar.
- Apr.-June
- July-Sept.
- Oct.-Dec.

Column 7: *Fill one circle for first three numbers*
- 186. 192.
- 187. 193.
- 188. 194.
- 189. 195.
- 190. 196.
- 191. 197.

Fill one circle for last number
- 0 5
- 1 6
- 2 7
- 3 8
- 4 9

Column 8: *Fill one circle*
- Now married
- Widowed
- Divorced
- Separated
- Never married

(Rows for persons numbered (1) through (8), each with Last name, First name, Middle initial.)

9. *If you used all 8 lines—* Are there any other persons in this household? Yes / No
Do not list the others; we will call to get the information.

10. Did you leave anyone out of Question 1 because you were not sure if he should be listed—for example, a new baby still in the hospital, or a lodger who also has another home? Yes / No
On back page, give name(s) and reason left out.

11. Did you list anyone in Question 1 who is away from home now—for example, on a vacation or in a hospital? Yes / No
On back page, give name(s) and reason person is away.

12. Did anyone stay here on Tuesday, March 31, who is not already listed? Yes / No
On back page, give name of each visitor for whom there is no one at his home address to report him to a census taker.

Please answer questions 10, 11, and 12 at the bottom of page 2.

80, 15, and 5 percent (100 percent)   Page 3

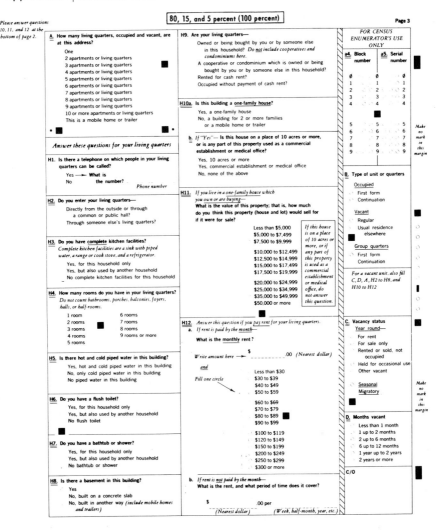

A. How many living quarters, occupied and vacant, are at this address?

- One
- 2 apartments or living quarters
- 3 apartments or living quarters
- 4 apartments or living quarters
- 5 apartments or living quarters
- 6 apartments or living quarters
- 7 apartments or living quarters
- 8 apartments or living quarters
- 9 apartments or living quarters
- 10 or more apartments or living quarters
- This is a mobile home or trailer

Answer these questions for your living quarters

H1. Is there a telephone on which people in your living quarters can be called?

Yes ⟶ What is
No   the number?
       Phone number

H2. Do you enter your living quarters—

- Directly from the outside or through a common or public hall?
- Through someone else's living quarters?

H3. Do you have complete kitchen facilities?
Complete kitchen facilities are a sink with piped water, a range or cook stove, and a refrigerator.

- Yes, for this household only
- Yes, but also used by another household
- No complete kitchen facilities for this household

H4. How many rooms do you have in your living quarters?
Do not count bathrooms, porches, balconies, foyers, halls, or half-rooms.

- 1 room   6 rooms
- 2 rooms   7 rooms
- 3 rooms   8 rooms
- 4 rooms   9 rooms or more
- 5 rooms

H5. Is there hot and cold piped water in this building?

- Yes, hot and cold piped water in this building
- No, only cold piped water in this building
- No piped water in this building

H6. Do you have a flush toilet?

- Yes, for this household only
- Yes, but also used by another household
- No flush toilet

H7. Do you have a bathtub or shower?

- Yes, for this household only
- Yes, but also used by another household
- No bathtub or shower

H8. Is there a basement in this building?

- Yes
- No, built on a concrete slab
- No, built in another way *(include mobile homes and trailers)*

H9. Are your living quarters—

- Owned or being bought by you or by someone else in this household? *Do not include cooperatives and condominiums here.*
- A cooperative or condominium which is owned or being bought by you or by someone else in this household?
- Rented for cash rent?
- Occupied without payment of cash rent?

H10a. Is this building a one-family house?

- Yes, a one-family house
- No, a building for 2 or more families or a mobile home or trailer

b. If "Yes"— Is this house on a place of 10 acres or more, or is any part of this property used as a commercial establishment or medical office?

- Yes, 10 acres or more
- Yes, commercial establishment or medical office
- No, none of the above

H11. If you live in a one-family house which you own or are buying—
What is the value of this property; that is, how much do you think this property (house and lot) would sell for if it were for sale?

- Less than $5,000
- $5,000 to $7,499
- $7,500 to $9,999
- $10,000 to $12,499
- $12,500 to $14,999
- $15,000 to $17,499
- $17,500 to $19,999
- $20,000 to $24,999
- $25,000 to $34,999
- $35,000 to $49,999
- $50,000 or more

If this house is on a place of 10 acres or more, or if any part of this property is used as a commercial establishment or medical office, do not answer this question.

H12. Answer this question if you pay rent for your living quarters.
a. If rent is paid by the *month*—

What is the monthly rent?

Write amount here ⟶ $ _____ .00 *(Nearest dollar)*

and

Fill one circle

- Less than $30
- $30 to $39
- $40 to $49
- $50 to $59
- $60 to $69
- $70 to $79
- $80 to $89
- $90 to $99
- $100 to $119
- $120 to $149
- $150 to $199
- $200 to $249
- $250 to $299
- $300 or more

b. If rent is *not paid* by the month—
What is the rent, and what period of time does it cover?

$ _____ .00 per _____
(Nearest dollar)   *(Week, half-month, year, etc.)*

FOR CENSUS ENUMERATOR'S USE ONLY

a4. Block number	a5. Serial number
Ø Ø Ø	
1 1 1	
2 2 2	
3 3 3	
4 4 4	
5 5 5	
6 6 6	
7 7 7	
8 8 8	
9 9 9	

Make no mark in this margin

B. Type of unit or quarters

Occupied
- First form
- Continuation

Vacant
- Regular
- Usual residence elsewhere

Group quarters
- First form
- Continuation

For a vacant unit, also fill C, D, A, H2 to H8, and H10 to H12

C. Vacancy status

Year round—
- For rent
- For sale only
- Rented or sold, not occupied
- Held for occasional use
- Other vacant

- Seasonal
- Migratory

Make no mark in this margin

D. Months vacant

- Less than 1 month
- 1 up to 2 months
- 2 up to 6 months
- 6 up to 12 months
- 1 year up to 2 years
- 2 years or more

C/O

Page 4

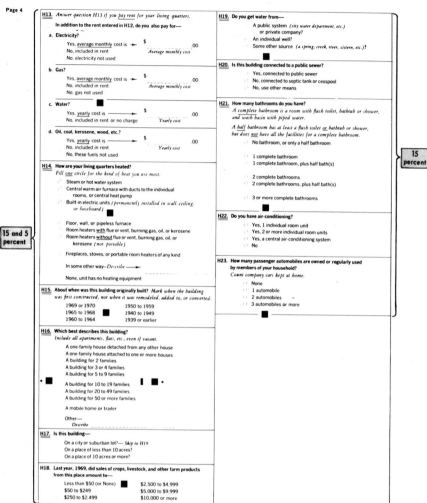

H13. *Answer question H13 if you pay rent for your living quarters.*

In addition to the rent entered in H12, do you also pay for—

a. Electricity?
- Yes, average monthly cost is → $ _____ .00 *Average monthly cost*
- No, included in rent
- No, electricity not used

b. Gas?
- Yes, average monthly cost is → $ _____ .00 *Average monthly cost*
- No, included in rent
- No, gas not used

c. Water?
- Yes, yearly cost is → $ _____ .00 *Yearly cost*
- No, included in rent or no charge

d. Oil, coal, kerosene, wood, etc.?
- Yes, yearly cost is → $ _____ .00 *Yearly cost*
- No, included in rent
- No, these fuels not used

H14. How are your living quarters heated?
Fill one circle for the kind of heat you use most.
- Steam or hot water system
- Central warm air furnace with ducts to the individual rooms, or central heat pump
- Built-in electric units *(permanently installed in wall, ceiling, or baseboard)*
- Floor, wall, or pipeless furnace
- Room heaters *with* flue or vent, burning gas, oil, or kerosene
- Room heaters *without* flue or vent, burning gas, oil, or kerosene *(not portable)*
- Fireplaces, stoves, or portable room heaters of any kind
- In some other way—*Describe* → _____
- None, unit has no heating equipment

H15. About when was this building originally built? *Mark when the building was first constructed, not when it was remodeled, added to, or converted.*
- 1969 or 1970
- 1965 to 1968
- 1960 to 1964
- 1950 to 1959
- 1940 to 1949
- 1939 or earlier

H16. Which best describes this building?
Include all apartments, flats, etc., even if vacant.
- A one-family house detached from any other house
- A one-family house attached to one or more houses
- A building for 2 families
- A building for 3 or 4 families
- A building for 5 to 9 families
- A building for 10 to 19 families
- A building for 20 to 49 families
- A building for 50 or more families
- A mobile home or trailer
- Other—
  Describe _____

H17. Is this building—
- On a city or suburban lot?— *Skip to H19*
- On a place of less than 10 acres?
- On a place of 10 acres or more?

H18. Last year, 1969, did sales of crops, livestock, and other farm products from this place amount to—
- Less than $50 (or None)
- $50 to $249
- $250 to $2,499
- $2,500 to $4,999
- $5,000 to $9,999
- $10,000 or more

H19. Do you get water from—
- A public system *(city water department, etc.)* or private company?
- An individual well?
- Some other source *(a spring, creek, river, cistern, etc.)*?

H20. Is this building connected to a public sewer?
- Yes, connected to public sewer
- No, connected to septic tank or cesspool
- No, use other means

H21. How many bathrooms do you have?
A complete bathroom is a room with flush toilet, bathtub or shower, and wash basin with piped water.
A half bathroom has at least a flush toilet or bathtub or shower, but does not have all the facilities for a complete bathroom.
- No bathroom, or only a half bathroom
- 1 complete bathroom
- 1 complete bathroom, plus half bath(s)
- 2 complete bathrooms
- 2 complete bathrooms, plus half bath(s)
- 3 or more complete bathrooms

H22. Do you have air-conditioning?
- Yes, 1 individual room unit
- Yes, 2 or more individual room units
- Yes, a central air-conditioning system
- No

H23. How many passenger automobiles are owned or regularly used by members of your household?
Count company cars kept at home.
- None
- 1 automobile
- 2 automobiles
- 3 automobiles or more

15 and 5 percent

15 percent

The 15-percent form contains the questions shown on page 4. The 5-percent form contains the questions shown in the first column of page 4 and the questions shown on page 5.

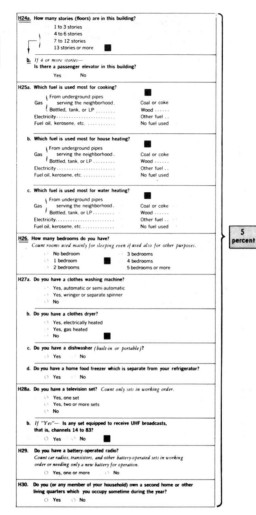

H24a. How many stories (floors) are in this building?

1 to 3 stories
4 to 6 stories
7 to 12 stories
13 stories or more ■

b. *If 4 or more stories—*
Is there a passenger elevator in this building?

Yes   No

H25a. Which fuel is used most for cooking? ■

Gas { From underground pipes serving the neighborhood.   Coal or coke
{ Bottled, tank, or LP . . . .   Wood . . . . . .
Electricity . . . .   Other fuel . .
Fuel oil, kerosene, etc. . . . .   No fuel used

b. Which fuel is used most for house heating? ■

Gas { From underground pipes serving the neighborhood .   Coal or coke
{ Bottled, tank, or LP . . . .   Wood . . . . . .
Electricity . . . .   Other fuel . .
Fuel oil, kerosene, etc. . . . .   No fuel used

c. Which fuel is used most for water heating? ■

Gas { From underground pipes serving the neighborhood .   Coal or coke
{ Bottled, tank, or LP . . . .   Wood . . . . . .
Electricity . . . .   Other fuel . .
Fuel oil, kerosene, etc. . . . .   No fuel used

H26. How many bedrooms do you have?
Count rooms used mainly for sleeping even if used also for other purposes.

No bedroom   3 bedrooms
1 bedroom ■   4 bedrooms
2 bedrooms   5 bedrooms or more

H27a. Do you have a clothes washing machine?

Yes, automatic or semi-automatic
Yes, wringer or separate spinner
No

b. Do you have a clothes dryer?

Yes, electrically heated
Yes, gas heated
No

c. Do you have a dishwasher *(built-in or portable)*?

Yes   No

d. Do you have a home food freezer which is separate from your refrigerator?

Yes   No

H28a. Do you have a television set? *Count only sets in working order.*

Yes, one set
Yes, two or more sets
No

b. *If "Yes"—* Is any set equipped to receive UHF broadcasts, that is, channels 14 to 83?

Yes   No ■

H29. Do you have a battery-operated radio?
Count car radios, transistors, and other battery-operated sets in working order or needing only a new battery for operation.

Yes, one or more   No

H30. Do you (or any member of your household) own a second home or other living quarters which you occupy sometime during the year?

Yes   No

5 percent

The 15-percent and 5-percent forms contain a pair of facing pages for each person in the household (as listed on page 2). Shown on each pair of pages in the 15-percent form are the questions designated as 15-percent here on pages 6, 7, and 8. Shown on each pair of pages in the 5-percent form are the questions designated as 5-percent here on pages 6, 7, and 8.

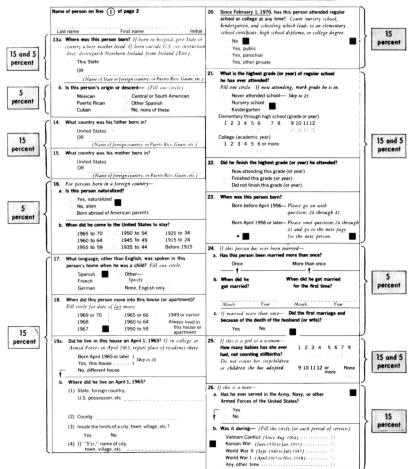

15 and 5 percent

Name of person on line ① of page 2

Last name   First name   Initial

13a. Where was this person born? *If born in hospital, give State or country where mother lived. If born outside U.S., see instruction sheet; distinguish Northern Ireland from Ireland (Eire).*

    This State

    OR

    (Name of State or foreign country; or Puerto Rico, Guam, etc.)

5 percent

b. Is this person's origin or descent— *(Fill one circle)*

    Mexican   Central or South American

    Puerto Rican   Other Spanish

    Cuban   No, none of these

15 percent

14. What country was his father born in?

    United States

    OR

    (Name of foreign country; or Puerto Rico, Guam, etc.)

15. What country was his mother born in?

    United States

    OR

    (Name of foreign country; or Puerto Rico, Guam, etc.)

5 percent

16. *For persons born in a foreign country—*

a. Is this person naturalized?

    Yes, naturalized

    No, alien

    Born abroad of American parents

b. When did he come to the United States to stay?

    1965 to 70   1950 to 54   1925 to 34

    1960 to 64   1945 to 49   1915 to 24

    1955 to 59   1935 to 44   Before 1915

17. What language, other than English, was spoken in this person's home when he was a child? *Fill one circle.*

    Spanish   Other—

    French   *Specify _____*

    German   None, English only

15 percent

18. When did this person move into this house (or apartment)? *Fill circle for date of last move.*

    1969 or 70   1965 or 66   1949 or earlier

    1968   1960 to 64   Always lived in

    1967   1950 to 59   this house or

                              apartment

19a. Did he live in this house on April 1, 1965? *If in college or Armed Forces in April 1965, report place of residence there.*

    Born April 1965 or later

    Yes, this house .... } *Skip to 20*

    No, different house

b. Where did he live on April 1, 1965?

    (1) State, foreign country, U.S. possession, etc. _____

    (2) County _____

    (3) Inside the limits of a city, town, village, etc.?

         Yes   No

    (4) *If "Yes,"* name of city, town, village, etc.

20. *Since February 1, 1970,* has this person attended regular school or college at any time? *Count nursery school, kindergarten, and schooling which leads to an elementary school certificate, high school diploma, or college degree.*

    No

    Yes, public

    Yes, parochial

    Yes, other private

15 percent

21. What is the highest grade (or year) of regular school he has ever attended?

Fill one circle. If now attending, mark grade he is in.

    Never attended school— *Skip to 23*

    Nursery school

    Kindergarten

Elementary through high school (grade or year)

    1 2 3 4 5 6   7 8   9 10 11 12

College (academic year)

    1 2 3 4 5 6 or more

22. Did he finish the highest grade (or year) he attended?

    Now attending this grade (or year)

    Finished this grade (or year)

    Did not finish this grade (or year)

15 and 5 percent

23. When was this person born?

    Born before April 1956— *Please go on with questions 24 through 41.*

    Born April 1956 or later— *Please omit questions 24 through 41 and go to the next page for the next person.*

24. *If this person has ever been married—*

a. Has this person been married more than once?

    Once   More than once

b. When did he   When did he get married

    get married?   for the first time?

    Month   Year   Month   Year

c. *If married more than once—* Did the first marriage end because of the death of the husband (or wife)?

    Yes   No

5 percent

25. *If this is a girl or a woman—*

How many babies has she ever   1 2 3 4   5 6 7 8

had, not counting stillbirths?

Do not count her stepchildren   9 10 11 12 or   None

or children she has adopted.   more

15 and 5 percent

26. *If this is a man—*

a. Has he ever served in the Army, Navy, or other Armed Forces of the United States?

    Yes

    No

b. Was it during— *(Fill the circle for each period of service.)*

    Vietnam Conflict *(Since Aug. 1964)* ....

    Korean War *(June 1950 to Jan. 1955)* ....

    World War II *(Sept. 1940 to July 1947)* ....

    World War I *(April 1917 to Nov. 1918)* ....

    Any other time ....

15 percent

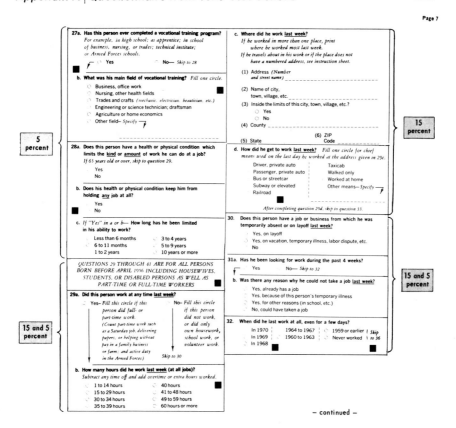

– continued –

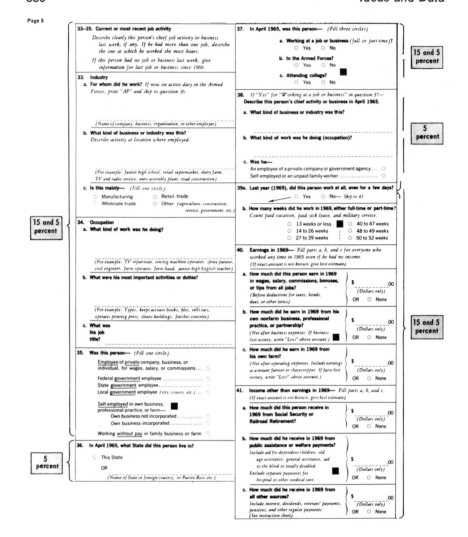

33–35. Current or most recent job activity

Describe clearly this person's chief job activity or business last week, if any. If he had more than one job, describe the one at which he worked the most hours.

If this person had no job or business last week, give information for last job or business since 1960.

33. Industry

a. For whom did he work? If now on active duty in the Armed Forces, print "AF" and skip to question 36.

(Name of company, business, organization, or other employer)

b. What kind of business or industry was this?
Describe activity at location where employed.

(For example: Junior high school, retail supermarket, dairy farm, TV and radio service, auto assembly plant, road construction)

c. Is this mainly— *(Fill one circle)*

- ○ Manufacturing
- ○ Wholesale trade
- ○ Retail trade
- ○ Other *(agriculture, construction, service, government, etc.)*

34. Occupation

a. What kind of work was he doing?

(For example: TV repairman, sewing machine operator, spray painter, civil engineer, farm operator, farm hand, junior high English teacher)

b. What were his most important activities or duties?

(For example: Types, keeps account books, files, sells cars, operates printing press, cleans buildings, finishes concrete)

c. What was his job title?

35. Was this person— *(Fill one circle)*

Employee of private company, business, or individual, for wages, salary, or commissions... ○

- Federal government employee .... ○
- State government employee.................. ○
- Local government employee *(city, county, etc.)*... ○

Self-employed in own business, ■
professional practice, or farm—
- Own business not incorporated .... ○
- Own business incorporated .... ○

Working without pay in family business or farm ○

36. In April 1965, what State did this person live in?

- ○ This State

OR

(Name of State or foreign country; or Puerto Rico, etc.)

37. In April 1965, was this person— *(Fill three circles)*

a. Working at a job or business *(full or part-time)?*
- ○ Yes   ○ No

b. In the Armed Forces?
- ○ Yes   ○ No   ■

c. Attending college?
- ○ Yes   ○ No

38. If "Yes" for "Working at a job or business" in question 37—
Describe this person's chief activity or business in April 1965.

a. What kind of business or industry was this?

b. What kind of work was he doing (occupation)?

c. Was he—
- An employee of a private company or government agency... ○
- Self-employed or an unpaid family worker .... ○

39a. Last year (1969), did this person work at all, even for a few days?
- ○ Yes   ○ No— *Skip to 41*

b. How many weeks did he work in 1969, either full-time or part-time? Count paid vacation, paid sick leave, and military service.

- ○ 13 weeks or less ■
- ○ 14 to 26 weeks
- ○ 27 to 39 weeks
- ○ 40 to 47 weeks
- ○ 48 to 49 weeks
- ○ 50 to 52 weeks

40. Earnings in 1969— Fill parts a, b, and c for everyone who worked any time in 1969 even if he had no income. *(If exact amount is not known, give best estimate.)*

a. How much did this person earn in 1969 in wages, salary, commissions, bonuses, or tips from all jobs?
(Before deductions for taxes, bonds, dues, or other items.)
$ _____ .00 *(Dollars only)*
OR ○ None

b. How much did he earn in 1969 from his own nonfarm business, professional practice, or partnership?
(Net after business expenses. If business lost money, write "Loss" above amount.) ■
$ _____ .00 *(Dollars only)*
OR ○ None

c. How much did he earn in 1969 from his own farm?
(Net after operating expenses. Include earnings as a tenant farmer or sharecropper. If farm lost money, write "Loss" above amount.)
$ _____ .00 *(Dollars only)*
OR ○ None

41. Income other than earnings in 1969— Fill parts a, b, and c. *(If exact amount is not known, give best estimate.)*

a. How much did this person receive in 1969 from Social Security or Railroad Retirement?
$ _____ .00 *(Dollars only)*
OR ○ None

b. How much did he receive in 1969 from public assistance or welfare payments?
Include aid for dependent children, old age assistance, general assistance, aid to the blind or totally disabled. Exclude separate payments for hospital or other medical care. ■
$ _____ .00 *(Dollars only)*
OR ○ None

c. How much did he receive in 1969 from all other sources?
Include interest, dividends, veterans' payments, pensions, and other regular payments. *(See instruction sheet.)*
$ _____ .00 *(Dollars only)*
OR ○ None

15 and 5 percent

5 percent

15 and 5 percent

5 percent

15 and 5 percent

15 and 5 percent

Appendix B

Portions of 1973 *Uniform Crime Report*

CRIME INDEX TOTALS

The offenses of murder, forcible rape, robbery, aggravated assault, burglary, larceny-theft, and auto theft are used to establish an Index in the Uniform Crime Reporting Program, to measure the trend and distribution of crime in the United States. These crimes are counted by law enforcement agencies as they become known and are reported on a monthly basis. The Crime Index offenses were selected as a measuring device because, as a group, they represent the most common local crime problem. They are all serious crimes, either by their very nature or due to the volume in which they occur. The offenses of murder, forcible rape, aggravated assault, and robbery make up the violent-crime category. The offenses of burglary, larceny-theft, and auto theft make up the property-crime category.

Law enforcement does not purport to know the total volume of crime because of the many criminal actions that are not reported to official sources. Estimates as to the level of unreported crime can be developed through costly victim surveys, but this does not eliminate the reluctance of the victim to report all criminal actions to law-enforcement agencies. In light of this situation, the best source for obtaining usable crime counts is the next logical universe, which are the offenses known to the police. The crimes used in the Crime Index are those considered to be most constantly reported and provide the capability to compute meaningful crime trends and crime rates.

The crime counts used in the Crime Index and set forth in this publication are based on actual offenses established by police investigation. When the law-enforcement agency receives a complaint of a criminal matter and the follow-up investigation discloses no crime occurred, it is "unfounded." On a national average, police investigations "unfound" 4 percent of the complaints concerning Crime Index offenses ranging from 2 percent in the larceny classification to 15 percent in the forcible-rape classification. These unfounded complaints are eliminated from the crime counts.

During calendar year 1973, an estimated 8,638,400 Crime Index offenses were reported to law-enforcement agencies. This includes total larceny-theft, which was used as an Index offense in 1973. Total larceny-theft replaces the "larceny $50 and over" offense category, which was previously utilized as an Index offense. All data in this publication uses total larceny-theft for comparative periods. There is a 6-percent increase in estimated volume of Index offenses, 1973 over 1972. The violent-crime category made up 10 percent of the Crime Index total and increased 5 percent in volume over 1972. Murder increased 5 percent, forcible rape 10 percent, and aggravated assault 7 percent. Robbery increased 2 percent. The voluminous property crimes as a group increased 6 percent. Auto theft increased 5 percent, larceny-theft increased 5 percent, and burglary was up 8 percent.

Since 1968, the violent crimes as a group have increased 47 percent and the property crimes 28 percent. Crime, as measured by the Crime Index offenses, has risen 30 percent in volume during this five-year period.

The estimated 1973 crime figures for the United States are set forth in the following table titled "National Crime, Rate, and Percent Change."

National Crime, Rate, and Percent Change

Crime Index Offenses	Estimated Crime 1973		Percent Change Over 1972		Percent Change Over 1968		Percent Change Over 1960	
	Number	Rate per 100,000 Inhabitants	Number	Rate	Number	Rate	Number	Rate
Total..........	8,638,400	4,116.4	+5.7	+4.9	+29.7	+23.5	+157.6	+120.2
Violent.........	869,470	414.3	+4.9	+4.1	+47.2	+40.2	+203.8	+159.6
Property........	7,768,000	3,702.1	+5.8	+5.0	+28.0	+21.9	+153.3	+116.5
Murder..........	19,510	9.3	+5.2	+4.5	+42.2	+34.8	+115.6	+86.0
Forcible rape	51,000	24.3	+9.7	+9.0	+62.4	+54.8	+199.2	+155.8
Robbery..........	382,680	182.4	+2.1	+1.3	+46.2	+39.2	+256.3	+204.5
Aggravated assault	416,270	198.4	+7.0	+6.2	+46.7	+39.7	+172.6	+132.9
Burglary...........	2,540,900	1,210.8	+8.0	+7.2	+38.0	+31.4	+181.3	+140.3
Larceny-theft	4,304,400	2,051.2	+4.7	+3.9	+24.8	+18.9	+134.3	+100.3
Auto theft.........	923,600	440.1	+4.7	+3.9	+18.5	+12.9	+183.0	+141.8

A study of the volume of crime, as measured by the Crime Index, reveals [that] the large core cities having population in excess of 250,000 recorded a 1-percent increase, while the suburban areas recorded a 9-percent increase over 1972. The rural areas of the United States registered a 10-percent increase. The cities over 1 million population reported a decrease of one-half of one percent from the previous year.

Regionally, in 1973, the Western states reported a 2-percent increase in crime, while the Northeastern states registered a 4-percent increase, the North Central states a 6 percent increase, and the Southern states recorded an increase of 9 percent.

CRIME AND POPULATION

Crime rates relate the incidence of reported crime to population. A crime rate should be considered a victim risk rate. Crime rates used are based on Crime Index offenses. The change in the level of the crime rates published in prior years is due to the utilization of total larceny-theft in 1973 rather than larceny $50 and over as an Index offense.

The Crime Index rate of the United States in 1973 was 4,116 per 100,000 inhabitants. This was a 5-percent increase from the crime rate of 3,925 per 100,000 inhabitants in 1972. The national crime rate, or the risk of being a victim of one of these crimes, has increased 24 percent since 1968. Many factors influence the nature and extent of crime in a particular community. A crime rate takes into consideration only the numerical factor of population and does not incorporate any of the other elements that contribute to the amount of crime in a given area. Tables disclose that the varying crime experiences, especially in large cities and suburban communities, are affected by a complex set of involved factors and are not solely related to numerical population differences.

The tables set forth on these pages reveal the variations in crime experience by geographic region, large cities, suburban, and rural areas.

The crime rates set forth in the "National Crime, Rate and Percent Change" table for each of the Crime Index offenses show a variation

Crime Rate by Region, 1973 (rate per 100,000 Inhabitants)

Crime Index Offenses	North-eastern States	North Central States	Southern States	Western States
Total	3,738.5	3,922.2	3,636.8	5,801.5
Violent	453.8	353.3	411.8	461.4
Property	3,284.7	3,568.9	3,225.1	5,340.1
Murder	7.6	7.6	12.9	7.8
Forcible rape	19.1	22.3	23.8	35.4
Robbery	253.7	166.8	141.6	183.5
Aggravated assault	173.4	156.7	233.4	234.6
Burglary	1,123.8	1,040.4	1,117.4	1,766.1
Larceny-theft	1,579.3	2,132.0	1,792.2	3,032.3
Auto theft	581.6	396.6	315.4	541.7

Crime Rate by Area, 1973 (rate per 100,000 Inhabitants)

Crime Index Offenses	Total U.S.	Cities over 250,000	Suburban	Rural
Total............	4,116.4	6,582.8	3,562.6	1,471.8
Violent	414.3	1,003.4	248.5	147.4
Property.........	3,702.1	5,579.5	3,314.1	1,324.4
Murder...........	9.3	20.7	5.1	7.5
Forcible rape	24.3	51.4	17.8	12.0
Robbery	182.4	571.5	76.1	17.7
Aggravated assault	198.4	359.9	149.5	110.2
Burglary	1,210.8	1,949.3	1,054.4	564.0
Larceny-theft	2,051.2	2,651.8	1,952.4	677.6
Auto theft..........	440.1	978.4	307.4	82.8

from a 9-percent increase in forcible rape to a 1-percent increase in robbery. The number of crimes per unit of population is highest in the large metropolitan centers.

The accompanying charts illustrate the trend of crime in the United States from 1968 through 1973 by showing percent changes in volume and crime rate together with the population increase. Separate charts provide similar information relative to crimes of violence and crimes against property. Since 1968, the violent-crime rate has increased 40 percent and the property-crime rate increased 22 percent. The violent-crime group includes murder, forcible rape, robbery, and aggravated-assault offenses. The property-crime category is made up of burglary, larceny-theft, and auto-theft offenses.

MURDER AND NONNEGLIGENT MANSLAUGHTER

This Crime Index offense is defined in Uniform Crime Reporting as the wilful killing of another. The classification in this offense, as in all of the other Crime Index offenses, is based solely on police investigation, as opposed to the determination of a court, medical examiner, coroner, jury, or other judicial body.

Deaths caused by negligence, suicide, accident, or justifiable homicide are not included in the count for this offense classification. Attempts to murder or assaults to murder are scored as aggravated assaults and not as murder.

Volume

In 1973 there were an estimated 19,510 murders committed in the United States. This represents a numerical increase of 960 over the 18,550

CHART 2
Crime and Population, 1968–1973 (percent change over 1968)
Crime = Crime Index Offenses
Crime Rate = Number of Offenses per 100,000 Inhabitants

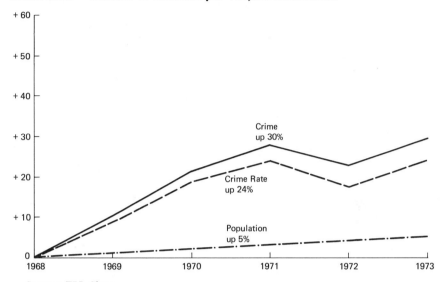

Source: FBI Chart.

CHART 3
Crimes of Violence, 1968–1973 (percent change over 1968)
Limited to Murder, Forcible Rape, Robbery, and Aggravated Assault

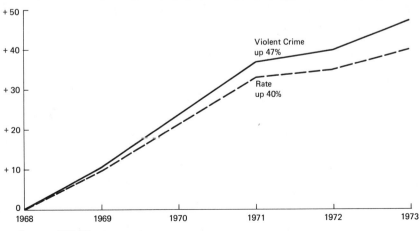

Source: FBI Chart.

CHART 4
Crimes Against Property, 1968–1973 (percent change over 1968)
Limited to Burglary, Larceny-Theft, and Auto Theft

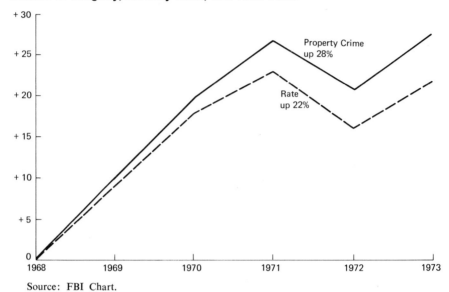

Source: FBI Chart.

estimated homicide offenses for 1972. The number of murders in 1973 is approximately 2 percent of the total for violent crime and less than one-half of one percent of the total of the seven Crime Index offenses.

An analysis of murder by month in 1973 shows that the summer months had the greatest frequency of murder, as compared to any other period of the year.

A geographical breakdown of murder by region showed 44 percent of the murders occurred in the Southern states, 22 percent in the North Central states, 19 percent in the Northeastern states, and 15 percent in the Western states.

Trend

The number of murders increased 5 percent in 1973 over 1972. The trend in this crime classification reveals an increase from 13,720 in 1968 to 19,510 in 1973. This is an increase of 42 percent.

Regionally, the number of murder offenses in 1973 increased 4 percent in the Western states, 4 percent in the Northeastern states, and 3 percent in the Southern states. The number of murders increased approximately 11 percent in the North Central states.

An analysis, by population grouping, of murder shows that large core cities of 250,000 or more inhabitants had a 5-percent increase in the

CHART 5
Murder, 1968–1973 (percent change over 1968)

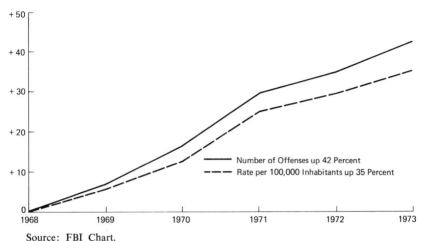

Source: FBI Chart.

number of murders in 1973, the suburban areas experienced a 9-percent increase in murder offenses, and the rural areas had a 0.2-percent increase.

Murder Rate

In 1973, there were 9.3 victims of murder for every 100,000 inhabitants in the nation. This was an increase of 4 percent over the murder rate of 8.9 per 100,000 inhabitants recorded in 1972.

By population grouping, the cities with 250,000 or more inhabitants reported a murder rate of 20.7 victims per 100,000 inhabitants, the suburban areas showed a rate of 5.1, and the rural areas a rate of 7.4 per 100,000 inhabitants.

The number of murder victims in proportion to population was highest in the Southern states, with 12.9 murders per 100,000 inhabitants. This is an increase of 2 percent over the murder rate of that region in 1972. In 1973, the Western states showed a murder rate of 7.8, an increase of 1 percent over the rate in 1972 for that region. The Northeastern states had a rate of 7.6, which was a 4-percent increase over the 1972 rate for those states. The North Central Region had a rate of 7.6, an increase of 12 percent, in comparison to the 1972 rate.

Nature of Murder

The law-enforcement agencies that participate in Uniform Crime Reporting cooperate in providing additional information regarding homi-

Age, Sex, and Race of Murder Victims, 1973

Age	Number	Percent	Sex		Race					
			Male	Female	White	Negro	Indian	Chinese	Japanese	All Others
Total	17,123	—	13,125	3,998	8,031	8,863	94	28	11	96
Percent	—	100.0*	76.7	23.3	46.9	51.8	.5	.2	.1	.6
Infant (under 1)	131	.8	71	60	82	42	1	—	—	6
1–4	329	1.9	183	146	182	139	4	—	—	4
5–9	150	.9	86	64	91	56	—	—	—	3
10–14	259	1.5	160	99	141	118	—	5	—	—
15–19	1,476	8.6	1,073	403	699	758	6	5	1	7
20–24	2,686	15.7	2,054	632	1,162	1,494	16	5	2	7
25–29	2,454	14.3	1,978	476	1,046	1,370	21	4	—	13
30–34	1,951	11.4	1,564	387	809	1,114	12	2	1	13
35–39	1,587	9.3	1,218	369	675	891	10	2	—	9
40–44	1,462	8.5	1,150	312	646	796	9	4	2	5
45–49	1,177	6.9	937	240	555	607	5	3	3	4
50–54	993	5.8	813	180	508	482	2	—	—	1
55–59	725	4.2	588	137	397	318	4	2	—	4
60–64	501	2.9	396	105	290	204	1	—	1	5
65–69	380	2.2	277	103	232	142	2	—	—	4
70–74	282	1.6	198	84	164	114	—	1	1	2
75 and over	334	2.0	184	150	256	76	1	—	—	1
Unknown	246	1.4	195	51	96	142	—	—	—	8

* Because of rounding, percentages may not add to total.

Murder Victims—Weapons Used, 1973

Age	Number	Gun	Cutting or Stabbing	Blunt Object (Club, Hammer, Etc.)	Personal Weapons (Hands, Fists, Feet, Etc.)	Poison	Explosives	Arson	Narcotics	Strangulation	Asphyxiation	Unknown Weapon or Weapon Not Stated
						Weapons						
Total	17,123	11,249	2,985	848	1,064	8	11	173	24	381	41	339
Infant (under 1)	131	9	6	11	66	1	–	3	–	7	6	22
1–4	329	44	14	25	177	–	2	26	1	15	4	21
5–9	150	55	19	12	20	–	–	12	3	21	4	4
10–14	259	151	33	12	17	1	1	9	1	20	1	13
15–19	1,476	1,005	271	58	46	2	2	4	3	50	2	33
20–24	2,686	1,934	487	78	58	1	–	14	7	56	7	44
25–29	2,454	1,797	416	76	81	–	3	11	5	31	2	32
30–34	1,951	1,431	326	69	74	–	1	10	–	21	1	18
35–39	1,587	1,136	273	67	62	–	–	12	1	18	2	16
40–44	1,462	1,006	278	61	66	2	1	9	1	22	2	14
45–49	1,177	757	220	81	56	1	–	13	–	25	–	24
50–54	993	630	189	75	74	–	–	7	1	13	2	22
55–59	725	421	146	63	55	–	–	5	1	17	1	16
60–64	501	285	110	38	44	–	–	4	–	9	2	9
65–69	380	202	68	35	44	–	–	9	–	12	1	9
70–74	282	137	53	28	32	–	1	7	–	15	–	9
75 and over	334	95	58	47	82	–	–	15	–	17	4	16
Unknown	246	154	38	12	10	–	–	3	–	12	–	17

cide so that a more in-depth analysis of this offense can be made. Through a supplemental reporting system, information is provided regarding the age, sex, and race of the victim; the weapon used in the murder; and the circumstances surrounding the offense.

The victims of murder in 1973 were male in approximately three out of four instances. This ratio of male to female victims is similar to the experience in the last several years. Approximately 47 out of 100 murder victims were white, 52 were Negro, and 1 percent other races. The largest number of murders occurring in any ten-year age bracket was in the 20-to-29 group with three of every ten murder victims.

In 1973, firearms again predominated as the weapon most often used in homicide in the nation. The accompanying chart illustrates a breakdown by type of weapon used in the commission of murder in the nation. Firearms were used more frequently in the Southern states than in any other region, with firearms used in more than seven of every ten murders. Nationwide, 67 percent of the homicides were committed through the use of firearms and 53 percent were committed with handguns. In 1972, 54 percent of the murders were through the use of handguns.

Cutting or stabbing weapons were used in 18 percent of the murders in the nation. The Northeastern states reported the greatest use of knives or cutting instruments, with three out of every ten murders being committed with this type of weapon. The North Central and Southern states had the least incidence of use of this type of weapon, with less than two out of every ten murders. Other weapons (blunt objects, poisons, explosives, arson, drowning, etc.) were used in 7 percent of the homicides and the remaining 9 percent of the murders were the result of use of personal weapons, such as hands, fists, feet, etc.

A comparative study for the past six years shows an increase from 65 percent of all homicides through use of firearms in 1968 to 67 percent of all homicides in 1973. A comparative analysis of weapons used to commit murder for 1968 through 1973 is shown in tabular form.

Murder, Type of Weapon Used, 1973 (percent distribution)

Region	Total All Weapons Used	Fire-arms	Knife or Other Cutting Instrument	Other Weapon (Club, Poison, Etc.)	Personal Weapons
Northeastern States.	100.0	51.3	29.0	8.4	11.3
North Central States	100.0	72.5	13.5	6.0	8.0
Southern States	100.0	74.0	14.0	5.3	6.7
Western States.	100.0	61.9	18.7	8.5	10.9
Total.	100.0	67.0	17.8	6.6	8.6

The circumstances that result in murder vary from family arguments to felonious activities. Criminal homicide is largely a societal problem which is beyond the control of police. The circumstances of murder serve to emphasize this point. In 1973, murder within the family made up approximately one-fourth of all murder offenses. Over one-half of these family killings involved spouse killing spouse. The remainder were parents killing children and other in-family killings. Felony murder in Uniform Crime Reporting is defined as those killings resulting from

Murder, Type of Weapon Used, 1968–1973 (percent distribution)

Year	Total Number	Total Percent	Firearms	Knife or Other Cutting Instrument	Other Weapon (Club, Poison, Etc.)	Personal Weapons
1968	13,720	100.0	65.4	18.7	8.3	7.6
1969	14,670	100.0	64.5	19.9	7.4	8.2
1970	15,890	100.0	65.4	18.9	7.6	8.1
1971	17,670	100.0	65.1	19.8	6.5	8.6
1972	18,550	100.0	66.2	19.0	6.6	8.2
1973	19,510	100.0	67.0	17.8	6.6	8.6

robbery, burglary, sex motive, gangland and institutional slaying, and all other felonious activities. Felony-type and suspected-felony-type murders in 1973 constituted 29 percent of all murders, whereas these two categories accounted for 25 percent of total murder in 1968. An analysis of felony murder reveals that 52 percent of these killings occurred in connection with robbery offenses. Prostitution and commercialized vice,

CHART 6
Murder, by Type of Weapon Used, 1973

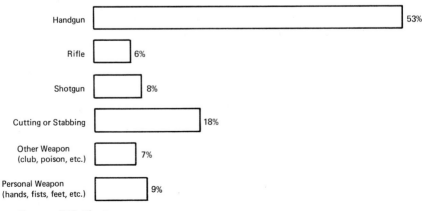

Handgun 53%
Rifle 6%
Shotgun 8%
Cutting or Stabbing 18%
Other Weapon (club, poison, etc.) 7%
Personal Weapon (hands, fists, feet, etc.) 9%

Source: FBI Chart.

rape, and sex offenses accounted for 9 percent of the total, while Narcotic Drug Law offenses comprised 6 percent of felony murder. Tables showing breakdown by geographical region for murder in 1973 and murder breakdown by circumstances for 1968–1973 accompany this section.

During 1973, 7 percent of the murders were the result of romantic triangles or lovers' quarrels. In murders involving husband and wife, the wife was the victim in 52 percent of the incidents and the husband the victim in the remaining 48 percent. In these incidents involving spouses, 49 percent of the victims were Negro, 50 percent white, and the remaining victims were of other races.

The victims of felony-type murder were 62-percent white, 37-percent Negro, and the remaining 1 percent of other race or race not reported.

Clearances

Nationally, police continue to be successful in clearing or solving by arrest a greater percentage of homicides than any other Crime Index offense. In 1973, 79 percent of the homicides were solved; however, in 1972, 82 percent of all murder offenses were solved. Persons under 18 years of age were involved in 6 percent of the willful killings solved by police.

Murder Circumstances, 1968–1973 (percent distribution)

Year	Total Number	Total Percent	Spouse Killing Spouse	Parent Killing Child	Other Family Killings	Romantic Triangle and Lovers' Quarrels	Other Arguments	Known Felony Type	Suspected Felony Type
1968	13,720	100.0	13.7	3.3	8.7	7.2	42.2	17.4	7.5
1969	14,670	100.0	13.1	3.7	8.4	7.0	41.3	19.3	7.2
1970	15,890	100.0	12.1	3.1	8.1	7.1	40.8	20.4	8.4
1971	17,870	100.0	12.8	3.5	8.4	6.3	41.5	20.4	7.1
1972	18,550	100.0	12.5	2.9	8.9	7.1	41.2	22.1	5.3
1973	19,510	100.0	12.3	3.2	7.7	7.5	40.3	21.6	7.4

Murder Circumstances, 1973 (percent distribution)

Region	Total	Spouse Killing Spouse	Parent Killing Child	Other Family Killings	Romantic Triangle and Lovers' Quarrels	Other Arguments	Known Felony Type	Suspected Felony Type
Northeastern States	100.0	9.7	3.1	5.6	5.7	41.1	26.6	8.2
North Central States	100.0	10.2	3.1	7.8	6.5	36.7	25.6	10.1
Southern States	100.0	14.1	2.6	9.3	9.2	43.2	16.4	5.2
Western States	100.0	14.1	4.9	5.9	6.0	36.8	24.0	8.3
Total	100.0	12.3	3.2	7.7	7.5	40.3	21.6	7.4

Since 1968, the clearance rate, nationwide, in homicide has decreased from 86 per 100 offenses to 79 per 100 offenses in 1973.

Persons Arrested

Based on reports submitted by law-enforcement agencies, 10 percent of all persons arrested for murder were under 18 years of age and 45 percent were under 25. During the period 1968–1973, there was a 59-percent increase in the number of persons under 18 years of age arrested for murder. The increase in adult arrests for murder offenses during this period was 39 percent. Numerically, the 20-to-24-year age group had the heaviest involvement during 1973 with 25 percent of the total arrests coming from within this age group. Negroes made up 58 percent of the arrests for murder in 1973 and 52 percent of the victims of homicide were also Negroes.

Persons Charged

Law-enforcement agencies' reports disclose that 66 percent of all adults arrested for murder in 1973 were prosecuted during the year. Forty-five percent of the adults prosecuted were found guilty as charged and 23 percent were convicted on some lesser charge. The remaining won release by acquittal or dismissal of the charges against them. Of all individuals processed for murder, 11 percent were juveniles who had their cases referred to juvenile-court jurisdiction.

Aggravated assault is defined as an unlawful attack by one person upon another for the purpose of inflicting severe bodily injury, usually accompanied by the use of a weapon or other means likely to produce death or serious bodily harm. Attempts are included since it is not necessary that an injury result when a gun, knife, or other weapon is used, which could and probably would result in serious personal injury if the crime were successfully completed.

Volume

In calendar year 1973, there were an estimated 416,270 aggravated assaults in the nation. This is a 7-percent increase, or 27,300 additional offenses, over 1972. This crime against the person made up 5 percent of the Crime Index offenses in 1973 and comprised 48 percent of the crimes of violence. Regionally, the Southern states reported 37 percent of the total count of these crimes, followed by the North Central states with 22 percent, the Northeastern states with 21 percent, and the Western states reported the remainder. As has been the experience in previous years, the summer months recorded the highest frequencies of aggravated assault during 1973.

Trend

In 1973, the volume of aggravated-assault offenses increased 7 percent over 1972 and 47 percent over 1968. Cities with over 250,000 inhabitants had an increase of about 1 percent. The suburban areas reported an increase of 14 percent and the rural areas an increase of 5 percent.

The North Central states had an increase of 10 percent, the Western states an increase of 9 percent, the Northeastern states had a 7 percent increase, and the Southern states an increase of approximately 4 percent.

Aggravated Assault Rate

For each 100,000 persons in the United States during 1973, there were 198 victims of aggravated assault. Large core cities with 250,000 or more inhabitants recorded a victim rate of 360 aggravated assaults per 100,000 inhabitants, suburban areas had 150, and rural areas 110. The victim rate for the nation for aggravated assault increased 6 percent over 1972 and 40 percent over 1968. The Western states were highest with a rate of 235 per 100,000, followed by the Southern and the North Central states 157.

Nature of Aggravated Assault

Most aggravated assaults occur within the family unit and among neighbors or acquaintances. The victim-offender relationship, as well as the nature of the attack, makes this crime similar to murder. In 1973, 26 percent of the serious assaults were committed with the use of a firearm. A knife or other cutting instrument was used in 25 percent of the assaults, 23 percent were committed with blunt objects or other dangerous weapons. The remaining assaults were with personal weapons, such as hands, fists, and feet. A comparison of the weapons used to commit assault from 1968 to 1973 indicates that assaults with firearms have increased 63 percent; assaults with a knife or other cutting instrument have risen 16 percent; assaults where blunt objects or other dangerous weapons are used increased 37 percent, and those assaults through use of personal weapons have climbed 83 percent. The table that follows demonstrates the regional experience of aggravated assault in 1973 by type of weapon used.

Clearances

Law-enforcement agencies were successful in solving 63 of each 100 cases of aggravated assault in 1973. This clearance rate decreased from 66 of each 100 cases in 1972. This relatively high solution rate is consistent with high solution rates in other crimes against the person. Persons under 18 years of age were identified in 10 percent of these clearances. Due to the nature of these crimes, arrests are frequently made upon the response of patrol units. This type of patrol call is hazardous to

Aggravated Assault, Type of Weapon Used, 1973 (percent distribution)

Region	Total All Weapons	Fire-arms	Knife or Other Cutting Instru-ment	Other Weapon (Club, Poison, Etc.)	Personal Weapons
Northeastern States.	100.0	20.1	30.6	26.1	23.2
North Central States	100.0	27.5	23.1	21.6	27.8
Southern States	100.0	29.6	24.3	20.1	26.0
Western States.	100.0	23.7	20.4	24.0	31.9
Total.	100.0	25.7	24.6	22.6	27.1

the officers. Since 1964, 125 officers have lost their lives responding to disturbance-type calls, which frequently involve family or neighborhood arguments.

CHART 7
Aggravated Assault, 1968–1973
Percent Change Over 1968

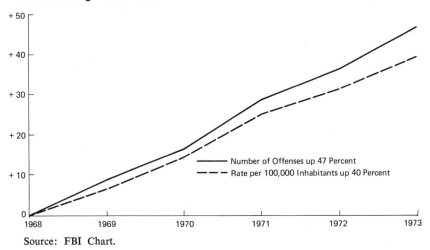

Number of Offenses up 47 Percent
Rate per 100,000 Inhabitants up 40 Percent

Source: FBI Chart.

Persons Arrested

Arrests for aggravated assault in 1973 increased 36 percent over 1968. Since 1968, arrests of persons 18 years of age and over for aggravated assault have increased 35 percent and arrests of persons under 18 years of age for this offense have increased 42 percent. As a group, persons 21 years of age and over accounted for 69 percent of the arrests for aggravated assault in 1973 and those under age 21 accounted for 31 percent. Arrests of males outnumbered females by about 7 to 1.

Persons Charged

Law-enforcement agencies have difficulty in obtaining convictions based on the original charge in the aggravated-assault category. The close family or other relationship that exists between victims and assailants in this category accounts for the victims' frequent unwillingness to testify for the prosecution. Acquittals and dismissals therefore continue to run high, accounting for 44 percent of the dispositions. Eighty-two out of every 100 adults arrested for aggravated assault in 1973 were prosecuted. Seventeen percent of the adults prosecuted for this offense were convicted of lesser charges. Seventeen percent of all persons processed were referred to juvenile court jurisdiction.

FORCIBLE RAPE

Forcible rape, as defined under this Program, is the carnal knowledge of a female through the use of force or the threat of force. Assaults to commit forcible rape are also included; however, statutory rape (without force) is not counted in this category. Crime counts in this offense classification are broken down by actual forcible rapes and attempted forcible rapes.

Volume

During 1973, there was an estimated total of 51,000 forcible rapes. Numerically, the volume increased by 4,520 offenses over 1972. Forcible rape continues, as in prior years, to comprise less than 1 percent of the Crime Index total. It makes up nearly 6 percent of the volume of crimes of violence. When viewed geographically, the Southern states recorded 31 percent of the total volume, while the Western and North Central states each reported 25 percent. The Northeastern states reported 19 percent of the volume.

A comparison of the month-to-month variations of forcible rape in 1973 with the long-term seasonally adjusted trend followed the pattern set for many years. Chart 7 reflects the month-to-month variations of forcible rape during 1973, as well as a comparison with the prior average 5-year experience.

Trend

The volume of forcible-rape offenses in 1973 increased 10 percent over 1972 and 62 percent over 1968. During 1973, this crime occurred most frequently in large cities with 250,000 or more inhabitants, which accounted for 44 percent of the forcible rapes. Forcible rape increased 8 percent in this group of cities and 7 percent in the suburban areas surrounding the large core cities. The rural areas registered a 6-percent increase. Geographically, all regions of the United States reported increases in this offense. The Northeastern and Southern states each reported increases of 12 percent in this offense, followed by the North Central states with a 10-percent increase and the Western states with a 5-percent increase.

Forcible-Rape Rate

A crime rate, in its proper perspective, is a victim risk rate since it equates the number of crimes per unit of population. In 1973, 47 out of every 100,000 females in this country were reported rape victims. Since 1968, the forcible-rape rate has increased 55 percent. In calendar year 1973, the forcible-rape rate increased 9 percent over 1972.

The 58 core cities with populations in excess of 250,000 experienced a victim risk rate of 100 per 100,000 females. This is in marked contrast to the suburban areas of the country where the risk rate for females was 35 per 100,000 and the rural area with a risk rate of 23. In the Western states, a rate of 69 per 100,000 females was recorded. Females residing in the Southern states were victims of forcible rape at the rate of 46 per 100,000. The North Central and Northeastern states recorded rates of 43 and 37 per 100,000 females, respectively.

Nature of Offenses

In 1973, 73 percent of all forcible rape offenses were actual rapes by force, while the remainder were attempts or assaults to commit forcible rape. This offense is a violent crime against the person, and of all the Crime Index offenses, law enforcement administrators recognize that this offense is probably one of the most under reported crimes due primarily to fear and/or embarrassment on the part of the victims. As a national average, 15 percent of all forcible rapes reported to police were determined by investigation to be unfounded. In other words, the police established that no forcible-rape offense or attempt occurred. This is caused primarily due to the question of the use or threat of force frequently complicated by a prior relationship between victim

CHART 8
Forcible Rape, 1968–1973 (percent change over 1968)

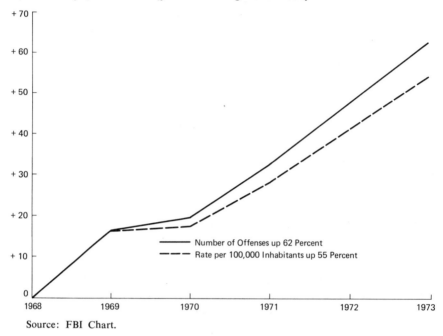

Source: FBI Chart.

and offender. Crime counts in this publication are limited to actual offenses established by police investigation.

Clearances

Of the total forcible rapes reported in 1793 to law enforcement, 51 percent were cleared by arrest. This is a 9-percent decrease over the clearance rate for 1972. The large cities with 250,000 or more people had a clearance rate of 50 percent. The suburban areas of the country reported a 52-percent rate, while the rural areas had a 66-percent clearance rate. Of the total clearances for forcible rape, 11 percent were by the arrest of persons under the age of 18.

Persons Arrested

The age grouping of males 16 to 24 years of age constituted the greatest concentration of arrests for forcible rape in 1973. Total arrests for this offense increased 12 percent with the arrest of persons under 18 years of age up 13 percent over 1972. Sixty-one percent of the arrests for forcible rape during the year were of persons under the age of

25. All arrests for forcible rape in 1973 compared to 1968 indicate an increase of 53 percent. Figures for the same years indicate that arrests of persons under 18 years of age have increased 52 percent. In 1973, 47 percent of the persons arrested for forcible rape were Negroes, 51 percent whites, and all other races comprised the remainder.

Persons Charged

Of all adults arrested for forcible rape in 1973, 76 percent were prosecuted for this offense. Prosecutive problems accounted for acquittals and/or dismissals in 47 percent of the cases. Thirty-six percent of the adults prosecuted were found guilty of the substantive offense and 17 percent were convicted of lesser offenses. Juvenile referrals amounted to 22 percent of the persons processed on forcible rape charges in 1973.

ROBBERY

Robbery is a vicious type of crime that takes place in the presence of the victim to obtain property or a thing of value from a person by use of force or threat of force. Assault to commit robbery and attempts are included. This is a violent crime and frequently results in injury to the victim. For crime-reporting purposes, information concerning robbery is collected for armed robbery where any weapon is used and strong-arm robbery where no weapon other than a personal weapon is used. The latter category includes crimes such as mugging, yoking, etc.

Volume

The volume of estimated robberies increased in 1973 by 7,890 offenses from the prior year. There was an estimated total of 382,680 robbery offenses committed in the United States in 1973. This offense makes up 4 percent of the total Crime Index and compromises 44 percent of the crimes of violence. In 1973, these offenses occurred most frequently during the month of December.

The heaviest volume of robbery offenses occurred in the Northeastern states, with 33 percent of the total. The North Central states experienced 25 percent, the Southern states 24 percent, and the remainder were reported in the Western states.

Trend

When the total robbery offenses occurring in 1973 is compared with the 1972 total, a 2-percent increase is noted. Since 1968, robbery has increased 46 percent.

Ideas and Data

Large core cities over 250,000 population reported a 2-percent de-crease in robbery offenses in 1973, when compared to the reported volume in 1972. Suburban areas surrounding the large core cities re-ported a 10-percent increase, while the rural areas recorded an upward trend of 6 percent.

Geographically, the Southern states experienced an 11-percent in-crease in robbery offenses. The Western and North Central states re-ported 5-percent and 1-percent increases, respectively. The Northeastern states reported a 4-percent decrease in robbery offenses.

The accompanying chart depicts the trend in the volume of robbery and the robbery rate, 1968–1973.

Robbery Rate

The 1973 robbery rate of 182 per 100,000 inhabitants was 1 percent above the 1972 rate. Robbery is primarily a large-city crime. American cities with more than 250,000 inhabitants accounted for two-thirds of all robberies that occurred in the United States during 1973.

CHART 9
Robbery, 1968–1973 (percent change over 1968)

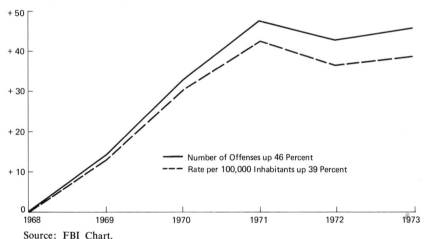

Source: FBI Chart.

Cities with over 250,000 inhabitants had a robbery rate of 571 victims per 100,000 people. There were 76 robbery victims per 100,000 in the suburban areas, up 5 percent over the preceding year. The rural areas experienced a rate of 18 victims per 100,000 people. Robbery rates in the larger cities were about eight times greater than the rates in the suburban areas.

This crime occurred most frequently in relation to population in the

Northeastern states, where the rate was 254 per 100,000 inhabitants. The Western states had a rate of 183, the North Central states 167, and the Southern states 142 per 100,000 people.

Nature of Robbery

Supplemental robbery information is obtained from law-enforcement agencies as a part of the monthly collection of statistical data under this Program. In 1973, these figures disclosed that half of the robberies were committed in the street. Nationally, bank-robbery offenses decreased from 2,618 offenses in 1972 to 2,521 in 1973. The average bank-robbery dollar loss increase from $3,529 in 1972 to $4,653 in 1973.

The 1968–1973 trends in robbery by type, as illustrated by the following charts, show bank robbery has increased 37 percent. During this same period, gas- or service-station holdups have decreased 6 percent; chain-store robberies increased 167 percent; street robberies 35 percent; robberies in residences 64 percent; and holdups of other commercial or business establishments rose 31 percent.

Armed perpetrators were responsible for 66 percent of the robbery offenses during 1973, while 34 percent were muggings, yokings, or other violent confrontations where personal weapons were used by the offender to subdue or overcome the victim. Since 1968, armed robbery has increased 60 percent and strong-arm robbery 24 percent.

Robbery by Geographic Region

	Total	North-eastern States	North Central States	Southern States	Western States
Armed—any weapon	65.9	67.4	65.2	67.6	61.8
Strong-arm—no weapon	34.1	32.6	34.8	32.4	38.2
Total.	100.0	100.0	100.0	100.0	100.0

Special surveys have indicated that approximately 63 percent of all armed robbery is committed with a firearm, 24 percent with a knife or other cutting instrument, and 13 percent with blunt objects such as clubs, etc.

As it has been pointed out in prior issues of this publication, the full impact of this violent crime on the victim cannot be completely measured in terms of dollar loss alone. While the object of the attack is money or property, many victims of the mugger and the strong-arm robber, as well as the armed robber, suffer serious personal injury as a result of the attack. During 1973, the average value loss in each robbery incident was $261, for a total loss of $100 million.

Clearances

In 1973, law-enforcement agencies were successful in clearing 27 percent of the robbery offenses reported. Eighty-two percent of the robberies that were cleared by arrest involved adults. Arrests of persons under 18 years of age figured in the clearance of 12 percent of the armed robberies and 29 percent of the strong-arm type.

Persons Arrested

Nationally, arrests for robbery increased 4 percent in 1973, when compared to 1972. The greatest volume of arrests occurred in cities and were up 3 percent. In the rural areas, arrests increased 21 percent and in the suburban areas arrests increased 17 percent.

Examination of arrest data discloses that 76 percent of the persons arrested for robbery were under 25 years of age and 56 percent were under 21 years of age. Of all persons arrested for robbery, 34 percent were under the age of 18. This greater proportion of youthful arrests, compared to clearances, is accounted for in part by the fact the young-age offenders frequently act in groups. Robbery arrests for this young-age group recorded a 12-percent increase in 1973 over 1972. In the suburban areas young persons made up 30 percent of the arrests for this offense. The rural areas reported young offenders made up 18 percent of the total arrests for robbery.

In 1973, 7 of every 100 persons arrested for robbery were females. Arrests of women for this offense rose 5 percent in 1973, when compared to 1972.

From a standpoint of race, 63 percent of those arrested were Negro, 35 percent were white, and all other races made up the remainder.

Persons Charged

In 1973, 72 percent of all adults arrested for robbery were prosecuted. Thirty-five percent of the persons processed for this crime were juveniles whose cases were referred to juvenile court jurisdiction. Of the adults prosecuted in 1973, 46 percent were convicted of the substantive offense, 16 percent were convicted for lesser charges, and the remainder were acquitted or their cases were dismissed.

BURGLARY

The Uniform Crime Reporting Program defines burglary as the unlawful entry of a structure to commit a felony or theft. The use of force to gain entry is not required to classify the crime as a burglary. The offense

CHART 10

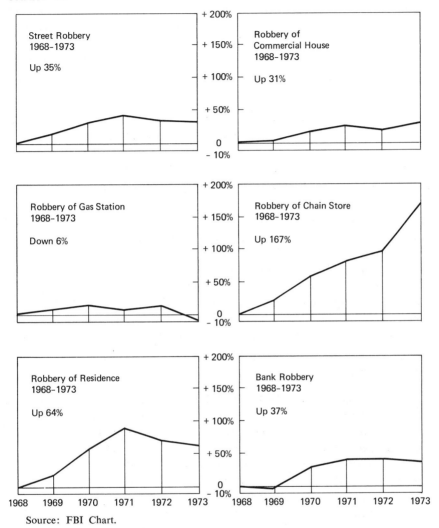

Source: FBI Chart.

of burglary in this Program is broken down into three subclassifications: forcible entry, unlawful entry where no force is used, and attempted forcible entry.

Volume

An estimated total of 2,540,900 burglaries occurred during 1973. The increase in the number of offenses from 1972 to 1973 was 188,100. In 1972, the large core cities over 250,000 inhabitants recorded 35 percent of the total burglary figure. For calendar year 1973, this decreased to 33 percent. Of the Crime Index offenses, burglary makes up 29 percent of the total. When viewed as a segment of property crime, burglary is found to comprise 33 percent of the total. Geographically, the Southern states reported 29 percent of the total volume, the Western states 25 percent, with the North Central states 24 percent and the Northeastern 22 percent.

Viewed monthly the highest volume of burglary occurred in December of 1973.

Trend

The five-year trend, 1968–1973, indicates burglary offenses have risen 38 percent during the period. In 1973, burglary increased 8 percent from 1972, as compared to a decrease of 1 percent, 1972 over 1971. Cities over 250,000 population reported an increase of 4 percent. In 1972, these cities experienced a decrease of 7 percent in volume. In 1973, the suburban and rural areas of the nation reported increases of 10 and 8 percent, respectively. Viewed regionally, the Southern states reported a 12-percent increase and the North Central states a 9-percent increase in burglary offenses. The Western states experienced a 6-percent increase and the Northeastern states a 4-percent increase for this offense.

Burglary Rate

The burglary rate in 1973 was 1,211 per 100,000 inhabitants. During the period of 1968–1973, this rate increased 31 percent. The burglary rate for 1973 increased 7 percent, when compared with 1972. The large core cities with over 250,000 inhabitants reported a rate of 1,949 burglaries per 100,000 people. The suburban areas experienced a rate of 1,054 offenses per 100,000 population in 1973. The rural areas recorded a rate of 564 offenses per 100,000 inhabitants.

The Western states again recorded the highest burglary rate in 1973 with 1,766 offenses per 100,000 inhabitants, followed by the Northeastern states with a rate of 1,124, the Southern states 1,117, and the North Central states 1,040.

Nature of Burglary

Burglary is generally accepted as a crime of stealth and opportunity. It is committed by both amateurs and professionals. In 1973, 75 percent of the burglaries involved forcible entry, 18 percent were unlawful entry (without force), and 7 percent were recorded as forcible-entry attempts. Residential burglaries decreased from 63 percent of the total burglaries in 1972 to 62 percent in 1973. Nonresidential offenses increased from 37 percent in 1972 to 38 percent in 1973. Daytime burglaries of residences increased 9 percent in 1973 and accounted for over half of the residential burglaries. Considering the period 1968–1973, there has been an increase of 56 percent in the volume of daytime residential burglaries.

Prevention and detection of the burglary offense poses a most difficult problem to law enforcement. Volume alone is an overriding factor, particularly as related to the number of officers available for this type investigation. Viewed as a group, nighttime burglary represents 61 percent of all burglaries.

Economically, the offense of burglary represents a substantial sum. Victims suffered a loss of $856 million in 1973 through the offense of burglary; this is an increase of about $134 million from the 1972 loss.

CHART 11
Burglary, 1968–1973 (percent change over 1968)

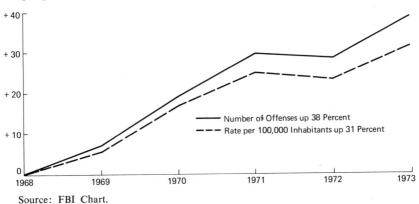

Source: FBI Chart.

During 1973, residential losses amounted to $543 million. In 1972, that loss amounted to $465 million. Nonresidential losses due to burglaries amounted to $313 million in 1973 and $258 million in 1972. In 1973, the average dollar loss per burglary was $337.

Clearances

As suggested earlier, burglary is a crime of stealth. This characteristic tends to make the detection of the perpetrator more difficult. In 1973, law enforcement was successful in clearing 18 percent of the total burglary offenses.

Adults were involved in 67 percent of all cases cleared, while young persons under 18 years of age were involved in 33 percent. Law-enforce-

406   *Ideas and Data*

CHART 12

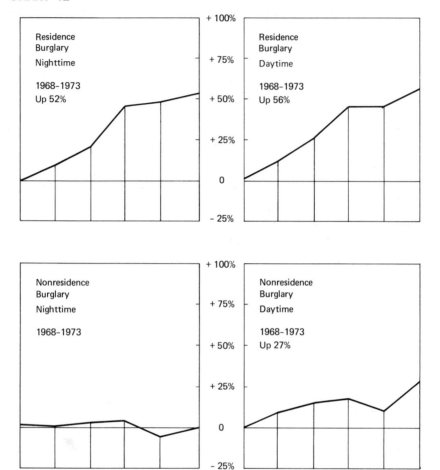

Source: FBI Chart.

ment agencies in cities 250,000 and above cleared 19 percent of these crimes in 1973. In the suburban areas 17 percent were solved, while 19 percent were cleared in the rural areas.

Persons Arrested

In this Program, the arrest of one person may account for the clearance of numerous offenses. Likewise, the arrest of several may clear only one offense. In the offense of burglary, it has been the experience of law enforcement that the arrest of one person frequently clears several reported offenses. In 1973, total arrests for burglary increased by 11 percent. Arrests of persons under the age of 18 increased 17 percent, while arrests of persons 18 years and over increased 4 percent. In the cities and suburban areas, increases of 9 and 17 percent, respectively, were reported. The rural areas experienced a 14-percent increase in total arrests for burglary.

In analyzing the 1968–1973 period, a 19-percent increase in burglary arrests is seen. Arrests of individuals under the age of 18 increased 18 percent, while the arrests of adult burglary offenders increased 20 percent.

Nationally, persons under 25 accounted for 84 percent of all arrests for burglary in 1973. Young persons under 18 accounted for 54 percent of all arrests for this crime. Females were involved in 5 of every 100 arrests for burglary during 1973. Arrests of whites outnumbered Negroes by 2 to 1.

Persons Charged

In 1973, 82 percent of the adults arrested for burglary were prosecuted. In 1972, this figure was 80 percent. Of the adults prosecuted, 49 percent were found guilty as charged. Conviction for lesser offenses accounted for 18 percent, and 33 percent were freed through acquittal or dismissal of charges. Juveniles referred to juvenile-court jurisdiction accounted for 55 percent of all persons processed for burglary in 1973.

LARCENY-THEFT

Larceny-theft is the unlawful taking or stealing of property or articles without the use of force, violence, or fraud. It includes crimes such as shoplifting, pocket-picking, purse-snatching, thefts from autos, thefts of auto parts and accessories, bicycle thefts, etc. In the Uniform Crime Reporting Program this crime category does not include embezzlement, "con" games, forgery, and worthless checks. Auto theft, of course, is excluded from this category for crime-reporting purposes inasmuch as it is a separate Crime Index offense.

Volume

In 1973, there were 4,304,400 offenses of larceny-theft, which is an increase from 4,109,600 such crimes in 1972. This offense makes up 50 percent of the Crime Index total. From a seasonal standpoint, the volume of larceny was highest during the summer months of 1973.

Geographically, the volume of larceny-theft was highest in the North Central states, which reported 29 percent of the total number, followed by the Southern states with 27 percent, the Western states with 26 percent, and the Northeastern states with 18 percent.

Trend

Larceny-theft increased 5 percent in 1973, when compared to the previous year. The large cities with over 250,000 inhabitants reported a decrease of less than 1 percent in the volume of this offense. The suburban areas reported an 8-percent increase in this offense and the rural areas showed an 11-percent increase. Nationwide, this offense has increased 25 percent since 1968.

Geographically, the Western states reported an increase of less than 1 percent and the Northeastern states reported a 4-percent increase. The North Central states had an increase of 6 percent and the Southern states recorded an increase of 8 percent.

Larceny Rate

During 1973, the larceny crime rate was 2,051 offenses per 100,000 inhabitants, an increase of 4 percent from the 1972 rate. The rate has increased 19 percent since 1968. In 1973, the large core cities registered a larceny rate of 2,652 per 100,000 inhabitants. The suburban larceny rate was 1,952 and the rural rate was 678. Viewed geographically, the Western states reported the highest larceny rate with 3,032 offenses per 100,000 inhabitants, which was 1 percent below 1972. The North Central states had a rate of 2,132, up 6 percent; the Southern states

CHART 13
Larceny-Theft, 1968–1973 (percent change over 1968)

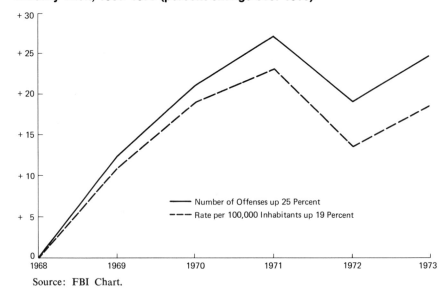

Source: FBI Chart.

1,792, up 6 percent; and the Northeastern states 1,579 reported, an increase of 5 percent in the rate.

Nature of Larceny-Theft

The average value of property stolen in each larceny in 1973 was $140, up from $100 in 1968 and $74 in 1960. When average value is applied to the estimated crimes in this category, the dollar loss to victims was $603 million. It is true that a portion of the goods stolen was recovered and returned to victims but the relatively low percentage of these crimes cleared by arrest and the lack of specific identification characteristics on such property indicates these recoveries did not materially reduce the overall loss. In addition, many offenses in this category, particularly where the value of the stolen goods is small, never come to police attention.

In 1973, the average value of goods and property reported stolen from victims of pickpockets was $101, by purse-snatchers, $62, by shoplifters $28, by thefts from autos $160, and by miscellaneous thefts from buildings $246.

The accompanying table presents distribution of larceny by type for large cities, suburban, and rural areas. Cities and suburban areas appear to have similar experience except for pocket-picking and purse-snatching,

Larceny Analysis, 1973 (percent distribution)

	Area			
Classification	*Total United States*	*Cities Over 250,000*	*Suburban*	*Rural*
Pocket-picking	1.0	2.1	0.4	0.3
Purse-snatching	2.2	4.0	0.9	0.4
Shoplifting	10.8	11.3	7.5	3.8
From autos (except accessories)	17.4	18.6	16.2	15.3
Auto accessories	16.0	18.8	17.1	11.2
Bicycles	16.9	11.7	17.3	5.3
From building	16.8	17.8	13.9	16.4
From coin-operated machines	1.3	1.0	1.4	1.3
All others	17.6	14.7	25.3	46.0
Total	100.0	100.0	100.0	100.0

which are considerably less in the suburban areas. This, of course, is to be expected as these theft opportunities flourish where population and business houses are highly concentrated. Thefts from autos made up 19 percent of larceny offenses in large cities over 250,000 in population, 16 percent in suburban areas, and 15 percent in rural areas.

From year to year, the distribution of larceny as to type of theft remains relatively constant. As in prior years, a major portion of these thefts, 33 percent, represented thefts of auto parts and accessories and other thefts from automobiles. Other major types of thefts that contributed to the large number of these crimes were thefts from buildings and stolen bicycles with 17 percent each. Miscellaneous types of larcenies, not falling into any of the specific categories for which data were collected, made up 18 percent of the total. The remainder was distributed among pocket-picking, purse-snatching, shoplifting, and thefts from coin-operated machines.

Clearances

The nature of larceny, a crime of opportunity, sneak thievery, and petty, unobserved thefts, makes it an extremely difficult offense for law-enforcement officers to solve. A lack of witnesses and the tremendous volume of these crimes work in the offender's favor. In 1973, 19 percent of all larceny offenses brought to police attention were solved. Involvement of the younger-age group is demonstrated by the fact that 37 percent of these crimes that were cleared in the nation's cities were solved by arrest of persons under 18 years of age. Juvenile clearance figures for suburban areas and rural areas were 40 percent and 27 percent, respectively.

The larceny clearance percentage for the cities over 250,000 inhabitants was 20 percent. The suburbs and rural areas reported a 17-percent clearance rate.

Persons Arrested

Forty-seven percent of the total arrests for Crime Index offenses in 1973 were for larceny. Arrests for this crime increased 3 percent, 1973 over 1972. Forty-eight percent of these arrests were of persons under 18 years of age and, when individuals under 21 were considered, the ratio rose to two-thirds. When examined by sex of arrested persons, it was determined that females comprised 32 percent of all arrests for larceny-theft and had a higher involvement in this offense than for any of the other Index offenses. In fact, women were arrested more often for larceny then any other offense in 1973.

Arrests of females rose 8 percent in 1973, while arrests of males increased 2 percent. Arrests of whites outnumbered Negroes by more than 2 to 1, with all other races comprising about 2 percent of the arrests for larceny-theft. The total volume of arrests for larceny-theft in 1973 as compared with the 1968 figures indicates a 29-percent increase. Arrests of individuals under 18 were 12 percent greater than 1968. The number

CHART 14

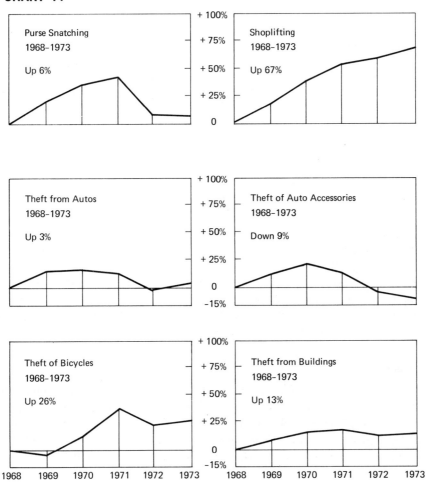

Souce: **FBI** Chart.

of adult arrests rose 50 percent over the number of arrests for this offense in 1968.

Persons Charged

As in prior years, law-enforcement agencies nationally charged more offenders for larceny-theft than for any other Crime Index Offense. Sixty-nine percent of the adults prosecuted for larceny-theft were found guilty of this offense, 6 percent were found guilty of a lesser charge, and 25 percent had their cases dismissed or were acquitted. Thirty-nine percent of persons processed in 1973 for larceny were referred to juvenile-court jurisdiction.

AUTO THEFT

In Uniform Crime Reporting, auto theft is defined as the unlawful taking or stealing of a motor vehicle, including attempts. This definition excludes taking for temporary use by those persons having lawful access to the vehicle.

Volume

In 1973, 923,600 motor vehicles were reported stolen. This is a 5-percent increase compared to 1972, when 882,200 motor vehicles were reported stolen.

Geographically, the volume of auto theft in 1973 was highest in the Northeastern states, which reported 31 percent of the total number, followed by the North Central states with 25 percent. The Southern states reported 23 percent and the Western states reported the remainder. This crime made up 11 percent of the total crime Index offense volume. Seasonal variations during 1973 disclosed the volume of auto theft was highest during the month of October.

Trend

The number of auto thefts in 1973 increased 5 percent, compared to 1972. The number of auto thefts has increased 19 percent since 1968.

Auto theft increased 1 percent in large cities with 250,000 or more inhabitants during 1973. The rural areas reported an increase of 15 percent in auto thefts, while the suburban areas had an increase of 10 percent.

Geographically, auto thefts were up 8 percent in the Southern states, the Northeastern states reported an increase of 7 percent, the North Central states an increase of 4 percent, and the Western states reported a decrease of 1 percent. The accompanying chart shows the trend in auto thefts, 1968–1973.

Auto-Theft Rate

The 1973 auto-theft rate of 440 offenses per 100,000 inhabitants is 4 percent higher than in 1972. Since 1968, the auto-theft rate has risen 13 percent. People in cities with over 1 million population were deprived more often of their motor vehicles in 1973 than in any other population group, with 11 thefts per 1,000 inhabitants.

Nationally, the auto-theft rate in large core cities with 250,000 or more inhabitants was 978. The suburban areas had an auto-theft rate of 307 per 100,000 inhabitants in 1973. The rural areas had an auto-theft rate of 83.

Regionally, the Northeastern states had the highest auto theft rate in 1973. This rate was 582, an increase of 8 percent from 1972. The Western states had a rate of 542 per 100,000 inhabitants, which was a decrease of 2 percent. The North Central states had a rate of 397, which was 4 percent higher than the prior year, and the Southern States reported an increase of 6 percent in the auto-theft rate to 315 per 100,000 inhabitants.

Across the nation in 1973, one of every 128 registered automobiles was stolen. Regionally, this rate was the highest in the Northeastern states, where 12 cars per 1,000 registered vehicles were stolen. In the other three regions the figures were 8 in the Western states, 7 in the North Central states, and 5 in the Southern states.

CHART 15
Auto Theft, 1968–1973 (percent change over 1968)

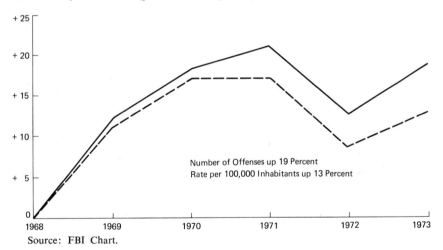

Number of Offenses up 19 Percent
Rate per 100,000 Inhabitants up 13 Percent

Source: FBI Chart.

Nature of Auto Theft

Auto-theft rates again clearly indicate that this crime is primarily a large-city problem, since the highest rates appear in the most heavily populated sections of the nation. In 1973, the average value of stolen automobiles was $1,095 at the time of theft.

Clearances

Law-enforcement agencies were successful in solving 16 percent of the auto thefts by arrest of the offender.

In the nation's largest cities, 14 percent of auto thefts were cleared during 1973. Police in the suburban areas were somewhat more successful, clearing 19 percent. Throughout the nation, auto-theft clearance percentages ranged from 22 percent in the South Atlantic states to 11 percent in the New England states.

In all geographic divisions and population groups, the participation of the young-age-group population is indicated by the high proportion of these clearances that were through the arrest of persons under 18 years of age. In the large core cities, 32 percent of the auto thefts cleared were cleared by arrests in this age group, while juveniles accounted for 38 percent of the solutions in the suburbs and 34 percent in the rural areas.

Persons Arrested

As in prior years, persons arrested for auto theft come primarily from the young-age-group population. In 1973, 56 percent of all persons arrested for this crime were under 18 years of age. When persons under 21 are included in the computations, the proportion of arrests rises to 74 percent.

The national trend in auto-theft arrests disclosed an increase of 5 percent in 1973, when compared to 1972. Adult arrests decreased less than 1 percent, while arrests of persons under 18 increased 10 percent. During the period 1968–1973, auto-theft arrests decreased 7 percent.

Females under 18 years of age recorded an increase of 14 percent in arrests for auto theft over 1973. White persons made up 66 percent of the arrests for auto theft, Negroes 32 percent, and all other races accounted for the remainder.

Persons Charged

Police reports disclosed that, of all persons formally processed for auto theft in 1973, 62 percent were referred to juvenile-court jurisdiction. No other Crime Index offense results in such a high percentage of juvenile referrals. When the remaining adult offenders were considered as a group, 43 percent of those prosecuted on charges of auto theft were found guilty as charged, 15 percent were convicted of lesser charges, and 42 percent were acquitted or their cases were dismissed.

NCIC Stolen Vehicle File

The National Crime Information Center (NCIC) is a computerized system operated by the FBI servicing law enforcement at all levels throughout the United States. The NCIC system's stolen-vehicle file provides law enforcement with the ability to immediately enter the auto-theft record information. These agencies also have the ability to immediately modify the record in the system when the stolen vehicle is recovered.

The NCIC system generally has on file approximately 869,000 active stolen-vehicle records.

SUMMARY OF UNIFORM CRIME REPORTING PROGRAM

Uniform Crime Reports provides a nationwide view of crime based on the voluntary submission of police statistics by city, county, and state law-enforcement agencies throughout the country. The extent of coverage as demonstrated by this publication is a tribute to the cooperative and dedicated spirit of the law-enforcement community in this country.

Historical Background

The Uniform Crime Reporting Program is the outgrowth of a need for a national and uniform compilation of law-enforcement statistics. A voluntary national Program of collection of crime counts was initiated in 1930 by the Committee on Uniform Crime Records of the International Association of Chiefs of Police (IACP). In that same year, the Federal Bureau of Investigation (FBI) was authorized by the Congress of the United States to serve as the national clearinghouse for statistical information on crime. Crime reports are obtained from law-enforcement agencies throughout the nation based on uniform classifications and procedures of reporting. Information regarding crime is available to law enforcement in a variety of data spheres, e.g., offenses, arrests, prosecutions, convictions, and confinements. In an effort to provide as complete a picture of crime in the United States as possible, the Commitee on Uniform Crime Records of the IACP chose to obtain data from offenses that became known to police. Greater numbers of these data were available than in any other category of reportable crime information. A meaningful overview of crime was available through examination of seven offenses which were selected because of their seriousness, frequency in occurrence, and likelihood of being reported to police. These offenses, known as the Crime Index offenses, were murder, forcible rape, robbery, aggravated assault, burglary, larceny-theft, and auto theft. To provide for uniformity nationwide in the reporting of these offenses, standardized definitions were adopted This standardization was necessary to overcome the variations in definitions of criminal offenses in the states and localities. Reporting agencies are required to interpret local criminal acts and law violations in the context of these definitions prior to submission of their counts to the FBI. The Uniform Crime Reporting definitions of these offenses are set forth later in this section. Because of the differences among the state codes, there is no possibility in a Program such as this to distinguish between crimes by designation such as "felony" or "misdemeanor."

The Committee on Uniform Crime Records, IACP, continues to serve in an advisory capacity to the FBI in the operation of this Program. In this connection, the Field Operations Division of the IACP is also playing an active and effective part in quality control through surveys of police records and crime-reporting systems. Dr. Peter P. Lejins, Director, Institute of Criminal Justice and Criminology, University of Maryland, College Park, Maryland, continues as a consultant to the FBI in the conduct of this Program.

The National Sheriff's Association (NSA) in June 1966, established a Committee on Uniform Crime Records to serve in an advisory capacity to the NSA membership and the national Uniform Crime Reporting Program. This Committee actively encourages sheriffs throughout the country to fully participate in this important Program.

Committees on Uniform Crime Reporting within state law-enforcement associations are active in promoting interest in the Uniform Crime Reporting Program, fostering widespread and more intelligent use of uniform crime statistics and lending assistance to contributors when the need exists.

In recent years, the FBI has actively assisted individual states in the development of statewide programs of police statistics compatible with the national system. These state statistical programs provide the advantage of increased coverage of law-enforcement agencies due to state mandatory reporting requirements. The state systems also can provide direct and frequent service to law-enforcement agencies in assuring completeness and quality of information provided by them. Through coordination by the state data-collection agency, information is more readily available for the use of the state. The collection and reporting machinery for the national Program also is substantially streamlined.

With the development of state Uniform Crime Reporting Programs, the FBI ceases collection of data directly from individual law-enforcement agencies within the state. Completed information from these agencies is forwarded to the national Program through the state Uniform Crime Reporting collection agency. There are 22 states now operating state Uniform Crime Reporting Programs. These include Arkansas, California, Delaware, Florida, Idaho, Illinois, Kentucky, Maine, Michigan, Minnesota, Nebraska, Nevada, New Jersey, New Mexico, North Carolina, Oklahoma, Oregon, Pennsylvania, Rhode Island, South Carolina, West Virginia, and Wisconsin. Several other states are in various stages of development. The conditions under which these systems are developed provide for consistency and comparability in the data submitted to the national Program. They also permit regular and timely reporting of the national crime data. These conditions are:

(1) The state Program must conform to the national Uniform Crime Reports standards, definitions, and information required. This, of course, does not prohibit the state from collecting other statistical data beyond the national collection. (2) The state criminal-justice agency must have a proven, effective, mandatory, statewide Program and have instituted acceptable quality-control procedures. (3) Coverage within the state by a state agency must be, at least, equal to that attained by *Uniform Crime Reports.* (4) The state agency must have adequate field staff assigned to conduct audits and to assist local units in record practices and crime-reporting procedures. (5) The state agency must furnish to the FBI all of the detailed data regularly collected by the FBI in the form of duplicate returns, computer printouts, and/or magnetic tape. (6) The state must have the proven capability (tested over a period of time) to supply all the statistical data required to the FBI in time to meet national *Uniform Crime Reports* publication deadlines. (7) The FBI will continue its internal procedures of verifying and reviewing individual agency reports for both completeness and quality. (8) The FBI will continue to have direct contact with individual reporting units within the state where necessary in connection with crime-reporting matters but will coordinate such contacts with the state agency. (9) Upon request, the FBI will continue its training programs within the state with respect to police records and crime-reporting procedures. For mutual benefit these will be coordinated with the state agency. (10) Should circumstances develop whereby the state agency cannot provide the data required by the national Program, the FBI will reinstitute a direct collection of *Uniform Crime Reports* from law-enforcement agencies within the state.

Objectives of Uniform Crime Reporting

The fundamental objective of the Uniform Crime Reporting Program is to produce a reliable set of criminal statistics on a national basis for use in law-enforcement administration, operation, and management. This compiled data is also intended for the use and information of other professionals and scholars who have an interest in the crime problem. At the same time, this information is important as a reference source for the public as an indicator of the crime factor in our society.

The means utilized to attain these objectives are:

(1) To measure the extent, fluctuation, distribution, and nature of serious crime in the United States through presentation of data on the seven Crime Index offenses.

(2) To measure the total volume of serious crime known to police.

(3) To show the activity and coverage of law-enforcement agencies through arrest counts and police employee strength data.

Reporting Procedure

In the national Uniform Crime Reporting Program, contributing law-enforcement agencies are wholly responsible for compiling their own crime reports and submitting them to the FBI. The FBI, in an effort to maintain quality and uniformity in the data received, furnishes to the contributing agencies, upon their request, training in Uniform Crime Reporting procedures. All contributors, also, are furnished with the *Uniform Crime Reporting Handbook*, which outlines in detail procedures for scoring and classifying offenses. The *Handbook* illustrates and discusses the monthly and annual reporting forms as well as the numerous tally sheets made available to facilitate the periodic tabulation of desired data.

The publication of the Uniform Crime Reporting "Newsletter," which was initiated in October 1963, has continued with issues published when pertinent. This "Newsletter" is utilized to explain revisions in the Program as well as to present information and instructional material to assist contributors.

A centralized record system is necessary to the sound operation of any law-enforcement agency. The record system is an essential basis for crime reporting by the agency. The FBI makes available upon request to any law-enforcement agency the *Manual of Police Records,* which can serve as a guide in the establishment or modification of a basic, nonautomated police-record system. Special Agents of the FBI are utilized to encourage new Uniform Crime Reporting contributors and to assist them in the established reporting procedures of Uniform Crime Reporting.

On a monthly basis, law-enforcement agencies (police, sheriffs, and state police) report the number of offenses that became known to them during the month in the following crime categories: murder and nonnegligent manslaughter, manslaughter by negligence, forcible rape, robbery, assault, burglary, larceny-theft, and auto theft. This count is taken from a record of all complaints of crime received by the law-enforcement agency from victims, other sources, and/or discovered by officers. Whenever complaints of crime are determined through investigation to be unfounded or false, they are eliminated from the actual count. The number of "actual offenses known" in these crime categories is reported to the FBI whether or not anyone is arrested for the crime; the stolen property is recovered; prosecution is undertaken; or any other restrictive consideration is in effect. Law-enforcement agencies, on a monthly basis, report the total number of these reported crimes that they clear either by arrest or exceptional means. A separate count of crimes cleared that involve only persons under the age of 18 is shown. The number of law-enforcement officers killed and assaulted and the value of the property stolen and recovered during the month are also reported.

Arrests are reported monthly for all criminal acts, except traffic violations, by crime category and include the age, sex, and race of each person arrested. A report is also submitted on an annual basis concerning the number of persons formally charged by crime classification and the disposition of such charges.

Law-enforcement-employee data specifically encompass the number of full-time sworn officers and other personnel. This information is collected as of October 31 of each calendar year. State Uniform Crime Reporting Programs are encouraged to maintain this same method and scope of data collection for a reasonable period before expanding their efforts. In January 1972, a monthly collection in the national Program was instituted concerning the number of law-enforcement officers assaulted by type of duty assignment. Additional information is collected relative to the type of weapon used, the circumstances of the assault, and whether the victim officer sustained injury.

Reporting Area

During calendar year 1973, crime reports were received from law-enforcement agencies representing 97 percent of the United States population living in the standard metropolitan statistical areas, 90 percent of the population in other cities, and 80 percent of the rural population. The combined coverage accounts for 93 percent of the total national population.

Presentation of crime data by areas as used in this publication follows as closely as practical the definitions used by the Office of Management and Budget and the Bureau of the Census for standard metropolitan statistical areas and other cities. There is, however, some deviation insofar as the rural area is concerned. For crime-reporting purposes, rural is generally the unincorporated portion of a county outside of standard metropolitan statistical areas. In addition, statistics are presented in certain tables relative to "suburban" areas. A suburban area consists of cities with population less than 50,000 together with counties that are within a standard metropolitan statistical area. In this use of suburban, the major core city is, of course, excluded. The suburban-area concept is used because of the particular crime conditions that exist in these communities surrounding the major core cities.

Standard metropolitan statistical areas are generally made up of an entire county or counties having at least one core city of 50,000 or more inhabitants, with the whole area having certain metropolitan characteristics. In New England, "town" instead of "county" is used to describe standard metropolitan statistical areas. These towns do not coincide generally with established reporting units; therefore, metropolitan state economic areas in New England are used in these areas' tabulations since they encompass an entire county or counties. Standard metropolitan statistical areas, as used in this publication, make up approximately 73 percent of the total United States population.

"Other cities" are urban places outside standard metropolitan statistical areas. Most of these places are incorporated and comprise 11 percent of the 1973 population. Rural areas are made up of the unincorporated portions of counties outside of urban places and standard metropolitan statistical areas and represent 16 percent of our national population. Throughout this Program, sheriffs, county police, and many state police report on crimes committed within the limits of the counties but outside cities, while local police report on crime committed within the city limits (urban places).

Verification Procedures

Uniformity of crime data collected under this Program is of primary concern to the FBI as the national clearinghouse. With the receipt of reports covering approximately 11,000 jurisdictions, the problems of attaining uniformity are readily apparent. Issuance of instructions does not complete the role of the FBI. On the contrary, it is standard operating procedure to examine each incoming report not only for arithmetical accuracy but also, and possibly of even more importance, for reasonableness as a possible indication of error.

Variations in the level and ratios among the crime classes established by previous reports of each agency are used as a measure of possible or probable incompleteness or changes in reporting procedures. Necessary arithmetic adjustments or unusual variations are brought to the attention of the submitting agency by correspondence. During 1973, 19,200 communications were addressed to contributors primarily as a result of editing and evaluation processes. Correspondence with contributors is the principal tool for supervision of quality. Not only are individual reports studied but also periodic trends for individual reporting units are prepared. Crime rates for all units are grouped for general comparability to assist in detecting variations and fluctuations possibly due to some reason other than chance. For the most part, the problem is one of keeping the contributors aware of the type of information necessary for the success of this Program.

The elimination of duplication in crime reporting by the various agencies is given constant attention. In addition to detailed instructions as to the limits of reporting jurisdictions between sheriffs and police in urban places, lists of urban places by county are furnished to sheriffs, county police, and, in some instances, state police organizations.

The FBI schedules Uniform Crime Reporting seminars and workshops throughout the country for law-enforcement personnel. Contacts by Special Agents of the FBI are utilized to enlist the cooperation of new contributors and to explain the purpose of this Program and the methods of assembling information for reporting. When correspondence, including specially designed questionnaires, do not elicit a response, Special Agents may be directed to visit the contributor to satisfactorily resolve the misunderstanding.

Variations from the desired reporting standard that cannot be resolved by the steps indicated above are brought to the attention of the Committee on Uniform Crime Records of the IACP. The Committee may designate a representative to make a personal visit to the local department to cooperatively assist in a needed revision of records and reporting methods.

Regardless of the extent of the statistical verification processes used by the FBI, the accuracy of the data assembled under this Program depends upon the sincere effort exerted by each contributor to meet the necessary standards of reporting. For this reason, the FBI is not in a position to vouch for the validity of individual agency reports.

The Crime Totals

Communities not represented by crime reports are relatively few. An examination of the tables that follow show 1973 crime totals for the Index classifications and the extent of coverage of the data in a particular table. The FBI conducts a continuing Program to further reduce the unreported areas. The continuing development and implementation of mandatory state Uniform Crime Reporting Programs will virtually eliminate unreported areas.

Within each of the three areas—standard metropolitan statistical, other urban, and rural—it is assumed that the unreported portion had the same proportionate crime experience as that for which reports were received. In lieu of figures for the entire year from those agencies, reports for as many as nine months are accepted as a sufficient data base on which to base estimates for the year. Estimates for unreported areas are based on the reported crime experience of similar areas. Certain refinements are made in this basic estimating procedure as the need arises.

Crime Trend

Crime data for trends are homogeneous to the extent that figures from identical reporting units are used for each of the periods tabulated. In all trend tabulations, only those reporting units are used that have provided comparable data for the period under consideration. National, geographic, and area trends are always established on the basis of two consecutive years. Exclusions from trend computations are made when figures from a reporting unit are obviously inaccurate for any period or when it is ascertained that unusual fluctuations are due to such variables as improved records procedures.

As a matter of standard procedure, crime trends for individual places are analyzed five times a year by the FBI. Any significant increase or decrease is made the subject of a special inquiry with the contributing agency. In 1973, for example, more than 2,500 letters were sent to police administrators of contributing agencies inquiring as to the reason for significant increases or decreases in pertinent crime classifications. The communication containing this inquiry specifically directs attention to possible changes in records or reporting procedures. When it is found that crime reporting procedures are in part responsible for the difference in the level of crime, the figures for specific crime categories or totals are excluded from the trend tabulations. Year-to-year trends in Uniform Crime Reports are valid and may be used to reasonably establish long-term trends as well as to reestimate crime volume and reconstruct crime trends for prior years. It can be assumed logically that the current year is the most complete in terms of volume. Trend or percent change as established by comparable units for each two-year period is then applied as the basis for reestimating the volume of crime for prior years.

On the other hand, crime-rate tables by state and standard metropolitan statistical area contain the most reliable reports available for the current year, and care should be exercised in any direct comparisons with prior issues. Changes in crime level may have been due in part to improved reporting or records procedures rather than to chance.

Population Data

In computing crime rates by state, geographic division, standard metropolitan statistical area, and the nation as a whole, population estimates released by the Bureau of the Census on July 1, 1973 were used. Population estimates for individual cities and counties were prepared using special census reports, state sources and estimates, commercial sources, and extrapolation where no other estimate was available. Complete 1973 population estimates for individual cities and counties were used from 14 states while official sources in other states provided limited data which was used selectively. The estimated United States population increase in 1973 was nearly 1 percent over 1972 according to the figures published by the Bureau of the Census.

Recent Developments in Uniform Crime Reporting

Collection of traffic-enforcement data by the national Uniform Crime Reporting Program was discontinued during 1972. This decision, upon advisement of the Committee on Uniform Crime Records of the IACP, was made in that this information is in part duplicative of broader and more detailed collections made at the state level and by the National Safety Council.

Since 1958, "larceny $50 and over in value" has been a Crime Index offense. The problem of dollar valuation of larceny has been the subject of discussion in the Committee on Uniform Crime Records meetings since 1963. During recent years, the Committee has considered modification in the definition of this offense due to problems of evaluation of stolen property and inflation factors in the $50 value which is basic to the definition of this offense. The Committee and the FBI have had mutual concern in this matter and have jointly discussed a variety of possible solutions, including increasing the dollar valuation from $50 to some higher dollar value. This suggestion was seen as only a temporary solution to the problem. In the latter part of 1972 consideration by the FBI, the Committee, the operating state programs, and several large city police departments resulted in the adoption of "total larceny-theft" as a replacement for the Crime Index offenses of "larceny $50 and over in value." This new classification includes the total number of larceny-theft offenses known to police without regard to value. The Index offense of "total larceny-theft" was instituted as of January 1973.

In the interest of maintaining comparability of data in this larceny classification, contributing agencies continued reporting larceny offenses with the $50 breakdown during 1973.

The IACP Committee on Uniform Crime Records adopted certain changes in the Program to be instituted in January 1974. Due to law enforcements' concern over the robbery problem, an expansion of the sub-breakdowns of robbery incidents was adopted. Prior to 1974, robbery was viewed as either armed or strong-armed. The breakdowns for 1974 information will be firearm, knife or cutting instrument, other dangerous weapons, and strong-arm. The collection of the data in this fashion will enhance the specificity of type of weapon used in this crime.

The category of auto theft has been renamed motor vehicle theft in 1974. To more fully present this problem, law enforcement has been asked to provide the type of vehicle stolen in three categories: autos, trucks and buses, and other vehicles.

Appendix C

Survey Questionnaire Used in NORC Spring 1975 General Social Survey

This copy of the questionnaire has interviewer specifications marked on it. These were not present on the actual questionnaires used by field interviewers. A split sample design was used in the 1975 General Social Survey. Half of the sample was multistage probability, with quotas (based on sex, age, and employment status) used by interviewers at the block level; the other half was a full multistage probability design with predesignated respondents. Questions 24–31 were asked only of the "block quota" half of the sample, since this information had been previously collected, in identical format, on a "Household Enumeration Folder" for the "probability" half of the sample.

QUESTION - BY - QUESTION
SPECIFICATIONS

Survey 4209
March, 1975

NATIONAL OPINION RESEARCH CENTER
University of Chicago

BEGIN DECK 01

☐☐☐☐☐ 01-05/

06/R

This is the cover for the White questionnaire

☐ 1 07/

GENERAL SOCIAL SURVEY

BLOCK QUOTA SAMPLE

INTRODUCTION TO PERSON WHO ANSWERS DOOR:

Hello. I'm (YOUR NAME) from the National Opinion Research Center of the University of Chicago. We're conducting a national survey concerning attitudes towards many current issues, and I am here to interview a (PERSON NEEDED TO FILL QUOTA).

Is there someone here who fits that description?

IF YES: PROCEED WITH INTERVIEW.

IF NO: RECORD CALL ON BSLS AND GO ON TO NEXT DU.

Be sure to enter the time AND circle AM or Pm

TIME
INTERVIEW_____ AM
BEGAN: PM
08-09/ 10/

*Note: Midnight = A.M.
Noon = P.M.*

Survey 4510
                                                              March, 1975

NATIONAL OPINION RESEARCH CENTER
University of Chicago

BEGIN DECK 01

01-05/

06/R

07/   [2]

This is the cover
for the green questionnaire

GENERAL SOCIAL SURVEY
AREA PROBABILITY SAMPLE

Be sure to enter
the time and circle
Am or P.M

TIME	
INTERVIEW	_____ AM
BEGAN:	PM

08-09/   10/

Note: Midnight = A.M.
Noon   = P.M.

Spex for Q.2
(continued)   EXAMPLE: *If the response to Item F, China,*
is "-5," you would circle code "10" in Row F.

Note: If R asks, "China" refers to
Mainland, or Red, China.

-2-   DECK 01

1. We are faced with many problems in this country, none of which can be solved
    easily or inexpensively. I'm going to name some of these problems, and for each
    one I'd like you to tell me whether you think we're spending too much money on it,
    too little money, or about the right amount. First (READ ITEM A) . . , are we
    spending too much, too little, or about the right amount on (ITEM)? *If R ANSWERS
    READ EACH ITEM; CODE ONE FOR EACH. *in terms different from categories
    Repeat categories as *(such as "enough") Repeat printed*
    necessary. Do not try to *categories as probes*
    explain or define categories
    for respondent.

		Too much	Too little	About right	Don't Know	
A.	Space exploration program	3	1	2	8	11/9
B.	Improving and protecting the environment	3	1	2	8	12/9
C.	Improving and protecting the · nation's health	3	1	2	8	13/9
D.	Solving the problems of the big cities	3	1	2	8	14/9
E.	Halting the rising crime rate	3	1	2	8	15/9
F.	Dealing with drug addiction	3	1	2	8	16/9
G.	Improving the nation's education system	3	1	2	8	17/9
H.	Improving the conditions of Blacks	3	1	2	8	18/9
I.	The military, armaments and defense	3	1	2	8	19/9
J.	Foreign aid	3	1	2	8	20/9
K.	Welfare	3	1	2	8	21/9

2. You will notice that the boxes on this card go from the highest position of "plus
    5" for a country which you like very much, to the lowest position of "minus 5"
    for a country you dislike very much. How far up the scale or how far down the
    scale would you rate the following countries? READ EACH ITEM, A THROUGH H.
    CODE ONE FOR EACH. *EXAMPLE; If R says, your answer to item C, ENGLAND, "+4"*
    you would circle code 02 in Row C, as it is the code
    for +4 on the scale.

	HAND CARD A	+5	+4	+3	+2	+1	-1	-2	-3	-4	-5	DK	
A.	Russia	01	02	03	04	05	06	07	08	09	10	98	22-23/99
B.	Japan	01	02	03	04	05	06	07	08	09	10	98	24-25/99
C.	England	01	(02)	03	04	05	06	07	08	09	10	98	26-27/99
D.	Canada	01	02	03	04	05	06	07	08	09	10	98	28-29/99
E.	Brazil	01	02	03	04	05	06	07	08	09	10	98	30-31/99
F.	China	01	02	03	04	05	06	07	08	09	(10)	98	32-33/99
G.	Israel	01	02	03	04	05	06 ·	07	08	09	10	98	34-35/99
H.	Egypt	01	02	03	04	05	06	07	08	09	10	98	36-37/99

3. Do you expect the United States to fight in another war within the next ten years?

                                          Yes 1   38/9

                                          No 2

                                          No opinion. 8

---

4. Do you think it will be best for the future of this country if we take an active
    part in world affairs, or if we stay out of world affairs?

                                          Active part 1   39/9

                                          Stay out 2

                                          Don't know. 8

---

5. Do you think our government should continue to belong to the United Nations, or
    should we pull out of it now?

                                          Continue to belong . . 1   40/9

                                          Pull out now 2

                                          Don't know 8

Tell me if you agree or disagree with these statements:

	Agree	Disagree	Not Sure	
6. Most men are better suited emotionally for politics than are most women	1	2	8	41/9
7. Women should take care of running their homes and leave running the country up to men.	1	2	8	42/9

---

8. Do you approve or disapprove of a married woman earning money in business or in-
    dustry if she has a husband capable of supporting her?

    Probe, if necessary: Approve 1   43/9
    "*In general*"....   Disapprove. 2

                                Don't know. 8

---

9. If your party nominated a woman for President, would you vote for her if she
    were qualified for the job?

                                          Yes 1   44/9
                                          No 2
                                          Don't know. 8

-4-   DECK   01

10. As you know, many older people share a home with their grown children. Do you think this is generally a good idea or a bad idea?

A good idea 1	45/9
Bad idea 2	
Depends. 3	
Don't know 8	

Next, I have a few factual questions about yourself.

11. Which of the categories on this card comes closest to the type of place you were living in when you were 16 years old?

> HAND
> CARD
> B

In open country but not on a farm 1   46/9
On a farm 2
In a small city or town (under 50,000) 3
In a medium-size city (50,000-250,000) 4
In a suburb near a large city. 5
In a large city (over 250,000) 6
Don't know 8

12. A. In what state or foreign country were you living when you were 16 years old?

EX: ARKANSAS =

REFER TO STATE CODES BELOW AND
ENTER CODE NUMBER IN BOX. . . . ➔ | 7 | 1 | 47-48/99

B. IF STATE NAMED IS SAME STATE R. LIVES IN NOW, ASK:

When you were 16 years old, were you living in this same (city/town/county)?

That is, SAME state in which you are conducting interview

Yes 1	49/9
No 2	

Read "city" if you are in a city, "town" if you are in a town AND "county" if you are interviewing in a rural area.

STATE CODES

Alabama 63	Louisiana 73	Oklahoma 72
Alaska 94	Maine 11	Oregon 92
Arizona 87	Maryland 52	Pennsylvania 23
Arkansas 71	Massachusetts . . . 14	Rhode Island 16
California 93	Michigan 34	South Carolina . . . 57
Colorado 86	Minnesota 41	South Dakota 45
Connecticut 15	Mississippi 64	Tennessee 62
Delaware 51	Missouri 43	Texas 74
Washington, D.C. . 55	Montana 81	Utah 85
Florida 59	Nebraska 46	Vermont 12
Georgia 58	Nevada 84	Virginia 54
Hawaii 95	New Hampshire . . . 13	Washington 91
Idaho 82	New Jersey 22	West Virginia . . . 53
Illinois 32	New Mexico 88	Wisconsin 31
Indiana 33	New York 21	Wyoming 83
Iowa 42	North Carolina . . 56	
Kansas 47	North Dakota . . . 44	Foreign country . .
Kentucky 61	Ohio 35	_____ 01

Including Suburbs

-5-   DECK 01

↳Please note this instruction And follow it.

13. Were you living with both your own mother and father around the time you were 16?
(IF NO: With whom were you living around that time?) (IF R. MARRIED OR LEFT HOME)
BY AGE 16, PROBE FOR BEFORE THAT.)

HAND CARD C	Both own mother and father (GO TO Q. 14) 1 50/9
	Father and stepmother. . . (ASK A) . . . . 2 If you Are
	Mother and stepfather. . . (ASK A) . . . . 3 Not sure how
	Father--no mother or stepmother . . .(ASK A). . 4 to code ..... RecorD VeR-
	Mother--no father or stepfather . . .(ASK A). . 5 baTim AND

"Before you (got married/left home were you living with your own mother AND father?"

Some other male relative (No female head)
(SPECIFY AND ASK A)_____
                                        6

do not code

Some other female relative (No male head)
(SPECIFY AND ASK A)_____

IF R was living with mother AND male Relative other than father (grandfather, uncle), code "other" AND Specify 8

→ With or without other people 7

Other arrangement with both male and female relatives (e.g., aunt and uncle, grandparents) . . . . (ASK A) . . 8

— The same applies for living with father AND other female Relative (Aunt, older sister, grandmother.)

Other (SPECIFY AND ASK A)
_____
                                        0

A. IF NOT LIVING WITH BOTH OWN MOTHER AND FATHER: What happened?

That is, what happened to your PAReNT(s), why weren't you living with them?

One or both parents died 1   51/9
Parents divorced or separated. 2
Father absent in armed forces. 3
One or both parents in institution . . . 4
Other (SPECIFY)

_____
                                        5
Don't know 8

Note these instructions

NOTE:	NOTE:
IF NOT LIVING WITH OWN FATHER: ASK Q'S. 14, 15 & 16 IN TERMS OF STEPFATHER, OR OTHER MALE SPECIFIED ABOVE.	IF NOT LIVING WITH OWN MOTHER: ASK Q'S. 17 & 18 IN TERMS OF STEPMOTHER, OR OTHER FEMALE SPECIFIED ABOVE.
IF NO STEPFATHER OR OTHER MALE, SKIP Q'S. 14, 15 & 16.	IF NO STEPMOTHER OR OTHER FE-MALE, SKIP Q'S. 17 & 18.
	NOTE SPECIAL INSTRUCTIONS BE-FORE Q. 19.

-6-　　　　　　　　　　　　　　　　　　　　DECK　01

ASK Q'S. 14, 15, & 16 ABOUT FATHER -- OF (FATHER SUBSTITUTE) (SEE Q. 13).

14.　A.　What kind of work did your (father/FATHER SUBSTITUTE) usually do while
　　　　you were growing up? That is, what was his job called? *If father (or*
　　　　substitute) had more than one kind of work, ask for work around
　　　　time R was 16. If more than one job at a time, probe for job he
　　　　OCCUPATION:　*usually spent most of his time at:*_____

　　　B.　IF NOT ALREADY ANSWERED, ASK: What did he actually do in that job? Tell
　　　　me, what were some of his main duties?

　　　　See box below Q13. If R did not
　　　　live with own father, read "step-
　　　　father" or other male R named

　　　C.　What kind of place did he work for?

　　　　　　　INDUSTRY:_____

　　　D.　IF NOT ALREADY ANSWERED, ASK: What did they (make/do)?

　　　　As always we need a complete description
　　　　of occupation AND industry. The order in
　　　　which you get the information in A-E does not
　　　　make any difference. The important thing is that
　　　　it is all there.

　　　E.　IF ALREADY ANSWERED, CODE WITHOUT ASKING: Was he self-employed, or did
　　　　he work for someone else?

　　　Do not miss this question　　　　Self-employed. . . . 1

　　　　　　　　　　　　　　　　　　　Someone else 2

　　　　　　　　　　　　　　　　　　　Don't know 8

　　　　　　　　　　　　　　　　　　　　　　　　　　·52-54/

　　　　　　　　　　　　　　　　　　　　　　　　　　.55-54/

　　　　　　　　　　　　　　　　　　　　　　　　　　.57-59/

15. When you were growing up, did your (father/FATHER SUBSTITUTE) think of himself
　　mostly as a Republican, Democrat, Independent, or what?

Code only one. If more　　　Republican . . . . 1　　60/9
than one response, probe　　Democrat 2
for ..... "Most of the time　Independent. 3
while you were growing　　Changed parties, shifted around. . . . 4
up."　　　　　　　　　　　Other or minor party 5
　　　　　　　　　　　　　　Didn't vote, apolitical 6
　　　　　　　　　　　　　　Wasn't a U.S. citizen 7
　　　　　　　　　　　　　　Don't know 8

　　　　　　　　　"Apolitical" = wasn't interested
　　　　　　　　　　　　　　　　　in politics

See Spex for Q102
                                    -7-   DECK 01
                           → see box below Q. 13.
16. What is the highest grade in elementary school or high school that your
     (father/FATHER SUBSTITUTE) finished and got credit for? CODE EXACT GRADE

```
                                       Follow All skip instructions
 HAND   No formal school . 00          CAREfully                    61-62/99
 CARD   1st grade  . . . . 01
  D     2nd grade  . . . . 02    GO TO Q. 17 ────────────────────────→
If NONE 3rd grade  . . . . 03
"WRite  4th grade  . . . . 04
 Not    5th grade  . . . . 05              9th grade . . . . 09
Applicable 6th grade . . . 06             10th grade . . . . 10   ASK
        7th grade  . . . . 07             11th grade . . . . 11   A & B
        8th grade  . . . . 08             12th grade . . . . 12
                                          Don't know . . . . 98
```

IF FINISHED 9TH - 12TH GRADE, OR D.K.:

A. Did he ever get a high school diploma or a GED certificate?

                              Yes . . . . (ASK B) . . . 1   63/9
                              No . . . . . (ASK B) . . . 2
                              Don't know . (ASK B) . . . 8

B. Did he ever complete one or more years of college for credit--not including
    schooling such as business college, technical or vocational school?

                              Yes . [ASK (1) & (2)] . . 1   64/9
                              No 2
    IF YES TO B: Don't know 8

    (1) How many years did he complete?

                                        1 year 13 65-66/99
                                        2 years . . . 14
                                        3 years . . . 15
                                        4 years . . . 16
                                        5 years . . . 17
                                        6 years . . . 18
                                        7 years . . . 19
                                        8+ years . . . 20
                                        Don't know . . 98
    (2) Does he have any college degrees?

                              Yes . . [ASK (3)] . . 1   67/9
                              No 2
                              Don't know 8
        (3) IF YES TO (2): What degree or degrees? CODE HIGHEST DEGREE EARNED.

                              Junior college 2   68/9
                              Bachelor's 3
                              Graduate 4
                              Don't know 8

-8-   *See box below* BEGIN DECK 02
Q.13.

ASK Q'S. 17 & 18 ABOUT MOTHER--OR (MOTHER SUBSTITUTE)(SEE Q. 13)

17. What is the highest grade in elementary school or high school that your (mother/
MOTHER SUBSTITUTE) finished and got credit for? CODE EXACT GRADE. *If none, write "Not Applicable"*

HAND CARD D		

No formal school . 00   *See spex for Q.102*   07-08/99
1st grade 01
2nd grade 02
3rd grade 03   GO TO Q. 18 ─────────────►
4th grade 04
5th grade 05   9th grade 09
6th grade 06   10th grade 10   ASK
7th grade 07   11th grade 11   A & B
8th grade 08   12th grade 12
                            Don't know 98

IF FINISHED 9TH - 12TH GRADE, OR D.K.:

A. Did she ever get a high school diploma or a GED certificate?

Yes . . . . (ASK B) . . . 1   09/9
No . . . . . (ASK B) . . . 2
Don't know . (ASK B) . . . 8

B. Did she ever complete one or more years of college for credit--not including schooling such as business college, technical or vocational school?

Yes . [ASK (1) & (2)] . . 1   10/9
No 2
Don't know 8

IF YES TO B:

(1) How many years did she complete?

1 year 13   11-12/99
2 years . . . 14
3 years . . . 15
4 years . . . 16
5 years . . . 17
6 years . . . 18
7 years . . . 19
8+ years . . . 20
Don't know . . 98

(2) Does she have any college degrees?

Yes . . [ASK (3)] . . 1   13/9
No 2
Don't know 8

(3) IF YES TO (2): What degree or degrees? CODE HIGHEST DEGREE EARNED.

Junior college. . . . 2   14/9
Bachelor's 3
Graduate 4
Don't know 8

-9-   DECK 02

18. When you were growing up, did your (mother/MOTHER SUBSTITUTE) think of herself
    mostly as a Republican, Democrat, Independent, or what?

See spex for Q. 15

Republican 1	15/9
Democrat 2	
Independent 3	
Changed parties, shifted around 4	
Other or minor party. 5	
Didn't vote, apolitical 6	
Wasn't a U.S. citizen 7	
Don't know 8	

ASK Q. 19 <u>ONLY</u> OF RESPONDENTS WHO LIVED WITH <u>OWN</u> MOTHER (SEE Q. 13):

19. Did your mother ever work for pay for as long as a year, after she was married?

Ask this question if R lived with own
mother (see Q.13) ..... Regardless of who
else was in the household. That is, if   Yes . . .(ASK A & B). . 1   16/9
                                                                  No 2
    IF YES: *Q13 was coded 1, 3, 5 or possibly 0 (for "other," if that*   Don't know 8
            included own mother.)
    A. Did she work for as long as a year before you started first grade?

Yes 1	17/9
No 2	
Don't know. 8	

    B. Did she work for as long as a year around the time you were 16?

Yes 1	18/9
No 2	
Don't know. 8	

ASK EVERYONE:

20. Thinking about the time when you were 16 years old, compared with American fami-
    lies in general then, would you say your family income was--far below average,
    below average, average, above average, or far above average? (PROBE: Just your
    best guess.)

Far below average . . . 1	19/9
Below average 2	
Average 3	
Above average 4	
Far above average . . . 5	
Don't know 8	

21. How many brothers and sisters did you have? Count those born alive, but no longer
    living, as well as those alive now. Also include stepbrothers and stepsisters,
    and children adopted by your parents.

This is Altogether —
Not at Age 16.

None 00	20-21/99
One 01	
Two 02	
Three. 03	
Four 04	
Five 05	
Six 06	
Seven. 07	
Eight. 08	
Nine 09	

If "none" or less than 10,
circle appropriate code.
If 10 or more, enter
exact # in boxes

Ten or more (ENTER
    EXACT NUMBER)

Don't know 98

-10-   DECK 02

22. From what countries or part of the world did your ancestors come? *Example: "Ireland" =*

IF SINGLE COUNTRY IS NAMED, REFER TO NATIONAL
CODES BELOW, AND ENTER CODE NUMBER IN BOXES: > . . . . ➤ [1 4]   22-23/99
IF MORE THAN ONE COUNTRY IS NAMED, ENTER
CODE 88 AND ASK A.

A. IF MORE THAN ONE COUNTRY NAMED: Which one of these countries do you feel
                                      closer to?

IF ONE COUNTRY NAMED, REFER TO CODES BELOW,
AND ENTER CODE NUMBER IN BOXES ⟩ . . ⟩ [|]   24-25/99
IF CAN'T DECIDE ON ONE COUNTRY, ENTER CODE 88

NATIONAL CODES *If R says "U.S."- Probe: "Before they came to the U.S." Note: There is a category for "American Indian"*

American Indian	 30	Mexico	17
Africa	01	Netherlands (Dutch/Holland)	18
Austria	02	Norway	19
Canada (French)	03	Philippines	20
Canada (Other)	04	Poland	21
China	05	Puerto Rico	22
Czechoslovakia	06	Russia (USSR)	23
Denmark	07	Scotland	24
England and Wales	08	Spain	25
Finland	09	Sweden	26
France	10	Switzerland	27
Germany	11	West Indies	28
Greece	12	Other (SPECIFY)	29
Hungary	13		
Ireland	14	More than one country/can't	
Italy	15	decide on one	88
Japan	16	Don't know	98

---

23. Are you currently--married, widowed, divorced, separated, or have you never been
    married?

If R asks: "Separated" (in this part of the question) includes informal separation as well as legal separation. By "informal separation" we mean the married couple live apart

Married . . . . (ASK A & B) . .	1 26/9
Widowed . . . . (ASK A & B) . .	2
Divorced . . . . (ASK A) . . .	3
Separated . . . (ASK A) . . .	4
Never married (GO TO Q. 24) . . .	5

Probe for approximate age, if necessary "About how old ....."

IF EVER MARRIED: *(see below)*

A. How old were you when you first married? ENTER EXACT AGE: [|]   27-28/99

B. ASK ONLY IF CURRENTLY MARRIED OR WIDOWED: Have you ever been divorced or
   ➤ *Ask only if Q23 is coded 1 or 2* legally separated?

Yes	1 29/9
No	2

And consider themselves separated but have not gone to court to make it legal. It does not mean that one of the married couple happens to be away temporarily: (ie husband in armed services or wife visiting relatives.)

Here we want only legal separation gained through a court.

Note instructions in BOX - pages 11 and 12 are for Block Quota
(White Quex) interviews, ONLY. The information collected on these pages is the same
as that collected for the Probability Sample households on the Household Enumeration Folder,
                                                          DECKS 02- 03

pages 2-3. See Ad-
ministrative Spex
> ASK Q'S 24-31 FOR BLOCK QUOTA (WHITE SPEX) R'S ONLY.   *for HEF Q's 2-11.*
> PROBABILITY SAMPLE (GREEN SPEX): SKIP TO Q. 32, p. 13   *Those instructions*
                                                          (continued) →

24. Now, just a few questions about this household.
     What are the names of the people who usually **live in** this household? Let's start
     with the head of the household. LIST ON LINES 01-10 BELOW.

	25. Have we forgotten anyone: such as babies or small children; roomers; people who usually live here but are away temporarily--on business trips, vacation, temporarily in a hospital, and so on?	27. *EXAMPLES OF RELATIONSHIPS:* "Mother" "Sister-in-law" "Grandson" "roomer" What is (PERSON)'s relationship to (HEAD OF HOUSEHOLD)? "houseguest" "live-in housekeeper"	28. CODE SEX (ASK IF NOT OB-VIOUS)	29. How old was (HEAD/PERSON) on (his/her) last birthday?

     Yes [ ] LIST ADDITIONAL PERSONS ON LINES 01-10 BELOW.
     No [ ] GO TO Q. 26.

26. Are there any people currently staying here--visitors,
     friends, or relatives--who do not _usually_ live here?

     Yes [ ] LIST VISITORS ON LINES 11-14 BELOW.
     No [ ] GO TO Q. 27.

     AFTER QS. 24-26, ASK QS. 27-30 FOR EACH PERSON.

	First Name	Last Name	M	F	
01	*Be sure to enter the "Head" on the first line →* (HEAD) 30		31	1 2	32-33
02	*For remainder of Household, be sure to get relationship* 37		38	1 2	39-40
03	*to the Head, not to the person giving you the information, or relationships between other* 44		45	1 2	46-47
04	*household members.* 51		52	1 2	53-54
05	58		59	1 2	60-61
06	65		66	1 2	67-68
07	*FOR EXAMPLES OF WHO SHOULD BE INCLUDED IN THIS LISTING, SEE "APPENDIX TO Q-BY-Q SPEX", pages 2+3.* BEGIN DECK 03 07		08	1 2	09-10
08	14		15	1 2	16-17
09	21		22	1 2	23-24
10	28		29	1 2	30-31
11	35		36	1 2	37-38
12	42		43	1 2	44-45
13	49		50	1 2	51-52
14	56		57	1 2	58-59

USUAL (label for lines 01-10)
VISITORS/OTHER (label for lines 11-14)

     IF MORE THAN 10 USUAL PERSONS AND/OR MORE THAN 4 VISITORS,
     USE A PLAIN SHEET FOR ADDITIONAL LISTINGS.
If it is necessary to use a plain sheet of paper for additional persons,
be sure to identify them as "usual household members" (lines 01-10) or Visitors"
(lines 11-14). Also, be sure to record information for them for Q's 27-31, as required.

(continued from p. 11)
apply to Q's 24-31 here,
<u>except</u> where differences
are noted.

-12- See Administrative Spex
for discussion of this question
(Q. 9, ON HEF).

DECKS 02-03

31.
Are any of the people we have listed (staying somewhere <u>else</u> right now?)

IF NO, CHECK BOX AND GO TO Q. 32 . . . . ☐

IF YES, ASK A BELOW.

30.

IF 13 YEARS OR OLDER, ASK:

Is (PERSON) now married, widowed, divorced, separated, or has (he/she) never been married?

A.
Who is staying somewhere else right now? CHECK (✓) LINE OF EACH PERSON WHO IS AWAY.

B.
ASK FOR EACH PERSON CHECKED (✓) IN A:
Where is (PERSON) living right now: is (PERSON) staying at another household; is (he/she) travelling; is (he/she) in some institution or dormitory--like at college or in a hospital or somewhere; or what? If it is not clear which category a person belongs in, probe for details and record verbatim. CIRCLE CODE BELOW

Marr	Wid	Div	Sep	Never Marr			Another House-hold	Travel-ling	Insti-tition	Other /DK	
1	2	3	4	5	34	35	1	2	3	4	36
1	2	3	4	5	41	42	1	2	3	4	43
1	2	3	4	5	48	49	1	2	3	4	50
1	2	3	4	5	55	56	1	2	3	4	57
1	2	3	4	5	62	63	1	2	3	4	64
1	2	3	4	5	69	70	1	2	3	4	71
1	2	3	4	5	11	12	1	2	3	4	13
1	2	3	4	5	18	19	1	2	3	4	20
1	2	3	4	5	25	26	1	2	3	4	27
1	2	3	4	5	32	33	1	2	3	4	34
1	2	3	4	5	39	40	1	2	3	4	41
1	2	3	4	5	46	47	1	2	3	4	48
1	2	3	4	5	53	54	1	2	3	4	55
1	2	3	4	5	60	61	1	2	3	4	62

AFTER Q. 30 FOR LAST
PERSON 13 OR OLDER,
ASK Q. 31.

Note the difference between Q. 31-B and Q. 11 of the HEF: on this form, you do <u>not</u> have to call the Sampling Dept. in unclear cases; just record the information. Also, on this form you do <u>not</u> have to cross out any persons entered; just circle the appropriate code.

-13-   DECK   03

32. Last week were you (working) full time, part time; going to school; keeping
     house; or what?

```
HAND    EX: If R has 2        CIRCLE ONE CODE ONLY    IF MORE THAN
CARD    jobs, one full-time,  ONE RESPONSE, GIVE PREFERENCE TO
        one part-time ...     SMALLEST CODE NUMBER THAT APPLIES.
        "code 1"
                              (Working full time) . . . (ASK A) . . 1      63/9
                              (Working part time) . . . (ASK A) . . 2
        Let R decide if he    With a job, but not at work because        EX: If R.
        was working full-        of temporary illness, vacation,        was working
        time or part-time.       strike . . . . . . . (ASK B) . . 3     part-time
        Do not try to define                                            and also
        these terms for R.    Unemployed, laid off, looking for         going to
                                 work . . . . . . (GO TO Q. 33) . . 4    school,
                                                                        circle
                              Retired . . . . . . . (ASK C) . . 5       code "2."
                              In school . . . . . . . (ASK C) . . 6
        EX: Might be disabled Keeping house . . . . . (ASK C) . . 7
        or too ill to work. 2 (Other) . . . (SPECIFY AND ASK C) . 8
```

A. IF WORKING, FULL OR PART TIME: How many hours did you work last week,
    at all (jobs?)

                                Hours: [|]   64-65/99

                        ┌─────────────────────┐
                        │ NOW GO TO Q. 33   │
                        └─────────────────────┘

B. IF WITH A JOB, BUT NOT AT WORK: How many hours a week do you usually
    work, at all (jobs?)

                                Hours: [|]   66-67/99

                        ┌─────────────────────┐
                        │ NOW GO TO Q. 33   │
                        └─────────────────────┘

C. IF RETIRED, IN SCHOOL, KEEPING HOUSE, OR OTHER: Did you ever work for
    as long as one year?

    BY "working" and "job" we mean: Yes . . (ASK Q. 33). . 1   68/9
    Working for pay at a job, or   No. .(SKIP TO INSTRUC-
    running his/her own business   TIONS BEFORE Q. 34) . 2
    or profession (or farm), or
    working without pay in R's
    family's farm or business.

-14-   BEGIN DECK 04

33. A. What kind of work do you (did you normally) do? That is, what (is/was)
         your job called?

         Only used if not currently working. This question Applies Also to people who may be Retired from one occupation, but ARE now working At something else. We want what they are doing NOW

     B. IF NOT ALREADY ANSWERED, ASK: What (do/did) you actually do in that job?
         Tell me, what (are/were) some of your main duties?

         If more than one job PROBE for job R usually spends more time AT.

     C. What kind of place (do/did) you work for?

                INDUSTRY: _____

     D. IF NOT ALREADY ANSWERED, ASK: What (do/did) they (make/do)?

         Also, see Appendix on job description.

     E. IF ALREADY ANSWERED, CODE WITHOUT ASKING: (Are/Were) you self-employed
         or (do/did) you work for someone else?

                                         Self-employed 1
                                         Someone else 2
                                                                  06-08/
                                                                  09-10/
                                                                  11-13/

    ┌──┐
    │ REFER TO Q. 32--   │
    │   │
    │ ASK Q. 34 IF R. . . . . WORKING; TEMPORARILY NOT WORKING; (OR KEEPING │
    │ HOUSE.) (CODES 1, 2, 3, or 7)   │
    │   │
    │ ALL OTHERS; SKIP TO INSTRUCTIONS BEFORE Q. 35.   │
    └──┘

34. On the whole, how satisfied are you with the work you do--would you say you are
     very satisfied, moderately satisfied, a little dissatisfied, or very dissatisfied?

     This question Refers to satisfaction   Very satisfied. 1   14/9
     with job itself---- Not R's feelings   Moderately satisfied. . . . 2
     About how well or poorly he does   A little dissatisfied . . . 3
     the job.   Very dissatisfied 4
                                                    Don't know 8
     *For R's who ARE "Keeping house"
     this question Refers to satisfaction
     with that work.*

-15-   DECK 04

IF (CURRENTLY MARRIED) ASK Q. 35.   → NOTE: *Currently married refers only to those coded "1" in Q. 23.*

OTHERS, SKIP TO Q. 37.

35.   Last week was your (wife/husband) working full time, part time; going to school; keeping house; or what?

| HAND CARD E |

CIRCLE ONE CODE ONLY. IF MORE THAN ONE RESPONSE, GIVE PREFERENCE TO SMALLEST CODE NUMBER THAT APPLIES.

Let R decide if spouse was working full-time or part-time. Do not try to define these terms

Working full time . . . . (ASK A) 1   15/9

Working part time . . . . (ASK A) 2

With a job, but not at work because of temporary illness, vacation, strike . . . . (ASK B) 3

Unemployed, laid off, looking for work . . . . . . (GO TO Q. 36) 4

EX.: If R's spouse was working part-time and also going to school, circle code 2.

Retired . . . . (ASK C) 5

In school . . . . (ASK C) 6

Keeping house . . . . . . (ASK C) 7

Other . . . . (SPECIFY AND ASK C) 8

A.   IF WORKING, FULL OR PART TIME: How many hours did (he/she) work last week, at all jobs?

Hours: [|]   16-17/99

NOW GO TO Q. 36

B.   IF WITH A JOB, BUT NOT AT WORK: How many hours a week does (he/she) usually work, at all jobs?

Hours: [|]   18-19/99

NOW GO TO Q. 36

C.   IF RETIRED, IN SCHOOL, KEEPING HOUSE, OR OTHER: Did (he/she) ever work for as long as one year?

Yes . . . . . . (ASK Q. 36) . . 1   20/9

No . . . . . . (SKIP TO Q.37) . . 2

Don't know. (SKIP TO Q. 37) . . . 8

→ *By "jobs" and "working" we mean: working for pay at a job, or running his/her own business or profession (or farm), or working without pay in family business (or farm.)*

-16- DECK 04

36. A. What kind of work (does (SPOUSE) (did [SPOUSE] normally) do? That is, what (is/was) (his/her) job called?

Read "husband" or "wife," as applicable.

OCCUPATION: _____

B. <u>IF NOT ALREADY ANSWERED, ASK</u>: What (does/did) (SPOUSE) actually do in that job? Tell me, what (are/were) some of (his/her) main duties?

Same instructions as for Q.33.

C. What kind of place (does/did) (SPOUSE) work for?

INDUSTRY: _____

D. <u>IF NOT ALREADY ANSWERED, ASK</u>: What (do/did) they (make/do)?

E. <u>IF ALREADY ANSWERED, CODE WITHOUT ASKING</u>: (Is/Was) (he/she) self-employed or (does/did) (he/she) work for someone else?

Self-employed . . . 1

Someone else 2

Don't know 8

21-23/
24-25/
26-28/

<u>ASK EVERYONE</u>

37. At any time during the last ten years, have you been unemployed <u>and</u> looking for work for as long as a month?

Be sure R hears whole question before you except his answer.

Yes 1   29/9

No 2

Don't know 8

38. Did you ever--because of sickness, unemployment, or any other reason--receive anything like welfare, unemployment insurance, or other aid from government agencies?

Yes	1	30/9
No	2	
Don't know	8	

39. Do you (or your [SPOUSE]) belong to a labor union? (Who?)

Read this phrase if R is currently married.
Read "husband" or "wife" as appropriate.

Yes, respondent belongs	1	31/9
Yes, spouse belongs	2	
Yes, both belong	3	
No, neither R. (nor spouse) belongs . .	4	

40. We are interested in how people are getting along financially these days. So far as you and your family are concerned, would you say that you are pretty well satisfied with your present financial situation, more or less satisfied, or not satisfied at all?

Pretty well satisfied	1	32/9
More or less satisfied.	2	
Not satisfied at all.	3	
Don't know	8	

41. During the last few years, has your financial situation been getting better, getting worse, or has it stayed the same?

If response is "up and down," probe..... "In general, would you say it has been getting better....."

Getting better	1	33/9
Getting worse	2	
Stayed the same. . . .	3	
Don't know	8	

42. Compared with American families in general, would you say your family income is-- far below average, below average, average, above average, or far above average? (PROBE: Just your best guess.)

Far below average . . . !	1	34/9
Below average	2	
Average	3	
Above average	4	
Far above average . . .	5	
Don't know	8	

43. If you were asked to use one of four names for your social class, which would you say you belong in: the lower class, the working class, the middle class, or the upper class?

Probe if necessary.... "Which class are you in... which comes closest to describing your class?"

Lower class	1	35/9
Working class	2	
Middle class	3	
Upper class	4	

-18-   DECK 04

44. I am going to name some institutions in this country. As far as the <u>people running</u> these institutions are concerned, would you say you have a great deal of confidence, only some confidence, or hardly any confidence at all in them? READ EACH ITEM; CODE ONE FOR EACH.

HAND CARD F	A great deal of confidence	Only some confidence	Hardly any confidence at all	Don't know	
A. First, how much confidence do you have in the people running the Executive branch of the federal government?	1	2	3	8	36/9
B. How about people running organized labor?	1	2	3	8	37/9
C. Press?	1	2	3	8	38/9
D. Military?	1	2	3	8	39/9
E. Major companies?	1	2	3	8	40/9
F. How about the people running organized religion?	1	2	3	8	41/9
G. Education?	1	2	3	8	42/9
H. Medicine?	1	2	3	8	43/9
I. TV?	1	2	3	8	44/9
J. U. S. Supreme Court?	1	2	3	8	45/9
K. How about the people running the Scientific community?	1	2	3	8	46/9
L. Congress?	1	2	3	8	47/9
M. Banks and financial institutions?	1	2	3	8	48/9

45. The United States Supreme Court has ruled that no state or local government may <u>require</u> the reading of the Lord's Prayer or Bible verses in public schools.

What are your views on this--do you approve or disapprove of the court ruling?

When R Responds "Approve" or "disApprove" probe as follows, to make sure R understands question:

Approve 1   49/9
Disapprove 2
No opinions . . . 8

"Then you (Approve/disApprove) of the Ruling that no government may Require Reading of prayers or Bible verses in public schools?"

-19-   DECK 04

46. How much of the time do you think you can trust the government in Washington to
     do what is right--just about always, most of the time, or only some of the time?

                                    Always 1   50/9

                                    Most of the time 2

                                    Some of the time 3

                                    None of the time
                                         (VOLUNTEERED) 4

                                    Don't know 8

47. Would you say the government is pretty much run by a few big interests looking
     out for themselves or that it is run for the benefit of all the people?

                                    Few big interests 1   51/9

                                    For benefit of all 2

                                    Other, depends, refused
                                         to choose 3

                                    Don't know 8

48. Some people seem to follow what's going on in government and public affairs,
     whether there is an election going on or not. Others aren't that interested.

     Would you say that you follow what's going on in government and public affairs
     most of the time, some of the time, only now and then, or hardly at all?

                                    Most of the time 1   52/9

                                    Some of the time 2

                                    Only now and then 3

                                    Hardly at all 4

                                    Don't know 8

49. In talking to people about the 1974 Congressional election, we found that a
     lot of people did not vote. How about you--did you vote in the November 1974
     election?

              Note: A and B are   Yes . . . (ASK A) 1   53/9
              on next page.   No . . (ASK B) 2

                                          Don't remember/don't know
                                               (GO TO Q. 50) 8

-20-   DECK 04

Note skip instructions and follow carefully.

49. Continued

A. **IF YES:** How about the vote for Congress--do you remember which candidate you
voted for? (Who?)

Remembers name (SPECIFY & ASK [2])

R might have voted for other offices in that election, but not for Congress.

_____ 1   54/9

Don't remember name (ASK [1]). . . . 2

Didn't vote for Congress
(GO TO Q. 50) 5

    [1] **IF DON'T REMEMBER NAME:** Do you remember which party that was?

Democratic party . . . (ASK [2]) . . 3   55/9
Republican party . . . (ASK [2]) . . 4
Don't remember . . . (GO TO Q. 50) . 8

    [2] **IF ANY CANDIDATE OR PARTY NAMED:** What would you say was the most
important reason for voting for (CANDIDATE/PARTY NAMED)? RECORD
VERBATIM. PROBE FOR ADDITIONAL REASON. Any other reasons?

Be sure to probe for clarity   56-57/
before going on to the probe   58-59/
for additional reasons.

| NOW GO TO Q. 50 |

B. **IF NO:** Could you tell me which one of these reasons best describes why you
did not vote.

Probe, if necessary, for one main reason.

HAND
CARD
G

I wasn't registered . . . . . (ASK [3]) . . .01   60-61/99
I was ill . . . . (GO TO Q. 50) .02
I forgot . . . . (GO TO Q. 50) .03   *Note:*
The weather was too bad . . . (GO TO Q. 50) .04   *Sub (3) is*
I was working . . . . (GO TO Q. 50) .05   *on next*
I had no transportation . . . (GO TO Q. 50) .06   *page.*
I am just tired of elections and politics
(GO TO Q. 50) 07
I didn't think that this election would
make any difference . . . (GO TO Q. 50) .08
I thought the candidates were too much
alike . . . . (GO TO Q. 50) .09
I never vote . . . . (GO TO Q. 50) .10

-21-   DECK 04

49. Continued

[3] <u>IF NOT REGISTERED</u>: Could you tell me which one of these reasons best
describes why you are not registered.

```
┌──────┐
│ HAND │     I was ill . . . . . . . . . . . . . . . . . . . . . . . . .1        62/9
│ CARD │     I forgot to register & missed the registration deadline . 2     *Probe, if*
│  H   │     I didn't know where to register or how to register  . . . 3     *necessary, for*
└──────┘     I couldn't get to the place of registration because it                *one main*
             was too far away and I didn't have transportation . . . 4          *reason.*
             I never register and I never vote . . . . . . . . . . . 5
             I didn't want to bother to register because I am tired
             of politics and elections . . . . . . . . . . . . . . 6
             Not eligible  . . . . . . . . . . . . . . . . . . . . 7
```

50. I'd like to talk with you about issues some people tell us are important. Please
look at Card I. Some people think that the government in Washington should do
everything possible to improve the standard of living of all poor Americans; they
are at Point 1 on this card. Other people think it is not the government's responsibility, and that each person should take care of himself; they are at Point 5.

```
┌──────┐     I STRONGLY                          I STRONGLY
│ HAND │     AGREE THE                           AGREE THAT
│ CARD │     GOVERNMENT                          PEOPLE
│  I   │     SHOULD            I AGREE           SHOULD
└──────┘     IMPROVE           WITH              TAKE CARE
             LIVING            BOTH              - OF           Don't
             STANDARDS         ANSWERS           THEMSELVES     know
```

As you READ this question, try to point to the Appropriate Numbers on the CARD.

A. Where would you   1   2   3   4   5   8   63/9
    place yourself
    on this scale,   *→ FOR Q.'s 50-56: If R has NOT made*
    or haven't you   *up his mind on an issue, code "don't*
    made up your   *know." This is an acceptable response...*
    mind on this?   *--- do not probe*

B. IF RESPONDENT CHOOSES 1 TO 5 ABOVE <u>AND</u> IF HE RESPONDED 'YES' TO Q. 49, ASK:

    In voting for (NAME OF CANDIDATE OR PARTY) for Congress, how important was
    this issue in your decision to vote for him, rather than for the other
    candidate? Was it . . . READ CATEGORIES (a) - (c).

         (a) One of the most important issues? . . . 1   64/9

         (b) An important issue? 2

         (c) Or, didn't you even think about this
              when you voted for him? 3

              Other response/don't know 8

See Q. 51 for additional instructions for Q.'s 50-56.

-22-   DECK 04

51. Now look at CARD J. Some people think that the government in Washington is trying to do too many things that should be left to individuals and private businesses. Others disagree and think that the government should do even more to solve our country's problems. Still others have opinions somewhere in between.

HAND CARD J	I STRONGLY AGREE THAT THE GOVERNMENT SHOULD DO MORE	I AGREE WITH BOTH ANSWERS	I STRONGLY AGREE THAT THE GOVERNMENT IS DOING TOO MUCH	Don't know	

A. Where would you place yourself on this scale, or haven't you made up your mind on this?

          1   2   3   4   5   8   65/9

B. IF RESPONDENT CHOOSES 1 TO 5 ABOVE AND IF HE RESPONDED 'YES' TO Q. 49, ASK:

In voting for (NAME OF CANDIDATE OR PARTY) for Congress, how important was this issue in your decision to vote for him rather than for the other candidate? Was it . . . READ CATEGORIES (a) - (c)

    (a) One of the most important issues? . . . 1   66/9

    (b) An important issue? 2

    (c) Or, didn't you even think about this when you voted for him? 3

    Other response/don't know 8

*√ See Q.49A .... If R Named the candidate he voted for .... use candidate's name here. If candidate not named, use party name here [from Q49A(I)]. If neither candidate nor party named, skip sub-question B. (This applies to Q.'s 50 — 56.)

If you are reading party name (because candidate was not named) read "it" rather than "him."

52. Look at CARD K. In general, some people think that it is the responsibility of
the government in Washington to see to it that people have help in paying for
doctors and hospital bills. Others think that these matters are not the responsibility of the federal government and that people should take care of these
things themselves.

HAND CARD K	I STRONGLY AGREE IT IS THE RESPONSIBILITY OF GOVERNMENT TO HELP		I AGREE WITH BOTH ANSWERS		I STRONGLY AGREE PEOPLE SHOULD TAKE CARE OF THEMSELVES	Don't know	

A. Where would   1   2   3   4   5   8   67/9
you place
yourself on
this scale,
or haven't
you made up
your mind
on this?

B. IF RESPONDENT CHOOSES 1 TO 5 ABOVE AND IF HE RESPONDED 'YES' TO Q. 49, ASK:

In voting for (NAME OF CANDIDATE OR PARTY) for Congress, how important was
this issue in your decision to vote for him rather than for the other
candidate? Was it . . . READ CATEGORIES (a) - (c).

        (a) One of the most important issues?. . . . 1   68/9

        (b) An important issue? 2

        (c) Or, didn't you even think about this
             when you voted for him? 3

             Other response/don't know 8

-24-   DECK 04

53. Look at CARD L. Some people think that the government in Washington ought to
     reduce the income differences between the rich and the poor--perhaps by raising
     the taxes of wealthy families or by giving income assistance to the poor. Others
     think that the government should not concern itself with reducing the income
     differences between the rich and the poor.

HAND CARD L		I STRONGLY AGREE GOVERNMENT SHOULD DO SOMETHING TO REDUCE INCOME DIFFERENCES BETWEEN RICH AND POOR	I AGREE WITH BOTH ANSWERS	I STRONGLY AGREE GOVERNMENT SHOULD NOT CONCERN ITSELF WITH REDUCING INCOME DIFFERENCES	Don't know

A. Where would   1   2   3   4   5   8   69/9
    you place
    yourself on
    this scale,
    or haven't
    you made up
    your mind
    on this?

B. IF RESPONDENT CHOOSES 1 TO 5 ABOVE AND IF HE RESPONDED 'YES' TO Q. 49, ASK:
    In voting for (NAME OF CANDIDATE OR PARTY) for Congress, how important was
    this issue in your decision to vote for him rather than for the other
    candidate? Was it . . . READ CATEGORIES (a) - (c).

              (a) One of the most important issues? . . . 1   70/9

              (b) An important issue? 2

              (c) Or, didn't you even think about this
                   when you voted for him? 3

                   Other response/don't know 8

54. Now look at CARD M. Some people think that (Blacks/Negroes) have been discrimi-
nated against for so long that the government has a special obligation to help
improve their living standards. Others believe that the government should not
be giving special treatment to (Blacks/Negroes).

HAND CARD M	I STRONGLY AGREE THE GOVERNMENT IS OBLIGATED TO HELP BLACKS		I AGREE WITH BOTH ANSWERS		I STRONGLY AGREE THAT GOVERNMENT SHOULDN'T GIVE SPECIAL TREATMENT	Don't know

A. Where would you place yourself on this scale, or haven't you made up your mind on this?

    1   2   3   4   5   8   71/9

B. IF RESPONDENT CHOOSES 1 TO 5 ABOVE AND IF HE RESPONDED 'YES' TO Q. 49, ASK:
In voting for (NAME OF CANDIDATE OR PARTY) for Congress, how important was
this issue in your decision to vote for him rather than for the other
candidate? Was it . . . READ CATEGORIES (a) - (c).

    (a) One of the most important issues? . . . 1   72/9

    (b) An important issue? 2

    (c) Or, didn't you even think about this
        when you voted for him? 3

    Other response/don't know 8

-26-   DECK 04

55. Now look at CARD N. Some people think that our domestic problems are so serious
that we should cut defense spending and spend more on problems at home. Others
think that we should maintain our defense spending at the present level.

		I STRONGLY AGREE WE SHOULD CUT DEFENSE SPENDING	I AGREE WITH BOTH ANSWERS	I STRONGLY AGREE THAT WE SHOULD MAINTAIN DEFENSE SPENDING	Don't know	
HAND CARD N						
A.	Where would you place yourself on this scale, or haven't you made up your mind on this?	1 2	3 4	5	8	73/9

B. IF RESPONDENT CHOOSES 1 TO 5 ABOVE AND IF HE RESPONDED 'YES' TO Q. 49, ASK:
In voting for (NAME OF CANDIDATE OR PARTY) for Congress, how important was
this issue in your decision to vote for him rather than for the other
candidate? Was it . . . READ CATEGORIES (a) - (c).

     (a) One of the most important issues? . . . 1   74/9

     (b) An important issue? 2

     (c) Or, didn't you even think about this
         when you voted for him? 3

        Other response/don't know 8

56. Now look at CARD O. Some people think that the government in Washington should see to it that black and white children go to the same schools, others feel that the government should stay out of this altogether.

HAND CARD O	GOVERNMENT SHOULD HELP INTEGRATE SCHOOLS		I AGREE WITH BOTH ANSWERS		GOVERNMENT SHOULD STAY OUT OF SCHOOL INTEGRATION	Don't know	
A. Where would you place yourself on this scale, or haven't you made up your mind on this?	1	2	3	4	5	8	07/9

B. IF RESPONDENT CHOOSES 1 TO 5 ABOVE AND IF HE RESPONDED 'YES' TO Q. 49, ASK: In voting for (NAME OF CANDIDATE OR PARTY) for Congress, how important was this issue in your decision to vote for him rather than for the other candidate? Was it . . . READ CATEGORIES (a) - (c).

(a) One of the most important issues? . . . 1   08/9

(b) An important issue? 2

(c) Or, didn't you even think about this when you voted for him? 3

Other response/don't know 8

-28-   DECK 05

57. Everything considered, would you say that, in general, you approve or disapprove
    of wiretapping?

                                        Approve 1   09/9
                                        Disapprove 2
                                        No opinion 8

58. Do you favor or oppose the death penalty for persons convicted of murder?

    If R says "it depends," probe   Favor 1   10/9
    by Repeating the question. If   Oppose 2
    R can't decide, code d.K.   Don't know 8

59. Would you favor or oppose a law which would require a person to get a police
    permit before he or she could buy a gun?

                                        Favor 1   11/9
                                        Oppose 2
                                        Don't know 8

60. In general, do you think the courts in this area deal too harshly or not
    harshly enough with criminals?

                                        Too harshly 1   12/9
    Do not Read   Not harshly enough 2
    this category ────────→ About right (VOLUNTEERED) . 3
    Code only if   Don't know 8
    volunteered.

61. Generally speaking, would you say that most people can be trusted or that you
    can't be too careful in dealing with people?

                                        Most people can be trusted 1   13/9
                                        Can't be too careful . . . 2
                                        Other, depends 3
                                        Don't know 8

62. Do you believe there is a life after death?

                                        Yes 1   14/9
                                        No 2
                                        Undecided 8

63. Do you think the use of marijuana should be made legal or not?

                                        Should 1   15/9
                                        Should not 2
                                        No opinion 8

64. Have you ever been punched or beaten by another person?

    This is meant to cover any   Yes . . . (ASK A & B) . . . 1   16/9
    circumstances, including in   No 2
    a fight.   Don't know 8

    IF YES:
    A. Did this happen to you as a child or as an adult?

                                        Child 1   17/9
                                        Adult 2
                                        Both 3
                                        Not sure 8

    B. How many times would you guess this has happened to you?
       Altogether   Once 1   18/9
                                        Two or three times . . 2
                                        Four or more times . . 3
                                        Not sure 8

65. Have you ever been threatened with a gun, or shot at?

If R Asks —this does include
Armed- Forces related incidents.

Yes . (ASK A & B) . 1   19/9
No 2
Don't know 8

IF YES:
A. Did this happen to you as a child or as an adult?

Child 1   20/9
Adult 2
Both 3
Not sure 8

B. How many times would you guess this has happened to you?

Altogether

Once 1   21/9
Two or three times . . 2
Four or more times . . 3
Not sure 8

66. Are there any situations that you can imagine in which you would approve of a
man punching an adult male stranger?

Yes . . . . (ASK A-E) . . . 1   22/9
No . . (GO TO Q. 67) . . . 2
Not sure . (ASK A-E) . . . 8

IF YES OR NOT SURE:
Would you approve of a man punching a stranger who:
Read each statement and code one
for each.

	Yes	No	Not sure	
A. ...was in a protest march showing opposition to the other man's views?	1	2	8	23/9
B. ...was drunk and bumped into the man and his wife on the street?	1	2	8	24/9
Would you approve a man punching a stranger who:				
C. ...had hit the man's child after the child accidentally damaged the stranger's car?	1	2	8	25/9
D. ...was beating up a woman and the man saw it?	1	2	8	26/9
E. ...had broken into the man's house?	1	2	8	27/9

67. Are there any situations you can imagine in which you would approve of a policeman striking an adult male citizen?

Yes . . . . (ASK A-D) . . . 1   28/9
No . . (GO TO Q. 68) . . . 2
Not sure . (ASK A-D) . . . 8

IF YES OR NOT SURE:
Would you approve of a policeman striking a citizen who:
Read each statement and code one for
each.

	Yes	No	Not sure	
A. ...had said vulgar and obscene things to the policeman?	1	2	8	29/9
B. ...was being questioned as a suspect in a murder case?	1	2	8	30/9
Would you approve of a policeman striking a citizen who:				
C. ...was attempting to escape from custody?	1	2	8	31/9
D. ...was attacking the policeman with his fists?	1	2	8	32/9

-30-   DECK 05

68. Now to a different subject.

<table>
<tr><td>HAND
CARD
P</td><td>A. The qualities listed on this card may all be important, but which <u>three</u>
would you say are the <u>most desirable</u> for a <u>child</u> to have? CIRCLE <u>THREE</u>
CODES ONLY IN COLUMN A.</td></tr>
</table>

B. Which <u>one</u> of <u>these three</u> is the <u>most</u> desirable of all? READ THE THREE R.
    CHOSE. CODE <u>ONE</u> ONLY IN COLUMN B.
            →*I N   A N S W E R   t o   A.*

C. All of the qualities on this card may be desirable, but could you tell me
    which <u>three</u> you consider <u>least important</u>? CIRCLE <u>THREE</u> CODES ONLY IN
    COLUMN C.

D. And which <u>one</u> of these three is <u>least important</u> of all? READ THE THREE R.
    CHOSE. CODE <u>ONE</u> ONLY IN COLUMN D.
            →*I N   A N S W E R   t o   C*

Note that the ANSWER to B must
be ONE of the three qualities
NAMEd iN A. Also, the ANSWER to
D must be ONE of the three
QuAlities NAMEd iN C.

	Most Desirable		Least Important		
	A. Three Most	**B.** One Most	**C.** Three Least	**D.** One Least	
1) that he has good manners.	2	1	4	5	33/9
2) that he tries hard to succeed.	2	1	4	5	34/9
3) that he is honest.	2	1	4	5	35/9
4) that he is neat and clean.	2	1	4	5	36/9
5) that he has good sense and sound judgment.	2	1	4	5	37/9
6) that he has self-control.	2	1	4	5	38/9
7) that he acts like a boy (she acts like a girl).	2	1	4	5	39/9
8) that he gets along well with other children.	2	1	4	5	40/9
9) that he obeys his parents well.	2	1	4	5	41/9
10) that he is responsible.	2	1	4	5	42/9
11) that he is considerate of others.	2	1	4	5	43/9
12) that he is interested in how and why things happen.	2	1	4	5	44/9
13) that he is a good student.	2	1	4	5	45/9

-31- DECK 05

69. What do you think is the ideal number of children for a family to have?

PRobe, if NECESSARY, "FoR most people ....."

None 00	46-47/99
One 01	
Two 02	
Three 03	
Four 04	
Five 05	
Six 06	
Seven or more 07	
As many as you want . . 08	
Don't know 98	

Use this Response only if A number is given (7 oR LARgeR number.) Not foR vAgue Responses like "dozens" oR "lots." Probe such vAgue Responses! ..... "Well About how many would you SAy?"

→ *Probe oNCe befoRe Accepting this ANSweR*

70. A. In some places in the United States, it is not legal to supply birth control information. How do you feel about this--do you think birth control information should be available to anyone who wants it, or not?

Stress the woRd "InfoRmation" So R does not thinK we ARe RefeRRing to supplying birth coNtRol devices.

Should be available . . 1	48/9
Should not be available 2	
No opinion 8	

B. Do you think birth control information should be available to teenagers who want it, or not?

Should be available . . 1	49/9
Should not be available 2	
No opinion 8	

71. Would you be for or against sex education in the public schools?

For 1	50/9
Against 2	
Don't know 8	

72. Should divorce in this country be easier or more difficult to obtain than it is now?

Easier 1	51/9
More difficult 2	
Stay as is 3	
No opinion 8	

-32-   DECK 05

73. Please tell me whether or not <u>you</u> think it should be possible for a pregnant
woman to obtain a <u>legal</u> abortion if . . . READ EACH STATEMENT, AND CIRCLE ONE
CODE FOR EACH.

Repeat question as necessary

	Yes	No	Don't know	
A. If there is a strong chance of serious defect in the baby?	1	2	8	52/9
B. If she is married and does not want any more children?	1	2	8	53/9
C. If the woman's own health is seriously endangered by the pregnancy?	1	2	8	54/9
D. If the family has very low income and cannot afford any more children?	1	2	8	55/9
E. If she became pregnant as a result of rape?	1	2	8	56/9
F. If she is not married and does not want to marry the man?	1	2	8	57/9

74. There's been a lot of discussion about the way morals and attitudes about sex are
changing in this country. If a man and a woman have sex relations before marriage,
do you think it is always wrong, almost always wrong, wrong only sometimes, or
not wrong at all?

                          Always wrong 1   58/9
                          Almost always wrong . . . 2
                          Wrong only sometimes . . . 3
                          Not wrong at all 4
                          Don't know 8

75. Have you seen an X-rated movie in the last year?

If R doesn't know what
an X-Rated movie is, code "Don't Know."   Yes 1   59/9
                                                 No 2
                                                 Don't know . 8

76. The next questions are about pornography--books, movies, magazines, and photographs
that show or describe sex activities.

    Which of these statements comes closest to your feelings about pornography laws?
    READ FIRST THREE CATEGORIES [(a) - (c)] ONLY. CIRCLE ONE CODE.

    (a) There should be laws against the distribution of
        pornography whatever the age 1   60/9

    (b) There should be laws against the distribution of
        pornography to persons under 18 2

    (c) There should be no laws forbidding the distribution of
        pornography 3

        Don't know (VOLUNTEERED) 8

    Do not Read to R.

If R asks, this refers to pornography as defined in the beginning of Q.76. DECKS 05-06

77. I am going to read some opinions about the effects of looking at or reading (such sexual materials) As I read each one, please tell me if you think sexual materials <u>do</u> or <u>do not</u> have that effect. READ EACH ITEM. CODE ONE FOR EACH.

Repeat question as necessary .....
"Do you think sexual materials do or do not have that effect?"

		Yes, do	No, do not	Don't know	
A.	Sexual materials provide information about sex.	1	2	8	61/9
B.	Sexual materials lead to breakdown of morals.	1	2	8	62/9
C.	Sexual materials lead people to commit rape.	1	2	8	63/9
D.	Sexual materials provide an outlet for bottled-up impulses.	1	2	8	64/9

If R asks: "Organizations" refers to groups that have characteristics such as: newsletters, dues, meetings, etc. BEGIN DECK 06

78. Now we would like to know something about the (groups and organizations) to which individuals belong. Here is a list of various kinds of organizations. Could you tell me whether or not you are a member of each type? READ EACH ITEM. CODE ONE FOR EACH.

			Yes	No	Don't know	
HAND CARD Q	A.	Fraternal groups	1	2	8	07/9
	B.	Service clubs	1	2	8	08/9
	C.	Veterans' groups	1	2	8	09/9
	D.	Political clubs	1	2	8	10/9
	E.	Labor unions	1	2	8	11/9
	F.	Sports groups	1	2	8	12/9
	G.	Youth groups	1	2	8	13/9
	H.	School service groups	1	2	8	14/9
	I.	Hobby or garden clubs	1	2	8	15/9
	J.	School fraternities or sororities	1	2	8	16/9
	K.	Nationality groups	1	2	8	17/9
	L.	Farm organizations	1	2	8	18/9
	M.	Literary, art, discussion, or study groups	1	2	8	19/9
	N.	Professional or academic societies	1	2	8	20/9
	O.	Church-affiliated groups	1	2	8	21/9
	P.	(Any other groups?)	1	2	8	22/9

Suggested Probe: "Are there any other kinds of organizations you belong to that you may not have mentioned already?"

23-24/

-34-   DECK 06

79. Would you use this card and tell me which answer comes closest to how often you do the following things . . . READ EACH ITEM. CODE ONE FOR EACH.

HAND CARD R	Almost every day	Once or twice a week	Several times a month	About once a month	Several times a year	About once a year	Never	Don't know	
A. Spend a social evening with relatives?	1	2	3	4	5	6	7	8	25/9
B. Spend a social evening with someone who lives in your neighborhood?	1	2	3	4	5	6	7	8	26/9
C. Spend a social evening with friends who live outside the neighborhood?	1	2	3	4	5	6	7	8	27/9
D. Go to a bar or tavern?	1	2	3	4	5	6	7	8	28/9

[handwritten by item A:] That is, Relatives who live outside R's household.

80. How often do you read the newspaper--every day, a few times a week, once a week, less than once a week, or never?

[handwritten:] Probe: "Usually, that is most of the time."

Every day 1   29/9
A few times a week . . 2
Once a week 3
Less than once a week . 4
Never 5

81. On the average day, about how many hours do you personally watch television?

[handwritten:] Probe: "On the AveRAGe, how mANy hours...."   ✓ RecoRD VeRbAtim ____ 30-31/99

82. Would you say that most of the time people try to be helpful, or that they are mostly just looking out for themselves?

[handwritten:] If necessARy, pRobe.... "In geNeRAl, would you sAy.... "Repeat Question

Try to be helpful 1   32/9
Just look out for themselves 2
Depends 3
Don't know 8

[handwritten:] Probe oNce befoRe AcceptiNg A "depends" ResponSe.

83. Do you think most people would try to take advantage of you if they got a chance, or would they try to be fair?

Would take advantage of you 1   33/9

Would try to be fair 2

Depends 3

Don't know 8

84. For each area of life I am going to name, tell me the number that shows how much **satisfaction** you get from that area. READ ITEMS A-E. CODE ONE FOR EACH.

HAND CARDS	*Repeat question as necessary..."How much satisfaction do you get from (area)."*	1. A very great deal	2. A great deal	3. Quite a bit	4. A fair amount	5. Some	6. A little	7. None	8. Don't know	
	A. The city or place you live in.	1	2	3	4	5	6	7	8	34/9
	B. Your non-working activities--hobbies and so on.	1	2	3	4	5	6	7	8	35/9
	C. Your family life.	1	2	3	4	5	6	7	8	36/9
	D. Your friendships.	1	2	3	4	5	6	7	8	37/9
	E. Your health and physical condition.	1	2	3	4	5	6	7	8	38/9

85. (ASK ONLY IF CURRENTLY MARRIED.) (OTHERS SKIP TO Q. 86.)

Taking things all together, how would you describe your marriage? Would you say that your marriage is very happy, pretty happy, or not too happy?

Very happy 1   39/9

Pretty happy . . . 2

Not too happy . . . 3

Don't know 8

86. ASK EVERYONE:

Taken all together, how would you say things are these days--would you say that you are very happy, pretty happy, or not too happy?

If necessary, probe: "In general, how happy are you these days....." And repeat the categories

Very happy 1   40/9

Pretty happy . . . 2

Not too happy . . . 3

87. Would you say your own health, in general, is excellent, good, fair, or poor?

Excellent 1   41/9

Good 2

Fair 3

Poor 4

Don't know 8

-36-   DECK 06

88. In general, do you favor or oppose the busing of (Negro/Black) and white school
children from one school district to another?

Read "Negro" or "Black"...... which   Favor 1   42/9
ever term you think R would be   Oppose 2
most comfortable with.   Don't know 8

IF R IS BLACK, SKIP TO Q. 95   (Q'S. 89-94 ARE ASKED OF NON-BLACKS ONLY.)

89. Would you yourself have any objection to sending your children to a school where
a few of the children are (Negroes/Blacks)?

Note this skip instruction—...   Yes . . (GO TO Q. 90) . 1   43/9
.... Important.   No . . . . (ASK A) . . 2
                                     Don't know (ASK A) . . 8

A. IF NO OR DON'T KNOW: Where half of the children are (Negroes/Blacks)?

See definition of Race in Appendix   Yes . . (GO TO Q. 90) . 1   44/9
to Q-by-Q spec (Q116). If you are not   No . . . [ASK (1)] . . 2
sure of R's race, you cannot ask at   Don't know [ASK (1)] . . 8   *in deciding*
this point. Use your best judgement of R's race *whether*
(1) IF NO OR DON'T KNOW TO A: Where more than half of the children are *to ask or*
(Negroes/Blacks)?   *skip this series.*
                                     Yes 1   45/9
                                     No 2
                                     Don't know 8

90. Do you think there should be laws against marriages between (Negroes/Blacks) and
whites?
                                     Yes 1   46/9
                                     No 2
                                     Don't know 8

91. Are there any (Negroes/Blacks) living in this neighborhood now?

R's definition of   Yes . . (ASK A-C) . . 1   47/9
"neighborhood"   No . . (GO TO Q. 92) . 2
                                     Don't know (GO TO Q.92). 8

IF YES:
A. Are there any (Negro/Black) families living close to you?
                                     Yes 1   48/9
                                     No 2

B. How many blocks (or miles) away do they (the [Negro/Black] families who live
closest to you) live?
                                     On this block (a few doors/houses away) . 1   49/9
In Rural Areas, 1-3 blocks away (under 1/4 mile) 2
Read this phrase 4-8 blocks away (1/4 to 1 mile) 3
Also   Over 8 blocks (over 1 mile) 4
                                     Don't know 8

C. Do you think this neighborhood will become all (Negro/Black) in the next few
years, or will it remain integrated?
                                     All Negro/Black 1   50/9
                                     Remain integrated . . . 2
                                     Don't know 8

-37-   DECK 06

92. If your party nominated a (Negro/Black) for President, would you vote for him if he were qualified for the job?

Yes 1   51/9
No 2
Don't know 8

93. Here is an opinion other people have expressed in connection with (Negro/Black)-white relations. Please tell me which statement on this card comes closest to how you, yourself, feel about it.

HAND CARD T

	Agree strongly	Agree slightly	Disagree slightly	Disagree strongly	No opinion
(Negroes/Blacks) shouldn't push themselves where they're not wanted.	1	2	3	4	8

52/9

94. Suppose there is a community-wide vote on the general housing issue. There are two possible laws to vote on: (READ CATEGORIES A & B) Which law would you vote for? *ONLY*

HAND CARD U

A. One law says that a homeowner can decide for himself who to sell his house to, even if he prefers not to sell to (Negroes/Blacks). 1   53/9

B. The second law says that a homeowner cannot refuse to sell to someone because of their race or color 2

Do not Read to R → Neither (VOLUNTEERED) 3
Don't know (VOLUNTEERED) 8

ASK EVERYONE

95. Have you ever been on active duty for military training or service for two consecutive months or more?

Yes . . (ASK A & B) . . 1   54/9
No 2

IF YES:
A. What was your total time on active duty?

Less than 2 years . . . 1   55/9
2-4 years 2
More than 4 years . . . 3

B. In what branch of the service was that?

Air Force Guard 1   56/9
Air Force (or Air Force Reserve). . . . 2
Navy (or Naval Reserve) 3
Army (or Army Reserve) 4
National Guard 5
U.S. Marine Corps (or Marine Reserve) . . 6
Coast Guard (or Coast Guard Reserve) . . 7

-38-   DECK 06

96. How many children have you ever had? Please count all that were born alive at
any time (including any you had from a previous marriage)

Refers to any children born to (or fathered by) R.

Omit this phrase if "Never married."

Ask everyone, regardless of age, sex, or marital status

None 0	57/9
One 1	
Two 2	
Three 3	
Four 4	
Five 5	
Six 6	
Seven 7	
Eight or more . . . 8	

ASK EVERYONE, UNLESS TOTALLY INAPPROPRIATE. *You may not want to ask this*
IF INAPPROPRIATE, CIRCLE CODE 4. *of a 70-yr. old widow, but do ask of everyone who could possibly have children in the future.*

97. Do you expect to have any (more) children?

Note: If R is an obviously pregnant woman, you may code "yes" without asking, then ask A and B.

Yes . . . (ASK A & B) . 1	58/9
No . . . . 2 *Regardless*	
Uncertain . . . . . 3 *of sex or*	
Not asked, inappropriate . . . . 4 *marital status.*	

IF YES:
A. How many (more)?   *If R has ever had any children, use this. See Q 96.*   59-60/99

B. How many (more) in the next five years? . . . _____   61/9

98. Generally speaking, do you usually think of yourself as a Republican, a Democrat,
an Independent, or what?

Republican . . . . (ASK A & B) . . . 1	62/9
Democrat . . . . (GO TO Q. 99) . . . 2	
Independent (SKIP TO Q 100) . . . 3	
Other . . . . (SKIP TO Q. 100) . . . 4	
No preference (SKIP TO Q. 100) . . . 5	

IF REPUBLICAN:
A. Would you call yourself a strong Republican or not a very strong Republican?

Strong 1	63/9
Not very strong 2	

B. Was there ever a time when you thought of yourself as a Democrat rather than
a Republican?

Yes . . (ASK [1]) 1	64/9
No . (SKIP TO Q. 101) . . . 2	

HAND
CARD
V

[1] IF YES TO B: When did you change from Democrat to Republican?

Example: Taft's Administration

If R answers "several times"— Probe ... "When was the most recent change?"

ENTER "PARTY CHANGE"
CODE NO. FROM CARD V → | 0 | 4 | ← 65-66/99
THEN SKIP TO Q. 101

Code numbers and categories for this card are shown on p. 39.

-39-   DECK 06

99. <u>ASK IF "DEMOCRAT."</u>
    A. Would you call yourself a <u>strong</u> Democrat or <u>not a very strong</u> Democrat?

                                              Strong 1   67/9
                                              Not very strong 2

    B. Was there ever a time when you thought of yourself as a Republican rather than
       a Democrat?

                                              Yes . . (ASK [1]) . . . 1   68/9
    Same as Q.98   No .(SKIP TO Q. 101) . 2

    ┌──────┐
    │ HAND │   [1] <u>IF YES TO B</u>: When did you change from Republican to Democrat?
    │ CARD │
    │ V   │   ENTER "PARTY CHANGE" ┌──┬──┐
    └──────┘   CODE NO. FROM CARD V; │ │ │   69-70/99
                                          THEN SKIP TO Q. 101 └──┴──┘

                          CATEGORIES ON CARD V:
                          CODES FOR PARTY CHANGE

                  Presidential Administration   <u>OR</u>   <u>Years</u>

       01 . . . . Before 1900 . . . 01
       02 . . . McKinley + T. Roosevelt . . . . 1901 - 1904 . . . 02
       03 . . . T. Roosevelt . . . . 1905 - 1908 . . . 03
       04 . . . Taft . . . . 1909 - 1912 . . . 04   *Note error*
       05 . . . Woodrow Wilson - first term . . . . 1913 - 1916 . . . 05   *in year;*
       06 . . . Woodrow Wilson - second term . . . . 1917 - 1920 . . . 06   *should be*
       07 . . . Harding + Coolidge . . . . 1920 < 1924 . . . 07   *1921.*
       08 . . . Coolidge . . . . 1925 - 1928 . . . 08   *The card*
       09 . . . Hoover . . . . 1929 - 1932 . . . 09   *has cor-*
       10 . . . FDR - first term . . . . 1933 - 1936 . . . 10   *rect*
       11 . . . FDR - second term . . . . 1937 - 1940 . . . 11   *date.*
       12 . . . FDR - third term . . . . 1941 - 1944 . . . 12
       13 . . . FDR + Truman . . . . 1945 - 1948 . . . 13
       14 . . . Truman . . . . 1949 - 1952 . . . 14
       15 . . . Eisenhower - first term . . . . 1953 - 1956 . . . 15
       16 . . . Eisenhower - second term . . . . . . 1957 - 1960 . . . 16
       17 . . . Kennedy + Johnson . . . . 1961 - 1964 . . . 17
       18 . . . Johnson . . . . 1965 - 1968 . . . 18
       19 . . . Nixon - first term . . . . 1969 - 1972 . . . 19
       20 . . . Nixon - second term + Ford . . . . . 1973 - 1974 . . . 20

       98 . . . Don't know 98

-40-   DECKS 06-07

100. ASK IF "INDEPENDENT," "OTHER," OR NO PREFERENCE:

Do you think of yourself as closer to the Republican or to the Democratic party?

Republican . . (ASK A) . . 1   71/9

Democratic . . (ASK B) . . 2

Neither   . . . (ASK C) . . 3

BEGIN DECK 07

A. IF CLOSER TO REPUBLICAN: Was there ever a time when you thought of yourself
    as closer to the Democratic party instead of the Republican party?

Same As Q 98   Yes . . . . (ASK [1]) . . . 1   07/9
                               No, never (GO TO Q. 101). . 2

[1] IF YES TO A: When did you change?

Note: Instruction omitted   ENTER "PARTY CHANGE"   [ ]   08-09/99
from questionnaire in   CODE NO. FROM CARD V;
error   THEN GO TO Q. 101

B. IF CLOSER TO DEMOCRATIC: Was there ever a time when you thought of yourself
    as closer to the Republican party instead of the Democratic party?

                               Yes . . . . (ASK [2]) . . . 1   10/9
                               No, never (GO TO Q. 101). . 2

HAND
CARD   [2] IF YES TO B: When did you change?
V
        Same as Q. 98   ENTER "PARTY CHANGE"   [ ]   11-12/99
                               CODE NO. FROM CARD V;
                               THEN GO TO Q. 101

C. IF CLOSER TO NEITHER: Was there ever a time when you thought of yourself as a
    Democrat or as a Republican? (IF YES: Which?)

                               Yes, Republican (ASK [3]) . 1   13/9
                               Yes, Democrat   (ASK [3]) . 2
                               No, never (GO TO Q. 101) . 3

HAND
CARD   [3] IF YES, REPUBLICAN OR DEMOCRAT: When did you change? (IF CHANGED MORE
V   THAN ONCE, PROBE FOR MOST RECENT CHANGE.)

        Same as Q. 98   ENTER "PARTY CHANGE"   [ ]   14-15/99
                               CODE NO. FROM CARD V;

101. We hear a lot of talk these days about liberals and conservatives. I'm going to
      show you a seven-point scale on which the political views that people might hold
      are arranged from extremely liberal--point 1--to extremely conservative--point 7.
      Where would you place yourself on this scale?   *stress*

                               1) Extremely liberal 1   16/9
HAND   2) Liberal 2
CARD   3) Slightly liberal. 3
W   4) Moderate, middle of the road. . . . 4
                               5) Slightly conservative 5
                               6) Conservative 6
                               7) Extremely conservative. 7
                                          Don't know 8

-41-   DECK 07

ASK EVERYONE:

102. **What is the highest grade in elementary school or high school that you** fin- **ished and got credit for?** CODE EXACT GRADE. *Includes schooling the person may have received in night school or special classes -- If credit was given towards a high school diploma. / Note: There are no "D.K." codes for R in this question.*

HAND CARD D	No formal school .	00	
	1st grade	01	
	2nd grade	02	GO TO Q. 103
	3rd grade	03	

If foreign schooling, probe for closest equivalent to U.S. grades. If R unsure, record country & probe for details on education.

4th grade	04
5th grade	05
6th grade	06
7th grade	07
8th grade	08

| 9th grade . . . . | 09 |
| 10th grade . . . . | 10 | ASK
| 11th grade . . . . | 11 | A & B
| 12th grade . . . . | 12 |

17-18/99

IF FINISHED 9TH - 12TH GRADE:

A. Did you ever get a high school diploma or a GED certificate?

Ask B regardless of answer to A. Yes . . . . (ASK B) . . 1   19/9
                                    No . . . . (ASK B) . . 2

B. Did you ever complete one or more years of college for credit (not including schooling such as business college, technical, or vocational school)

Earning credit toward an academic degree.   Yes . [ASK (1) & (2)] . 1   20/9
                                              No 2

IF YES TO B:

(1) How many years did you complete?   21-22/99

If you cannot decide whether a person's schooling was regular college (toward an academic degree)-or technical or vocational training; record description verbatim, record how many years of what, and do not code.

If "Nursing" find out how many years of training, if any, counted for credit towards college degree.

1 year	13
2 years . . .	14
3 years . . .	15
4 years . . .	16
5 years . . .	17
6 years . . .	18
7 years . . .	19
8+ years . . .	20

(2) Do you have any college degrees?
                                    Yes . . [ASK (3)] . . 1   23/9
                                    No 2

(3) IF YES TO (2): What degree or degrees? CODE HIGHEST DEGREE EARNED.

If not sure how to code, record verbatim.   Junior college . . . 2   24/9

                                              Bachelor's 3

                                              Graduate 4

-42-   DECK 07

IF CURRENTLY MARRIED, ASK Q.103. *If R is not currently married, write "Not Applicable" and go to Q.104.*

103. What is the highest grade in elementary school or high school that your (husband/wife) finished and got credit for? CODE EXACT GRADE.

HAND CARD D		
No formal school .	00	
1st grade	01	
2nd grade	02	GO TO Q. 104
3rd grade	03	
4th grade	04	
5th grade	05	
6th grade	06	
7th grade	07	
8th grade	08	

SEE SPEX FOR Q. 102   25-26/99

9th grade 09
10th grade 10   ASK
11th grade 11   A & B
12th grade 12
Don't know 98

IF FINISHED 9TH - 12TH GRADE, OR DK:

A. Did (he/she) ever get a high school diploma or a GED certificate? *Equivalency diploma*

       Yes . . . . (ASK B) . . . 1   27/9
       No . . . . . (ASK B) . . . 2
       Don't know . (ASK B) . . . 8

B. Did (he/she) ever complete one or more years of college for credit--not including schooling such as business college, technical, or vocational schools?

       Yes . [ASK (1) & (2)] . . 1   28/9
       No 2
       Don't know 8

IF YES TO B:

(1) How many years did (he/she) complete?

       1 year 13   29-30/99
       2 years . . . 14
       3 years . . . 15
       4 years . . . 16
       5 years . . . 17
       6 years . . . 18
       7 years . . . 19
       8+ years . . . 20
       Don't know . . 98

(2) Does (he/she) have any college degrees?

       Yes . . [ASK (3)] . . 1   31/9
       No 2
       Don't know 8

(3) IF YES TO (2): What degree or degrees? CODE HIGHEST DEGREE EARNED.

       Junior college . . . 2   32/9
       Bachelor's 3
       Graduate 4
       Don't know 8

-43-   DECK 07

104. In 1972, you remember that McGovern ran for President on the Democratic ticket
      against Nixon for the Republicans. Do you remember for sure whether or not you
      voted in that election?

                                             Voted . . . . .(ASK A). . 1   33/9
                                             Did not vote . .(ASK B). . 2
                                             Ineligible . . .(ASK B). . 3
                                             Refused. 4
                                             Don't know/can't remember. 8

      A. IF VOTED: Did you vote for McGovern or Nixon?

                                             McGovern 1   34/9
                                             Nixon 2
                                             Other candidate 3
                                             Didn't vote for president. . . . . .(ASK B). . 4
                                             Don't know/can't remember. 8

      B. IF DID NOT VOTE OR INELIGIBLE: Who would you have voted for, for President,
                                          if you had voted?

          *If R says "I wouldn't
          have voted for either
          one, that's why I didn't   McGovern 1   35/9
          vote" — Record verbatim   Nixon 2
          and don't code.*   Other 3
                                          Don't know/can't remember. 8

105. What is your religious preference? Is it Protestant, Catholic, Jewish, some
      other religion, or no religion?

          Refers to Roman Catholic Only.   Protestant . . .(ASK A). . 1   36/9
          Greek Orthodox or other Eastern   Catholic. 2
          Catholic Churches should be coded Jewish 3
          as "other" and recorded verbatim. None . (SKIP TO Q. 107). . 4
          If "other" be sure to ask for full Other (SPECIFY RELIGION
          name of religion,   AND/OR CHURCH AND
          church or denomination.   DENOMINATION). 5

      A. IF PROTESTANT: What specific denomination is that, if any?

                                             Baptist 1   37/9
                                             Methodist. 2
                                             Lutheran 3
                          Includes Anglicans Presbyterian 4
                                             Episcopalian 5
                                             Other (SPECIFY). 6
                                             No denomination given or
                                               non-denominational
                                               church 7

                                                              38-39/

-44-   DECK 07

ASK EVERYONE WITH ANY RELIGIOUS PREFERENCE NAMED IN Q. 105

106. Would you call yourself a strong (PREFERENCE NAMED IN Q. 105 OR 105-A) or a not very strong (PREFERENCE NAMED IN Q. 105 OR 105-A)?

EX: If R is Catholic, read "Catholic."
If R is a Protestant and Names
a denomination in Q105-A, read
the name of the denomination.
If R is Protestant but doesn't
name any particular denomination or says non-denominational,
read "Protestant."

Strong 1   40/9
Not very strong. 2
Somewhat strong. 3
(VOLUNTEERED)
Don't know 8

ASK EVERYONE

107. In what religion were you raised?

If R answers "same"..... Referring
to answer to Q105, circle the same
code or codes here as in Q105.
If anything is written in in Q.105,
write note to coders directing
them to answers in Q.105.

Protestant . . .(ASK A). . 1   41/9
Catholic 2
Jewish 3
None 4
Other (SPECIFY RELIGION
AND/OR CHURCH AND
DENOMINATION) 5

   A. IF PROTESTANT: What specific
      denomination is that, if any?

Baptist 1   42/9
Methodist. 2
Lutheran 3
Presbyterian 4
Episcopalian 5
Other (SPECIFY). 6

No denomination given or
non-denominational
church 7
                          43-44/

108. How often do you attend religious services? (USE CATEGORIES AS PROBES, IF NECESSARY.)

If R gives some vague
answer, or answer that
can't be fitted into the
categories.

Never 0   45/9
Less than once a year. 1
About once or twice a year . . . 2
Several times a year 3
About once a month 4
2-3 times a month. 5
Nearly every week. 6
Every week 7
Several times a week 8

470   *Ideas and Data*

-45-   DECK 07

IF R. IS CURRENTLY MARRIED, AS Q. 109. (OTHERS, SKIP TO Q. 111.)

109. What is your (SPOUSE'S) religious preference? Is it Protestant, Catholic,
      Jewish, some other religion, or no religion?

See spex for Q105.

        Protestant . . . .(ASK A). . 1   46/9
        Catholic 2
        Jewish 3
        None 4
        Other (SPECIFY RELIGION AND/OR
        CHURCH AND DENOMINATION) 5

      A. IF PROTESTANT: What specific denomination is that, if any?

        Baptist. 1   47/9
        Methodist. 2
        Lutheran 3
        Presbyterian 4
        Episcopalian 5
        Other (SPECIFY). 6
        No denomination given or non-
        denominational church. 7
                                                        48-49/

110. In what religion was your (husband/wife) raised?

        Protestant . . . .(ASK A). . 1   50/9
See spex for. Q107   Catholic 2
        Jewish 3
        None 4
        Other (SPECIFY RELIGION AND/ OR
        CHURCH AND DENOMINATION). 5

        Don't know 8

      A. IF PROTESTANT: What specific denomination is that, if any?

        Baptist. 1   51/9
        Methodist. 2
        Lutheran 3
        Presbyterian 4
        Episcopalian 5
        Other (SPECIFY). 6

        No denomination given or non-
        denominational church 7
                                                        52-53/

-46-   DECK 07

111. Now just a few questions about this household. . .

(IF ONE-PERSON HOUSEHOLD, DO NOT READ PHRASE IN PARENTHESES. ALL OTHERS,
DO READ IT.)

(Just thinking about your (family) now--those people in the household who are
related to you. . .) How many persons in the family (including yourself) earned
any money last year--1974--from any job or employment?

This question is designed to get total number of wage earners in the household who are related to R. "Family" refers only to persons related to R who are living in household.

☐ 54/9

If no one, enter "0" in Box.

112. In which of these groups did your total family income, from all sources, fall
last year--1974--before taxes, that is? Just tell me the letter.

This question is designed to get total income for All family members in the household, from all sources. In addition to earned income (income from employment), other kinds of income could be: interest or dividends, rent, social security, other pensions, Alimony or child support, unemployment compensation, Public Aid (welfare), Armed Forces or Veteran Administration Allotment. The time period is last year ... 1974

HAND CARD X

A. Under $1,000 01   55-66/99
B. $ 1,000 to 2,999 02
C. $ 3,000 to 3,999 03
D. $ 4,000 to 4,999 04
E. $ 5,000 to 5,999 05
F. $ 6,000 to 6,999 06
G. $ 7,000 to 7,999 07
H. $ 8,000 to 9,999 08
I. $10,000 to 14,999 09
J. $15,000 to 19,999 10
K. $20,000 to 24,999 11
L. $25,000 or over 12
    Refused 13
    Don't know. 98

SEE Q. 34 (PAGE 14). IF ANY OCCUPATION RECORDED, ASK Q. 113.
Note Instruction. OTHERS, SKIP TO Q. 114.

113. Did you earn any income from ((OCCUPATION) DESCRIBED IN Q. 34)) in 1974?

Read job title from Q34

Yes . . . .(ASK A). . 1   57/9
No 2

A. IF YES: In which of these groups did your earnings from ((OCCUPATION IN
Q. 34)) for last year--1974--fall? That is, before taxes or other
deductions. Just tell me the letter.

This question is concerned with any income R earned from occupation described in Q34 ... not any other income R may have earned from any other jobs, or income from other sources ... or income of other family members.

HAND CARD X

A. Under $1,000. 01   58-59/99
B. $ 1,000 to 2,999 02
C. $ 3,000 to 3,999 03
D. $ 4,000 to 4,999 04
E. $ 5,000 to 5,999 05
F. $ 6,000 to 6,999 06
G. $ 7,000 to 7,999 07
H. $ 8,000 to 9,999 08
I. $10,000 to 14,999 09
J. $15,000 to 19,999 10
K. $20,000 to 24,999 11
L. $25,000 or over 12
    Refused 13
    Don't know. 98

This question is concerned with occupation rather than specific job or employer. EX: In Q34 R was "Waitress." You would ask here about R's total income in 1974 as a waitress ..... Even if she worked in several different places during the year.

-47-   DECK 07

114. In what year were you born?

    If R is not sure, probe for closest estimate.   ☐☐☐☐   60-63/99

---

115. CODE RESPONDENT'S SEX:

    Don't forget this!!

                       Male 1   64/9

                       Female. 2

---

116. CODE WITHOUT ASKING <u>ONLY</u> IF THERE IS <u>NO</u> DOUBT IN YOUR MIND.

    What race do you consider yourself? RECORD VERBATIM <u>AND</u> CODE.

    If there is no doubt as to R's race,   *See Appendix for Census definition of race.*
    code without asking. If you have
    <u>any</u> doubt, ask. If you do ask, be   White 1   65/9
    sure to check box.
                       Black 2
                       Other (SPECIFY) . . . 3

        NOTE: IF YOU <u>ASKED</u> R'S RACE, CHECK BOX . . . ☐   66/

(IF YOU ALREADY HAVE PHONE NO. RECORDED ON HEF, (GREEN QUEX), SKIP TO Q. 118.)

ALL OTHERS (WHITE QUEX OR GREEN QUEX, NO PHONE ON HEF), ASK:

117. Thank you very much for your time and help.

    May I have your name and telephone number just in case my office wants to verify
    this interview? ENTER NAME AND PHONE NUMBER. IF NO PHONE OR REFUSED, CIRCLE
    APPROPRIATE CODE NUMBER.

                             TELEPHONE
    RESPONDENT'S NAME: _____   NUMBER: _____
                                AREA   NUMBER
                                CODE/

                     No phone number 1   67/9
                     Refused phone number . . . 2

    IF TELEPHONE NUMBER IS GIVEN, ASK A:

    A. Is this phone located in your own home?

                         Yes 3
                         No (SPECIFY WHERE PHONE IS
                            LOCATED) 4

    If this is a White (Block Quota) interview, ask Q 117.

    *If this is a Green (Probability) interview, and a phone number
    was obtained at the time of the household enumeration, you
    may skip Q.117. If the phone number was not obtained (refused,
    not asked, etc.), then ask Q117 now.*

-48-   DECK 07

118. CODE DAY OF WEEK OF INTERVIEW:

Monday . . . . . (ASK A) . . 1		68/9
Tuesday . . . . . (ASK A) . . 2		
Wednesday . . . . (ASK A) . . 3		
Thursday . . . . (ASK A) . . 4		
Friday . . . . . (ASK A) . . 5		
Saturday . . . . (ASK B) . . 6		
Sunday . . . . . (ASK B) . . 7		

Note Skips: Go to A

Go to B

A. **IF MONDAY-FRIDAY:** We are always interested in improving our survey methods. For statistical purposes, we would like to estimate what our chances were of finding you at home today. Think for a moment about where you were at this time--that is at TIME INTERVIEW BEGAN, TO NEAREST HOUR--during the last four weekdays, not counting today. For how many of those four days--READ APPROPRIATE DAYS--were you at home at this time? PROBE FOR BEST GUESS.

Round to the nearest hour.
EX: If interview began at 9:25, read "9 O'Clock."
EX: If interview began at 7:50, read "8 O'Clock."

Read the 4 most recent weekdays.
EX: If interview is conducted on a Tuesday, say: "Yesterday, Monday ... And last Wednesday, Thursday and Friday."

None 1		69/9
One 2		
Two 3		
Three 4		
Four 5		
Refused 6		

B. **IF SATURDAY OR SUNDAY:** We are always interested in improving our survey methods. For statistical purposes, we would like to estimate what our chances were of finding you at home today. Think for a moment about where you were at this time--that is at TIME INTERVIEW BEGAN, TO NEAREST HOUR--during the last four Saturdays/Sundays, not counting today. For how many of those four Saturdays/Sundays were you at home at this time? PROBE FOR BEST GUESS.

If R is reluctant to answer Q118, reassure him that these answers are for statistical purposes only, and are not identified with any individual. Do not continue probing, but accept a refusal if this does not convince him to respond.

Read appropriate day only. If interview is conducted on Saturday, read "Saturday." If interview is conducted on Sunday, read "Sunday."

None 1		70/9
One 2		
Two 3		
Three 4		
Four 5		
Refused 6		

Thank you.

Do not forget to enter time and circle A.M. or P.M.

TIME INTERVIEW ENDED:	_____	AM PM

```
                              -49-                          BEGIN DECK 08

                        INTERVIEWER REMARKS

         (TO BE FILLED OUT AS SOON AS POSSIBLE AFTER LEAVING RESPONDENT)

A.  Length of interview:    [0] [7] [5]  Minutes    1 hour 15 min. =,
                              07-09/

B.  Date of interview:   [0] [3]    [1] [8]    EXAMple:
                         Month       Day        MARch 18 =,
                         10-11/      12-13/
```

C. In general, what was the respondent's attitude toward the interview? CODE ONE.

Friendly and interested	1	14/9
Cooperative but not particu- larly interested	2	
Impatient and restless	3	
Hostile	4	

D. Was respondent's understanding of the questions . . . CODE ONE.

Good?	1	15/9
Fair?	2	
Poor?	3	

IF BLOCK QUOTA SAMPLE (WHITE QUEX), RECORD INFORMATION FROM THE BLOCK SAMPLE
LISTING SHEET.   Note: If this is a Block Quota
                                                           INteRView (White Quex.), you must
(SKIP TO F IF PROBABILITY SAMPLE [GREEN] QUEX.) fill in this information!

```
                         PSU #         SEG. #        LINE #
E.  (1)                 [   ]         [   ]         [   ]
                         16-18/        19-21/        22-24/
```

     (2) CIRCLE CODE FOR QUOTA THIS CASE APPLIES TO:

Male, 18-34	1	25/
Male, 35+	2	
Female, Unemployed	3	
Female, Employed	4	

F. INTERVIEWER'S SIGNATURE: _____

```
G.  INTERVIEWER'S NUMBER:    [   ]
                              26-30/
```

H. COMMENTS:

National Opinion Research Center
University of Chicago

Survey 4209/4510
March, 1975

APPENDIX TO QUESTION-BY-QUESTION SPECIFICATIONS

Job Descriptions - Q's. 14, 33, and 36:

It is important to get the kind of business or industry, and to get it
crystal clear. The name of the company or employer is not necessary and
in most instances will not tell us what the respondent actually does in
his job. The kind of business or industry is crucial to our properly
classifying the job.

It is important that we have detailed information concerning the kind of
business. A description such as "automobiles" is far from sufficient--
this could mean an auto factory, a new car dealership, a used car lot, a
car rental agency, a car wash, a car repair shop, an automobile importer,
or something else. Probe fully using sub-questions A through E to find
out exactly what kind of business or industry it is.

Respondents, of course, have no way of knowing that the classifying of
occupations is very difficult and we need all the information we can get.
It is your job to obtain the information. To give you an idea of the
difficulty involved, the Bureau of the Census lists 91 different types
of "laborers." How can we properly classify the respondent if all we have
to go on is "laborer" as a job description? If you find out just what it
is he does as a "laborer," then we can properly classify him.

Don't be content with a job title. "Maintenance man" could mean a person
who maintains large and complicated machinery, or a janitor, or something
else. Find out what he does as a maintenance man. "Office work" can mean
supervising typists, being a typist, being a file clerk, supervising the
entire office, or something else. Find out what he does in the office.

"Farmer" is definitely not a good job description. It is incomplete because the person may . . .

--own a farm,

--or rent a farm,

--or be a sharecropper (working on someone else's land for a
     share of the crop or a share of the value of the crop),

--or work without pay on his family's farm,

--or be a farm laborer for wages,

--or be a foreman on a farm.

When you receive the response "farmer," find out which of these possibilities applies to the person, so we can properly classify his occupation.

-1-

-2-

Q. 116. Please study the following guidelines for classification of race, as
derived from Census definitions. If, in the interview situation, you
have <u>any</u> reason to be unsure of the respondent's race, according to
the definitions given here, <u>ask</u> the question as printed in the quex.
Then record the response <u>verbatim</u> and circle the appropriate code, and
<u>check the box provided</u>.

A person should be classified as <u>OTHER</u> only if he is American Indian,
Japanese, Chinese, Filipino, Asian Indian, Korean, Polynesian,
Indonesian, Hawaiian, Aleut, or Eskimo.

A person is classified as <u>BLACK</u> only if he is American Negro; or if
he is African, West Indian, or Puerto Rican, and <u>also</u> appears to be
black.

All other persons are classified as <u>WHITE.</u> This includes Mexicans;
Spaniards; and also Africans, West Indians, or Puerto Ricans who
appear to be white.

<u>Questions Requiring the Use of Show Cards (Cards A-X)</u>

This study utilizes 24 show cards. In order to keep them from getting separated
or lost, they are hole-punched and are to be kept together on a ring. It is part
of your job to hand the appropriate card to the respondent at the appropriate
time. <u>You</u> should keep possession of the set of cards at all times that the
respondent is not actually referring to one.

When a show card instruction appears in the questionnaire, you should <u>turn to</u>
the correct card and <u>hand it</u> to the respondent; when the question has been
answered, <u>take the set of cards back</u>. Do not leave the set in the respondent's
hands. If they are holding the cards, respondents tend to look through them;
this is a bad procedure for several reasons: It distracts the respondent from
what you are saying; it gives him advance information on questions that are
coming up later, it discourages him from reading through the card carefully
at the right time, and it makes it very difficult for you to be sure he is looking at the appropriate card for the question you are reading.

You must pay close attention to the respondent when he is answering the first
few card questions. If he cannot read, or appears to be having difficulty
reading, you will have to read the card categories out loud to him for all the
card questions. To accomplish this, you can say something like: "I will
read the categories as you look at the card." If this is said in a matter-of-
fact way, the respondent should assume this is the usual procedure. In some
cases, if the respondent has poor eyesight, he may just ask you to read them
to him.

Appendix D

The *Code of Hammurabi*

NOTES ON THE *CODE OF HAMMURABI*

When developing a coding scheme for the following laws, you may find it helpful to know that silver and corn formed the basis for the monetary system in Babylonia. Silver was in the form of bullion and was thus weighed. A table of weights used for silver was: 180 grains = 1 shekel; 60 shekels = 1 mana; and 60 manae = 1 talent. The measures for corn were as follows: 60 gan = 1 ka and 300 ka = 1 gur.

The following translation is from Robert Francis Harper, published by the University of Chicago Press, Callaghan and Company, Luzac and Company, 1904. There are numerous other translations. The one done by Chilperic Edwards, Kennikat Press, 1904, reissued 1971, provides useful notes on translation for your reference.

TRANSLATION

§1. If a man bring an accusation against a man, and charge him with a (capital) crime, but cannot prove it, he, the accuser, shall be put to death.

§2. If a man charge a man with sorcery, and cannot prove it, he who is charged with sorcery shall go to the river, into the river he shall throw himself and if the river overcome him, his accuser shall take to himself his house (estate). If the river show that man to be innocent and he come forth unharmed, he who charged him with sorcery shall be put to death. He who threw himself into the river shall take to himself the house of his accuser.

§3. If a man, in a case (pending judgement), bear false (threatening) witness, or do not establish the testimony that he has given, if that case be a case involving life, that man shall be put to death.

§4. If a man (in a case) bear witness for grain or money (as a bribe), he shall himself bear the penalty imposed in that case.

§5. If a judge pronounce a judgment, render a decision, deliver a verdict duly signed and sealed and afterward alter his judgment, they shall call that judge to account for the alteration of the judgment which he had pronounced, and he shall pay twelvefold the penalty which was in said judgment;

477

and, in the assembly, they shall expel him from his seat of judgment, and he shall not return, and with the judges in a case he shall not take his seat.

§6. If a man steal the property of a god (temple) or palace, that man shall be put to death; and he who receives from his hand the stolen (property) shall also be put to death.

§7. If a man purchase silver or gold, manservant or maid servant, ox, sheep or ass, or anything else from a man's son, or from a man's servant without witnesses or contracts, or if he receive (the same) in trust, that man shall be put to death as a thief.

§8. If a man steal ox or sheep, ass or pig, or boat—if it be from a god (temple) or a palace, he shall restore thirtyfold; if it be from a freeman, he shall render tenfold. If the thief have nothing wherewith to pay, he shall be put to death.

§9. If a man, who has lost anything, find that which was lost in the possession of (another) man; and the man in whose possession the lost property is found say: "It was sold to me, I purchased it in the presence of witnesses;" and the owner of the lost property say: "I will bring witnesses to identify my lost property": if the purchaser produce the seller who has sold it to him and the witnesses in whose presence he purchased it, and the owner of the lost property produce witnesses to identify his lost property, the judges shall consider their evidence. The witnesses in whose presence the purchase was made and the witnesses to identify the lost property shall give their testimony in the presence of god. The seller shall be put to death as a thief; the owner of the lost property shall recover his loss; the purchaser shall recover from the estate of the seller the money which he paid out.

§10. If the purchaser do not produce the seller who sold it to him, and the witnesses in whose presence he purchased it (and) if the owner of the lost property produce witnesses to identify his lost property, the purchaser shall be put to death as a thief; the owner of the lost property shall recover his loss.

§11. If the owner (claimant) of the lost property do not produce witnesses to identify his lost property, he has attempted fraud (has lied), he has stirred up strife (calumny), he shall be put to death.

§12. If the seller have gone to (his) fate (i.e., have died), the purchaser shall recover damages in said case fivefold from the estate of the seller.

§13. If the witnesses of that man be not at hand, the judges shall declare a postponement for six months; and if he do not bring in his witnesses within the six months; that man has attempted fraud, he shall himself bear the penalty imposed in that case.

§14. If a man steal a man's son, who is a minor, he shall be put to death.

§15. If a man aid a male or female slave of the palace, or a male or female slave of a freeman to escape from the city gate, he shall be put to death.

§16. If a man harbor in his house a male or female slave who has fled from the palace or from a freeman, and do not bring him (the slave) forth at the call of the commandant, the owner of that house shall be put to death.

§17. If a man seize a male or female slave, a fugitive, in the field and bring that (slave) back to his owner, the owner of the slave shall pay him two shekels of silver.

§18. If that slave will not name his owner, he shall bring him to the palace and they shall inquire into his antecedents and they shall return him to his owner.

§19. If he detain that slave in his house and later the slave be found in his possession, that man shall be put to death.

§20. If the slave escape from the hand of his captor, that man shall so declare, in the name of god, to the owner of the slave and shall go free.

§21. If a man make a breach in a house, they shall put him to death in front of that breach and they shall thrust him therein.

§22. If a man practice brigandage and be captured, that man shall be put to death.

§23. If the brigand be not captured, the man who has been robbed, shall, in the presence of god, make an itemized statement of his loss, and the city and the governor, in whose province and jurisdiction the robbery was committed, shall compensate him for whatever was lost.

§24. If it be a life (that is lost), the city and governor shall pay one mana of silver to his heirs.

§25. If a fire break out in a man's house and a man who goes to extinguish it cast his eye on the furniture of the owner of the house, and take the furniture of the owner of the house, that man shall be thrown into that fire.

§26. If either an officer or a constable, who is ordered to go on an errand of the king, do not go but hire a substitute and dispatch him in his stead, that officer or constable shall be put to death; his hired substitute shall take to himself his (the officer's) house.

§27. If an officer or a constable, who is in a garrison of the king, be captured, and afterward they give his field and garden to another and he conduct his business—if the former return and arrive in his city, they shall restore to him his field and garden and he himself shall conduct his business.

§28. If an officer or a constable, who is in a fortress of the king, be captured (and) his son be able to conduct the business, they shall give to him the field and garden and he shall conduct the business of his father.

§29. If his son be too young and be not able to conduct the business of his father, they shall give one-third of the field and of the garden to his mother, and his mother shall rear him.

§30. If an officer or a constable from the beginning of (or, on account of) (his) business neglect his field, his garden, and his house and leave them uncared for (and) another after him take his field, his garden, and his house, and conduct his business for three years; if the former return and desire (or, would manage) his field, his garden, and his house, they shall not give them to him; he, who has taken (them) and conducted the business shall continue (to do so).

§31. If he leave (them) uncared for but one year and return, they shall give him his field, his garden, and his house and he himself shall continue his business.

§32. If a merchant ransom either an officer or a constable who has been captured on an errand of the king, and enable him to reach his city; if there be sufficient ransom in his house, he shall ransom himself; if there be not sufficient ransom in his house, in the temple of his city he shall be ransomed; if there be not sufficient ransom in the temple of his city, the palace shall ransom him. In no case shall his field or his garden or his house be given for his ransom.

§33. If a governor or a magistrate take possession of the men of levy (or, pardon a deserter) or accept and send a hired substitute on an errand of the king, that governor or magistrate shall be put to death.

§34. If a governor or a magistrate take the property of an officer, plunder an officer, let an officer for hire, present an officer in a judgment to a man of influence, take the gift which the king has given to an officer, that governor or magistrate shall be put to death.

§35. If a man buy from an officer the cattle or sheep which the king has given to that officer, he shall forfeit his money.

§36. In no case shall one sell the field or garden or house of an officer, constable or tax-gatherer.

§37. If a man purchase the field or garden or house of an officer, constable or tax-gatherer, his deed-tablet shall be broken (canceled) and he shall forfeit his money and he shall return the field, garden or house to its owner.

§38. An officer, constable or tax-gatherer shall not deed to his wife or daughter the field, garden or house, which is his business (i.e., which is his by virtue of his office), nor shall he assign them for debt.

§39. He may deed to his wife or daughter the field, garden or house which he has purchased and (hence) possesses, or he may assign them for debt.

§40. A woman, merchant or other property holder may sell field, garden or house. The purchaser shall conduct the business of the field, garden or house which he has purchased.

§41. If a man have bargained for the field, garden or house of an officer, constable or tax-gatherer and given sureties, the officer, constable or tax-gatherer shall return to his field, garden, or house and he shall take to himself the sureties which were given to him.

§42. If a man rent a field for cultivation and do not produce any grain in the field, they shall call him to account, because he has not performed the work required on the field, and he shall give to the owner of the field grain on the basis of the adjacent (fields).

§43. If he do not cultivate the field and neglect it, he shall give to the owner of the field grain on the basis of the adjacent (fields); and the field which he has neglected, he shall break up with hoes, he shall harrow and he shall return to the owner of the field.

§44. If a man rent an unreclaimed field for three years to develop it, and neglect it and do not develop the field, in the fourth year he shall break up the field with hoes, he shall hoe and harrow it and he shall return it to the owner of the field and shall measure out ten GUR of grain per ten GAN.

§45. If a man rent his field to a tenant for crop-rent and receive the crop-rent of his field and later Adad (i.e., the Storm God) inundate the field and carry away the produce, the loss (falls on) the tenant.

§46. If he have not received the rent of his field and he have rented the field for either one-half or one-third (of the crop), the tenant and the owner of the field shall divide the grain which is in the field according to agreement.

§47. If the tenant give the cultivation of the field into the charge of another—because in a former year he has not gained a maintenance—the owner of the field shall not interfere. He would cultivate it, and his field has been cultivated and at the time of harvest he shall take grain according to his contracts.

§48. If a man owe a debt and Adad inundate his field and carry away the produce, or, through lack of water, grain have not grown in the field, in that year he shall not make any return of grain to the creditor, he shall alter his contract-tablet and he shall not pay the interest for that year.

§49. If a man obtain money from a merchant and give (as security) to the merchant a field to be planted with grain and sesame (and) say to him: "Cultivate the field, and harvest and take to thyself the grain and sesame which is produced"; if the tenant raise grain and sesame in the field, at the time of harvest, the owner of the field shall receive the grain and sesame which is in the field and he shall give to the merchant grain for the loan which he had obtained from him and for the interest and for the maintenance of the tenant.

§50. If he give (as security) a field planted with [grain] or a field planted with sesame, the owner of the field shall receive the grain or the sesame which is in the field and he shall return the loan and its interest to the merchant.

§51. If he have not the money to return, he shall give to the merchant [grain or] sesame, at their market value according to the scale fixed by the king, for the loan and its interest which he has obtained from the merchant.

§52. If the tenant do not secure a crop of grain or sesame in his field, he shall not cancel his contract.

§53. If a man neglect to strengthen his dike and do not strengthen it, and a break be made in his dike and the water carry away the farmland, the man in whose dike the break has been made shall restore the grain which he has damaged.

§54. If he be not able to restore the grain, they shall sell him and his goods, and the farmers whose grain the water has carried away shall share (the results of the sale).

§55. If a man open his canal for irrigation and neglect it and the water carry away an adjacent field, he shall measure out grain on the basis of the adjacent fields.

§56. If a man open up the water and the water carry away the improvements of an adjacent field, he shall measure out ten GUR of grain per GAN.

§57. If a shepherd have not come to an agreement with the owner of a field to pasture his sheep on the grass; and if he pasture his sheep on the field without the consent of the owner, the owner of the field shall harvest his field, and the shepherd who has pastured his sheep on the field without the consent of the owner of the field shall give over and above twenty GUR of grain per ten GAN to the owner of the field.

§58. If, after the sheep have gone up from the meadow and have crowded their way out (?) of the gate into the public common, the shepherd turn the sheep into the field, and pasture the sheep on the field, the shepherd shall oversee the field on which he pastures and at the time of harvest he shall measure out sixty GUR of grain per ten GAN to the owner of the field.

§59. If a man cut down a tree in a man's orchard, without the consent of the owner of the orchard, he shall pay one-half mana of silver.

§60. If a man give a field to a gardener to plant as an orchard and the gardener plant the orchard and care for the orchard four years, in the fifth year the owner of the orchard and the gardener shall share equally; the owner of the orchard shall mark off his portion and take it.

§61. If the gardener do not plant the whole field, but leave a space waste, they shall assign the waste space to his portion.

§62. If he do not plant as an orchard the field which was given to him, if corn be the produce of the field, for the years during which it has been neglected, the gardener shall measure out to the owner of the field (such produce) on the basis of the adjacent fields, and he shall perform the required work on the field and he shall restore it to the owner of the field.

§63. If the field be unreclaimed, he shall perform the required work on the field and he shall restore to the owner of the field and he shall measure out ten GUR of grain per ten GAN for each year.

§64. If a man give his orchard to a gardener to manage, the gardener shall give to the owner of the orchard two-thirds of the produce of the orchard, as long as he is in possession of the orchard; he himself shall take one-third.

§65. If the gardener do not properly manage the orchard and he diminish the produce, the gardener shall measure out the produce of the orchard on the basis of the adjacent orchards.

§100. . . . . he shall write down the interest on the money, as much as he has obtained, and he shall reckon its days and he shall make returns to his merchant.

§**101.**   If he do not meet with success where he goes, the agent shall double the amount of money obtained and he shall pay it to the merchant.

§**102.**   If a merchant give money to an agent as a favor, and the latter meet with a reverse where he goes, he shall return the principal of the money to the merchant.

§**103.**   If, when he goes on a journey, an enemy rob him of whatever he was carrying, the agent shall take an oath in the name of God and go free.

§**104.**   If a merchant give to an agent grain, wool, oil or goods of any kind with which to trade, the agent shall write down the value and return (the money) to the merchant. The agent shall take a sealed receipt for the money which he gives to the merchant.

§**105.**   If the agent be careless and do not take a receipt for the money which he has given to the merchant, the money not receipted for shall not be placed to his account.

§**106.**   If an agent obtain money from a merchant and have a dispute with the merchant (i.e., deny the fact), that merchant shall call the agent to account in the presence of God and witnesses for the money obtained and the agent shall give to the merchant threefold the amount of money which he obtained.

§**107.**   If a merchant lend to an agent and the agent return to the merchant whatever the merchant had given him; and if the merchant deny (receiving) what the agent has given to him, that agent shall call the merchant to account in the presense of God and witnesses and the merchant because he has had a dispute with his agent, shall give to him sixfold the amount which he obtained.

§**108.**   If a wine seller do not receive grain as the price of drink, but if she receive money by the great stone, or make the measure for drink smaller than the measure for corn, they shall call that wine seller to account, and they shall throw her into the water.

§**109.**   If outlaws collect in the house of a wine seller, and she do not arrest these outlaws and bring them to the palace, that wine seller shall be put to death.

§**110.**   If a priestess who is not living in a MAL.GE.A, open a wine shop or enter a wine shop for a drink, they shall burn that woman.

§**111.**   If a wine seller give 60 KA of drink . . . on credit, at the time of harvest she shall receive 50 KA of grain.

§**112.**   If a man be on a journey and he give silver, gold, stones or portable property to a man with a commission for transportation, and if that man do not deliver that which was to be transported where it was to be transported, but take it to himself, the owner of the transported goods shall call that man to account for the goods to be transported which he did not deliver, and that man shall deliver to the owner of the transported goods fivefold the amount which was given to him.

§**113.**   If a man hold a [debt of] grain or money against a man, and if he take grain without the consent of the owner from the heap or the granary, they shall call that man to account for taking grain without the consent of the owner from the heap or the granary, and he shall return as much grain as he took, and he shall forfeit all that he has lent, whatever it be.

§114. If a man do not hold a [debt of] grain or money against a man, and if he seize him for debt, for each seizure he shall pay one-third mana of silver.

§115. If a man hold a [debt of] grain or money against a man, and he seize him for debt, and the one seized die in the house of him who seized him, that case has no penalty.

§116. If the one seized die of abuse or neglect in the house of him who seized him, the owner of the one seized shall call the merchant to account; and if it be a man's son [that he seized] they shall put his son to death; if it be a man's servant [that he seized] he shall pay one-third mana of silver and he shall forfeit whatever amount he had lent.

§117. If a man be in debt and sell his wife, son or daughter, or bind them over to service, for three years they shall work in the house of their purchaser or master; in the fourth year they shall be given their freedom.

§118. If he bind over to service a male or female slave, and if the merchant transfer or sell such slave, there is no cause for complaint.

§119. If a man be in debt and he sell his maid servant who has borne him children, the owner of the maid servant (i.e., the man in debt) shall repay the money which the merchant paid (him), and he shall ransom his maid servant.

§120. If a man store his grain in bins in the house of another and an accident happen to the granary, or the owner of the house open a bin and take grain or he raise a dispute about (or deny) the amount of grain which was stored in his house, the owner of the grain shall declare his grain in the presence of God, and the owner of the house shall double the amount of the grain which he took and restore it to the owner of the grain.

§121. If a man store grain in the house of another, he shall pay storage at the rate of five KA of grain per GUR each year.

§122. If a man give to another silver, gold or anything else on deposit, whatever he gives he shall show to witnesses and he shall arrange the contracts and (then) he shall make the deposit.

§123. If a man give on deposit without witnesses or contracts, and at the place of deposit they dispute with him (i.e., deny the deposit), that case has no penalty.

§124. If a man give to another silver, gold or anything else on deposit in the presence of witnesses and the latter dispute with him (or deny it), they shall call that man to account and he shall double whatever he has disputed and repay it.

§125. If a man give anything of his on deposit, and at the place of deposit either by burglary or pillage he suffer loss in common with the owner of the house, the owner of the house who has been negligent and has lost what was given to him on deposit shall make good (the loss) and restore (it) to the owner of the goods; the owner of the house shall institute a search for what has been lost and take it from the thief.

§126. If a man have not lost anything, but say that he has lost something, or if he file a claim for loss when nothing has been lost, he shall declare his (alleged) loss in the presence of god, and he shall double and pay for the (alleged) loss the amount for which he had made claim.

§127. If a man point the finger at a priestess or the wife of another and cannot justify it, they shall drag that man before the judges and they shall brand his forehead.

§128. If a man take a wife and do not arrange with her the (proper contracts, that woman is not a (legal) wife.

§129. If the wife of a man be taken in lying with another man, they shall bind them and throw them into the water. If the husband of the woman would save his wife, or if the king would save his male servant (he may).

§130. If a man force the (betrothed) wife of another who has not known a male and is living in her father's house, and he lie in her bosom and they take him, that man shall be put to death and that woman shall go free.

§131. If a man accuse his wife and she has not been taken in lying with another man, she shall take an oath in the name of God and she shall return to her house.

§132. If the finger have been pointed at the wife of a man because of another man, and she have not been taken in lying with another man for her husband's sake, she shall throw herself into the river.

§133. If a man be captured and there be maintenance in his house and his wife go out of her house, she shall protect her body and she shall not enter into another house.

§133A. [If] that woman do not protect her body and enter into another house, they shall call that woman to account and they shall throw her into the water.

§134. If a man be captured and there be no maintenance in his house and his wife enter into another house, that woman has no blame.

§135. If a man be captured and there be no maintenance in his house, and his wife openly enter into another house and bear children; if later her husband return and arrive in his city, that woman shall return to her husband (and) the children shall go to their father.

§136. If a man desert his city and flee and afterward his wife enter into another house; if that man return and would take his wife, the wife of the fugitive shall not return to her husband because he hated his city and fled.

§137. If a man set his face to put away a concubine who has borne him children or a wife who has presented him with children, he shall return to that woman her dowry and shall give to her the income of field, garden and goods and she shall bring up her children; from the time that her children are grown up, from whatever is given to her children they shall give to her a portion corresponding to that of a son and the man of her choice may marry her.

§138.   If a man would put away his wife who has not borne him children, he shall give her money to the amount of her marriage settlement and he shall make good to her the dowry which she brought from her father's house and then he may put her away.

§139.   If there were no marriage settlement, he shall give to her one mana of silver for a divorce.

§140.   If he be a freeman, he shall give her one-third mana of silver.

§141.   If the wife of a man who is living in his house, set her face to go out and play the part of a fool, neglect her house, belittle her husband, they shall call her to account; if her husband say "I have put her away," he shall let her go. On her departure nothing shall be given to her for her divorce. If her husband say: "I have not put her away," her husband may take another woman. The first woman shall dwell in the house of her husband as a maid servant.

§142.   If a woman hate her husband, and say: "Thou shalt not have me," they shall inquire into her antecedents for her defects; and if she have been a careful mistress and be without reproach and her husband have been going about and greatly belittling her, that woman has no blame. She shall receive her dowry and shall go to her father's house.

§143.   If she have not been a careful mistress, have gadded about, have neglected her house and have belittled her husband, they shall throw that woman into the water.

§144.   If a man take a wife and that wife give a maid servant to her husband and she bear children; if that man set his face to take a concubine, they shall not countenance him. He may not take a concubine.

§145.   If a man take a wife and she do not present him with children and he set his face to take concubine, that man may take a concubine and bring her into his house. That concubine shall not rank with his wife.

§146.   If a man take a wife and she give a maid servant to her husband, and that maid servant bear children and afterward would take rank with her mistress; because she has borne children, her mistress may not sell her for money, but she may reduce her to bondage and count her among the maid servants.

§147.   If she have not borne children, her mistress may sell her for money.

§148.   If a man take a wife and she become afflicted with disease, and if he set his face to take another, he may. His wife, who is afflicted with disease, he shall not put away. She shall remain in the house which he has built and he shall maintain her as long as she lives.

§149.   If that woman do not elect to remain in her husband's house, he shall make good to her the dowry which she brought from her father's house and she may go.

§150.   If a man give to his wife field, garden, house or goods and he deliver to her a sealed deed, after (the death of) her husband, her children cannot make claim against her. The mother after her (death) may will to her child whom she loves, but to a brother she may not.

§151. If a woman, who dwells in the house of a man, make a contract with her husband that a creditor of his may not hold her (for his debts) and compel him to deliver a written agreement; if that man were in debt before he took that woman, his creditor may not hold his wife, and if that woman were in debt before she entered into the house of the man, her creditor may not hold her husband.

§152. If they contract a debt after the woman has entered into the house of the man, both of them shall be answerable to the merchant.

§153. If a woman bring about the death of her husband for the sake of another man, they shall impale her.

§154. If a man have known his daughter, they shall expel that man from the city.

§155. If a man have betrothed a bride to his son and his son have known her, and if he (the father) afteward lie in her bosom and they take him, they shall bind that man and throw him into the water.

§156. If a man have betrothed a bride to his son and his son have not known her but he himself lie in her bosom, he shall pay her one-half mana of silver and he shall make good to her whatever she brought from the house of her father and the man of her choice may take her.

§157. If a man lie in the bosom of his mother after (the death of) his father, they shall burn both of them.

§158. If a man, after (the death of) his father, be taken in the bosom of the chief wife (of his father) who has borne children, that man shall be cut off from his father's house.

§159. If a man, who has brought a present to the house of his father-in-law and has given the marriage settlement, look with longing upon another woman and say to his father-in-law, "I will not take thy daughter"; the father of the daughter shall take to himself whatever was brought to him.

§160. If a man bring a present to the house of his father-in-law and give a marriage settlement and the father of the daughter say, "I will not give thee my daughter"; he (i.e., the father-in-law) shall double the amount which was brought to him and return it.

§161. If a man bring a present to the house of his father-in-law and give a marriage settlement, and his friend slander him; and if his father-in-law say to the claimant for the wife, "My daughter thou shalt not have," he (the father-in-law) shall double the amount which was brought to him and return it, but his friend may not have his wife.

§162. If a man take a wife and she bear him children and that woman die, her father may not lay claim to her dowry. Her dowry belongs to her children.

§163. If a man take a wife and she do not present him with children and that woman die; if his father-in-law return to him the marriage settlement which that man brought to the house of his father-in-law, her husband may not lay claim to the dowry of that woman. Her dowry belongs to the house of her father.

§164. If his father-in-law do not return to him the marriage settlement, he may deduct from her dowry the amount of the marriage settlement and return (the rest) of her dowry to the house of her father.

§165. If a man present field, garden or house to his favorite son and write for him a sealed deed; after the father dies, when the brothers divide, he shall take the present which the father gave him, and over and above they shall divide the goods of the father's house equally.

§166. If a man take wives for his sons and do not take a wife for his youngest son, after the father dies, when the brothers divide, they shall give from the goods of the father's house to their youngest brother, who has not taken a wife, money for a marriage settlement in addition to his portion and they shall enable him to take a wife.

§167. If a man take a wife and she bear him children and that woman die, and after her (death) he take another wife and she bear him children and later the father die, the children of the mothers shall not divide (the estate). They shall receive the dowries of their respective mothers and they shall divide equally the goods of the house of the father.

§168. If a man set his face to disinherit his son and say to the judges: "I will disinherit my son," the judges shall inquire into his antecedents, and if the son have not committed a crime sufficiently grave to cut him off from sonship, the father may not cut off his son from sonship.

§169. If he have committed a crime against his father sufficiently grave to cut him off from sonship, they shall condone his first (offense). If he commit a grave crime a second time, the father may cut off his son from sonship.

§170. If a man's wife bear him children and his maid servant bear him children, and the father during his lifetime say to the children which the maid servant bore him: "My children," and reckon them with the children of his wife, after the father dies the children of the wife and the children of the maid servant shall divide the goods of the father's house equally. The child of the wife shall have the right of choice at the division.

§171. But if the father during his lifetime have not said to the children which the maid servant bore him: "My children"; after the father dies, the children of the maid servant shall not share in the goods of the father's house with the children of the wife. The maid servant and her children shall be given their freedom. The children of the wife may not lay claim to the children of the maid servant for service. The wife shall receive her dowry and the gift which her husband gave and deeded to her on a tablet and she may dwell in the house of her husband and enjoy (the property) as long as she lives. She cannot sell it, however, for after her (death) it belongs to her children.

§172. If her husband have not given her a gift, they shall make good her dowry and she shall receive from the goods of her husband's house a portion corresponding to that of a son. If her children scheme to drive her out of the house, the judges shall inquire into her antecedents and if the children be in the wrong, she shall not go out from her husband's house. If the woman set her face to go out, she shall leave to her children the gift which her husband gave her; she shall receive the dowry of her father's house, and the husband of her choice may take her.

§173. If that woman bear children to her later husband into whose house she has entered and later on that woman die, the former and the later children shall divide her dowry.

§174. If she do not bear children to her later husband, the children of her first husband shall receive her dowry.

§175. If either a slave of the palace or a slave of a freeman take the daughter of a man (gentleman) and she bear children, the owner of the slave may not lay claim to the children of the daughter of the man for service.

§176. And if a slave of the palace or a slave of a freeman take the daughter of a man (gentleman); and if, when he takes her, she enter into the house of the slave of the palace or the slave of the freeman with the dowry of her father's house; if from the time that they join hands, they build a house and acquire property; and if later on the slave of the palace or the slave of the freeman die, the daughter of the man shall receive her dowry, and they shall divide into two parts whatever her husband and she had acquired from the time they had joined hands; the owner of the slave shall receive one-half and the daughter of the man shall receive one-half for her children.

§ 176A. If the daughter of the man had no dowry they shall divide into two parts whatever her husband and she had acquired from the time they joined hands. The owner of the slave shall receive one-half and the daughter of the man shall receive one-half for her children.

§177. If a widow, whose children are minors, set her face to enter another house, she cannot do so without the consent of the judges. When she enters another house, the judges shall inquire into the estate of her former husband and they shall entrust the estate of her former husband to the later husband and that woman, and they shall deliver to them a tablet (to sign). They shall administer the estate and rear the minors. They may not sell the household goods. He who purchases household goods belonging to the sons of a widow shall forfeit his money. The goods shall revert to their owner.

§178. If (there be) a priestess or a devotee to whom her father has given a dowry and written a deed of gift; if in the deed which he has written for her, he have not written "after her (death) she may give to whomsoever she may please," and if he have not granted her full discretion; after her father dies her brother shall take her field and garden and they shall give her grain, oil and wool according to the value of her share and they shall make her content. If her brothers do not give her grain, oil, and wool according to the value of her share and they do not make her content, she may give her field and garden to any tenant she may please and her tenant shall maintain her. She shall enjoy the field, garden or anything else which her father gave her as long as she lives. She may not sell it, nor transfer it. Her heritage belongs to her brothers.

§179. If (there be) a priestess or a devotee to whom her father has given a dowry and written a deed of gift; if in the deed which he has written for her, he have written "after her (death) she may give to whomsoever she may please," and he have granted her full discretion; after her father dies she may give it to whomsoever she may please after her (death). Her brothers may not lay claim against her.

§180. If a father do not give a dowry to his daughter, a bride or devotee, after her father dies she shall receive as her share in the goods of her father's house the portion of a son, and she shall enjoy it as long as she lives. After her (death) it belongs to her brothers.

§181. If a father devote a votary or NU.PAR to a god and do not give her a dowry, after her father dies she shall receive as her share in the goods of her father's house one-third of the portion of a son and she shall enjoy it as long as she lives. After her (death), it belongs to her brothers.

§182. If a father do not give a dowry to his daughter, a priestess of Marduk of Babylon, and do not write for her a deed of gift; after her father dies she shall receive as her share with her brothers one-third the portion of a son in the goods of her father's house, but she shall not conduct the business thereof. A priestess of Marduk, after her (death), may give to whomsoever she may please.

§183. If a father present a dowry to his daughter, who is a concubine, and give her to a husband and write a deed of gift; after the father dies she shall not share in the goods of her father's house.

§184. If a man do not present a dowry to his daughter, who is a concubine, and do not give her to a husband; after her father dies her brothers shall present her a dowry proportionate to the fortune of her father's house and they shall give her to a husband.

§185. If a man take in his name a young child as a son and rear him, one may not bring claim for that adopted son.

§186. If a man take a young child as a son and, when he takes him, he is rebellious toward his father and mother (who have adopted him), that adopted son shall return to the house of his father.

§187. One may not bring claim for the son of a NER.SE.GA, who is a palace guard, or the son of a devotee.

§188. If an artisan take a son for adoption and teach him his handicraft, one may not bring claim for him.

§189. If he do not teach him his handicraft, that adopted son may return to his father's house.

§190. If a man do not reckon among his sons the young child whom he has taken for a son and reared, that adopted son may return to his father's house.

§191. If a man, who has taken a young child as a son and reared him, establish his own house and acquire children, and set his face to cut off the adopted son, that son shall not go his way. The father who reared him shall give to him of his goods one-third the portion of a son and he shall go. He shall not give to him of field, garden or house.

§192. If the son of a NER.SE.GA, or the son of a devotee, say to his father who has reared him, or his mother who has reared him: "My father thou art not," "My mother thou art not," they shall cut out his tongue.

§193. If the son of a NER.SE.GA or the son of a devotee identify his own father's house and hate the father who has reared him and the mother who has reared him and go back to his father's house, they shall pluck out his eye.

§194. If a man give his son to a nurse and that son die in the hands of the nurse, and the nurse substitute another son without the consent of his father or mother, they shall call her to account, and because she has substituted another son without the consent of his father or mother, they shall cut off her breast.

§195. If a son strike his father, they shall cut off his fingers.

§196. If a man destroy the eye of another man, they shall destroy his eye.

§197. If one break a man's bone, they shall break his bone.

§198. If one destroy the eye of a freeman or break the bone of a freeman, he shall pay one mana of silver.

§199. If one destroy the eye of a man's slave or break a bone of a man's slave he shall pay one-half his price.

§200. If a man knock out a tooth of a man of his own rank, they shall knock out his tooth.

§201. If one knock out a tooth of a freeman, he shall pay one-third mana of silver.

§202. If a man strike the person of a man (i.e., commit an assault) who is his superior, he shall receive sixty strokes with an oxtail whip in public.

§203. If a man strike another man of his own rank, he shall pay one mana of silver.

§204. If a freeman strike a freeman, he shall pay ten shekels of silver.

§205. If a man's slave strike a man's son, they shall cut off his ear.

§206. If a man strike another man in a quarrel and wound him, he shall swear: "I struck him without intent," and he shall be responsible for the physician.

§207. If (he) die as the result of the stroke, he shall swear (as above), and if he be a man, he shall pay one-half mana of silver.

§208. If (he) be a freeman, he shall pay one-third mana of silver.

§209. If a man strike a man's daughter and bring about a miscarriage, he shall pay ten shekels of silver for her miscarriage.

§210. If that woman die, they shall put his daughter to death.

§211. If, through a stroke, he bring about a miscarriage to the daughter of a freeman, he shall pay five shekels of silver.

§212. If that woman die, he shall pay one-half mana of silver.

§213.   If he strike the female slave of a man and bring about a miscarriage, he shall pay two shekels of silver.

§214.   If that female slave die, he shall pay one-third mana of silver.

§215.   If a physician operate on a man for a severe wound (or make a severe wound upon a man) with a bronze lancet and save the man's life; or if he open an abscess (in the eye) of a man with a bronze lancet and save that man's eye, he shall receive ten shekels of silver (as his fee).

§216.   If he be a freeman, he shall receive five shekels.

§217.   If it be a man's slave, the owner of the slave shall give two shekels of silver to the physician.

§218.   If a physician operate on a man for a severe wound with a bronze lancet and cause the man's death; or open an abscess (in the eye) of a man with a bronze lancet and destroy the man's eye, they shall cut off his fingers.

§219.   If a physician operate on a slave of a freeman for a severe wound with a bronze lancet and cause his death, he shall restore a slave of equal value.

§220.   If he open an abscess (in his eye) with a bronze lancet, and destroy his eye, he shall pay silver to the extent of one-half of his price.

§221.   If a physician set a broken bone for a man or cure his diseased bowels, the patient shall give five shekels of silver to the physician.

§222.   If he be a freeman, he shall give three shekels of silver.

§223.   If it be a man's slave, the owner of the slave shall give two shekels of silver to the physician.

§224.   If a veterinary physician operate on an ox or an ass for a severe wound and save its life, the owner of the ox or ass shall give to the physician, as his fee, one sixth of a shekel of silver.

§225.   If he operate on an ox or an ass for a severe wound and cause its death, he shall give to the owner of the ox or ass one-fourth its value.

§226.   If a brander, without the consent of the owner of the slave, brand a slave with the sign that he cannot be sold, they shall cut off the fingers of that brander.

§227.   If a man deceive a brander and he brand a slave with the sign that he cannot be sold, they shall put that man to death, and they shall cast him into his house. The brander shall swear: "I did not brand him knowingly," and he shall go free.

§228.   If a builder build a house for a man and complete it, (that man) shall give him two shekels of silver per SAR of house as his wage.

§229.   If a builder build a house for a man and do not make its construction firm, and the house which he has built collapse and cause the death of the owner of the house, that builder shall be put to death.

§230.   If it cause the death of a son of the owner of the house, they shall put to death a son of that builder.

§231.   If it cause the death of a slave of the owner of the house, he shall give to the owner of the house a slave of equal value.

§232. If it destroy property, he shall restore whatever it destroyed, and because he did not make the house which he built firm and it collapsed, he shall rebuild the house which collapsed from his own property (i.e., at his own expense).

§233. If a builder build a house for a man and do not make its construction meet the requirements and a wall fall in, that builder shall strengthen that wall at his own expense.

§234. If a boatman build a boat of 60 GUR for a man, he shall give to him two shekels of silver as his wage.

§235. If a boatman build a boat for a man and he do not make its construction seaworthy and that boat meet with a disaster in the same year in which it was put into commission, the boatman shall reconstruct that boat and he shall strengthen it at his own expense and he shall give the boat when strenghtened to the owner of the boat.

§236. If a man hire his boat to a boatman and the boatman be careless and he sink or wreck the boat, the boatman shall replace the boat to. the owner of the boat.

§237. If a man hire a boatman and a boat and freight it with grain, wool, oil, dates or any other kind of freight, and that boatman be careless and he sink the boat or wreck its cargo, the boatman shall replace the boat which he sank and whatever portion of the cargo he wrecked.

§238. If a boatman sink a man's boat and refloat it, he shall give silver to the extent of one-half its value.

§239. If a man hire a boatman, he shall give him six GUR of grain per year.

§240. If a boat under way strike a ferryboat (or boat at anchor), and sink it, the owner of the boat whose boat was sunk shall make declaration in the presence of God of everything that was lost in his boat and (the owner) of (the vessel) under way which sank the ferryboat shall replace his boat and whatever was lost.

§241. If a man seize an ox for debt, he shall pay one-third mana of silver.

§242, §243. If a man hire (an ox) for a year, he shall give to its owner four GUR of grain as the hire of a draught ox, (and) three GUR of grain as the hire of an ox (?).

§244. If a man hire an ox or an ass and a lion kill it in the field, it is the owner's affair.

§245. If a man hire an ox and cause its death through neglect or abuse, he shall restore an ox of equal value to the owner of the ox.

§246. If a man hire an ox and he breaks its foot or cut its hamstring (?), he shall restore an ox of equal value to the owner of the ox.

§247. If a man hire an ox and destroy its eye, he shall pay silver to the owner of the ox to the extent of one-half its value.

§248. If a man hire an ox and break its horn or cut off its tail or injure the flesh (through which) the ring (passes), he shall pay silver to the extent of one-fourth of its value.

§249. If a man hire an ox and a god strike it and it die, the man who hired the ox shall take an oath before God and go free.

§250. If a bull, when passing through the street, gore a man and bring about his death, this case has no penalty.

§251. If a man's bull have been wont to gore and they have made known to him his habit of goring, and he have not protected his horns or have not tied him up, and that bull gore the son of a man and bring about his death, he shall pay one-half mana of silver.

§252. If it be the servant of a man, he shall pay one-third mana of silver.

§253. If a man hire a man to oversee his farm and furnish him the seed grain and entrust him with oxen and contract with him to cultivate the field, and that man steal either the seed or the crop and it be found in his possession, they shall cut off his fingers.

§254. If he take the seed grain and overwork the oxen, he shall restore the quantity of grain which he has hoed.

§255. If he let the oxen of the man on hire, or steal the seed grain and there be no crop in the field, they shall call that man to account and he shall measure out 60 GUR of grain per 10 GAN.

§256. If he be not able to meet his obligation, they shall leave him in that field with the cattle.

§257. If a man hire a field laborer, he shall pay him 8 GUR of grain per year.

§258. If a man hire a herdsman, he shall pay him 6 GUR of grain per year.

§259. If a man steal a watering-machine in a field, he shall pay 5 shekels of silver to the owner of the watering machine.

§260. If a man steal a watering bucket or a harrow, he shall pay 3 shekels of silver.

§261. If a man hire a herdsman to pasture oxen or sheep, he shall pay him 8 gur of grain per year.

§262. If a man, an ox or a sheep to . . . .

§263. If he lose an ox or sheep which is given to him, he shall restore to their owner ox for ox, sheep for sheep.

§264. If a shepherd, to whom oxen or sheep have been given to pasture, receive as his hire whatever was agreed upon (?) and be satisfied, and he let the cattle or sheep decrease in number, or lessen the birth rate, according to his contracts he shall make good the birth rate and the produce.

§265. If a shepherd, to whom oxen or sheep have been given to pasture, have been dishonest or have altered their price, or sold them, they shall call him to account, and he shall restore to their owner oxen and sheep tenfold what he has stolen.

§266. If a visitation of God happen to a fold, or a lion kill, the shepherd shall declare himself innocent before God, and the owner of the fold shall suffer the damage.

§267. If a shepherd be careless and he bring about an accident in the fold, the shepherd shall make good in cattle and sheep the loss through the accident which he brought about in the fold and give them to their owner.

§268. If a man hire an ox to thresh, 20 KA of grain is its hire.

§269. If he hire an ass to thresh, 10 KA of grain is its hire.

§270. If he hire a young animal (goat) to thresh, 1 KA of grain is its hire.

§271. If a man hire oxen, a wagon and a driver, he shall pay 180 KA of grain per day.

§272. If a man hire a wagon only, he shall pay 40 KA of grain per day.

§273. If a man hire a laborer, from the beginning of the year until the fifth month, he shall pay 6 SE of silver per day; from the sixth month till the end of the year he shall pay 5 SE of silver per day.

§274. If a man hire an artisan, the wage of a . . . is 5 SE of silver; the wage of a brickmaker (?) is 5 SE of silver; the wage of a tailor is 5 SE of silver; the wage of . . . is . . . SE of silver; the wage of a . . . is . . . SE of silver; the wage of a . . . is . . . SE of silver; the wage of a carpenter is 4 SE of silver; the wage of a (?) is 4 SE of silver; the wage of a (?) is . . . SE of silver; the wage of a mason is . . . SE of silver; so much per day shall he pay.

§275. If a man hire a . . . its hire is 3 SE of silver per day.

§276. If he hire a sailboat(?), he shall pay 2½ SE of silver per day as its hire.

§277. If a man hire a boat of 60 GUR (tonnage), he shall pay ⅙ of a shekel of silver as its hire per day.

§278. If a man sell a male or female slave, and the slave have not completed his month, and the bennu fever fall upon him, he (the purchaser) shall return him to the seller and he shall receive the money which he paid.

§279. If a man sell a male or female slave and there be a claim upon him, the seller shall be responsible for the claim.

§280. If a man purchase a male or female slave of a man in a foreign country, and if, when he comes back to his own land, the (former) owner of the male or female slave recognize his male or female slave—if the male or female slave be a native of the land, he shall grant them their freedom without money.

§281. If they be natives of another land, the purchaser shall declare before God the money which he paid (for them), and the owner of the male or female slave shall give to the merchant the money which he paid out, and he (the owner) shall receive into his care his male or female slave.

§282. If a male slave say to his master: "Thou art not my master," his master shall prove him to be his slave and shall cut off his ear.

Appendix E

Translation for the Computer

A very useful tool for the analysis of data is the computer. This is true not only for such data as responses to structured questionnaires but also the content of conversations, news media, and open-ended interviews. In addition, "simulation models" may be constructed to analyze the practical implications of specified alternatives. The process of transferring raw information into a form usable by the computer once again involves you in translation, this time translation from the language of measurement strategies to the language of the computer.

CODING

This process of translation is referred to as coding. Coding usually involves the assignment of a number to various responses or pieces of information that have been collected.

Before we pursue this process of coding further, you should know something about the structure of computer cards. Computer cards are in a standard format of 80 columns with 12 single punches possible in each column. By producing combinations of multiple punches in a single column it is possible to expand the range of information beyond 12 to various symbols and alphabetic characters. Some of the possibilities are shown in Exhibit E.1. You can see that the letters S through Z are signaled by a "0" punch coupled with a second punch of "2" through "9." When devising your coding scheme and your codebook (these are discussed next), the standard format of the computer card should be kept in mind.

As an example of the coding process, the first page from a questionnaire given to third year law school students is reprinted in Exhibit E.2. The initial question was open-ended and, hence, we went through each of the questionnaires and developed a content-analysis scheme whereby the responses could be categorized. Once this was done, these categories of responses were assigned numbers as follows: (1) Social influence; (2) Inherent interest; (3) Flexibility; (4) Self-gain other; (5) Altruistic;

EXHIBIT E.1
Computer Card with Selected Punches

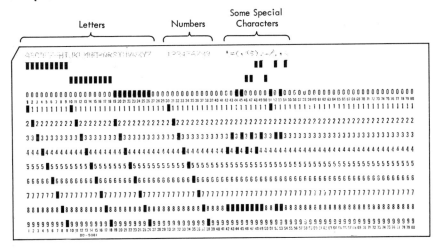

(6) Draft avoidance; (7) Continue education; (8) Lack of better alternative; and (9) Other.

It should be apparent from this that numbers are not "numbers" in the usual sense of the term. Rather, they are simply designations for certain responses for purposes of analysis. When analysis is completed, it is a simple matter to go back and retranslate the numbers into what they signify. To facilitate this translation you should construct a *codebook*. A codebook is a set of rules for translating answers to questions into numbers or other symbols to be processed by the computer. In the codebook for the questionnaire in Exhibit E.2, it was indicated that columns 1 through 5 on the computer card were to be reserved for identification purposes and for the designation of the card number on which the information was to be "stored." Eventually, seven cards for each respondent were used. Columns 6 through 8 were to be reserved for responses to the closed-ended questions, with "Great Importance" being coded 1, "Some Importance" coded 2, and "No Importance" coded 3. "Checks" were indicated by a "4." In column 33 the timing of the decision to study law was coded with "Before High School" 1, "During High School" 2, "Freshman or Soph Year College" 3, "Junior or Senior Year College" 4, and "After College Graduation" 5. The final question on this page, the respondent's LSAT score, was given three columns, 34–36, and coded as reported.

Working from this codebook, the "coder" simply took each of the returned questionnaires and wrote the appropriate number beside each response where necessary. The numbers beside the parentheses are the

EXHIBIT E.2
First Page of Questionnaire Administered to Third-year Law Students

I. 1. What were your most important reasons for coming to law school? **C1**
        (If you state more than one reason, please rank them in order of
        importance, assigning "1" to the most important, "2" to the next
        most, etc.)

        _____

        _____
        _____   **6–8**
        _____

    2. Regardless of your answer to the previous question, please indi-
        cate the effect of the following factors on your decision to enter
        law school. Use: great importance (1); some importance (2);
        no importance (3).

Lawyers in family ..... 9( )   Wanted to be of service
Influence of teacher or   to underprivileged ... 21( )
   friend .... 10( )   Desired varied work .... 22( )
Wanted opportunity to   Wanted to go into
   work with members   business later .... 23( )
   of family .... 11( )   Wanted to go to Wall
Interested in subject   Street .... 24( )
   matter .... 12( )   Wanted to go into legal
Desired intellectual   education .... 25( )
   stimulation .... 13( )   Wanted to go into
Professional training ... 14( )   government service ... 26( )
Liked to argue and   Financial rewards ...... 27( )
   debate .... 15( )   Wanted to postpone
Prestige of profession ... 16( )   military service ...... 28( )
Wanted to help   Felt I needed further
   restructure society ... 17( )   education to get a job .. 29( )
Desired to handle other   Family wanted me to ... 30( )
   people's affairs ...... 18( )   Was uncertain of career
Desired independence .. 19( )   plans, law seemed like
Wanted to become a   good bet .... 31( )
   politician .... 20( )
Other .... 32( )

    3. At what time did you make a reasonably firm decision to study
        law?
        A. Before High School .... ( )
        B. During High School .... ( )
        C. Freshman or Soph Year College .... ( )
        D. Junior or Senior Year College .... ( )
        E. After College Graduation .... ( )
    4. What was your highest LSAT score? _____   **34–36**

columns of the computer card into which the information was to be punched. The "*C1*" in the upper right-hand margin was printed on each questionnaire as a signal to the keypuncher that the following information was to be placed in the first card for each individual. Later in the questionnaire, "*C2*", "*C3*", . . . "*C7*" informed the keypuncher that a new card was to be started. Each law student's responses, then, were "stored" on seven computer cards for later analysis.

Three rules of thumb should be kept in mind when devising a coding scheme—maximize detail, no multiple punches in a single column, and use blanks to indicate nonresponse only when absolutely necessary. It is a good idea to maximize detail in terms of the number of categories utilized in that categories can always be collapsed in later analysis. It is more difficult and generally impossible to recreate information you have left out. Multiple punches in single columns will signal information that is different than you intended. For example, if you have a question on age and punch the years in a single column, obvious difficulties arise. As shown in Exhibit E.1, a "38" will be interpreted as an equals sign. Even if this were not the case, it would be impossible to tell the difference between "38" and "83." Therefore, if you need more than ten categories (0 through 9), use two or more columns, depending on the number of categories involved.

The third rule of thumb has to do with the use of blanks. The most usual situation in which this question arises is when persons skip over questions and you need to code "No Response." The tendency is to code these as "Blank." However, many computer programs (we will get to this topic shortly) will confuse blank responses and may stop processing the data when blanks are encountered. This is not necessarily the case, but it is likely enough to make the use of blanks an undesirable practice. "No Response" can be coded "0" if this has not been used for some other option. Another commonly used alternative, when "0" is used for something like "Uncertain," is to code nonresponses with some "Out of Range" value, such as "9."

THE MECHANICS OF TRANSFER

Once coded, the information is ready to be transferred to computer cards. This often is accomplished by way of a keypunch machine. A keypunch machine is much like a typewriter, though it punches holes in cards as well as typing letters, numbers, and other symbols. Keypunch operators may work directly from the questionnaire if it has been "precoded" ahead of time. That is, if you have taken time in the construction of the questionnaire to indicate responses via the numbers to be punched and if you have provided certain "benchmarks" in the form of indicating the columns into which responses are to be punched, keypunch operators can work directly from the research instrument. If you have not done this, or if you are working with material less susceptible to "precoding," such as content analysis of novels, then there are forms available, such as the one in Exhibit E.3, which correspond to the columns on a computer card. Each line on this form corresponds to one computer card. You simply transfer the information onto the form by writing the appropriate number in the column you have designated in your codebook. The keypunch operator works from this form instead of from the research instrument.

Another option involves the use of mark sense sheets. These are forms similar to the one in Exhibit E.4. Instead of writing the appropriate code in the corresponding column, you darken in the appropriate number with a pencil. These forms, each one of which corresponds to a single card, are then fed into an optical scanner, which automatically punches cards. Where available, these forms are to be recommended for both their efficiency and greater accuracy over the forms in Exhibit E.3. They are more efficient than manual keypunching for perhaps obvious reasons. They are also more accurate if you have taken care when making the marks in the appropriate spots.

Of somewhat more limited utility are mark sense sheets given directly to the respondent. Instead of marking answers on the questionnaire, responses are marked on sheets such as the one in Exhibit E.5. These forms can be fashioned for particular studies and have the virtue of eliminating the necessity of transferring the information from a questionnaire to another form before the production of cards. They have the disadvantage of being unfamiliar to many respondents and an additional source of possible confusion in a mail-out questionnaire. Nevertheless, if questionnaires are being administered in group sessions where instructions can be given and where confusion can be cleared up, these forms may prove useful.

USING CANNED PROGRAMS

Once responses have been transferred to computer cards, you are in a position to utilize the computer. Although the specific additional steps that must be taken vary from one computer center to another, there are general categories that recur.

Many computer centers have a series of "packages" available that allow you to manipulate the information collected in a number of ways. If none are available and you still wish to use the computer for analysis, you will either be called on to learn "programming" or employ a programmer. We will discuss only the use of existing packages—programs already written by others.

EXHIBIT E.3

YALE COMPUTER CENTER

80 COLUMN CODING SHEET

PROGRAMMER

PROBLEM

DATE

PAGE ___ OF ___

	5	6	10	11	15	16	20	21	25	26	30	31	35	36	40	41	45	46	50	51	55	56	60	61	65	66	70	71	73	80

EXHIBIT E.4
General Coding Form

Source: Optical Scanning Corporation, Newtown; Pa. © Optical Scanning Forms™.

PRINTED IN U.S.A.

EXHIBIT E.5

SCHOOL _____ CITY _____

INSTRUCTOR _____ GRADE _____ TEST _____

PRINT YOUR NAME IN THE BOXES PROVIDED, THEN BLACKEN THE LETTER BOX BELOW WHICH MATCHES EACH LETTER OF YOUR NAME.

YOUR LAST NAME | YOUR FIRST NAME | MI

TEACHER ONLY: STUDENT ABSENT FOR PART: I II III IV

SEMESTER: FALL, SPRING — A, B

FORM OF THIS TEST IS: A 1, B 2, C 3, D 4

GRADE: 1 2 3 4 5 6

BIRTH DATE MO/YEAR

SEX

STUDENT NUMBER

I
1 A B C D E   6 A B C D E   11 A B C D E   16 A B C D E   21 A B C D E   26 A B C D E   31 A B C D E   36 A B C D E
2 A B C D E   7 A B C D E   12 A B C D E   17 A B C D E   22 A B C D E   27 A B C D E   32 A B C D E   37 A B C D E
3 A B C D E   8 A B C D E   13 A B C D E   18 A B C D E   23 A B C D E   28 A B C D E   33 A B C D E   38 A B C D E
4 A B C D E   9 A B C D E   14 A B C D E   19 A B C D E   24 A B C D E   29 A B C D E   34 A B C D E   39 A B C D E
5 A B C D E   10 A B C D E   15 A B C D E   20 A B C D E   25 A B C D E   30 A B C D E   35 A B C D E   40 A B C D E

II
41 A B C D E   46 A B C D E   51 A B C D E   56 A B C D E   61 A B C D E   66 A B C D E   71 A B C D E   76 A B C D E
42 A B C D E   47 A B C D E   52 A B C D E   57 A B C D E   62 A B C D E   67 A B C D E   72 A B C D E   77 A B C D E
43 A B C D E   48 A B C D E   53 A B C D E   58 A B C D E   63 A B C D E   68 A B C D E   73 A B C D E   78 A B C D E
44 A B C D E   49 A B C D E   54 A B C D E   59 A B C D E   64 A B C D E   69 A B C D E   74 A B C D E   79 A B C D E
45 A B C D E   50 A B C D E   55 A B C D E   60 A B C D E   65 A B C D E   70 A B C D E   75 A B C D E   80 A B C D E

III
81 A B C D E   86 A B C D E   91 A B C D E   96 A B C D E   101 A B C D E   106 A B C D E   111 A B C D E   116 A B C D E
82 A B C D E   87 A B C D E   92 A B C D E   97 A B C D E   102 A B C D E   107 A B C D E   112 A B C D E   117 A B C D E
83 A B C D E   88 A B C D E   93 A B C D E   98 A B C D E   103 A B C D E   108 A B C D E   113 A B C D E   118 A B C D E
84 A B C D E   89 A B C D E   94 A B C D E   99 A B C D E   104 A B C D E   109 A B C D E   114 A B C D E   119 A B C D E
85 A B C D E   90 A B C D E   95 A B C D E   100 A B C D E   105 A B C D E   110 A B C D E   115 A B C D E   120 A B C D E

IV
121 A B C D E   126 A B C D E   131 A B C D E   136 A B C D E   141 A B C D E   146 A B C D E   151 A B C D E   156 A B C D E
122 A B C D E   127 A B C D E   132 A B C D E   137 A B C D E   142 A B C D E   147 A B C D E   152 A B C D E   157 A B C D E
123 A B C D E   128 A B C D E   133 A B C D E   138 A B C D E   143 A B C D E   148 A B C D E   153 A B C D E   158 A B C D E
124 A B C D E   129 A B C D E   134 A B C D E   139 A B C D E   144 A B C D E   149 A B C D E   154 A B C D E   159 A B C D E
125 A B C D E   120 A B C D E   135 A B C D E   140 A B C D E   145 A B C D E   150 A B C D E   155 A B C D E   160 A B C D E

STANDARD ANSWER SHEET-A   PRINTED IN U.S.A.   DS 1120-A

Source: Optical Scanning Corporation, Newtown; Pa. © Optical Scanning Forms™.

To use existing programs, five general categories of instructions usually are submitted to the computer. "Submitting" most often simply involves handing a deck of appropriately punched computer cards to a person who will then perform the physical task of feeding them to the computer. The first of these categories tells the computer to "Get ready because here I come." The specifics of these cards will differ from one center to another. They include bookkeeping information, which tells the computer who to bill for the time used, how long the run is likely to take, and how much "output" (e.g., pages of computer paper) will be required. On the basis of this information, many computer centers have a set of priorities for performing the requested tasks. Short jobs are run before long ones, professors before students or students before professors, and so forth. In addition, included in this set of instructions is a card that tells the computer which "package" is going to be utilized.

A second set of cards defines various aspects of the information being submitted. Here, the computer is told which columns contain various responses, what labels to give categories within each variable, how many cases there are, and the name of this particular "run."

A third set of cards specifies the manipulations the computer is to perform. It specifies the subroutines of the package that are to be utilized. You might want a frequency count of the number of persons who are married, the number of veterans, and so forth. You might want to know whether being married or serving in the Armed Forces is associated with various attitudes or behavior. In this latter case you might choose between a "cross-tabulation" of information or a "regression-analysis" subroutine of the package. In any event, this set of cards tells the computer what operations to perform on the data you have coded.

The fourth set of cards includes the data that have been collected. If there are 500 individuals in your survey study and each individual's responses are punched on two cards, then this set of cards will number 1,000. Information on cards generally is transferred to "tape," in which case you simply specify the identification number for the tape.

Finally, the fifth set of cards tells the computer "Goodbye." A signal is given to end the job so the computer can move on to the next run. Further details on the specific instructions for existing programs are available in their accompanying manuals. Once you become familiar with available programs, you will be surprised at just how simple an operation it is.

The entire operation of using an existing program is really quite simple—so simple that "real" computer buffs often use the derogatory term of "canner" to signify those who engage in such a mundane enterprise. Derogation notwithstanding, the individual interested primarily in the empirical pursuit of ideas will do well to learn how to use "canned" programs. You often can go a long way into analysis with these tools. A note of caution should be interjected at this point, however. Be careful that you do not let the limitations of an existing program determine your style of analysis. The starting point for analysis should be grounded in the set of ideas pursued rather than in the limits set by the program.

Author Index

Subject Index

*This book has been set in 10 and 9 point
Caledonia, leaded 2 points. Chapter numbers
are 24 and 36 point Scotch Roman and chapter titles are 18 point Scotch Roman. The size
of the type page is 27 x 45½ picas.*